'V'RSITIES AT MEDW'

HANDBOOK OF AGRICULTURAL ECONOMICS
VOLUME 2B

HANDBOOKS
IN
ECONOMICS

18

Series Editors

KENNETH J. ARROW
MICHAEL D. INTRILIGATOR

ELSEVIER

AMSTERDAM · BOSTON · LONDON · NEW YORK · OXFORD · PARIS
SAN DIEGO · SAN FRANCISCO · SINGAPORE · SYDNEY · TOKYO

HANDBOOK OF AGRICULTURAL ECONOMICS

VOLUME 2B
AGRICULTURAL AND FOOD POLICY

Edited by

BRUCE L. GARDNER
University of Maryland, College Park

and

GORDON C. RAUSSER
University of California, Berkeley

2002

ELSEVIER

AMSTERDAM · BOSTON · LONDON · NEW YORK · OXFORD · PARIS
SAN DIEGO · SAN FRANCISCO · SINGAPORE · SYDNEY · TOKYO

ELSEVIER SCIENCE B.V.
Sara Burgerhartstraat 25
P.O. Box 211, 1000 AE Amsterdam, The Netherlands

First edition 2002

Library of Congress Cataloging in Publication Data
A catalog record from the Library of Congress has been applied for.

British Library Cataloguing in Publication Data
A catalogue record from the British Library has been applied for.

ISBN: 0-444-51081-8 (set, comprising vols. 2A & 2B)
ISBN: 0-444-51080-X (vol. 2A)
ISBN: 0-444-51079-6 (vol. 2B)
ISSN: 0169-7218 (Handbooks in Economics Series)

⊗ The paper used in this publication meets the requirements of ANSI/NISO Z39.48-1992 (Permanence of Paper).
Printed in The Netherlands.

INTRODUCTION TO THE SERIES

The aim of the *Handbooks in Economics* series is to produce Handbooks for various branches of economics, each of which is a definitive source, reference, and teaching supplement for use by professional researchers and advanced graduate students. Each Handbook provides self-contained surveys of the current state of a branch of economics in the form of chapters prepared by leading specialists on various aspects of this branch of economics. These surveys summarize not only received results but also newer developments, from recent journal articles and discussion papers. Some original material is also included, but the main goal is to provide comprehensive and accessible surveys. The Handbooks are intended to provide not only useful reference volumes for professional collections but also possible supplementary readings for advanced courses for graduate students in economics.

KENNETH J. ARROW and MICHAEL D. INTRILIGATOR

PUBLISHER'S NOTE

For a complete overview of the Handbooks in Economics Series, please refer to the listing at the end of this volume.

CONTENTS OF THE HANDBOOK

VOLUME 2A

VOLUME 2B

PART 5 – AGRICULTURAL AND FOOD POLICY

INTRODUCTION

The subject matter of agricultural economics has both broadened and deepened in recent years, and the chapters of this Handbook present the most exciting and innovative work being done today. The field originated early in the twentieth century with a focus on farm management and commodity markets, but has since moved far into analysis of issues in food, resources, international trade, and linkages between agriculture and the rest of the economy. In the process agricultural economists have been pioneering users of developments in economic theory and econometrics. Moreover, in the process of intense focus on problems of economic science that are central to agriculture – market expectations, behavior under uncertainty, multimarket relationships for both products and factors, the economics of research and technology adoption, and public goods and property issues associated with issues like nonpoint pollution and innovations in biotechnology – agricultural economists have developed methods of empirical investigation that have been taken up in other fields.

The chapters are organized into five parts, contained in two volumes. Volume 1 contains Part 1, "Agricultural Production", and Part 2, "Marketing, Distribution and Consumers". These two parts include much of the traditional scope of agricultural economics, emphasizing advances in both theory and empirical application of recent years. Volume 2 consists of three parts: "Agriculture, Natural Resources and the Environment", "Agriculture in the Macroeconomy", and "Agricultural and Food Policy". Although agricultural economists have always paid attention to these topics, research devoted to them has increased substantially in scope as well as depth in recent years.

A large-scale effort to review and assess the state of knowledge in agricultural economics was previously undertaken by the American Agricultural Economics Association (AAEA), with publication in four volumes from 1977 to 1992.[1] Those earlier survey volumes have strikingly different subject-matter content from that of the present Handbook, especially considering that they described the same field only 20 years ago. The AAEA volumes have extensive coverage of farm management issues, costs of production in agriculture, and estimates of efficiency of marketing firms. In our judgment little in any fundamental way has been added to our knowledge in these areas, and applications have become routine rather than imaginative research. The largest AAEA volume was devoted entirely to agriculture in economic development. This remains a

---

[1] *A Survey of Economics Literature*, Lee Martin, ed., Minneapolis: University of Minnesota Press. Volume 1, Traditional Field of Agricultural Economics (1977); Volume 2, Quantitative Methods in Agricultural Economics (1977); Volume 3, Economics of Welfare, Rural Development, and Natural Resources (1981); Volume 4, Agriculture in Economic Development (1992).

most important topic, but we cover it in only one complete chapter and parts of several others. This reflects in part the integration of work on developing countries with mainstream applied work. For example, our chapters on production economics, expectations, and risk management also encompass applications to agriculture in developing economies.

That integration points to another gradual but notable change in agricultural economists' research. The AAEA surveys had most of the chapters of one volume devoted to quantitative methods. We do not have any separate methodological chapters. In contrast, we have several chapters with substantial development of economic theory. This reflects an evolution in the research priorities of leading agricultural economists who, following the earlier work of Nerlove on supply and Griliches on technological change, are working at the theoretical frontiers and simultaneously undertaking empirical work – not just purveying new theories to their more "applied" colleagues.

As its title indicates, the AAEA volumes were surveys of literature, and aimed at completeness of coverage within their subject matter. We asked our authors to be selective, to focus on what they saw as the main contributions to the area they covered, and to assess the state of knowledge and what remains to be learned. This approach has left some gaps in our coverage, and has given us some chapters that are perhaps more idiosyncratic than is usual for a survey chapter. In order to pull things together at a higher level of aggregation, we commissioned five "synthesis" chapters, one for each of the five parts of the Handbook. And, to provide our own even broader overview, the editors have written closing syntheses of each volume. Because these syntheses provide capsule summaries of each Handbook chapter, we will not present further description of content here.

Although advances in research in agricultural economics are increasingly being made in many countries, our authors and coverage of applied topics is heavily U.S.-weighted (only six authors work outside of the U.S.: two in Europe, two in Australia, one in Canada, and one in Israel). Of those in the U.S., however, six are economists at the World Bank, an international rather than American institution. Probably in another twenty years or so one will have to become more international to capture the most interesting and exciting developments in the field, but that day has not arrived yet.

Among the many debts we have accrued in the preparation of this Handbook, the most important was Rachael Goodhue. She not only assessed the substance of many chapters, but she persuaded many reviewers and authors alike to complete their assigned responsibilities. Other critical contributors include the dedicated staff who provided support at the University of California, Berkeley, and at the University of Maryland. At Maryland, Liesl Koch served as copy editor and guided the authors' final revisions and preparation of the manuscript with sure judgment and a firm but diplomatic hand, a job best likened to driving a herd of cats. Coordination of correspondence with authors and reviewers was organized and carried out at Berkeley with exemplary efficiency and organizational skill by Jef Samp, Jessica Berkson, and Jennifer Michael, under the direction of Nancy Lewis.

We also want to recognize the comments and suggestions received from 45 reviewers of chapter drafts: Julian Alston, Jock Anderson, Richard Barichello, Eran Beinenbaum, Michael Boehlje, Dan Bromley, Steve Buccola, Allan Buckwell, David Bullock, Michael Caputo, Jean-Paul Chavas, John Connor, Klaus Deininger, Jeffrey Dorfman, Marcel Fafchamps, Gershon Feder, Joe Glauber, Dan Gilligan, Rachael Goodhue, Tom Grennes, Zvi Griliches, Geoff Heal, Eithan Hochman, Matt Holt, Wallace Huffman, D. Gale Johnson, Zvi Lerman, Erik Lichtenberg, Ethan Ligon, Alan Love, Jill McCluskey, Mario Miranda, Arie Oskam, Dick Perrin, Mark Rosegrant, Vern Ruttan, Ed Schuh, Kathleen Segerson, Larry Sjaastad, Spiro Stefanou, Jo Swinnen, Frans van der Zee, Finis Welch, Abner Womack, and Jacob Yaron.

BRUCE GARDNER
GORDON RAUSSER

CONTENTS OF VOLUME 2B

PART 5

AGRICULTURAL AND FOOD POLICY

Chapter 33

THE INCIDENCE OF AGRICULTURAL POLICY

JULIAN M. ALSTON

Department of Agricultural and Resource Economics, University of California, Davis

JENNIFER S. JAMES

Department of Agricultural Economics and Rural Sociology, The Pennsylvania State University

Contents

Handbook of Agricultural Economics, Volume 2, Edited by B. Gardner and G. Rausser
© 2002 Elsevier Science B.V. All rights reserved

Abstract

This chapter first discusses what economists mean by "the incidence of agricultural policy" and why we care about it. Then it reviews models of the determinants of the differential incidence of different policies among interest groups such as suppliers of factors of production, consumers, middlemen, taxpayers, and others. Results are represented in terms of Marshallian economic surplus, and surplus transformation curves. After reviewing the results from standard models under restrictive assumptions, certain assumptions are relaxed in order to analyze the effects of imperfect supply controls, variability, cheating and imperfect enforcement of policies, and the dynamics of supply.

Keywords

agricultural policy, welfare analysis, incidence, efficient redistribution

JEL classification: Q18

1. Introduction

Why study policy incidence? One reason is that the economic welfare effects of policies are intrinsically interesting. In addition, the distribution of the resulting benefits and costs is central to understanding why particular policies are chosen; and it is also useful, in some settings, for prescribing policies. Whether we are interested primarily in the causes or in the consequences of policies, it is often appropriate to go beyond the most aggregative summary measures reported in some studies, such as Harberger triangles of deadweight loss, to consider the welfare effects on particular groups in society.

In the analysis of agricultural commodity policies, for instance, it is common to distinguish between the effects on welfare of agricultural producers and the effects on other economic agents. The economic effects of policies are then represented in terms of the costs and benefits to producers as a group and to other groups in society (i.e., the distributional effects), and the net effects on society as a whole (the sum of the effects on producers and others). When we talk about the incidence of agricultural policy, then, we usually mean the distribution of the costs and benefits of the policy among different interest groups, defined in terms of their roles as consumers, taxpayers, or producers (or suppliers of factors of production).

It is conventional in commodity policy analysis to use Marshallian consumer surplus as a measure of consumer welfare change, as an approximation of the more theoretically correct Hicksian welfare measures, implicitly presuming the bias is small, based on arguments from Willig (1976). In addition, it is conventional to explicitly or implicitly invoke Harberger's (1971) "Three Postulates" of applied welfare economics.[1] When these assumptions are valid, the consumer benefits from consumption may be measured as the area beneath the ordinary demand curve, so that net changes in consumer welfare may be measured using Marshallian consumer surplus, and the area beneath the supply curve is a measure of total costs, so that changes in the net welfare of producers may be measured using producer surplus or quasi-rent.[2]

One of the key points to be made in the pages that follow is that supply conditions, especially elasticities of factor supply but also factor cost shares and elasticities of substitution among factors, are primary determinants of the incidence of policies. Supply analysis is difficult in a range of dimensions, including the inherent dynamics, uncertainty, and the role of expectations. Here, we abstract completely from the truly

---

[1] These postulates are (a) that the competitive demand price for a given unit measures the value of that unit to the demander, (b) that the competitive supply price for a given unit measures the value of that unit to the supplier, and (c) that when evaluating the net benefits or costs of a given policy action, the costs and benefits should be added without regard to the individual(s) to whom they accrue. Harberger (1971) also discusses the implications of multiple market distortions in general equilibrium for these welfare measures and provides a multiple-distortion deadweight-loss measure.

[2] In a comprehensive review of empirical approaches to the measurement of welfare, Slesnick (1998) reviewed the literature documenting the shortcomings of Marshallian consumer surplus as a measure of consumer welfare and social welfare.

dynamic and uncertain nature of agricultural supply response and, for the most part, consider comparative-static analysis with a given supply curve. But we do consider the implications of an increasing elasticity of supply, with increasing length of run, for the longer-run incidence of policy – the evolution of the incidence with the evolution of supply response. Notably, one of the first empirical studies of agricultural policy incidence was by Nerlove (1958) in a study titled *The Dynamics of Supply*.

A related issue concerns the degree of aggregation across markets. As we aggregate across commodities, supply becomes less elastic, in particular because the inelasticity of the total supply of land becomes increasingly more relevant as a constraint. For the most part, here, we will be considering policies for individual commodities, commodities for which it is not appropriate to regard the supply of land as absolutely fixed (even if it were appropriate for a nation as a whole, when considering all agricultural commodities together). Only if we are considering changes in a policy that affects all of the commodities together is it reasonable to consider the market for an aggregate agricultural commodity with a fixed supply of land. Even then, a multimarket model, taking appropriate account of the differences among commodities, is likely to be more meaningful, unless the commodities all experience the same policy effects.

Many policies affect agriculture. However, attention here will be limited to policies that are applied directly through farm commodity markets or input markets with a view to raising returns to producers.[3] In Section 2, we consider output subsidies and output quotas in the context of a single-market, closed-economy model. Since international trade is important in most agricultural commodity markets, in Section 3 we extend the discussion to consider markets and policies for traded goods. We limit our coverage of those aspects, though, since international trade and trade policy are the subject of another chapter. In Section 4, we consider vertical linkages in multimarket models, which allows us to extend the set of instruments to consider subsidies or quotas on inputs. While we consider small multimarket models, the analysis here is restricted to partial equilibrium models.

In all of these models, for each instrument, we consider the effects on prices and quantities of output (and, where relevant, inputs) and, accordingly, on economic welfare and its distribution among taxpayers, consumers, and producers (and, where relevant, input suppliers). We consider both simple policies and policies involving combinations of instruments, and we compare policies in terms of their transfer efficiency, using conventional stylized models of policies and markets. In addition, we maintain the assumptions that imply that changes in producer and consumer surplus are appropriate measures of welfare change: static supply and demand, perfect knowledge, perfect competition, and perfect and costless enforcement of policies.

In the subsequent sections we consider some extensions to the above models, including some more realistic characterizations of supply controls (Section 5), variability and stabilization issues (Section 6), the role of imperfect enforcement and other costs

---

[3] The same procedures could be used to evaluate transfers to consumers [e.g., Alston et al. (1999)].

of administering policies (Section 7), and some implications of the dynamics of supply response for the incidence of different policies (Section 8). Importantly, however, throughout the chapter we retain the assumption of perfect competition. Finally, Section 9 concludes the chapter.

2. Single-market models of policy incidence in commodity markets

Discussions of the formal analysis of the welfare consequences of agricultural policy often begin with Wallace (1962). Other influential articles in this area, published around the same time, include Nerlove (1958), Parish (1962), Floyd (1965), Johnson (1965), Dardis (1967), and Dardis and Learn (1967). Much of this work can be traced to the University of Chicago.

2.1. The basic model

Wallace (1962) compared the effects of two stylized policies in a competitive market for a non-traded commodity: (1) a marketing quota (which he called the "Cochrane proposal"), and (2) a target price and deficiency payments (which he called the "Brannan plan"). These two policies are depicted in Figure 1, where D represents demand, S represents supply, and the initial equilibrium occurs at the price, P_0, and corresponding quantity, Q_0. The policies are designed to generate a given price, P_1, for producers. This is done either by fixing a quota of Q_1, or by fixing a producer target price at P_1, allowing the corresponding production of Q_2 to be sold at a consumer price, P_2, and paying producers a deficiency payment of $P_1 - P_2$ per unit. In this static setting the latter policy is identically equivalent to paying producers a per unit subsidy of $P_1 - P_2$, and for simplicity we refer to it below as a subsidy. Both policies result in the same producer price of P_1, but the quota reduces the quantity produced and consumed to Q_1, while the subsidy increases it to Q_2.

The size and distribution of the welfare effects differ between the two policies, as shown in Table 1 (as is conventional practice, for this analysis it is assumed that quota rents accrue to producers and are included in producer surplus). An important distinction between the two policies is their effects on consumers and taxpayers. The quota policy benefits producers at the expense of consumers, with no effect on taxpayers, while the subsidy policy benefits consumers as well as producers, all at the expense of taxpayers. Producer benefits are greater under the subsidy, since area $A + B + C$ is greater than area $A - (G + K)$. The net social cost or deadweight loss from the quota ($DWL_q = -\Delta NS = $ area $B + G + K$, where ΔNS is the change in net social welfare) may be greater or smaller than that for the subsidy ($DWL_s = $ area E), depending on the relative sizes of supply and demand elasticities.

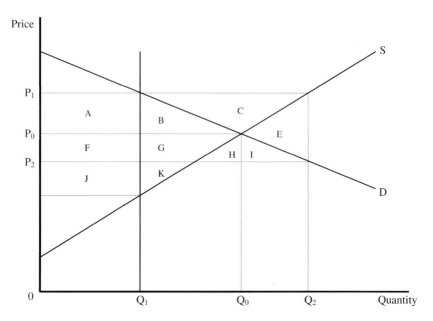

Figure 1. Welfare effects of a quota and a subsidy.

Table 1
Welfare effects of a quota and a subsidy

Changes in	Marketing quota	Production subsidy
Producer Surplus (ΔPS)	$A - (G + K)$	$A + B + C$
Consumer Surplus (ΔCS)	$-(A + B)$	$F + G + H + I$
Taxpayer Surplus (ΔTS)	0	$-(A + B + C + E + F + G + H + I)$
National Surplus (ΔNS = −DWL)	$-(B + G + K)$	$-E$

Note: The entries in this table refer to areas on Figure 1 associated with each policy applied to generate the given increase in the producer price.

The relationship between the deadweight loss measures for the two policies can be seen by approximating the social cost of each policy, using linear approximations of supply and demand. These approximate social cost areas are given by:

$$\text{DWL}_q = \frac{1}{2} P_0 Q_0 \tau^2 \eta^2 \left(\frac{\varepsilon + \eta}{\varepsilon \eta} \right); \qquad \text{DWL}_s = \frac{1}{2} P_0 Q_0 \tau^2 \varepsilon^2 \left(\frac{\varepsilon + \eta}{\varepsilon \eta} \right),$$

where τP_0 is the increase in price, ε is the supply elasticity, and η is the absolute value of the demand elasticity at the initial equilibrium. The social cost of either policy increases with the size of the induced quantity change, and the size of the price wedge associated with that change. Intuitively, the quantity response to the subsidized price increases as supply becomes more elastic, and a more restrictive quota will be required to reach the target price as demand becomes more elastic. Thus, the social cost of the quota increases with increases in the demand elasticity and with reductions in the supply elasticity, while the converse is true for the subsidy. As summarized by Wallace (1962), $\mathrm{DWL}_q \geqslant \mathrm{DWL}_s$ when $\eta \geqslant \varepsilon$, and vice versa. So, if demand is more elastic than supply (as depicted in Figure 1), the social cost of a quota is greater than that of a subsidy policy, for a given effect on producer price.

A weakness of this analysis is that, in comparing the instruments, it may not be appropriate to hold the producer *price* effect constant. More recent work, which has its roots in articles by Nerlove (1958), Dardis (1967), and Josling (1969), has developed a more useful basis for comparing policies.[4] Rather than comparing social costs for a given increase in price or gross revenue, policies are compared in terms of their efficiency of redistribution, or transfer efficiency.

2.2. Efficient redistribution

Measures of transfer efficiency provide a means for comparing the benefits to producers with the combined costs to consumers and taxpayers, and to society as a whole. Several such measures have their roots in literature described above, but the idea was popularized by Gardner (1983, 1987a, 1987b). Gardner (1983) linked various measures of transfer efficiency to the graphical representation of agricultural policy incidence developed by Josling (1974) and showed how the results depend on elasticities. Using this approach, alternative policies can be compared graphically in terms of their efficiency in meeting a particular goal.

The graphical comparison of policies is facilitated by the use of surplus transformation curves, which are typically attributed to Josling (1974). The surplus transformation curve (STC) for a particular policy instrument typically shows the range of combinations of welfare of producers versus consumers and taxpayers that can be achieved using that instrument.[5] Several STCs, one for each policy instrument under consideration, may be drawn in a single graph. Then, given some target level of producer benefits or some acceptable cost to consumers and taxpayers, policies may be compared easily in terms of one of several efficiency measures that are defined below. These graphical representations allow us to compare policy consequences, to prescribe more efficient policies, and to understand policy choices.

---

[4] Nerlove (1958) expressed welfare losses per net increment to producer surplus as did Dardis (1967), Dardis and Dennisson (1969), and Dardis and Learn (1967). Josling (1969) considered two objectives – increasing farm income and displacing imports – and compared policies in terms of the marginal and average costs per unit of each objective.

[5] The axes need not be defined this way. Reducing the problem to two dimensions is helpful but not necessary, and for some problems it may be appropriate to aggregate consumers with producers versus taxpayers, or producers with taxpayers versus consumers.

2.2.1. Redistribution using an output quota

The STC for a production quota indicates the combinations of producer and consumer surplus attained when the quota quantity is varied. An example is shown in Figure 2. When the quota is set at the initial equilibrium quantity, Q_0 in Figure 1, the competitive equilibrium is reached, with a distribution of surplus represented by point E in Figure 2. Movement along the STC to the left of point E shows how much producer surplus increases and consumer surplus decreases as the quota quantity is progressively reduced. At point L in Figure 2, if PS_1 and CS_1 are those resulting from the quota quantity Q_1 in Figure 1, then ΔPS and ΔCS in Figure 2 correspond to the areas $A - (G + K)$ and $A + B$, respectively, in Figure 1.

The deadweight loss (DWL) associated with quota quantity Q_1 is also shown in Figure 2. For any value of CS, the total DWL is seen graphically as the vertical distance from the STC to the 45° line through point E, while for any value of PS, the total DWL is seen as the horizontal distance from the STC to the 45° line. Thus, the vertical or horizontal distance from point L to the 45° line corresponds to area $(B + G + K)$, the DWL associated with a quota quantity of Q_1. As noted above, the DWL associated with a quota increases as the quantity distortion increases, so the DWL is always increasing as one moves further to the left from point E.

DWL is a useful measure for comparing policies when the objective is to increase producer surplus by a certain amount. However, when benefits to producers vary across

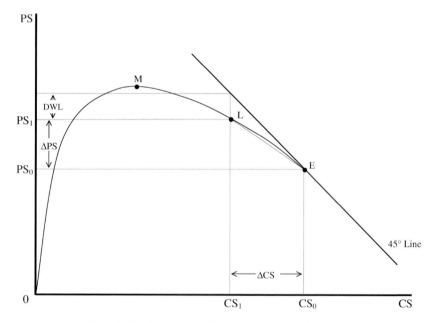

Figure 2. Surplus transformation curve for a production quota.

policies, a measure of average transfer efficiency may be more appropriate (although comparisons are meaningful only if we hold constant either producer benefits or costs to others). One such measure is what Dardis (1967) referred to as the Relative Social Cost (RSC) of a policy, which is defined as the change in total social welfare (i.e., the negative of the DWL) per dollar transferred to producers (i.e., $-\text{DWL}/\Delta\text{PS}$). RSC is inversely related to the average efficiency measure used by Gardner (1983), the average producer benefit for each dollar foregone by consumers and taxpayers – i.e., $\Delta\text{PS}/\Delta(\text{CS} + \text{TS})$, which he called "total redistribution". The primary advantage of Gardner's measure is that it can be seen graphically as the slope of the line going through point E and the relevant point on the STC. Because the STC is concave, Gardner's average efficiency measure is always decreasing (in absolute value) as we move away from the competitive equilibrium. Furthermore, because of the inverse relationship between average transfer efficiency (ATE) and the RSC of a policy (i.e., $\text{ATE} = 1/(\text{RSC} - 1)$), the DWL per dollar transferred to producers increases as we move along the STC to the left of point E.

A final group of efficiency measures evaluates the marginal efficiency of the transfer to producers. The marginal efficiency of a transfer indicates how much of the next dollar taken from consumers (and taxpayers) will actually be received by producers, and is equal to the absolute value of the slope of the STC at a given point. Similarly, the marginal DWL of a dollar taken from consumers and taxpayers is equal to one minus the marginal efficiency. Finally, the inverse of the marginal efficiency can be interpreted as the marginal cost to consumers and taxpayers of transferring another dollar to producers, and one minus this marginal cost is equal to the absolute value of the marginal RSC of an additional dollar transferred to producers. Because the first of these marginal efficiency measures is most clearly seen in graphs of STCs, it will be the focus of the following discussion.

The marginal efficiency of the first dollar transferred to producers is equal to the slope of the STC at the no-intervention equilibrium, point E, which is -1, reflecting the negligible DWL associated with a small restriction in quota. As the quota is reduced, each incremental dollar of welfare loss to consumers yields a smaller incremental producer surplus gain: the marginal gain in producer surplus diminishes and the STC flattens. This continues until the point is reached where the slope of the STC is zero (its tangent is horizontal), which occurs when the quota quantity equals the output quantity for a monopolist (point M in Figure 2). Further reductions in quota will reduce both producer and consumer surplus.

The relationship between marginal transfer efficiency and average efficiency is also of interest. Consider point L, where the tangent line is flatter than the line connecting points L and E. This relationship indicates that average efficiency is greater than marginal efficiency, and that the decreasing marginal efficiency of additional transfers is pulling down the average efficiency. Because the STC is concave, as one moves away from the competitive equilibrium, both marginal and average efficiencies fall with increases in transfers to producers.

2.2.2. Redistribution using a subsidy

The STC for a subsidy is derived as above, by evaluating the combinations of producer, consumer, and taxpayer welfare associated with different settings of the subsidy. Unlike the quota policy, however, taxpayers are affected by the implementation of a subsidy. In order to reduce the STC to two dimensions, consumers and taxpayers are typically treated as one group, and consumer and taxpayer surplus are added together. Movement to the left along the STC in this case corresponds to an increase in the per unit subsidy. The shape of the STC for a subsidy differs slightly from that for a quota. While both STCs are concave, the slope of the STC for the subsidy is always negative over the relevant range of CS + TS, since producers can always be made better off at the expense of consumers and taxpayers – producer welfare always increases as the subsidy is increased. This is the primary difference between the subsidy and quota, since producer welfare cannot be increased once a quota has reached the monopolist's quantity. Otherwise, the interpretation and graphical representations of the various efficiency measures are the same for the STCs of the two policy instruments.

2.2.3. Comparing quotas and subsidies

In comparing the STCs for the two policies, the same types of relationships can be seen as were discussed above in the comparison of the two policies while holding the price effects equal. Here, however, we compare the policies for a given benefit to producers. The position of the STC for a subsidy relative to that of the STC for a quota is determined by the elasticities of supply and demand. When demand is more elastic than supply at the undistorted equilibrium (or when the two elasticities are equal), the STC for the subsidy lies entirely above that for the quota. In this case, for any PS, the subsidy will have a smaller DWL, and will be a more efficient means for transferring income to producers, on both an average and a marginal basis.

Figure 3 shows a more interesting case in terms of policy performance. Here, supply is more elastic than demand at the competitive equilibrium. For a given relatively small transfer to producers, the DWL associated with a subsidy policy is larger than that of a quota, and both marginal and average efficiency measures favor the quota. However, when the transfer to producers is increased, the marginal efficiency of the subsidy eventually exceeds that of the quota. At some higher PS, the two STCs intersect, and the average efficiencies are equal. For transfers beyond that PS amount, the subsidy will have a smaller DWL and more favorable measures of average and marginal efficiency. Furthermore, producer surplus in excess of the monopolist's PS can be attained only by use of a subsidy. The main point, here, is that the relative efficiency of the two policies will depend on the size of the transfer as well as the supply and demand elasticities.

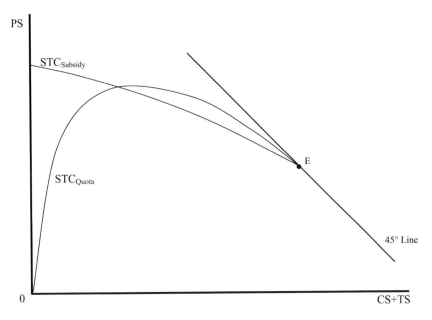

Figure 3. Surplus transformation curves: quota versus subsidy.

2.3. Multiple instruments

Alston and Hurd (1990) extended Gardner's (1983) analysis to show what happens when the policies are not mutually exclusive and may be combined efficiently. If a quota set equal to the competitive quantity were combined with a subsidy, transfers from taxpayers to producers could be made without any distortions in production or consumption because the quota would prevent supply response to the subsidy. Thus, the efficient STC for this problem is the 45° line in Figure 3 since, by combining the two instruments, the equivalent of a lump-sum transfer is achieved.

The idea that combining instruments can increase transfer efficiency has been formalized and extended in several recent articles, going beyond two interest groups and two policies. One issue is the number of policy instruments required to achieve a Pareto-efficient outcome, given a particular number of interest groups. Bullock (1994, 1995) has analyzed this issue. Bullock and Salhofer (1998a) provided theoretical and empirical results on measuring the costs of suboptimal combinations of policy instruments, and Bullock and Salhofer (1998b) showed that under the usual assumptions, in general, the addition of another instrument cannot reduce transfer efficiency. A number of recent studies have measured the transfer efficiency of different simple and combined policies, including Kola (1993), Salhofer (1996, 1997), and Alston and Gray (1998). In earlier work, Just (1984), Innes and Rausser (1989), and Gisser (1993) considered the welfare implications of combined policies, but did not measure transfer efficiency. Bullock, Salhofer and Kola (1999) present a synthesis and review of these and related studies.

2.4. The marginal social opportunity cost of funds

The analysis above rests on the conventional assumption that a dollar of government spending involves a loss of taxpayer surplus of one dollar. In developing the STC for a subsidy, Gardner (1983) considered the effects when the social opportunity cost of one dollar of government spending is greater than one dollar, owing to the distortions involved in general taxation measures. Thus the marginal taxpayer cost of a subsidy expenditure can be represented as $1 + \delta$ times that amount, where δ is the marginal excess burden or deadweight loss involved in generating the revenue to finance the subsidy. This excess burden includes the deadweight losses from distortions in the markets from which the tax revenue is raised (primarily, the labor market) along with taxpayer costs of compliance, and costs to the treasury, including revenue collection costs and other costs of administration and enforcement of the tax policy.

Most studies of the deadweight costs of general taxation refer only to the distortions in the labor market associated with income taxes. One issue in the literature has been the appropriate value for the relevant labor supply elasticity, which may depend on assumptions about what is to be done with the tax revenue. The response of the quantity of labor supplied to the imposition of a tax can be partitioned into substitution and income effects which work in opposite directions so that the uncompensated labor supply curve, including both effects, is less elastic than the compensated supply curve, including only the substitution effect. If all tax revenues were effectively returned to taxpayers – through either a lump-sum payment or the provision of public good – then the income effect would be eliminated. When the income effect is eliminated, the tax-induced distortion in quantity and the deadweight costs of taxation are larger.

An extensive literature documents measures of the deadweight losses from income taxation and discusses the interpretation of the estimates. Relatively recently, Fullerton (1991) reconciled a wide range of previous estimates of the marginal social cost of public funds in the United States in terms of their treatment of the income effect. He suggested values for the marginal cost of public funds ranging from $1.07, when the income effect is included, to $1.25 when the income effect has been eliminated. Campbell and Bond (1997) reported corresponding estimates for Australia of $1.19 and $1.24;[6] similar estimates were obtained by Diewert and Lawrence (1995) for New Zealand. A value for δ in the range of 10 to 25 percent seems plausible. In the context of benefit-cost analysis of the provision of public goods, Campbell and Bond (1997) and Campbell (1997) argue for using the larger value. They note that measures of the benefits from projects funded with taxes generally do not include income effects, and so neither should the measures of the costs.

---

[6] Findlay and Jones (1982) and Freebairn (1995) provide a wider range of estimates for Australia that may be more comparable to the range from Fullerton (1991) and the other U.S. studies.

2.4.1. Implications of δ > 0

To show the effects of $\delta > 0$, Figure 4 replicates the curves in Figure 3. If a dollar of subsidy payments reduces taxpayer surplus by $1 + \delta$ dollars, the STC for a subsidy alone is shifted down from b to b', while the STC for a quota is unaffected. This increases the likelihood that an all-or-nothing choice between production controls and subsidies will favor production controls. The reasoning is straightforward. For very small transfers, the distortion associated with a quota is infinitesimal and the marginal transfer efficiency of a quota is almost one. However, a one dollar lump-sum payment now costs the economy $1 + \delta$ dollars, owing to the excess burden of taxation. This deadweight cost of taxation, in addition to the deadweight loss in the commodity market caused by the subsidy, means that the slope of the STC for the subsidy must be less than $-1/(1 + \delta)$, even for very small transfers.

Consider, again, a subsidy combined with a quota fixed at the competitive quantity. The surplus transformation curve for this policy is no longer the line, c, with slope -1, but, rather, the line, d, with slope $-1/(1 + \delta)$. This line, d, is also the STC for a lump-sum transfer, as described above. However, when $\delta > 0$, the policy of combining a quota of Q_0 and a subsidy is no longer efficient. As shown by Alston and Hurd (1990), a superior option would be to combine a subsidy with a production quota set at the quantity corresponding to point F, where the slope of the STC for production controls equals $-1/(1 + \delta)$, and the marginal deadweight cost from further reductions

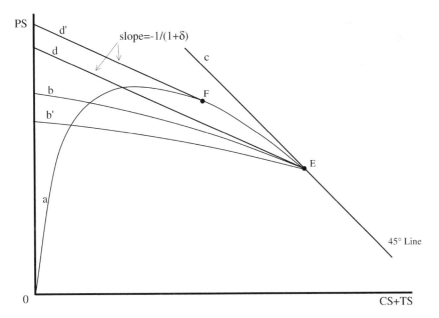

Figure 4. Surplus transformation curves and marginal social opportunity cost.

in quantity equals the marginal deadweight cost of taxation. This option is shown by d' which is parallel to d, but above it. Thus, the curve EFd' shows the efficient STC for this problem, and it may be efficient to specialize in production controls or to use a mix of policies, depending on the size of the transfer to producers, and the values of δ and the other parameters. For small transfers (i.e., points to the right of F), a quota alone is superior, but for larger transfers (i.e., points to the left of F), a quota combined with a subsidy is superior.[7]

3. Implications of international trade for incidence

While the above models can be applied to any commodity, most agricultural commodities are traded internationally, and if we fail to account explicitly for international markets the aggregate welfare measures may not be accurate or relevant as a measure of national welfare. In addition, analysts could use inappropriately small values for elasticities if they failed to recognize that the total supply to the market includes relatively elastically supplied imports, or that the total demand includes relatively elastic demand for exports. Elasticities matter for both the total welfare effects and the international as well as domestic distribution of the effects.

The introduction of international trade changes both the relevant elasticities and the computation of domestic, as compared with global, benefits and costs. It also increases the number of potential policy instruments, since instruments may distinguish among different groups of consumers, or producers, or both. Further, international trade expands geometrically the possibilities for combinations of policies. For instance, U.S. grain policies in recent years combined supply controls with target prices and deficiency payments as well as export subsidies, food aid, and government stocks policies. Since most commodities are actually or potentially tradeable, policies that may appear to be primarily domestic are often made possible only through concomitant trade barriers – e.g., domestic milk market policies are often sustained by an embargo against imports.

We cannot deal effectively here with the full range of the many different and interesting trade-oriented or trade-distorting policies used in agricultural commodity markets. However, the extension of the analysis of quotas and subsidies to the case of traded goods is straightforward and interesting, especially in case of a large-country exporter. This leads naturally to a consideration of export subsidies and price-discrimination, revenue-pooling schemes, in comparison both with one another and with the alternative of a simple output subsidy.

---

[7] Chambers (1995) extended the analysis of Alston and Hurd (1990) and Gardner (1983) to general equilibrium, and found that partial equilibrium measures tend to overstate the welfare effects of stereotypical commodity policies when general equilibrium feedback is important, as may happen in less-developed countries.

3.1. Market power in trade

Large-country trading nations, by definition, can influence the world market price by changing their quantities traded. Hence, as nations they have market power in the international market and can improve net domestic welfare by exploiting their monopoly power in export markets or their monopsony power in import markets. In order to obtain the greatest possible national benefits from production and consumption, a large-country importer might tax imports with an "optimal tariff" while a large-country exporter might charge an "optimal export tax".

To see how this works, consider Figure 5 in which panel a represents the domestic market (with domestic supply, S, and domestic demand, D) and panel b represents the export market (with supply of exports, ES, and demand for exports, ED). The export supply curve is given by the horizontal difference between domestic demand and supply – i.e., at any price, the quantity on ES is equal to the quantity on S minus the quantity on D (similarly, ED is derived, implicitly, as the difference between demand and supply in the rest of the world). With free trade, the equilibrium is given by the intersection of ED and ES, resulting in a price of P_0, so that the quantity produced domestically is Q_0, the quantity consumed domestically is C_0, and the quantity exported is E_0, equal to $Q_0 - C_0$. From the home country's point of view, welfare is maximized when the marginal revenue from sales on the export market (MR in panel b of Figure 5) is equal to the marginal (opportunity) cost of exports, measured by ES. This outcome is achieved when the quantity exported is equal to E_1, which could be achieved by imposing either

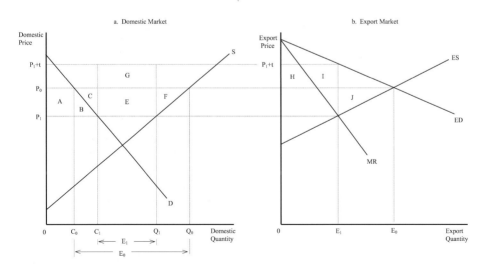

Figure 5. Optimal export tax for a large country.

an export quota equal to E_1 or an export tax equal to t per unit (and at the optimum, t would be equal to the reciprocal of the elasticity of export demand).[8]

With the export tax, the equilibrium price paid by foreigners increases to $P_1 + t$, but the domestic price falls to P_1, so that the quantity produced domestically is Q_1, the quantity consumed domestically is C_1, and the quantity exported is E_1, equal to $Q_1 - C_1$. The welfare effects can be seen in panel a. Domestic consumer surplus increases by area $A + B$, domestic producer surplus falls by area $A + B + C + E + F$, but taxpayers gain revenue of $tE_1 =$ area $G + E$. Thus, the net effect on domestic welfare is a gain equal to area $G - (C + F)$ (equal to area $H + I - J$ in panel b), and this amount is positive and maximized when t is set "optimally". An export quota set at E_1 would have the same effects on producers, consumers, and domestic welfare; the only difference would be that area $G + E$ would be quota rent (going to those given the licenses to export) rather than tax revenue.

Corresponding results apply for an importable good, for which there is an optimal tariff, which equates the marginal cost of imports and the domestic consumer and producer prices (with the tariff rate equal to the reciprocal of the elasticity of supply of imports), and an equivalent optimal import quota. Terms of trade effects also arise through the operation of any other instruments that affect traded quantities in a large-country trader, including quotas and subsidies applied to total production.

3.2. Output quotas for traded goods

An output quota alone cannot be a useful policy for transferring income to producers in a small open economy. When we see an output quota applied by an importing or exporting country that is a price taker in the world market, it is always in conjunction with some other trade-restricting policy. In these cases, trade restrictions prevent international arbitrage from undermining the quota's intended effects: to raise producer returns by restricting supply and thereby raising domestic consumer prices. For instance, milk quotas are generally accompanied by barriers against imports and, when these quotas apply at a sub-national level, barriers to interprovincial or interstate trade.

In a large-country case, where the country can influence the world price, a production quota still does not make much sense for an importer that aims to assist producers. A restriction of domestic output may drive up the domestic and world price for the commodity, but it would be a very inefficient policy, since producers in the rest of the world would benefit without having to restrict their production. In this case, producers could be protected instead by an import quota or a tariff, possibly with an increase rather than a decrease in domestic welfare, since the policy would work to the disadvantage of the rest of the world. Import barriers have been extensively applied as part of the

---

[8] The algebra and diagrams for "optimal" import tariffs and export taxes and related discussion can be found in Corden (1997). Other distortions in the economy may change the optimum trade taxes, as will allowing for $\delta > 0$, which, in this case, implies that the marginal social value of trade tax revenue is greater than one.

protective umbrella for domestic agricultural producers in most countries that protect agriculture, whether they have market power in trade or not.

For a large-country exporter, an output quota offers similar benefits to an export quota (or export tax), but is less efficient since the output quota distorts domestic consumption. A case in point is the farm program for U.S. tobacco, which has been analyzed in these terms by Johnson (1965), Johnson and Norton (1983), Johnson (1984), Sumner and Alston (1984), and Alston and Sumner (1988). These authors all concluded that the U.S. tobacco quota had generated net benefits to the U.S. economy – the U.S. benefits from monopolistic exploitation of the markets in the rest of the world outweighed the losses from distortions in U.S. production and consumption. While not as efficient as an export tax, which is ruled out by the U.S. Constitution, the output quota had achieved many of the same benefits. Clearly, in such setting, a quota is a more efficient means of transferring income to producers than any form of output or export subsidy, which must entail deadweight losses – especially when $\delta > 0$.

3.3. Comparing subsidies on output versus exports

Following Gardner (1983), Alston and Hurd (1990) compared a range of instruments in terms of their costs of achieving a given benefit to producers in the case of a small-country importer or exporter. The results parallel those for the closed economy case. They showed that the introduction of $\delta > 0$ changes the comparison between policies that involve different amounts of government spending as well as between those that involve spending and those that do not, overturning some conventional wisdom that is based on an implicit assumption that $\delta = 0$.

A conventional view is that trade-distorting policies cannot be preferred to a production subsidy as a means of supporting domestic producer income. However, Alston and Hurd (1990) showed that, in the case of a small-country importer, a tariff combined with a quota and an output subsidy might be more efficient than an output subsidy alone, depending on the relative slopes of supply and demand. Moreover, the rankings of policies may change completely when $\delta > 0$. Certainly some tax on trade will be superior to free trade when δ is positive, even in this small-country case. Indeed, an import tariff could yield net social benefits when a dollar of tariff revenue is worth $1 + \delta$ dollars of taxpayer surplus.

It is not possible to rank all policies unambiguously from theory alone. As in the case of a closed economy, the ranking of policies in an open economy depends on the size of the transfer, elasticities of supply and demand, the marginal value of government revenue, as well as the share of production that is traded. Alston, Carter and Smith (1993) compared subsidies on output and exports for both large- and small-country cases. As they showed, the comparison of an export subsidy and an output subsidy for a given producer benefit depends on the difference between the cost of distortions in domestic consumption under the export subsidy and the deadweight losses from additional taxation to fund the additional outlays for the output subsidy. The social cost of consumption distortions is infinitesimal for small transfers, but grows geometrically with rising subsidies. A result that is surprising to some is that, for large values of δ or relatively small transfers, an export subsidy could be more efficient than a subsidy on all output.[9] As well as changing the efficiency ranking of policy instruments, different values of δ change the measure of the taxpayer costs and the net social costs.

3.4. Price discrimination and pooling schemes

A common policy has been to establish statutory authorities (such as marketing boards or state trading enterprises) that are empowered to price discriminate among markets. Some discriminate between fresh and processing uses of a commodity (e.g., various milk marketing authorities) and others between different geopolitical markets (e.g., domestic versus export markets). Among the best-known examples are the Australian and Canadian wheat boards. These types of policies have been studied extensively in general terms [e.g., Alston and Freebairn (1988)] as well as in particular instances [e.g., Parish (1963), Ippolito and Masson (1978), Longworth and Knopke (1982), Sieper (1982)]. A key feature of such schemes is that they are self-financing – i.e., no taxpayer expenditure is required. Rather, different segments of the total market are separated and charged different discriminatory prices, the resulting revenue is pooled, and producers receive and respond to a unit price equal to the average revenue thus obtained.

The simplest case, with a perfectly elastic export demand and a downward-sloping domestic demand, is shown in Figure 6. In this case, the domestic price is set above the export price, since domestic demand is less elastic than export demand, and the producer price (P_p) is equal to a share-weighted average of the domestic price (P_d) and the export price (P_e). The pooled price line is defined such that the pooled revenue for any quantity to producers exactly exhausts the revenue earned from the domestic and export markets. At the equilibrium, this means that total revenue (area $B + C + E + F + G$) equals the revenue from the domestic market (area $A + B + F$) plus revenue from the export market (area G). Hence, area $A = $ area $C + E$.

Alston and Freebairn (1988) extended the analysis to a large-country exporter. Alston, Carter and Smith (1993), following Sieper (1982) and others, argued that such a policy of regulated pricing and revenue pooling could be regarded as the equivalent of either (a) an output subsidy of $P_p - P_e$ per unit financed by a domestic consumption tax of $P_d - P_e$ per unit, or (b) an export subsidy of $P_p - P_e$ per unit financed by a domestic consumption tax of $P_d - P_p$ per unit. In this sense, price-discriminatory, revenue-pooling schemes can be considered as export subsidy programs financed by a tax on a particular group (consumers of the subsidized commodity), rather than on society as a whole. [Alston, Carter and Smith (1995) and Gardner (1995) elaborate on whether this perspective is reasonable.]

---

[9] As discussed by Alston, Carter and Smith (1993), other studies have justified export subsidies as a second-best correction for some other distortion in the economy – e.g., Itoh and Kiyono (1987), Feenstra (1986), and Abbott, Paarlberg and Sharples (1987).

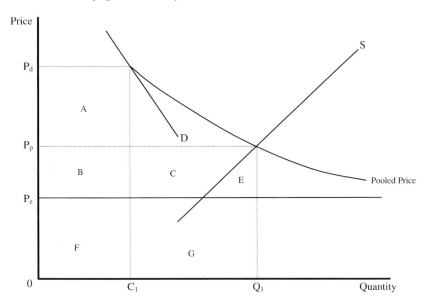

Figure 6. Price discrimination and revenue pooling.

The conclusions drawn from the simplest case – price discrimination and revenue pooling in a small country – apply also to a more general setting with multiple separate markets and market power in trade. For example, Alston and Gray (1998) compared an export subsidy against price discrimination and revenue pooling by a state trader having sole export powers (exemplified by the Canadian Wheat Board, CWB) as alternative ways of achieving a given benefit to producers. They showed that the effective export subsidy per unit must be greater under the policy of a state trader discriminating against the domestic market (since production would be the same under both policies but the domestic price would be lower and domestic consumption greater under the export subsidy). They also found that transfer efficiency was likely to have been greater under the actual CWB policies in 1994 than if an equivalent export subsidy had been used.

4. Multimarket models

The conventional supply and demand model, while powerful, has some limitations. In particular, participants in the commodity market are characterized as either producers or consumers, and their welfare is aggregated accordingly. Even when we disaggregate horizontally, between domestic and foreign producers and consumers, we have still aggregated vertically across various suppliers of factors of production and final consumers.

Our choice of which market to analyze implicitly defines how welfare measures are aggregated. For instance, if we study policy incidence in a retail market, benefits accruing to middlemen are combined with those accruing to all other input suppliers in "producer" surplus; if we study incidence in the market for the farm product, however, benefits to middlemen are part of "consumer surplus". Vertical disaggregation of markets and the resulting welfare measures is important if we are to accurately describe, prescribe, and explain policy choices when the goal of policy is to transfer benefits to specific resource owners or interest groups (such as landowners or agribusiness firms). To disaggregate these measures of policy incidence into more useful subaggregates requires a more elaborate model of supply and demand.

At one extreme, we can envision a totally disaggregated general equilibrium model, in which consumption expenditures are endogenous and depend on factor payments as well as endowment incomes. At the other extreme, we have the single commodity market model, as discussed above. In between lie many intermediate cases with different degrees of elaboration of the vertical structure and factor markets, and the horizontal structure in terms of different commodities and spatial aggregates. Modeling several linked markets allows us to take account of cross-market effects, which may be important for accurately measuring the incidence in the market for the commodity in question, as well as for studying the spillover effects into the related commodity markets.[10]

In what follows we consider small, essentially partial equilibrium, multimarket settings, to see the implications of the vertical structure for incidence among factors. Similar models can also be used to consider the incidence of policy in a multi-output setting – where, when commodities interact in either production or consumption, policies applied in the market for one commodity can have implications for producers and consumers of related commodities. This type of multimarket structure was modeled by Buse (1958) and more recently by Piggott (1992) in terms of the equilibrium prices and quantities. Just, Hueth and Schmitz (1982), Thurman (1991, 1993), Bullock (1993), and Brännlund and Kriström (1996) discuss welfare measures and their interpretations in this type of setting. An early study in this vein was by Hushak (1971).

4.1. Aggregation of goods and welfare

Welfare aggregations for vertically and horizontally linked markets are summarized graphically in Figure 7. Here, land, labor, and other (purchased) farm inputs are used to produce a farm product, and the farm product is used with other (marketing) inputs to produce a retail product. Each of these farming and marketing inputs earns a quasi-rent or producer surplus that can be measured from its supply function, and consumer surplus can be measured from the retail demand function. The interpretation of the area of producer surplus (and, indeed, the associated consumer surplus) in terms of the

---

[10] Such intercommodity interactions are involved in sector-wide (but nevertheless *partial* equilibrium) models of the agricultural sector, such as the USDA's SWOPSIM model, as well as in *general equilibrium* models [such as Higgs (1986)], and are reflected in the results when those models are used to measure the welfare effects of policy.

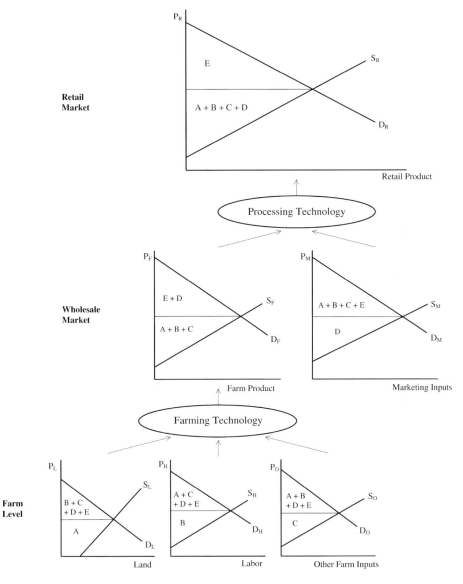

Figure 7. Distribution of welfare in a multimarket model.

underlying surpluses accruing to factors of production and consumers depends on which market is being studied.

The welfare measures defined in each market are related in precise and interesting ways, as proven by Just and Hueth (1979). Provided that all inputs are necessary, and that a positive shutdown price exists for output, the total surplus (the sum of consumer and producer surplus) is equal to area $A + B + C + D + E$ in every market. This means that we can measure the total economic surplus in any of the markets and get the correct answer. However, the interpretations differ among the markets. In the retail market, the consumer surplus accrues to purchasers of the final product and the producer surplus includes the surpluses accruing to all the inputs. Area D accrues to suppliers of marketing inputs, and area $A + B + C$, the sum of the surpluses across inputs used to produce the farm product (area A to landowners, area B to farm labor, and area C to suppliers of purchased farming inputs), accrues to the farm product supplier.

The supply of the farm product at wholesale is derived from the underlying supply functions for inputs used in farming and the farming technology. The demands for the farm product and marketing inputs are derived demands, each depending on retail demand, the processing technology, and the supply of the other. Accordingly, consumer surplus in the farm product market includes retail consumer surplus and the producer surplus accruing to marketing input suppliers, while consumer surplus in the market for marketing inputs includes retail consumer surplus and farm product producer surplus. The demands for all of the inputs used in farming are derived demands, each depending on the demand for the farm product (which is itself a derived demand) and the supplies of the other inputs used in farming. Consumer surplus in each of the farm input markets includes the consumer surplus in the market for the farm product and the quasi-rents accruing to the other farm inputs.[11]

Similar relationships among the surplus measures can be seen in all vertically and horizontally linked markets, so long as the issue is not confounded by price feedback effects (i.e., so long as any endogenous prices of one input are not arguments of supply for another input). In any given market, "consumer" surplus includes the consumer surplus of the market directly above it in the production process (i.e., the market for which it is an input) as well as the quasi-rent accruing to suppliers of other inputs used at the same stage of production. The area of producer surplus in any market includes the quasi-rent accruing to suppliers of all inputs used to produce the product supplied to that market (e.g., farm product and marketing inputs for retail; land, labor, and other inputs for farm product).

A policy that is introduced in the market for any of the factors, or the output, affects the factor suppliers by inducing a shift in the demand for their factor. Hence, for example, whether suppliers of land to the industry in question benefit from a subsidy on purchased inputs (such as, say, a fertilizer subsidy) depends on whether the derived

---

[11] In some settings, general-equilibrium type feedback of price effects into supply and demand equations means that one cannot disentangle the total surplus in such a fashion [for instance, see Thurman (1991, 1993)]. In the meat industry, if supplies of hogs and chickens are related (i.e., if they compete for and both influence the price of feed grains) and the demands are related for pork and poultry, then we have multiple sources of general equilibrium feedback and the producer and consumer surplus areas do not have welfare significance. Here, since all of the underlying factor supply functions and the final demand function are independent of one another, no such problems arise.

demand for land is induced to rise or fall. This depends in turn on a complex set of induced changes in the demands and thus prices of all the other factors, and the cross-elasticities of demand for land with respect to those prices.[12] Thus, as shown in Figure 8, a fertilizer subsidy could lead to an increase in demand for land, but reduced demand for farm labor, an increased supply of the farm product, an increased demand for marketing inputs, and an increased retail supply. In this hypothetical case, landowners, fertilizer suppliers, middlemen, and consumers all gain, but suppliers of labor (i.e., farmers) lose. Producer surplus measured in the market for the agricultural product increases, but within that aggregate, there is a hidden loss to suppliers of farm labor.

In this section we develop some more formal models of policy incidence in multimarket models, to establish the determinants of the types of results illustrated in Figure 8. The distribution of producer surplus among the factors of production is most readily seen in the most basic example, which is presented first, that of two inputs used in fixed proportions to produce a single output. We then relax the assumption of fixed factor proportions.

4.2. Two factors with fixed factor proportions

Figure 9 shows the markets for a retail product (panel a), and the marketing inputs (panel b) and farm product (panel c) used to produce it. Since we have fixed proportions between the farm product (F) and the marketing inputs (M) in the production of the retail product (R), we can choose appropriate quantity units (so that one unit of output is produced using one unit of each of the inputs), and arrange the panels vertically as shown, so that the quantities of the inputs and output change together in lock step.[13]

Given the demand for the retail product (D_R), the technology of production (the fixed factor proportions), and the supply functions for marketing inputs (S_M) and the farm product (S_F), we can derive demand functions for each of the two inputs (D_M and D_F) and the supply function for the retail product (S_R). For any given quantity of output, the willingness to pay for the corresponding quantity of one input is equal to the price per unit of the retail product minus the marginal cost of the other input. Thus, the demand for each input is simply the vertical difference between the retail product demand and the supply of the other input. Similarly, the marginal cost at retail is equal to the sum of the marginal costs of the two inputs per unit of output, so that the retail supply function is simply the vertical sum of the two factor supply functions. These derived supply

---

[12] In the limiting case, when all the other factor prices are exogenous (i.e., the supplies are all perfectly elastic), the issue reduces to whether land and purchased inputs are substitutes or complements; otherwise it is more complicated (although it is essentially the same idea) to establish whether an increase in supply of one factor leads to an increase in demand for another, holding constant the supply functions of the other factors. This can be thought of as a "total" cross-price elasticity of factor demand in the terminology of Buse (1958); also, see Piggott (1992).

[13] Friedman (1976) describes a model of the production of knives using blades and handles in fixed proportions, which was first used by Marshall (1949, pp. 383–384).

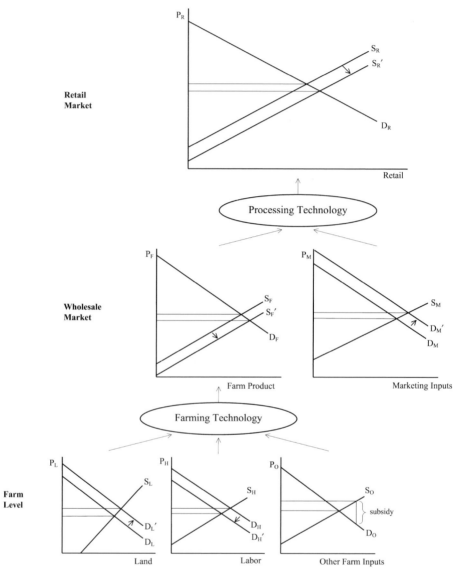

Figure 8. Hypothetical incidence of a subsidy on purchased inputs in a multimarket model.

and demand relationships show how the elasticities of the three underlying functions, and the factor shares, determine the elasticities of output supply and derived demand. Increasing the elasticity of supply of either input increases the elasticity of supply of output and the elasticity of demand for the other input, and increasing the elasticity of demand for output increases the elasticities of demand for both inputs.

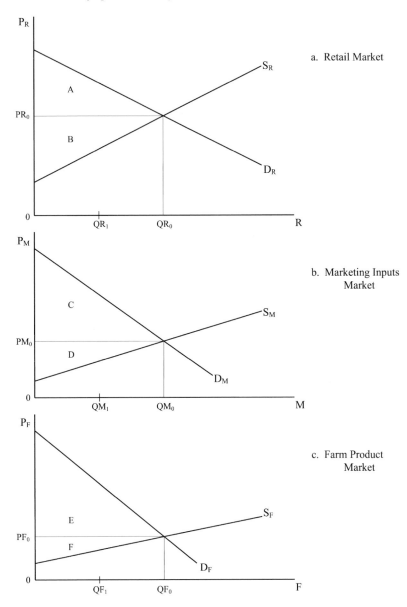

Figure 9. Surplus distribution in a model with two factors used in fixed proportions.

Equilibrium in the retail market is given by the intersection of D_R and S_R, with a quantity of QR_0 and a price of PR_0. Corresponding to this are equilibria in the other markets with quantities and prices of marketing inputs, QM_0 and PM_0, and of the

Table 2
Surplus distribution in a model with two factors used in fixed proportions

Market	Producer surplus (PS)	Consumer surplus (CS)	Total (net) surplus (NS)
Retail	$B = D + F$	A	$A + B = A + D + F$
Marketing input	D	$C = A + F$	$C + D = A + D + F$
Farm product	F	$E = A + D$	$E + F = A + D + F$

Note: The entries in this table refer to areas in Figure 9.

farm product, QF_0 and PF_0. As above, our measures of producer, consumer, and total economic surplus (PS, CS, and NS) depend on which market we look at. Table 2 lists the surplus measures for each market, and shows how they relate to one another, in accordance with the above discussion of vertical markets.

The two-factor, fixed-proportions model can be used to consider the incidence of policies applied in the different markets; for instance, a subsidy or quota in the farm or retail markets. It can easily be seen in the model in Figure 9 that the incidence does not depend on whether a per unit subsidy or quota applies to output or an input when we have fixed factor proportions; only the elasticities of factor supply and retail demand, and factor shares matter. The assumption of fixed factor proportions means a quota, QR_1, in the output market is identically equivalent to the same quota in either input market (QF_1 or QM_1). Similarly, a per unit subsidy on either input would have the exact same price, quantity, and welfare effects as would result if the same per unit subsidy were applied to the output market. Nevertheless, if we choose to study incidence in only one market, we must choose that market with a view to isolating the welfare effects of particular interest. The equivalence of the effects of a policy (quota or subsidy), regardless of whether it applies to an input or output, is a direct consequence of the assumption of fixed factor proportions. In the next section we relax this assumption, and see that the incidence of a policy depends on where it is implemented.

4.3. Two factors with variable factor proportions

Variable factor proportions in production is more realistic and adds some interesting dimensions to the analysis. In this section, we use a market displacement model to consider policy incidence in an output market and two input markets. We can define the output as either a farm product or a retail product. In the first case, the relevant inputs would be land and other farming inputs, whereas, in the second case, inputs would include the farm product and marketing inputs. If we were interested in the effects of a policy on landowners, we must choose the first structure. Similarly, if we were interested in the effects of a policy on middlemen (e.g., processors), we would choose the latter structure.

Two-factor, one-output models of agricultural commodity markets have been of two types. Some have assumed a relatively simple (and restrictive) explicit functional form for the production function, such as the Cobb-Douglas or constant-elasticity-of-substitution (CES) form, or the Leontief fixed-proportions form shown above). Gisser (1993) provides a recent example using a CES model. Others have taken a local linear approximation to a general function, and modeled displacements from an initial equilibrium. Floyd (1965) exemplifies this approach, although he used explicit constant elasticity models for factor supply and final demand rather than leaving those functions in general form. Muth (1964) provides a more complete set of solutions for essentially the same model – without imposing any specific functional forms. This approximation approach is in some senses more general than using explicit functional forms (since it admits more general forms of production technology). It is also usually easier, especially when we extend the analysis to allow for more than two factors or more than one output (although cases may be found where specific functional forms are easier to solve or have other advantages in more accurately representing particular policies).

4.3.1. Equations of the model

In all of these two-factor models, the basic structure includes a final demand, two factor supply equations, a production function (or a cost function) to represent the technology for production of a homogeneous product, Q, using two factors of production, X_1 and X_2, and equations imposing competitive market clearing.[14] Thus, we can model the market equilibrium of a competitive industry in terms of the following six equations:

$$Q = D(P, A) \tag{1a}$$

$$C = c(W_1, W_2)Q \tag{1b}$$

$$X_1 = c_1(W_1, W_2)Q \tag{1c}$$

$$X_2 = c_2(W_1, W_2)Q \tag{1d}$$

$$X_1 = g_1(W_1, B_1) \tag{1e}$$

$$X_2 = g_1(W_2, B_2) \tag{1f}$$

The first equation expresses quantity of the product demanded, Q, as a function of its price, P, and an exogenous demand shifter, A. The second equation shows the industry total cost function, which is assumed to be characterized by constant returns to scale. Thus, unit costs, $c(W_1, W_2) = C/Q$, depend on the two factor prices, and, under competition, factor payments exhaust the total product [i.e., $P = c(W_1, W_2)$]. The third and fourth equations are derived by the application of Shephard's lemma to the cost function, and are Hicksian (output constant) demands for the two factors of

---

[14] In his version of this model, Muth (1964), like Floyd (1965), characterized the technology using a production function instead of a cost function. A cost function is easier to apply, especially for more than two factors [e.g., see Wohlgenant (1982), and Alston, Norton and Pardey (1995)].

production so that $c_i = \partial c(\cdot)/\partial W_i$. The fifth equation expresses the quantity of X_1 supplied as a function of its own price and an exogenous supply shifter, B_1; the sixth equation is the supply of X_2. The endogenous variables are the prices and quantities of the output and inputs (i.e., P, W_1, W_2, Q, X_1, X_2), and the exogenous shifters are A, B_1, and B_2.[15]

Totally differentiating equations (1a–f) and expressing the results in relative change terms (i.e., $dX/X = d\ln X$) yields equations in terms of relative changes and elasticities:[16]

$$d\ln Q = -\eta \, d\ln P + \alpha \tag{1a$'$}$$

$$d\ln P = k_1 \, d\ln W_1 + k_2 \, d\ln W_2 \tag{1b$'$}$$

$$d\ln X_1 = -k_2\sigma \, d\ln W_1 + k_2\sigma \, d\ln W_2 + d\ln Q \tag{1c$'$}$$

$$d\ln X_2 = k_1\sigma \, d\ln W_1 - k_1\sigma \, d\ln W_2 + d\ln Q \tag{1d$'$}$$

$$d\ln X_1 = \varepsilon_1 \, d\ln W_1 + \beta_1 \tag{1e$'$}$$

$$d\ln X_2 = \varepsilon_2 \, d\ln W_2 + \beta_2 \tag{1f$'$}$$

In these equations, α, β_1, and β_2 express the effects of shift variables on demand and supply as general shifts in the quantity direction, in relative change terms. As before, η is the absolute value of the own-price elasticity of output demand, ε_i is the elasticity of supply of factor i, k_i is the cost share of factor i, and σ is the elasticity of substitution between the two factors.[17] This system could be solved either by repeated substitution or by using matrix algebra methods.[18] The solution consists of linear equations expressing relative changes in endogenous prices and quantities as functions of the parameters and the exogenous shifters.

We can use this general model to represent specific price policies that operate through either input or output markets.[19] The shift variables take particular forms to represent the price and quantity effects of a subsidy on an output or an input; they take different values, combined with extreme elasticity assumptions, to represent a quota on an output or an input. For simplicity we will drop one of the input supply shifters by setting $\beta_2 = 0$. The results are summarized in Table 3 and explained below.

---

[15] Muth (1964) also included shifters to represent neutral and biased technical changes, but these are omitted since technical change is not the focus of this analysis.

[16] This derivation uses the fact that the Hicksian factor demand elasticities can be represented in terms of the elasticity of substitution and the factor shares as follows: $\eta_{11}^H = -k_2\sigma$, $\eta_{12}^H = k_2\sigma$, $\eta_{21}^H = k_1\sigma$, $\eta_{22}^H = -k_1\sigma$.

[17] The elasticity of substitution is defined mathematically for the case of constant returns to scale as $\sigma = \sigma_{12} = \sigma_{21} = c_{12}c/c_1c_2$ where c_{12} is the second cross-partial derivative of the cost function, $c(W_1, W_2)$, and c_1 and c_2 are its first derivatives. For perfect substitutes, $\sigma = \infty$, while for fixed factor proportions, $\sigma = 0$.

[18] See Alston, Norton and Pardey (1995, pp. 258–260) for details.

[19] Gardner (1975) used an essentially identical model to analyze marketing margins, and Gardner (1987b) used related methods to analyze various agricultural policies.

Table 3
Price and quantity effects of subsidies or quotas on output or an input in a two-factor model

	Output subsidy (τ_Q)	Input subsidy (τ_1)	Output quota (δ_Q)	Input quota (δ_1)
dln Q	$\dfrac{\eta[\varepsilon_1\varepsilon_2 + \sigma(k_1\varepsilon_1 + k_2\varepsilon_2)]}{D}\tau_Q$	$\dfrac{k_1\varepsilon_1\eta(\sigma+\varepsilon_2)}{D}\tau_1$	$-\delta_Q$	$-\dfrac{k_1\eta(\sigma+\varepsilon_2)}{D''}\delta_1$
dln P	$\dfrac{\eta(\sigma+k_2\varepsilon_1+k_1\varepsilon_2)}{D}\tau_Q$	$-\dfrac{k_1\varepsilon_1(\sigma+\varepsilon_2)}{D}\tau_1$	δ_Q/η	$\dfrac{k_1(\sigma+\varepsilon_2)}{D''}\delta_1$
dln X_1	$\dfrac{\eta\varepsilon_1(\sigma+\varepsilon_2)}{D}\tau_Q$	$\dfrac{[(k_2\sigma+k_1\eta)\varepsilon_2+\eta\sigma]\varepsilon_1}{D}\tau_1$	$-\dfrac{\varepsilon_1(\sigma+\varepsilon_2)}{D'}\delta_Q$	$-\delta_1$
dln X_2	$\dfrac{\eta\varepsilon_2(\sigma+\varepsilon_1)}{D}\tau_Q$	$-\dfrac{k_1(\sigma-\eta)\varepsilon_1\varepsilon_2}{D}\tau_1$	$-\dfrac{\varepsilon_2(\sigma+\varepsilon_1)}{D'}\delta_Q$	$\dfrac{k_1(\sigma-\eta)\varepsilon_2}{D''}\delta_1$
dln W_1	$\dfrac{\eta(\sigma+\varepsilon_2)}{D}\tau_Q$	$-\dfrac{(k_1\sigma+k_2\eta+\varepsilon_2)\varepsilon_1}{D}\tau_1$	$-\dfrac{(\sigma+\varepsilon_2)}{D'}\delta_Q$	$\dfrac{(k_1\sigma+k_2\eta+\varepsilon_2)}{D''}\delta_1$
dln W_2	$\dfrac{\eta(\sigma+\varepsilon_1)}{D}\tau_Q$	$-\dfrac{k_1(\sigma-\eta)\varepsilon_1}{D}\tau_1$	$-\dfrac{(\sigma+\varepsilon_1)}{D'}\delta_Q$	$\dfrac{k_1(\sigma-\eta)}{D''}\delta_1$

$D = \sigma(k_1\varepsilon_1 + k_2\varepsilon_2 + \eta) + \eta(k_2\varepsilon_1 + k_1\varepsilon_2) + \varepsilon_1\varepsilon_2 > 0$, $D' = \sigma(k_1\varepsilon_1 + k_2\varepsilon_2) + \varepsilon_1\varepsilon_2 > 0$, and $D'' = \sigma\eta + \varepsilon_2(k_1\eta + k_2\sigma) > 0$.

4.3.2. Output subsidy

An output subsidy at a rate $100\tau_Q$ percent can be represented as an upwards shift of demand. Thus, setting $\tau_Q = 0.1$ gives the effects of a 10 percent output subsidy. In the model, the demand shifter, α, operates in the quantity direction, so we set $\alpha = \eta\tau_Q$ to represent an output subsidy of τ_Q. The relative changes in quantities and prices as a result of an output subsidy are given in the first column of Table 3. The subsidy results in an increase in both the quantity and *producer* price of output, while the change in *consumer* price is a decrease: dln $P - \tau_Q$. At the same time, with the increase in production, the demands for both factors of production have increased, reflected in increases in both the quantity and price of each factor.

Given the price and quantity changes in Table 3, we can estimate the changes in consumer and producer welfare in any of the three markets, provided that both inputs are necessary and that a positive shut-down price exists in the output market. For simplicity, we can approximate the changes in consumer (or producer) surplus using the percentage change in the relevant price, multiplied by the initial value of consumption (or production). These approximations measure the rectangle of surplus (given by the price change on the initial quantity) but leave out the triangle associated with the policy-induced change in quantity. For small changes in prices, the rectangle is very large relative to the triangle, and the approximation error is small.

The benefits to consumers are approximately equal to the relative change in the consumer price multiplied by the value of initial consumption – i.e., $\Delta CS \approx -(\text{dln } P - \tau_Q)PQ = (\text{dln } Q/\eta)PQ = \text{dln } Q(PQ/\eta)$. Similarly, the benefits to producers can be approximated by $\Delta PS \approx (\text{dln } P)PQ = \text{dln } Q(PQ/\varepsilon)$.[20] This amount is equal to the sum of the increases in producer surplus for the two factor suppliers. The benefit from an output subsidy to suppliers of input i is approximately equal to the relative change in supplier price multiplied by the initial value of that input – i.e., $\Delta PS_i \approx (\text{dln } W_i)W_i X_i = \text{dln } X_i (W_i X_i/\varepsilon_i) = \text{dln } X_i (k_i PQ/\varepsilon_i)$. In other words, benefits to consumers, producers, and input suppliers are approximately proportional to the increases in their respective quantities consumed and supplied.

The benefits to suppliers of input 1 relative to suppliers of input 2, $\Delta PS_1/\Delta PS_2$, can be approximated as $k_1(\sigma + \varepsilon_2)/k_2(\sigma + \varepsilon_1)$. Clearly, a greater share of the benefits goes to a factor as it becomes more important (accounting for a larger share of costs) or less elastically supplied. Let input 1 be land and consider the extreme case where $\varepsilon_1 = 0$ (i.e., the supply of land is fixed), and consider the benefits to landowners relative to other input suppliers: $k_1(\sigma + \varepsilon_2)/k_2\sigma$. If all the benefits of an output subsidy went to landowners, as is often claimed, this ratio would be ∞. However, this can occur only in one of two extreme cases: either the price of input 2 is fixed and there is no producer surplus for its suppliers ($\varepsilon_2 = \infty$), or factor proportions are fixed ($\sigma = 0$).

The conditions under which all of the benefits from an output subsidy accrue to landowners are extreme, but may be appropriate at some levels of aggregation. However, it is often not adequately recognized that both factor supply conditions and policies differ importantly between agriculture in aggregate and particular agricultural industries. For instance, in his analysis of policies for individual commodities, Gisser (1993) assumed a fixed supply of land for each individual crop while all other inputs were perfectly elastically supplied. These assumptions are clearly inappropriate for individual commodities, and guarantee that all of the benefits would go to landowners. Such assumptions are more reasonable for agriculture as a whole. For instance, Rosine and Helmberger (1974) assumed a fixed supply of land and a perfectly elastic supply of other inputs except labor (which had a large supply elasticity of 2.6), and concluded that 92 percent of the benefits from U.S. farm programs went to landowners, and the other 8 percent went to suppliers of labor. The problem with this analysis is that Rosine and Helmberger (1974) modeled agriculture as a single industry, as though a single uniform policy applied to every commodity. The assumptions made in either study may be appropriate in some context or at some level of aggregation, but Gisser (1993) failed to match his parameters to his commodity aggregates, and Rosine and Helmberger (1974) could not match their policy instrument to theirs.

4.3.3. Input subsidy

To represent an input subsidy of τ_1 per unit on input 1, we set $\alpha = 0$ and $\beta_1 = \varepsilon_1 \tau_1$. The corresponding relative changes in prices and quantities are shown in the second column in Table 3. Because the subsidy reduces the price output suppliers must pay for the

---

[20] ε is the elasticity of output supply: $\varepsilon = \{\varepsilon_1\varepsilon_2 + \sigma(k_1\varepsilon_1 + k_2\varepsilon_2)\}/\{\sigma + k_1\varepsilon_2 + k_2\varepsilon_1\}$.

input, the marginal cost of output production is reduced and the output supply function shifts down. In turn, this shift implies an increase in output quantity, a decrease in the output price, and an increase in consumer welfare. A subsidy on X_1 unambiguously increases the quantity of X_1 demanded, by lowering the price paid by output producers (dln $W_1 < 0$). The change in price received by suppliers of X_1, including the subsidy, is dln $W_1 + \tau_1 > 0$, giving rise to benefits to suppliers of X_1.

The effects on the X_2 market are ambiguous, hinging on whether the inputs are substitutes or complements in production. If the two inputs are gross complements (i.e., $\sigma < \eta$), the lower price of X_1 results in an increase in demand for X_2, and the quantity, price, and producer surplus for suppliers of X_2 all increase. If the two inputs are gross substitutes (i.e., $\sigma > \eta$), however, a lower price of X_1 causes a reduction in demand for X_2, and consequent reductions in price, quantity, and producer surplus in the X_2 market. Thus, an input subsidy aimed at transferring income to suppliers of X_1 could either confer benefits or impose costs on suppliers of X_2.

The output and input subsidies can be compared in terms of their effectiveness at achieving particular effects for a given subsidy expenditure since, for equal subsidy expenditures, $\tau_Q P Q = \tau_1 W_1 X_1$, so that $\tau_Q = k_1 \tau_1$. From the equation for dln Q, the output effect of a τ_Q subsidy on output is greater than the effect of spending the same amount as a τ_1 subsidy on input 1 if $\varepsilon_2 > \varepsilon_1$ (so long as $\sigma > 0$ and $\varepsilon_1 > 0$).[21] Hence, for the same taxpayer cost, consumers will benefit more from a subsidy on output than from a subsidy on X_1 only if X_1 is relatively inelastically supplied. On the other hand, making the same substitution (such that $\tau_Q = k_1 \tau_1$) in the equation for dln X_1, suppliers of X_1 necessarily benefit more from a subsidy on X_1 than from an output subsidy with the same taxpayer cost, unless we have fixed factor proportions ($\sigma = 0$). In this case, X_1 suppliers are indifferent between the two subsidies. Finally, using the equation for dln X_2, suppliers of X_2 will always prefer a subsidy on output over a subsidy on the other input (again, unless $\sigma = 0$, in which case suppliers of X_2 are indifferent between the two policies).

4.3.4. Quotas on output or an input

The same model can be used to explore the implications of quantitative restrictions on inputs or on output, as done by Floyd (1965), for example. The effects of introducing a quota on output can be analyzed using the solutions above, by making the effective demand perfectly inelastic (by setting $\eta = 0$ in the solutions) and defining the displacement as a quantity reduction using $\alpha = -\delta_Q$ (where δ_Q is the proportional reduction in quantity from the competitive solution) so that (1a') becomes dln $Q = -\delta_Q$. The effects on price and consumer surplus are obtained using dln $P = -$ dln Q/η, where

---

[21] Parish and McLaren (1982, p. 12) report an equivalent result, although they were identifying the least-cost way of achieving a given effect on output, an output subsidy or an input subsidy. They considered a case where one of the inputs was supplied by a decreasing-cost industry.

η is the actual demand elasticity (in absolute value terms). Similarly, the effects of introducing a quota on one input, X_1, can be analyzed by making the effective supply of that factor perfectly inelastic ($\varepsilon_1 = 0$) and defining the displacement as a quantity shift by $\beta_1 = -\delta_1$ (where δ_1 is the proportional reduction from the competitive solution) so that (1d′) becomes dln $X_1 = -\delta_1$. The last two columns in Table 3 show the effects of a quota that reduces output by a fraction δ_Q, and a quota that reduces the quantity of X_1 by a fraction δ_1, respectively.

An output quota raises the consumer price and reduces the demand for both inputs, harming consumers and suppliers of both inputs. These effects are offset partially by the quota rents accruing to quota owners: only quota owners benefit, and their benefits are smaller than the costs imposed on consumers and input suppliers. The consumer share of the cost of the output quota depends on the elasticity of demand relative to the elasticity of output supply. The distribution of the cost between input suppliers can be seen in terms of the ratio, $\Delta PS_1/\Delta PS_2$, which is approximately equal to $k_1(\sigma + \varepsilon_2)/k_2(\sigma + \varepsilon_1)$. This is identical to the ratio of the benefits to the input suppliers from an output subsidy, only now the effects are negative: suppliers of an input bear more of the cost of an output quota, the less elastic is the supply of the input or the bigger is its share of costs.

An input quota also raises the output price, resulting in losses to consumers. Assuming that they own the quota, suppliers of input 1 gain from a quota on X_1 (in the relevant range of quota quantities, their losses as suppliers of X_1 from the reduction in quantity are more than offset by their gains in quota rent).[22] Suppliers of the other input, X_2, may gain or lose, depending on whether the two inputs are gross substitutes ($\sigma > \eta$), in which case they gain, or gross complements ($\sigma < \eta$), in which case they lose. These results are opposite those for a subsidy on X_1: when the two inputs are gross substitutes, suppliers of X_2 lose as a result of a subsidy on X_1 but gain when the quantity of X_1 is restricted by a quota. Thus, for example, landowners are likely to favor acreage allotments over output quotas, and they may be supported in this view by suppliers of other inputs that are close substitutes for land.

4.3.5. Combining instruments

As discussed above, single instruments are likely to be less efficient than multiple instruments combined. In the single-market model, we saw that an output quota at the competitive quantity, combined with an output subsidy, would be equivalent to a lump-sum transfer to producers (more precisely, to whoever owns the quotas). We also saw that it would be more efficient to set the quota below the competitive quantity if the social opportunity cost of government spending were $1 + \delta$ dollars per dollar of spending. The same ideas apply in the same ways in the context of the two-factor model,

---

[22] The effects on W_1 in the case of an input quota are obtained assuming suppliers of X_1 own the quota and the quota rents are included in W_1. The price of X_1 excluding the quota rent, V_1, can be deduced using dln $V_1 = -$ dln X_1/ε_1, where ε_1 is the actual supply elasticity. These two effects can be combined to determine the size of the quota rent.

with a less-aggregated view of producer surplus. That is, if the objective of a policy were to transfer income to suppliers of X_1, an efficient policy would be to combine an input quota on X_1 (set so its marginal cost per dollar of benefit to the input suppliers is $1 + \delta$) with a subsidy on X_1.

The effects of combining an output subsidy with an input quota, a common policy in the United States, can be seen by combining the elements in the first and last columns of Table 3. The elements in the first column have to be adjusted to reflect the fixed supply of land, by setting $\varepsilon_1 = 0$, before they are added to the elements in the last column. In a typical representation, the effects on output and producer prices are likely to be in the same direction as with an output subsidy alone (i.e., both quantity and producer price increase), but the magnitudes of changes are reduced by the input quota. Of course, an input quota could be set such that output is less than the competitive quantity, more than offsetting the effects of the subsidy on quantity produced. Thus the effect on consumption and the consumer price is ambiguous, depending on parameter values and the size of the transfer. The effect of the combined policy on the rental price for land is unambiguously positive. If the two inputs were gross substitutes ($\sigma > \eta$), then the input quota on land and the output subsidy both would act to increase the demand for X_2, causing its price and quantity to rise with benefits to the suppliers. If land and X_2 were gross complements, however, X_2 and W_2 may rise or fall.

Understanding some subtler policy choices may require a finer disaggregation into a larger number of groups that have distinct interests. Some [e.g., Babcock, Carter and Schmitz (1990)] have suggested that agribusiness interests (including both suppliers of inputs purchased by farmers and suppliers of inputs combined with farm products in processing) are politically influential, and thus there is merit in considering the incidence of policy alternatives on agribusiness in attempting to understand policy choices. To do this requires a less aggregative model.[23]

5. Supply controls – some extensions to the analysis

Thus far, the welfare effects of policies have been analyzed under a number of assumptions. We now begin to consider how the results may change when some of these assumptions are relaxed, and more realistic policy and market characteristics are introduced. First, in the present section (Section 5), we consider the implications for the analysis of quotas when we allow for limits on transferability, endogenous quality, quotas on inputs (as a proxy for output), and quotas under variability. Then, in subsequent sections we consider some further extensions to models for a more general set of policies, including other aspects of variability (Section 6), enforcement costs (Section 7), and dynamic responses (Section 8).

---

[23] For instance, Alston, Carter and Wohlgenant (1989) extended the two-factor model to a three-factor model of a competitive agricultural commodity market, which they used to derive and illustrate the conditions under which agribusiness firms (i.e., middlemen or farm input suppliers) may gain or lose from different types of farm policies.

5.1. Quota ownership and transferability

In the analysis above, it was assumed that quota was given to producers, so that quota rents may be included in producer surplus. This assumption may be accurate for a new quota scheme, since quota is usually allocated to producers based on past production so that initially, quota owners are also producers. When the quota is freely transferable by lease or sale, as is often assumed, the interests of quota owners and producers become increasingly disparate over time. This arises because the original quota recipients receive a windfall gain of the quota rents accruing over the life of the policy (or the equivalent value by selling the quota), regardless of whether they continue to produce or continue to own the quota. On the other hand, producers who purchase or lease quota incur quota rents as a cost of production. As a result, in many instances, it is appropriate to treat quota rents separately from quasi-rents accruing to the suppliers of other inputs.

The distinction between producers and quota owners adds one complication to the standard analysis of a quota. Another is introduced when restrictions on the transferability of quota are imposed. There are usually limits on who may buy or lease quota, whether they are allowed to lease or must buy the asset, and how much quota an individual may own or use. In addition, there are often rules that make transfers inefficient (e.g., regulated rental or purchase prices, restrictions on when transfers may occur or the size of transactions, or a requirement that all transfers must be made through a regulatory agency). If any of the restrictions are binding, then quota will not be allocated to the most efficient producers, costs will not be minimized, and the unrestricted marginal cost curve is no longer relevant. Higher production costs arising from restrictions on quota ownership or use may mean a reduction in producer quasi-rents, a reduction in quota rents, or both, but unambiguously reduce both the sum of quasi-rents and quota rents, and net social welfare.[24] Barichello and Cunningham-Dunlop (1987) documented comprehensively the nature of the restrictions on quota ownership and transfer in Canadian agriculture and the sources of efficiency loss that they entailed.

The efficiency loss resulting from restrictions on quota transfer has been the subject of several empirical studies, but has been more often ignored in both theoretical and empirical analysis of quotas in agriculture. Alston (1986) estimated that limits on transferability of hen quota increased the costs of producing eggs in Victoria, Australia, by approximately 20 percent. Rucker, Thurman and Sumner (1995) evaluated the implications of restrictions on inter-county transfers of U.S. flue-cured tobacco quota. They found that a move to free transferability would increase quota rents by 3.5 percent, but would also entail a 2.1 percent loss of producer surplus accruing to growers. Bureau et al. (1997) found that cross-border transferability of sugar quota in the European Union would result in a very substantial redistribution of production with important effects on net welfare and quota rents – even *within* country transferability would confer

---

[24] In addition, going beyond the static analysis, Lermer and Stanbury (1985) suggested that restrictions on who may own quota increase the risk associated with owning quota, since such restrictions mean quota is held in relatively undiversified portfolios, and this cost of risk is leveled against the quota rents.

considerable benefits. A number of studies have considered the implications of transferable quotas for milk. The issue of milk quota transferability in New South Wales was modeled by Neutze (1961), Parish (1963), Lloyd (1971), and more recently measured by Lembit et al. (1988), Tozer (1993), and Drynan et al. (1994). Milk quotas were introduced in the European Community in 1984 and have been much analyzed since, beginning with Burrell (1989). Recent studies measuring the benefits of transferable quotas include Guyomard et al. (1996) for French milk, and Boots, Oude-Lansink and Peerlings (1997) for Dutch milk.

Despite the deadweight costs associated with limits on transferability, imperfectly transferable quotas continue to be the norm. Sieper (1982, p. 65) suggested that the law of restricted quota transferability "may be as well established as the law of demand" and hence, such restrictions should not be assumed away lightly when analyzing quota policies.

5.2. Quotas and quality

The typical policy analysis assumes that the commodity of interest is homogeneous. However, commodities are rarely homogeneous, and output controls can lead to distortions in the mix of qualities produced. That the United States produces and exports high-quality flue-cured tobacco, while importing low-quality tobacco, is thought to be – at least in part – a response to the tobacco marketing quotas. Such quality responses to quantity controls can be seen in terms of the Alchian and Allen (1964) theorem and Barzel's (1976) alternative approach to taxation.

The Alchian and Allen theorem concerns the effects of per unit costs on the relative consumption of high-quality and low-quality goods. The original example concerned "good" and "bad" grapes grown in California. From an individual consumer's perspective, prices are fixed, and the price of each quality of grapes for a consumer in, say, New York increases by the transportation cost. Thus, good grapes become relatively cheaper for a consumer in New York, and hence, a New Yorker will consume a larger proportion of good grapes compared with a person in California who has identical preferences and means. An analogous result holds for producers, as described by Borcherding and Silberberg (1978) in their analysis of why Washington apple growers "ship the good apples out". The Alchian and Allen theorem holds for individual consumers and producers under certain conditions, and applies for any per unit cost that meets criteria described by Umbeck (1980). Such costs include per unit taxes and quota rents, the only difference being that the tax rate is exogenous while quota rent is endogenously determined by the interactions of supply and demand, given the quota quantity.

Barzel (1976) addressed a similar phenomenon at the market level in his alternative approach to taxation. Barzel noted that every commodity is more or less a bundle of characteristics. If a per unit tax is imposed, the tax statute will use a subset of characteristics to define the commodity, assuming that an exhaustive description is either impossible or very costly. As a result, the per unit tax is actually taxing the defining characteristics. In maximizing their profits subject to the tax, producers may alter the characteristics included in their units of production. Barzel (1976) showed that the quantity of the defining characteristics (specified in the tax statute) will decrease, and the other characteristics will increase on a per unit basis.

Just as the specification of a per unit tax will use some characteristics to define a "unit", so will the specification of a production quota. In general, a quota will be specified in terms of the commodity's physical characteristics, e.g., weight. Quota rents act as a per unit tax, so that Barzel's model can be applied and used to predict that, although the physical quantity of a commodity is restricted by the quota, other characteristics of the commodity, which implicitly define its quality, will increase. Thus, a quota will lead to an increase in quality.

To estimate the welfare effects of quality responses to an output quota, James (2000) specified a model of two qualities of the same commodity, and imposed a quota to be allocated between the two markets. The average quality, measured as the proportion of production and consumption in the high-quality market, increased as the quota quantity was reduced. The increase in quality increased the producer benefits (exclusive of quota rent) and decreased the consumer losses from a given quota quantity, relative to the case where quality was held constant. However, the quota rent generated by a given quota quantity was smaller than that generated in the constant-quality case, reducing the efficiency of the policy as a means of transferring income to producers. When producers alter the quality of their production in response to a quota policy, the actual transfer achieved from a given quota is smaller and a more restrictive quota must be imposed in order to achieve the desired transfer, relative to the case where quality remains unchanged.

5.3. Output versus input controls and slippage

Production quotas as such are rarely observed. Usually, quotas restrict quantities marketed rather than those produced, and are typically found in industries where production is relatively controllable (e.g., tobacco, where weather effects on yields are relatively small) or in industries where marketing is controlled and a secondary market or storage is available to absorb excess production (e.g., manufacturing milk markets absorb production in excess of fluid milk quotas). When output quotas have been used for commodities for which production or marketing is not controlled, producers have found ways to subvert the quota, either legally or illegally. For instance, a marketing quota on feedgrains can be subverted by vertically integrating a grain enterprise with a livestock enterprise. Some response of this type occurred during the Australian experiment with wheat delivery quotas during 1969–1975.

The difficulty of controlling production or marketing of output may explain, in part, the importance of input quotas in agriculture, especially acreage limitations on crops. Input controls may have been used as a proxy for output controls. In many cases, inputs are easier to control and measure than output. For instance, hen quotas were used to control supply in the Australian and Canadian egg industries because the raw farm product in that industry is ready for final consumption, making production virtually impossible to monitor.

Although input controls may be easier to enforce, they can be less effective as a control over production, and less efficient than output quotas in other senses.[25] Given an input restriction, producers will inevitably alter their production decisions in order to make the costs of that restriction less binding. The most immediate response may be to use the highest quality of the restricted input (e.g., the most fertile land) so that the average productivity of that input increases. In addition, producers will likely intensify their use of other inputs, so that production is greater than it would have been if input proportions had remained unchanged. In the longer run, new varieties or production technologies may be adopted in order to increase output given the input restriction. All of these effects reduce the effectiveness of an input quota in restricting output, a phenomenon often referred to as "slippage".

With acreage controls, slippage is manifested in yield increases. The extent of slippage under acreage restrictions is governed by the elasticity of substitution between land and other inputs. If this elasticity is zero, output is reduced in proportion to the reduction in land use, and there is no slippage. If it is not zero, output is reduced by a smaller proportion than land is, and in order to achieve a given effect on output, an even tighter restriction on the input is necessary. Some studies have found slippage to be quite substantial.

The combination of acreage restrictions with price supports may have encouraged the adoption of varieties and cultural practices that increased yield at the expense of quality, as noted by Brandow (1977, pp. 258). For instance, Foster and Babcock (1990, 1993) estimated that the use of acreage allotments for tobacco had a very significant effect on both the level and the growth rate of tobacco yields, as was shown after the switch to poundage (marketing) quotas in 1965, when yields fell by 12 percent. Tobacco quality is said to have fallen under input allotments and risen under poundage quotas [e.g., Seagraves (1983)]. Similarly, James and Alston (2002) found a statistically significant reduction in an index of French wheat quality in response to set-asides implemented as part of the 1992 reform of the Common Agricultural Policy.

Environmental externalities associated with agricultural production may have implications for the choice between input controls and output controls.[26] When input quotas provide a second-best correction for another distortion, such as an environmental externality, they may be more efficient than output controls; indeed, they could improve net welfare. Input controls that lead to intensification of production in order to increase

---

[25] We can use the equilibrium displacement model presented in Section 4 to compare an input quota on X_1, and an output quota, both of which reduce output and raise output price by the same amount, by fixing $\delta_Q = k_1 \eta (\sigma + \varepsilon_2) \delta_1 / D''$.

[26] Lichtenberg and Zilberman (1986) modeled the effects of a target-price cum deficiency-payment scheme in the presence of environmental externalities.

yields (e.g., output per cow, per hen, or per acre) might reduce or increase externalities associated with agricultural production. For instance, an acreage control *will* lead
to an increase in the intensity of chemical use on the restricted acreage and *may* lead to
an overall increase or decrease in agricultural chemical use (depending on the relative
sizes of the scale and substitution effects). Therefore, an acreage control may increase or
decrease the potential for externalities from agricultural chemicals. An increase seems
more likely than a decrease in this case, especially since it seems likely that some externalities are a function of the intensity of use of a polluting input, more than a function
of the total use.[27] Alternatively, if a quota were applied to chemical inputs, rather than
to land or output, output would be reduced and there would be a clear advantage of
reduced chemical pollution. Similarly, hen quotas are likely to reduce any externalities
associated with effluent disposal and might reduce them better than would an output
quota that resulted in the same quantity of eggs produced.

5.4. Quotas and variability

A number of studies have examined the effect of variability of supply or demand on
the impacts of quotas. Variability in supply or demand can change the market outcomes
under a quota, and may accordingly alter the effects of the quota on welfare and its
distribution. A marketing (or production) quota insulates input suppliers from the effects
of demand variability, but exacerbates the effects of demand variability on output price
(by making supply perfectly inelastic). As a result, consumer welfare and quota rent
have to absorb all of the variability from demand. By the same token, consumers are
insulated from variability in supply (or marginal cost), which is absorbed entirely by
changes in producer welfare and quota rent.

Variability may also influence the producers' planned production choices under
marketing quotas. Alston and Quilkey (1980) presented some heuristic arguments,
suggesting that risk-neutral producers would be expected to aim to overproduce,
on average, when production is uncertain. More recent studies have formalized and
extended this analysis, with mixed results [e.g., Fraser (1986, 1995), Babcock (1990),
and Borges and Thurman (1994)].

Variability may also imply some response by policymakers when markets change.
When demand grows under a quota, either price must rise to clear the market, or
the quota quantity must increase, or some combination of the two must happen.
How the policy is allowed to adjust to accommodate the changes in the market has
distributional implications. Sumner and Wohlgenant (1985) raised this issue in relation
to the incidence of cigarette taxes on the U.S. tobacco market, Sumner and Alston
(1984) elaborate on the same point in relation to more general shifts in demand for
tobacco, and Brown and Martin (1996) provide some further results.

---

[27] Hertel (1989) suggested that, without environmental targeting, acreage set-asides likely exacerbate the
chemical pollution of streams and groundwater.

6. Variability, stabilization, and policy risk

The inherent variability in agricultural markets is widely recognized. In fact, it is often used as a justification for government intervention. Many policies have been implemented in the guise of stabilization but have their primary effect on raising the average returns to producers. As well as influencing the goals and rationale for policies, variability may change the incidence of a given policy. Policies that have the same incidence in a static sense, or the same incidence when supply and demand are at their expected values, may have entirely different incidence when supply or demand shift, or when actual values are realized. This section discusses issues related to variability, its effects on the typical static welfare analysis, and the trade-off between market risk and policy risk created by government intervention.

6.1. The stabilization trade-off

As was shown above for the case of a production quota, in general, policies that stabilize one dimension of the market (e.g., quantity) will inevitably increase the variability in some other dimension (e.g., price, quota rent, producer welfare, or consumer welfare). This is a common theme in the literature on stabilization policies. Policies that reduce price variability or output variability at the farm level are likely to destabilize some other variable, such as gross or net revenue, which may be a more relevant target for stabilization. Indeed, some policies might reduce the year-to-year variation in prices while increasing the odds of a market collapse.[28] Some such policies have stabilized prices, quantities, gross revenues, or net incomes for some market participants, but in doing so they have increased the variability experienced by others.

Several studies have examined this phenomenon in the context of trade policies and the variability of international prices. Johnson (1975, 1991) analyzed worldwide impacts of domestic agricultural policies and concluded, as Josling (1977) did, that freer world trade would lessen international price variability for most agricultural products. Sarris and Freebairn (1983) showed that, in the case of wheat, free trade would provide generally much higher and less variable world prices.[29] These studies showed that variability must be accommodated by adjustments somewhere in the market, and if one avenue for adjustment is closed (e.g., prices in one country), others must carry more of the burden. The variable import levies implemented as part of the Common Agricultural Policy in the European Union provide an excellent example. Under this policy, import tariffs were varied in order to offset changes in the world price, so that internal commodity prices in the European Union were held constant. However, this policy increased the variability of world prices by two means. First, none of the

---

[28] Brian Wright (personal communication) likened a buffer stock scheme to eliminating the minor bumps in the road in exchange for introducing a 100-foot drop somewhere down the road; an odd notion of stabilization.

[29] See studies in Sumner (1988), especially cautionary comments by Bruce Gardner (pp. 170–173).

variability originating from other countries was accommodated by the European Union. Second, the policy meant that any variability in EU supply and demand had to be absorbed by international markets.

6.2. Welfare analysis in variable markets

A number of issues arise when we modify the typical static welfare analysis to account for variation in a market. One such issue is that the equivalence between certain policies in a static setting may break down. For instance, in our initial discussion of a target-price deficiency payments program, we noted that in a static setting this would be equivalent to a per unit subsidy (of $P_1 - P_2$ in Figure 1). However, this is not true when supply or demand changes.

Consider a parallel, outward shift in demand. In the case of a target-price policy, producer price, and thus production, remain unchanged, while the consumer price increases and taxpayer costs are reduced, with a reduction in deadweight loss. In the case of a constant per unit subsidy, the same demand shift results in increased producer and consumer prices, increases in production and consumption, and an increase in taxpayer costs, but no change in deadweight loss. After demand has shifted, a smaller per unit subsidy is required to achieve the same effect on producer welfare as the original target price policy. In other words, the equivalence among instruments is conditional on a given set of market conditions.[30]

In addition to leading to a breakdown of equivalence among policy instruments, variability means that the expected (ex ante) incidence of policy will differ from the actual (ex post) incidence. Furthermore, because measures of policy incidence are nonlinear functions of random variables (prices and quantities), the expected incidence may differ from the incidence when markets are at their expected values. Those engaged in measuring assistance to agriculture often look backwards at the actual income redistribution conferred by a policy rather than what may have been intended or anticipated before market conditions were realized. In some settings, or for some questions, the ex post measure may be misleading.

A floor price scheme is a good example. Suppose the government guarantees producers a minimum price for their commodity. In the typical ex post analysis, if the price floor had not been binding, it would be concluded that the policy had not conferred any benefits on producers, as if the policy had not existed. However, an ex ante measure would take into account the implicit assistance from the policy, which is based on the probability that the floor price would be binding. Bardsley and Cashin (1990), following Gardner (1977), suggested that the assistance provided by a government minimum price guarantee is equal to the value of an equivalent put option, and this value can be assessed

---

[30] In addition to domestic demand and supply conditions, when the commodity of interest is traded, changes in export demand or import supply may also break down the equivalence of policies applied domestically or at the border [e.g., see Tyers and Falvey (1988), Falvey and Lloyd (1991)].

using the Black-Scholes formula. Thus, whether the price floor is binding or not, the possibility that it will bind amounts to a transfer of benefits to producers from taxpayers. Bardsley and Cashin (1990, p. 219) estimated that the underwriting assistance provided an implicit transfer from Australian taxpayers to Australian wheat growers worth about A\$20–40 million per year from 1979/80 through 1985/86, equivalent to a subsidy rate of about 2–4 percent.

6.3. Producer and policy responses

Variability and policies that affect the degree of market variability also have indirect effects. Risk averse producers may respond systematically to policies that change price variability. In addition, changes in market conditions may provoke policy responses.

Innes and Rausser (1989) considered the implications of price stabilization for the incidence of the stereotypical U.S. commodity programs. They argued that if producers are risk averse and contingent claim (e.g., insurance) markets are incomplete, price stabilization will induce a supply response. As a result, producers may produce more for a given guaranteed price than they would for the same expected price. This producer response will modify the incidence of the policy. In addition, a policy that stabilizes prices or net incomes can confer welfare gains even when there is no behavioral response, under certain assumptions about risk attitudes [see also Moschini (1984) and Innes (1990)]. Innes and Rausser (1989) suggested that these effects could be so large that the conventional welfare implications of a target price with deficiency payments are reversed: producers can be made worse off, and society as a whole, better off. The authors also derived conditions under which production controls would improve net social welfare, but they showed that, in this case, the static effects on producers and consumers would not be reversed by the introduction of risk and risk aversion.

As noted above, market variability alters the incidence of policies. From a policy-maker's perspective, then, a policy must adjust to market conditions and the induced producer responses in order for it to have the intended effects. Some studies have allowed for endogenous policy responses to changes in market conditions [e.g., Rausser and Freebairn (1974), Sarris and Freebairn (1983), Rausser and Foster (1990)] and, indeed, some have advocated the adoption of flexible policy rules so that policies would adapt optimally when market conditions change [e.g., Just (1984, 1985), Love and Rausser (1997)]. Of course, perfect adjustment for market variation requires perfect foresight regarding supply or demand shocks, producer responses to policies, and the hypothetical price and quantity at which the market would clear if it were undistorted. The danger of designing a policy whose operation and success depends on such perfect foresight is exemplified by buffer stock schemes, which have all, ultimately, collapsed.[31]

Under buffer stock schemes, government purchases are made when the market price is expected to be "too low", and stocks are released when the market price is expected

---

[31] Wright (1993) discusses the dynamic incidence of agricultural policies generally, with some emphasis on floor-price schemes.

to be "too high". The success of such schemes, then, relies on the ability of government operators to beat the market. While this may be possible in some time periods, Wright and Williams (1988) and Williams and Wright (1991, pp. 396–397) note that budgetary constraints will eventually bind, either because of imperfect foresight or because of prolonged periods requiring government purchases. Bardsley (1994) documented the 1989 collapse of the Australian wool reserve price scheme (essentially a buffer stock scheme). Before its collapse, the scheme eliminated A\$1.8 billion of reserve funds, and left wool growers with a debt of A\$2.7 billion and a wool stockpile, much of which remained unsold ten years later.

6.4. Policy risk

A hypothetical benevolent government might introduce agricultural policies to reduce price variability experienced by producers, making risk averse producers and society better off, as suggested by Moschini (1984) and by Innes and Rausser (1989). However, the same intervention introduces another source of risk, *policy risk*: the risk that producers will experience a loss arising from changes in policy or a policy-induced market collapse. Hence, any government intervention in a commodity market is likely to involve elements of policy risk, and any policy designed to mitigate market risk will entail at best a trade-off between market risk and policy risk.

Just and Rausser (1984, p. 129) presented a comprehensive discussion of how the design of policies can affect producer uncertainty and concluded that, "The inherent instability and riskiness of the U.S. food and agriculture system is the market-failure justification for U.S. agricultural policy. The implementation of policies to address such market failures is often confronted with government failure. Political-administrative instabilities resulting from government failure can exceed the inherent instabilities of the private sector".

Evidence about policy risk has been inferred by some from the rates of capitalization of quota rents into quota asset prices. For instance, Lermer and Stanbury (1985) estimated that costs of policy risk offset half or more of potential producer benefits from supply management for eggs, broilers, and turkeys in Canada. Lermer and Stanbury (1985) attributed all of the premium in the quota rental rate (rents as a percentage of the quota value), above a risk-free rate of return, to diversifiable risk, which would not exist if quota were held in fully diversified portfolios; hence, it represents an unnecessary cost of "insurance" against loss of the quota income stream. Alston (1992), however, suggested that some of the premium must reflect the equivalent of actuarially fair insurance, so that Lermer and Stanbury (1985) probably overstated the cost of unnecessary risk-bearing from limited quota transferability.[32]

---

[32] Seagraves (1969) may have been the first to raise these issues. Also, see Barichello (1981, 1996), Barichello and Cunningham-Dunlop (1987), and Johnson (1991) for further discussion on the capitalization of quota rents into quota values.

Other studies have sought to identify the capitalization of commodity programs into land prices. Various authors have proposed that government payments may be discounted more heavily than income from the market, when they are capitalized into land values [e.g., Just and Miranowski (1993), Clark, Klein and Thompson (1993), Schmitz (1995), Weersink et al. (1999)]. This could simply reflect an expectation that government program payments will not persist, which may have been an accurate prediction, and need not imply any risk premium as such, nor any waste of the type identified by Lermer and Stanbury (1985). On the other hand, the discounting could contain an element of policy risk and excessive risk costs.

7. Costs of administration and enforcement

All of the analysis above ignores the costs of administration and enforcement of policies. Once we allow for these costs, taxpayers as an interest group are affected by regulatory instruments such as quotas, not just the instruments that involve subsidies and taxes. Taxpayers bear the costs of administration and enforcement and receive as benefits revenues raised from fines imposed as penalties. These costs therefore change the qualitative implications of policies, as well as their quantitative implications, in terms of the distribution of benefits and costs, optimal instrument combinations and settings, and transfer efficiency.

Costs of administration and enforcement may be quite substantial, and may differ among policies. The processes of initially allocating quota and dealing with the inevitable appeals for reallocation can be very costly, as is well known to anyone who has witnessed them at close hand; every producer (or other presumptive quota owner) must be dealt with on an individual basis. Similarly, substantial costs of negotiation and rent-seeking arise whenever the elimination of a quota is seriously contemplated by government. The processes involved in introducing or eliminating a subsidy, on the other hand, are much simpler (and presumably less expensive). The costs of introducing or modifying policies may be more important than the conventional measures of deadweight costs, yet we usually have no information on these costs and leave them out of the analysis.

Once policies have been introduced, the administrative costs may be relatively low, so long as producers and consumers willingly comply. But some policies create incentives for producers or consumers to break the policy rules, and there is some evidence that participants in agricultural commodity markets will respond to such incentives.[33] We need to extend our models to account for optimizing behavior in those cases where it is profitable to break the rules, or where accounting for cheating will lead to significant changes in implications of policies. This requires taking into account the market incentives to break the rules, the odds of being caught, and the penalties. In addition, many

---

[33] For instance, when the egg market in the state of Victoria, Australia, was supposedly being controlled by hen quotas, it was estimated that the black market accounted for 10–30 percent of all eggs [Alston (1986)].

aspects of enforcement are chosen by policymakers when they choose how vigorously to enforce policies and what penalties to apply to those who are caught in violation, and this too can be modeled. Finally, the direct costs of enforcement must be added.

At one level, this calls for no more than a routine application of the economics of crime and punishment for which there is an extensive literature, beginning with Becker (1968). Surprisingly, perhaps, the literature on agricultural policy has had very little to say on these matters. Some recent work by Giannakas (1998), and Giannakas and Fulton (2000a, 2000b, 2001a, 2001b) has redressed a significant part of this deficiency, but much remains to be done. As will be seen below, the economic problem of analyzing a policy with cheating and enforcement costs, where the policy rules and enforcement effort are endogenous, along with the settings of the instruments, has many dimensions. Dealing with all of those dimensions makes for an intractable problem; assuming them away restricts the generality of the results. Here we will add some components of imperfect enforcement, but restrict attention to some special, comparatively easy cases.

7.1. Quotas and cheating

Suppose we have an output quota policy with costly (and, therefore, probably incomplete) enforcement [this policy is modeled in detail by Giannakas and Fulton (2001a)]. In Figure 10, the unregulated supply and demand are represented by S and D. If effective, a quota of Q_Q would result in supply of S_Q, yielding a price of P_1. At this price, producers would want to produce Q_1, which is more than the competitive quantity, Q_0. How much they will produce beyond their quota will depend not only on the odds of being caught and the penalty imposed if they are caught, but also on how those odds and penalties vary with the size of over-quota production. In addition, producers may be able to influence the odds of being caught by taking certain precautions, at a cost. Taking all these considerations into account, we can imagine a regulated supply function, S_R, that coincides with the unregulated supply function for quantities less than the quota, but lies above it for over-quota production, reflecting the costs of cheating (including costs of avoiding detection and expected costs of punishment), added to the ordinary costs of production.[34]

As the regulated supply curve is drawn in Figure 10, the marginal costs of crime and punishment perceived by producers are initially infinitesimally small (perhaps reflecting that the odds of being caught or that the penalties when caught are negligible for small amounts of over-quota sales) but rise with the size of over-quota production. This could reflect a positive effect of increasing over-quota production on either the chance of being caught, the costs of avoiding detection, or the penalty per unit of over-quota production.

---

[34] Alston and Smith (1983) drew a similar diagram to represent the consequences of incompletely enforced price floor regulations. The details of the nature of the shift from S to S_R to the right of Q_Q – pivotal as drawn in Figure 10 or more nearly parallel as drawn by Giannakas and Fulton (2000a, Figure 1) or some other form – will depend on the nature of the relationship between cheating, the odds of being caught, and the penalty once caught.

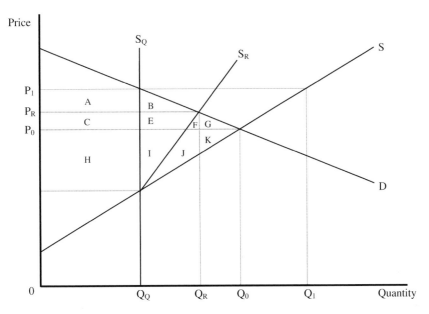

Figure 10. Output quota with imperfect enforcement.

Table 4
Welfare effects of a quota with and without cheating

Changes in	Quota with no cheating	Quota with cheating	Effect of cheating
Producer Surplus (ΔPS)	$A + C - (I + J + K)$	$C + E - (J + K)$	$E + I - A$
Consumer Surplus (ΔCS)	$-(A + B + C + E + F + G)$	$-(C + E + F + G)$	$A + B$
National Surplus (ΔNS = −DWL)	$-(B + E + F + G + I + J + K)$	$-(F + G + J + K)$	$B + E + I$

Note: The entries in this table refer to areas in Figure 10.

Thus, the regulated output that is actually sold on the market, Q_R, is between the competitive quantity and the quota quantity, and the corresponding regulated price, P_R, is between the competitive price and the quota price. Several interesting welfare effects can be seen in this figure, as summarized in Table 4. Under the perfectly (and costlessly) enforced output quota, producers (who are assumed also to own the quota) would gain area $(A + C) - (I + J + K)$. If producers cheat and expand their production to Q_R, they gain only area $(C + E) - (J + K)$. Producer benefits are lower by $A - (E + I)$ when the quotas are imperfectly enforced. However, the black market returns, area $E + I$, do not necessarily go to quota owners. In addition, area $E + I$ represents net returns after deducting the expected taxpayer benefits from fines (which also should be deducted from the deadweight losses). Consumer losses are smaller, by area $A + B$, as are net social costs, by area $B + E + I$.

How does cheating affect transfer efficiency? If we were able to impose a fully enforceable output quota of Q_R it would achieve greater producer benefits than the imperfectly enforceable quota set at Q_Q, with a smaller deadweight loss. For the same reason, then, for a given producer benefit, transfer efficiency is lower under an imperfectly enforced output quota than under a perfectly enforced output quota. In addition, the net costs of enforcement must be added to the other deadweight losses, further reducing the efficiency of transfers (even more so when tax revenues with a marginal cost of $1 + \delta$ are used to fund enforcement efforts). Policymakers can make the policy more like a perfectly enforced quota by increasing enforcement effort (which would shift S_R further towards S_Q), but this is simply a trade-off between the costs of enforcement and the deadweight losses in the commodity market. If that trade-off has been optimized already, then S_R represents the least-cost regulated supply function.

Figure 10 could also be used to represent the contrast between an output quota (set at Q_Q) and an input quota set at the quantity that would be used to produce Q_Q in the absence of intervention.[35] In this case, however, the difference between S and S_R reflects the increased cost of production under an input quota arising from the intensification of the use of other (nonquota) inputs, or slippage. In both cases, what we see is evidence of producers incurring expenses in order to circumvent the constraint of the quota, either the costs of cheating or the costs of distorting the input mix. This observation makes it easier to understand how input quotas are sometimes chosen over output quotas to achieve the same goal. Holding enforcement costs constant, an input quota would be preferred if $S_{\text{R-INPUT QUOTA}}$ is closer to S_Q than $S_{\text{R-OUTPUT QUOTA}}$. This would be likely if producer costs of cheating under an output quota were relatively low (reflecting small penalties or difficult detection) or if slippage were relatively low (reflecting low input substitution possibilities). The odds are pushed further in favor of input quotas if they are easier to enforce than output quotas.

7.2. *Deficiency payments and cheating*

Consider a target-price and deficiency-payments scheme, where the cheating takes the form of producers overstating the amount of their production in order to receive larger deficiency payments [this policy is modeled by Giannakas and Fulton (2001b)]. This situation is represented in Figure 11. Given a target price of P_T and no cheating, relative to the competitive equilibrium (P_0, Q_0) producers gain area $A + B$, consumers gain area $E + F + G$, and taxpayers lose area $A + B + C + E + F + G$, so that there is a deadweight loss of area C. If producers cheat, however, and claim to have produced Q_2 when in fact they produced only Q_1, then they receive additional benefits of H, against which they must count any expected costs of penalties for cheating that is detected. But, as pointed out by Giannakas (1998), this additional amount is a lump-sum transfer from taxpayers and does not involve any additional distortions in production or

---

[35] See Alston (1981, 1986) for some discussion of this scenario.

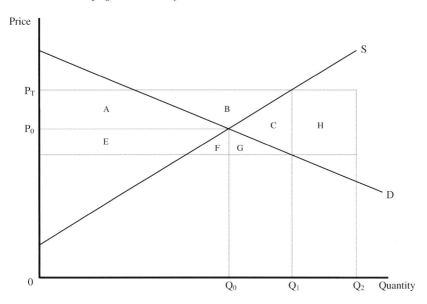

Figure 11. Cheating with a target price and deficiency payments.

consumption. Alternatively, if a total transfer of $A + B$ were intended, and producers cheat by overstating their production, then the target price could be set lower than P_T and the taxpayer costs and net social costs would be reduced (i.e., reduce the target price until the area corresponding to $A + B + H$ is reduced to the size of $A + B$ in Figure 11). Ironically, cheating increases the transfer efficiency of a target-price and deficiency-payments policy. Of course, this assessment has not factored in the costs of enforcement, which will reduce the transfer efficiency, and some enforcement will be necessary in order to limit the total amount being transferred. Nor has it accounted for the deadweight losses from taxation to finance the policy and its enforcement. In addition, the existence of cheating means that the benefits will be shifted towards those who have a higher propensity for cheating, which may not be consistent with the goals of the policy.

These results show that, even in a very stylized representation of the problem, cheating may increase or reduce the efficiency of transfers. Given a quota quantity, cheating is likely to reduce the total producer benefit, the total deadweight loss, and transfer efficiency. With a target-price and deficiency-payments scheme, cheating enhances transfer efficiency, increasing producer benefits but with no effect on deadweight loss (if $\delta = 0$), or with an increase in deadweight loss but a reduction in the average deadweight loss (if $\delta > 0$). A more complete understanding of the effects of cheating and costs of enforcement and administration requires a more complete specification of the details of the penalties and so on. Once these details have been specified, empirical estimates of the implications of cheating may be simulated or estimated econometrically.

8. Dynamics of factor and product supply, and policy incidence

The analysis in Section 3 showed how the incidence of policy turns on the conditions of supply of output and, ultimately, inputs. Understanding supply response is critical to understanding policy incidence. The models used above are based on static supply functions, and typify models used commonly in the analysis of commodity programs. Hence, in these models, policy incidence is static, too, and is determined by the elasticities that characterize the static supply functions. In contrast, in econometric models of supply response, the most challenging elements relate to the treatment of uncertainty and expectations, the lags between decisions and their consequences, and the dynamic evolution of supply response.[36] Thus, there is little connection between the typical static representation of supply in commodity policy models and econometric models of agricultural supply response, the most conspicuous features of which are dynamics and uncertainty. Questions arise, accordingly, about the interpretation of measures of policy incidence based on static supply models.

In a classic article, Cassels (1933) identified the key issues in analyzing agricultural supply response, and these have remained largely unchanged in spite of the major advances in theory, availability of detailed data, computing power, and econometric estimation techniques. A significant proportion of the rather extensive literature on supply analysis during the past 65 years has concerned treatments for problems raised by Cassels (1933).[37] Primarily these efforts have related to the dynamics of response and the formation of expectations, beginning with Nerlove (1958). That the essential problems persist can be seen in the more recent reviews by Colman (1983) and Just (1993). Both of these authors discussed the issues in choosing between models in which results from the (static) theory of the firm can be imposed as restrictions (e.g., static econometric models based on cost functions or profit functions, or programming models) and other models that connect less closely to that set of theory but, at the same time, are more realistic in their use of other theory related to dynamics and expectations (i.e., the so-called ad hoc single-equation econometric models). These discussions centered on the development of models with a view to econometric estimation and prediction, rather than policy analysis, but the same types of arguments can be made for policy models. There is a trade-off between the different types of model characteristics (consistency with static producer theory versus incorporation of

---

[36] In particular, biological processes in agricultural production take time, so that decisions about the commitment of inputs and planned production are based on incomplete information about weather and other events during the growing season (or several seasons), and about what prices will be when products become available for sale. These biological lags can involve several years in certain livestock industries, and much longer for some perennial crops and forestry. In addition, responses to given price changes and other events evolve over time, increasing with length of run as more things become more variable.

[37] Alston et al. (1995, pp. 18–19) provide a summary overview of that literature, including documentation of a number of more comprehensive reviews.

dynamics and expectations), the dimensions of which will vary depending on the types of questions being addressed and availability of data and so on.

If we decide that we must use a more realistic representation of supply response, going beyond the simple static model used above, we also have to reconsider the criterion for the welfare analysis. Changes in producer surplus can reasonably be used to represent changes in profit in the simple static model. However, in a model with dynamics and uncertainty, we may have to define a different measure of producer welfare change and we may have to aggregate over multiple periods. Such approaches may be too difficult for many problems.

8.1. Evolution of supply response

As characterized by Cassels (1933) and many writers since, there is no such thing as *the* supply function but, rather, there is a family (or fan) of supply curves for a particular commodity – more elastic supply curves for longer lengths of run. By choosing a particular supply elasticity for a commodity we are, implicitly, choosing a particular length of run.

Why does the supply elasticity increase with increases in length of run? In the theory of the (competitive) firm, factors are often defined as either fixed or variable (with fixed prices), so that the firm faces factor supply functions that are either perfectly inelastic (for the fixed factors) or perfectly elastic (for the variable factors). In the context of this theory, length of run is defined in terms of the numbers of factors that are fixed: at longer lengths of run, fewer factors are fixed. When more factors are variable, the firm has more dimensions for economizing on inputs as it increases its output in response to a price increase and, accordingly, marginal costs do not rise as quickly. This can be seen as a special case of a more general view in which firms face upward-sloping supplies of all factors of production (some of which may be highly elastic), that become more elastic as length of run increases. It is the evolution of these factor supply functions, becoming more elastic with increases in the length of run (or, equivalently, the reduction in the importance of quasi-fixed factors), that gives rise to the increasing elasticity of the output supply function. At the industry level, factor supply functions are likely to slope up even when prices are exogenous to individual firms. Here, too, the source of upward-sloping output supply is upward-sloping input supply, including the supply of firms themselves, and with increases in length of run the factor supply functions become more elastic, as does the output supply function.

8.2. Implications of dynamic output supply response

When we use comparative statics to measure the welfare implications of commodity policies, we are taking a static approximation to a dynamic problem. Figure 12 depicts a family of supply curves with increasing length of run and elasticity as we go from the market period (S_M) to the short run (S_{SR}), intermediate run (S_{IR}), and long run (S_{LR}).

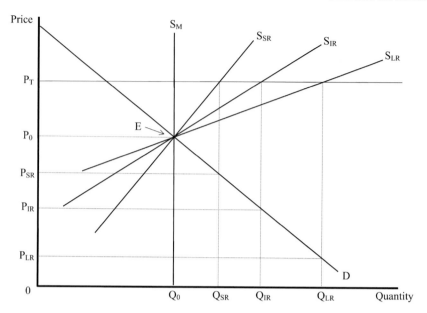

Figure 12. Supply elasticity and length of run.

These discrete alternatives represent a selection from a continuum of supply curves that all pass through the current equilibrium of supply with demand at point E in Figure 12.

Suppose a target price is applied to the market for the commodity in Figure 12 at P_T. In the current market period no supply response is possible, everything is fixed, and the effect is to make a lump-sum transfer from taxpayers to producers equal to $(P_T - P_0)Q_0$. In the short run, some supply response is possible, output increases to Q_{SR} and price falls to P_{SR}, leading to benefits to consumers, an increase in benefits to producers, and an increase in the burden on taxpayers, with an associated deadweight loss. The supply response to the increase in price from P_0 to P_T progressively expands to Q_{IR} in the intermediate run, and Q_{LR} in the long run, and the effects on price and welfare are progressively amplified.

Given that the producer welfare effects change with the length of run being considered, which is the "correct" measure? Just, Hueth and Schmitz (1982) suggest two measures, each of which is a discounted sum of the changes in producer surplus over the life of the policy. When the relevant production function is intertemporally separable, the benefit to producers from a target-price policy is equal to the sum of discounted producer surplus changes, where the change in producer surplus for each future period is measured from a supply function of the corresponding (incrementally increasing) length of run. An alternative measure that does not require intertemporal separability is the sum of discounted changes in producer surplus, as measured using the short-run supply curve for each period, less the present value of expenditures on investment in fixed assets. Bullock, Garcia and Lee (1996) extend the formal analysis presented by Just, Hueth and Schmitz (1982, Appendix C) to allow for different (i.e., other than "naive") expectations processes in the evaluation of welfare change under a dynamically evolving supply response.

The time path of measures of policy incidence will vary among policy instruments. For instance, with a target-price and deficiency-payments policy, the evolution of supply response involves ever-greater benefits to both producers and consumers, at the expense of ever-greater taxpayer costs and deadweight losses. In contrast, with a conventional per unit subsidy, the benefits may initially go entirely to producers but, with the evolution of supply response, may later shift toward consumers – and will end up entirely as a benefit to consumers when long-run supply response is perfectly elastic. On the other hand, with a quota, the evolution of supply response might not change the cost to consumers, and does not eliminate producer benefits in the long run, though it does reduce the quota rents and producer benefits over time.[38] This helps account for why quotas, and not subsidies, are more often found in industries for which the long-run supply is highly elastic, such as tobacco, eggs, poultry, and fresh milk.

8.3. Evolution of factor supply and policy incidence

As the length of run increases, the incidence shifts not only between producers and consumers; as supply becomes more elastic relative to demand, it also shifts among the factors. Some factors are relatively fixed in the short run and relatively variable in the long run. As a result, short-run incidence may differ qualitatively as well as quantitatively from longer-run incidence, particularly if the policy induces technological change.

For instance, consider the nature of the response of California's milk supply to a policy-induced increase in price. Ultimately, a permanent increase in production might imply a proportional increase in the use of all inputs. But it may take farmers in the industry two years after deciding to increase output in response to a higher price to add any additional cows to the total milking herd (although some short-term adjustments could be made by delaying culling). Additional output could be achieved perhaps by intensifying the use of other inputs such as purchased feed or growth hormones. In the short run, in which the number of milking cows is essentially fixed (corresponding to less than two years), the supply of feed to the dairy industry is likely to be highly elastic so that feed (or land) is not the limiting factor; cows are. In the intermediate run, however, say two to five years, the dairy industry can supply itself with additional milking cows at approximately constant cost. The cows are no longer the critical specialized factor. In some industries, and this might be an instance, processing capacity may be less elastically supplied than other inputs over the short and intermediate lengths of run, although it would be expected to be highly elastically supplied in the long run.

---

[38] Another possibility is that quota restrictions may imply a slower rate of technological change than would arise otherwise [e.g., see Alston (1986)].

In the intermediate and longer lengths of run, it may be managerial capacity that limits industry supply response more than other things.

Thus, the incidence of policies in the dairy industry will change with length of run. In the short run, but not in the longer run, for instance, the primary beneficiaries of a subsidy may be the owners of milking cows, not always the same people as those who supply other inputs such as land, feed, or equipment used in dairy farming. The differential dynamic incidence of policy is even more readily apparent for specific instances such as the U.S. whole-herd buyout program, where compensating some dairy producers for exiting the industry, and eliminating their herds, benefited those remaining in the industry who owned cows, but only in the period before replacement cows could be (and were) raised [e.g., see Chambers (1987)].

These types of issues are relatively important where dynamics in supply response are relatively important. Perennial crops provide good examples. Alston et al. (1995) provide a comprehensive analysis of the California almond industry and its reserve policy. In the almond industry, like many other tree crops, after a decision has been made to expand production by planting new trees there will be long lags before those new plantings come into production (say four years), and even longer lags before they reach their productive potential (say eight years), which can be maintained for a long time (up to twenty-five years). In the very short run, there cannot be any significant production response to a price increase. The Almond Board of California has exploited that fact in diverting some production from edible uses (a type of price discrimination strategy) in order to drive up the market price for edible uses. In the short run this policy cannot be undermined by supply response to the higher average revenue that results from the diversion. In the long run, however, the supply of almonds is likely to be highly elastic (there is an abundant supply of land and other resources suitable for almond production and no evidence of decreasing returns to industry scale, and the policy does not limit entry or production). While this policy can raise average revenues and profits in the short run, in the longer run it stimulates entry and raises industry productive capacity, depressing prices.

8.4. Dynamic evolution of markets in response to policy

The farm program for U.S. tobacco provides another good example of the dynamic evolution of markets in response to policy, with some surprising implications for the incidence of the policy. As documented by Johnson (1984), when the farm program for U.S. flue-cured tobacco was first introduced during the 1930s, the U.S. industry dominated the world market. From 1940, supply was controlled (initially using acreage allotments; since 1965 using poundage quotas), which held up the domestic and world price for U.S. tobacco. Over time, in response to the higher price of U.S. tobacco, production in other countries increased and export demand facing the United States fell.

In an analysis of the dynamic effects of the policy, Seagraves (1983) reported that during 1935–39, the United States produced 64 percent of the world's flue-cured tobacco and 83 percent of the world's net exports. By 1980–82, these numbers had fallen so that the United States produced only 17 percent of world production, and only 21 percent of exports. In recent years, the United States has been importing roughly one-third of tobacco used in cigarette production in the United States, while exporting one-half of the tobacco grown in the United States.

Alston and Sumner (1988) estimated the static welfare effects in 1987, and concluded that the quota was close to the quantity that would maximize the net U.S. gains in that year.[39] But over time, the potential U.S. market power has been progressively eroded, as a result of some market power being exercised through the quota. Whether the policy has been *dynamically* optimal, so as to maximize the present value of U.S. benefits over time, has not been evaluated.[40]

Any policy by a large exporter that restricts supply to the world market (as for U.S. tobacco and almonds) raises the world price along with the domestic one, and confers benefits on overseas producers, to some extent at the future expense of U.S. producers: today's domestic producers may be gaining at the expense of tomorrow's. Conversely, policies that lead to greater output and exports of, say, wheat would be expected to have dynamic domestic consequences arising from their negative effects on competing wheat producers overseas. Domestic supply responses to subsidies on output (or exports) increase with length of run. At the same time, foreign supply response to lower world prices also increases with increases in length of run, which means that the demand for wheat exports also becomes more elastic with increases in length of run. Dynamic responses such as these account for the (surprising to some) shift of the European Union from being an importer, before the Common Agricultural Policy was first introduced, to being the world's largest exporter of wheat 30 years later, with significant political and budgetary problems arising from the larger-than-anticipated responses to the policy. Like U.S. tobacco, and California almonds, dynamic responses to the EU wheat policy progressively undermined the effectiveness of the policy as a means of transferring income to producers efficiently.

9. Conclusion

The incidence of agricultural policy depends on the details of the policies and the contexts in which they are applied, especially concerning the conditions of supply of factors of production to the industries concerned. It is necessary to account for these details that vary from one setting to the next. Hence, we cannot generally make the

---

[39] Sumner (1996) summarizes the main results.

[40] Studies have looked at the optimal time path of trade taxes, and the same types of issues are likely to arise here. For instance, see Gaskins (1971) and Karp (1987). Alston et al. (1995, Ch. 7), analyze a very similar problem for the almond industry, although the competitive fringe here includes domestic as well as foreign entrants.

types of broad generalizations that we may wish to make, such as that farm program benefits are ultimately capitalized into land, based on theory alone.

The literature on the incidence of agricultural policies includes two main types of studies. Specific studies of particular policies (such as the U.S. tobacco program) or particular events (such as the collapse of the Australian wool reserve price scheme) sometimes tell us a great deal about incidence. However, not many of the empirical studies that have been done have characterized the policies, or the markets in which they apply, in sufficient detail to provide much information about policy incidence beyond the distinction between domestic and international, or producer and consumer welfare effects. In particular, few studies of commodity policies have provided clear statements about the elasticities of supply of different factors of production to the industry in question, which is a central determinant of incidence among factors of production. The other main type of study takes a more general look either at certain policy issues (e.g., broad-brush comparisons of particular instruments), or at agricultural industries (e.g., overall assessments of the effects of agricultural policy in the United States). While the latter types of study can teach us much about the determinants of incidence, they usually forsake too much of the necessary detail to offer much empirically, if our claims about the importance of details are valid.

Two important elements of realism are often lacking from studies of commodity policies and their incidence. These are (1) a realistic representation of the policy instruments, and (2) an appropriate representation of the conditions of factor supply and product demand, and technology. In relation to the instruments, quite substantial differences in incidence can be found as a result of apparently innocuous details – such as whether a quota applies to inputs or outputs or is transferable, or whether we have a subsidy versus a target price with deficiency payments – especially when we allow for market variability and dynamics.

In this chapter we have emphasized two main types of domestic commodity policy instruments, supply control policies (output or input quotas) and subsidies. For each of these instruments we have identified a real-world departure from the common theoretical characterization, which has potentially profound implications for the evaluation of each, and for the comparison between them. First, real-world quotas, whether applied to inputs or outputs, are typically not transferable, and this has very serious implications for the social costs of supply controls. Second, allowing for the deadweight costs of taxation to finance subsidies means that subsidies involve much greater deadweight losses, and a much heavier burden on taxpayers, than a conventional analysis would indicate. In addition, both subsidies and supply controls are costly to introduce, administer, and enforce. These costs, and the effects of producer responses to the incentives to cheat, also change the deadweight losses from each of the policies, their distributional consequences, and their efficiency as means of transferring income to producers.

The second set of concerns relates to the (mis-)representation of the market context in which a policy is applied. We often see policies analyzed using unrealistic combinations of assumptions about supply and demand conditions and policy instruments. For instance, often in the literature, policies that apply to individual commodities, or groups of commodities, are analyzed as though they apply to agriculture in aggregate; and elasticities that are relevant for agriculture as a whole are used as thought they apply to individual commodities. One form of fallacy of composition is to conduct an analysis of U.S. agriculture that treats the entire industry as though it has the same policy as the wheat industry has; another is the use of a perfectly inelastic supply of land, as may be a good approximation for U.S. agriculture, in the analysis of the U.S. wheat price-support policy. There are few policy questions for which either of these approximations will be reasonable. Another common failing is the use of elasticities, especially for demand, that reflect a failure to account for the role of international trade. If the results are to be meaningful, we must match elasticities to both the length of run and the market of interest.

As well as being intrinsically interesting, understanding the effects of policies is also a first step to understanding why certain policies are chosen, and to prescribing policies. While we have made considerable progress in theoretical models that help us think about these issues, we have relatively little to show in terms of empirical understanding of incidence of farm commodity policies. More meaningful empirical analysis requires better measures of the conditions of supply of different factors of production in particular industries, taking into account the level of aggregation and length of run, better empirical estimates of the *relevant* commodity supply and demand elasticities, and more realistic representation of policy instruments. Important elements of the unfinished agenda for work in this area also include further theoretical development and empirical work on dynamic incidence of policy, policy risk, endogenous quality, the costs of administration and enforcement of policies, and the consequences of cheating.

Acknowledgements

The authors are grateful for helpful comments from David Bullock, Dinos Giannakas, Roley Piggott, Klaus Salhofer, Daniel Sumner and Jo Swinnen, as well as comments from anonymous reviewers and the editors.

References

Abbott, P.C., P.L. Paarlberg and J.A. Sharples (1987), "Targeted export subsidies and social welfare", American Journal of Agricultural Economics 69:723–732.

Alchian, A.A., and W.R. Allen (1964), University Economics (Wadsworth, Belmont, CA).

Alston, J.M. (1981), "A note on the effects of non-transferable quotas on supply functions", Review of Marketing and Agricultural Economics 49:189–197.

Alston, J.M. (1986), "Consequences of deregulation in the Victorian egg industry", Review of Marketing and Agricultural Economics 54:33–43.

Alston, J.M. (1992), "Economics of commodity supply controls", in: T. Becker, R. Gray and A. Schmitz, eds., Improving Agricultural Trade Performance under the GATT (Wissenschaftsverlag Vauk, Kiel KG) Chapter 7.

Alston, J.M., H.F. Carman, J.E. Christian, J. Dorfman, J.-R. Murua and R.J. Sexton (1995), Optimal Reserve and Export Policies for the California Almond Industry: Theory, Econometrics and Simulations, Giannini Foundation Monograph No. 42 (Giannini Foundation of Agricultural Economics, Berkeley).

Alston, J.M., C.A. Carter and V.H. Smith (1993), "Rationalizing agricultural export subsidies", American Journal of Agricultural Economics 75:1000–1009.

Alston, J.M., C.A. Carter and V.H. Smith (1995), "Rationalizing agricultural export subsidies: Reply", American Journal of Agricultural Economics 77:209–213.

Alston, J.M., C.A. Carter and M.K. Wohlgenant (1989), "Who determines farm programs? Agribusiness and the making of farm policy", International Agricultural Trade Research Consortium Working Paper No. 89-1.

Alston, J.M., and J.W. Freebairn (1988), "Producer price equalization", Review of Marketing and Agricultural Economics 56:306–339.

Alston, J.M., and R.Gray (1998), "Export subsidies and state trading: Theory and application to Canadian wheat", in: T. Yildirim, A. Schmitz and W.H. Furtan, eds., World Agricultural Trade (Westview Press, Boulder, CO) 281–298.

Alston, J.M., and B.H. Hurd (1990), "Some neglected social costs of government spending in farm programs", American Journal of Agricultural Economics 72:149–156.

Alston, J.M., G.W. Norton and P.G. Pardey (1995), Science under Scarcity: Principles and Practice for Agricultural Research Evaluation and Priority Setting (Cornell University Press, Ithaca).

Alston, J.M., and J.J. Quilkey (1980), "Insurance milk", Australian Journal of Agricultural Economics 24:283–290.

Alston, J.M., and V.H. Smith (1983), "Some economic implications of minimum pricing: The case of wine grapes in Australia – comment", Review of Marketing and Agricultural Economics 51:180–189.

Alston, J.M., V.H. Smith, A. Acquaye and S. Hosseini (1999), "Least-cost cheap-food policies: Some implications of international food aid", Agricultural Economics 20:191–201.

Alston, J.M., and D.A. Sumner (1988), "A new perspective on the farm program for U.S. tobacco", Mimeo (Department of Agricultural Economics, University of California, Davis).

Babcock, B.A. (1990), "Acreage decisions under marketing quotas and yield uncertainty", American Journal of Agricultural Economics 72:958–965.

Babcock, B.A., C.A. Carter and A. Schmitz (1990), The political economy of U.S. wheat legislation, Economic Inquiry 28:335–353.

Ballard, C.L., and D. Fullerton (1992), "Distortionary taxes and the provision of public goods", Journal of Economic Perspectives 6:117–131.

Bardsley, P. (1994), "The collapse of the Australian wool reserve price scheme", The Economic Journal 104:1087–1105.

Bardsley, P., and P. Cashin (1990), "Underwriting assistance to the Australian wheat industry – an application of option pricing theory", Australian Journal of Agricultural Economics 34:212–222.

Barichello, R.R. (1981), "The economics of Canadian dairy industry regulation", Technical Report E/1/2, March (Economic Council of Canada and the Institute for Research on Public Policy, Ottawa).

Barichello, R.R. (1996), "Capitalizing government program benefits: Evidence of the risk associated with holding farm quotas", in: J.M. Antle and D.A. Sumner, eds., The Economics of Agriculture Volume 2, Papers in Honor of D. Gale Johnson (University of Chicago Press, Chicago) Chapter 16.

Barichello, R.R., and C. Cunningham-Dunlop (1987), "Quota allocation and transfer schemes in Canada", Working Paper 8/87 (Department of Agricultural Economics, University of British Columbia, Vancouver).

Barzel, Y. (1976), "An alternative approach to the analysis of taxation", Journal of Political Economy 84:1177–1197.

Becker, G.S. (1968), "Crime and punishment: An economic approach", Journal of Political Economy 76:169–217.

Boots, M., A. Oude-Lansink and J. Peerlings (1997), "Efficiency loss due to distortions in Dutch milk quota trade", European Review of Agricultural Economics 24:31–46.

Borcherding, T.E., and E. Silberberg (1978), "Shipping the good apples out: The Alchian and Allen theorem reconsidered", Journal of Political Economy 86:131–138.

Borges, R.B., and W.N. Thurman (1994), "Marketing quotas and random yields: Marginal effects of inframarginal subsidies on peanut supply", American Journal of Agricultural Economics 76:809–817.

Brandow, G.E. (1977), "Policy for commercial agriculture, 1945–1971", in: L.R. Martin, ed., A Survey of Agricultural Economics Literature, Vol. 1 (University of Minnesota Press, Minneapolis).

Brännlund, R., and B. Kriström (1996), "Welfare measurement in single and multimarket models: Theory and application", American Journal of Agricultural Economics 78:157–165.

Brown, A.B., and L.L. Martin (1996), "Price versus quota reductions: U.S. flue-cured tobacco policy", Journal of Agricultural and Applied Economics 28:445–452.

Bullock, D.S. (1993), "Welfare implications of equilibrium supply and demand curves in an open economy", American Journal of Agricultural Economics 75:52–58.

Bullock, D.S. (1994), "In search of rational government: What political preference function studies measure and assume", American Journal of Agricultural Economics 76:347–361.

Bullock, D.S. (1995), "Are government transfers efficient? An alternative test of the efficient redistribution hypothesis", Journal of Political Economy 103:1236–1274.

Bullock, D.S., P. Garcia and Y.-K. Lee (1996), "Towards producer welfare measures in a dynamic, stochastic framework", Mimeo (Department of Agricultural Economics, University of Illinois, Urbana/Champaign).

Bullock, D.S., and K. Salhofer (1998a), "Measuring the social costs of suboptimal combinations of policy instruments: A general framework and an example", Agricultural Economics 18:249–259.

Bullock, D.S., and K. Salhofer (1998b), "A note on the efficiency of income redistribution with simple and combined policies", Agricultural and Resource Economics Review 27:266–269.

Bullock, D.S., K. Salhofer and J. Kola (1999), "The normative analysis of agricultural policy: A general framework and review", Journal of Agricultural Economics 50:512–535.

Bureau, J.-C., H. Guyomard, L. Morin and V. Requillart (1997), "Quota mobility in the European sugar regime", European Review of Agricultural Economics 24:1–30.

Burrell, A. (ed.) (1989), Milk Quotas in the European Community (CAB International, Wallingford).

Buse, R.C. (1958), "Total elasticities – a predictive device", Journal of Farm Economics 40:881–891.

Campbell, H. (1997), "Deadweight loss and the cost of public funds in Australia", Agenda 4:231–236.

Campbell, H.F., and K.A. Bond (1997), "The cost of public funds in Australia", The Economic Record 73:22–34.

Cassels, J.M. (1933), "The nature of statistical supply curves", Journal of Farm Economics 15:378–387.

Chambers, R.G. (1987), "Designing producer financed farm programs, or should we save the cows?", Working paper (University of Maryland).

Chambers, R.G. (1992), "On the design of agricultural policy mechanisms", American Journal of Agricultural Economics 74:646–654.

Chambers, R.G. (1995), "The incidence of agricultural policies", Journal of Public Economics 57:317–335.

Clark, J.S., K.K. Klein and S.J. Thompson (1993), "Are subsidies capitalized into land values? Some time series evidence from Saskatchewan", Canadian Journal of Agricultural Economics 41:155–168.

Colman, D. (1983), "A review of the arts of supply response analysis", Review of Marketing and Agricultural Economics 51:201–230.

Corden, W.M. (1997), Trade Policy and Economic Welfare (Clarendon Press, Oxford).

Dardis, R. (1967), "The welfare cost of grain protection in the United Kingdom", Journal of Farm Economics, 49:597–609.

Dardis, R., and J. Dennisson (1969), "The welfare cost of alternative methods of protecting raw wool in the United States", American Journal of Agricultural Economics 51:303–319.

Dardis, R., and E. Learn (1967), "Measures of the degree and cost of economic protection of agriculture in selected countries", USDA-ERS Technical Bulletin No. 1384 (Economic Research Service, U.S. Department of Agriculture, Washington, DC).

Diewert, W.E., and D.A. Lawrence (1995), "The excess burden of taxation in New Zealand", Agenda 2:27–34.

Drynan, R.G., M. Perich, R.L. Batterham and S.P. Whelan (1994), "The effects of policy changes in the production and sales of milk in New South Wales", Review of Marketing and Agricultural Economics 62:231–245.

Falvey, R.E., and P.J. Lloyd (1991), "Uncertainty and the choice of protective instrument", Oxford Economic Papers 43:463–478.

Feenstra, R.C. (1986), "Trade policy with several goods and 'market linkages' ", Journal of International Economics 20:249–267.

Findlay, C.C., and R.L. Jones (1982), "The marginal cost of Australian income taxation", Economic Record 58:253–262.

Floyd, J.E. (1965), "The effects of farm price supports on the returns to land and labor in agriculture", Journal of Political Economy 73:148–158.

Foster, W.E., and B.A. Babcock (1990), "The effect of government policy on flue-cured tobacco yields", Tobacco Science 34:4–8.

Foster, W.E., and B.A. Babcock (1993), "Commodity policy, price incentives, and the growth in per-acre yields", Journal of Agricultural and Applied Economics 25:253–265.

Fraser, R. (1986), "Uncertainty and production quotas", The Economic Record 62:338–342.

Fraser, R. (1995), "A note: Clarification of the role of yield uncertainty in influencing over-quota production", Australian Journal of Agricultural Economics 39:165–169.

Freebairn, J. (1995), "Reconsidering the marginal welfare cost of taxation", The Economic Record 71:121–131.

Friedman, M. (1976), Price Theory (Aldine Publishing Company, Chicago).

Fullerton, D. (1991), "Reconciling recent estimates of the marginal welfare cost of taxation", American Economic Review 81:302–308.

Gardner, B.L. (1975), "The farm-retail price spread in a competitive food industry", American Journal of Agricultural Economics 57:399–409.

Gardner, B.L. (1977), "Commodity options for agriculture", American Journal of Agricultural Economics 59:986–992.

Gardner, B. (1983), "Efficient redistribution through commodity markets", American Journal of Agricultural Economics 65:225–234.

Gardner, B.L. (1987a), "Causes of U.S. farm commodity programs", Journal of Political Economy 95:290–310.

Gardner, B.L. (1987b), The Economics of Agricultural Policies (Macmillan, New York).

Gardner, B.L. (1995), "Rationalizing agricultural export subsidies: Comment", American Journal of Agricultural Economics 77:205–208.

Gaskins, D.W. Jr. (1971), "Dynamic limit pricing: Optimal pricing under the threat of entry", Journal of Economic Theory 3:306–322.

Giannakas, K. (1998), "Agricultural policy analysis under costly enforcement: An economic analysis of cheating", Unpublished Ph.D. dissertation (University of Saskatchewan).

Giannakas, K., and M. Fulton (2000a), "Efficient redistribution using quotas and subsidies in the presence of misrepresentation and cheating", American Journal of Agricultural Economics 82:347–359.

Giannakas, K., and M. Fulton (2000b), "The economics of coupled farm subsides under costly and imperfect enforcement", Agricultural Economics 22:75–90.

Giannakas, K., and M. Fulton (2001a), "The economics of output quotas in the presence of cheating", Working Paper WP029 (Center for Agricultural and Food Industrial Organization, University of Nebraska, Lincoln).

Giannakas, K., and M. Fulton (2001b), "The economics of decoupled farm subsidies under costly and imperfect enforcement", Working Paper WP023 (Center for Agricultural and Food Industrial Organization, University of Nebraska, Lincoln).

Gisser, M. (1993), "Price support, acreage controls, and efficient redistribution", Journal of Political Economy 101:584–611.

Goodwin, B.K., and F. Ortalo-Magne (1992), "The capitalization of wheat subsidies into agricultural land values", Canadian Journal of Agricultural Economics 40:37–54.

Guyomard, H., X. Delache, X. Irz and L.-P. Mahe (1996), "A microeconometric analysis of milk quota transfer: Application to French producers", Journal of Agricultural Economics 47:206–223.

Harberger, A.C. (1971), "Three basic postulates for applied welfare economics: An interpretive essay", Journal of Economic Literature 9:785–797.

Hertel, T.W. (1989), "Ten truths about supply control", National Center for Food and Agricultural Policy and Food and Agriculture Committee, Resources for the Future, Discussion Paper Series FAP89-05, July.

Hertel, T.W. (1991), "Factor market incidence of agricultural trade liberalization: Some additional results", Australian Journal of Agricultural Economics 35:81–107.

Higgs, P.J. (1986), Adaptation and Survival in Australian Agriculture: A Computable General Equilibrium Analysis of the Impact of Economic Shocks Originating Outside the Agricultural Sector (Oxford University Press, Melbourne).

Hushak, L.J. (1971), "A welfare analysis of the voluntary corn diversion program, 1961 to 1966", American Journal of Agricultural Economics 53:173–181.

Innes, R. (1990), "Uncertainty, incomplete markets and government farm programs", Southern Economic Journal 57:47–65.

Innes, R., and G.C. Rausser (1989), "Incomplete markets and government agricultural policy", American Journal of Agricultural Economics 71:915–931.

Ippolito, R.A., and R.T. Masson (1978), "The social cost of government regulation of milk", Journal of Law and Economics 21:33–65.

Itoh, M., and K. Kiyono (1987), "Welfare-enhancing export subsidies", Journal of Political Economy 95:115–137.

James, J.S. (2000), "Quality responses to commodity policies", Unpublished Ph.D. dissertation (University of California, Davis).

James, J.S., and J.M. Alston (2002), "Seeds of progress? French wheat production, quality, and policy", Paper presented at the 46th Annual conference of the Australian Agricultural and Resource Economics Society.

Johnson, D.G. (1963), "Efficiency and welfare implications of United States agricultural policy", Journal of Farm Economics 45:331–342.

Johnson, D.G. (1975), "World agriculture, commodity policy, and price variability", American Journal of Agricultural Economics 57:823–838.

Johnson, D.G. (1991), World Agriculture in Disarray, 2nd edn. (St Martin's Press, New York).

Johnson, P.R. (1965), "The social cost of the tobacco program", Journal of Farm Economics 47:242–255.

Johnson, P.R. (1984), The Economics of the Tobacco Industry (Praeger, New York).

Johnson, P.R., and D.T. Norton (1983), "Social cost of the tobacco program redux", American Journal of Agricultural Economics 65:117–119.

Josling, T. (1969), "A formal approach to agricultural policy", Journal of Agricultural Economics 20:175–195.

Josling, T. (1974), "Agricultural policies in developed countries: A review", Journal of Agricultural Economics 25:229–264.

Josling, T. (1977), "Government price policies and the structure of international agricultural trade", Journal of Agricultural Economics 28:261–278.

Just, R.E. (1984), "Automatic adjustment rules for agricultural policy controls", AEI Occasional Papers (American Enterprise Institute for Public Policy Research, Washington, DC).

Just, R.E. (1985), "Automatic adjustment rules in commodity programs", in: B.L. Gardner, ed., U.S. Agricultural Policy: The 1985 Farm Legislation (American Enterprise Institute for Public Policy Research, Washington, DC) 355–377.

Just, R.E. (1993), "Discovering production and supply relationships: Present status and future opportunities", Review of Marketing and Agricultural Economics 61:11–40.

Just, R.E., and D.L. Hueth (1979), "Welfare measures in a multimarket framework", American Economic Review 69:947–954.

Just, R.E., D.L. Hueth and A. Schmitz (1982), Applied Welfare Economics and Public Policy (Prentice-Hall, Englewood Cliffs, NJ).

Just, R.E., and J.A. Miranowski (1993), "Understanding farmland price changes", American Journal of Agricultural Economics 75:156–168.

Just, R.E., and G.C. Rausser (1984), "Uncertain economic environments and conditional policies", in: G.C. Rausser and K.R. Farrell, eds., Alternative Agricultural and Food Policies for the 1985 Farm Bill (Giannini Foundation of Agricultural Economics, Berkeley) Chapter 5.

Karp, L.S. (1987), "Consistent tariffs with dynamic supply response", Journal of International Economics, 23:369–376.

Kola, J. (1993), "Efficiency of supply control programmes in income redistribution", European Review of Agricultural Economics 20:183–198.

Lembit, M.J., V. Topp, G. Williamson and S. Beare (1988), "Gains from a negotiable milk quota scheme for New South Wales", Quarterly Review of the Rural Economy 10:255–260.

Lermer, G., and W.T. Stanbury (1985), "Measuring the cost of redistributing income by means of direct regulation", Canadian Journal of Economics 18:190–207.

Lichtenberg, E., and D. Zilberman (1986), "The welfare economics of price supports in U.S. agriculture", American Economic Review 76:1135–1141.

Lloyd, A.G. (1971), "Quotas: Some general issues with reference to the dairy industry", Paper presented to the Australian Agricultural Economics Society conference, February.

Longworth, J.W., and P. Knopke (1982), "Australian wheat policy, 1948–79: A welfare evaluation", American Journal of Agricultural Economics 64:642–654.

Love, H.A., and G.C. Rausser (1997), "Flexible public policy: The case of the United States wheat sector", Journal of Policy Modeling 19:207–236.

Marshall, A. (1949), Principles of Economics, 8th edn. (Macmillan, London).

Moschini, G. (1984), "Quota values and price uncertainty", Canadian Journal of Agricultural Economics 32:231–234.

Muth, R.F. (1964), "The derived demand curve for a productive factor and the industry supply curve", Oxford Economic Papers 16:221–234.

Nerlove, M. (1958), The Dynamics of Supply: Estimation of Farmers' Response to Price (Johns Hopkins Press, Baltimore).

Neutze, G.M. (1961), "Saleable city milk supply quotas", Australian Journal of Agricultural Economics 5:136–137.

Parish, R. (1962), "The costs of protecting the dairy industry", Economic Record 38:167–182.

Parish, R. (1963), "On marketing quotas for fluid milk", Australian Journal of Agricultural Economics 71:61–78.

Parish, R., and K. McLaren (1982), "Relative cost-effectiveness of input and output subsidies", Australian Journal of Agricultural Economics 26:1–13.

Piggott, R.R. (1992), "Some old truths revisited", Australian Journal of Agricultural Economics 36:117–140.

Rausser, G.C., and W.E. Foster (1990), "Political preference functions and public policy reform", American Journal of Agricultural Economics 72:641–652.

Rausser, G.C., and J.W. Freebairn (1974), "Estimation of policy preference functions: An application to U.S. beef import quotas", Review of Economics and Statistics 56:437–449.

Rosine, J., and P.G. Helmberger (1974), "A neoclassical analysis of the U.S. farm sector, 1948–1970", American Journal of Agricultural Economics 56:717–729.

Rucker, R.R., and W.N. Thurman (1990), "The economic effects of supply controls: The simple analytics of the U.S. peanut program", Journal of Law and Economics 33:483–515.

Rucker, R.R., W.N. Thurman and D.A. Sumner (1995), "Restricting the market for quota: An analysis of tobacco production rights with corroboration from Congressional testimony", Journal of Political Economy 103:142–175.

Salhofer, K. (1996), "Efficient redistribution for a small country using optimal combined instruments", Agricultural Economics 13:191–199.

Salhofer, K. (1997), Efficiency of Income Redistribution Through Agricultural Policy: A Welfare Analysis (Peter Lang, Frankfurt).

Sarris, A.H., and J. Freebairn (1983), "Endogenous price policies and international wheat prices", American Journal of Agricultural Economics 65:214–224.

Schmitz, A. (1995), "Boom/bust cycles and Ricardian rent", American Journal of Agricultural Economics 77:1110–1125.

Schultz, T.W. (1945), Agriculture in an Unstable Economy (McGraw Hill, New York).

Schultz, T.W. (1978), "On economics and politics of agriculture", in: T.W. Schultz, ed., Distortions in Agricultural Incentives (Indiana University Press, Bloomington).

Seagraves, J.A. (1969), "Capitalized values of tobacco allotments and the rate of return to allotment holders", American Journal of Agricultural Economics 51:320–334.

Seagraves, J.A. (1983), "The life-cycle of the flue-cured tobacco program", Faculty Working Paper No. 34 (Department of Economics and Business, North Carolina State University, Raleigh).

Sieper, E. (1982), Rationalising Rustic Regulation (The Centre for Independent Studies, St. Leonards).

Slesnick, D.T. (1998), "Empirical approaches to the measurement of welfare", Journal of Economic Literature 36:2108–2165.

Sumner, D.A. (ed.) (1988), Agricultural Stability and Farm Programs: Concepts, Evidence, and Implications (Westview Press, Boulder, CO).

Sumner, D.A. (1996), "Tobacco supply management: Examples from the United States and Australia", in: A. Schmitz, G. Coffin and K.A. Rosaasen, eds., Regulation and Protectionism under GATT: Case Studies in North American Agriculture (Westview Press, Boulder, CO) Chapter 10.

Sumner, D.A., and J.M. Alston (1984), "Consequences of elimination of the tobacco program", North Carolina Agricultural Research Service Bulletin No. 469 (NCSU).

Sumner, D.A., and M.K. Wohlgenant (1985), "Effects of an increase in the federal excise tax on cigarettes", American Journal of Agricultural Economics 67:235–242.

Sumner, D.A., and C.A. Wolf (1996), "Quotas without supply control: Effects of dairy quota policy in California", American Journal of Agricultural Economics 78:354–366.

Thurman, W.N. (1991), "Applied general equilibrium welfare analysis", American Journal of Agricultural Economics 73:1508–1516.

Thurman, W.N. (1993), "The welfare significance and nonsignificance of general equilibrium demand and supply curves", Public Finance Quarterly 21:449–469..

Tozer, P.R. (1993), "Efficiency aspects of transferable dairy quotas in New South Wales: A linear programming approach", Review of Marketing and Agricultural Economics 61:141–155.

Tyers, R., and R. Falvey (1988), "Border price changes and domestic welfare in the presence if subsidised exports", Oxford Economic Papers 41:434–451.

Umbeck, J. (1980), "Shipping the good apples out: Some ambiguities in the interpretation of 'fixed charge' ", Journal of Political Economy 88:199–208.

Wallace, T.D. (1962), "Measures of social costs of agricultural programs", Journal of Farm Economics 44:580–594.

Weersink, A., S. Clark, C.G. Turvey and R. Sarkar (1999), "The effect of agricultural policy on farmland values", Land Economics 75:425–439.

Weiss, C.R. (1992), "The effect of price reduction and direct income support policies on agricultural input markets in Austria", Journal of Agricultural Economics 43:1–13.

Williams, J.C., and B.D. Wright (1991), Storage and Commodity Markets (Cambridge University Press, Cambridge).

Willig, R.D. (1976), "Consumer's surplus without apology", American Economic Review 66:589–597.

Wohlgenant, M.K. (1982), "The farm-retail price ratio in a competitive food industry with several marketing inputs", Working Paper No. 12 (Department of Economics and Business, North Carolina State University).

Wright, B.D. (1993), "Dynamic perspectives on agricultural policy issues", American Journal of Agricultural Economics 75:1113–1125.

Wright, B.D., and J.C. Williams (1988), "The incidence of market stabilising price support schemes", Economic Journal 98:1183–1198.

Chapter 34

INFORMATION, INCENTIVES, AND THE DESIGN OF AGRICULTURAL POLICIES

ROBERT G. CHAMBERS

Department of Agricultural and Resource Economics, University of Maryland, College Park, MD, and Agricultural and Resource Economics, University of Western Australia, WA

Contents

Handbook of Agricultural Economics, Volume 2, Edited by B. Gardner and G. Rausser

Abstract

This chapter surveys studies that have used the methods of mechanism design, optimal taxation, nonlinear pricing, and principal-agent analyses in the analysis of agricultural policy. The optimal design and reform of agricultural policy are studied under the presumption that agricultural producers are better informed about their technology or their actions than agricultural policy makers. The existence of these information asymmetries creates incentive problems that must be tackled in the design of an optimal agricultural policy. Two basic types of information asymmetries are studied, those associated with hidden knowledge and those with hidden action. Hidden knowledge occurs when the farmer has exact information about his technology, but the regulator does not. Hidden action occurs when only the farmer has exact information on the conditions, including the state of Nature and the farmer's actions, under which production takes place.

Keywords

agricultural policy, mechanism design, asymmetric information, incentives, hidden action, hidden knowledge

JEL classification: Q18

1. Introduction

Historically, agriculture has been a closely regulated sector in the industrialized economies. Consequently, economists have long studied the relative efficiency of different farm-policy implements in achieving farm-policy goals. This work is capably surveyed elsewhere in this volume, but I would be remiss if I didn't mention the fundamental contributions of Nerlove (1958), Wallace (1962), and Gardner (1983). These studies and their derivative literature have two essential characteristics: They only consider a fixed menu of policy implements (e.g., support prices, deficiency payments, acreage retirement). And they operate exclusively in terms of representative producers and consumers, thus ignoring the informational differences that exist between the regulator (typically national governments) and the regulated (farmers) and the obvious incentive problems that these informational differences incur. So, while these models do a good job of describing the relative deadweight losses of various agricultural policies, they are hard pressed to explain farm policies that differentially favor different sectors of the farm economy. They also carry the silent, if not overt, implication that if the farm regulator had enough willpower or political savvy, he or she could achieve the first-best and then redistribute resources efficiently through lump-sum transfers.

This chapter surveys a set of studies that have followed another path: They presume that important informational asymmetries exist between the government and farmers, and that these informational asymmetries can prevent the government from achieving the first best. The methods used by these studies are those of mechanism design, optimal taxation, nonlinear pricing, and principal-agent analyses. This alternative path is not long and encompasses a remarkably short list of studies, especially when compared to its huge parent literature in the areas of public economics and industrial organization. That shortness has both advantages and disadvantages. It permits me to be rather complete in a thankfully few number of pages, but the possibilities explored are still rather rudimentary.

My discussion is broken into two parts. The first considers the design of farm programs in the pure hidden-knowledge model using the principles of mechanism design developed by Mirrlees (1971), Baron and Myerson (1982), Guesnerie and Seade (1982), Guesnerie and Laffont (1984), and Weymark (1986). The second considers the design of risk-specific and all-risk agricultural insurance programs using the techniques of principal-agent analysis for the hidden-action model. As a number of other surveys of these more general areas [a short list would include Besanko and Sappington (1986), Caillaud et al. (1988), and Baron (1989)] exist, I will try to keep matters as simple as possible while focusing on the elements of each problem that appear peculiar to agriculture. So in Section 2, I start with the basics of mechanism design in the simplest of all possible worlds (two separate types of farmers), and using a mixture of graphical and nonlinear programming arguments based upon the reduced-form approach of Weymark (1986), I demonstrate how the solutions to the optimal agricultural policy problem under hidden information vary with two different government objectives: a budget-constrained, weighted-utilitarian redistribution model due to Lee (1986) and Chambers (1987, 1992); and social-surplus maximization with political-economy constraints due to Lewis, Feenstra and Ware (1989). After that, I extend the discrete two-type model to a continuous distribution of farmer types and discuss recent developments in the literature.

Much of what is said in Section 2 has direct precedents in the literatures on regulation of natural monopolies and optimal income taxation under asymmetric information. In general, however, the analysis follows the taxation literature more closely than the regulatory literature. Where the regulatory literature focuses on a single firm with private knowledge of its type, the optimal taxation literature focuses on the taxation of a distribution of individuals of differing ability types each with private knowledge of her type. While there are many formal similarities between the two problems, there are important differences in the results that emerge from the two specifications. For example, in the regulatory literature a standard result is that the optimal regulatory scheme should involve no marginal subsidies or taxes at the top of the firm efficiency distribution. In the optimal taxation literature and the analysis below, the parallel result is that optimal policy should involve no marginal subsidies or taxes at one of the two ends of the distribution of individual types. The difference in the results emerges from the fact that in the regulatory literature, the efficiency distribution of the firm provides a unique ordering of types. In the taxation literature, the efficiency distribution and the government's preferences over individuals of different abilities convolute to determine an ordering of producer types.

Section 3 opens with a brief discussion of the agricultural insurance problem under conditions of production uncertainty but symmetric information [Nelson and Loehman (1987)]. Then I turn to a state-contingent model of production uncertainty with perfect observability of states of nature but hidden action on the part of the farmer. Here I show one reason why risk-specific (e.g., hail insurance) agricultural insurance programs can work well even in the presence of hidden action by the farmer. Although the explanation is obvious, it is important because the stylized fact of the agricultural insurance literature is that risk-specific agricultural insurance can operate on a commercial basis with little or no government intervention, but all-risk (multiple-peril) agricultural insurance requires government subsidies and intervention [Gardner and Kramer (1986)]. This analysis unambiguously demonstrates that it is the convolution of hidden action and hidden knowledge (in the form of *ex post* unobservability of the states of nature by the regulator or insurance company) that creates the moral hazard typically associated with all-risk agricultural insurance programs and not the unobservability of hidden action. This leads to the treatment of two distinct hidden-action problems: The first follows Chambers and Quiggin (1996) and considers the design of all-risk agricultural insurance programs in a multi-task, principal-agent setting where the government has direct preferences on an unobservable action variable (nonpoint-source pollutants) and can observe the state of nature that occurs but cannot observe the farmer's commodity output. Section 3 then closes with what I think is a new discussion of the multi-task principal-agent problem where the government again has direct preferences over an unobservable action variable (nonpoint-source pollutants) and can observe farm output but not the state of nature.

2. Mechanism design with hidden knowledge

Our starting point is the simplest hidden-knowledge problem: There are two types of farmers of differing abilities. Each farmer knows his or her type, but the regulating authority either cannot discern a farmer's ability or is prevented by legal or political means from using its knowledge of types to discriminate among farmers.[1] I shall refer to these two types of farmers as high-cost and low-cost farmers. Following Mirrlees (1971) and Spence (1977), it is assumed that the differences between the two types of farmer are purely technical with low-cost farmers having everywhere lower marginal cost than high-cost farmers. Farmers possess twice-differentiable cost functions $c : \Re_+ \times \Theta \to \Re_+$ where $\Theta = \{\theta^1, \theta^2\}$ is the set of farm-type indexes. These cost functions are strictly increasing and strictly convex over $\Re_+$ and have no fixed costs so that $c(0, \theta) = 0$. In what follows, the convention is that subscripts on functions denote partial derivatives:

ASSUMPTION 1. Farm types θ^1 (high-cost) and θ^2 (low-cost) are ranked according to $c_q(q, \theta^2) < c_q(q, \theta^1)$ for all $q \in \Re_+$.

The government's problem is to achieve its objective in the face of the information asymmetry caused by the farmers knowing their farm type, but the government either not knowing it or being unable to use it overtly as a basis for discrimination. Because the farmers realize that knowledge of their type may have economic value they have no selfish reason to reveal it. Perhaps an example illustrates: Suppose the government is prepared to design farm policy in accordance with the principle that the better-off in life should help the less well off. The low-cost farmers, knowing this, would also know that revealing their type would make them candidates for implicit, if not explicit, taxation. Hence, they have no incentive to disclose this information. On the other hand, the high-cost farmers would want to reveal their type to qualify for these extra benefits. Therefore, in running its program, the government cannot rely upon a set of rules predicated upon farmers voluntarily revealing their type. The essence of mechanism design is for the government to come as close as possible to achieving its objective while accounting for these incentives.

---

[1] This latter distinction is important because a standard criticism of the mechanism-design approach to farm policy formulation is that once the government designs and offers an incentive-compatible contract which the farmer accepts and acts upon, the farmer's type is revealed. Hence, if the sole reason that the government does not discriminate directly among farmers is hidden information, a rational farmer would have to realize this and change his or her actions accordingly. This naturally leads to a repeated-game problem. A basic result [Laffont and Tirole (1993, Chapter 10)] in such settings is that the regulator can do no better than to commit at the beginning to implementing the optimal static contract in each period. Typically, however, this optimal commitment scheme will not be renegotiation proof [see, for example, Laffont and Tirole (1993, Chapter 10)].

The analysis of such problems has been greatly facilitated by the *revelation principle* [Dasgupta, Hammond and Maskin (1979), Harris and Townsend (1981), Myerson (1979)]. The basic intuition behind the revelation principle is very similar to Samuelson's notion of revealed preference: A person's economic actions will reflect his or her personal tastes and preferences as well as his or her private information provided the individual acts rationally. The key insight is that for any allocation rule or set of market rules, an observationally equivalent mechanism exists which operates on the principle that individual agents send a truthful message about their private information. Formally, this is referred to as a *truthful direct revelation mechanism* (DRM). This equivalent DRM must always be constructed so that it is in each agent's interest to report his or her private information accurately. This constraint prevents the government or the regulating authority from achieving its objective in an unfettered fashion.

An example illustrates. Suppose that prior to government intervention, agricultural producers face a given market price, p, for their commodity and act as price takers. Presuming that they maximize profit, then both producer types choose to produce where marginal cost equals price. The amount each farmer of type θ^i supplies, $q^*(\theta^i)$, would, therefore, be determined by the implicit solution to the following condition:

$$p - c_q\big(q^*(\theta^i), \theta^i\big) = 0.$$

Under Assumption 1, $q^*(\theta^2) > q^*(\theta^1)$. Low-cost farmers also earn both a higher revenue and a higher profit from the market than high-cost farmers.

Now suppose that the government wants to supplant this market with a DRM that achieves the same level of supply and returns to both producers. Can it do so? The answer is yes. All it would need to do is to announce a payment–production schedule $S(\Theta) = \{B(\theta), q(\theta) : \theta \in \Theta\}$ which is interpretable in the following fashion. If a farmer reports $\theta \in \Theta$ to the government, then he or she is allowed to sell $q(\theta)$ to the government in return for a payment of $B(\theta)$ which the government in turn resells to consumers at the going price of p. The trick is to choose this payment–production schedule appropriately. If it is chosen so that $q(\theta^i) = q^*(\theta^i)$, $B(\theta^i) = pq^*(\theta^i)$, then each farmer will honestly report his or her type to the government. To see why, notice that it must follow for type θ^1, for example, that

$$B(\theta^1) - c\big(q(\theta^1), \theta^1\big) = pq^*(\theta^1) - c\big(q^*(\theta^1), \theta^1\big)$$
$$\geqslant B(\theta^2) - c\big(q(\theta^2), \theta^1\big)$$
$$= pq^*(\theta^2) - c\big(q^*(\theta^2), \theta^1\big).$$

If the inequality here were violated high-cost farmers would have chosen to produce $q^*(\theta^2)$ prior to the government's intervention. But this contradicts rationality. The government can design a DRM for which the farmers' dominant strategy is to tell the truth and which implements the free market outcome. Hence, in considering the design of farm policies, we can always narrow consideration to payment schedules of the same general form as $S(\Theta)$. However, in the presence of an information asymmetry, we must restrict consideration to the $S(\Theta)$ that satisfy the following *incentive compatibility constraints*:

$$
\begin{aligned}
B(\theta^1) - c(q(\theta^1), \theta^1) &\geqslant B(\theta^2) - c(q(\theta^2), \theta^1), \\
B(\theta^2) - c(q(\theta^2), \theta^2) &\geqslant B(\theta^1) - c(q(\theta^1), \theta^2).
\end{aligned}
\tag{1}
$$

Any $S(\Theta)$ satisfying expression (1) elicits truthful revelation of the farmer's cost type. Expression (1) is the mathematical manifestation of the constraints that the information asymmetry places upon the government in designing farm programs. Expressions (1) imply

$$
\begin{aligned}
c(q(\theta^2), \theta^1) - c(q(\theta^1), \theta^1) &\geqslant B(\theta^2) - B(\theta^1) \\
&\geqslant c(q(\theta^2), \theta^2) - c(q(\theta^1), \theta^2).
\end{aligned}
\tag{2}
$$

The outer parts of the inequalities can be rewritten in integral form as

$$
\int_{q(\theta^1)}^{q(\theta^2)} c_q(q, \theta^1) - c_q(q, \theta^2)\, dq \geqslant 0.
$$

By using Assumption 1, it follows that $q(\theta^2) \geqslant q(\theta^1)$ while the second inequality in (2) implies $B(\theta^2) \geqslant B(\theta^1)$. We state this fundamental result on incentive-compatible mechanisms as a lemma for future reference.

LEMMA 1. *Any $S(\Theta)$ satisfying* (1) *must satisfy*

$$
\begin{aligned}
q(\theta^2) &\geqslant q(\theta^1), \\
B(\theta^2) &\geqslant B(\theta^1).
\end{aligned}
$$

In the sections that follow, we shall consider design of agricultural policy mechanisms under two separate objectives: weighted utilitarian income redistribution and welfare maximization subject to political economy constraints. However, before doing so, it is worthwhile to discuss briefly some of the limitations implicit in the analysis that follows. For example, when viewed from a gaming perspective, the type of game being considered is a one-off, leader–follower game, where the government plays the role of the leader. Thus, we are brushing under the carpet a number of potentially complex strategic interactions between the government and the farmer. For example, the use of a DRM implies that once a farmer adopts a production–payment pair, the government will know his or her type. Hence, if the relationship between the government and farmers extended over multiple periods, the farmers realizing this would have another incentive to diverge from the production–payment pairs intended for them. And accordingly, the analysis would have to be adapted to account for such strategic behavior.

One way to adapt the analysis is to assume explicitly that the government is prevented by constitutional or other political-social reasons from exploiting such knowledge when it exists. Another is to endow the government with the ability to commit at the beginning of the game to a firm policy that will not be changed as time passes. When the latter alternative is followed, results broadly similar to the ones found below will be obtained.

2.1. Income redistribution and farm-program design

This section follows a trail initially blazed by Lee (1986) in her study of optimal lending practices for farm lenders. Lee's work constitutes the first application of mechanism design methods to an agricultural policy problem. Following Mirrlees (1971) and Spence (1977), Lee deployed a nonlinear pricing framework, but as Guesnerie and Laffont (1984) have shown, all nonlinear pricing problems involving hidden information can be recast as truthful direct revelation mechanisms. Well before others examined the issue, she demonstrated that placing differential weights on farmers resulted in distinct patterns of allocating credit. Following on her work, Chambers (1987, 1992) systematically related government concerns about different farm groups to specific types of farm policies.

The analysis in this section is based on the premise that the objective of government farm policy is to maximize a weighted sum of farmer producer surplus. The assumption that the government acts to maximize a weighted sum of farmer producer surplus is sufficiently general to encompass more standard formulations which assume that the government has preferences over the simple sums of farmers' incomes while still allowing the government to pursue policies targeted towards specific kinds of farmers. Its weights, therefore, depend upon the farmer's type, and any policy must satisfy the incentive-compatibility constraints (1) and two other constraints: First, farmers should participate in farm programs voluntarily, and second, farm program outlays must meet a government budget constraint. The first constraint is reflected in the presumption that farmers must receive a positive return from participating in the farm program. The farm program is viewed as being designed *tabula rasa* and to encompass all aspects of marketing the farm commodity including its distribution to consumers. In contrast with the treatment in, for example, Chambers (1987, 1992) and Bourgeon, Jayet and Picard (1995), there is no presumption that the farmer sells his or her commodity to consumers under some type of linear pricing arrangement. However, all the optimal outcomes identified below can be implemented by such a mechanism augmented by other program provisions. Formally, we require that

$$
\begin{aligned}
B(\theta^1) - c(q(\theta^1), \theta^1) &\geqslant 0, \\
B(\theta^2) - c(q(\theta^2), \theta^2) &\geqslant 0.
\end{aligned}
\tag{3}
$$

We need only consider the first of the constraints in (3) because by Assumption 1,

$$B(\theta^1) - c(q(\theta^1), \theta^2) \geqslant B(\theta^1) - c(q(\theta^1), \theta^1) \geqslant 0.$$

Applying the second incentive compatibility constraint in (1) establishes that the second constraint in (3) is always satisfied if the first constraint is. In what follows, I shall refer to (3) as the farmers' participation constraints. The government's budget constraint is written as

$$\underline{B} \geqslant \sum_{i=1}^{2} g(\theta^i) B(\theta^i) - U\left(\sum_{i=1}^{2} g(\theta^i) q(\theta^i)\right),$$

where $\underline{B} > 0$ is the upper limit on government expenditures on farm programs and $U : \Re_+ \to \Re_+$ is the consumer's, or more generally society's, valuation of the total amount of the agricultural commodity that is produced. U is a differentiable, strictly increasing, and strictly concave function. Here the notion is that the government makes up any difference between farmer returns and consumer willingness to pay for the commodity.

The government's redistributional preferences are reflected by a weighted utilitarian objective function:

$$w(\theta^1) g(\theta^1) \pi(\theta^1) + w(\theta^2) g(\theta^2) \pi(\theta^2),$$

where $w(\theta^i) \geqslant 0$ is the weight attached to the profits earned by farmers of type i, $g(\theta^i)$ is the number of farmers of type i, and $\pi(\theta^i) = B(\theta^i) - c(q(\theta^i), \theta^i)$. The total number of farmers of both types is given by $N = g(\theta^1) + g(\theta^2)$. With these definitions and using Lemma 1, we can now state the government's mechanism design problem formally as

$$\underset{B(\theta^i) \in \vec{B}, \, q(\theta^i) \in \vec{q}}{\text{Max}} \left\{ \sum_{i=1}^{2} g(\theta^i) w(\theta^i) \pi(\theta^i) \right\},$$

$$\text{s.t.} \quad \pi(\theta^1) \geqslant B(\theta^2) - c(q(\theta^2), \theta^1),$$

$$\pi(\theta^2) \geqslant B(\theta^1) - c(q(\theta^1), \theta^2),$$

$$\pi(\theta^1) \geqslant 0,$$

$$\underline{B} \geqslant \sum_{i=1}^{2} g(\theta^i) B(\theta^i) - U\left(\sum_{i=1}^{2} g(\theta^i) q(\theta^i)\right),$$

where

$$\vec{B} = \left\{ (B(\theta^1), B(\theta^2)) : B(\theta^2) \geqslant B(\theta^1) \right\}$$

and

$$\vec{q} = \{(q(\theta^1), q(\theta^2)): q(\theta^2) \geqslant q(\theta^1)\}.$$

This problem can be solved in a stepwise fashion. In particular, note that it can also be written as

$$\underset{q(\theta^i) \in \vec{q}}{\text{Max}} \left\{ \Pi(q(\theta^1), q(\theta^2), \underline{B}) - \sum_{i=1}^{2} g(\theta^i) w(\theta^i) c(q(\theta^i), \theta^i) \right\},$$

where

$$\Pi(q(\theta^1), q(\theta^2), \underline{B}) = \underset{B(\theta^i) \in \vec{B}}{\text{Max}} \left\{ \sum_{i=1}^{2} g(\theta^i) w(\theta^i) B(\theta^i) \right\}, \tag{4}$$

$$\text{s.t.} \quad \pi(\theta^1) \geqslant B(\theta^2) - c(q(\theta^2), \theta^1),$$
$$\pi(\theta^2) \geqslant B(\theta^1) - c(q(\theta^1), \theta^2),$$
$$\pi(\theta^1) \geqslant 0,$$
$$\underline{B} \geqslant \sum_{i=1}^{2} g(\theta^i) B(\theta^i) - U\left(\sum_{i=1}^{2} g(\theta^i) q(\theta^i) \right).$$

For fixed output levels, finding the solution to the first-stage problem, $\Pi(q(\theta^1), q(\theta^2), \underline{B})$, is a simple linear program.

2.1.1. The solution to the first-stage problem

I first show that the budget constraint must always bind. Suppose that it didn't: then both $B(\theta^i)$ could be increased by a small, but strictly positive, amount while preserving the incentive compatibility constraints. But this change strictly increases the value of the objective function. Hence,

LEMMA 2. *In any solution to the first-stage problem, the government budget constraint is binding:*

$$\underline{B} = \sum_{i=1}^{2} g(\theta^i) B(\theta^i) - U\left(\sum_{i=1}^{2} g(\theta^i) q(\theta^i) \right).$$

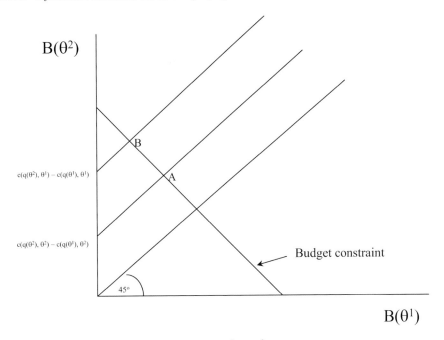

Figure 1. $\Pi(q(\theta^2), q(\theta^2), B)$.

The budget constraint is illustrated graphically in Figure 1 by a negatively sloped line segment with slope

$$\frac{\mathrm{d}B(\theta^2)}{\mathrm{d}B(\theta^1)} = -\frac{g(\theta^1)}{g(\theta^2)}.$$

If a solution to this first-stage problem exists, it must occur somewhere on this line segment. Lemma 1 further allows us to restrict attention to that portion lying above the 45° ray (the bisector) emanating from the origin. The next set of constraints considered are the incentive compatibility constraints. By (2), the feasible region satisfies

$$c\big(q(\theta^2), \theta^1\big) - c\big(q(\theta^1), \theta^1\big) + B(\theta^1) \geq B(\theta^2),$$
$$B(\theta^2) \geq B(\theta^1) + c\big(q(\theta^2), \theta^2\big) - c\big(q(\theta^1), \theta^2\big).$$

Figure 1 illustrates by the two line segments parallel to and above the bisector with vertical intercepts of $c(q(\theta^2), \theta^1) - c(q(\theta^1), \theta^1)$ and $c(q(\theta^2), \theta^2) - c(q(\theta^1), \theta^2)$, respectively. I have drawn these line segments under the presumption that $q(\theta^2) > q(\theta^1)$. If $q(\theta^2) = q(\theta^1)$, this restriction reduces to

$$B(\theta^1) \geq B(\theta^2) \geq B(\theta^1)$$

implying, of course, that $B(\theta^1) = B(\theta^2)$, i.e., both producer types are treated the same, or, in other words, are *bunched*. The pairs of total payments to the farmers that meet both the incentive compatibility constraints and the budget constraint are those lying on the budget constraint but between these two lines lying parallel to the bisector. The final constraint is the farmer-θ^1 participation constraint, portrayed pictorially by a line segment parallel to the $B(\theta^2)$ axis with horizontal intercept equaling $c(q(\theta^1), \theta^1)$. There are at least two possibilities: the high-cost farmer's participation constraint cuts the budget constraint to the right and below point A in Figure 1. In that instance, the feasible set for the first-stage linear program is empty and so we set its optimal value to $-\infty$. Next, the high-cost farmer's participation constraint may cut the budget constraint to the left and above point A in Figure 1, so that the feasible set for the first-stage linear program is nonempty. Its solution value will depend upon two things: where the high-cost farmer's participation constraint cuts the budget constraint, and on the relative weights that the government places upon the two farmer types in making its redistributional decisions. The case that we analyze is the most interesting and, fortuitously, the least complicated: The high-cost farmer's participation constraint cuts the budget constraint to the left and above point B in Figure 1.[2]

2.1.1.1. High-cost farmers weighted the most. Suppose, to start, that the government's objective is progressive in that a higher weight is placed upon high-cost farmer profit than upon low-cost farmers. Then the solution to the first-stage problem is obviously at point A in Figure 1: This represents the highest possible return to high-cost producers that is consistent with the budget constraint, the incentive compatibility constraints, and the high-cost farmer's participation constraint. The solution to the first-stage linear program, thus, solves the two linear equations:

$$\sum_{i=1}^{2} g(\theta^i) B(\theta^i) = \underline{B} + U\left(\sum_{i=1}^{2} g(\theta^i) q(\theta^i)\right),$$

$$B(\theta^2) - B(\theta^1) = c(q(\theta^2), \theta^2) - c(q(\theta^1), \theta^2).$$

There are several observations to make. First, the farm program has the characteristic that the low-cost farmers are just indifferent between the payment–production pair intended for the high-cost farmers and the payment–production pair intended for them. In Guesnerie and Seade's (1982) terminology, there is a *downward link* in the payment–production schedule. Intuitively, this result is pleasing because the incentive problem is

---

[2] As will be clear from the arguments that follow, if the high-cost farmer's participation constraint cuts the budget constraint to the right of point B, but to the left of point A, and low-cost farmers are weighted more heavily than high-cost farmers, it is possible that the first-best can be implemented by making the high-cost farmer just indifferent between participating and not participating. However, this can only happen when the budget available for farm programs is relatively small, and so the government's best strategy is to let the free market rule.

to keep the low-cost farmers from adopting the payment–production pair intended for the more favored high-cost farmers. Second, because we are specifically considering the case where the high-cost farmer's participation constraint is not effective, both types of farmers make strictly positive returns from the farm program. And third,

LEMMA 3. *If* $w(\theta^1) > w(\theta^2)$, *then*

$$\Pi(q(\theta^1), q(\theta^2), \underline{B}) = \overline{w}\left(\underline{B} + U\left(\sum_{i=1}^{2} g(\theta^i)q(\theta^i)\right)\right)$$
$$+ g(\theta^1)(\overline{w} - w(\theta^1))(c(q(\theta^2), \theta^2) - c(q(\theta^1), \theta^2)),$$

where

$$\overline{w} = \frac{\sum_{i=1}^{2} g(\theta^i)w(\theta^i)}{N}$$

is the average weight attached to farmers.

2.1.1.2. Low-cost farmers weighted the most.   The next alternative occurs when the government's objective is regressive in that it weights the returns to low-cost farmers more than it does the returns to high-cost farmers. In this instance, the solution to the first-stage linear program occurs at point B in Figure 1: Here, revenues to low-cost producers are as high as possible and still consistent with the budget constraint and the incentive compatibility constraints. The optimal producer payments solve the following pair of linear equations:

$$\sum_{i=1}^{2} g(\theta^i)B(\theta^i) = \underline{B} + U\left(\sum_{i=1}^{2} g(\theta^i)q(\theta^i)\right),$$
$$c(q(\theta^2), \theta^1) - c(q(\theta^1), \theta^1) = B(\theta^2) - B(\theta^1).$$

High-cost farmers are offered a payment–production bundle that leaves them just indifferent to adopting the payment–production pair intended for the now more favored low-cost farmers. We may think of the optimal contract structure as containing an *upward link*. Both producers continue to make nonnegative profit, and

LEMMA 4. *If* $w(\theta^2) > w(\theta^1)$, *then*

$$\Pi(q(\theta^1), q(\theta^2), \underline{B}) = \overline{w}\left(\underline{B} + U\left(\sum_{i=1}^{2} g(\theta^i)q(\theta^i)\right)\right)$$
$$+ g(\theta^2)(w(\theta^2) - \overline{w})(c(q(\theta^2), \theta^1) - c(q(\theta^1), \theta^1)).$$

2.1.1.3. Both types weighted equally. The final case considered is when the government weights both producer types equally. In this instance, there exists an infinity of
solutions to the first-stage linear programming problem, each corresponding to a particular point on the budget constraint between points A and B. Because points that lie in
the interior of this region do not require either of the incentive compatibility constraints
to be binding, without loss of generality, we have

LEMMA 5. *If* $w(\theta^2) = w(\theta^1)$, *then*

$$\Pi\left(q\left(\theta^1\right), q\left(\theta^2\right), \underline{B}\right) = \overline{w}\left(\underline{B} + U\left(\sum_{i=1}^{2} g\left(\theta^i\right) q\left(\theta^i\right)\right)\right).$$

2.1.2. Optimal redistributive farm programs

We shall consider these three cases in the reverse order from which they were presented
in the previous section.

2.1.2.1. Both types weighted equally. When the government weights both types of
farmers equally, by Lemma 5 the optimal farm policy mechanism solves

$$\underset{q(\theta^i)\in\bar{q}}{\text{Max}}\left\{\overline{w}\left(\underline{B} + U\left(\sum_{i=1}^{2} g\left(\theta^i\right) q\left(\theta^i\right)\right)\right) - \sum_{i=1}^{2} g\left(\theta^i\right)\overline{w}c\left(q\left(\theta^i\right), \theta^i\right)\right\}.$$

This problem can be reduced to a simple unconstrained nonlinear program by defining
the auxiliary variable $\alpha \geqslant 0$ by

$$q\left(\theta^2\right) = q\left(\theta^1\right) + \alpha.$$

The first-order condition for the nonnegative auxiliary variable is

$$\overline{w}g\left(\theta^2\right)\left(U'\left(\sum_{i=1}^{2} g\left(\theta^i\right) q\left(\theta^i\right)\right) - c_q\left(q\left(\theta^2\right), \theta^2\right)\right) \leqslant 0, \quad \alpha \geqslant 0,$$

in the usual complementary-slackness notation, while the first-order condition for $q(\theta^1)$
is

$$\overline{w}\sum_{i=1}^{2} g\left(\theta^i\right)\left(U'\left(\sum_{i=1}^{2} g\left(\theta^i\right) q\left(\theta^i\right)\right) - c_q\left(q\left(\theta^i\right), \theta^i\right)\right) \leqslant 0, \quad q\left(\theta^1\right) \geqslant 0.$$

Subject to relatively mild conditions on the consumer valuation and cost structures, an
interior solution to these conditions exists as the joint solution to the following two

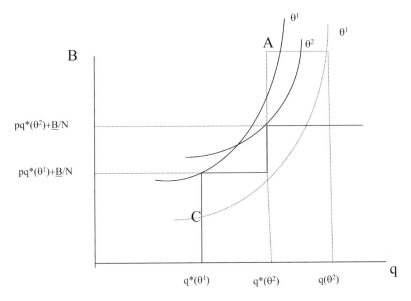

Figure 2. A decoupled policy mechanism.

equations:

$$U'\left(\sum_{i=1}^{2} g(\theta^i)q^*(\theta^i)\right) = c_q\left(q^*(\theta^1), \theta^1\right),$$

$$(5)$$

$$U'\left(\sum_{i=1}^{2} g(\theta^i)q^*(\theta^i)\right) = c_q\left(q^*(\theta^2), \theta^2\right).$$

Thus, when both producer types weigh equally in the government's preference function, the optimal farm-policy mechanism requires that marginal consumer valuation of the commodity be equated to the marginal cost of production for both types of farmers. An incentive-compatible market mechanism that will achieve this production pattern is a competitive market with linear price corresponding to $p = U'(\sum_{i=1}^{2} g(\theta^i)q^*(\theta^i))$ and government side payments to producers chosen so as not to violate incentive compatibility (for example, equal lump-sum payments to all producers in the amount $\underline{B}/N$). This particular mechanism is illustrated in Figure 2. There the solid curve labeled θ^1 represents the indifference curve for a high-cost farmer. The indifference curve's slope is given by high-cost farmer marginal cost; points above the curve represent higher levels of profit. Similarly, the curve labeled θ^2 represents the indifference curve for a low-cost farmer. As drawn, both farmer types willingly adopt the production pattern associated with the competitive market mechanism while receiving additional lump-sum payments from the government. Hence, when the government has no clear redistributive goals among farmer types, the optimal farm-policy mechanism need not interfere in the operation of the competitive market either on the producer or the consumer side, and government resources are allocated to farmers in a fashion that does not distort production incentives. In the jargon of agricultural policy, such a policy mechanism is called *decoupled* because the link between income support for farmers and farm production has been broken.

PROPOSITION 6. *When $w(\theta^2) = w(\theta^1)$, a competitive market mechanism with decoupled payments to farmers implements the preferred policy outcome.*

Decoupled farm programs are the type most frequently recommended by economists on efficiency grounds. This result clearly demonstrates why. When the government is not trying to re-distribute income, it can do no better than to allow farmers to go it alone and to rely upon the marketplace for their returns. This allows them to generate maximal productive surplus at minimal budgetary cost to the government. The reason, of course, is that the producers' objectives and the government's objective coincide in this instance. Hence, the informational asymmetries between the producers and the government have no important role to play in the analysis. However, when the government wants to re-distribute income, its objective only coincides with those of a subset of the farm population, the ones to whom it wants to re-distribute income. The government's objective clashes with those of the remaining farmers from whom the government intends to re-distribute income. Informational asymmetries will have an important role to play in such circumstances because the unfavored producers can exploit these informational asymmetries to their own advantage while inhibiting the government from achieving its redistributive goals.

So when the government wants to redistribute farm incomes, it must find some way of circumventing these informational problems. Given the structure of our model, this necessarily entails directly interfering with their productive decisions so that, generally speaking, optimal redistributive policies will not be decoupled.

2.1.2.2. Low-cost farmers weighted the most. When $w(\theta^2) > w(\theta^1)$, Lemma 4 implies that the optimal farm program solves

$$
\max_{q(\theta^1),\alpha} \left\{
\begin{array}{l}
\overline{w}\left(\underline{B} + U\left(\sum_{i=1}^{2} g(\theta^i)q(\theta^i)\right)\right) \\
+ g(\theta^2)\left(w(\theta^2) - \overline{w}\right)\left(c(q(\theta^2),\theta^1) - c(q(\theta^1),\theta^1)\right) \\
- \sum_{i=1}^{2} w(\theta^i)g(\theta^i)c(q(\theta^i),\theta^i)
\end{array}
\right\}.
$$

Here the first-order condition for the auxiliary variable after some minor manipulation can be written

$$
\overline{w}g(\theta^2)\left(U' - c_q(q(\theta^2),\theta^2)\right)
$$
$$
- g(\theta^2)\left(w(\theta^2) - \overline{w}\right)\left(c_q(q(\theta^2),\theta^2) - c_q(q(\theta^2),\theta^1)\right) \leqslant 0, \quad \alpha \geqslant 0,
$$

while the first-order condition for $q(\theta^1)$ is expressible as

$$\overline{w}\sum_{i=1}^{2}\left(g(\theta^i)U' - c_q(q(\theta^i),\theta^i)\right)$$

$$- g(\theta^2)(w(\theta^2)-\overline{w})(c_q(q(\theta^2),\theta^2) - c_q(q(\theta^2),\theta^1)) \leqslant 0, \quad q(\theta^1) \geqslant 0.$$

We first consider the case where there exists an interior solution to both of these first-order conditions. In that case the optimal production pattern satisfies

$$U' = c_q(q(\theta^1),\theta^1),$$

$$U' - c_q(q(\theta^2),\theta^2) = \frac{g(\theta^2)(w(\theta^2)-\overline{w})}{\overline{w}g(\theta^2)}(c_q(q(\theta^2),\theta^2) - c_q(q(\theta^2),\theta^1)). \tag{6}$$

By Assumption 1, the right-hand side of the second expression in (6) is a negative number implying that

$$c_q(q(\theta^2),\theta^2) > U'\left(\sum_{i=1}^{2}g(\theta^i)q(\theta^i)\right) = c_q(q(\theta^1),\theta^1). \tag{7}$$

So, when low-cost farmers weigh more heavily in the government's preference function than high-cost farmers, an optimally designed farm-policy mechanism involves high-cost farmers producing at the point where their marginal cost exactly equals the consumer marginal willingness to pay for an additional unit of the farm commodity, but low-cost farmers produce at a point where their marginal cost exceeds the consumer marginal willingness to pay. Hence, if all producer returns had to be financed solely from consumer payments, low-cost farmers would be overproducing at the margin in the following sense: If the production of high-cost farmers were held constant, consumers would be unwilling to pay the marginal cost of an additional unit of low-cost production.

In a moment, I shall show that an optimal farm policy mechanism characterized by (6) involves overproduction relative to what occurs in the competitive market mechanism, and that low-cost farmers are asked to produce more than in the competitive market mechanism while high-cost farmers are asked to produce less than in the competitive market mechanism. But before demonstrating that result, following Mirrlees (1971), Seade (1977), and Lee (1986), it is worth observing that the redistributive policy followed by the government involves having the relatively unfavored, high-cost farmers produce efficiently at the margin. Their marginal subsidy over and above what consumers are willing to pay is zero. (This does not mean, however, that their total subsidy is zero.) There are two reasons this happens: First, because of the linear weight structure, the government wants to transfer all producer surplus realized by high-cost farmers to the now more favored low-cost farmers. Having said this, the government also

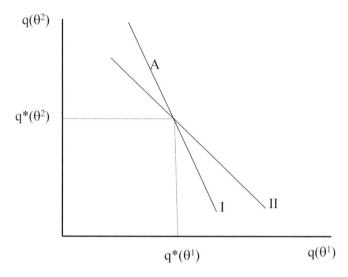

Figure 3. Overproduct and underproduction.

wants these high-cost farmers to produce as efficiently as possible. This maximizes the amount of high-cost producer surplus to be transferred while also diminishing the high-cost producers' reliance on the government's budget to fund its reservation profit level.

This result represents a marked departure from the type of result that one would expect to find in the nearly parallel literature on the regulation of a single firm whose type is its own private knowledge. As mentioned in the introduction, a naive application of results from that literature to the current problem might suggest that the optimal farm policy would require no departures at the margin from efficient production for the low-cost producers and departures from efficient production for high-cost producers.[3] But that would ignore the redistributional aspects of the farm policy, and at the margin it would lower the amount of surplus that could be transferred from high-cost to low-cost farmers.

To understand why overproduction is optimal in this case, consider the locus of points in $(q(\theta^1), q(\theta^2))$ space as illustrated by the curve labeled I in Figure 3. These are the points which are consistent with the first equality in expression (5) holding. The slope of this curve is given by

$$\frac{dq(\theta^2)}{dq(\theta^1)} = \frac{c_{qq}(q(\theta^1), \theta^1) - g(\theta^1)U''}{g(\theta^2)U''},$$

---

[3] This turns out to be true when high-cost farmers are weighted the most in the government's objective function.

while the slope of the curve (illustrated by the curve labeled II in the figure) tracing out the locus of points consistent with the second equality in (5) holding is

$$\frac{dq(\theta^2)}{dq(\theta^1)} = \frac{-g(\theta^1)U''}{g(\theta^2)U'' - c_{qq}(q(\theta^2), \theta^2)}.$$

As illustrated, curve II cuts curve I from below; the competitive market outcome is at the point of intersection between the two curves. Points lying above each curve correspond to situations where marginal cost exceeds consumer marginal willingness to pay. Points lying below the curves correspond to situations where marginal cost is less than consumer marginal willingness to pay. By expression (7), when low-cost farmers receive more weight in the government's objective function, the production allocation associated with the optimal farm-policy mechanism must be at a point like A in Figure 3. We conclude that

$$q(\theta^2) > q^*(\theta^2) > q^*(\theta^1) > q(\theta^1). \tag{8}$$

Now, using this fact, the convexity of the cost functions, and expression (7) implies

$$U'\left(\sum_{i=1}^{2} g(\theta^i) q(\theta^i)\right) = c_q(q(\theta^1), \theta^1) < c_q(q^*(\theta^1), \theta^1)$$

$$= U'\left(\sum_{i=1}^{2} g(\theta^i) q^*(\theta^i)\right).$$

The strict concavity of the consumer valuation function now leads us to conclude that

$$\sum_{i=1}^{2} g(\theta^i) q(\theta^i) > \sum_{i=1}^{2} g(\theta^i) q^*(\theta^i).$$

When low-cost farmers are favored, an optimal farm-policy mechanism involves a *spreading* of the output distribution as compared to the competitive market output distribution. The reason this happens can be easily understood by returning to Figure 2. Suppose that the government tried to achieve its policy goals by maintaining the competitive market mechanism but attempted to redirect its budget towards low-cost farmers. This would entail increasing the lump-sum transfer to low-cost producers while reducing the transfer to high-cost producers. Figure 2 illustrates by moving the low-cost producer payment–production pair to, say, a point like A and the high-cost producer payment–production pair to a point like C. This attempted reallocation is not incentive-compatible as high-cost farmers now strictly prefer the payment–production pair intended for low-cost farmers to their own. Hence, they would adopt it. So if the government wants to raise the return to low-cost farmers to a level like that associated with point A, it must be prepared to also increase the production required for that payment by moving the payment–production pair horizontally to the right of A. Low-cost farmers are required to produce at least the amount $q(\theta^2)$ illustrated there. Similarly, if the government were to move the payment–production pair intended for low-cost farmers horizontally to the left of C, it can ensure that the high-cost farmers will not prefer the payment–production pair intended for the low-cost farmers. On balance, the increased production realized from low-cost farmers will outweigh the decreased production from high-cost farmers.

Also note that the form of the optimal farm-policy mechanism has important implications for consumers as well. In most hidden-information models of farm policy, consumers are simply assumed to be price takers. Here, we allow for more general behavior. Because total output is now higher than in the competitive market mechanism, if the commodity is distributed to them via linear pricing, as would be the case for example with a Brannan-type policy, they would be strictly better off. They can consume more at a lower price than in the competitive market mechanism with the balance being paid by taxpayers.

PROPOSITION 7. *If $w(\theta^2) > w(\theta^1)$, the optimal farm-policy mechanism involves low-cost farmers producing where their marginal cost exceeds the consumer marginal valuation of the commodity, and high-cost producers producing where their marginal cost equals the consumer marginal valuation. Relative to the competitive market mechanism, low-cost farmers produce more while high-cost farmers produce less, and overall market production is higher. If the commodity is disbursed to consumers via a linear price, consumers are strictly better off than in the competitive market mechanism.*

A specific mechanism which can implement this policy outcome is a modified cost-recovery scheme. This is most easily demonstrated in the case where consumer demand is perfectly elastic so that the marginal valuation of another unit of the commodity for consumption is the constant p. Now suppose that for all units of production less than or equal to the $q(\theta^1)$ that solves (6) producers are required to sell in the market at the going rate of p, but for units in excess of this amount but no greater than the $q(\theta^2)$ which solves (6) producers are allowed to recover costs according to the high-cost farmer's cost structure

$$c(q, \theta^1) - c(q(\theta^1), \theta^1).$$

The reward scheme for farmers could then be written as in terms of a nonlinear pricing schedule

$$B^*(q) = \begin{cases} b + pq, & q \leqslant q(\theta^1), \\ b + pq(\theta^1) + c(q, \theta^1) - c(q(\theta^1), \theta^1), & q(\theta^1) < q \leqslant q(\theta^2), \end{cases}$$

where b is a lump-sum payment granted to all farmers. Faced with this nonlinear pricing schedule, high-cost farmers always weakly prefer $q(\theta^1)$ while low-cost farmers strongly prefer $q(\theta^2)$ because they are allowed to recover costs for production in excess of $q(\theta^1)$ at the rate at which they would be incurred by a high-cost farmer. This guarantees them a positive profit on each extra unit of output produced. Accordingly, this nonlinear pricing structure would implement the desired policy outcome in (weakly) dominant strategies.

So far we have simply presumed that the optimal level of the auxiliary variable is greater than zero, i.e., there does not exist any bunching of producer types. I now reconfirm a result originally due to Guesnerie and Seade (1982) that an optimal farm-policy mechanism with only two types cannot involve bunching. The only case that we consider is the only one of practical relevance, when bunching requires both types of farmers to produce the same positive amount of output, $q(\theta^1)$, and receive the same payment

$$B(\theta^1) = B(\theta^2) = \frac{B + U(Nq(\theta^1))}{N}.$$

A necessary condition for bunching to occur is that

$$\overline{w}g(\theta^2)(U' - c_q(q(\theta^1), \theta^2))$$
$$< g(\theta^2)(w(\theta^2) - \overline{w})(c_q(q(\theta^1), \theta^2) - c_q(q(\theta^1), \theta^1))$$

and

$$g(\theta^2)(w(\theta^2) - \overline{w})(c_q(q(\theta^1), \theta^2) - c_q(q(\theta^1), \theta^1))$$
$$= \overline{w}g(\theta^2)(U' - c_q(q(\theta^1), \theta^2)) + \overline{w}g(\theta^1)(U' - c_q(q(\theta^1), \theta^1)).$$

The first inequality follows from the first-order condition for the auxiliary variable while the equality is required for an interior solution for $q(\theta^1)$. By Assumption 1 and the presumption that low-cost farmers receive higher weight, the right-hand side of the inequality is negative, implying that the left is as well. Now adding the inequality and the equality yields $U' - c_q(q(\theta^1), \theta^1) > 0$, which with the fact that $U' - c_q(q(\theta^1), \theta^2) < 0$ contradicts Assumption 1. Hence, there can be no bunching and the auxiliary variable must always be positive.

2.1.2.3. High-cost farmers weighted the most. We now turn to the final case to be considered in this section, when high-cost farmers weigh more heavily in the government's social calculus than low-cost farmers. By Lemma 3, the optimal farm-policy mechanism solves

$$\underset{q(\theta^1), \alpha}{\text{Max}} \left\{ \begin{array}{l} \overline{w}(\underline{B} + U(\sum_{i=1}^{2} g(\theta^i)q(\theta^i))) \\ + g(\theta^1)(\overline{w} - w(\theta^1))(c(q(\theta^2), \theta^2) - c(q(\theta^1), \theta^2)) \\ - \sum_{i=1}^{2} w(\theta^i)g(\theta^i)c(q(\theta^i), \theta^i) \end{array} \right\}.$$

The first-order condition for the auxiliary variable can be written after some manipulation as

$$\overline{w}g(\theta^2)(U' - c_q(q(\theta^2), \theta^2)) \leqslant 0, \quad \alpha \geqslant 0,$$

while the first-order condition for high-cost farmer production is

$$\overline{w}\sum_{i=1}^{2} g(\theta^i)(U' - c_q(q(\theta^i), \theta^i))$$

$$+ g(\theta^1)(\overline{w} - w(\theta^1))(c_q(q(\theta^1), \theta^1) - c_q(q(\theta^1), \theta^2)) \leqslant 0, \quad q(\theta^1) \geqslant 0.$$

An argument very similar to the one that was made when low-cost farmers weighed more heavily in the government's objective function than high-cost farmers will reveal that it is only optimal to bunch these producer types if the optimal farm-policy mechanism entails both types producing nothing. Hence, so long as high-cost farm types produce something the optimal farm policy mechanism must satisfy

$$U' = c_q(q(\theta^2), \theta^2),$$

$$U' - c_q(q(\theta^1), \theta^1) = \frac{g(\theta^1)(w(\theta^1) - \overline{w})}{\overline{w}g(\theta^1)}(c_q(q(\theta^1), \theta^1) - c_q(q(\theta^1), \theta^2)).$$

$$(9)$$

The first expression in (9) reveals that an optimal farm policy now requires low-cost farmers to equate their marginal cost to consumer marginal valuation. However, by Assumption 1, the expression on the right-hand side of the second equality in (9) is positive, indicating that high-cost farmers are required to produce at a point where their marginal cost is smaller than the consumer marginal valuation of the farm commodity. Therefore, consumers would willingly pay for an output expansion by high-cost farmers, but not by low-cost farmers.

This last result accords closely with the kind of results that emerge from the literature on the regulation of a single firm under asymmetric information. As mentioned earlier, there one always finds it optimal to have no departures from efficiency at the top of the firm's efficiency distribution. Here we are getting a parallel result because it ensures the government a larger surplus pool from which to draw in transferring revenues to the high-cost farmers.

Using arguments very similar to those used in the case when low-cost farmers weigh more heavily in the government's social calculus, we can establish that an optimal farm-policy mechanism requires the output distribution to satisfy expression (8). However, because we now require low-cost farmers to equate marginal cost to the consumer marginal valuation of the commodity, the strict convexity of the producer cost structures implies

$$U'\left(\sum_{i=1}^{2} g(\theta^i)q(\theta^i)\right) = c_q(q(\theta^2), \theta^2) > c_q(q^*(\theta^2), \theta^2)$$

$$= U'\left(\sum_{i=1}^{2} g(\theta^i)q^*(\theta^i)\right).$$

And using the concavity of the consumer evaluation function we conclude

$$\sum_{i=1}^{2} g(\theta^i)q(\theta^i) < \sum_{i=1}^{2} g(\theta^i)q^*(\theta^i).$$

When government preferences are tilted in favor of high-cost farmers, the optimal farm policy mechanism entails producing less than in the competitive market mechanism. So if a linear pricing scheme is used to distribute the commodity to consumers, they will be strictly worse off than under the competitive market mechanism, or the optimal policy mechanism that prevails when low-cost farmers are relatively more favored.

Hueth (2000), in a closely related model that allows for countervailing incentives, has shown that a production pattern similar to that required here can be implemented by using a stylized version of an agricultural subsidy scheme found in the United States. There, producers sold what they produced in a competitive market, and in turn they were eligible for production subsidies. But total, per-farm subsidy payments were capped at a fixed dollar amount (typically $50,000). More recently, Bourgeon and Chambers (2000b) have shown that simultaneous payment of production and acreage retirement subsidies can be rationalized in a limiting version of this model where the goal of farm policy is to ensure that high-cost farmers achieve a parity income.

A closely related mechanism can now implement the payment–production schedule. The only difference is that a side-payment is required from low-cost farmers to ensure incentive compatibility and mechanism optimality. This is most easily illustrated for the case where consumer demand for the commodity is perfectly elastic at the constant price p, i.e., $U'(\sum_{i=1}^{2} g(\theta^i)q(\theta^i)) = p$ over the entire domain of the marginal valuation function. Suppose the government offers the following payment schedule to producers, $B(q)$, relating their returns to output:

$$B(q) = \begin{cases} (p+s)q, & q \leqslant q(\theta^1), \\ (p+s)q(\theta^1) + p(q - q(\theta^1)) - t, & q > q(\theta^1), \end{cases}$$

where the production subsidy, s, is chosen so that

$$(p+s)q(\theta^1) = B(\theta^1)$$

$$= \frac{B + p(g(\theta^1)q(\theta^1) + g(\theta^2)q^*(\theta^2)) - g(\theta^2)(c(q^*(\theta^2), \theta^2) - c(q(\theta^1), \theta^2))}{N},$$

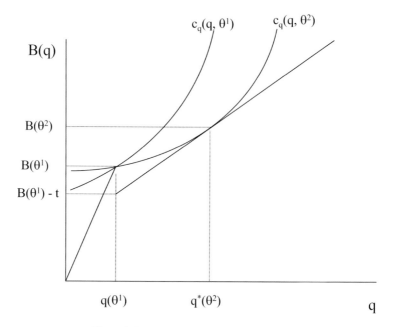

Figure 4. Production subsides and payments cap.

and the side payment, t, which equals the difference in market profit the low-cost firm can make from producing and selling $q^*(\theta^2)$ instead of $q(\theta^1)$, is chosen to satisfy the incentive compatibility conditions

$$t = pq^*(\theta^2) - c(q^*(\theta^2), \theta^2) - (pq(\theta^1) - c(q(\theta^1), \theta^2)).$$

(Note that because of the constant marginal consumer valuation of the commodity, the low-cost producers optimally produce $q^*(\theta^2)$.) This payment schedule corresponds to a producer subsidy with a total payment cap equaling $sq(\theta^1)$. Pictorially, it is represented in Figure 4 by the discontinuous policy schedule that starts as a ray emanating from the origin and going to the point $(B(\theta^1), q(\theta^1))$ with slope equal to $p + s$. At that point, the payment schedule jumps down discontinuously to $(B(\theta^1) - t, q(\theta^1))$ and after that increases linearly with slope equaling p. Production over and above $q(\theta^1)$ incurs no subsidy outlays.

PROPOSITION 8 [Hueth (2000)]. *If $w(\theta^1) > w(\theta^2)$, a deficiency payment scheme with a total cap on subsidy payments and incentive-compatible side payments can implement the most preferred payment–production schedule.*

One of the curiosities of modern farm programs is that they frequently resort to schemes which actually pay producers not to produce. In essence, certain farmers are given government monies simply because they are, or have been, farmers. And like most other welfare programs in the United States, to qualify for these government payments, individuals have to refrain in some way from earning income. For example, the Food Security Act of 1986 mandated a program called the Dairy Termination Program that involved total buyouts of dairy farmers [Chambers (1992)]. At the time it was introduced it was popularly viewed as an "early retirement" package for older dairy farmers. When $w(\theta^2) > w(\theta^1)$, the only way such a program could be the result of an optimally designed policy is if it were optimal to have all producers not produce. However, in the case of progressive welfare weights $w(\theta^1) > w(\theta^2)$, it is quite easy to see, following arguments originally made in Chambers' (1989c) study of workfare and welfare, that a scientifically designed farm program can entail having low-cost farmers producing where their marginal cost equals marginal consumer valuation of the commodity and high-cost producers not producing at all.

From the first-order conditions, this production pattern can only occur if

$$U'\big(g(\theta^2)q(\theta^2)\big) = c_q\big(q(\theta^2), \theta^2\big)$$

and

$$c_q\big(q(\theta^2), \theta^2\big) < c_q\big(0, \theta^1\big) + \frac{w(\theta^1) - \overline{w}}{\overline{w}}\big(c_q\big(0, \theta^1\big) - c_q\big(0, \theta^2\big)\big).$$

The right-hand side of the second expression here is strictly positive and strongly increasing in $w(\theta^1)$. Hence, if the weight on high-cost farmers grows unboundedly large, the optimally designed farm-policy mechanism will involve a buyout of the high-cost farmers. Moreover, the rate at which the right-hand side approaches infinity as the weight on high-cost farmers rises depends critically upon the marginal cost differences between high- and low-cost farmers at the origin. The larger these cost differences are, the more rapidly the right-hand side will approach infinity as $w(\theta^1)$ rises. Intuitively, therefore, a buyout program for high-cost producers is more likely to be optimal if there are relatively large cost differences between the two types or if high-cost producers receive a much higher weight than low-cost producers in the government's welfare calculus. The reason that this is true is apparent. When the marginal cost differences at the origin are quite large, the low-cost farmer's opportunity cost of the buyout is relatively high compared to the high-cost farmer's. So, in this case producing nothing becomes a relatively cheap way for the high-cost farmer to signal that he or she is worthy of the benefits intended for him or her. On the other hand, the low-cost farmer's cost of mimicking the high-cost farmer's production practices become unreasonably large in this instance.

Another interesting case emerges when the government places little or no weight upon low-cost farmers, and there are relatively few high-cost farmers. In this instance, $(w(\theta^1) - \overline{w})/\overline{w}$ goes toward infinity as the number of high-cost farmers goes to zero, and again a buyout could be optimal.

PROPOSITION 9. *If $w(\theta^1) > w(\theta^2)$, there is a weight structure which makes total buyouts of high-cost farmers an optimal farm policy.*

2.2. Agricultural policy reform

Mechanism design is usually viewed as a way to design policies *tabula rasa*. For example, in the previous section we explored the best forms of agricultural policies to achieve the government's distributional objectives. However, mechanism design is also useful in analyzing the reform of agricultural policies. The reform of agricultural policies is of more than just theoretical interest. For example, heavy government involvement in the agricultural sectors of both the United States and the European Community during the 1980s severely stressed those economies' fiscal budgets. And as a result, both economies experienced pressure to reform their agricultural policies. In the United States, the pressure was to return agriculture to a free-market footing and culminated in the 1995 Farm Bill that broke many of the remaining linkages between government programs and producers' decisions. The European Community, on the other hand, has elected to follow a page from U.S. agricultural policy history and has turned to acreage retirement programs, to limit the amount of output on which export refunds are paid.

Lewis, Feenstra and Ware (1989) examined optimal agricultural policy reform subject to the constraint that the majority of the farmers adopt the reform voluntarily. Bourgeon, Jayet and Picard (1995) examined the optimal redesign of the European Community's pricing and acreage retirement programs subject to the constraints that farmers voluntarily participate in the new program. Both models were developed for a continuum of producer types, so in this section I shall not attempt to replicate their analysis. Instead I shall use the platform set by the Lewis, Feenstra and Ware (1989) approach to illustrate some of the salient issues that a mechanism-design approach to policy reform raises. The reader should note that the mechanism-design approach, unlike the more standard analysis of policy reform, focuses on reforms which the government can implement in a given information setting. Therefore, the problem is not to find a reform that minimizes deadweight loss, but to find a policy reform that is both efficient and implementable. A conundrum that the more standard deadweight loss approach to policy reform has never addressed successfully is why agricultural policies are not immediately converted into programs involving lump-sum transfers. Because lump-sum transfers are Pareto efficient, it is easy to see that they can be designed to satisfy the political economy constraint of leaving farmers no worse off. However, in the face of informational differences lump-sum transfers are not generally incentive-compatible and, therefore, may not be feasible.

The informational structure of the model is the same as before, but now it is presumed that a set of farm programs already exist, farmers collect real economic rents from these programs, and reforming these farm programs will require the tacit support of at least some of these farmers (or their supporters in the legislature). It is no longer assumed that the government is driven by a redistributional objective. Instead its goal is to maximize the social surplus associated with farm programs. This latter presumption requires some discussion: Here, it is assumed that social surplus is the difference between consumer valuation of the farm product and producer cost less the social value of any government expenditures that are required to implement the payment–production schedule. If there is no deadweight loss associated with the government raising tax revenues, then this definition of social surplus reduces to the more usual notion of social surplus as the unweighted sum of consumer surplus (the difference between consumer valuation for the commodity and their payments for it) and producer surplus. If there is a deadweight loss associated with the government raising tax revenues, represented mathematically by the budget weight exceeding one, then this identity disappears. And with it frequently goes the ability to achieve the first-best in a world of asymmetric information.

So net social surplus is

$$
U\left(\sum_{i=1}^{2} g(\theta^i) q(\theta^i)\right) - \sum_{i=1}^{2} g(\theta^i) c(q(\theta^i), \theta^i)
$$

$$
- w_B\left(\sum_{i=1}^{2} g(\theta^i) B(\theta^i) - U\left(\sum_{i=1}^{2} g(\theta^i) q(\theta^i)\right)\right),
$$

where $w_B \geqslant 1$ represents the marginal social cost of raising government revenues. The presumption, of course, when $w_B > 1$ is that the government funds any excess payments to farmers that are over and above consumer willingness to pay.

To keep the political economy constraints as simple as possible, we will suppose that a majority of the farmers must support the proposed reform, and that they will support the reform only when their post-reform returns are at least as large as their pre-reform returns.[4] Denote the pre-reform returns of farmer type θ^i by $h(\theta^i) > 0$. A tyranny of the majority is specifically excluded: No farm type can be forced to accept negative returns for positive production. Therefore, there are two cases to consider: The first occurs when the high-cost farmers are in the majority, and the second when the low-cost farmers are in the majority. When the high-cost farmers are in the majority the optimal reform is designed according to

$$
\underset{B(\theta^i)\in \tilde{B},\ q(\theta^i)\in \tilde{q}}{\text{Max}} \left\{ \begin{array}{c} U\left(\sum_{i=1}^{2} g(\theta^i) q(\theta^i)\right) - \sum_{i=1}^{2} g(\theta^i) c(q(\theta^i), \theta^i) \\ - w_B\left(\sum_{i=1}^{2} g(\theta^i) B(\theta^i) - U\left(\sum_{i=1}^{2} g(\theta^i) q(\theta^i)\right)\right) \end{array} \right\},
$$

$$
\text{s.t.} \quad \pi(\theta^1) \geqslant B(\theta^2) - c(q(\theta^2), \theta^1),
$$

$$
\pi(\theta^2) \geqslant B(\theta^1) - c(q(\theta^1), \theta^2),
$$

$$
\pi(\theta^1) \geqslant h(\theta^1).
$$

---

[4] Of course, this is only one of many possible political economy constraints. And, in particular, it does not do justice to the true richness of the model presented by Lewis, Feenstra and Ware (1989). They model the political economy constraint in a more general fashion that allows for more sophisticated voting behavior. Readers interested in the details of their analysis should consult their paper directly.

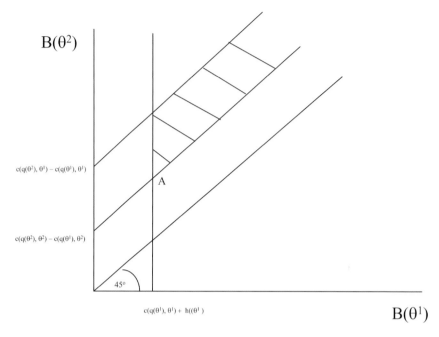

Figure 5. Political-economy constraints.

As before, this program can be solved in stages: In the first stage, the government minimizes the cost of achieving an incentive-compatible policy reform for a given production distribution. We restrict attention again to production patterns consistent with incentive compatibility so that the first-stage program can be written as the following linear program:

$$\underset{B(\theta^i)\in \bar{B}}{\text{Min}} \left\{ \sum_{i=1}^{2} g(\theta^i) B(\theta^i) \right\},$$

$$\text{s.t.} \quad \pi(\theta^1) \geqslant B(\theta^2) - c(q(\theta^2), \theta^1),$$

$$\pi(\theta^2) \geqslant B(\theta^1) - c(q(\theta^1), \theta^2),$$

$$\pi(\theta^1) \geqslant h(\theta^1).$$

The feasible set for this linear program is represented in Figure 5 by all payment combinations in the shaded area. Given the government's goal of minimizing the cost of implementing this policy reform, the solution is at point A in Figure 5. The optimal value of the government's first-stage objective function is

$$N(h(\theta^1) + c(q(\theta^1), \theta^1)) + g(\theta^2)(c(q(\theta^2), \theta^2) - c(q(\theta^1), \theta^2)),$$

so that the government's overall objective can be written as

$$(1 + w_B)\left(U - \sum_{i=1}^{2} g(\theta^i) c(q(\theta^i), \theta^i)\right)$$
$$- w_B g(\theta^2)(c(q(\theta^1), \theta^1) - c(q(\theta^1), \theta^2)) - w_B N h(\theta^1).$$

Following the methods developed above, the first-order condition for the auxiliary variable is

$$(1 + w_B) g(\theta^2)(U' - c_q(q(\theta^2), \theta^2)) \leqslant 0, \quad \alpha \geqslant 0,$$

while the first-order condition for $q(\theta^1)$ is

$$(1 + w_B) \sum_{i=1}^{2} g(\theta^i)(U' - c_q(q(\theta^i), \theta^i))$$
$$- w_B g(\theta^2)(c_q(q(\theta^1), \theta^1) - c_q(q(\theta^1), \theta^2)) \leqslant 0, \quad q(\theta^1) \geqslant 0.$$

As before it's never optimal to treat both producer types identically in the reformed farm program at any positive level of production.

Not surprisingly, the structure of $S(\Theta)$ under the optimal policy reform closely resembles the optimal redistributive farm policy derived when the government favors high-cost farmers in its political calculus. The main difference that emerges is that the politically dominant, high-cost farmers receive their reservation utility – their pre-reform returns from farming. Effectively, the political majority is bribed to ensure adoption of the new reform. Low-cost farmers are not so lucky. They produce efficiently at the margin, and while they receive more than high-cost farmers under the pre-reform policy, the difference is only enough to maintain incentive compatibility. Hence, in many reform scenarios, the low-cost farmers could lose. Consumers can also lose. Take, for example, the situation considered most closely by Lewis, Feenstra and Ware (1989)[5] – the pre-reform alternative is a target-price, deficiency payment scheme which would encourage overproduction relative to the competitive market on the part of both low-cost and high-cost farmers. The reform policy, however, requires

$$\sum_{i=1}^{2} g(\theta^i) q(\theta^i) < \sum_{i=1}^{2} g(\theta^i) q^*(\theta^i).$$

---

[5] Lewis, Feenstra and Ware (1989) voting structure is much more complicated than the current analysis suggests, but their basic result is similar to the one that emerges here. Optimal policy reform does not generally entail decoupling.

Total production is below the competitive outcome, and thus total product must have fallen from the pre-reform case. If, after the reform, the commodity is disbursed to consumers via linear pricing, then their welfare obviously falls because they end by paying a higher price for a lower quantity.

A mechanism, which would approximately implement this reform, might involve an increase in the target price (to ensure the high-cost farmers' compliance) and the introduction of total payment caps chosen to ensure that low-cost farmer production over and above that of high-cost farmers is consistent with marginal production efficiency. However, the ultimate policy implication, as emphasized by Lewis, Feenstra and Ware (1989), is that the optimal reform policy in this instance does not involve decoupling of farm programs.

The reason that decoupling does not emerge as the optimal policy reform is fairly intuitive. Because the political reality dictates that surplus must, in effect, be transferred from low-cost toward high-cost farmers, the government now needs to spread the production distribution in order to ameliorate the problems associated with the presence of information asymmetries between it and farmers. If it pursued a completely decoupled policy with lump-sum transfers, there would be no way for it to ensure that funds were effectively transferred from the politically weak, low-cost farmers to the politically strong, high-cost farmers.

Turning to the case where low-cost farmers are in the majority, $g(\theta^2) > g(\theta^1)$, the first-stage problem needs to be rewritten to reflect the new political economy constraint as

$$\underset{B(\theta^i)\in\bar{B}}{\text{Min}}\left\{\sum_{i=1}^{2}g(\theta^i)B(\theta^i)\right\},$$

$$\text{s.t.}\quad \pi(\theta^1) \geqslant B(\theta^2) - c(q(\theta^2),\theta^1),$$

$$\pi(\theta^2) \geqslant B(\theta^1) - c(q(\theta^1),\theta^2),$$

$$\pi(\theta^2) \geqslant h(\theta^2),$$

$$\pi(\theta^1) \geqslant 0.$$

Here it is again emphasized that there cannot be a complete tyranny of the majority: The political minority cannot be forced to make negative profits. The situation, here, is somewhat more complex than when low-cost farmers are in the majority because simultaneously making the farm policy politically acceptable, incentive-compatible, and individually rational permits a range of cases. At least three distinct possibilities emerge as solutions to the first-stage problem: If the low-cost farmers' political economy constraint intersects the individual rationality constraint for the high-cost farmers anywhere below point A in Figure 6, the first-stage solution will be at point A. If the political-economy constraint intersects the high-cost farmers' individual rationality constraint above A but below point B, the solution to the first-stage problem is at the point of in-

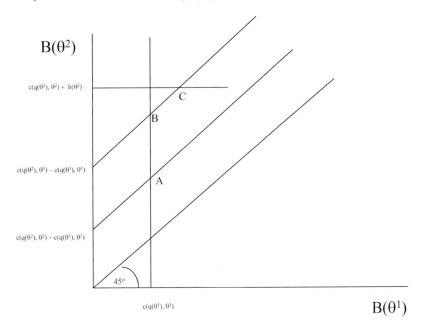

Figure 6. Political-economy with efficient majority.

tersection between these two constraints. And if the political-economy constraint intersects the high-cost farmers' individual rationality constraint above point B in Figure 6, the solution to the first-stage problem will be at the point of intersection between the political economy constraint and the incentive compatibility constraint for the high-cost farmers as illustrated by point C.

Depending upon the parameters of the problem (in particular, the pre-reform income of the low-cost farmers), the optimal solution to the farm-policy mechanism design problem can correspond to any of these three first-stage solutions. We won't bother to consider the mathematics of each case in detail here, because they are broadly similar to what we have already done above. In the order introduced, they will correspond successively to: underproduction relative to the competitive market mechanism with low-cost farmers producing efficiently at the margin and low-cost farmers making a strictly positive return over their pre-reform alternative; the same production pattern as in the competitive market mechanism with both types of farmers producing efficiently at the margin and low-cost farmers making the same return as in the pre-reform case with high-cost farmers receiving their reservation return of zero; and finally overproduction relative to the competitive market mechanism with high-cost farmers producing efficiently at the margin and high-cost farmers making a strictly positive profit and low-cost farmers making the same return as in the pre-reform situation.

The middle case, where the reform involves both producer types producing efficiently at the margin at competitive market levels, is particularly interesting because it suggests that the first-best production pattern can be achieved as a result of an incentive-compatible policy reform if low-cost farmers are in the majority. When high-cost farmers are in the majority, this possibility does not exist.

In this instance, low-cost farmers receive exactly their reservation returns, i.e., they are left indifferent between producing $q^*(\theta^2)$ and their pre-reform alternative, so that their total payment equals

$$B(\theta^2) = h(\theta^2) + c(q^*(\theta^2), \theta^2),$$

while high-cost farmers are driven to their participation constraint. So, *an additional* necessary condition for the competitive market production pattern to be incentive-compatible and politically palatable is that

$$c(q^*(\theta^2), \theta^1) - c(q^*(\theta^2), \theta^2) \geqslant h(\theta^2) \geqslant c(q^*(\theta^1), \theta^1) - c(q^*(\theta^1), \theta^2).$$

The budgetary cost of implementing this production pattern is

$$g(\theta^2)(h(\theta^2) + c(q^*(\theta^2), \theta^2)) + g(\theta^1)c(q^*(\theta^1), \theta^1) - U\left(\sum_{i=1}^{2} g(\theta^i)q^*(\theta^i)\right).$$

Together these expressions imply that the competitive market allocation can be implemented at nonnegative budget cost if

$$U\left(\sum_{i=1}^{2} g(\theta^i)q^*(\theta^i)\right) - g(\theta^2)c(q^*(\theta^2), \theta^2) - g(\theta^1)c(q^*(\theta^1), \theta^1) \geqslant g(\theta^2)h(\theta^2).$$

The first condition requires that the low-cost producers' cost advantage in producing their first-best output be larger than their pre-reform returns, and that these pre-reform returns exceed the low-cost producer cost advantage in producing the high-cost producer first-best output. This joint incentive-compatibility, political-economy constraint is satisfied, for example, if in the competitive market, low-cost farmers would produce much more than high-cost farmers at a substantial cost savings, but the pre-reform policy prevents the low-cost farmers from realizing the advantages that large-scale production could afford them. The budgetary condition simply says that first-best social surplus should exceed low-cost producer pre-reform returns.

To illustrate this possibility suppose that the pre-reform market regulation involves effective supply control at relatively low levels of output, and that low-cost producers are much more efficient technically than high-cost farmers. Examples from U.S. policy experience might include pro-rate regulations in several vegetable and fruit market orders and other marketing quotas arrangements. If demand is less than perfectly elastic, supply control increases producer prices. The cost of compliance, of course, is producing and selling less for the market. Because high-cost producers would produce relatively little (if anything) in the competitive market, their cost of compliance would be relatively small, while their gains from the pre-reform policy might be large. Low-cost producers on the other hand would be forced to forego a significant percentage of their competitive market sales by the pre-reform policy. Thus, their costs of compliance with the high-cost policy would be quite high compared to the price gains they realize on a relatively small output. Hence, a policy reform which granted them open access to a freer market would be quite attractive as it would enable them to realize the natural efficiency advantages that their more efficient cost structure confers on them.

2.3. The continuous case

So far, the presumption has been that there are only two types of farmers. Reality, of course, is quite different, and one expects to find a multiplicity of types. There are at least two ways to generalize: The first is to move to the consideration of N distinct farmer types. As the developments of Guesnerie and Seade (1982), Weymark (1986), and Chambers (1989a) have shown, this approach can be highly tractable.[6] However, an alternative generalization has proven more popular. That generalization is largely associated with the names of Baron and Myerson (1982) and Guesnerie and Laffont (1984) and assumes farmer types are distributed along a continuum $\Theta = (\underline{\theta}, \overline{\theta}) \in \Re$ according to a strictly increasing and continuously differentiable distribution function $G : \Theta \to \Re_+$.[7] Here $G(\theta)$ is usually taken to be the number of farmers in the interval $(\underline{\theta}, \theta)$, and the total number of farmers is normalized so that $G(\overline{\theta}) = 1$. To complete our transit from the discrete to the continuous case, we next alter our assumption on the physical differences between farm types to suit the continuous case. The presumption is the same as in the discrete case: the higher the farmer's index, the lower his or her marginal cost:

ASSUMPTION 2. $c(q, \theta)$ is twice-differentiable on $\Theta \times \Re_+$, strictly increasing and strictly convex on $\Re_+$, with $c_{q\theta}(q, \theta) < 0$ for all $q \in \Re_+, \theta \in \Theta$.

Any elements of the payment–production schedule $S(\Theta)$[8] must continue to be incentive-compatible in the sense that $S(\Theta)$ must satisfy

$$B(\theta^k) - c(q(\theta^k), \theta^k) \geq B(\theta^j) - c(q(\theta^j), \theta^k),$$
$$B(\theta^j) - c(q(\theta^j), \theta^j) \geq B(\theta^k) - c(q(\theta^k), \theta^j),$$

---

[6] I would also argue that it makes the inherent character of the incentive problem more intuitively transparent.

[7] In a slight abuse of notation, we here call the interval defining the range of farm types by the same name as the set of farm types in the two-type case. There should be no confusion.

[8] Recall our redefinition of Θ.

for any realizations of the information parameter $\theta^k, \theta^j \in \Theta$. Proceeding as before, these expressions can be rearranged to obtain an expression analogous to (2):

$$c\big(q\big(\theta^k\big), \theta^j\big) - c\big(q\big(\theta^j\big), \theta^j\big)$$
$$\geqslant B\big(\theta^k\big) - B\big(\theta^j\big) \geqslant c\big(q\big(\theta^k\big), \theta^k\big) - c\big(q\big(\theta^j\big), \theta^k\big). \tag{10}$$

Assumption 2 and expression (10) together imply that incentive compatibility requires for $\theta^k > \theta^j$ that $q(\theta^k) \geqslant q(\theta^j)$ and $B(\theta^k) \geqslant B(\theta^j)$. Any implementable payment–production schedule must have both the output and the farmer payment nondecreasing in the information parameter. Assuming that $\theta^k > \theta^j$ and dividing through in expression (10),

$$\frac{c(q(\theta^k), \theta^j) - c(q(\theta^j), \theta^j)}{\theta^k - \theta^j} \geqslant \frac{B(\theta^k) - B(\theta^j)}{\theta^k - \theta^j}$$
$$\geqslant \frac{c(q(\theta^k), \theta^k) - c(q(\theta^j), \theta^k)}{\theta^k - \theta^j}.$$

Letting $\theta^k \to \theta^j$ gives almost everywhere

$$B'(\theta) = \frac{dB(\theta)}{d\theta} = c_q\big(q(\theta), \theta\big)\frac{dq(\theta)}{d\theta} = c_q\big(q(\theta), \theta\big)q'(\theta). \tag{11}$$

Expression (11) is intuitively interpreted as the first-order condition for the type-revelation problem:

$$\max_{\hat{\theta}}\big\{B(\hat{\theta}) - c\big(q(\hat{\theta}), \theta\big)\big\}.$$

Hence, expression (11) requires that $S(\Theta)$ must be designed so that farmers maximize their returns by truthfully revealing their types, and in turn it implies almost everywhere that

$$\pi'(\theta) = \frac{d\pi(\theta)}{d\theta} = -c_\theta\big(q(\theta), \theta\big). \tag{12}$$

The economic interpretation of (12) is perhaps best understood in terms of the first-stage optimization problems encountered in the discrete case. There we found that the pattern of linking contracts depended critically upon the government's objective function. For example, in the weighted redistributive case when the government favored high-cost farmers over low-cost farmers, the equilibrium first-stage contracts were always linked downward. When the weights were regressive, the equilibrium first-stage contracts were upward linked. Expression (12) shows, however, that in the continuous case it must always be true that farmers of type $\hat{\theta}$, say, be just indifferent between their payment–production pair $(B(\hat{\theta}), q(\hat{\theta}))$ and the payment–production pair intended for the next highest cost farmer as well as that for the next lowest cost farmers.

These arguments imply that monotonicity of the payment–production schedule and expression (11) are necessary conditions for $S(\Theta)$ to be incentive-compatible in the continuous case. However, Baron and Myerson (1982) and Guesnerie and Laffont (1984) have shown that for the model at hand, they are not only necessary but sufficient as well. Therefore, we have

LEMMA 10. *$S(\Theta)$ is incentive-compatible under Assumption 2 if and only if*

$$\pi'(\theta) = -c_\theta(q(\theta), \theta),$$
$$q'(\theta) \geqslant 0.$$

To illustrate the use of the continuous version of the model, without re-covering ground already traversed, I choose an objective function of surplus maximization subject to providing a subgroup of farmers with a target income. The supposition is that farm programs endeavor to achieve as much economic efficiency as possible while ensuring the survival of this subclass of farmers. The government's inherent values are progressive in that it is farmers at the high end of the cost spectrum, those with type $\theta \in (\underline{\theta}, \hat{\theta})$, who must be ensured a profit of at least $\underline{\pi} > 0$. Under Assumption 2, incentive compatibility then implies that all farmers must receive a profit of at least $\underline{\pi}$. (The reasoning here is similar to that in the discrete case.) Hence, the main change in the government's problem is that any solution must satisfy a more extreme version of the participation constraint in the sense that highest-cost farmers must strictly prefer the government program to not producing at all. Consequently, the government's farm-policy mechanism-design problem is

$$\max_{q(\theta), B(\theta)} \left\{ U\left(\int_\Theta q(\theta) \, dG(\theta) \right) - \int_\Theta c(q(\theta), \theta) \, dG(\theta) \right.$$
$$\left. - w_B \left(\int_\Theta B(\theta) \, dG(\theta) - U\left(\int_\Theta q(\theta) \, dG(\theta) \right) \right) \right\},$$

s.t. $\pi(\underline{\theta}) \geqslant \underline{\pi}$,
$$\pi'(\theta) = -c_\theta(q(\theta), \theta),$$
$$q'(\theta) \geqslant 0.$$

The first constraint, of course, reflects the government's desire to ensure a minimum income to farmers on the high end of the cost spectrum. The remaining constraints are those associated with incentive compatibility.

As in the discrete case, the analysis of the government's problem can be simplified somewhat by proceeding in stages. Recalling our definition of profit and applying the fundamental theorem of calculus yields

$$B(\theta) = \pi(\underline{\theta}) - \int_{\underline{\theta}}^{\theta} c_\theta\big(q(\hat{\theta}), \hat{\theta}\big)\, d\hat{\theta} + c\big(q(\theta), \theta\big),$$

upon using Lemma 10. Using this last expression allows writing the total payments to farmers as (after integrating by parts)

$$\int_\Theta B(\theta)\, dG(\theta) = \pi(\underline{\theta}) + \int_\Theta c\big(q(\theta), \theta\big)\, dG(\theta) - \int_\Theta \big(1 - G(\theta)\big)c_\theta\big(q(\theta), \theta\big)\, d\theta.$$

Defining an auxiliary variable $\beta \geqslant 0$ by $\pi(\underline{\theta}) = \underline{\pi} + \beta$ then gives the following expression for the objective function:

$$(1 + w_B)\left(U\left(\int_\Theta q(\theta)\, dG(\theta) \right) - \int_\Theta c\big(q(\theta), \theta\big)\, dG(\theta) \right)$$

$$- w_B(\underline{\pi} + \beta) + w_B \int_\Theta \big(1 - G(\theta)\big)c_\theta\big(q(\theta), \theta\big)\, d\theta.$$

In what follows, I shall refer to this as the *concentrated objective function*. The concentrated objective function incorporates the first-order condition for truthful revelation of types as embedded in the envelope relationship. But it does not include the monotonicity condition on the farmers' outputs. There are two possible ways to proceed: The first is to introduce a co-state variable for each of the separate constraints $q'(\theta) \geqslant 0$ and then use standard optimal-control arguments to develop an augmented version of the current objective function that incorporates these constraints on the motion of the farmers' output. Another approach is to first maximize the concentrated objective function ignoring these motion constraints, and then check to see if the motion constraints are satisfied by the solution. If they are not, then the solution to the unconstrained problem must be suitably altered to satisfy these motion constraints. The second approach is by far the most popular and so that is the approach that we shall follow.

The first-order condition for the auxiliary variable β is

$$-w_B \leqslant 0, \qquad \beta \geqslant 0,$$

which, of course, implies $\beta = 0$. Therefore, the optimal mechanism always involves the highest-cost farmers just receiving the guaranteed profit. The first-order conditions for each $q(\theta)$ are

$$(1 + w_B)g(\theta)\big(U' - c_q\big(q(\theta), \theta\big)\big) + w_B\big(1 - G(\theta)\big)c_{\theta q}\big(q(\theta), \theta\big) \leqslant 0,$$

$$q(\theta) \geqslant 0.$$

The easiest way to interpret these first-order conditions is to notice that the first term,

$$(1 + w_B)g(\theta)\big(U' - c_q\big(q(\theta),\theta\big)\big),$$

corresponds to the marginal change in social welfare associated with changes in the θ-type's output. But, as we know, changing the θ-farmer's output creates an incentive problem by making it more attractive for higher-cost farmers to misrepresent themselves as θ-farmers. The second term in the first-order condition represents the social value of the budgetary cost of making a uniform transfer to higher-cost farmers that will restore incentive compatibility. As such, it represents the economic loss associated with the information asymmetry between farmers and the government for small output changes.

At an interior solution,

$$U' - c_q\big(q(\theta),\theta\big) = \frac{-w_B(1 - G(\theta))}{(1 + w_B)g(\theta)}c_{\theta q}\big(q(\theta),\theta\big) \geqslant 0.$$

By Assumption 2, this expression has the following interpretation: Only one type of farmer produces efficiently at the margin – the lowest-cost farmers. All other farmers produce at a point where marginal consumer valuation exceeds their marginal cost of production. Hence, this result corresponds in a broad sense to the results that were found in the discrete case when there were only two types of farmers, and the government pursued a weighted redistributive scheme placing a higher weight on high-cost than low-cost farmers. Relative to the competitive-market mechanism, there will be underproduction of the agricultural commodity.

Because of the nonlinear consumer valuation function, the concentrated objective function is not separable across farm types. Consequently, it will be quite difficult to determine whether the monotonicity constraint on farm production is satisfied for the payment–production plan that solves the first-order conditions associated with the concentrated objective function. Things are a little less complex if it is presumed that the marginal consumer valuation of the commodity is a constant p. In that case, we might think of rewriting the first-order conditions in the simplified notation

$$H_q(q,\theta) \leqslant 0, \quad q \geqslant 0,$$

where $\int_\Theta H(q,\theta)\, d\theta$ is the government's concentrated objective function. Second-order conditions for an optimum require

$$H_{qq}(q,\theta) \leqslant 0,$$

from which it follows immediately that the monotonicity condition will be satisfied at an interior solution to the first-order conditions for the concentrated objective function if and only if $H_{q\theta}(q,\theta) \geqslant 0$. An example illustrates. Suppose that farmer types are uniformly distributed and that a farmer of type θ's cost function can be represented by

$$c(q,\theta) = bq + (\bar{\theta} - \theta)\hat{c}(q),$$

where $b > 0$ and $\hat{c}(q)$ is a strictly increasing, strictly convex differentiable function. Simple calculation then verifies that $H_{q\theta}(q,\theta) > 0$, and the solution to the first-order conditions for the concentrated objective function represents an implementable payment–production schedule.

More generally, however, it cannot be guaranteed that the solution to the first-order conditions satisfies the monotonicity condition. For example, in a framework very similar to the current model, Hueth (2000) has shown that if the government places extra value on the production from the higher-cost farmers, then even the last restriction on the cost function and the distribution of farm types will not ensure monotonicity. In effect, the government objective function changes from that of maximizing social surplus to one of maximizing social surplus plus the government's greater valuation of high-cost production.

What happens if the monotonicity constraint is not satisfied? Formally, the problem is identical to planning the optimal investment decisions of a firm when investment is irreversible. This problem has been treated in detail by Arrow and Kurz (1970) in the context of public investment, in Clark (1976) in the context of fisheries management, and in the principal-agent context by Guesnerie and Laffont (1984). While we will not go into details here,[9] the basic idea is simple enough: Θ can be subdivided into intervals for which the solution to the first-order conditions satisfies monotonicity. Refer to these as free intervals. The optimal solution will stay as close to these free intervals as possible, and when it departs from it, there will be a "blocked interval" where $q'(\theta) = 0$ for all θ in the interval. Figure 7 illustrates for an hypothetical set of solutions to the first-order conditions for the concentrated objective function. As drawn there, that solution first increases in accordance with monotonicity, peaks, declines and eventually turns back up. The optimal trajectory would be the one that stays as close as possible to the original trajectory without violating monotonicity, but finding its precise location requires a fair bit of mathematical manipulation that we need not go into here. However, the fact that the solution to the first-order conditions for the concentrated objective function is not monotonic implies the existence of a blocked interval between θ' and θ'' in which all farmers produce the same output and receive the same payment for their production. These producers are bunched.

2.4. Applications of the continuous model

A number of studies have used the basic techniques developed for the continuous case to analyze a variety of agricultural policy problems ranging from the appropriate design of operating credit price schedules [Lee (1986)] to the optimal design of an acreage-retirement *cum* variable levy policy by Bourgeon, Jayet and Picard (1995). Neither time nor space permits me to give a detailed analysis of their findings, but in the next few paragraphs, I do provide a synopsis of their results.

---

[9] The interested reader can refer to the cited references for details.

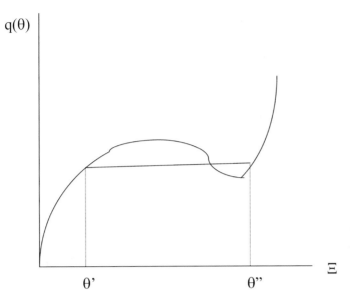

Figure 7. Blocked interval and bunching.

Lee's (1986) pioneering study was prompted by the farm credit crisis the United States experienced in the mid 1980s. Her analysis specifically focused on the Farm Credit System (FCS), a provider of long-term and operating credit to farmers. Originally funded by the U.S. government, by the time of Lee's work the FCS was an independent entity that operated with 'agency' status in credit markets. And at the time of Lee's study, there were serious proposals for the federal government to bail out the beleaguered lender. Lee showed how a provider of short-term operating credit could optimally discriminate amongst borrowers of differing farming abilities, and how the pattern of discrimination would change as the lender's objective changed. Thus, Lee's work presaged much of what has been said here. One of her more interesting results was the discovery that for a cooperative lender, like the FCS, average-cost pricing could approximately implement the optimal lending schedule under reasonable objectives. One of the most serious charges that critics had leveled against the FCS was that by average-cost pricing of its loans, the FCS effectively penalized borrowers of higher farming abilities and encouraged them to migrate to more commercially oriented lenders who were pricing loans at or near their marginal cost. Although it has been overlooked by many later authors because it remains unpublished to this day, Lee's study set the stage for the studies of Chambers (1987, 1992) and Smith (1992, 1995) and the literature that followed these studies.

Smith's (1992, 1995) investigation was also motivated by a practical policy problem: How to optimally manage the Conservation Reserve Program mandated by the Food Security Act of 1985. Unlike Lee (1986), who had relied upon nonlinear pricing methods, Smith (1992, 1995) studied this problem in the context of a continuous DRM under the presumption that the government or regulator could not observe a farmer's true farming efficiency. By interviewing the bureaucrats charged with implementing the Conservation Reserve, Smith determined that their intent was to achieve the Act's mandated acreage conservation at minimal budget cost.[10] His analysis, therefore, focused on the minimal cost design of an optimal conservation acreage reserve program. In effect, he analyzed the Conservation Reserve Program as a buyers' auction.

Smith's (1995) model differed in one major way from the models considered to this point. While he segmented farmers by efficiency, Smith considered a more complicated participation constraint for each farmer type. In particular, Smith required that participation in the Conservation Reserve Program be entirely voluntary so that the farmer's participation constraint required not that the farmer make a nonnegative return from farming and participating in the program, but that the farmer be no worse off participating in the program than he or she would have been if they had continued to farm but not participated in the acreage reserve program. While this considerably complicated Smith's analysis, the basic form of the results that he identified remain broadly similar to those that we have identified here: Any implementable mechanism would have acreage retired declining in farming efficiency, and government retirement payments had to adjust to maintain incentive compatibility in accordance with the first-order conditions for the optimality of truthful revelation.

The Conservation Reserve Program, as run by the United States Department of Agriculture, had been severely criticized by the General Accounting Office (GAO) for being too costly. The gist of GAO's criticism was that instead of being run properly as an auction, the Conservation Reserve Program had been run as an "offer system" whereby the government in each region established a single eligible price, easily discoverable by farmers, at which it would stand ready to pay for the retirement of as many eligible acres as were offered to it in that region. Smith (1992) showed that just such an offer system would implement the same equilibrium outcomes as a least-cost auction if the farmer's per-acre reservation values were independent of the number of acres retired. In essence, an offer system of the type run by USDA could be an optimal auction. However, Smith's study also included some numerical results suggesting that USDA spent approximately $600 million more on an annual basis than required to implement the level of mandated retirement.

Wu and Babcock (1996) studied the optimal design of environmental stewardship programs in a very similar setting. They assume that farmers have private information about their land quality which prevents the government from implementing a first-best input reward scheme that accounts for the environmental impacts of input utilization. Working in a scalar input case, they show that farmers with higher land quality will always use more input in any implementable mechanism and that the environmental input side payment will depend critically upon the divergence between marginal productivity

---

[10] Land entered into the acreage reserve was to be held out of production for a period of ten years.

and the prevailing market price for inputs. In a fashion similar to Smith (1992, 1995) they require that the environmental stewardship program be purely voluntary. Because they are specifically interested in environmentally damaging input use, Wu and Babcock (1996) assume that input utilization is scalar-valued, observable, and contractible. However, as a practical matter this seems far-fetched: First, it is unrealistic to assume farmers only use a single input; and second, it requires a degree of governmental monitoring of production practices at the farm level that would be prohibitively costly. Finally, as Chambers and Quiggin (1996) argue in the case of non-point source pollution, how a farm pollutes and damages the environment depends upon many more factors than just its input utilization,[11] even if pollution comes in the form of runoff or leaching of an input applied.

As an alternative, consider the following simple specification along the lines of Chambers and Quiggin (1996) as modified for a nonstochastic technology: Suppose that each farmer of type θ's technology is represented by an input correspondence $V : \Re_+^2 \times \Theta \to \Re_+^n$ defined by

$$V(q, e, \theta) = \{\mathbf{x}\colon \mathbf{x} \text{ can produce } (q, e) \text{ given } \theta\}.$$

Here q continues to denote output, θ is the unknown efficiency or land quality parameter, e is the level of environmental emission or pollution from farming, and $\mathbf{x}$ is a vector of inputs used in production. Dual to this input correspondence is a well-behaved cost function, which dropping price arguments, can be written $C(q, e, \theta)$ and represents the farmer's minimal cost of producing outputs q and e given the farmer's efficiency parameter. Faced with a market price for output of p, rational farmers maximize their profit from a given quantity of the farm output by choosing emissions to minimize cost. Hence, a rational farmer's returns are

$$pq - \min_e C(q, e, \theta) = pq - c(q, \theta).$$

If marginal environmental damages are constant at t then the social surplus from a θ-farmer producing at level q is given by

$$pq - te(q, \theta) - c(q, \theta),$$

where $e(q, \theta)$ is the cost-minimizing pollution level for a given output and efficiency parameter. Denoting the environmental side payment by $s(\theta)$ yields the following social-surplus maximization problem for the government:

$$\max_{q(\theta), s(\theta)} \left\{ \int_\Theta pq - te(q, \theta) - c(q, \theta) - w_B s(\theta) \, dG(\theta) \right\},$$

---

[11] Moreover, it seems hard to rationalize the government being able to observe the amount of inputs being applied to the land, but not being able to observe the actual quality of the land itself.

subject, of course, to individual participation constraints and incentive compatibility. Incentive compatibility requires that lower-cost farmers produce more, just as before, and the only other formal change in the incentive compatibility constraints is that

$$s'(\theta) = -\left(p - c_q\big(q(\theta), \theta\big)\right)q'(\theta)$$

replaces the monotonicity condition placed on the payments scheme before. (This expression corresponds to (b) in Lemma 1 in Wu and Babcock (1996).) However, it's also easy to see that despite this change, the rest of Lemma 10 continues to apply so that with minor modifications, analysis of this model proceeds as above in the continuous case.

Bourgeon, Jayet and Picard (1995), following Lewis, Feenstra and Ware (1989), studied the optimal design of set-aside mechanisms to achieve agricultural supply reduction. Their analysis is specifically targeted at the policies pursued by the European Community in response to budgetary pressures arising from export refunds under the Common Agricultural Policy. In a model that allows for a complex interplay between differing farm efficiencies and differing productivities of plots of land, Bourgeon, Jayet and Picard (1995) analyze two distinct sets of policies: incentive-based voluntary set-asides and mandated percentage reductions of available land. Unlike the models that we have considered here, they are specifically interested in modeling the trade dimension of the agricultural policy problem, and their objective function places a separate weight on the balance of trade for the commodity being regulated. By including a separate weight for the trade balance in their objective function, they are able to show that an optimal policy reform could include both set-asides and subsidized production.

Although not formally an agricultural policy problem, a cooperative's pricing rule can be affected by divergent interests of heterogeneous members. When such competing interests are present and informational asymmetries exist, preceding results might suggest that cooperative production decisions will depart from the first-best optimum. In particular, the traditionally recommended marginal cost pricing rule cum fee/rebate may no longer be implementable. Vercammen, Fulton and Hyde (1996) study such departures assuming a continuum of producer types and a non-discriminating management board in a framework broadly similar to the one considered here. In particular, they conduct a simulation analysis which, contrary to intuition, suggests that even in the presence of informational asymmetries the first-best cooperative pricing rule may be implementable. However, their theoretical analysis seems to suggest that the norm will be departures from first-best pricing. Working in a discrete framework, Bourgeon and Chambers (1999) have shown that this surmise is wrong. Reality may accord closely with the simulation results of Vercammen, Fulton and Hyde (1996). So long as there exists broadly symmetric bargaining power between producers of different types, then the first-best cooperative pricing rule will be implementable for the Nash bargaining equilibrium even in the presence of asymmetric information between producers of different types.

3. Mechanism design with hidden action in a stochastic world

A vast literature is devoted to agricultural hidden-action models. However, virtually all of it analyzes agrarian contracts in peasant societies using a theoretical model that is so stylized as to be devoid of insight for most practical policy problems in developed agriculture. Relatively few studies have considered how the presence of hidden action and the incentive problems it creates impinges on the design of agricultural policy. Those, that have, have focused primarily on public provision of crop insurance [Nelson and Loehman (1987), Chambers (1989b), Miranda (1991), Vercammen and van Kooten (1994)].

There has been a growing interest in the environmental impacts of agricultural support programs and, more broadly, agricultural production practices. Because farmer choices about polluting inputs (typically fertilizers and pesticides) in a world of uncertainty are likely closely related to their risk attitudes, agricultural pollution control and public support of agriculture appear closely linked. For example, chemical fertilizers are often identified as a primary source of non-point-source nitrogen runoff, and are usually characterized as risk-complementary inputs. If so, then policies fostering agricultural insurance programs might affect chemical fertilizer runoff. It's not implausible that such programs, by removing the need for farmer self-insurance, could increase the use of risk-complementary inputs, such as fertilizers, and thereby increase non-point-source pollution problems.

This section is devoted to an analysis of agricultural mechanism design in the presence of hidden action which, for expository purposes, is cast in the metaphor of public provision of multiple-peril crop insurance *cum* non-point-source pollution control. Formally, therefore, it considers a multi-task, principal-agent problem in the sense defined by Holmström and Milgrom (1987). Some may find this metaphor limiting because it does not focus on more traditional agricultural policies. However, this concern is misdirected because the production-insurance problem formulated below is general enough to subsume all traditional agricultural policies in a stochastic world. In particular, in a stochastic world, the general problem of all-risk or multiple-peril encompasses all the traditional problems at which agricultural policy is directed, including income support, price stabilization, and income stabilization.[12] The basic approach here is the same as in the previous section. Instead of focusing on particular policy instruments, the discussion is in terms of equilibrium policy outcomes. Suitable re-interpretation will show that the outcomes described below can be achieved by the specification of appropriate policy mechanisms.

So in what follows, I discuss the problem of crop insurance as articulated by Sanderson (1943), Lee (1953), and much later, the Farm Income Protection Insurance

---

[12] This may not be apparent to some readers used to viewing all-risk crop insurance as a supplement to other forms of income support and price stabilization. However, it is easy to see that the state-contingent premia discussed below are most appropriately interpreted as including these other forms of more traditional agricultural programs and payments.

Task Force (1983), Nelson and Loehman (1987), and Chambers (1989b).[13] I first consider a world where there is no hidden action or hidden knowledge, and then I turn to various aspects of these problems when some degree of hidden-action *cum* hidden-knowledge exists. In what follows, the discussion revolves around a representation of stochastic production by Chambers and Quiggin (1992, 1996, 1997, 2000), and some of what I say closely follows their treatment of the crop insurance problem [Chambers and Quiggin (2000)].

3.1. The state-contingent technology and farmer preferences

I start my discussion of crop insurance by introducing an Arrow–Debreu state-contingent model of stochastic production as articulated by Chambers and Quiggin (1992, 2000). The state-contingent model used here represents a clear departure from virtually all existing hidden-action models which rely on a stochastic production function representation of production uncertainty. The departure is made for a number of reasons.[14] Most important, the existing literature on hidden action typically treats production relations that relate a single stochastic output to a single non-stochastic input, euphemistically referred to as effort, and a stochastic input or variable. Hence, the modeled production structure bears no relation to actual agricultural production technologies, and accordingly severely limits the number of actual policy situations that can be analyzed. In particular, as a result of its restrictive nature, it is severely circumscribed in its ability to model multi-dimensional policy problems.[15] The state-contingent production model is specified in such a manner that it easily handles multiple inputs and outputs without placing any severe limitations upon the underlying technology.

The production model is intended to portray the following stylized situation: Farmers, who can be characterized by a representative farmer, are producing a crop[16] using a technology that leaves them uncertain about their production levels once inputs are committed. In addition, the production of this crop involves a by-product that can be thought of most conveniently as runoff or leaching and which we shall mnemonically refer to as "pollution". Uncertainty is modeled by "Nature" making a choice from a finite set of alternatives. Each of these alternatives is called a "state" and is indexed by a finite set of the form

$$\Omega = \{1, 2, \ldots, S\}$$

---

[13] Ahsan, Ali and Kurian (1982) studied the optimal provision of crop insurance under adverse selection. Although the details differ, their analysis can be recast in terms of the methods used in Section 2.1 of this paper.

[14] Chambers and Quiggin (2000), in particular Chapter 9, provide a thorough criticism of the axiomatic specification of such models.

[15] Particularly compelling examples of the limitations of this model come from the closely related field studying agricultural policy incidence in the presence of production uncertainty [e.g., Ramaswami (1993), Hennessy (1998)].

[16] The generalization to multiple crops is straightforward [Chambers and Quiggin (2000)].

where S denotes the number of states of nature. Once the index is given, all possible factors affecting production and contracting decisions (e.g., weather, market conditions) are known. However, all production decisions must take place before the index is given, i.e., before the state of nature is known.

Production relations are governed by a state-contingent technology set (known to both the farmers and the government)

$$T = \{(\mathbf{x}, \mathbf{p}, \mathbf{z}): \mathbf{x} \text{ can produce } (\mathbf{p}, \mathbf{z})\},$$

where $\mathbf{x} \in \Re_+^n$ is a vector of inputs committed prior to Nature choosing the state of nature, and $\mathbf{p}, \mathbf{z} \in \Re_+^s$ are vectors of state-contingent outputs of pollution in the form of agricultural runoff and agricultural output, respectively. The most appropriate interpretation of T is as an *ex ante* technology: $(\mathbf{x}, \mathbf{p}, \mathbf{z}) \in T$ implies that if the input vector $\mathbf{x}$ is committed and Nature picks $j \in \Omega$, then the jth elements of $\mathbf{p}$ and $\mathbf{z}$ will be the amount of pollution and agricultural output realized, respectively, after the resolution of uncertainty. Although our general production technology allows both pollution and agricultural output to be stochastic, in what follows for the sake of simplicity we shall assume that pollution is nonstochastic so that instead of being an S-dimensional vector, pollution is scalar-valued, i.e., $p \in \Re_+$.

The preferences of the representative farmer over returns and inputs are given by the von Neumann–Morgernstern utility function,

$$w(y, \mathbf{x}) = u(y) - g(\mathbf{x}),$$

where y represents *ex post* returns, u is a twice-differentiable, strictly increasing and strictly concave function, and g is a nonnegative, continuous, and convex function of the inputs.[17] In short, farmers are strictly risk averse.

Two different indirect representations of the state-contingent technology set T will prove very useful in developing analytical results. The first is the *effort-cost function* defined by

$$c(p, \mathbf{z}) = \min_x \{g(\mathbf{x}): (\mathbf{x}, \mathbf{p}, \mathbf{z}) \in T\}$$

if there is an input vector $\mathbf{x}$ that is feasible for given $(p, \mathbf{z})$, and ∞ otherwise. In words, $c(p, \mathbf{z})$ represents the least costly way for the farmer to produce a given state-contingent pollution and output vector. Chambers and Quiggin (1992, 1996, 1997, 2000) show that if T is convex and satisfies free disposability of state-contingent outputs $\mathbf{z}$, then $c(p, \mathbf{z})$

---

[17] I have chosen to represent farmer preferences as being additively separable in returns and effort. This assumption is needed to facilitate the discussion of moral hazard and production and is almost universal in that literature. However, all the basic results that I develop on production in the presence of *ex post* knowledge of the state of nature on the part of the government are robust to relaxation of this assumption [Chambers and Quiggin (2000)].

will be nondecreasing and convex in those state-contingent outputs and convex in p. Consonant with the approach in Chambers and Quiggin (1996), we strengthen these properties to require that $c(p, \mathbf{z})$ be twice continuously differentiable in both pollution and state-contingent outputs.

The second indirect representation of the technology considered is the farmer's *private-cost function* defined by

$$C(\mathbf{z}) = \min_{p}\{c(p, \mathbf{z})\}.$$

Associated with the private-cost function is the private-cost minimizing pollution choice:[18]

$$p(\mathbf{z}) = \arg\min_{p}\{c(p, \mathbf{z})\}.$$

Social damage caused by pollution is represented by the nondecreasing and convex function $m(p)$. Attention is focused on two special cases: where pollution causes no external damage,[19] i.e., $m'(p) = 0$ for all p, and where pollution causes a strictly positive level of damage, i.e., $m'(p) > 0$ for all p.

3.2. Crop insurance with no hidden information and pollution harmless

This section provides a point of comparison for the more realistic problems that follow. Here we presume that the government can observe the farmer's actions in preparing for the crop and the state of nature that actually occurs, and that agricultural runoff imposes no burden upon society. *Ex ante*, all individuals (farmers and the government) share common beliefs about which state of nature will occur. These beliefs are summarized by a vector of probabilities, $\boldsymbol{\pi} \in \Pi \subset \Re_{++}^{S}$ (no state occurs with zero probability) such that

$$\sum_{k=1}^{S} \pi_k = 1.$$

For simplicity's sake, we restrict attention to the case where the price of the agricultural output is nonstochastic and normalized to one.[20] Although cast in a state-contingent

---

[18] Assume, for simplicity, that $p(\mathbf{z})$ is unique.

[19] The analysis then reduces to the standard crop insurance problem as posed by Nelson and Loehman (1987) and Chambers (1989b).

[20] In a state-contingent framework, considering the case of price and production uncertainty is quite easy once one develops a revenue-indirect cost function analogous to the effort-cost function developed below. For such a formulation, see Chambers and Quiggin (2000, Chapters 4 and 7).

context, this specification represents the symmetric-information, crop-insurance problem studied in a continuous context by Nelson and Loehman (1987).

The government's problem is to design a crop insurance program that maximizes net social surplus from the production of the agricultural output. In doing so, it can make its net indemnity (net premium) to the farmer contingent upon the level of realized (*ex post*) output, the state of nature, and the farmer's action or effort vector, all of which are assumed observable and thus contractible. Formally, therefore, its problem can be written as one of choosing inputs, a state-contingent vector of outputs, pollution, and a state-contingent vector of net premia to maximize net social surplus:[21]

$$\max_{x,z,p,I}\left\{\sum_{k=1}^{S}\pi_k\big(u(z_k - I_k) - g(\mathbf{x}) + I_k\big): (\mathbf{x}, \mathbf{p}, \mathbf{z}) \in T\right\}.$$

Here $\mathbf{I} \in \Re^S$ denotes the vector of net insurance premia paid by the farmer to the government. (Net premia can be either positive or negative. If the net premium is positive, it means that the state-contingent indemnity associated with that particular state is less than the premium. If the net premium is negative, it means that the state-contingent indemnity associated with that state is greater than the premium.) By the principle of conditional optimization this problem can be rewritten as

$$\max_{z,I}\left\{\sum_{k=1}^{S}\pi_k\big(u(z_k - I_k) + I_k\big) - C(\mathbf{z})\right\}.$$

The government's crop insurance problem in this case reduces to that of picking a vector of state-contingent net premia and outputs to present to private-cost minimizing farmers. Because society does not directly value either inputs or pollution independently of the farmer's valuation, once a state-contingent vector of outputs is settled upon, a farmer's valuation of the inputs and pollution matches society's. Thus farmers have the correct incentives to choose the appropriate inputs and pollution. This slightly generalizes the Harris and Raviv (1979) result that optimal incentive contracts can be made independent of the level of effort.[22]

The government's problem, therefore, is a simple concave programming problem whose optimal value is characterized by the first-order conditions

$$1 - u'(z_k - I_k) = 0,$$

$$\pi_k u'(z_k - I_k) - C_k(\mathbf{z}) \leqslant 0, \quad z_k \geqslant 0, \quad k = 1, 2, \ldots, S,$$

---

[21] More correctly, net social surplus should be expressed in terms of the producer's certainty equivalent. The current formulation doesn't substantively change results and has the advantage of making the comparison between first-best and second-best outcomes more transparent.

[22] If one interprets pollution as an input, then this result can be recognized as a multi-input generalization of the Harris and Raviv (1979) result for scalar effort.

in the notation of complementary slackness.[23] The first S conditions require that net premia are chosen to equate the farmer's marginal utility from the net premium in each state to society's marginal valuation of the net premium in that state. Because u is strictly increasing and strictly concave, these conditions imply that social optimality involves stabilizing the farmer's net returns at the level r which is the implicit solution to the equation

$$u'(r) = 1.$$

Put another way, the net premium schedule is chosen to insure the farmer fully against the revenue risk that he or she faces. Using this result in the second S conditions yields

$$\pi_k - C_k(\mathbf{z}) \leqslant 0, \quad z_k \geqslant 0.$$

The interpretation of these S first-order conditions is now straightforward and manifests Borch's (1962) rule for optimal risk-sharing. The government's optimal policy, as originally demonstrated by Nelson and Loehman (1987), is to insure the farmer completely against his or her production uncertainty while requiring the now locally[24] risk-neutral farmer to produce at the point where the expected profit of the crop is maximized. If we let $\mathbf{z}^*$ denote the vector of state-contingent outputs which maximizes the expected profit from the farmer's crop, then the optimal net premia ($\mathbf{I}^*$) and the farmer's sure return are determined jointly by

$$1 - u'(r) = 0,$$
$$z_k^* - I_k^* = r, \quad k = 1, 2, \ldots, S.$$

Figure 8 illustrates this result pictorially using Hirshleifer's (1965) state-contingent diagram. The curve labeled isocost in that figure represents the level curve of the private-cost function as evaluated at the optimal level of state-contingent production. Because the private-cost function is convex, this curve is drawn as concave to the origin. It is drawn as tangent to the *fair-odds line*, whose slope is given by minus the ratio of the probabilities, at the optimal state-contingent production point (z_1^*, z_2^*). Pictorially, this represents the optimal solution to the last S first-order conditions. Two observations are especially relevant here: First, as we have said above, this is the production pattern that a risk-neutral producer facing the same probabilities would choose. And second, note the similarity between this pictorial representation and that for the multi-output producer facing a non-stochastic technology. The producer's

---

[23] More generally, all the results that are derived below for the symmetric-information, crop-insurance problem can be deduced by dominance arguments for much more general preference structures than used here without resorting to the calculus [Chambers and Quiggin (2000), especially Chapter 7].

[24] In the neighborhood of the optimum.

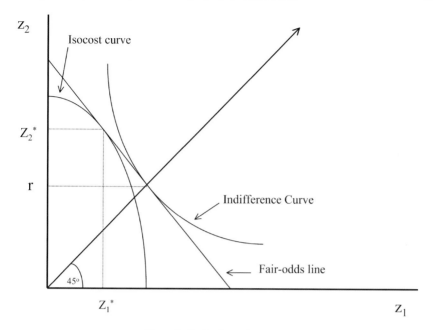

Figure 8. Optimal crop insurance.

ultimate revenue is illustrated by the point where the fair-odds line is tangent to the producer's indifference curve. As Hirshleifer shows, under the expected-utility hypothesis, this will always occur along the bisector. The net indemnity in each state can then be measured off of the horizontal and vertical axes, respectively, as the difference between r and the respective state-contingent outputs. Summarizing, this discussion we have:

PROPOSITION 11 [Nelson and Loehman (1987)]. *If there is no hidden action on the part of the farmer and the pollution externality is non-existent, the optimal crop-insurance program fully insures the farmer. The farmer produces in the same pattern as a risk-neutral farmer facing the same technology and probabilities.*

An important result follows immediately: So long as the government can observe the state of nature, the government need not observe the level of inputs or the *ex post* output to implement the optimal crop-insurance program. Rather, the government can implement this crop insurance program by specifying a state-contingent vector of net premia corresponding to I^* while allowing the farmer to optimize privately. Here the way that the crop insurance program would operate is particularly simple: The government offers to pay (receive) I_k^* in the event that state k occurs. Because the government can observe which state of nature occurs, such a contract is feasible. Farmers facing such a state-contingent net premia schedule privately optimize by solving

$$\max_{x,z,p}\left\{\sum_{k=1}^{S}\pi_k\left(u\left(z_k - I_k^*\right) - g(\mathbf{x})\right): (\mathbf{x}, \mathbf{p}, \mathbf{z}) \in T\right\}$$

$$= \max_{z}\left\{\sum_{k=1}^{S}\pi_k u\left(z_k - I_k^*\right) - C(\mathbf{z})\right\}.$$

Effectively, therefore, farmers have been made the residual claimants of the social surplus, and solving this last problem leads them to choose $\mathbf{z}^*$. And because farmers automatically choose the socially optimal state-contingent vector of outputs, they automatically choose the socially optimal input utilization and pollution level. Hence, we obtain:

PROPOSITION 12. *If the government can observe the state of nature and pollution is harmless, the government can implement the socially optimal crop insurance program even if it does not observe the level of inputs and ex post output.*

In evaluating this last result, which extends the Harris and Raviv (1979) result to state-contingent outputs, it is important to understand what it means from an informational perspective to be able to specify a state-contingent net premia schedule. The government can do so only if *ex post* it can verify what "Nature's" choice actually was. That is, it must be able to ascertain the exact conditions under which production took place. This does not require the government to have perfect foresight about the resolution of uncertainty, only perfect hindsight. When endowed with perfect hindsight, the government can implement the socially optimal crop insurance program without relying upon information about the farmer's choice of inputs, the pollution level chosen, or the level of state-contingent output that actually occurs. All it needs to be able to do is to verify the state of nature. Hence, so long as there is no hidden farmer knowledge in the form of the government not being able to observe the state of nature, the presence of hidden action on the part of the farmer does not impede implementation of a socially optimal crop insurance program.

This realization brings with it an obvious but important observation. The easier it is for the government to verify the state of nature that occurs, the easier it will be for it to implement the socially optimal crop insurance program. An obvious corollary, of course, is that it will also be more likely that there will be some private provision of optimal crop insurance. It is frequently observed that all-risk crop insurance programs have required government support and have virtually never been provided successfully on a commercial basis [Gardner and Kramer (1986)], while risk-specific (e.g., drought or hail insurance) commercial agricultural insurance programs have frequently thrived. The reason is apparent: The more specific the risk, generally the easier it is for the provider of insurance to ascertain the exact conditions under which production took place, and the easier it is to provide the appropriate net premium. When risk is not very specific, it is hard to ascertain the exact conditions, i.e., the state of nature, under which production takes place and to provide the appropriate net premia.[25]

From an agricultural policy perspective, these results show that acquiring exact information on the state of nature is sufficient to ensure the ability to achieve the first-best policy outcome. Therefore, it also suggests that government efforts at obtaining information on the farmer's on-farm actions, for example, in determining whether or not the farmer is adhering to best-management practice standards, may be misplaced when it is easier to obtain information on the state of nature.

3.3. Crop insurance with no hidden information but pollution not harmless

In the preceding section, we investigated the traditional crop insurance problem when there are no informational or incentive problems. In this section, we slightly complicate that problem by presuming that pollution from the agricultural production operation is no longer harmless, but that the government can still perfectly observe the farmer's actions and the state of Nature that occurs. The government's problem is now to design a crop insurance program that maximizes the net social surplus from the production of the crop recognizing that the run-off pollution from the crop imposes a cost on the rest of society. The associated optimization problem is

$$\max_{x,p,z,I} \left\{ \sum_{k=1}^{S} \pi_k \left(u(z_k - I_k) - g(\mathbf{x}) + I_k \right) - m(p): (\mathbf{x}, \mathbf{p}, \mathbf{z}) \in T \right\}.$$

By the principle of conditional optimization, we can rewrite this problem as

$$\max_{z,I,p} \left\{ \sum_{k=1}^{S} \pi_k \left(u(z_k - I_k) + I_k \right) - c(p, \mathbf{z}) - m(p) \right\}.$$

Hence, the main difference between this problem and the immediately preceding one is that in designing the socially optimal problem, we cannot entrust the optimal pollution choice problem to farmers because their marginal valuation of the cost of pollution is zero while society's is not. However, if farmers can somehow be induced by the government to produce an appropriate state-contingent output vector and pollution level, the choice of the remaining inputs can be entrusted completely to them because their private valuation of those inputs matches society's. Mathematically, the reflection of this fact is that we must use the effort-cost function and not the private-cost function in obtaining the socially optimal crop-insurance program. So we emphasize again that input monitoring is inessential so long as information can be obtained on the state of

---

[25] Lee (1953) makes a closely related point in arguing the superiority of temperature insurance over frost insurance for citrus products.

nature. Under our assumptions, this problem reduces to a simple concave programming problem whose solution is characterized by the first-order conditions

$$1 - u'(z_k - I_k) = 0, \quad k = 1, 2, \ldots, S,$$

$$\pi_k u'(z_k - I_k) - c_k(p, \mathbf{z}) \leqslant 0, \quad z_k \geqslant 0, \quad k = 1, 2, \ldots, S,$$

$$-c_p(p, \mathbf{z}) - m'(p) \leqslant 0, \quad p \geqslant 0.$$

These first-order conditions differ slightly from those uncovered in the previous section in that the socially optimal level of pollution no longer corresponds to $p(\mathbf{z})$, the level that farmers would choose as a result of solving their private-cost minimization problem. Here the farmer's cost reduction associated with emitting runoff pollution is balanced against the social damage that this run-off pollution incurs. Hence, the solution to these first-order conditions will not correspond to the solution identified in the previous section.

However, these first-order conditions are similar to those in the preceding section in that the social optimum continues to require that farmers be fully insured against production risk [Borch's (1962) rule for optimal risk-sharing], and that farmers choose their state-contingent output vector to maximize expected profit. But in the present case, social optimality requires that farmers maximize expected profit conditional on their producing a level of pollution that does not exceed the socially optimal amount.

Denote the solution to these first-order conditions as $(\hat{\mathbf{z}}, \hat{\mathbf{I}}, \hat{p})$. Provided that the level of pollution that the farmer emits is observable, then the socially optimal crop insurance program that balances farmer cost savings associated with pollution emission against its environmental damage can be implemented in the following fashion. The government specifies a state-contingent net premia schedule corresponding to $\hat{I}$ while simultaneously imposing the Pigouvian pollution tax:

$$m'(\hat{p})(p - \hat{p}).$$

A farmer facing this net premia *cum* pollution tax insurance scheme chooses his vector of inputs, state-contingent outputs, and pollution in accordance with

$$\max_{x, p, z} \left\{ \sum_{k=1}^{S} \pi_k \left(u(z_k - \hat{I}_k) - g(\mathbf{x}) - m'(\hat{p})(p - \hat{p}) \right) : (\mathbf{x}, \mathbf{p}, \mathbf{z}) \in T \right\}$$

$$= \max_{p, z} \left\{ \sum_{k=1}^{S} \pi_k u(z_k - \hat{I}_k) - c(p, \mathbf{z}) - m'(\hat{p})(p - \hat{p}) \right\}.$$

The associated first-order conditions for this private optimization problem are

$$\pi_k u'(z_k - \hat{I}_k) - c_k(p, \mathbf{z}) \leqslant 0, \quad z_k \geqslant 0, \quad k = 1, 2, \ldots, S,$$

$$-c_p(p, \mathbf{z}) - m'(\hat{p}) \leqslant 0, \quad p \geqslant 0.$$

Provided that the marginal pollution tax and the state-contingent net premia have been set correctly, the farmer solving these first-order conditions will choose the socially optimal level of runoff pollution and state-contingent outputs. Hence:

PROPOSITION 13 [Chambers and Quiggin (1996)]. *If the government can observe the state of nature and the level of pollution, it can implement a socially optimal crop insurance program even in the absence of knowledge of the level of inputs and output that occurs.*

As in the preceding section, the implication of this result is that so long as the state of nature is verifiable and the level of pollution is observable, the government need not base its crop insurance program on the amount of output that is produced or on the level of inputs utilized. Hence, hidden input action does not impinge on the formulation of an optimal crop insurance program. By specifying the state-contingent premia and the pollution tax appropriately, the government effectively makes the farmer the residual claimant for his or her actions.

3.4. Crop insurance with pollution and output unobservable to the government

In the two preceding sections, it was assumed that the government and the representative farmer share the same information. Thus, there was no scope for hidden action or hidden knowledge and the only difference in the analysis, so far, has revolved around whether or not pollution bears an external cost that is not appropriately internalized by the farmer in solving his or her private-cost problem. This section considers the case where there is hidden action and hidden knowledge: The level of pollution, the inputs deployed, and the *ex post* output that the farmer produces are not observable by the government. We continue, however, to assume that the government can observe the conditions under which production takes place, i.e., it can observe the state of nature. This situation corresponds to the multi-task non-point source pollution model studied by Chambers and Quiggin (1996).[26]

To distinguish the case studied here from those studied in the two previous sections, we shall refer to the problems where no informational asymmetry exists between the government and the farmer as being *first-best*. In general, the informational asymmetry between the government and the farmers prevents the first-best crop insurance program from being implementable. The informational asymmetry only allows the government to specify a payment schedule that is based upon what it can actually observe. In this instance, the only "observable" is the state of nature. However, an immediate consequence of the results in the two previous sections is:

---

[26] Chambers and Quiggin (1996) extend and generalize the earlier analysis by Segerson (1988) by considering stochastic production and risk aversion.

PROPOSITION 14 [Chambers and Quiggin (1996)]. *If the government cannot observe the farmer's choice of inputs, the ex post output, or pollution, the government can only implement the first-best crop insurance contract if the marginal social damage of pollution is always zero, or if the marginal social damage of pollution is strictly positive but $p(\mathbf{z}) = 0$ for the first-best state-contingent output vector.*

The intuition behind this result is simple given the results of the previous sections. There it was seen that the first-best crop insurance program could be implemented solely by specifying the appropriate set of state-contingent net premia and the appropriate Pigouvian tax, if necessary, for the level of pollution emitted. In the case under consideration, the government always has the ability to specify a set of state-contingent net premia that corresponds to the pattern that would be associated with the first best. When pollution is not socially damaging, this is all that is required to achieve the first best. And in the case where pollution is socially damaging but the farmer voluntarily chooses not to pollute because he or she does not realize a positive return from doing so, the farmer's private-cost minimization solution corresponds to what is socially optimal.

Unfortunately, the preceding case will generally not be relevant to most real-world situations as even the most casual empiricism establishes that farmers solving a private-cost minimization problem generally choose to pollute at a nonzero level.[27] In fact, we have:

PROPOSITION 15 [Chambers and Quiggin (1996)]. *If the government cannot observe the farmer's choice of inputs, the ex post output, or pollution, and the marginal social damage of pollution is strictly positive, the government cannot implement the first-best crop insurance program if $p(\mathbf{z}) > 0$ for the first-best state-contingent output vector.*

Again the heuristic explanation of this result is relatively straightforward: Even if the government can induce farmers to choose the first-best state-contingent output vector, privately rational farmers will solve the private-cost minimization problem by choosing the pollution level that minimizes their cost of producing that state-contingent output vector. Hence, while they may do what is first-best on the state-contingent output side, they will not do what is first-best on the pollution side because the private-cost minimization problem involves them choosing $p(\hat{\mathbf{z}})$ so that

$$-c_p\big(p(\hat{\mathbf{z}}), \hat{\mathbf{z}}\big) = 0,$$

instead of setting this same expression to $m'(p(\hat{\mathbf{z}})) > 0$ as required.

The only state-contingent outputs and pollution that are going to be implementable using an insurance contract that can only specify state-contingent net premia are ones

---

[27] See, for example, the study by Brossier et al. (1992) documenting the percolation of nitrogen run-off into the Vittel mineral water supply.

consistent with the self-interested maximizing behavior of farmers. Thus, given a vector of state-contingent net premia $I \in \Re^S$, the only implementable state-contingent output vectors (and implicitly pollution level) satisfy

$$\mathbf{z} \in \arg\max_z \left\{ \sum_{k=1}^{S} \pi_k u(z_k - I_k) - C(\mathbf{z}) \right\}.$$

Therefore, in designing its crop insurance program the government's formal problem is to choose $I \in \Re^S$, $\mathbf{z} \in \Re_+^S$ to

$$\max_{z,I} \left\{ \sum_{k=1}^{S} \pi_k u(z_k - I_k) + \pi_k I_k - C(\mathbf{z}) - m\big(p(\mathbf{z})\big): \right.$$

$$\left. \mathbf{z} \in \arg\max_z \left\{ \sum_{k=1}^{S} \pi_k u(z_k - I_k) - C(\mathbf{z}) \right\} \right\}.$$

Subject to suitable regularity conditions that ensure the existence of interior solutions to the farmer's individual optimization problem [see Chambers and Quiggin (1996), for details], the government's crop insurance problem can be solved in stages in a fashion similar to that used to solve the hidden-knowledge, mechanism-design problem considered earlier. The approach is based on the recognition that the order of optimization is irrelevant. One can always fix the action vector, here the vector of state-contingent outputs and the associated pollution level, and then choose the vector of state-contingent net premia to maximize the government's objective function. Doing so yields

$$\max_z \left\{ \max_I \left\{ \sum_{k=1}^{S} \pi_k u(z_k - I_k) + \pi_k I_k: \right. \right.$$

$$\left. \left. \mathbf{z} \in \arg\max_z \left\{ \sum_{k=1}^{S} \pi_k u(z_k - I_k) - C(\mathbf{z}) \right\} \right\} - C(\mathbf{z}) - m\big(p(\mathbf{z})\big) \right\},$$

which can be rewritten

$$\max_z \left\{ R(\mathbf{z}) - C(\mathbf{z}) - m\big(p(\mathbf{z})\big) \right\},$$

where

$$R(\mathbf{z}) = \max_I \left\{ \sum_{k=1}^{S} \pi_k u(z_k - I_k) + \pi_k I_k: \mathbf{z} \in \arg\max_z \left\{ \sum_{k=1}^{S} \pi_k u(z_k - I_k) - C(\mathbf{z}) \right\} \right\}.$$

The solution to the first-stage of the government's problem is easily solved by recognizing that the farmer's private optimization problem is a concave programming problem whose interior optima are characterized by the first-order conditions

$$\pi_i u'(z_i - I_i) - C_i(\mathbf{z}) = 0, \quad i = 1, 2, \ldots, S.$$

Hence, if a given vector of state-contingent outputs, $\mathbf{z}$, represents the farmer's optimal reaction to the state-contingent crop insurance program, the state-contingent net premia that must have engendered this reaction can be found by implicitly solving these first-order conditions for these state-contingent net premia in terms of $\mathbf{z}$ to obtain

$$I_i(\mathbf{z}) = z_i - v\left(\frac{C_i(\mathbf{z})}{\pi_i}\right), \quad i = 1, 2, \ldots, S,$$

where v is a strictly decreasing differentiable function satisfying

$$v'\left(\frac{C_i(\mathbf{z})}{\pi_i}\right) = \frac{1}{u''(z_i - I_i)}.$$

Consequently,

$$\begin{aligned}
\frac{\partial I_i(\mathbf{z})}{\partial z_i} &= 1 - \frac{C_{ii}(\mathbf{z})/\pi_i}{u''(z_i - I_i)} \geqslant 1, \\
\frac{\partial I_i(\mathbf{z})}{\partial z_j} &= -\frac{C_{ij}(\mathbf{z})/\pi_i}{u''(z_i - I_i)},
\end{aligned} \tag{13}$$

where the inequality in the first expression follows from the convexity of the private-cost function and the concavity of *ex post* utility. So long as all outputs are gross substitutes for one another ($C_{ij}(\mathbf{z}) \geqslant 0$), these facts imply that an increase in any state-contingent output is matched by an increase in all the state-contingent net premia. Moreover, to induce the farmer to raise, say, the ith state-contingent output by one unit, the net premium must rise by at least one unit. If the marginal cost of producing one state-contingent output is independent of the other state-contingent outputs ($C_{ij}(\mathbf{z}) = 0$), the state-contingent net premium for state i, say, depends only upon the ith state-contingent output. [Chambers and Quiggin (1996) refer to this case as *no effort economies of scope*.] In what follows, we shall always presume that state-contingent outputs are at least weak gross substitutes for one another.

The net premia, $I_i(\mathbf{z})$, can be thought of as the net premia that would rationalize a privately optimizing farmer choosing the vector of state-contingent outputs given by $\mathbf{z}$. One should notice that these net premia have the characteristic that, all else constant, the more risk-averse the farmer, the closer they will come to fully insuring the farmer by providing him or her a fixed return in each state, i.e.,

$$\frac{\partial I_i(z)}{\partial z_i} = 1, \qquad \frac{\partial I_i(z)}{\partial z_k} = 0, \quad k \neq i.$$

This is as it should be: The first-best crop insurance contracts fully insure the farmer. But fully insuring a risk-averse farmer does not give the appropriate incentives to control the now non-observable pollution runoff, especially if pollution is associated with the use of a risk-complementary input. Hence, the ability to pollute without being observed means that the incentive contract that emerges must balance efficiency gains obtained from manipulating the incentive scheme against losses in risk-sharing that emerge from not fully insuring the farmer. An optimal incentive contract in the presence of this form of hidden action requires the farmer to self-insure, and this requires the farmer to bear some of the production risk. However, the more risk-averse the farmer, the larger will be the social losses that arise from not fully insuring the farmer, and the more closely the optimal incentive contract should be designed so as to leave the farmer with a fixed return in each state of nature.

Using these net premia permits rewriting the second stage of the government's crop insurance *cum* pollution control problem as

$$\max_z \left\{ \sum_{k=1}^{S} \pi_k u\left(z_k - I_k(\mathbf{z})\right) + \pi_k I_k(\mathbf{z}) - C(\mathbf{z}) - m\left(p(\mathbf{z})\right) \right\}.$$

After using the farmer's first-order conditions for optimality, the first-order conditions for a strictly interior solution here are

$$\sum_{k=1}^{S} \pi_k \left(1 - u'\left(z_k - I_k(\mathbf{z})\right)\right) \frac{\partial I_k(\mathbf{z})}{\partial z_j} = m'\left(p(\mathbf{z})\right) \frac{\partial p(\mathbf{z})}{\partial z_j}, \qquad j = 1, 2, \dots, S. \tag{14}$$

The right-hand side of (14) represents the marginal pollution damage caused by altering the state-j contingent production of the agricultural commodity. Note, increasing z_j, say, can lower pollution and hence pollution damage so that the right-hand side can be negative. Manipulation of the solution to the farmer's private-cost minimization problem shows that $p(\mathbf{z})$ is increasing in z_j, say, if and only if increasing p decreases the marginal cost of producing the jth state-contingent output. The expression on the left-hand side of (14) is the inner product of the differences between society's marginal utility of the crop and the farmer's *ex post* marginal utility of the crop and the vector $\{\partial I_k(\mathbf{z})/\partial z_j\}$.

The first-best crop insurance contract requires that the farmer be fully insured: Full insurance requires

$$1 = u'\left(z_k - I_k(\mathbf{z})\right).$$

Hence, the first-order conditions in (14) represent a generalization of the well-known "inverse-elasticity" rule familiar from the theory of public pricing. Divergences from the first-best pattern of perfect risk-sharing are inversely related to the vector $\{\partial I_k(\mathbf{z})/\partial z_j\}$. It also follows from expression (14) that if there is no pollution externality in the sense that $m'(p) = 0$, then complete risk-sharing is consistent with the first-order conditions for an optimally designed crop insurance program because a zero divergence from first-best risk-sharing is orthogonal to all vectors. This result is consonant with Propositions 11 and 13.

When the cost structure exhibits no effort economies of scope, the connection between the inverse-elasticity rule and the necessary conditions for an optimal crop insurance program is more apparent. Then

$$\left(1 - u'\left(z_j - I_j(\mathbf{z})\right)\right)\frac{\partial I_j(\mathbf{z})}{\partial z_j} = m'\left(p(\mathbf{z})\right)\frac{\partial p(\mathbf{z})/\partial z_j}{\pi_j}, \quad j = 1, 2, \ldots, S.$$

This expression implies that the divergence from optimal risk-sharing and the marginal externality associated with z_j must have the same sign. So if the marginal cost of producing the jth state-contingent output is increasing in pollution, then at the optimum $1 - u'(z_j - I_j(\mathbf{z})) < 0$. The farmer's net return in the jth state is less than the amount that he or she would have been provided in the first best. Moreover, it also follows that the larger is $\partial I_j(\mathbf{z})/\partial z_j$, the smaller is the divergence from optimal risk-sharing required to accommodate a given marginal pollution externality. $\partial I_j(\mathbf{z})/\partial z_j$ is bounded below by one, but varies inversely with the farmer's degree of risk aversion. Using (13) in the last expression allows us to rewrite it more informatively as

$$\left(1 - u'\left(z_j - I_j(\mathbf{z})\right)\right)\left(\pi_j - \frac{C_{jj}(\mathbf{z})}{u''(z_j - I_j)}\right) = m'\left(p(\mathbf{z})\right)\frac{\partial p(\mathbf{z})}{\partial z_j}.$$

When the farmer is very risk-averse, the left-hand term approaches $\pi_j(1 - u'(z_j - I_j(\mathbf{z})))$ implying that the probability weighted divergence from optimal risk-sharing for the jth state approximates the marginal pollution externality caused by varying production of the jth state-contingent output. The intuitive explanation is that when the farmer is quite risk-averse, subtle changes in the net premia schedule that he or she faces will evoke relatively large changes in the state-contingent production pattern. In this case, varying the farmer's net premium provides an effective way of controlling the externality caused by pollution. When the farmer isn't very risk-averse, changes in the net premia schedule are then ineffective in eliciting changes in the farmer's production pattern. Consequently, the net-premia schedule is then ineffective in controlling the pollution externality.

The basic relationships driving the formulation of an optimal crop insurance policy are most stark where there are no effort economies of scope and $\Omega = \{1, 2\}$. The first-order conditions for the optimal crop insurance program are then

$$
\pi_1\big(1 - u'(z_1 - I_1(\mathbf{z}))\big)\frac{\partial I_1(\mathbf{z})}{\partial z_1} = m'(p(\mathbf{z}))\frac{\partial p(\mathbf{z})}{\partial z_1},
$$
$$
\pi_2\big(1 - u'(z_2 - I_2(\mathbf{z}))\big)\frac{\partial I_2(\mathbf{z})}{\partial z_2} = m'(p(\mathbf{z}))\frac{\partial p(\mathbf{z})}{\partial z_2}.
$$

(15)

Now suppose that pollution lowers the marginal cost of producing one state-contingent output, for concreteness' sake say state 1, while increasing the marginal cost of the other state-contingent output. Then it follows easily that

$$
1 - u'(z_1 - I_1(\mathbf{z})) > 0
$$

and

$$
1 - u'(z_2 - I_2(\mathbf{z})) < 0.
$$

By the strict concavity of u, the immediate implication is that the optimal crop insurance program satisfies $z_2 - I_2(\mathbf{z}) < r < z_1 - I_1(\mathbf{z})$. *Ex post* optimal returns to the farmer are left higher relative to the first best in the state where pollution lowers the marginal cost of that state's output, and are lower in the state where pollution raises the marginal cost of that state's output.

Intuitively, for a strictly risk-averse farmer, raising the *ex post* returns of a state in which pollution reduces marginal cost lowers the *ex post* marginal utility a farmer realizes by increasing output (thereby increasing pollution) in that state. On the other hand, lowering the *ex post* returns of a state in which pollution increases marginal cost provides a greater marginal incentive for increasing that state-contingent output (thereby diminishing pollution).

More generally, subtracting the second line of (15) from the first line gives, after some minor manipulation,

$$
u'(z_2 - I_2(\mathbf{z})) - u'(z_1 - I_1(\mathbf{z}))
$$
$$
= \frac{m'(p(\mathbf{z}))}{\partial I_2(\mathbf{z})/\partial z_2}\left(\frac{\partial p(\mathbf{z})/\partial z_1}{\pi_1}\frac{\partial I_2(\mathbf{z})/\partial z_2}{\partial I_1(\mathbf{z})/\partial z_1} - \frac{\partial p(\mathbf{z})/\partial z_2}{\pi_2}\right).
$$

So, in this case, optimal *ex post* returns are greater in state 1 than in state 2 if and only if

$$
\frac{\partial p(\mathbf{z})/\partial z_1}{\pi_1}\frac{\partial I_2(\mathbf{z})/\partial z_2}{\partial I_1(\mathbf{z})/\partial z_1} - \frac{\partial p(\mathbf{z})/\partial z_2}{\pi_2} > 0.
$$

(16)

To understand the economic content of this expression, it is helpful to consider how a multiplicative mean-preserving spread of the state-contingent output vector affects the farmer's pollution decision. Suppose that $z_2 > z_1$, then increasing the second state-contingent output marginally by $\delta > 0$, while decreasing the first state-contingent output marginally by $-\pi_2/\pi_1\delta$ leaves the expected value of the state-contingent output vector unchanged. However, it also does two other things: First, it represents an increase in the riskiness of the state-contingent output in the sense of Rothschild and Stiglitz (1970) because it increases the spread between high-output and low-output outcomes without changing the mean. Any risk-averter whose preferences can be represented by an expected-utility functional would always prefer the first pair of state-contingent outputs to the second pair [Rothschild and Stiglitz (1970)].[28] Second, producing this riskier output bundle leads the farmer to alter his or her pollution decision. Pollution emission changes by

$$\left(\frac{\partial p(\mathbf{z})/\partial z_2}{\pi_2} - \frac{\partial p(\mathbf{z})/\partial z_1}{\pi_1}\right)\pi_2\delta.$$

Therefore, the farmer's pollution emission increases as the riskiness (in the Rothschild–Stiglitz sense) of the state-contingent output increases if and only if

$$\left(\frac{\partial p(\mathbf{z})/\partial z_2}{\pi_2} - \frac{\partial p(\mathbf{z})/\partial z_1}{\pi_1}\right) \geqslant 0.$$

More generally:

LEMMA 16 [Chambers and Quiggin (1996)]. *Pollution emission increases as the riskiness of the state-contingent output increases if and only if*

$$\left(\frac{\partial p(\mathbf{z})/\partial z_2}{\pi_2} - \frac{\partial p(\mathbf{z})/\partial z_1}{\pi_1}\right)(z_2 - z_1) \geqslant 0.$$

If pollution emission increases as the riskiness of the state-contingent output vector increases, we shall refer to it as being *risk-complementary*, while if pollution emission decreases as the riskiness of the output vector increases we shall refer to it as being *risk-substituting*. The intuitive notions of risk complementarity and risk substitutability are quite analogous to the notions of risk-increasing and risk-reducing inputs.

Returning to expression (16) and supposing for the moment that

$$\frac{\partial I_2(\mathbf{z})/\partial z_2}{\partial I_1(\mathbf{z})/\partial z_1} = 1,$$

---

[28] More generally, Chambers and Quiggin (2000) show that any individual with generalized Schur concave preferences will prefer the original state-contingent output pair to the one arrived at by taking the multiplicative mean-preserving spread.

then the key determinant of which state has the highest *ex post* net income for the farmer is whether pollution is risk-complementary or risk-substituting. Suppose, as before, that $z_2 > z_1$ in the optimal crop-insurance program. If pollution is risk-complementary, the optimal crop insurance program leaves *ex post* returns higher in state 2 than state 1. The rationale is straightforward: If pollution is risk-complementary, it will tend to be associated with riskier production patterns. Therefore, to encourage the farmer to reduce pollution, the regulator would want him to arrange for a less risky pattern of production.

By raising the farmer's *ex post* return in state 2, the insurer diminishes a risk-averse farmer's marginal incentive to expand output in the high-output state. In terms of real-world implications, one might consider two types of inputs that are associated with pollution problems, but which play different roles in the farmer's risk management. Fertilizers (as in the Vittel mineral water example cited earlier) are usually thought to be risk-complementary inputs while pesticides are thought to be risk-substituting inputs. So if the government is trying to cope with pesticide contamination and crop insurance simultaneously, the optimal response is likely to provide farmers with a high degree of returns insurance to ensure that they do not overutilize pesticides in an attempt to self-insure. On the other hand, coping optimally with a nitrogen runoff problem requires a lower level of crop insurance to provoke the farmer into providing self-insurance by using less of the risk-complementary inputs.

3.5. Crop insurance with pollution and state of nature not observable

The traditional moral-hazard formulation assumes that output from a stochastic production process is observable by the government, but that the exact conditions under which production takes place, including the amount of effort used and the state of nature, are not. Moreover, it is typically assumed that the government has direct preferences over only the output from the production process and no direct preferences over any of the other producer decision variables. The preceding section examined the case where the government could observe the state of nature but not the output produced, and hence departs from the standard moral-hazard formulation. In this section, we return to the more standard formulation by assuming that the farmer's output but not the state of nature is observable. However, we continue to presume that the government cannot observe and, therefore, directly regulate either the farmer's utilization of inputs or the amount of pollution he or she emits. Hence, the current case encompasses both hidden action (input committal) and hidden knowledge (the state of nature that occurs) on the part of the farmer.[29] However, because pollution damages the environment, the government, in contrast to the more usual moral-hazard formulation, does have preferences over this action variable.

---

[29] My thinking on the formulation and specification of this version of the crop insurance problem was originally stimulated by several conversations with Rita Curtis on a closely related problem in fisheries regulation.

At this juncture, it is worthwhile to discuss briefly the implications of the various assumptions on what is and is not observable by the government. I am using observable as synonymous with contractible. That is, if the government can observe something then it can base its crop insurance payments upon it. So, for example, in previous sections, the assumption that the state of nature was observable permitted the specification of state-contingent net premia. Here, the state of nature is not directly observable. Consequently, the government can only enforce degenerate state-contingent net premia, i.e., a constant net premium for each state of nature. If the government specifies a non-degenerate distribution of net premia, a rational farmer *ex post* will claim that the state associated with the lowest net premium occurred. The government, lacking the knowledge of which state occurred, would have no choice but to award that payment to the farmer. Realizing that a pattern of differential state-contingent net premia would not work, the government would commit itself only to the degenerate state-contingent net premia. What is observable in the current case is *ex post* output. Therefore, the government can base its net premia on realized output.

I restrict attention to the simplest possible stochastic case, i.e., where $\Omega = \{1, 2\}$. It also turns out to be convenient to work in terms of farmer net revenues (y) rather than indemnities. The government's task now is to design a contract structure that awards the farmer on the basis of realized output while coming as close as possible, given the informational constraints of the model, to maximizing social surplus.

Let S be the class of all functions $s : \Re_+ \to \Re$ that the government can choose from in designing a farmer reward scheme.[30] The reward scheme works as follows: If the farmer realizes an output of z then his or her net revenue is set at $s(z)$ by the government. In picking such a reward scheme, the government must realize that if it wants to implement a particular state-contingent production structure (z_1, z_2), that state-contingent production structure must be both technically feasible and consistent with the agent's private optimization in the sense that

$$(z_1, z_2) \in \arg\max \{\pi_1 u(s(z_1)) + \pi_2 u(s(z_2)) - C(z_1, z_2)\}.$$

Notice, in particular, that here we use the farmer's private-cost function because pollution is not observable or contractible.

An interesting result emerges immediately: The payment scheme must be nondecreasing in realized output. To see why, suppose to the contrary that the government wanted to implement a state-contingent production structure where $z_2 > z_1$, while using a contract decreasing in output. Then because the farmer's private cost is nondecreasing in state-contingent outputs,

$$u(s(z_1)) - C(z_1, z_1) > \pi_1 u(s(z_1)) + \pi_2 u(s(z_2)) - C(z_1, z_2),$$

---

[30] As with our analysis of the hidden-knowledge model, the actual mechanism is left unspecified. Special cases of such reward schemes would include linear pricing, subsidized linear pricing, as well as a host of other alternatives.

thus violating rationality. Hence, we conclude:

LEMMA 17. *A contract $s : \Re_+ \to \Re$ can be implemented only if it is nondecreasing in ex post output. If cost is strictly increasing in state-contingent outputs, a contract $s : \Re_+ \to \Re$ can be implemented only if it is strictly increasing in ex post output.*

The socially optimal crop insurance *cum* pollution control problem can now be formulated as

$$\max_{s \in S} \left\{ \begin{array}{l} \pi_1 u\big(s(z_1)\big) + \pi_2 u\big(s(z_2)\big) - C(z_1, z_2) + \pi_1\big(z_1 - s(z_1)\big) \\ + \pi_2\big(z_2 - s(z_2)\big) - m\big(p(z_1, z_2)\big): \\ (z_1, z_2) \in \arg\max\{\pi_1 u\big(s(z_1)\big) + \pi_2 u(s(z_2)) - C(z_1, z_2)\} \end{array} \right\} \tag{17}$$

for technically feasible **z**. As in previous problems, it is analytically convenient to solve this problem in stages. To that end, notice that the maximization problem can be rewritten as

$$\max_{s \in S, \bar{u}} \left\{ \begin{array}{l} \bar{u} + \pi_1\big(z_1 - s(z_1)\big) + \pi_2\big(z_2 - s(z_2)\big) - m\big(p(z_1, z_2)\big): \\ (z_1, z_2) \in \arg\max\{\pi_1 u\big(s(z_1)\big) + \pi_2 u\big(s(z_2)\big) - C(z_1, z_2)\}, \\ \pi_1 u\big(s(z_1)\big) + \pi_2 u\big(s(z_2)\big) - C(z_1, z_2) \geqslant \bar{u} \end{array} \right\}.$$

Under relatively weak conditions [Quiggin and Chambers (1998)], this version of the government's crop insurance problem is equivalent to designing a state-contingent insurance structure subject to a set of constraints which make it privately rational for the farmer to pick the state-contingent production structure that corresponds to the solution to the above crop insurance problem. As discussed by Quiggin and Chambers (1998), the crop insurance scheme operates in the following way: When the farmer realizes an *ex post* output of, say, z she receives an *ex post* payment of y_1 if $z = z_1$, a payment of y_2 if $z = z_2$, and an arbitrarily large negative payment otherwise. Formally, the government's problem becomes

$$\max_{\bar{u}, y, z} \left\{ \begin{array}{l} \bar{u} + \pi_1(z_1 - y_1) + \pi_2(z_2 - y_2) - m\big(p(z_1, z_2)\big): \\ \pi_1 u(y_1) + \pi_2 u(y_2) - C(z_1, z_2) \geqslant \bar{u}, \\ \pi_1 u(y_1) + \pi_2 u(y_2) - C(z_1, z_2) \geqslant u(y_1) - C(z_1, z_1), \\ \pi_1 u(y_1) + \pi_2 u(y_2) - C(z_1, z_2) \geqslant u(y_2) - C(z_2, z_2), \\ \pi_1 u(y_1) + \pi_2 u(y_2) - C(z_1, z_2) \geqslant \pi_1 u(y_2) + \pi_2 u(y_1) - C(z_2, z_1) \end{array} \right\}.$$

The last three constraints in this problem ensure that the farmer finds it privately rational to pick the state-contingent production structure in return for the state-contingent reward structure offered by the government.

An immediate implication of this reformulation of the crop insurance problem and Lemma 17 is:

COROLLARY 18. *Any solution to the optimal crop insurance problem must satisfy*

$$(y_1 - y_2)(z_1 - z_2) \geqslant 0.$$

Even in this form, it is difficult to obtain meaningful results without further assumptions on the technology. I choose ones that limit attention to cases where there is a naturally "good" and a naturally "bad" state of nature [Chambers and Quiggin (2000, Chapter 9)]. Limiting the range of outcomes in this way removes some of the generality of the model, but greatly enhances our ability to obtain clear-cut economic results. To that end:

ASSUMPTION 3. $C(z_1, z_2)$ is positively linearly homogeneous, and in the first best, $z_2 \geqslant z_1$.

This assumption ensures that the second state is the good state of nature and that state 1 is the bad state of nature in the sense that a risk-neutral individual facing this technology and these probabilities would always choose to produce more output in the second state than in the first state. Under this assumption, following the approach of Quiggin and Chambers (1998) while using Corollary 18, one can show that the government's optimal crop insurance problem can now be rewritten as

$$\max_{\bar{u}, z} \{\bar{u} + \pi_1 z_1 + \pi_2 z_2 - m(p(z_1, z_2)) - Y(z_1, z_2, \bar{u}) : z_2 \geqslant z_1\}, \tag{18}$$

where $Y(z_1, z_2, \bar{u})$ represents what Quiggin and Chambers (1998) term the *agency-cost function* and is defined as the least costly way in an expected value sense for the government to get the farmer to adopt (z_1, z_2). Mathematically,

$$Y(z_1, z_2, \bar{u}) = \min_{y} \left\{ \begin{array}{l} \pi_1 y_1 + \pi_2 y_2 : \\ \pi_1 u(y_1) + \pi_2 u(y_2) - C(z_1, z_2) \geqslant \bar{u}, \\ \pi_1 u(y_1) + \pi_2 u(y_2) - C(z_1, z_2) \geqslant u(y_1) - C(z_1, z_1), \\ \pi_1 u(y_1) + \pi_2 u(y_2) - C(z_1, z_2) \geqslant u(y_2) - C(z_2, z_2), \\ \pi_1 u(y_1) + \pi_2 u(y_2) - C(z_1, z_2) \\ \qquad \geqslant \pi_1 u(y_2) + \pi_2 u(y_1) - C(z_2, z_1) \end{array} \right\}.$$

By making a change of variables, $u_i = u(y_i)$, whence $y_i = u^{-1}(u_i) = h(u_i)$, this agency-cost problem can be translated into a simple convex programming problem subject to four linear constraints [Grossman and Hart (1983), Quiggin and Chambers (1998)]. Using techniques that parallel those used in our earlier treatment of the hidden-knowledge, mechanism-design problem, Quiggin and Chambers (1998) isolate the following explicit solution:

$$Y(z_1, z_2, \bar{u}) = \pi_1 h(\bar{u} + C(z_1, z_1)) + \pi_2 h\left(\bar{u} + \frac{C(z_1, z_2)}{\pi_2} - \frac{\pi_1}{\pi_2} C(z_1, z_1)\right). \tag{19}$$

$h(u_i)$ is a strictly increasing and strictly convex function. Thus, $u_1 = \bar{u} + C(z_1, z_1)$ represents the farmer's optimal *ex post* utility in state 1, and $u_2 = \bar{u} + C(z_1, z_2)/\pi_2 - \pi_1/\pi_2 C(z_1, z_1)$ the same in state 2.

Using (19) in (18) and introducing the auxiliary variable $\gamma \geqslant 0$,

$$z_2 = z_1 + \gamma,$$

gives the following first-order conditions for the government's optimal crop insurance program:

$$1 - \pi_1 h'(u_1) - \pi_2 h'(u_2) = 0,$$

$$1 - m'\big(p(z_1, z_2)\big)\big(p_1(z_1, z_2) + p_2(z_1, z_2)\big) - Y_1(z_1, z_2, \bar{u}) - Y_2(z_1, z_2, \bar{u}) \leqslant 0,$$

$$z_1 \geqslant 0,$$

$$\pi_2 - m'\big(p(z_1, z_2)\big)p_2(z_1, z_2) - Y_2(z_1, z_2, \bar{u}) \leqslant 0, \quad \gamma \geqslant 0,$$

in the usual complementary slackness notation.

In interpreting these conditions, it helps to compare them with the first best. Recall that in the first best, farmer revenues are stabilized, and that the farmer bears the marginal cost of his or her pollution emission. Revenues are stabilized at the point r where

$$u'(r) = 1.$$

By the implicit function theorem,

$$h'(u_i) = \frac{1}{u'(y_i)},$$

so that the first-best crop insurance program requires: $h'(u_1) = 1 = h'(u_2)$. The current first-order condition, together with Corollary 18, requires that

$$h'(u_2) > 1 > h'(u_1),$$

or expressed in terms of net revenues,

$$y_2 > r > y_1,$$

implying that the farmer is not perfectly insured. In the good state of nature, state 2, the farmer receives more net revenue from production than in the first best, but in the bad state he or she receives less than in the first best. The reason is that insuring the farmer perfectly against risk, in the absence of an ability to monitor the state of nature, always gives the farmer an incentive to claim that the state associated with the lowest *ex post* output occurred. The farmer does this by arranging to produce the low-state output

in both states of nature. Doing so cuts his or her production cost while not imping-
ing upon his or her returns. To counteract these adverse incentives, the optimal crop
insurance contract requires the farmer to bear some revenue risk. Because the farmer
bears some risk, he or she will now find it advantageous to self-insure by adjusting their
state-contingent outputs and effort.

The first-best crop insurance program also has the farmer bear the marginal societal
pollution damage. Now, however, the informational structure ensures that the farmer
always solves his or her private-cost problem. As a result, the government cannot
directly implement a contract requiring him or her to pollute efficiently at the margin.
For any given state-contingent output vector, the farmer always emits pollution at the
point where its shadow cost is zero. Hence, government must control pollution indirectly
through its manipulation of the state-contingent payment and production scheme.

In the first best,[31]

$$\frac{\pi_2}{\pi_1} = \frac{c_2(\hat{p}, \hat{\mathbf{z}})}{c_1(\hat{p}, \hat{\mathbf{z}})} = \frac{C_2(\hat{z}_1, \hat{z}_2)}{C_1(\hat{z}_1, \hat{z}_2)},$$

whence

$$\frac{C_2(\hat{z}_1, \hat{z}_2)}{\pi_2} - \frac{C_1(\hat{z}_1, \hat{z}_2)}{\pi_1} = 0.$$

Under Assumption 3, this condition determines a unique first-best, state-contingent
output mix, $\hat{z}_2/\hat{z}_1$. In Figure 9, this state-contingent output mix is given by the slope
of the ray connecting the origin and the point of tangency between the fair-odds line
and the level set for the private-cost curve. (By homogeneity all of these level sets are
parallel.)

Some manipulation of the first-order conditions will show that in the case of a strictly
interior solution for γ and z_1, the optimal crop insurance program production pattern
now satisfies

$$\frac{C_2(z_1, z_2)}{\pi_2} - \frac{C_1(z_1, z_2)}{\pi_1} = \frac{h'(u_1) - h'(u_2)}{h'(u_2)} \left(C_1(z_1, z_1) + C_2(z_1, z_1) \right)$$

$$+ \frac{m'(p(z_1, z_2))}{h'(u_2)} \left(\frac{p_1(z_1, z_2)}{\pi_1} - \frac{p_2(z_1, z_2)}{\pi_2} \right). \tag{20}$$

Consider first the case where pollution is not socially damaging. Then expression
(20), upon using the fact that the farmer is no longer fully insured, establishes that

$$\frac{C_2(z_1, z_2)}{\pi_2} < \frac{C_1(z_1, z_2)}{\pi_1}$$

---

[31] The second equality follows by applying the envelope theorem to the private-cost minimization problem.

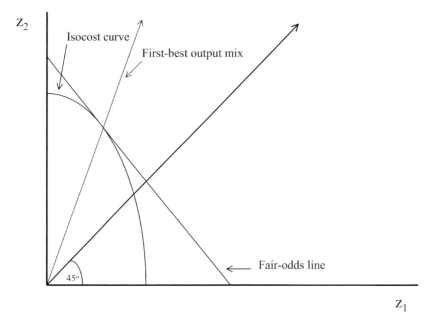

Figure 9. Production with moral hazard.

for the optimal crop insurance contract. It follows immediately from the curvature and homogeneity properties of the private-cost function that $z_2/z_1 < \hat{z}_2/\hat{z}_1$. In terms of Figure 9, the optimal output mix is given by a ray lying closer to the bisector (the 45° ray emanating from the origin) than that for the first best.[32] I will refer (z_1, z_2) as being *less dispersed* than $(\hat{z}_1, \hat{z}_2)$. Coping with moral hazard involves a crop insurance program having farmers produce a less risky state-contingent output mix than in the first best. The reasoning is as follows: The government would always prefer the farmer to produce at the point where his or her expected returns from farming are maximized. However, to get a risk-averse farmer to produce in such a fashion in the first best, the government must provide full insurance. Now, in the presence of asymmetric information, full insurance provides the farmer with adverse incentives to shirk. Hence, to combat these incentives the government must have the farmer bear some production risk. Once a risk-averse farmer is asked to bear some production risk, he or she will respond by self-insuring in the form of producing a less risky output mix than in the first best.

PROPOSITION 19. *If pollution is not socially damaging, the optimal crop insurance program involves a less dispersed state-contingent output mix than in the first best.*

---

[32] Note the bisector is the degenerate case where there is no production uncertainty.

Now consider what happens when pollution is socially damaging. By Lemma 16 and the fact that $z_2 > z_1$, pollution is risk-complementary if and only if

$$\frac{p_1(z_1, z_2)}{\pi_1} - \frac{p_2(z_1, z_2)}{\pi_2} < 0,$$

and risk-substituting if the inequality is reversed. From this observation and (20), we have:

PROPOSITION 20. *If pollution is socially damaging and risk-complementary, the optimal crop insurance program involves a less dispersed state-contingent output mix than when pollution is not socially damaging. If pollution is socially damaging and risk-substituting, then the optimal crop-insurance program involves a more dispersed output mix than when pollution is not socially damaging. The optimal crop insurance program always involves a more dispersed state-contingent output mix when pollution is risk-substituting than when it is risk-complementary.*

The intuition is similar to the case where the state of nature is unobservable. There the only way that the government can effect changes in pollution practices is by manipulating the state-contingent payment schedule to give the farmer less incentive to pollute. Here, the only tool the government has to influence the pattern of pollution is the slope of the output reward scheme. When pollution is a risk-complementary input, as casual observation suggests it is in the Vittel mineral water case discussed earlier, the government acts to blunt the farmer's marginal incentives to pollute by requiring the farmer to produce a less risky output mix than if pollution were not socially damaging or if it were risk-substituting. The farmer in producing this less risky state-contingent output mix will have less incentive to pollute if pollution is risk-complementary. Similarly, if pollution is risk-substituting and the government induces the farmer to produce a more risky state-contingent output mix, this gives the farmer less incentive to pollute at the margin. In fact, if pollution is risk-substituting and the marginal social damage from pollution is quite large, the government could conceivably have the farmer produce a riskier output pattern than in the first best. If pollution is of overwhelming importance to society, then its negative effects can completely outweigh the gains from insuring the farmer against production risk.

Chambers and Quiggin (2001) have recently used this model to show that an incentive contract consisting of a production standard with a fixed payment to the producer is only optimal if pollution is risk substituting in the neighborhood of certainty and if in the absence of agency considerations, the negative effects associated with runoff pollution would be severe enough to reverse the rank ordering of state-contingent outputs dictated by the farmer's private cost function under Assumption 3.

3.6. Related work

This discussion has focused narrowly on a mechanism design approach to optimal crop insurance while treating crop insurance as a metaphor for public support of agriculture in a stochastic world. Necessarily, therefore, a number of contributions to the crop insurance literature have been overlooked as their emphasis was different than the main thrust of this chapter. In the remainder of this section, I will briefly discuss some of these contributions.

Ahsan, Ali and Kurian (1982) considered the optimal design of crop insurance in the presence of adverse selection. Nelson and Loehman (1987) formulated and solved the first-best crop insurance program and considered some of the problems associated with insurance markets that prevent actual insurance contracts from attaining the first best. These problems include both hidden action and hidden knowledge. They prescribe designing agricultural contracts using the best information available to policy makers while recognizing the incentive problems associated with the presence of asymmetric information. Following on their work, Chambers (1989b) studied moral hazard in the public provision of crop insurance while paying particular attention to whether agricultural markets were actually "insurable", i.e., whether agricultural contracts exist which make both insurer and insuree better off than in the absence of insurance. Chambers (1989b) characterized second-best insurance contracts under moral hazard and derived sufficient conditions for agricultural markets to be insurable. More recently, Chambers and Quiggin (2000) have used a state-contingent approach to examine farmers' optimal reaction to both actuarially fair and actuarially unfair crop insurance while paying particular attention to conditions under which farmers will fully insure even in the presence of actuarially unfair insurance.

Chambers' (1989b) moral hazard results apply for the case where the moral hazard facing insurance providers cannot be resolved. The key for optimally removing the moral hazard associated with hidden action is either an ability to observe the farmer's actual production practice or an ability to observe and write contracts contingent on which state of nature occurs. However, a number of authors have suggested insurance schemes for resolving some of the problems associated with the provision of insurance under moral hazard that depend upon neither observing the farmer's action nor the state of nature. Essentially, these schemes work by specifying insurance contracts contingent on some partition of the state space that is observable and hence contractible to the insurer. For example, rather early on, Lee (1953) suggested that the provision of temperature insurance in place of frost insurance might help resolve some of the moral hazard associated with the provision of insurance to citrus producers because temperature could be more easily verified than actual frost damage. Much later, Miranda (1991), building on early work by Halcrow (1949), suggested that area-based yield insurance, in which indemnities are based on divergences between the area yield for the geographic region surrounding the farmer and some predetermined critical yield, would effectively eliminate moral hazard. Mahul (1999) has recently characterized optimal area-yield insurance policies. Because both of these types of insurance contracts do not completely resolve the problems associated with the unobservability of the state of nature, neither area-based yield insurance or temperature insurance generally represents an optimal response to the presence of hidden action. While they control for moral hazard, they generally will not have the optimal risk-sharing characteristics of optimal incentive contracts. This is most easily observed by noting that our optimal contracts typically have the farmer's indemnification scheme vary with his observed output. Neither area-based yield insurance nor temperature insurance has this characteristic. Moreover, Bourgeon and Chambers (2000a) demonstrate that the optimal area-based yield insurance scheme designed by Mahul (1999) can be subject to adverse selection problems if insurance loading costs are sufficiently large.

A number of studies have examined either theoretically or empirically the design of various crop insurance provisions [Lee (1953), Skees and Reed (1986), Miranda (1991)] as well as farmer reaction to various crop insurance program provisions [King and Oamek (1983), Goodwin (1993), Ramaswami (1993), Horowitz and Lichtenberg (1993), Vercammen and van Kooten (1994), Vandeveer and Loehman (1994), Smith (1995), Lee, Harwood and Somwaru (1997)], and the environmental impacts of crop insurance provisions [Innes and Ardila (1994)]. Unfortunately space and the focus of this chapter do not permit the more thorough review that these studies deserve.

4. Summary

This paper surveys agricultural policy studies which have taken as their motivating theme the existence of information asymmetries between agricultural producers and those in charge of formulating agricultural policy. It has typically been assumed that the information asymmetries run in a single direction with the agricultural producers being better informed about their technology or their actions than the policy makers. The existence of these asymmetries creates incentive problems that must be tackled in the design of an optimal agricultural policy.

We have studied two basic types of information asymmetries, those associated with hidden knowledge and those with hidden action. In the context studied here, hidden knowledge occurs when the farmer has exact information about his technology but the regulator does not. Hidden action occurs when only the farmer has exact information on the conditions under which production takes place. Specifically, it is assumed that the farmer alone knows what productive actions he takes and the state of nature that occurs.

In analyzing both types of information asymmetries, the current paper has made a significant departure from more traditional analyses of farm policies in several ways. Most important, it has adopted a mechanism-design approach instead of the more familiar practice which typically restricts itself to evaluating the relative desirability of a limited menu of policy tools with desirability being judged by measuring the area of "deadweight" loss triangles. The more neutral mechanism-design approach has a number of advantages over the "triangle" approach. Most important, it is free of a bias inherent in any approach that *a priori* limits itself to considering a finite number of alternatives. And, that is, any judgment as to which is the most preferred policy outcome is obviously limited to being one of the alternatives considered.[33] While the "triangle"

---

[33] As a result, a veritable cottage industry has evolved of agricultural policy economists questioning or criticizing the findings of previous studies on the basis that previous studies ignored a particular policy

approach may do a relatively fine job of calculating the relative deadweight loss of a specific mix of farm policies, it is simply incapable of accurately evaluating the complex array of existing policies in even the simplest economy imaginable.

Even more importantly, however, the comparison of different alternatives blurs an important shortcoming of this approach: It simply cannot explain why the most efficient means are not used to achieve policy objectives. In the informational setting most commonly studied by these means, it is virtually tautological that lump-sum transfers should be made. In fact, most welfare comparisons made in terms of "deadweight" loss use lump-sum transfers as the basis upon which welfare loss calculations are made.

A primary lesson of the hidden-knowledge formulation is that the incentive problems created by the presence of asymmetric information can prevent a regulator with redistributional objectives from implementing first-best farm policies. While obvious once the model is formulated, this result lies in stark contrast to much of the existing literature on agricultural policy which simply cannot explain why redistributional goals are not achieved efficiently. While it is unreasonable to argue that such informational asymmetries are the true, or perhaps even a primary, cause of the departure from first-best policies, this finding suggests that the traditional yardstick by which differing policies are evaluated may be in need of a severe redefinition of units and perhaps even of its origin. If lump-sum policies are simply not possible, then the seemingly natural presumption that "bestness" should be judged in terms of departures from lump-sum policies is potentially flawed.

Another important insight that emerges from the study of the hidden-knowledge formulation is that the existence of asymmetric information about farmer ability creates an incentive for an efficient regulator to design policies that cope with its presence. Typically, this means that the regulator will need to alter the desired output distribution away from that achieved in competitive market. For the simple discrete models, this implies a spreading of the output distribution. In an optimally designed policy, high-cost farmers are never asked to produce more than they would in the competitive market and low-cost farmers are never asked to produce less than they would in the competitive market. And when the government disproportionately favors low-cost producers in its welfare calculus, this spreading of the output distribution results in policies that lead to overproduction as compared to the competitive market outcome. When the government favors high-cost farmers, this spreading effect results in policies which entail underproduction relative to the competitive market outcome.

The spreading of the output distribution is the government's optimal response to the incentive problems caused by the presence of asymmetric information. By distorting the production pattern away from the competitive outcome, it makes it cheaper for the government to design redistributional programs that separate out unfavored farmers from favored farmers. Although using stylized theoretical models to make inferences

---

component, and that the conclusions would change if the policy component were considered. Because the number of existing policy instruments is quite large, simple combinatorics suggests that the number of such possible papers is quite large and may even approach infinity for practical purposes.

about real-world practices is tricky at best, on this basis, one is naturally tempted to identify production-retirement programs with programs targeted toward benefiting high-cost farmers and heavy government production subsidies with programs targeted toward benefiting low-cost farmers.

The study of the hidden-action policy problem emphasizes a different set of incentive problems than the hidden-knowledge formulation. Instead of presuming that the regulator does not know the farmer's technology, it is assumed that the regulator does know the farmer's technology but that he or she cannot observe the producer's actions or the state of nature that determine the producer's stochastic output. So, for example, a policy maker observing a low farm output cannot be sure whether it results from Nature making a bad draw for the farmer or from the farmer working less efficiently. If the government does not concern itself about low returns to farmers in bad times, this unobservability of action has no policy consequences. More typically, however, if governments are less risk-averse than individual farmers, it is optimal to allow the more risk-averse farmers to transfer some of the production risk they face to the government by providing them some form of production insurance. But if there exists hidden action, providing insurance dampens a producer's incentives to take productively efficient actions. Hence, the design of government-provided insurance schemes must take these incentive effects into account.

The problem governments face is complicated by the further realization that policies can have cross-cutting effects on farmers' incentives. For example, forcing a farmer to bear additional production risk in an attempt to ensure that he or she take productively efficient actions may induce the farmer to overutilize inputs directed at controlling the riskiness of production, e.g., pesticides. If these inputs have negative environmental effects, then the incentive effects of the insurance scheme will have to be modulated to account for the negative environmental impact of heavy pesticide use. How the incentives are structured depends critically upon what is and what is not observable, and thus contractible, to the farm policy maker. For example, if the state of nature is not observable then the policy maker cannot freely prescribe state-contingent contracts without taking into account individual incentive effects. On the other hand, when the state of nature is observable and contractible, the regulator is free to make contracts state-contingent, but if there are unobservable actions for which the farmer is not or cannot be the residual claimant, then even state-contingent contracts will generally not be first best.

The nexus between the first and the second parts of the paper is the recognition that appropriate design of agricultural policy depends critically upon the informational setting in which policy is actually made. Traditionally it has been assumed that the maker of farm policy is, in effect, omniscient. In the real world, decision makers face simultaneously both types of information asymmetries modeled here. Recognizing the obvious fallacy of this assumption about the policy maker's omniscience brings with it the further recognition that policies must be suitably tuned and refined to reflect this lack of omniscience. Unfortunately, at present, we have only the most rudimentary understanding of which direction this tuning and refining should take.

References

Ahsan, S., A. Ali and N. Kurian (1982), "Toward a theory of agricultural insurance", American Journal of Agricultural Economics 64:510–529.

Arrow, K.J., and M. Kurz (1970), Public Investment, the Rate of Return, and Optimal Fiscal Policy (Johns Hopkins University Press, Baltimore, MD).

Baron, D. (1989), "Design of regulatory mechanisms and institutions", in: R. Schmalensee and R. Willig, eds., Handbook of Industrial Organization, Vol. 2 (North-Holland, New York).

Baron, D.P., and R.B. Myerson (1982), "Regulating a monopolist with unknown costs", Econometrica 50:911–930.

Besanko, D., and D.E.M. Sappington (1986), Designing Regulatory Policy With Limited Information (Harwood, New York).

Borch, K. (1962), "Equilibrium in a reinsurance market", Econometrica 30:424–444.

Bourgeon, J.-M., and R.G. Chambers (1999), "Producer organizations, bargaining, and asymmetric information", American Journal of Agricultural Economics 81:602–609.

Bourgeon, J.-M., and R.G. Chambers (2000a), "Optimal area-yield crop insurance reconsidered" (Department of Agricultural and Resource Economics, University of Maryland).

Bourgeon, J.-M., and R.G. Chambers (2000b), "Stop-and-go agricultural policies", American Journal of Agricultural Economics 82:1–13.

Bourgeon, J.-M., P.-A. Jayet and P. Picard (1995), "An incentive approach to land set-aside programs", European Economic Review 39:1487–1509.

Brossier, J., M. Benoit, F. Falloux and Ph. Pierre (1992), "Agricultural practices, underground water quality, and research-development project", 24th EAAE Seminar Paper.

Caillaud, B., R. Guesnerie, P. Rey and J. Tirole (1988), "Government intervention in production and incentives theory: a review", Rand Journal of Economics 19:1–26.

Chambers, R.G. (1987), "Designing producer financed farm programs, or 'should we save the cows?'", Working paper (University of Maryland).

Chambers, R.G. (1989a), "Concentrated objective functions for nonlinear tax models", Journal of Public Economics 39:365–375.

Chambers, R.G. (1989b), "Insurability and moral hazard in agricultural insurance markets", American Journal of Agricultural Economics 71:614–626.

Chambers, R.G. (1989c), "Workfare or welfare?", Journal of Public Economics 40:79–97.

Chambers, R.G. (1992), "On the design of agricultural policy mechanisms", American Journal of Agricultural Economics 74:646–654.

Chambers, R.G., and J. Quiggin (1992), "A state-contingent approach to production under uncertainty", Working paper 92-03 (University of Maryland).

Chambers, R.G., and J. Quiggin (1996), "Nonpoint-source pollution control as a multi-task principal-agent problem", Journal of Public Economics 59:95–116.

Chambers, R.G., and J. Quiggin (1997), "Separation and hedging results with state-contingent production", Economica 64:187–210.

Chambers, R.G., and J. Quiggin (2000), Uncertainty, Production, Choice, and Agency: The State-Contingent Approach (Cambridge University Press, New York).

Chambers, R.G., and J. Quiggin (2001), "Incentives and standards in agency contracts", Working paper (University of Maryland).

Clark, C.W. (1976), Mathematical Bioeconomics: The Optimal Management of Renewable Resources (Wiley–Interscience, New York).

Dasgupta, P., P. Hammond and E. Maskin (1979), "The implementation of social choice rules: some general results on incentive compatibility", Review of Economic Studies 46:185–216.

Farm Income Protection Insurance Task Force (1983), Farm Income Protection Insurance: A Report to the U.S. Congress (Washington, DC).

Gardner, B.L. (1983), "Efficient redistribution through commodity markets", American Journal of Agricultural Economics 65:225–234.

Gardner, B.L., and R. Kramer (1986), "Experience with crop insurance in the United States", in: P. Hazell, C. Pomareda and A. Valdes, eds., Crop Insurance for Agricultural Development: Issues and Experience (Johns Hopkins University Press, Baltimore, MD).

Goodwin, B. (1993), "An empirical analysis of the demand for multiple-peril crop insurance", American Journal of Agricultural Economics 75:425–434.

Grossman, S., and O. Hart (1983), "An analysis of principal-agent problems", Econometrica 51:7–46.

Guesnerie, R., and J.-J. Laffont (1984), "A complete solution of a class of principal-agent problems with an application to the control of the self-managed firms", Journal of Public Economics 25:329–370.

Guesnerie, R., and J. Seade (1982), "Nonlinear pricing in a finite economy", Journal of Public Economics 17:157–179.

Halcrow, H.G. (1949), "Actuarial structures for crop insurance", Journal of Farm Economics 21:418–443.

Harris, M., and A. Raviv (1979), "Optimal incentives with imperfect information", Journal of Economic Theory 20:231–259.

Harris, M., and R.M. Townsend (1981), "Resource allocation under asymmetric information", Econometrica 49:33–64.

Hennessy, D. (1998), "The production effects of income support policies under uncertainty", American Journal of Agricultural Economics 80:46–57.

Hirshleifer, J. (1965), "Investment decision under uncertainty: choice-theoretic approaches", Quarterly Journal of Economics 79:509–536.

Holmstrom, B., and P. Milgrom (1987), "Aggregation and linearity in the provision of intertemporal incentives", Econometrica 55:303–328.

Horowitz, J.K., and E. Lichtenberg (1993), "Insurance, moral hazard, and chemical use in agriculture", American Journal of Agricultural Economics 75:926–935.

Hueth, B. (2000), "Further observations on the design of agricultural-policy mechanisms", American Journal of Agricultural Economics 82:13–22.

Innes, R., and S. Ardila (1994), "Agricultural insurance and soil depletion in a simple dynamic model", American Journal of Agricultural Economics 76:371–384.

King, R., and G. Oamek (1983), "Risk management by Colorado dryland farmers and the elimination of the disaster assistance program", American Journal of Agricultural Economics 65:247–255.

Laffont, J.-J., and J. Tirole (1993), A Theory of Incentives in Procurement and Regulation (MIT Press, Cambridge, MA).

Lee, H. (1986), "Optimal nonlinear agricultural credit pricing", Ph.D. thesis (University of Maryland).

Lee, H., J. Harwood and A. Somwaru (1997), "Implications of disaster assistance reform for non-insured crops", American Journal of Agricultural Economics 79:419–429.

Lee, I.M. (1953), "Temperature insurance – an alternative to frost insurance in citrus", Journal of Farm Economics 35:15–28.

Lewis, T., R. Feenstra and R. Ware (1989), "Eliminating price supports: a political economy perspective", Journal of Public Economics 40:159–185.

Mahul, O. (1999), "Optimum area yield crop insurance", American Journal of Agricultural Economics 81:75–82.

Miranda, M.J. (1991), "Area-yield crop insurance reconsidered", American Journal of Agricultural Economics 73:233–242.

Mirrlees, J.A. (1971), "An exploration in the theory of optimum income taxation", Review of Economic Studies 38:175–208.

Myerson, R.B. (1979), "Incentive compatibility and the bargaining problem", Econometrica 47:61–74.

Nelson, C., and E. Loehman (1987), "Further toward a theory of agricultural insurance", American Journal of Agricultural Economics 69:523–531.

Nerlove, M. (1958), The Dynamics of Supply: Estimation of Farmers' Response to Price (Johns Hopkins University Press, Baltimore, MD).

Quiggin, J., and R.G. Chambers (1998), "A state-contingent production approach to principal-agent problems with an application to point-source pollution control", Journal of Public Economics 70:441–472.

Ramaswami, B. (1993), "Supply response to agricultural insurance: risk reduction and moral hazard", American Journal of Agricultural Economics 75:914–925.

Rothschild, M., and J.E. Stiglitz (1970), "Increasing risk I: A definition", Journal of Economic Theory 2:225–243.

Sanderson, F. (1943), "A specific-risk insurance scheme for wheat crop insurance", Journal of Farm Economics 25:759–776.

Seade, J.K. (1977), "On the shape of optimal tax schedules", Journal of Public Economics 7:203–235.

Segerson, K. (1988), "Uncertainty and incentives in nonpoint pollution control", Journal of Economics and Environmental Management 15:87–98.

Skees, J., and M. Reed (1986), "Rate making for farm-level crop insurance: Implications for adverse selection", American Journal of Agricultural Economics 68:653–659.

Smith, R.B.W. (1995), "The conservation acreage reserve program as a least-cost land-retirement program", American Journal of Agricultural Economics 77:93–105.

Smith, R.B.W. (1992), On Designing a Optimal Conservation Reserve Program (University of Maryland).

Spence, A.M. (1977), "Nonlinear prices and welfare", Journal of Public Economics 8:1–18.

Vandeveer, M.L., and E.T. Loehman (1994), "Farmer response to modified crop insurance: a case study of corn in Indiana", American Journal of Agricultural Economics 76:128–140.

Vercammen, J., M. Fulton and C. Hyde (1996), "Nonlinear pricing schemes for agricultural cooperatives", American Journal of Agricultural Economics 78:572–584.

Vercammen, J., and G.C. van Kooten (1994), "Moral-hazard cycles in individual-coverage crop insurance", American Journal of Agricultural Economics 76:250–261.

Wallace, T.D. (1962), "Measurement of social costs of agricultural programs", Journal of Farm Economics 44:580–594.

Weymark, J. (1986), "A reduced-form optimal income tax problem", Journal of Public Economics 30:199–217.

Wu, J.-J., and B.A. Babcock (1996), "Contract design for the purchase of environmental goods from agriculture", American Journal of Agricultural Economics 78:935–944.

Chapter 35

MARKET FAILURES AND SECOND-BEST ANALYSIS WITH A FOCUS ON NUTRITION, CREDIT, AND INCOMPLETE MARKETS

ROBERT INNES

Department of Agricultural and Resource Economics, University of Arizona, Tucson

Contents

Handbook of Agricultural Economics, Volume 2, Edited by B. Gardner and G. Rausser

Abstract

This chapter studies second-best models of nutritional externalities, credit, and incomplete markets for risk, developing implications for welfare-improving government policy using primitive economic building blocks. Using a simple model of altruism wherein the rich obtain utility from the nourishment of the poor, the analysis describes efficiency properties of alternative food subsidy policies, with and without enforcement costs of targeting subsidies to the poor. In three models of imperfect information in credit markets, the chapter characterizes equilibrium financial contracts and policy remedies to inefficiencies. Finally, welfare properties of stereotypical agricultural policies are developed in a stochastic production economy with incomplete markets.

Keywords

market failures, second best analysis, nutrition, credit, incomplete risk markets

JEL classification: Q18

1. Introduction

Governments intervene in agricultural and food markets in a wide variety of ways. In the U.S., for example, farmers' production activities have been subsidized with direct (deficiency) payment and price subsidy policies. Farmers are offered subsidized insurance that protects them from the risk of low crop yields; price support programs provide additional insurance against short-term declines in crop prices. Some farmers can obtain government-subsidized credit, both short-term and long-term, and all farmers can benefit from government backing of the Farm Credit System. A variety of government programs are designed to protect the environment from potentially harmful agricultural activities (including land set-aside programs and policies regulating water pollution and pesticide use). Poor consumers are supported with food stamps and other government feeding programs (including the school lunch and WIC programs). The risk of contaminated food is combatted by government food inspection systems, standards for public food handling, and regulation of pesticide residues. And the government directly invests in agricultural research, extension and education.

Many of these activities are responses to "market failures", circumstances that prevent unfettered competitive markets from achieving the Pareto optimum described in the Fundamental Theorems of Welfare Economics. Economists have identified a number of distinct types of market failures, none mutually exclusive and all of which have relevance to agriculture:

Externalities arise when one agent makes choices that directly affect another agent's well-being, but does not have to "pay" for these effects. Environmental pollution is the classic example, with unfettered polluters not bearing the costs of their pollution to others and over-polluting as a result. Examples of externalities in agriculture are numerous, including nutrient runoff and leaching that contaminates ground and surface waters; increased water salinity from agricultural irrigation that harms downstream users; depletion of the stratospheric ozone layer due to evaporation of the fumigant methyl bromide; odors, spills, and nutrient runoff from the handling of livestock waste; and consumer harm from hidden pesticide residues on fresh food products.

Public goods are those for which consumption is non-rival, so that one person's consumption of the good does not reduce the amount available to anyone else. Since any one person receives only a tiny fraction of the gains from a public good's provision, too little of these goods are provided in unfettered markets. Prominent examples of public goods in agriculture are health and nutrition of the poor, water quality, knowledge advanced by agricultural research, and public information about (and standards for) the health and safety attributes of the foods that we eat.

Incomplete contingent claim markets can prevent free trading across states of nature and thereby prevent fully efficient (first-best) risk-sharing. Government policies, by implicitly prompting trades across states of nature, may potentially improve efficiency.[1]

---

[1] While some economists have stressed the use of financial securities to complete markets and thereby improve efficiency [Ross (1976)], Hart (1983) has shown that the addition of state-contingent claim markets

Because agricultural activities are so risky, policy approaches to the achievement of risk-sharing benefits in agriculture have been of particular interest to both governments and economic scholars. Among agricultural policies that may potentially yield risk-trading benefits are commodity price stabilization and support programs.

Imperfect information is typically partitioned into two forms: hidden attributes (asymmetric information) and hidden action (moral hazard). Asymmetric information can give rise to either costly signalling behavior or "adverse selection", when agents with different attributes are "pooled" and receive common treatment. For example, in insurance markets, risk averse farmers may be high or low risk. Low risk farmers may either signal their type by under-insuring or be pooled with high-risk types in an insurance contract that bears higher premiums than are actuarially fair for the low risk types; the high premiums also prompt farmers to under-insure. Moral hazard, in contrast, prevents agents from considering the effects of their *actions* on other parties to a contractual arrangement. For example, an insured farmer may have little incentive to reduce risk when it is the insurance company that benefits; incomplete insurance will emerge to counter such incentives, at the cost of imperfect risk-sharing. Problems of imperfect information arise in many contexts that are important in agriculture, including non-point-source pollution control, insurance markets, and credit contracting. [See Chambers (2002), this Handbook, for a full treatment of insurance problems.]

Imperfect competition can prompt a wide variety of inefficient economic behavior, including underproduction, over-pricing of output, under-pricing of inputs, and over-investment in entry deterrence [see Sexton and Lavoie (2001), this Handbook].

In discussing potential failures in agricultural and food markets, this chapter has, necessarily, a very circumscribed objective. While market failures can motivate government policy, the correction of such failures is almost never free. Governments may be subject to some of the same primitive forces that drive inefficiencies in private markets. And the administration and enforcement of government policies can be costly.[2] The modeling of such costs and constraints on government behavior can be important to characterizing an efficient design for government policies to correct market failures. In this chapter, I will illustrate this type of second-best modeling – and its potential policy implications – for three areas which are important in agriculture, namely, nutrition, credit, and incomplete markets for risk.

The methodological theme of the chapter is that second-best analyses, to be persuasive in motivating policy and its design, must begin with primitive economic phenomena and not presumed economic outcomes that are otherwise inconsistent with model

---

need not increase welfare when markets are not fully completed. Nor need unfettered private actors necessarily have incentives to create efficiency-enhancing markets. Hence, market creation is not a panacea for mitigating welfare costs of incomplete risk trading, motivating (in part) economists' focus on other policy strategies to the achievement of risk-sharing gains.

[2] Government subsidies also come at the cost of raising taxes, a process that can be both directly costly and indirectly distorting [e.g., see Fullerton (1991)]. Kaplow (1997) has recently disputed the huge indirect costs that economists typically attribute to taxes.

foundations. For example, many analyses of credit markets assume fixed contractual arrangements between borrowers and lenders that are not privately optimal; in doing so, such analyses build upon assumed economic *outcomes* and not upon *primitive phenomena*. As a result, the conclusions they derive about market inefficiencies, and the potential scope for beneficial government policy, are potentially driven by the inexplicable presumption of private actors' irrationality. A coherent economic foundation for policy requires instead the premise of privately rational responses to primitive economic forces.

In what follows, this methodological message is illustrated in all three applications. In the case of nutrition, the analysis builds upon primitive premises of nutritional externalities (i.e., utility benefits that the general public obtains from the nourishment of the poor) and a government inability to costlessly detect fraud in the acquisition and use of subsidies targeted to the poor (i.e., enforcement costs). Both premises are shown to have important implications for the design of food policy. In the case of credit markets, the analysis builds upon primitive premises of private information (about a borrower's profits, profit distribution, or borrower-controlled inputs into the enterprise), combined with natural liability limits. These primitive forces are shown to drive privately optimal behavior in the design of credit contracts and the selection of inputs in a production enterprise. Despite privately optimal behavior, market outcomes are shown to be socially inefficient, and the analysis develops implications for welfare-improving government interventions. And in the case of incomplete contingent claim markets, the analysis focuses on stereotypical agricultural policies which are consistent with unmodeled problems in securities trading that prevent complete and efficient unfettered markets [Radner (1970)].

While modeling constraints that confine government behavior, the following presentation abstracts from the political-economic considerations that affect the *government's* incentives to behave efficiently or not. Rather, the focus here is on understanding how a government *can* behave efficiently in second-best environments.

The balance of the chapter is organized as follows. Section 2 develops and analyzes a simple model of nutritional externalities. Section 3 then turns to the analysis of credit markets under imperfect information, followed in Section 4 by a study of typical agricultural policies in a stochastic production economy with incomplete markets. Finally, concluding comments on the nature of second-best analysis are presented in Section 5. Proofs of all propositions and lemmas are contained in Appendix A. Topical sections of the chapter (Sections 2, 3, and 4) are written to stand on their own so that readers interested in a specific application can refer to the relevant section without loss.

2. Nutritional externalities: Optimal food policy with and without asymmetric information

Arguably, we all benefit – in a direct way – when all in our community, including the poorest, are well-nourished. This simple premise implies that the nutrition-related choices of those who may potentially be under-nourished, namely, the poor, have external effects on others in society that will not be taken into account in an unfettered competitive economy. In principle, the government can enter the breach by raising the nutritional well-being of the poor, reaping the external benefits (to the non-poor), and thereby improving economic efficiency. This section develops this public good motivation for policy, and analyzes its potential implications for policy design, all in the simplest possible model.

2.1. The case of costless information

In seminal work by Mark Pauly and others in the early 1970s,[3] the primitive economics of such consumption externalities were studied.[4] Specifically, let us suppose that a nation's population can be divided into two homogeneous groups, the rich (R) and the poor (Q). Agents in each group have utility defined on consumption of "food", x, and a numeraire good, y. In addition, however, the rich benefit from increased consumption of "food" by the poor. Utility is thus generated as follows:

$$U_R = U_R(x_R, y_R, x_Q), \quad \text{and} \quad U_Q = U_Q(x_Q, y_Q), \tag{1}$$

where U_R and U_Q are both MISC functions with a positive cross-effect, $U_{ixy} \geqslant 0$ for $i \in \{Q, R\}$.[5] For simplicity, I will suppose that
   (1) the economy has a fixed endowment of the numeraire good, Y;
   (2) domestic "food" X is produced at the numeraire cost, $C(X)$; and
   (3) "food" is freely exported at a constant international price P_E.
   A Pareto optimum is then achieved as a solution to the following problem, where n_R and n_Q denote the respective numbers of rich and poor people in the population, and X_E is the volume of food exports:

$$\max_{\{x_R, y_R, x_Q, y_Q, X_E\}} U_R = U_R(x_R, y_R, x_Q) \tag{2}$$

$$\text{s.t. } U_Q(x_Q, y_Q) \geqslant \overline{U}_Q, \tag{2a}$$

$$C(n_R x_R + n_Q x_Q + X_E) + n_R y_R + n_Q y_Q \leqslant Y + P_E X_E. \tag{2b}$$

Problem (2) maximizes the utility of the rich subject to constraints on the utility of the poor and feasibility of the consumption allocation. First order necessary conditions for a solution to problem (2) imply that the consumption of food by the poor, x_Q, must satisfy:

$$n_R \frac{\partial U_R/\partial x_Q}{\partial U_R/\partial y_R} + n_Q \frac{\partial U_Q/\partial x_Q}{\partial U_Q/\partial y_Q} - n_Q C'( ) = 0. \tag{3}$$

---

[3] See Pauly (1970), Rodgers (1973), Olsen (1971), for example.
[4] Perrin and Scobie (1981), Knudsen and Scandizzo (1982), and Scandizzo and Knudsen (1996) implicitly appeal to consumption externalities as motivation for their studies on alternative market interventions for the achievement of improved nutrition.
[5] $U_{ixy} \geqslant 0$ ensures that food is a weakly normal good.

Because the poor's food consumption has value to both the poor and the rich, an optimum equates the marginal cost of this consumption ($n_Q C'(\ )$) with the sum of its "direct" marginal monetary value to the poor ($n_Q \text{MRS}_Q$) and its "indirect" marginal monetary value to all of the rich ($n_R \text{MRS}_R^{x_Q}$).

In an unfettered competitive economy, in contrast, the poor choose their food consumption to equate its direct marginal monetary value, to themselves, with its price:

$$\text{MRS}_i = \frac{\partial U_i/\partial x_i}{\partial U_i/\partial y_i} = C'(\ )(= P_E = \text{price of food}), \quad \text{for } i = Q. \tag{4}$$

Because the poor do not obtain the extra benefits of their food consumption in enhancing the well-being of the rich, they eat too little.

2.1.1. Policies to achieve a first-best

There are two ways to restore efficiency:

2.1.1.1. Price subsidies to the poor. Suppose that the poor are offered a per-unit-food price subsidy that is set as follows:

$$s = \text{price subsidy} = (n_R/n_Q)\frac{\partial U_R/\partial x_Q}{\partial U_R/\partial y_R}. \tag{5}$$

By equating their marginal value of food consumption, MRS_Q, with its now-subsidized price, $P_E - s$, the poor will satisfy the optimality condition in (3). The subsidy in (5) gives to the poor the "indirect" marginal benefits that accrue to the rich from their food consumption; efficiency is thereby restored.

2.1.1.2. Food vouchers for the poor. Under a voucher program, the government gives each poor person vouchers that are good for the free purchase of a given amount of food, x_v; in return, the recipient must pay the government a fixed amount of money (that is less than the market cost of the food). The voucher offer is a "take-it-or-leave-it" proposition, so that the recipient can choose not to participate in the program, but cannot choose to "buy" less than the full complement of vouchers for a proportionately lower payment.

Figure 1 illustrates a voucher policy. Without any government intervention – and when the poor each have income I_Q – the poor optimize by finding the tangency between their indifference curve, IC_Q^0, and their "unfettered" budget line (where condition (4) holds). The voucher program aims to increase the poor's food consumption from its unfettered level, x_Q^0, to x_v by offering poor consumers a lump-sum dollar subsidy for the purchase of this food. The minimum subsidy that makes a poor person willing to participate in the program is $S_{\min}$ such that, with the subsidy and the x_v

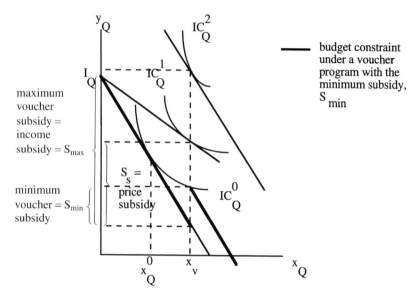

Figure 1. A voucher program.

consumption level, the poor person obtains exactly the same utility as without the vouchers:

$$\text{Unfettered utility} = V_Q(P_E, I_Q) = \max_{x_Q} U_Q(x_Q, I_Q - P_E x_Q)$$

$$= U_Q(x_v, I_Q + S_{\min} - P_E x_v) = \text{Utility with vouchers.}$$

By an appropriate choice of x_v and subsidy level S, the government can both prompt the poor's participation in a voucher program and achieve efficiency.

Figure 1 also illustrates a price-subsidy policy that achieves the same level of food consumption as does the voucher program, x_v. The price subsidy elicits increased levels of food consumption by rotating the budget line outward until a tangency is reached between the poor's indifference curve, IC_Q^1, and the "subsidized" budget line, at x_v. The total government subsidy required under this policy is S_s, as depicted in the figure.

An immediate implication here is that *a given consumption level, x_v, can be achieved at lower subsidy cost under a voucher policy ($S_{\min}$) than under a price-subsidy policy (S_s)* [Pauly (1970)]. A second implication of the graphical analysis is that any voucher subsidy between $S_{\min}$ and $S_{\max}$, the maximum subsidy that elicits consumption of x_v, will elicit both program participation by the poor and the target consumption level x_v. Note that, as shown in Figure 1, $S_{\max}$ is greater than S_s.

2.1.2. Policies that do not achieve a first-best

Prominent alternative policies do not, in general, achieve the Pareto optimum described above:

2.1.2.1. Income subsidies to the poor.

Income subsidies can raise the food consumption of the poor (assuming, as done here, that food is a normal good). However, in general, such subsidies do not provide the poor with correct *marginal* incentives for food consumption. The poor continue to solve their private optimization condition (4), ignoring the external benefits to the rich of increasing their food intake.

However, if the nutritional externality is characterized by a "threshold effect", this conclusion can be reversed. Suppose, for example, that the rich only obtain marginal benefits from the poor's food intake when this intake is below x_v. Then an income subsidy that elicits consumption at or above the x_v threshold will achieve a Pareto optimum.

Even with threshold effects, an income subsidy policy is a costly means to achieve a target food consumption level. As indicated in Figure 1, the income subsidy required to achieve a given x_v is S_{max}, a higher government cost than is required using either price-subsidies (S_s) or vouchers (S_{min}) [Pauly (1970)].

2.1.2.2. Uniform price subsidies.

If a price subsidy cannot be targeted to the poor, and instead must be made available to all, the poor can be prompted to internalize the external benefits of their food consumption (per condition (3)), but the rich will also increase their food consumption in response to the subsidy – inefficiently consuming food beyond the point at which their marginal monetary consumption benefits equal the marginal cost of food production. Hence, Pareto optimality (which requires that x_R satisfy condition (4) for $i = R$) will not be achieved.

However, as I will discuss in considerable depth below, offering a price subsidy (or voucher opportunity) to only a subset of the population creates incentives for those who are not the targets of the program to obtain the subsidies; to mitigate such incentives requires the investment of resources in program enforcement/administration that would not be required with a uniform price subsidy. Therefore, it is worth considering the merits of uniform price subsidies in a "second-best" setting in which targeted subsidies are presumed to be infeasible – or sufficiently costly to administer that they are inefficient. In such a setting, the following conclusion holds:

PROPOSITION 1. *In the absence of targeted food subsidies, there exists a positive uniform food price subsidy which will increase economic welfare.*

The intuition for Proposition 1 is quite simple. Consider raising a uniform price subsidy marginally above zero. The benefit of the marginal subsidy is that it raises food consumption by the poor; because the poor consume strictly less than is optimal without the subsidy, their increased consumption generates a strictly positive welfare gain. The cost of the marginal subsidy is that it also raises food consumption of the rich above its efficient level by confronting them with a price that is less than the marginal cost of production; however, for a marginal subsidy (one which is arbitrarily close to zero), the deviation of price from marginal cost is approximately zero – and so too, therefore, is the welfare cost from the marginal consumption distortion. In sum, the marginal subsidy generates a strictly positive welfare gain by dint of its effect on the poor, and a negligible welfare cost by dint of its effect on the rich, for a net positive welfare benefit.

In principle, a uniform food price subsidy can be effectively implemented on either the demand or the supply side of the market. Consumers can be provided a subsidy directly. Alternately, producers can be provided the subsidy on domestic sales using, for example, a per-unit-output subsidy combined with an equal export tax.

2.2. Asymmetric information and enforcement

While the foregoing analysis describes potential economic benefits of targeted food subsidies, it neglects costs of ensuring that targeted subsidies get to their target – the poor. Such costs not only affect the relative economic merits of targeted approaches to realizing external nutritional benefits; they are also important to the efficient design of targeted food policies. In this section, I take a preliminary pass at modeling the "enforcement costs" for targeted food subsidies, and studying their implications for policy design.

Two types of enforcement problems will be considered here. First, rich people may be able to "masquerade" as poor people and thereby qualify for subsidies on offer to the poor. Second, poor people can sell their subsidies to rich people on a black-market. The incentive for such trades is due to the different food consumption levels of the rich and the poor, which make price subsidies and food vouchers more valuable to the rich. For example, a voucher program compels the poor to consume more food than they would otherwise choose to consume, reducing the value of the vouchers to them; the rich, on the other hand, consume more food than can be obtained with the vouchers alone, permitting them to reap the vouchers' full subsidy value. For both types of enforcement problem, the government can invest resources to catch and penalize cheaters.

For the rich attempting to defraud the government, let us suppose (for simplicity) that there are no direct costs to the pretenders from claiming to be poor; however, if caught "pretending", a rich person can be fined (by the government) as much as f_R. The government cannot freely "catch" pretenders; rather, it catches them with probability q_P by investing $e_1(q_P)$ in enforcement, where more resources are required for a higher catch probability, $e_1'( ) > 0$.[6]

---

[6]   An implicit premise here is that the costs of achieving a given "catch rate", q_P, do not depend upon the type of targeted subsidy program that is enacted; it is neither more nor less costly to catch those who fraudulently claim voucher entitlements as it is to catch those who fraudulently claim price subsidy entitlements. Similarly, costs of catching black-market traders are assumed to be the same under voucher and price subsidy programs. Such premises are reasonable if mechanisms for allocating and dispensing subsidies are the same under the two approaches.

In the black-market, let us again suppose (for simplicity) that there are no direct costs of trade, but that each party bears the risk of being caught trading, and being fined accordingly. The maximum fine is f_Q for the poor (and, again, f_R for the rich). Black-market traders (even poor subsidy sellers) can also be denied vouchers. The government can catch subsidy sellers (the poor) with probability q_Q, and subsidy buyers (the rich) with probability q_R, by investing $e_2(q_Q, q_R)$ in enforcement. More resources are again required for higher "catch rates", $\partial e_2(\ )/\partial q_i > 0$ for $i = Q, R$.

In this simple enforcement model, three issues will be addressed. First, I will evaluate the relative efficiency of voucher and price-subsidy approaches to the provision of targeted food subsidies. Recall that, without enforcement costs, either of these two approaches can be used to achieve fully Pareto optimal outcomes. However, in the presence of enforcement costs, I will argue that vouchers are always more efficient than price subsidies as a mechanism to deliver food subsidies targeted to the poor. Second, I will explore the implications of enforcement costs for the optimal setting of the voucher program's two parameters, the subsidy level S and the food consumption target x_v. And third, I will consider whether the presence of enforcement costs argues for the use of another policy instrument – a uniform price subsidy to all consumers – *in concert* with a voucher program.

2.2.1. Vouchers vs. price subsidies

The government's objective in its enforcement policy is to deter, at minimum cost, both black-market trades and fraud in the acquisition of subsidies. Following the logic of Becker (1968), this objective calls for *maximizing the penalty to agents who are "caught"*; for a given enforcement policy, such penalties minimize the incentive for illegal behavior and thereby permit the deterrence of such behavior with minimal probabilities of apprehension, (q_P, q_Q, q_R).

In view of this observation, let us now compare the government's enforcement costs under two policies that are otherwise equivalent: (1) a price subsidy of s per-unit-food that elicits food consumption by the poor of x_v, and (2) a program that issues vouchers for x_v units of food, with implicit (lump-sum) subsidy of $S = sx_v$. Assuming the (subsidy-free) income levels for rich and poor are unaffected by the choice between the two alternative policies,[7] let us first consider the constraints which the government must satisfy in order to deter fraud. Under the price subsidy policy, the "no-fraud" constraint is

$$(1 - q_P)V_R(P_E - s, I_R) + q_P V_R(P_E, I_R - f_R) \leqslant V_R(P_E, I_R), \tag{NF$_s$}$$

---

[7] In essence, I am considering the following (logical) thought experiment. Let the government tax the rich to cover subsidy and enforcement costs under the price subsidy. Now, if the government switches to an equivalent voucher policy, taxes as before, and saves enforcement costs, then it can increase welfare using its enforcement cost savings to invest in beneficial public goods that do not affect incentives for fraud or black-market trading.

where I_R and V_R are, respectively, the income and indirect utility function of the rich.[8] The left-hand side of (NF$_s$) gives the rich person's expected utility when behaving fraudulently (pretending to be poor); when the person is caught, he faces the maximal penalty f_R and thereby obtains the utility payoff $V_R(P_E, I_R - f_R)$; when he is not caught, he obtains the subsidy payoff $V_R(P_E - s, I_R)$. The right-hand side of (NF$_s$) gives the rich person's payoff when behaving honestly (not pretending to be poor). The inequality in (NF$_s$) thus requires (and ensures) that the rich person weakly prefers to behave honestly.

Similarly, under the voucher policy, the "no-fraud" constraint is[9]

$$(1 - q_P)V_R(P_E, I_R + S) + q_P V_R(P_E, I_R - f_R) \leqslant V_R(P_E, I_R). \tag{NF$_v$}$$

Comparing (NF$_s$) and (NF$_v$), it is easily seen that (NF$_s$) requires a higher q_P catch rate, and hence higher enforcement costs, if the reward to unpunished fraud is higher under the price subsidy policy than under the voucher program, i.e., if

$$V_R(P_E - s, I_R) > V_R(P_E, I_R + S) \quad \text{(where } S = sx_v). \tag{6}$$

Inequality (6), in turn, follows from a simple revealed preference argument. In essence, the price subsidy policy permits the rich person to obtain the same consumption bundle that is optimal for him or her under the voucher policy; but it also offers additional consumption possibilities that are preferred.

A similar argument applies to the deterrence of black-market trades. Replacing a price subsidy policy with an equivalent voucher program lowers the rich buyer's potential black-market payoff, thereby permitting the deterrence of black-market trades with a lower (less costly) probability of apprehension q_R.

PROPOSITION 2. *Enforcement costs of deterring both fraud and black-market trades are higher under a price subsidy policy than under an equivalent voucher program. Therefore, in the presence of enforcement costs, a voucher program is a more efficient vehicle for the delivery of targeted food subsidies.*

2.2.2. The enforcement costs of a voucher program

The two parameters of a voucher program, the subsidy S and the voucher quantity x_v, can affect the level of enforcement expenditures needed to deter fraud and black-market trades. Specifically, we will find that, in the absence of other price interventions,

---

[8] For simplicity (and without loss of generality), the x_Q argument in $V_R(.)$ is suppressed at this juncture. Later, when getting to effects of x_v on enforcement costs, a separability assumption will be made and $V_R(.)$ reinterpreted as R's indirect *sub*utility function.

[9] Implicit in (NF$_v$) is the premise that the rich demand at least as much food, with price P_E and income $I_R + S$, as the voucher quantity x_v. The violation of such a premise would imply that the government – and the rich – want the poor to consume more food than the rich, an unreasonable state of affairs that I rule out.

a higher level of x_v will raise enforcement costs, while a higher S has offsetting effects – generally raising costs of deterring fraud, but often lowering costs of deterring black-market trades. Because of these effects, enforcement costs will imply a lower optimal level of x_v than would occur in a "first-best" world without such costs, and either a higher or lower optimal subsidy level, depending upon which enforcement cost effects are stronger.

Before developing these results, a few conceptual issues should be discussed. First, on a technical front, I will keep matters simple by invoking the following premise:

ASSUMPTION 1. *The rich have a "no income effect" utility function that is linearly separable in x_Q:*

$$U_R(x_R, y_R, x_Q) = \alpha(x_Q) + \beta(x_Q)u_R^0(x_R, y_R), \tag{7a}$$

$$u_R^0(x_R, y_R) = y_R + u_R^1(x_R). \tag{7b}$$

Separability in x_Q implies that incentives of the rich for fraud and black-market trades are unaffected by the poor's level of food consumption. The premise that there is no income effect on the food demand of the rich also simplifies the enforcement constraints by implying a constant marginal utility of income for the rich, whether they behave honestly or dishonestly. Given Assumption 1, I can redefine the indirect utility function $V_R(P, I)$ as follows (for simplicity and without loss of generality):

$$V_R(P, I) = \max u_R^0(x_R, I - Px_R).$$

Second, because I will later consider the imposition of uniform price subsidies, it is useful to modify the enforcement constraints at this juncture to account for such subsidies (or taxes). In particular, holding the subsidy to the poor constant at S, a uniform price subsidy of s per-unit-food (a) lowers food prices to $P_E - s$, and (b) lowers the nominal subsidy that must be afforded by food vouchers to $S - sx_v$. The "no-fraud" constraint, (NF$_v$), thus becomes (for example),

$$G_F(q_P; S, x_v, s) = (1 - q_P)V_R(P_E - s, I_R + S - sx_v)$$
$$+ q_P V_R(P_E - s, I_R - f_R) - V_R(P_E - s, I_R) \leqslant 0. \tag{8}$$

Third, there is the question of who pays taxes to support costs of both food voucher subsidies and any uniform price subsidies. In a general two-agent model of the type considered here, it is natural to suppose that the rich pay these taxes and that these tax effects must therefore be incorporated in the constraints that define incentives of the rich for fraud and black-market trades. Specifically, when the rich have pre-tax income of I_R^0, their post-tax income will be as follows:

$$I_R = I_R(S, s): I_R = I_R^0 - (n_Q/n_R)S - sx_R^*(P_E - s), \tag{9}$$

where $x_R^*(P) = \operatorname{argmax} u_R^0(x_R, I - Px_R)$. As indicated in (9), the rich must each pay taxes of $(n_Q/n_R)S$ to support the S subsidy to the poor, and must refund their own price subsidy receipts to the government, in lump-sum taxes.

Finally, two issues arise in thinking about the enforcement constraints. In the "no fraud" constraint, Equation (8) with $I_R = I_R(S, s)$, I focus on incentives for fraud in the acquisition of food vouchers, not in the tax process; hence, when a rich person successfully obtains vouchers, he/she still pays the taxes assessed on the rich and thereby reaps a pre-voucher income of $I_R(S, s)$.[10] Moreover, when caught cheating, either in the acquisition of vouchers or in the black-market, the penalty to the rich is assumed to be fixed at f_R – and not to depend upon the available income, $I_R(S, s)$.[11] While reasonable starting points at this initial stage of modeling, both premises may merit relaxation in further work.

2.2.2.1. Costs of deterring fraud.

For a relevant range of x_v (i.e., less than the food consumption of the rich), inspection of the no-fraud constraint, (8) above, reveals that the voucher quantity only affects the enforcement costs of deterring fraud when the price subsidy s is non-zero. Armed with vouchers, the rich person is not constrained by x_v and, hence, has an incentive to obtain the vouchers that depends only upon the subsidy that the vouchers carry with them, $S - sx_v$. A higher subsidy, in fact, raises the incentives for fraudulent behavior (the left-hand side of (8)) and thereby requires a higher "catch and penalty" probability q_P to deter such behavior.

PROPOSITION 3. *Enforcement costs of deterring fraudulent attempts to obtain food vouchers are higher when the vouchers contain a higher S subsidy level. When the untargeted per-unit price subsidy s is equal to zero, these enforcement costs are unaffected by the voucher quantity x_v; however, if $s > 0$ (< 0), these costs fall with (rise with) x_v.*

2.2.2.2. Costs of deterring a black-market.

Effects on black-market deterrence are somewhat more complex. For simplicity, let us suppose that a poor voucher recipient either sells all of his vouchers, or none.[12] Letting P_v denote the black-market price for the x_v vouchers, the following equations describe, respectively, the gains to the rich from voucher purchases and the gains to the poor from voucher sales:

---

[10] A reasonable alternative view of fraud deterrence would have the rich either pretending to be poor, or behaving honestly, in *both* tax payment and voucher eligibility contexts.

[11] An alternative premise would set the maximum penalty so that net income falls to some fixed level (perhaps zero), $I_R^0 - f_R$.

[12] If the probability of apprehending a black-market trader does not depend upon the volume of traded vouchers, then any black-market trade of vouchers will be of the all-or-nothing variety for the following reason: Given that it is optimal for the government to maximally penalize caught culprits [per the logic of Becker (1968)], all-or-nothing trades maximize the expected gains from the trade to the trading parties.

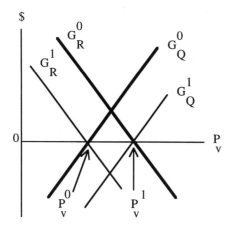

Figure 2. Black-market pricing.

$$G_R(q_R, P_v; S, x_v, s) = (1 - q_R)V_R(P_E - s, I_R - P_v + S - sx_v)$$

$$+ q_R V_R(P_E - s, I_R - f_R) - V_R(P_E - s, I_R), \qquad (10a)$$

$$G_Q(q_Q, P_v; S, x_v, s) = (1 - q_Q)V_Q(P_E - s, I_Q + P_v)$$

$$+ q_Q V_Q(P_E - s, I_Q - f_Q) - U_Q(x_v, I_Q - P_E x_v + S). \qquad$$

$$(10b)$$

In each case, the gains from trade equal the expected payoff from trade (given the possibility that the trader will be "caught" and a maximum penalty then assessed), less the payoff that is achieved without the trade.

A trade occurs if and only if there is a price P_v such that both the rich and the poor gain from the trade, $G_R > 0$ and $G_Q > 0$. For example, Figure 2 graphs some possible G_R and G_Q functions, (G_R^0, G_Q^0), for which a black-market voucher price between P_v^0 and P_v^1 will prompt trades. *To deter such trades*, the government must either

(i)   raise its rich-person "catch rate" q_R so that G_R shifts down from G_R^0 to G_R^1,

(ii) raise its poor-person "catch rate" q_Q so that G_Q shifts down from G_Q^0 to G_Q^1, or

(iii) raise both q_R and q_Q in tandem so that G_R and G_Q shift down to intersect at a price where both take on a zero value.

Such changes in enforcement policy ensure that there is no black-market voucher price at which both the rich and poor can gain from trading.

In the absence of any enforcement effort, black-market trades of vouchers can be advantageous to rich buyers and poor sellers when and only when the rich attach a higher value to the vouchers. For example, if vouchers do not bind the poor's food consumption (because the poor would consume more food anyway), then the value of the vouchers to rich and poor alike is simply their monetary subsidy value. In this case, the voucher program acts as a pure cash transfer and there is no black-market – because there is no gain from trade – even with no enforcement effort.

However, the more interesting case is one in which vouchers serve the purpose of raising food consumption by the poor above what it would otherwise be. Then the value of the vouchers to the poor is less than the monetary subsidy; and because the program will not be designed to elicit more food consumption by the poor than by the rich (i.e., the rich will choose to consume more food than x_v), the value of the vouchers to the rich will be higher, equal to the monetary subsidy. In this case, positive enforcement effort is required to deter the black-market and an optimal black-market-deterrence policy solves the following problem (assuming interior optima, $q_i \in (0, 1)$, $i \in \{R, Q\}$):[13,14]

$$\min e_2(q_R, q_Q) \quad \text{s.t.} \tag{11}$$

$$G_R(q_R, P_v; S, x_v, s) = 0 \quad \text{and} \quad G_Q(q_Q, P_v; S, x_v, s) = 0. \tag{12}$$

Given a q_R (for example), Equation (12) defines a poor-person catch rate q_Q (and associated "intersection price" P_v) such that black-market trades are just deterred, $q_Q(q_R; S, x_v, s)$. Implicitly, then, Equation (11) chooses q_R (and the associated black-market deterring $q_Q(\ )$) to minimize enforcement costs.

The effect of changes in the voucher parameters, x_v and S, on the minimal enforcement costs in Equation (11) can now be inferred from the parameter effects on $q_Q(q_R; S, x_v, s)$ (as defined implicitly in (12)):

$$\frac{de_2(q_R^*, q_Q^*)}{dz} = \frac{de_2(q_R^*, q_Q(q_R^*; S, x_v, s))}{dz}$$

$$= \left(\frac{\partial e_2(\ )}{\partial q_Q}\right)\left(\frac{\partial q_Q(\ )}{\partial z}\right) \overset{S}{=} \frac{\partial q_Q(\ )}{\partial z} \tag{13}$$

for $z = S, x_v, s$, where "$\overset{S}{=}$" denotes "equals in sign". Armed with Equation (13), we can complete our analysis of the black-market by totally differentiating (12) to obtain[15]

$$\frac{\partial q_Q(\ )}{\partial x_v} \overset{S}{=} -\frac{dU_Q(x_v, I_Q - P_E x_v + S)}{dx_v}$$

$$- s(1 - q_Q)V_{QI}(P_E - s, I_Q + P_v), \tag{14a}$$

$$\frac{\partial q_Q(\ )}{\partial S} \overset{S}{=} (1 - q_Q)V_{QI}(P_E - s, I_Q + P_v) - U_{Qy}(x_v, I_Q - P_E x_v + S). \tag{14b}$$

---

[13] Strictly speaking, the constraints in (12) should be in "less-than-or-equal-to" form. However, whenever one of such inequality constraints in slack, q_R or q_Q can be lowered without prompting black-market trades. Hence, any solution to (11) involves the constraints in (12) binding as stated.

[14] The results that follow can be extended to cases in which one or the other non-negativity constraints on q_i bind. For example, if costs of catching voucher sellers are much higher than costs of catching voucher buyers, an optimal black-market-deterrence policy may call for setting $q_Q = 0$.

[15] For their derivation, Equations (14a) and (14b) draw upon Assumption 1 conditions (7a) and (7b).

Equations (13) and (14) imply the following:

PROPOSITION 4. *Suppose that there is no non-targeted price subsidy ($s = 0$) and that there are positive costs of black-market deterrence (because $x_v > x_Q^*(P_E, I_Q + S) = $ argmax $U_Q(x_Q, I_Q - P_E x_Q + S)$). Then enforcement costs of deterring black-market trades fall with (a) a decrease in the voucher quantity x_v, and/or (b) an increase in the voucher subsidy S.*

To understand Proposition 4, consider first the effect of a decrease in the "voucher volume" x_v. When a voucher program serves to raise food consumption by the poor above what it would be with an equivalent cash transfer, a marginal reduction in the voucher quantity reduces the "penalty" to the poor of voucher-required overconsumption. It thereby reduces the incentive of the poor to sell vouchers on the black-market. Because the poor gain less from trading vouchers (ceteris paribus), such trades can be deterred with a lower probability of apprehension q_Q and, hence, lower enforcement costs (Proposition 4(a)).

A higher subsidy level S can also lower incentives for black-market trades for the following reason. When the subsidy rises, the black-market price of the vouchers rises by the increased subsidy value (in order for the rich to be still just willing to buy). The benefit to the poor from selling vouchers rises by this price increase – though only for the proportion of the time that a seller is not "caught", $(1 - q_Q)$. However, the benefit from selling also falls by the increased subsidy value that is foregone when the vouchers are handed over – a cost that is borne with probability one. In sum, the increased subsidy raises the cost to a voucher seller of losing the subsidy when the seller is caught and penalized; it thereby lowers incentives to sell.[16] As before, the reduced incentive to trade permits the government to deter trade with a lower q_Q catch rate, and, hence, lower enforcement costs (Proposition 4(b)).

2.2.3. Enforcement cost effects of an untargeted price subsidy

To determine the effect of an untargeted price subsidy on costs of deterring fraud, we can differentiate the "no fraud" constraint (8) (and appeal to Assumption 1) as follows:

$$\partial G_F(\ )/\partial s = -(1 - q_P)V_{RI}(P_E - s, I_R + S - s x_v)x_v < 0. \tag{15}$$

Fixing the absolute level of subsidy to the poor at S, a non-targeted price subsidy reduces the relative (poor vs. rich) subsidy level, $S - s x_v$, and thereby reduces the incentive of the rich to behave fraudulently (inequality (15)). As a result, a non-targeted subsidy permits the government to lower its q_P enforcement effort and still deter fraud.

---

[16] This argument also requires that marginal subsidy dollars have at least the same value to a prospective voucher seller when no sale occurs as when a sale successfully occurs (so that $V_{QI} \leqslant U_{Qy}$ in Equation (14b)). The proof of Proposition 4 derives this inequality.

Effects of an untargeted subsidy on black-market deterrence costs can be ascertained by differentiating the minimal black-market-deterring q_Q catch rate implicitly defined in (12):

$$\partial q_Q(\ )/\partial s \overset{S}{=} -(1 - q_Q)\big(x_v - x_Q^{*a}\big) + \big(V_{QI}^b/V_{QI}^a\big)q_Q x_Q^{*b}, \tag{16}$$

where the superscript "a" evaluates functions at the poor's "successful sell" outcomes, $(P_E - s, I_Q + P_v)$; the superscript "b" evaluates functions at the poor's "unsuccessful sell" outcomes, $(P_E - s, I_Q - f_Q)$; and $x_Q^*(P, I) = \operatorname{argmax} U_Q(x_Q, I - P x_Q)$. If the minimal q_Q catch rate goes down with an untargeted subsidy – so that the derivative in (16) is negative – then enforcement costs of black-market deterrence also decline (by Equation (13) above).

In intuitive terms, a price subsidy lowers the incentive for black-market trades by reducing the discrepancy between the poor's voucher-required consumption, x_v, and their preferred food choice (with the subsidy), the discrepancy that makes the vouchers less valuable to the poor than to the rich. (The first term in Equation (16) reflects this effect.) However, a price subsidy also creates an offsetting incentive for the poor to sell the vouchers by lowering the penalty to being caught selling; the higher subsidy lowers the food price faced by caught culprits and thereby raises their penalty payoff, $V_Q(P_E - s, I_Q - f_Q)$. (The second term in (16) captures this effect.) If a seller's probability of apprehension q_Q is small, then this second effect – the added incentive to sell vouchers because of the raised "penalty payoff" – is also small. In such cases, a higher price subsidy will then lower incentives for black-market trades and thereby permit their deterrence with lower enforcement costs. In summary:

PROPOSITION 5. *Raising a non-targeted food price subsidy, while preserving the absolute subsidy to the poor,* (a) *lowers costs of deterring fraud,*[17] *and* (b) *lowers any positive costs of deterring a black-market if there are sufficiently high costs to catching voucher sellers that q_Q is set sufficiently low.*[18]

2.2.4. Second-best policy: The optimal design of a voucher program

The foregoing describes properties of the minimum enforcement costs needed to deter fraud and black-market trades. Denoting these minimum cost functions by $e_1^*(S, x_v, s)$ and $e_2^*(S, x_v, s)$, respectively, we can construct a Paretian choice problem

---

[17] If fraud by a rich person also frees the person from taxes required to support subsidy programs (contrary to the premise made in this paper), then Proposition 5(a) is generally reversed. Equation (15) then becomes: $\partial G_F(\ )/\partial s = (1 - q_P)V_{RI}(x_R^*(P_E - s) - x_v)$, with $x_R^*(P_E - s)$ larger than x_v for the reasons stated earlier (see note 9).

[18] The proof of Proposition 4 establishes that $x_v > x_Q^{*a}$ whenever there are positive costs of deterring a black-market. Proposition 5(b) thus follows directly from Equation (16).

to characterize constrained efficient levels of the policy parameters, (S, x_v, s). Given Assumption 1, this problem is

$$\max_{\{S, x_v, s, X_E\}} n_R U_R(\ ) = n_R \{\alpha(x_v) + \beta(x_v) V_R(P_E - s, I_R)\}$$

$$\text{s.t. } U_Q(x_v, I_Q - P_E x_v + S) \geqslant \overline{U}_Q, \tag{17}$$

where

$$n_R I_R = n_R I_R^0 + P_E(X_E + n_Q x_v) - C\left(n_R x_R^*(P_E - s) + n_Q x_v + X_E\right)$$
$$\qquad - n_Q S - e_1^*(S, x_v, s) - e_2^*(S, x_v, s), \tag{18}$$

$$x_R^*(P) = \text{argmax}\{u_R^0(x_R, I - P x_R) = I - P x_R + u_R^1(x_R)\}. \tag{19}$$

Equation (18) gives the net income of the rich after (i) adding revenue from production sales (in exports and to the poor), less costs of production, and (ii) subtracting tax costs of paying subsidies to the poor and covering enforcement costs.

Necessary conditions for a solution to (17) are:

$$X_E: \quad P_E - C' = 0, \tag{20}$$

$$x_v: \quad n_R(\partial U_R/\partial x_v) + \phi_Q(dU_Q/dx_v)$$
$$\qquad - \beta(x_v)\{(\partial e_1^*/\partial x_v) + (\partial e_2^*/\partial x_v)\} = 0, \tag{21}$$

$$S: \quad -\beta(x_v)n_Q + \phi_Q U_{Qy} - \beta(x_v)\{(\partial e_1^*/\partial S) + (\partial e_2^*/\partial S)\} = 0, \tag{22}$$

$$s: \quad \beta(x_v)n_Q(\partial x_R^*/\partial P)s - \beta(x_v)\{(\partial e_1^*/\partial s) + (\partial e_2^*/\partial s)\} = 0, \tag{23}$$

where ϕ_Q is the Lagrange multiplier for problem (17), and (23) relies upon (19) and (20).

Conditions (21)–(23) all contain the enforcement cost effects, $-\beta(x_v)\{(\partial e_1^*/\partial z) + (\partial e_2^*/\partial z)\}$. These terms imply that, if raising (or lowering) the level of a policy variable can reduce enforcement costs, the policy variable will be optimally set at a higher (lower) level than would satisfy the optimality condition in the absence of enforcement costs. For example:

- If, at $s = 0$, an increase in the price subsidy lowers enforcement costs (per Proposition 5), then *a positive uniform price subsidy* will be optimal as a complement to a food voucher program.
- Suppose that the effects of the subsidy level S on the costs of deterring fraud are dominant, so that enforcement costs rise with higher subsidy levels (per Propositions 3 and 4). Then an optimal S will be lower to account for this effect (ceteris paribus). Moreover, if $s = 0$, conditions (21) and (22) will together imply that an optimal food voucher quantity will not solve the "first-best" condition (3), instead setting this derivative *above zero* by circumscribing the voucher quantity. By lowering the voucher quantity below a first-best level, enforcement costs can be saved (by Propositions 3 and 4) and welfare thereby raised.

2.3. Section overview and outstanding issues

In the foregoing analysis, I have explored implications of nutritional externalities for optimal allocations of food and money between "the rich" and "the poor"; how these allocations can and cannot be achieved by the government; and effects of enforcement costs – those costs needed to deter fraudulent and black-market behaviors that undermine the purpose of government transfer programs – for the optimal design of policies intended to reap external nutritional benefits. The analysis generally identifies economic merits of a voucher approach to the provision of food subsidies to the poor; suggests that, if enforcement costs of transfer programs are sufficiently high, a positive uniform price subsidy will be called for as a substitute for such programs (Proposition 1); identifies distinct costs of deterring fraud and deterring black-market trades in transfer entitlements (vouchers) that can potentially motivate a food policy that simply transfers cash to the poor – rather than tying the transfer to minimum levels of food consumption – when costs of black-market deterrence are sufficiently high; and describes links between policy parameters and enforcement costs that affect optimal settings for these parameters, arguing (for example) that a uniform price subsidy may be called for as an optimal complement to a voucher program.

As a preliminary pass at modeling enforcement costs in the provision of food subsidies, the foregoing embeds some primitive premises that merit scrutiny in future work. But, more fundamentally, the general two-agent two-good framework considered here, while providing a natural benchmark for the analysis of food policy, abstracts from some important issues in the modeling of public nutrition programs, such as:

(1) *Who are the poor?* Aside from questions of whose food consumption has external effects on whom (is it anyone poorer than me or only the "very poor", about whose definition we can all agree), "the poor" may be endogenous, at least at the margin. If so, policy-makers (and advising analysts) must be concerned with program-created incentives to become "poor", as well as a definition of "the poor" that may reduce costs of deterring fraud.[19]

(2) *How is nutrition produced?* In fact, there is no obvious simple relationship between some measure of food purchases (such as expenditures) and "nutritional well-being".[20] With many different food products contributing in many different ways to "nutrition", the logic of nutritional externality modeling is likely to favor more targeted approaches to the provision of food subsidies, with those foods that afford a greater "nutritional bang" targeted for a higher subsidy. However, the potential hazards in this are many. For example, can vouchers for specific classes of food be used and, if so, how does one design them to account for multiple food products in a given "nutritional

---

[19] Interesting recent work [Chambers (1989)] considers mechanisms for deterring fraud using self-selection devices such as food-for-work programs.

[20] Indeed, a central focus of recent work in nutritional economics focuses on the effects of food stamps on nutritional intake, both from the equivalent income that food stamps transfer and additional (e.g., voucher-induced overconsumption) effects [e.g., Butler and Raymond (1996), Gawn et al. (1993), Devaney and Moffitt (1991), Subramanian and Deaton (1996), and many others]. Conclusions from this work are mixed.

class" that have different cost and taste attributes? Do price subsidies for a class of food increase consumption within this class or merely shift consumption to more expensive products? Are administrative/enforcement costs of regulating and monitoring multiple class-specific subsidies huge?

While nutritional economics has made great strides in the theoretical and empirical modeling of the nutrient intake process, economics also has potentially valuable insights to deliver on the efficient design of nutrition policy, addressing such questions as posed in this section. On this front, there is much rigorous thought that is yet to be done.

3. Imperfect information in credit markets

When entrepreneurs (such as farmers) need investment funds from others in order to undertake their desired production activities, imperfect information about the prospective profitability and management of these activities can have important implications both for the design of the investment contract and for the economic efficiency of production outcomes. In this section, I explore some of these implications in financial contracting models that embed two general types of imperfect information, hidden attributes (or asymmetric information), and hidden action (or moral hazard).

Arguably, the informational imperfections examined here represent natural departures from the perfect markets premise that underpins the Fundamental Theorems of Welfare Economics; unlike the unencumbered Neoclassical model, each model analyzed necessarily elicits entrepreneurs' optimal use of debt-type financial contracts to raise investment capital (rather than equity instruments or other contractual forms).

What is more, the endogenization of financial contract forms in this section embodies the overarching methodological message of this chapter: To be persuasive as motives for policy, second-best models must build upon *primitive* economic phenomena. In the present section, the posited primitive phenomena are underlying information imperfections, combined with natural liability limits. To build upon such phenomena, a necessary first step is the characterization of their effects on unfettered behavior, namely, the privately optimal financial contracts that arise in response to informational asymmetries. It is *absolutely crucial* – not just the obsession of meticulous scholars – that an analysis of optimal contracting *precede* an analysis of second-best credit market policy; without understanding how private agents can and will deal with imperfect information, there is no logical basis for concluding that unfettered markets are incapable of surmounting the attendant challenges to economic efficiency.

In evaluating the efficiency properties of a free market equilibrium, two questions can be asked:

(1) Can economy-wide net expected economic surplus from entrepreneurial investment and production be increased?

(2) Can Pareto improvements be made?

In the models developed here, the answer to the second question may sometimes be "yes". However, in *all* of the models, free market equilibria diverge from first-best (perfect information) outcomes and, as a result, the answer to the first question will be shown to be affirmative. In view of these inefficiencies, the analysis below will consider how the government can improve upon the market equilibrium.

3.1. Asymmetric information in credit contracting

Consider a population of risk-neutral entrepreneurs, each of whom can invest in his farm today and realize a net worth (also called profit) tomorrow of $\pi = \pi(A, \varepsilon; x)$, where A denotes the total investment today, $\varepsilon \in [0, \bar{\varepsilon}]$ is a random variable with continuous density (distribution) $h(\varepsilon)$ ($H(\varepsilon)$), and x is a non-stochastic variable to be defined in a moment. The total investment, A, is financed by external funds of I, and a given amount, $A - I$, of an entrepreneur's own wealth. In the two model variants analyzed below, it can be shown that an entrepreneur will invest all of his own financial resources in his firm. Therefore, $A - I$ can be treated as fixed. Moreover, when relevant (and without loss in generality), the population of entrepreneurs will be defined to have a common level of initial wealth/collateral, $I - A = W_0$. The external investment, I, will then determine A, and we can define the probability density and distribution functions for π by $f(\pi; I, x)$ and $F(\pi; I, x)$, respectively. $f(\ )$ is assumed to be strictly positive on $[0, K(I, x)]$ and zero elsewhere.

"External" investors are assumed to be risk neutral, rational, and competitive in the sense that they are willing to sign financial contracts which yield them an expected return of ρ, the return on a risk-free bond. The investment contract specifies both the external investment level, I, and the entrepreneur's payment to the external investors for each possible realization of π, $B(\pi)$. Due to the entrepreneur's limited liability, $B(\pi)$ cannot exceed π, a constraint which rules out a fixed payment contract.

"In a first-best" world without any information problems, an optimal $B(\pi)$ can take any form that satisfies limited liability and that yields the investors their required expected return, ρ. Further, a "first-best" setting will yield an investment level, I^*, which solves the following maximization:

$$\max_I E(\pi; I, x^*) - (1 + \rho)I,$$

where E is the expectation operator for π, x^* will be defined appropriately in what follows and $E(\pi; I, x)$ is concave in (I, x).

I now turn to an analysis of two different information structures which are consistent with the emergence of standard debt contracts – financial contracts which yield investors the minimum of a fixed promised payment (i.e., interest and return of principal) and firm assets/profits (when the firm is effectively bankrupt).

3.1.1. Model 1: Ex-post asymmetric information[21]

Following the development in Gale and Hellwig (1985) [also see Townsend (1979), Diamond (1984), and Williamson (1987)], suppose that external investors cannot observe

---

[21] This section borrows from Innes (1990a).

ex-post profit, π, or the state of nature, ε, unless they incur an observation cost of $c(I, \varepsilon)$, where $\forall (I, \varepsilon) \gg 0$, $c > 0$, $c_I \geqslant 0$, and $c_{II} \geqslant 0$. Ex-post profits here are simply $\pi(A, \varepsilon)$ (without x), with $\pi(\ )$ assumed to have the following properties: $\pi_A > 0$, $\pi_\varepsilon > 0$, $\pi_{AA} < 0$, $\pi_{A\varepsilon} > 0$, and $\pi(A, 0) = 0$.

After profits are realized (i.e., after the value of ε is determined), the entrepreneur will report a profit (or ε) level to the external investors. In principle, the farmer's report may or may not be honest. However, from the Revelation Principle, a contract which sometimes elicits dishonest reports is equivalent to another which *always* elicits honest reports [e.g., see Harris and Townsend (1985)]. Restricting attention to the latter *incentive compatible* contracts, the financial agreement will specify the set of profit (or ε) reports for which investor observation occurs. If N represents the set of ε realizations wherein investors do *not* observe π, then $\forall \varepsilon \in N$, the entrepreneur can and will pay investors the minimum level of $B(\pi)$ consistent with $\varepsilon \in N$, namely, $B_N = \min_{\varepsilon \in N} B(\pi(A, \varepsilon))$. Thus, for incentive compatibility, $B(\pi(A, \varepsilon)) = B_N$ $\forall \varepsilon \in N$. In addition, if $B(\pi(A, \varepsilon))$ were greater than B_N for some $\varepsilon_0 \notin N$, then the entrepreneur would never report ε_0; therefore, for incentive compatibility, $B(\pi(A, \varepsilon)) \leqslant B_N$, $\forall \varepsilon \notin N$. Given the entrepreneur's limited liability, these incentive compatibility requirements imply that the investors must observe profits in *some* states of nature in order to *ever* obtain a positive payoff. For a given I, an optimal financial contract will minimize the expected costs of investor observation subject to the incentive compatibility, limited liability, and investor return requirement constraints. A debt contract achieves this minimum by setting $N = \{\varepsilon: \varepsilon \geqslant \varepsilon^*, \text{ some } \varepsilon^* > 0\}$ and $B(\pi(A, \varepsilon)) = \pi(A, \varepsilon)$, $\forall \varepsilon < \varepsilon^*$, thereby maximizing the payments in observation states and minimizing the probability of observation that is needed to yield the investor her required expected return. Thus, we have:

PROPOSITION 6. *In Model* 1, *equilibrium contracts take a standard debt form*,

$$B(\ ) = \min\bigl(\pi(A, \varepsilon), B_N = \pi(A, \varepsilon^*)\bigr), \quad N = \{\varepsilon: \varepsilon \geqslant \varepsilon^*\}.$$

Note that, with debt contracts, the farmer gives up all firm assets to the investor whenever investor observation occurs; hence, $c(\ )$ could be interpreted as a bankruptcy cost.

Given Proposition 6, the entrepreneur's investment choice problem is as follows:

$$\max_{I, \varepsilon^*} \int_{\varepsilon^*}^{\bar{\varepsilon}} \bigl(\pi(W_0 + I, \varepsilon) - \pi(W_0 + I, \varepsilon^*)\bigr) h(\varepsilon)\, d\varepsilon \quad \text{s.t.} \tag{24}$$

$$G(I, \varepsilon^*; \rho) = \int_0^{\varepsilon^*} \bigl(\pi(W_0 + I, \varepsilon) - c(I, \varepsilon)\bigr) h(\varepsilon)\, d\varepsilon$$

$$+ \pi(W_0 + I, \varepsilon^*)\bigl(1 - H(\varepsilon^*)\bigr) - (1 + \rho)I \geqslant 0. \tag{25}$$

Substituting from (25), problem (24) can be rewritten as

$$\max_{I,\varepsilon^*} J(I, \varepsilon^*; \rho) = \left\{ E(\pi; I) - (1 + \rho)I \right\} - \int_0^{\varepsilon^*} c(I, \varepsilon) h(\varepsilon) \, d\varepsilon \tag{26}$$

subject to (25). The solution to problem (26) will be denoted $\hat{I}, \hat{\varepsilon}, \hat{\lambda}$, where λ corresponds to the Lagrange multiplier for constraint (25).

Because problem (26) is constructed as a constrained optimization of one agent's utility subject to another agent's achievement of a given expected payoff, its solution is constrained Pareto optimal (i.e., a Pareto improvement is not possible). However, this solution is not "first-best". For example, when investment is raised, investors require a higher expected payoff that is achieved by raising the payment promised to investors and, in doing so, increasing the number of states-of-nature in which "bankruptcy" occurs; that is, ε^* must rise.[21] Therefore, there is an additional cost to marginal investment – raising expected observation/bankruptcy costs – that leads to a lower optimal investment level than would occur in a world without bankruptcy costs. In sum:

PROPOSITION 7. *Equilibrium investment is less than "first-best"*: $\hat{I} < I^*$ *if* $\hat{\varepsilon}^* < \bar{\varepsilon}$.

The deviation of $\hat{I}$ from I^* admits the possibility that government policy can increase total net expected payoffs in the credit market. For example, if the government simply gave the entrepreneur I^* dollars today, the entrepreneur would choose the "first-best" investment, finance it entirely with his own funds, and thereby save the economy the investor observation cost. However, such lump sum transfers may be costly to achieve for a variety of reasons, including the incentives that they create for non-entrepreneurs to "seek" the transfer rents. Therefore, it is of interest to examine the scope for another policy instrument, interest subsidies, to yield gains in total expected payoffs.

Letting ρ now denote the *un*subsidized cost of funds, a marginal interest subsidy of s yields the subsidized cost of funds, $\rho - s$. Since $J(I, \varepsilon^*; \rho)$ (from (26)) represents the economy-wide net expected payoff from farm investment, a marginal interest subsidy will be welfare-improving if $J(\hat{I}(\rho - s), \hat{\varepsilon}^*(\rho - s); \rho)$ is larger than $J(\hat{I}(\rho), \hat{\varepsilon}^*(\rho); \rho)$, where the dependence of J, $\hat{I}$, and $\hat{\varepsilon}^*$ on ρ is now made explicit. The following propositions can now be derived:

PROPOSITION 8. *Suppose that* $\hat{\varepsilon}^*(\rho - s) \leqslant \hat{\varepsilon}^*(\rho) < \bar{\varepsilon}$ *so that a marginal interest subsidy does not lead to an increase in the probability of firm bankruptcy and, in the absence of subsidies, the firm does not always go bankrupt. Then some subsidy on* ρ, $s > 0$, *will increase overall economic welfare (i.e., it will increase the total economy-wide net expected payoff from firm investment).*

---

[21] If a marginal increase in I above $\hat{I}$ did not require ε^* to rise, this increase in I would unambiguously raise the value of the entrepreneur's objective function in (24) and $\hat{I}$ could not be optimal.

PROPOSITION 9. *Suppose $\hat{\varepsilon}^*(\rho) < \bar{\varepsilon}$. Overall economic welfare will be raised by an interest subsidy, $s > 0$, that is not available on investment amounts above the following $\bar{I}$ level*:

$$\bar{I} = \min\left(I_J^*\left(\hat{\varepsilon}^*(\rho); \rho\right), I_G\left(\hat{\varepsilon}^*(\rho); \rho - s\right)\right) > \hat{I}(\rho),$$

where $I_G(\varepsilon^*, \rho)$ solves and

$$G(I, \varepsilon^*; \rho) = 0 \quad and \quad I_J^*(\varepsilon^*; \rho) = \operatorname{argmax} J(I, \varepsilon^*; \rho).$$

By reducing the investor's required return, a subsidy on ρ has the direct effect of reducing the probability of bankruptcy, ε^*. However, the subsidy is also likely to elicit an increase in investment, which raises the probability of bankruptcy. If the first "direct" effect dominates the second "investment" effect (as assumed in Proposition 8), then the subsidy has two beneficial consequences:

(1) it leads to a level of investment which is closer to that which maximizes economy-wide net expected payoffs (given ε^*), and

(2) it reduces the probability of bankruptcy, thereby saving the economy some bankruptcy costs.

However, even if the "investment" effect dominates the "direct" effect, benefits from a subsidy policy can be ensured by limiting the subsidy to investment levels that do *not* increase the probability of bankruptcy. Proposition 9 defines such a policy.

3.1.2. Model 2: Ex-ante asymmetric information[23]

Consider a setting in which there are no profit observation costs, but there is asymmetric information about the quality, q, of an entrepreneur's profit distribution. Each entrepreneur is either high ($q = H$) or low ($q = L$) quality and is assumed to know his own quality type. However, external investors cannot directly observe an entrepreneur's q and, in the absence of borrower signaling, can only infer that a given borrower is high quality with probability θ, where θ is the proportion of high quality borrowers in the population of loan applicants. Borrower signaling/self-selection can occur if two financial contracts emerge in equilibrium, one of which is preferred by high quality entrepreneurs and the other of which is preferred by low quality entrepreneurs.

In this model, the variable x corresponds to q, the entrepreneur's quality type. Higher levels of q and I are assumed to elicit "better" profit distributions in the sense of the monotone likelihood ratio property, MLRP [see Milgrom (1981)], and first order stochastic dominance, FOSD, respectively.[24] In addition, the investor payoff function $B(\pi)$

---

[23] This section borrows from Innes (1991).

[24] The MLRP has become standard in the agency literature [e.g., see Jewitt (1988), Rogerson (1986)] and is a somewhat stronger condition than FOSD. The principal economic distinction between the the two constructs

is assumed to be monotone non-decreasing both because this weak restriction is consistent with all varieties of observed financial instruments and because non-monotonic contracts can create perverse incentives that rule them out [e.g., see Innes (1993b)].[25]

Following Wilson (1977), equilibrium in this model is a set of contracts, $(B_q(\pi), I_q)$, $q = L, H$, which maximizes the net expected payoff of the high quality entrepreneur subject to three constraints:

(E1) *Investor return requirement*: Investors earn non-negative expected profits on each distinct contract;

(E2) *Incentive compatibility*: Low quality farmers weakly prefer their own contract; and

(E3) *Low quality payoff*: Low quality farmers earn an expected payoff at least as high as on their perfect information contract.

(E1)–(E3) represent feasibility constraints on the equilibrium. Moreover, since investors are competitive, any contracts which satisfy (E1)–(E3) but do not solve the posited high quality entrepreneur maximization problem will be supplanted by investor offers of the contracts that do solve this problem; the latter solutions will attract the business of at least the high quality entrepreneurs, thereby earning the investors that offer them no less than (and possibly greater than) their required expected return.[26,27]

For this specification, the following result is proven in Innes (1993b):

---

is as follows: Any agent that likes an outcome variable y (i.e., who has utility that is increasing in y) prefers a probability distribution for y, call it A, that first order stochastically dominates another distribution for y, call it B. Now consider restricting y outcomes to an arbitrary subset, S, of all possible y outcomes, $Y \supset S$. Any von Neumann–Morgenstern agent that likes y will prefer the conditional probability distribution for y under A, given $y \in S$, to the corresponding conditional distribution under B if and only if A exhibits the MLRP relative to B, i.e., $g_A(y)/g_B(y)$ is increasing in y, where $g_A(y)$ and $g_B(y)$ are the probability densities for y under A and B, respectively. See Whitt (1980) for further discussion of this distinction.

[25] For example, investors may be able to "sabotage" the firm ex-post without penalty. If so, they will do so whenever realized output is in a decreasing segment of their payoff function. In order to prevent investor sabotage, the entrepreneur will always choose to have a contract which is everywhere non-decreasing in output. It is worth noting here that "sabotage" need not take the form of a criminal act. For example, investors are generally able, by legal right, to compel the firm to "prove" its output level to an impartial outsider (via a costly audit) or to bear other legal or bankruptcy-related costs; these costs have the effect of reducing, or "sabotaging", the firm output that is available for distribution to firm claimants.

[26] See Hellwig (1987), DeMeza and Webb (1989), Innes (1991) for a more complete motivation of the Wilson equilibrium.

[27] With some plausible restrictions on investors' out-of-equilibrium beliefs [restrictions akin to those of Cho and Kreps (1987)], Wilson outcomes emerge as a stable equilibrium to the following three-stage game: First, each investor announces a set of contract offers. Next, each entrepreneur applies for one contract out of the set of contracts on offer. Finally, after observing entrepreneurial credit applications, each investor decides whether to accept or reject each application that he has received. In other game structures, other equilibria are possible. Most notably, an alternative game yields a Miyazaki-type [Miyazaki (1977)] equilibrium in which the high quality entrepreneur's payoff is maximized subject to constraints (E2), (E3), and the following revised investor return requirement: (E1') Investors earn non-negative profits on the *set* of market contracts. The difference between Wilson and Miyazaki outcomes is that the latter allow for cross-subsidized contracts, on one of which the investor loses money and on the other of which he makes money. This distinction is important because constrained inefficiencies in Wilson equilibria are due to precisely the implicit preclusion

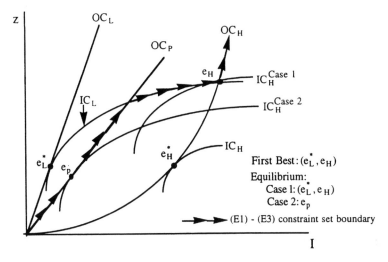

Figure 3. Model 2: Equilibrium.

PROPOSITION 10. *In Model 2, any equilibrium contract either takes a standard debt form, $B_q(\pi) = \min(\pi, z_q)$, or is equivalent to one that does.*

In essence, debt contracts maximize investor payoffs in low entrepreneurial profit states of nature. Since low quality types have probability weight concentrated in these states, high quality agents, by taking a debt contract, can minimize the low quality type's incentive to masquerade. The incentive compatibility constraint (E2) is thereby relaxed, permitting higher net expected profits for the high quality entrepreneur. Thus Proposition 10 emerges and a contract can be completely described by a pair, (I, z).

Two graphical constructs now permit a simple characterization of the equilibrium (see Figure 3):

(1) Entrepreneur indifference curves (IC_q), which give the (I, z) contracts that yield a quality q entrepreneur a given (constant) net expected payoff,

$$\mathrm{IC}_q: \int_z^{K(\ )} (\pi - z) f(\pi; I, q)\, d\pi = \text{constant.}$$

of cross-subsidized contracting. However, for small borrowers, the game underpinning Wilson equilibria is arguably a more plausible representation of credit market play. Miyazaki outcomes require a game in which entrepreneurs begin play by offering investors a menu of contracts (one for each quality type); the investor either agrees to offer the menu or not; and, if the investor agrees, the entrepreneur then selects a single contract from among those on offer. Such a game requires the entrepreneurs to have a great deal of information about the entire market, which may be plausible when entrepreneurs are "large", but unlikely when they are "small". Readers interested in Miyazaki-type credit market equilibria should see Innes (1992), where it is shown that neutral (non-distorting) taxation renders even Miyazaki outcomes constrained inefficient.

(2) Investor offer curves, which give the (I, z) contracts that yield investors exactly their required expected return when (i) the contracts are taken by a quality q farmer (OC_q) and (ii) the contracts are taken by both types of entrepreneur (OC_p, where p is for "pooling"),

$$OC_q: \; E\big(\min(\pi, z) \mid I, q\big) = (1 + \rho)I.$$

$$OC_p: \; \theta E\big(\min(\pi, z) \mid I, H\big) + (1 - \theta)E\big(\min(\pi, z) \mid I, L\big) = (1 + \rho)I.$$

Since entrepreneurs "like" investment, I, and "dislike" payments to investors, z, indifference curves are upward-sloping and lower curves (in Figure 3) correspond to higher entrepreneur payoffs. In addition, it is assumed that high quality indifference curves are *steeper* than low quality indifference curves due to "superior" high quality marginal investment returns.[28] Since investors "like" z and "dislike" I, offer curves are also upward-sloping. Further, OC_H is below OC_L due to "better" high quality profit distributions.

The "first-best" in this model is the set of tangencies between IC_q and OC_q for $q = L, H$. To make the analysis interesting, it is assumed that these contracts violate incentive compatibility in that the low quality farmer prefers the high quality type's "first-best" contract to his own (see Figure 3). Two types of equilibria are then possible.

Case 1: As shown in Figure 3, the equilibrium high quality contract corresponds to the point on the (E1)–(E3) constraint set (as indicated by arrows) that is on the lowest IC_H; in Case 1, this contract is e_H, which exactly deters adverse selection by low quality entrepreneurs.

Case 2: When the high quality entrepreneur prefers his favorite "pooling" contract, e_p, to e_H, e_p emerges in equilibrium.

The following proposition is now graphically evident:

PROPOSITION 11.
   (i) *In a Model 2 pooling equilibrium (Case 2), $I_L > I_L^*$ and $I_H < I_H^*$, where I_q^* is the first-best investment level for a quality q entrepreneur.*
   (ii) *In a Model 2 separating equilibrium (Case 1), $I_L = I_L^*$ and $I_H > I_H^*$ (i.e., the high quality entrepreneur over-invests in order to signal his type).*

Given the equilibrium's deviation from a first-best, it is of interest to evaluate the prospective welfare benefits of typical policy interventions. For example, consider the government's direct offer of a subsidized credit contract that is designed for low quality entrepreneurs. In Figure 4, a subsidized contract, e_L^S, is constructed so that low quality

---

[28] Milde and Riley (1988) construct a model in which *low* quality indifference curves are steeper due to identical high and low quality marginal investment returns. Implications of this alternative specification are discussed in Innes (1991).

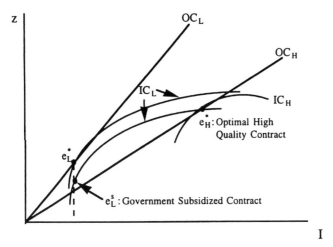

Figure 4. Proposed government debt subsidy policy.

entrepreneurs invest at their first-best level and are indifferent between e_L^S and the first-best high quality contract, e_H^*. It is assumed that either (i) e_L^S is above OC_H so that high quality entrepreneurs would not choose to take e_L^S and obtain supplemental private financing, or (ii) the government offer of e_L^S is combined with a requirement that any takers of this contract obtain *no* supplemental financing. Then the government offer of e_L^S will elicit a first-best equilibrium by reducing the low quality entrepreneur's incentive to "masquerade" as high quality, thereby relaxing the incentive compatibility constraint which is driving the free market inefficiency. Overall economic welfare will thereby be raised by the intervention.[29]

3.2. Moral hazard in credit markets

Let us now turn to potential economic implications of moral hazard in credit markets. To do so, I will suppose that there are no informational asymmetries about profit realizations or about the attributes of an entrepreneur's investment project, but that the entrepreneur makes an effort choice which affects his profit distribution and is unobservable to external investors. Because the effort level, e, is hidden, the investment contract cannot specify e and, in setting financial contract parameters, investors must infer effort choices from the entrepreneur's underlying choice problem. Thus, a standard principal agent problem emerges. In this section, I will study this problem in detail, taking explicit account for linkages between output markets and credit arrangements.

---

[29] Notably, Model 2 competitive equilibria can often be improved upon in the Pareto sense as well. See Innes (1991) for discussion of this point, as well as an analysis of other common credit market interventions (including loan guarantees, lump sum grants, and interest rate subsidies).

The analytical structure – and the conceptual issues that it can address – differs from the models above and most other work on credit markets in that entrepreneurial activities have primitive effects on outputs, not profits, with output prices affecting and affected by entrepreneurial investment contracts.[30]

Formally [drawing from Innes (1993a)], consider the following two-date model. N identical risk neutral entrepreneurs produce a random time 1 output of $y \in R_+$ using two time 0 inputs: (i) investment funds and (ii) entrepreneurial effort, $e \in R_+$. The investment funds consist of the entrepreneur's own wealth (equity) and the investment from outsiders, I. For notational simplicity, I will fix the equity level in the background and represent investment effects with I.[31]

The random output obeys the production relation, $y = y(I, e, \varepsilon_i)$. ε_i is a random shock that has positive support on the interval, $[\underline{\varepsilon}, \bar{\varepsilon}]$, and has two components, $\varepsilon_i = \theta + \eta_i$ for $i = 1, \ldots, N$. θ is the systematic shock common to all entrepreneurs and the η_i are idiosyncratic i.i.d. random variables. For all relevant I and e, the output function $y(\ )$ is increasing and concave with $y(I, 0, \varepsilon) = 0$ $\forall \varepsilon$ (effort is necessary for production), $y(I, e, \underline{\varepsilon}) = 0$ (zero output is always possible), and for a finite $e_{\max}$, $y_e(I, e_{\max}, \varepsilon) = 0$ $\forall \varepsilon$ (bounding e at $e_{\max}$). In addition, $y_I(0, e, \varepsilon)$ is assumed to be sufficiently large that positive borrowing is always privately and socially optimal.

Ex-post firm "profits" are the product of the firm's output, y, and the output price, $P(Y)$, where $Y = \sum_i y_i$ is economy-wide output and $P' < 0$.[32] The entrepreneur is competitive in that, from his or her point of view, the probability distribution of P is fixed. This probability distribution is denoted by $H(P)$, where the density function is $h(P)$.

Given the effort level e and the output price P, the probability density and distribution functions for firm output y will be denoted by the twice differentiable functions, $g(y \mid I, e, P)$ and $G(y \mid I, e, P)$. For all possible price realizations, higher effort levels yield superior output distributions in the sense of the MLRP (see note 24):

$$\frac{\partial}{\partial y}\left(\frac{g_e(\ )}{g(\ )}\right) > 0 \quad \forall(y, I, e, P): g(\ ) > 0. \tag{27}$$

---

[30] This line of thought is most closely related to Brander and Spencer (1989), who focus on the implications of debt-contract-induced moral hazard for competitive and monopolistic firms' input and output choices, but do not endogenize the form of the financial contract. Other recent papers have also linked financial structure choices with output market behavior, but do so in the presence of imperfect output market competition and under the assumption that financial contracts take certain prespecified forms, such as debt and equity [e.g., see Bolton and Scharfstein (1990), Brander and Lewis (1986), Poitevin (1989), Titman (1984), and, for a survey, Ravid (1988)].

[31] Implicit in this specification is an assumption that the entrepreneur's current consumption is fixed and that his investment opportunities outside of the firm are the same as those available to prospective outside investors. Under these circumstances, the opportunity cost of the entrepreneur's own investment in the firm (i.e., his own equity) is the same as that for the outside investors and it can be shown that the entrepreneur will optimally invest all of his own available wealth in his firm before raising any funds from outside sources [e.g., see Eswaran and Kotwal (1989)].

[32] For simplicity, I abstract from random demand shocks.

As before, the outside investors are competitive and risk neutral. The investors cannot observe the effort choice, e, and, therefore, cannot sign a contract which specifies e. However, they can infer the entrepreneur's effort choice from his utility maximization problem. Therefore, the investors require an expected return of ρ on their investment I, considering the inferred effort choice effects of contract terms.

The investors' return is obtained by ex-post producer payments which depend upon the observables, P (output price) and y (firm output). This payment function will be denoted $B(P, y)$ and assumed to be (i) piecewise differentiable, (ii) subject to the entrepreneur's limited liability, $B(\ ) \leqslant Py$, and (iii) non-decreasing in output, $B_y(\ ) \geqslant 0$ everywhere.[33]

Subject to the differentiability, limited liability, monotonicity and investor return constraints, each entrepreneur will choose a contract that gives him maximal utility. Formally, the entrepreneur has the following utility function in his time 1 dollar payoff, $w = Py - B(P, y)$, and effort:

$$U(w, e) = w - v(e), \tag{28}$$

where $v(e)$ is an increasing and convex disutility of effort function.[34]

Given a pre-chosen investment level I and a fixed $B(\ )$ function, the entrepreneur will choose effort to solve the following problem:

$$\max_e V(e, B, I) \equiv E\{U(Py - B(P, y), e) \mid I, e\}$$

$$= \int_P \int_y (Py - B(P, y)) g(y \mid I, e, P) \, dy \, h(P) \, dP - v(e),$$

$$\text{s.t. } e \in [0, e_{\max}]. \tag{29}$$

In view of the effort choice problem (29), the entrepreneur's contractual choice problem can be stated as follows (for a given level of I):

$$\max_{e, B} V(e, B, I) \quad \text{s.t. (a) } E(B(P, y) \mid I, e) \geqslant (1 + \rho)I, \tag{30}$$

$$\text{(b) } B(P, y) \leqslant Py, \ B_y(\ ) \geqslant 0, \ \forall (P, y) \in R_2^+,$$

$$\text{(c) } e \text{ solves (29).}$$

Condition (a) gives the investor return requirement; (b) gives the limited liability and monotonicity constraints on the contract form; and (c) gives the key effort choice constraint that creates the moral hazard problem in this model.

---

[33] The monotonicity constraint is imposed for the same reasons as in Section 1.1.2 above. For example, see note 25.

[34] Entrepreneurial risk neutrality implies that $U(w, e)$ takes the form $U = a(e)w - v(e)$. Allowing $a(e)$ to vary with e complicates the analysis, but alters nothing that follows. Therefore, for simplicity, I restrict attention to the utility function in (28), as has become standard in the principal-agent literature.

3.2.1. First-best contracts

Problem (30)'s first-best analog – (30) subject only to the investor return requirement (30a) – can be written as follows:

$$\max_{e} V^*(e, I) \equiv E\{U(Py - (1+\rho)I, e) \mid I, e\}$$

$$= E\{Py \mid I, e\} - (1+\rho)I - v(e). \tag{31}$$

Given concavity of $[E\{Py \mid I, e\} - v(e)]$ in e, problem (31) yields a unique first-best effort level, $e^*(I) > 0$.[35]

Turning now to the entrepreneur's optimal contract problem when there *is* a moral hazard problem but *not* the limited liability restriction, $B(\ ) \leqslant Py$, the following results are immediate [e.g., see Shavell (1979)]:

PROPOSITION 12. *When there is no limited liability restriction, the fixed payment contract, $B(\ ) = (1+\rho)I$, is feasible, elicits the first-best effort choice $e^*(I)$, and is optimal. Also feasible and optimal in the absence of a limited liability constraint is any contract which* (i) *specifies payments that are invariant to output and* (ii) *meets the investor return requirement, (30a), with equality. However, no output-invariant-payment contract is feasible when the producer has limited liability.*

When the producer's payments to the investor do not depend on output, they are also unaffected by the producer's effort choice; therefore, with an output-invariant-payment contract, the producer receives all of the expected profit gains that result from a marginal increase in effort and the first-best effort choice results. However, the producer's limited liability, together with the possibility of a zero output level, implies that the entrepreneur will not be able to make a positive fixed payment in low output states of nature. Therefore, output-invariant-payment contracts are infeasible here. This cost of limited liability is crucial; as we will see in a moment, it is the source of market inefficiency here, without which there would be no motive for government policy.

3.2.2. Equilibrium contracts

Due to the entrepreneur's limited liability, the investor payoff on the contract $B(\ )$ must be zero when the entrepreneur's output is zero. Thus, since $B(\ )$ is non-decreasing in output y, $B_y(\ )$ must be strictly positive on some interval of positive measure in order for the investor to receive a positive expected payoff and, hence, for the investor return constraint (30a) to be satisfied.

---

[35] $E(Py \mid I, e)$ can be written as the expectation (over P and ε) of $Py(I, e, \varepsilon)$, where the joint probability of (P, ε) is invariant to e. Thus, the concavity of $E\{Py \mid I, e\} - v(e)$ ($= E_{\varepsilon, P}(Py(I, e, \varepsilon)) - v(e)$) in e follows from the concavity of $y(I, e, \varepsilon)$ in e and the convexity of $v(e)$.

Now note that, due to condition (27), marginal effort shifts probability weight from lower outputs to higher outputs. Therefore, since the investor payoff function is everywhere non-decreasing in output – and somewhere increasing – increases in entrepreneurial effort shift probability weight from low investor payoff states of nature to higher investor payoff states of nature, thereby increasing the investor's expected payoff, $E\{B(\ )\mid I, e\}$. The entrepreneur thus gives up some of the benefits from marginal effort to the investor, while still bearing its full disutility cost, $v_e(e)$. As a result, we have:

PROPOSITION 13. *For any I, a solution to problem* (30) *specifies an effort level,* $\hat{e}(I)$, *which is strictly less than the first-best effort level,* $e^*(I)$.[36]

Of course the entrepreneur would like to be able to commit to an effort level that is as close to $e^*(I)$ as possible. It is this desire that motivates the following contracting result:

PROPOSITION 14. *Any contract that solves problem* (30), $\widehat{B}$, *earns the investor exactly the required expected return,* ρ, *and takes the form of a price-contingent commodity bond,*

$$\widehat{B}(P, y) = P \min(y, \bar{y}(P)). \tag{32}$$

Because marginal effort shifts probability weight from low output levels to high output levels, the entrepreneur can maximize his incentives to exert effort – and thereby permit himself to implicitly commit to a higher level of e – by choosing a contract form that maximizes his own payoffs in high output states. Among all possible monotonic contract forms, commodity bonds give the entrepreneur the highest possible payoffs in high output states of nature, thereby minimizing the disparity between $\hat{e}(I)$ and $e^*(I)$.[37]

3.2.3. Partial equilibrium effort, investment, and output

Having described the equilibrium contract form, I now turn to the characterization of e, I, and y, with the primary objective being to relate these choices to those that would be

---

[36] Proposition 13 generalizes similar conclusions of Myers (1977), Brander and Spencer (1989), and Innes (1990b). See Innes (1993a) for formal proofs of Propositions 13 and 14.

[37] The price-contingent commodity bond is a form of debt contract. A standard debt contract requires a dollar payment equal to the minimum of the entrepreneur's actual revenue, Py, and a promised payment, z. The commodity bond in Equation (32) describes such a contract, but specifies a promised dollar payment that depends, in general, upon the realized output price, $\bar{z}^*(P) = P\bar{y}^*(P)$. Innes (1993a) shows that such a contract can be replicated using a combination of a standard debt instrument, a commodity futures contract, and a continuum of commodity call options, with the investor guaranteeing the producer's position on futures and options markets. If investors can observe an entrepreneur's revenue, but not both his output and price (perhaps because there are multiple products or grades or timing of sales that complicate such observations), then financial contracts will be contingent on revenues, Py. Under these circumstances, a pure debt contract will emerge in equilibrium due to the same logic that underlies Proposition 14 [see Innes (1990b)].

made in the absence of moral hazard and thereby to gain a better understanding of the inefficiencies that moral hazard introduces. I begin this endeavor by considering *partial equilibrium* relationships that are obtained for a *given* set of "market input levels", $\bar{I}$ and $\bar{e}$. In the next section, $\bar{I}$ and $\bar{e}$ are endogenized in order to describe market equilibrium relationships. Two cases will be of special interest in this undertaking:

(1) when e and I are complements in production, requiring

$$\frac{\partial^2 E(y \mid I, e, P)}{\partial I \partial e} > 0 \quad \forall (I, e, P)$$

and, somewhat more strictly,

$$\int_{\bar{y}}^{\infty} G_{eI}(y \mid I, e, P)\, dy \leqslant 0 \quad \forall (I, e, P, \bar{y});$$

and

(2) when e and I are substitutes, requiring

$$\frac{\partial^2 E(y \mid \cdot)}{\partial I \partial e} < 0$$

everywhere and, somewhat more strictly,

$$\int_{\bar{y}}^{\infty} G_{eI}(y \mid I, e, P)\, dy \geqslant 0 \quad \forall (I, e, P, \bar{y}).^{38}$$

3.2.3.1. Inputs.   Given $(\bar{I}, \bar{e})$, relevant "first-best" (i.e., no moral hazard) input choices are e^* and I^* that solve $e^* = e^*(I^*) = \mathrm{argmax}_e V^*(e, I^*)$ and $I^* = I^*(e^*) \equiv \mathrm{argmax}_I V^*(e^*, I)$, where $V^*(\ )$ is the producer surplus defined in Equation (31) and the $(e^*(\ ), I^*(\ ))$ functions are "quasi-first-best" constructs that will be useful as we proceed.

Corresponding solutions to the entrepreneur's "moral-hazard-constrained" choice problem will be denoted by $\hat{e}$ and $\hat{I}$. In choosing his level of investment (and borrowing), each entrepreneur will consider the effects of the investment choice on his induced effort level, $\hat{e}(I)$. Formally, with the entrepreneur paying exactly the investor's cost of funds $(1 + \rho)I$ (from Proposition 14 above), he will choose $\hat{I}$ to solve

$$\max_{I} V^*(e, I) \quad \text{s.t. } e \leqslant \hat{e}(I). \tag{33}$$

Assuming that (33) has a unique interior solution, we have:

---

[38] A sufficient condition for complementarity (substitutability) is that $G_{eI} \leqslant 0$ ($\geqslant 0$) everywhere (with strict inequality on sets of positive measure), which states that higher (lower) effort levels yield first order stochastically dominant output payoffs from *marginal* investment.

PROPOSITION 15. *The partial equilibrium investment level $\hat{I}$ is less than (greater than) its quasi-first-best counterpart $I^*(\hat{e})$ when the effort choice is negatively (positively) related to the investment level: $\hat{I} < (=, >)I^*(\hat{e})$ when $d\hat{e}(\hat{I})/dI < (=, >)0$.*

When a higher investment level prompts increased effort, it helps to mitigate the under-exertion cost of contracting, imparting an extra benefit to marginal investment that is absent in a first-best setting. Conversely, when extra investment prompts lower effort, it bears the additional cost of worsening the moral hazard problem. These extra benefits and costs of investment yield the relationships described in Proposition 15. A more precise interpretation of these relationships derives from the following observation:

PROPOSITION 16. *When e and I are substitutes (complements), $d\hat{e}(\hat{I})/dI < 0 \; (\gtrless 0)$.*

A higher investment level has two effects on incentives to exert effort. First, it changes the marginal product of effort directly. And second, it requires higher promised payments to investors, which lead, in turn, to reduced incentives for effort. When effort and investment are substitutes, higher investment *lowers* the marginal product of effort, and effort incentives are unambiguously reduced. However, when effort and investment are complements, the two effects are offsetting.

Drawing on Propositions 13, 15, and 16, Figures 5 and 6 depict possible relationships between the "first-best" functions, $e^*(\;)$ and $I^*(\;)$, and the moral-hazard-constrained effort choice function, $\hat{e}(I)$.[39] Together, Proposition 15 and the figures indicate that there are competing influences on effort and investment choices that render unambiguous comparisons between $(\hat{I}, \hat{e})$ and (I^*, e^*) difficult. For example, when (e, I) are substitutes, a lower effort level leads to a higher marginal product of investment; as a result, moral-hazard induced reductions in effort directly favor an investment level which is higher than I^*. However, since $d\hat{e}(\hat{I})/dI < 0$ in the case of substitutes, the choice of a *lower* investment level helps to mitigate the moral hazard problem by implicitly committing the entrepreneur to a higher level of e.

Despite these conflicting influences, an unambiguous relationship between $(\hat{I}, \hat{e})$ and (I^*, e^*) can be derived in two cases: (1) when (e, I) are complements and $d\hat{e}(\hat{I})/dI < 0$, which implies that $\hat{I} < I^*$ and $\hat{e} < e^*$, and (2) when $y_{Ie} = 0$ everywhere (e.g., when $y(\;) = \alpha(e, \varepsilon) + \beta(I, \varepsilon)$), which also implies that $\hat{I} < I^*$ and $\hat{e} < e^*$. The latter case is particularly interesting in that it illustrates the linkage between input choices that is engendered by the financial contract, despite a *technological* independence between

---

[39] The figures also reflect the following derivative relationships:

$$\frac{de^*(I)}{dI} \underset{\underline{S}}{\ge} \frac{dI^*(e)}{de} \underset{\underline{S}}{\ge} \int_P \frac{\partial^2 E(y \mid I, e, P)}{\partial I \partial e} Ph(P)\, dP \underset{\underline{S}}{\ge} \left[\left(\frac{dI^*(e)}{de} \right)^{-1} - \frac{de^*(I)}{dI} \right],$$

where the last sign equality holds at any point of intersection between $I^*(e)$ and $e^*(I)$.

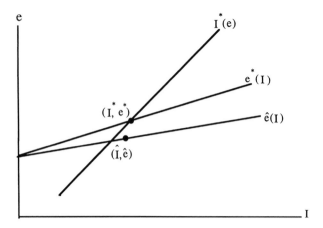

Figure 5. Equilibria with and without moral hazard when e and I are complements.

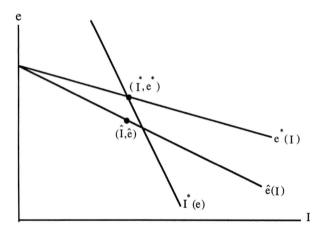

Figure 6. Equilibria with and without moral hazard when e and I are substitutes.

the inputs. To be more specific, when $y_{Ie} = 0$, an investment level which is less than I^* is optimal because it permits reductions in promised output payments under the entrepreneur-investor financial contract; these promised payment reductions in turn permit the entrepreneur to commit to an effort level which is closer to e^*.

3.2.3.2. Output.   Although unambiguous relationships between $(\hat{I}, \hat{e})$ and (I^*, e^*) are difficult to obtain in general, the following weak separability restriction on technology helps to relate *output* choices with and without moral hazard:

$$y(I, e, \varepsilon) = F(\phi(I, e), \varepsilon),$$ (R)

where F and ϕ are increasing and concave, and ϕ exhibits decreasing marginal factor productivity along its level sets. Condition (R) permits the analysis to focus on the single output index, $\phi(\ )$, which is monotonically related to output in all states of nature.

PROPOSITION 17. *If* (R) *holds, then* $\phi(\hat{I},\hat{e}) < \phi(I^*,e^*)$ *if either* (a) $\hat{I} \leqslant I^*$ *or* (b) $d\hat{e}(\hat{I})/d\hat{I} \leqslant 0$.

If equilibrium investment is lower than in a first-best, then moral hazard curbs output both by indirectly inducing the investment cutback and by directly reducing effort incentives. Moreover, when the moral hazard problem gets worse as investment and output rise (i.e., when $d\hat{e}(\hat{I})/d\hat{I} \leqslant 0$), the marginal cost of output is higher than in a first-best/perfect information setting, and equilibrium output is lower as a result. Together, Propositions 16 and 17 imply that moral hazard spurs lower output whenever effort and investment are weak substitutes in production.

3.2.4. Government policy in a partial equilibrium

In the partial equilibrium characterized here, the entrepreneur's expected utility is maximized subject to the other relevant agents (i.e., the investors) receiving a given expected payoff. As a result, this equilibrium is "second best" (i.e., constrained efficient). However, the deviation from a "first-best" allocation permits policy interventions to increase the sum of all agents' expected payoffs.

PROPOSITION 18. *The following conditions are sufficient for a policy measure, G, to increase overall economic welfare in the partial (fixed $(\bar{I},\bar{e})$) equilibrium: The policy* (i) *raises the entrepreneurial effort levels, $\hat{e}(I)$, for all I, and* (ii) *preserves the entrepreneur's objective function in problem* (33).

Now consider the following two policies: (1) an ex-post government grant to the entrepreneur of $G > 0$, where G is not large enough to fully cover the entrepreneur's loan obligations at the post-grant equilibrium, and (2) an interest subsidy, $s > 0$, on investment levels no greater than I_s, where I_s is less than the post-subsidy (partial) equilibrium level of I. When $sI_s = G$, these two policies are equivalent, each yielding an augmented investor return requirement of $(1 + \rho)I - G$.

By lowering the investor's required return, either policy permits a given investment level to be achieved with lower promised output payments, $\bar{y}(P)$. Because lower promised output payments raise the entrepreneur's incentives to exert effort, the government subsidy permits a higher effort solution to the entrepreneur's contractual choice problem (30), that is, a higher $\hat{e}(I)$. The policies thereby satisfy the requirements of Proposition 18, raising overall economic welfare. In essence, they do so by reducing the investor's claim on the entrepreneur's profit distribution and thereby relaxing the moral hazard constraint (in (33)) by reducing the marginal effort benefits that must be given up to the investor.

3.2.5. Market equilibrium

So far, we have fixed the market-level input (and output) choices, $(\bar{I}, \bar{e})$, in the background. To endogenize these choices, I will continue to assume that condition (R) holds. Market level output (per firm) and firm-specific output can then be represented by the indices, $y_E = \phi(\bar{I}, \bar{e})$ and $\hat{y} = \phi(\hat{I}, \hat{e})$, respectively. With θ denoting the systematic output shock described at the outset, realized aggregate market output becomes

$$Y = \sum_i F(y_E, \varepsilon_i) = Y(y_E, \theta), \tag{34}$$

and corresponding market prices are (abusing notation somewhat) $P(Y) = P(y_E, \theta)$.[40]

It is instructive at this juncture to characterize the partial equilibrium, and its dependence on market-level outcomes, in terms of the output index $\hat{y}$. Given an output choice of $\hat{y}$ and market-level output of y_E, firm revenue is

$$R(\hat{y}; y_E) = \int_\theta P(y_E, \theta) E\{y; \hat{y}, \theta\} q(\theta) \, d\theta, \tag{35}$$

where $E\{y; \hat{y}, \theta\}$ is the conditional expectation of firm output and $q(\theta)$ denotes the probability density of θ.[41] The corresponding firm cost of output is

$$C(\hat{y}; y_E) = \min_{I,e} \{(1 + \rho)I + v(e)\}$$

$$\text{s.t. (a) } \phi(I, e) \geq \hat{y}, \quad \text{(b) } e \leq \hat{e}(I; y_E). \tag{36}$$

(36) minimizes the sum of investment and effort costs subject to (a) achieving a given level of output and (b) incentive-compatibility of the effort choice.[42] A partial equilibrium choice of the output index, $\hat{y}$, solves the profit maximization,

$$\max_{\hat{y}} R(\hat{y}; y_E) - C(\hat{y}; y_E), \tag{37}$$

which I will assume to have a unique interior solution, $\hat{y}(y_E)$. A symmetric market equilibrium solves the identity $\hat{y}(y_E) = y_E$, the solution to which I will denote $\hat{y}^*$.

---

[40] I implicitly invoke my premise of atomistic firms by specifying the invariance of aggregate output to idiosynchratic variations in individual firm outputs, $\sum_i F(y_E, \varepsilon_i) = N E_\eta(F(y_E, \theta + \eta)) = Y(y_E, \theta)$, where E_η is the expectation operator over the idiosynchratic output shock η.

[41] In terms of our primitive function and variable definitions, $E\{y; \hat{y}, \theta\} = E_\eta(F(\hat{y}, \theta + \eta))$.

[42] With the primitive stochastic shock θ taking the place of the random price P in our prior analysis, promised output payments and output densities take the forms, $\bar{y}(\theta, y_E, I)$ and $g(y; I, e, \theta)$. The entrepreneur's effort choice can thus be written as

$$\hat{e}(I; y_E) = \operatorname{argmax} \int_\theta P(y_E, \theta) \int_{\bar{y}(\theta, y_E, I)}^\infty \left(y - \bar{y}(\theta, y_E, I)\right) g(y; I, e, \theta) \, dy \, q(\theta) \, d\theta - v(e).$$

The corresponding market equilibrium investment level will be denoted $\hat{I}^*$ (the solution to (36) with $\hat{y} = y_E = \hat{y}^*$).

Important properties of the "moral-hazard-constrained" effort choice and cost functions are as follows:

PROPOSITION 19. *A higher level of market output leads to* (i) *less effort,* $\partial\hat{e}(I; y_E)/\partial y_E < 0$, *and* (ii) *a higher firm-level cost of output,* $\partial C(\hat{y}; y_E)/\partial y_E > 0$.

A higher level of market supply, y_E, lowers market prices and thereby requires that investors be paid higher levels of promised output in order to meet their investment return requirements. Higher promised output payments imply, in turn, that the entrepreneur must give up more marginal effort benefits to the investor, thus reducing incentives to exert effort, worsening the moral hazard problem, and thereby raising the costs required to achieve a given level of the output measure $\hat{y}$.

3.2.5.1. Relating equilibrium output to first-best output.   In a first-best world (without moral hazard), the parallel to the "partial equilibrium" choice problem of Equation (37) is

$$\max_{y^*} R(y^*; y_E) - C^*(y^*), \quad \text{with}$$

$$C^*(y^*) = \min_{I,e}\{(1+\rho)I + v(e)\} \quad \text{s.t. } \phi(I,e) \geqslant y^*. \tag{38}$$

The solution to (38) will be denoted $y^*(y_E)$, and its market equilibrium counterpart by $y^{**} = y_E$: $y^*(y_E) = y_E$. Comparing problems (37) and (38) reveals the following:

PROPOSITION 20. *If* (R) *holds and* $\partial\hat{e}(\hat{I}^*; \hat{y}^*)/\partial I \leqslant 0$, *then a symmetric market equilibrium yields lower output than would occur in a first-best world,* $\hat{y}^* < y^{**}$.

The logic of this result is simple: If output were higher under moral hazard, then prices would be lower. But, under the prior conditions of Proposition 20, both moral hazard and low prices inhibit production, yielding the contradiction of lower output.

3.2.5.2. Relating equilibrium output to "second-best" output.   Following Brander and Spencer (1989), let us turn to the question of whether an altruistic social planner would choose a different level of output than emerges in the equilibrium. For simplicity, let us assume that consumer utility is quasi-linear in aggregate output Y and expenditure on other goods, m: $U_c = u(Y) + m$.[43] Then expected aggregate welfare is the expected utility from good Y less production costs:[44]

---

[43] Brander and Spencer (1989) make the same assumption in order to abstract from income effects, aggregation problems, and second-best effects from distortions in other sectors.

[44] Brander and Spencer (1989) define welfare also as a function of financial structure parameters. Here, such parameters have been chosen optimally and implicitly embedded in the welfare function.

$$W(\hat{y}) = \int_{\theta} u\big(Y(\hat{y}, \theta)\big) q(\theta) \, d\theta - NC(\hat{y}; \hat{y}), \tag{39}$$

where aggregate output $Y(\;)$ is as described in (34) above. A "second-best" output level maximizes the welfare function in (39), $\hat{y}^{**} = \operatorname{argmax} W(\hat{y})$, by solving the first order condition,

$$
\begin{aligned}
W'(\hat{y}) &= \int_{\theta} u'(\;)\big[\partial Y(\;)/\partial\hat{y}\big] q(\;) \, d\theta - N\big(dC(\;)/d\hat{y}\big) \\
&= \int_{\theta} P(\hat{y}, \theta) N \big[\partial \mathrm{E}(y; \hat{y}, q)/\partial\hat{y}\big] q(\;) \, d\theta - N\big(dC(\;)/d\hat{y}\big) \\
&= N \left\{ \left. \frac{\partial R(\hat{y}; y_E)}{\partial\hat{y}} \right|_{y_E=\hat{y}} - \left. \frac{\partial C(\hat{y}; y_E)}{\partial\hat{y}} \right|_{y_E=\hat{y}} - \left. \frac{\partial C(\hat{y}; y_E)}{\partial y_E} \right|_{y_E=\hat{y}} \right\} = 0. \tag{40}
\end{aligned}
$$

The first equality in (40) follows from consumer utility maximization and expansion of the aggregate output derivative, $\partial Y(\;)/\partial\hat{y}$, while the second equality recalls the definition of firm revenue $R(\;)$ in Equation (35). Evaluating $W'(\;)$ at $\hat{y}^*$ (the equilibrium output choice defined in Equation (37)), we have

$$W'(\hat{y}^*) = -N \left. \frac{\partial C(\hat{y}^*; y_E)}{\partial y_E} \right|_{y_E=\hat{y}^*} < 0, \tag{41}$$

where the inequality follows from Proposition 19. Assuming the second order condition $W'' < 0$ holds in a relevant region, Equation (41) gives us:

PROPOSITION 21. *Equilibrium output is higher than is second-best, $\hat{y}^* > \hat{y}^{**}$.*

In the presence of moral hazard, higher output levels have an external cost that is not considered by competitive producers. By lowering market prices, higher outputs raise investors' required claim on each entrepreneur's output distribution, reducing incentives to exert effort, worsening the moral hazard problem, and thereby raising costs of production. Because they fail to consider this external cost, competitive entrepreneurs produce more than is efficient in a second-best sense.[45]

Conceptually, the "second-best" output choice described here represents that of a benevolent welfare-maximizing regulator who can observe and control investment and financing decisions, but not entrepreneurial effort. Deviation from the "second-best" does not necessarily imply that the equilibrium is constrained inefficient – i.e., that

---

[45] Contrary to Proposition 21, Brander and Spencer (1989) conclude that the competitive equilibrium is second-best and, hence, constrained efficient (see their Proposition 7). However, in coming to this conclusion, these scholars ignore precisely the external effect of investment (and output) that gives rise to the inefficiency identified here.

Pareto-improving policy interventions are possible. The reason is that compensatory taxes on entrepreneurs – those taxes needed to compensate consumers for consumer surplus losses that occur when output is reduced – affect the equilibrium if they reduce the resources that the entrepreneur has available for either investment (if the taxes are ex-ante) or loan repayment (if the taxes are ex-post). However, if such compensatory redistributions come from entrepreneurial resources that are not available for investment or loan repayments (e.g., bankruptcy-protected wages), then the redistributions are non-distorting and the deviation from the second-best does imply constrained inefficiency.

The market equilibrium effects identified here may also diminish the partial equilibrium welfare gains from lump-sum government subsidies to entrepreneurs (such as those described following Proposition 18 above). If subsidies spur increased output (by prompting output choices that are closer to first-best levels), then the resulting reduction in output prices will worsen the moral hazard problem. Interestingly, this logic may argue for the provision of subsidies in a form that does not permit the welfare-depleting costs of market effects. For example, offering subsidies in a "target price" form (whereby entrepreneurs receive any positive difference between a given target price and the market price) partially decouples entrepreneurs' revenues from market price declines and thereby limits the adverse effects of lowered market prices on moral hazard. Tying payments from target price programs to production restrictions will, in turn, have dual advantages, limiting output expansion incentives from above-market prices and potentially permitting contraction in output to second-best levels. Market effects can thus have important implications for the appropriate design of subsidy programs.

3.3. Section overview

In this section, I have discussed implications of imperfect information for the design of credit contracts, the efficiency properties of market equilibria, and the potential scope for government interventions to improve economic welfare, all in simple two-date models that illustrate modeling methods and conceptual issues that arise in this context (and that are developed in recent related research). While all of the model frameworks admit a positive (welfare-improving) role for some form of government subsidy to entrepreneurial borrowers, I want to stress the illustrative nature of the analysis and, in doing so, suggest avenues for extension. A number of phenomena that are not modeled here may have implications for credit market equilibria and their efficiency properties, among them: interactions between the different varieties of imperfect information [e.g., see Vercammen (1995)]; the effects of market power in credit supply [e.g., see Brander and Spencer (1989), Besanko and Thakor (1987)]; an alternative information structure in which banks (investors) have better information than do borrower/entrepreneurs [e.g., DeMeza and Southey (1996)]; an ability of prospective lenders to "screen" applicants into different quality types at a cost [e.g., DeMeza and Webb (1988)], combined with costly mechanisms for borrower signalling; borrower entry effects when there is asymmetric information and many potential qualities of borrower projects [e.g., DeMeza and Webb (1987, 1989)]; market equilibrium effects in asymmetric information models; and, of course, dynamics [e.g., Webb (1991)].

Despite the many avenues for further inquiry, the modeling in this section poses a challenge to conventional economic premises of free market utopia in credit markets, and gives reason to doubt the associated conviction that government can only make matters worse when striving to support those who may be most equity-constrained – and therefore most subject to the prospective efficiency costs of contracting described here.

4. Government agricultural policy when contingent claim markets are incomplete

Absent other market failures, Arrow (1971) and Debreu (1959) long ago showed how the Fundamental Theorems of Welfare Economics extend to risky environments; all that is needed is a complete set of markets for *state-contingent* income, income that is specific to the realization of a particular state of nature. For example, given a full set of spot commodity markets, Debreu showed that markets will be complete if, for every state of nature, there is a traded Arrow–Debreu security that yields a payoff of one dollar in the given state of nature and zero otherwise. However, if there is not a complete set of Arrow–Debreu markets, the competitive equilibrium is, in general, inefficient [e.g., Borch (1968)], even in a constrained sense [Newbery and Stiglitz (1982a), Hart (1983)]. The reason is that, with incomplete markets, agents' indifference curves need not be tangent in state-contingent income space; as a result, there can be trades of state-contingent incomes that would make all agents better off. From a policy perspective, the possibility of Pareto-improving trades is important because a policy measure may be able to implicitly elicit such trades and thereby increase economic welfare.

In this section, I will explore potential implications of incomplete markets for a stereotypical agricultural policy, namely, a target price/deficiency payment program (the so-called "Brannan Plan") with and without complementary production controls (the "Cochrane Plan").[46] A target price program pays farmers any positive difference between the target price and the prevailing market price for their output. Under certainty and perfect competition, such an intervention benefits producers, hurts consumers/taxpayers, and causes a net (Harberger triangle) welfare loss.[47] However, in

---

[46] The analysis borrows from Innes (1990d) [see also Innes (1990c), Innes and Rausser (1989)]. Innes and Rausser (1989) also consider the effects of acreage controls (rather than production controls). By focusing on production risk and the resulting variability in output prices, these analyses raise issues which are familiar to the extensive literature on price stabilization [e.g., see Campbell and Turnovsky (1985), Helms (1985), Miranda and Helmberger (1988), Newbery and Stiglitz (1981, 1982b), Wright (1979)], though this literature does not consider the agricultural policies of interest here. Myers (1988) has also studied the implications of incomplete markets for welfare-improvement in agriculture, focusing on benefits of fully completing markets.

[47] See Wallace (1962), Gardner (1983) for the classic works on agricultural policy in non-stochastic environments.

a simple Diamond-type [Diamond (1980)] closed economy with stochastic production, incomplete contingent claim markets, and rational agents, I will argue here that all of these conclusions can be reversed under conditions that are generally thought to hold for staple food markets, viz, producer risk aversion and low price and income elasticities of consumer demand. In essence, a target price program improves welfare by implicitly prompting trades of state-contingent income between farmers and consumers/taxpayers that, because contingent claim markets are absent, place the economy inside a lens of mutual advantage. What is more, production controls are shown to be optimal as a complement to a Brannan Plan, with a joint target price/production control policy optimal under less onerous conditions than is a target price program on its own.

As in other second-best analyses, the strength of the argument hinges upon both the objective merit and the internal consistency of the underlying premises. Here, the central premise is that complete markets are not present in the unfettered economy. For example, Ross (1976) shows that call options can be used to complete contingent-claim markets. Indeed, in the two-state model developed below, a single commodity price option would suffice to complete markets. However, there may be good reasons that farmers use such options only sparingly and, hence, that the agricultural economy behaves as if such markets are absent. For instance, there is likely to be asymmetric information of the kind described by Radner (1970), with large option traders on one side of the market (e.g., large commodity marketing companies) having better information about commodity prices than do small farmer traders on the other side of the market; option trades will then be rationally deterred.[48] The analysis that follows is consistent with such a failure in private markets. Nevertheless, I want to caution the reader that the specific policy conclusions derived here, while important in illustrating the analysis and impact of risk and imperfect risk trading in the evaluation of agricultural policy, must be tempered by both the empirical merits of the posited market failure and real-world departures from the assumed absence of international commodity trading, intertemporal income smoothing, and deadweight costs of taxation.

4.1. The incomplete markets model

Consider a static two-good closed economy in which the two goods are a food commodity (x) and a numeraire (y). Food production is characterized by a representative (aggregate) farmer who is price-taking and has the following multiplicative-risk production technology [as in Diamond (1980), Newbery and Stiglitz (1982b)]:

$$\tilde{x} = \tilde{\theta} f(y_x, k). \tag{42}$$

In (42), $\tilde{x}$ is the random ex-post food output; $\tilde{\theta}$ is the random output coefficient with expectation, $E(\tilde{\theta}) = 1$; $f()$ is an increasing and weakly concave production function; k

---

[48] For evidence on risk problems and lack of perfect risk trading in agriculture, see Barry (1984).

is a fixed factor of production in the agricultural sector (say, land and/or human capital); and y_x is the numeraire input in food production.[49]

The input, y_x, must be chosen before the actual (ex-post) realization of either $\tilde{\theta}$ or the market food price, $\tilde{P}$, is known. However, in choosing y_x, the farmer is assumed to know the *equilibrium* probability distribution of the pair $(\tilde{\theta}, \tilde{P})$. In other words, the farmer has rational expectations about food price, the construction of which will be made precise in a moment.

Given the fixed factor, k, choice of the input y_x is equivalent to choice of "expected output", which will be denoted by $z \equiv f(y_x, k)$. The cost of producing the "expected output" z (in terms of the numeraire) is simply the associated input level y_x; this cost will be denoted by

$$C(z) \equiv \min(y_x : f(y_x, k) \geqslant z). \tag{43}$$

By construction, $C(\ )$ is increasing ($C' > 0$) and convex ($C'' > 0$).

This development leads to stochastic farmer profits of

$$\tilde{\pi} \equiv \tilde{P}^R \tilde{\theta} z - C(z) - t, \tag{44}$$

where $\tilde{P}^R$ represents the random food price *received* by the farmer for his output, and t denotes a *fixed* (i.e., nonstochastic) government tax on the farmer. With a target price program, the target price, P^T, sets a *floor* on the price which the farmer may receive. If the realized market food price is higher than P^T, the farmer receives the market price. Otherwise, he receives P^T. Thus, $\tilde{P}^R = \max(\tilde{P}, P^T)$.

Due to his price-taking behavior, the farmer treats the probability distribution of $\tilde{P}^R$ as fixed when he makes his choice of z. The government, on the other hand, will *choose* the target price, P^T, and infer the effects of this choice on the distribution of market price, $\tilde{P}$.

The farmer is assumed to have von Neumann–Morgenstern preferences so that his utility can be represented by the function, $EU(\tilde{\pi})$, where E now denotes the expectation operator over $(\tilde{\theta}, \tilde{P})$, and $U(.)$ is a twice-differentiable ex-post utility function with $U'(\ ) > 0$ and $U''(\ ) \leqslant 0$. In the absence of production controls, the farmer will choose his "expected output" level, z, to maximize $EU(\tilde{\pi})$.

It should be noted at this point that this specification implicitly reflects an absence of contingent-claim markets. The farmer is not permitted to trade on security or insurance markets in order to augment his profit distribution. Rather, he must bear the risk implicit in the distribution of $\tilde{\pi}$ that results from his choice of z. In what follows, the consumer will also be precluded from trading in relevant contingent claims. This absence of risk-trading between farmers and consumers permits

---

[49] Throughout this section, tildes will be used to indicate random variables (e.g., $\tilde{\theta}$), while specific realizations of random variables will lack tildes (e.g., θ).

government policy to implicitly elicit trades that private agents cannot achieve on their own.[50]

Turning to the consumption side of the market, *I* assume that the economy has a fixed endowment of the numeraire good, $\overline{Y}$, which is owned by a representative consumer. This consumer has the ex-post indirect utility function $V(P, Y)$, where P is the realized market price of food, Y is the realized (ex-post) level of aggregate consumer income, and $V(.)$ is twice differentiable with $V_P < 0$, $V_Y > 0$, and $V_{YY} \leqslant 0$. His demand for food, $x^d(P, Y) \equiv -V_P(P, Y)/V_Y(P, Y)$, is downward-sloping in price. In addition, the consumer obeys the standard rationality axioms of choice under uncertainty, so that his ex-ante utility can be represented by $EV(\widetilde{P}, \widetilde{Y})$.

In the absence of taxes, Y is just the numeraire endowment, $\overline{Y}$, and is thus nonstochastic. However, the government balances its budget by levying two types of taxes. The first tax is levied on the consumer in order to pay the full ex-post costs of any target price program. The consumer's bill from this tax is stochastic since the costs of the farm program depend on food output and price realizations. The second type of tax/subsidy represents a fixed (i.e., *non*stochastic) transfer between the farmer and the consumer, namely, t. This second tax instrument permits the government to realize any distributional objectives that it may have without resort to intervention in the food market.

Given these taxes, the consumer's random income is as follows:

$$\widetilde{Y} = \overline{Y} - \left(P^T - \min\left(\widetilde{P}, P^T \right) \right) \tilde{\theta} z + t. \tag{45}$$

Since a target price program pays farmers any positive difference between P^T and P, the second term in (45) gives the governmental costs of the target price program, and t represents the government transfer from the farmer to the consumer.

It is now possible to characterize an equilibrium in the closed economy model. In doing so in the subsequent analysis, the following simplifying assumption will be made: $\tilde{\theta}$ takes one of *two* possible values, θ_1 and θ_2, with *equal* probability. The indices, $s \in \{1, 2\}$, will be used to represent the "states of nature" that elicit the corresponding θ values. Since this economy is closed and has only the one source of uncertainty (i.e., $\tilde{\theta}$), there is a one-to-one correspondence between the ex-post production level, $\theta_s z$, and the ex-post market price, P_s. Thus, associated with each "state of nature" is a pair, (θ_s, P_s). Without loss in generality, θ_1 is assumed to exceed θ_2 (i.e., farm output is higher in state 1). The latter condition implies (given downward-sloping food demand) that state 1 is the low-food-price state of nature (i.e., $P_1 < P_2$).

Now suppose that there are no production controls so that the farmer can choose his expected output level, z. Further, since a target price set below P_1 (and, hence, below

---

[50] This government capability in no way negates the informational considerations that explain a lack of contingent claim markets.

P_2) is equivalent to one set equal to P_1, it will be assumed that $P^T \geqslant P_1$ without loss in generality. The farmer's utility maximization problem can then be written as

$$\max_z .5 \left[U \left(P^T \theta_1 z - C(z) - t \right) + U \left(\max(P_2, P^T) \theta_2 z - C(z) - t \right) \right], \tag{46}$$

with first order condition (assuming an interior solution)

$$.5 \left[U_1' \left(P^T \theta_1 - C' \right) + U_2' \left(\max(P_2, P^T) \theta_2 - C' \right) \right] = 0, \tag{47}$$

where U_s' denotes the state s derivative, $U'(\pi_s)$. From Equation (47), the farmer's optimal z, z^*, is a function of the prices which the farmer receives for his output in the two states of nature, P^T and $\max(P_2, P^T)$, as well as the fixed tax t. Therefore, given rational farmer expectations, market prices are determined by the equilibrium conditions

$$x^d \left(P_s, Y_s(P^T, t) \right) \equiv -V_P \left(P_s, Y_s(P^T, t) \right) / V_Y \left(P_s, Y_s(P^T, t) \right)$$
$$= \theta_s z^* \left(P^T, \max(P_2, P^T), t \right), \quad s = 1, 2, \tag{48}$$

where, using (45), $Y_s(P^T, t) = \bar{Y} - (P^T - \min(P_s, P^T)) \theta_s z^*(P^T, \max(P_2, P^T), t) + t$.
$P_1(P^T, t)$ and $P_2(P^T, t)$ will denote the solutions to (48), which are assumed to exist and to be unique, stable (in the Walrasian sense) and differentiable at the point $P^T = P_1^{ce}$, where P_s^{ce} denotes the no-program competitive equilibrium price in state s.[51] Given these solutions, the producer's equilibrium choice of "expected output" can be represented as a function of P^T and t alone:

$$z^{**}(P^T, t) \equiv z^* \left(P^T, \max(P_2(P^T, t), P^T), t \right). \tag{49}$$

4.2. Target price intervention

For the stochastic production economy described above, the following proposition is proven in Innes (1990c):

PROPOSITION 22. *If*
   (a) *demand is price inelastic for* $P \in [P_1^{ce}, P_2^{ce}]$,
   (b) *farmers are risk averse,*
   (c) $x_Y^d(P_2^{ce}, \bar{Y}) \approx 0 \approx x_p^d(P_2^{ce}, \bar{Y})$ *(where subscripts denote partial derivatives), and*

---

[51] Walrasian stability implies that, with price responding positively to excess demand, excess demand declines (increases) as price rises (falls) from equilibrium.

(d) $\eta \equiv d\ln x^d(P, Y)/d\ln Y$ *(the consumer's income elasticity of demand) is less than* $\phi^* \equiv d\ln V_Y(P, Y)/d\ln Y$ *(the consumer index of relative risk aversion) for* $P \in [P_1^{ce}, P_2^{ce}], Y = \overline{Y}$,

then there is a positive target price, $P^T = P_o^T > P_1^{ce}$, *such that:*

  (I) *With* $t = 0$, *the farmer is worse off when* $P^T = P_o^T$ *than when* $P^T = P_1^{ce}$.
  (II) *With* $t = 0$, *the consumer is better off when* $P^T = P_o^T$ *than when* $P^T = P_1^{ce}$.
  (III) *For some* t_o, *both the consumer and producer are better off with the policy pair* $P^T = P_o^T$ *and* $t = t_o$ *than with* $P^T = P_1^{ce}$ *and* $t = 0$.

Prospective welfare benefits of a target price program (i.e., result (III)) have a rather straightforward motivation. Consider Figure 7, which depicts a pure exchange analog to our incomplete market economy. Because of the absence of contingent claim markets, the consumer and producer indifference curves are not tangent at e_0 (the competitive equilibrium) and there is a region for mutually beneficial trade. The question now

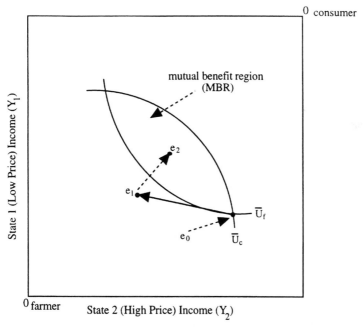

e_0 = competitive (no-program) equilibrium allocation

$\overline{U}_f$ = farmer indifference curve for the utility generated
     by allocation e_0

$\overline{U}_c$ = consumer indifference curve for the utility
     generated by allocation e_0

Figure 7. Exchange representation of incomplete markets.

is whether or not a target price/deficiency payment program can push the economy inside this "mutual benefit region" (MBR) when the program is complemented by some non-stochastic compensation, t. The following observations will help to answer this question:

(I) Suppose that there is price inelastic demand for "food" and no government intervention in the "food" market. Then the producer will have higher profits in the high price (vs. low price) state. Therefore, so long as the farmer is risk averse, the following inequality will hold: $U_2' < U_1'$. The consumer, on the other hand, will have the same income in both states, $\overline{Y}$, but will face a higher food price, and hence a lower "real" income, in state 2. With consumer risk aversion, it is to be expected that a lower "real" income will elicit a larger marginal utility of income for the consumer, V_{sy}. The following expansion formalizes this correspondence [e.g., see Newbery and Stiglitz (1982b)]:[52]

$$V_{YP}(P, Y) = (Vy/P)\alpha(\phi^* - \eta),\tag{50}$$

where α is the consumer's food expenditure share. From (50), V_{2y} will exceed V_{1y} so long as the consumer's income elasticity of demand, η, is less than his index of relative risk aversion, ϕ^*, over a relevant range of price-income pairs. Thus, given the conditions required by Proposition 22, we have the following relationship between marginal rates of substitution at the no-program equilibrium:

$$\mathrm{MRS}_{consumer} = V_{2y}/V_{1y} > U_2'/U_1' = \mathrm{MRS}_{producer}.\tag{51}$$

Equation (51) implies that the MBR is to the northwest of e_0 (as depicted in Figure 7).

(II) A target price program directly transfers income from consumers to producers in low price states of nature. In the high price states, positive supply response to the program yields higher "real" income for consumers and lower profits to producers. In terms of Figure 7, these exchanges imply a move in the northwestern direction.

In summary, target price intervention can push the economy in the same general direction as the MBR. Moreover, nonstochastic compensation leads to movement up or down a 45-degree line (such as from e_1 to e_2 in Figure 7). Therefore, with appropriate complementary compensation, movement in the same general direction as the MBR is all that is necessary to achieve a Pareto improvement. For example, Proposition 22 implies that producers can be made worse off by a target price program, implying that the post-program allocation, e_1, lies outside of the MBR. If condition (51) is satisfied, Figure 7 reveals that nonstochastic compensation can complement a target price program to push the economy inside the MBR (to e_2) even if the post-program allocation without compensation (e_1) is outside this region.

---

[52] Equation (50) is obtained by differentiating the identity, $x^d(P, Y) = -V_P(D, Y)/V_y(P, Y)$, with respect to Y.

The distributional results described in Proposition 22 also have intuitive explanations: Since a sufficiently low target price will not be effective in the high price state of nature (state 2), farmers can be made worse off by a target price program if their supply response elicits a sufficiently large drop in the state 2 output price.[53] Consumers, on the other hand, get the benefits of this state 2 price drop without having to bear any state 2 program cost; if these free benefits are large enough (and they will be with a sufficiently large price drop), they will outweigh the net consumer cost of the program in state 1.

The principal requirements of Proposition 22 – consumer and farmer risk aversion, and low price and income elasticities of demand – are well established properties of staple food markets in which target price programs have actually been employed [Innes (1990d)]. However, Proposition 22's condition (c) is arguably rather restrictive and is certainly its least plausible requirement. It states that when the food price is P_2^{ce} (i.e., the high-price-state no-program level) and consumer income is $\overline{Y}$, consumer demand is approximately invariant to small changes in price and income. When the government is permitted to limit production, the social optimality of target price intervention can be proven without this requirement.

4.3. Joint target price/production control

I now turn to the joint employment of target price and production control instruments. Under certainty, a production control is always an optimal complement to a target price program, since the former can prevent the allocational distortion (i.e., overproduction) caused by the latter. In this section's stochastic production economy, it turns out, a production control is also an optimal complement to a target price program. Intuitively, you may expect this outcome for the following reason: Under certain circumstances, a target price program yields welfare benefits by way of the interstate income transfers it produces, but at the cost of giving producers a wrong incentive price in at least one state of nature. Suppose, for example, that a target price program is used to achieve full equality between consumers' and producers' marginal rates of substitution for state-contingent incomes; that is, an optimal no-supply-response target price is chosen. In this case, the farmer has the "right" marginal utilities in his first order condition but at least one "wrong" price; in fact, the wrong price is too high and, therefore, the output choice will also be too high. Consequently, a production control will be called for.

---

[53] As observed elsewhere [e.g., Newbery and Stiglitz (1982b), Just and Zilberman (1986)], such a divergence in the directional shifts of output and producer utility is made possible by two phenomena: (i) price-taking behavior and (ii) risk aversion. Due to price-taking, farmers do not consider the adverse price effects of increased output choices in their optimization calculus. Due to risk aversion, there is a non-monotonic relationship between *marginal* utility (which governs output choices) and *total* utility.

To treat this issue formally, define z^c as the controlled level of "expected output". A welfare-maximizing government will then have the following choice problem:

$$\max_{\{t,P^T,z^c\}} W(t,P^T,z^c) = \sum_{s=1}^{2} .5\Big[U\big(\max(P^T,P_s(t,P^T,z^c))\theta_s z^c - C(z^c) - t\big)$$

$$+ \lambda V\big(P_s(t,P^T,z^c),\overline{Y}+t$$

$$- \big(P^T - \min(P^T,P_s(t,P^T,z^c))\big)\theta_s z^c\big)\Big], \quad (52)$$

where $P_s(t,P^T,z^c)$ solves

$$x^d\big(P_s,\overline{Y}+t - (P^T - \min(P^T,P_s))\theta_s z^c\big) = \theta_s z^c$$

and $\lambda \geq 0$ is an arbitrary weight. The government will maximize a weighted sum of the farmer's and consumer's expected utilities, thereby achieving an allocation which is on the economy's utility-possibility frontier. The solution to problem (52) will be denoted by $\{t_+, P_+^T, z_+^c\}$, which yields market prices $\{P_s^+\}$ and aggregate consumer incomes $\{Y_s^+\}$, $s \in \{1,2\}$.

In characterizing the solutions to problem (52), the following questions will be of interest: (1) If and when a target price program is optimal, will a production control be an optimal complement? (2) When will a target price program be optimal?

In question (1), the term "production control" refers to a government choice of z^c which restricts farm output in the sense that the farmer would prefer an expected output level which is higher than z^c. Formally, a "production control" is characterized by a level of z^c which satisfied the inequality, $z^c < z^{**}(P^T,t)$, where $z^{**}()$ corresponds to the farmer's expected output choice in the absence of controls.

To determine whether the latter inequality is satisfied with the government's optimal policy choices, we must evaluate the necessary conditions for the solutions to problem (52). In expressing these conditions, note that the government may choose P^T to be either above or below P_2. Therefore, there are two cases to consider:

Case 1: $P^T < P_2$: After some simplification (using Roy's identity),

$$\partial W/\partial z^c = E\big(U'(\max(P^T,P)\theta - C')\big) + (\theta_2 P_2/\gamma_2)(\lambda V_{2Y} - U_2')$$

$$- \lambda V_{1Y}(P^T - P_1)\theta_1 = 0, \quad (53a)$$

$$\partial W/\partial t = \big[\lambda E(V_Y) - E(U')\big] - .5(\alpha_2\eta_2/\gamma_2)(\lambda V_{2Y} - U_2') = 0, \quad (54a)$$

$$\partial W/\partial P^T = .5\theta_1 z^c(U_1' - \lambda V_{1Y}) \leq 0, = 0 \quad \text{if } P^T > P_1. \quad (55a)$$

In (53a) and (54a), α_s, η_s, and γ_s represent, respectively, the consumer's food expenditure share, income elasticity of food demand, and price elasticity of food demand, all in state s.

Case 2: $P^T > P_2$: Again using Roy's identity to simplify,

$$\partial W/\partial z^c = \mathrm{E}\big(U'(P^T\theta - C')\big) - \lambda \mathrm{E}\{V_Y(P^T - P)\theta\} = 0, \tag{53b}$$

$$\partial W/\partial t = \lambda \mathrm{E}(V_Y) - \mathrm{E}(U') = 0, \tag{54b}$$

$$\partial W/\partial P^T = \mathrm{E}\{\theta z^c(U' - \lambda V_Y)\} = 0. \tag{55b}$$

Using Equations (53)–(55), the following proposition can now be proven:

PROPOSITION 23. *A production control is optimal whenever it is optimal to set a positive target price:* If $P_+^T > P_1^+$, *then* $z_+^c < z^{**}(P_+^T, t_+)$.

To determine when the optimal target price, P_+^T, is above P_1, suppose $P_+^T = P_1(t_o, 0, z_o^c)$ with t_o and z_o^c chosen to satisfy (54a) and (53a). If the (55a) derivative is positive with these values of P^T, t, and z^c, the necessary condition given by (55a) cannot be satisfied at $P^T = P_1$ and, therefore, the solution to problem (54) must set P_+^T above P_1; given Proposition 23, the solution to problem (52) must then entail a joint target price/production control program. Following this logic, the next proposition can be proven:

PROPOSITION 24. *When the following conditions are satisfied, a joint target price/production control policy will be optimal:* (i) *farmers are everywhere risk averse, and* (ii) *for* $P \in [P_1(t_o, 0, z_o^c), P_2(t_o, 0, z_o^c)]$, $Y = \overline{Y} + t_o$, *consumer food demand is price inelastic and the consumer index of relative risk aversion,* ϕ^*, *is greater than the income elasticity of food demand,* η.

4.4. Section overview

This section has analyzed some stereotypical agricultural policy interventions in a simple closed economy model with stochastic production and no markets for contingent claims. The analysis indicates that policies which are typically viewed as income transfer mechanisms (with allocational costs) also have implications for risk-bearing. These implications, in fact, can alter the programs' distributional and welfare properties in fundamental ways.

When consumer demand is price inelastic, for example, target price intervention reduces variability in both farmer profits and consumers' "real" income. For farmers, price inelastic demand implies lower profits in the high output (low price) states of nature and it is in these states that a target price program yields farm subsidies; likewise, inelastic demand implies higher profits in the low output (high price) states and it is in these states that supply response to a target price program curtails farm revenues. Symmetrically, consumers benefit from target price intervention in the high price (and, hence, low "real" income) states and lose in the low price (high "real" income) states. Welfare benefits result from these risk reduction effects. Absent compensation, distributional effects of the Brannan Plan can also be the opposite of those that would be experienced in a non-stochastic economy: Farmers can be made worse off if the supply response to the program is sufficiently large (or the demand curve sufficiently steep) that profits fall far in those high-price states in which program subsidies do not occur. Similarly, consumers can be made better off because of the "free" price declines in those same high-price states of nature.

Notwithstanding the welfare benefits of a Brannan Plan program, farmers face an above-market price when the target price is effective; as a result, production will be higher than is constrained efficient, and a production control, in concert with a Brannan Plan, will raise economic welfare. What is more, the production control will reduce the cost to farmers, in low output (high price) states-of-nature, of the supply-response and attendant market price decline that results from a target price program; the production control can thus turn a welfare-improving policy that may harm farmers (absent compensation) to one which benefits farmers (with or without compensation).[54]

As noted at the outset, these findings are limited to some extent by the premises that underpin them. By design, this chapter has explored the effects of certain specific policy interventions in the simplest possible stochastic production model, abstracting (for example) from intertemporal income smoothing and international commodity trading, and implicitly embedding a market failure, the empirical merits of which merit close scrutiny. These limitations argue for some caution in the use, for policy prescription, of this section's specific conclusions. However, by fundamentally reversing standard "perfect markets" implications of stereotypical agricultural policies, the results presented here also argue for careful economic thinking and analysis of agricultural policy effects in light of real world risks and market imperfections.

5. Conclusion

This chapter has discussed "second-best" policies designed to correct market failures in three domains that are important in agriculture: nutrition, credit, and incomplete markets for risk. Underpinning the analytical approaches taken in the chapter is a general theme. While *primitive economic forces drive inefficiencies in markets* – inefficiencies that argue for government corrections – the nature of the market inefficiencies and *primitive difficulties in achieving government corrections* have effects on the desired structure of policy. To achieve targeted food subsidies, the government must confront primitive enforcement problems. In striving to improve efficiency in credit markets, the government is subject to the same primitive economic forces – the same informational

---

[54] In a numerical analysis that embeds empirically plausible parameter values, Innes (1990d) shows that gains in economic welfare from an optimal Brannan plan can be large relative to sectoral welfare, and that the principal effect of a complementary production control is not to raise welfare (which it does slightly) but rather to shift program benefits from consumers to producers.

imperfections – that drive free market contractual arrangements. And in improving upon incomplete markets, stereotypical government agricultural policies do not suffer from the informational problems that hinder the formation and use of complete private markets.

I stress the word "primitive" here, not only to endorse work that posits fundamental premises that are natural building blocks for economic modeling and thinking, but to contrast this type of work with analyses built upon premises that there are *inefficient outcomes* rather than *primitive phenomena that can potentially cause inefficiencies*. If we presume an inefficient outcome, on what basis can we argue that a "corrective policy" which reduces the inefficiency is "good" (in the usual economic sense of advancing economic welfare), when another policy that removes the premise – correcting the presumed inefficiency – may be available? Only if the premise can be *explained by primitive phenomena* can we understand the constraint structure in which policies are designed and make positive statements about the merits of alternative courses of action.

Two examples may help to illustrate this distinction. It has been argued in agricultural policy debates that the governmental and welfare costs of commodity programs may be reduced by additional government subsidies. For instance, Sumner (1995) describes (but does not endorse) arguments that agricultural export subsidies may reduce the government costs of farm support programs by taking product off of the domestic market, thereby raising domestic market prices and reducing the government payments required to support given price targets. The deadweight economic costs of these support programs may also be reduced by export subsidies, it is argued, if the resulting market price increases prevent the government from implementing acreage set-asides that come into play when market prices are sufficiently low. Acreage set asides directly restrict an input in agricultural production, land, and have attendant costs in reducing production efficiency. A similar case has been made for ethanol subsidies that increase the demand for domestic corn and thereby, it is claimed, reduce costs of government feed grain programs. While the objective merits of these arguments are suspect, the arguments are also built upon a premise of an inefficient policy outcome; without an internal explanation for the inefficiency, what logical foundation is there for any economic advice other than removal of the offending policy (in this case, the acreage set-asides)?

A second (more subtle) example is analyses of credit market imperfections in which the form of the financial contract is assumed, but cannot be explained by primitive phenomena that are internally consistent with the analyses. For instance, Stiglitz and Weiss (1981), Gale (1990), Mankiw (1986) and others assume that standard debt instruments are used by lenders/investors in models that, were financial contracts endogenous, would produce equity contracts. With debt contracts, inefficient market equilibria arise; with equity contracts, however, the inefficiencies are corrected.

The strength of second-best modeling rests on the merits of its building blocks – the posited primitive phenomena that cause market inefficiencies. Only when the underlying premises are internally consistent can the resulting logical arguments be persuasive.

Acknowledgments

I owe thanks to Bruce Gardner, Glynis Gawn, Gordon Rausser, and an anonymous referee for very helpful comments on an earlier draft of this chapter.

Appendix A

A.1. Section 2 propositions

PROOF OF PROPOSITION 1. Without targeted subsidies – and the possibility of a uniform price subsidy – a constrained Pareto optimum is characterized by the solution to problem (2) subject to two additional constraints that the rich and poor, respectively, satisfy their private optimality condition for choice of food consumption:

$$\text{MRS}_R = P_E - s, \tag{A.1a}$$

$$\text{MRS}_Q \geqslant P_E - s, \tag{A.1b}$$

where $s =$ price subsidy and, for analytical reasons (and without loss of generality), I state a (weaker) inequality version of the poor person's constraint. Denoting the Lagrange multipliers for constraints (A.1a), (A.1b), (2a), and (2b) by λ_R, λ_Q, ϕ_Q, and ϕ_B, respectively, the Lagrangian function for this constrained Paretian problem is

$$\begin{aligned} L(\ ) &= U_R(x_R, y_R, x_Q) + \phi_Q(U_Q(x_Q, y_Q) - \overline{U}_Q) \\ &\quad + \phi_B\big(Y + P_E X_E - C(n_R x_R + n_Q x_Q + X_E) - n_R y_R - n_Q y_Q\big) \\ &\quad + \lambda_R\big(\text{MRS}_R - (P_E - s)\big) + \lambda_Q\big(\text{MRS}_Q - (P_E - s)\big). \end{aligned} \tag{A.2}$$

To prove the proposition, it suffices to show that, at a zero price subsidy, $s = 0$, the optimized value of the Lagrangian function rises with a marginal increase in the subsidy, $\partial L(\ )/\partial s > 0$. Two observations are needed to derive this result:

(1) With $s = 0$, λ_R equals zero. Differentiating (A.2) gives the following necessary conditions for an optimum:

$$\partial L(\ )/\partial x_R = \partial U_R(\ )/\partial x_R - \phi_B C'(\ )n_R - \lambda_R(\partial \text{MSR}_R/\partial x_R) = 0, \tag{A.3a}$$

$$\partial L(\ )/\partial y_R = \partial U_R(\ )/\partial y_R - \phi_B n_R - \lambda_R(\partial \text{MSR}_R/\partial y_R) = 0. \tag{A.3b}$$

Dividing (A.3a) by (A.3b), substituting for $C'(\ ) = P_E$, and using (A.1a), we have:

$$\text{MSR}_R = \frac{\phi_B P_E n_R + \lambda_R(\partial \text{MSR}_R/\partial x_R)}{\phi_B n_R + \lambda_R(\partial \text{MSR}_R/\partial y_R)} = P_E. \tag{A.4}$$

Multiplying through Equation (A.4) by the middle denominator and simplifying gives

$$\lambda_R \{(\partial \text{MSR}_R / \partial x_R) - P_E(\partial \text{MSR}_R / \partial y_R)\} = 0. \tag{A.4$'$}$$

The bracketed term in (A.4$'$), after substituting from (A.1a), is seen to be the change in the slope of R's indifference curve as x_R is increased:

$$(\partial \text{MSR}_R / \partial x_R) - \text{MSR}_R(\partial \text{MSR}_R / \partial y_R) = \left. \frac{d\text{MSR}_R}{dx_R} \right|_{\text{IC}_R} > 0. \tag{A.5}$$

Together, (A.4$'$) and (A.5) imply that $\lambda_R = 0$, as claimed.

(2) With $s = 0$, λ_Q is positive. Because (A.1b) is an inequality constraint, the Kuhn–Tucker Conditions (KTC) imply that λ_Q is non-negative. Moreover, if λ_Q were zero, then (given Observation (1)) the KTC for an optimum would be identical to those that characterize the solution to the unconstrained Paretian problem (2). But one of those conditions, Equation (3) (together with the production optimality requirement, $C'(\ ) = P_E$), implies that constraint (A.1b) is violated, contradicting the premise that λ_Q is zero.

From Observation (2), constraint (A.1b) binds (as do (2a) and (2b)). Together, Observations (1) and (2) thus yield

$$\partial L(\ ) / \partial s = \lambda_Q + \lambda_R > 0,$$

which completes the proof. □

PROOF OF PROPOSITION 2. It suffices to prove the first statement of the proposition, from which the second follows directly. To this end, consider each of the two enforcement problems:

(1) *Costs of deterring fraud.* To establish inequality (6) – and hence, that costs of deterring fraud are higher under a targeted price subsidy regime – it suffices to show that the rich person's optimal consumption bundle under the voucher policy, (x_R^v, y_R^v), is feasible under the price-subsidy policy, but not chosen; then the utility of the rich person's chosen (optimal) consumption bundle, $V_R(P_E - s, I_R)$, must be greater than the utility of the unchosen bundle, $U_R(x_R^v, y_R^v) = V_R(P_E, I_R + S)$. Feasibility of (x_R^v, y_R^v) follows from:

Cost of (x_R^v, y_R^v) under the price-subsidy policy

$$= (P_E - s)x_R^v + y_R^v = (P_E x_R^v + y_R^v) - sx_R^v$$
$$= (I_R + sx_v) - sx_R^v = I_R + s(x_v - x_R^v) \leqslant I_R. \tag{A.6}$$

The second equality in (A.6) follows from satisfaction of the (voucher-program) budget constraint, with the voucher subsidy $S = sx_v$; the final inequality follows from $x_v \leqslant x_R^v$ (see note 9). If the inequality in (A.8) is strict (i.e., $x_v < x_R^v$), then (6) follows immediately from the above argument (because the price subsidy policy permits consumption of $(x^v_R, y^v_R + d)$, $d > 0$). If (A.6) is satisfied with equality (i.e., $x_v = x^v_R$), then by concavity of U_R, (x^v_R, y^v_R) will not be chosen under the price subsidy policy even though it is feasible; again, (6) is implied.

(2) *Costs of deterring a black-market.* Under a price subsidy policy, the rich and poor gain the following expected benefit from a black-market trade at price P_v.

$$G^s_R(q_R, P_v; s) = (1 - q_R)V_R(P_E - s, I_R - P_v)$$
$$+ q_R V_R(P_E, I_R - f_R) - V_R(P_E, I_R), \tag{A.7a}$$
$$G^s_Q(q_Q, P_v; s) = (1 - q_Q)V_Q(P_E, I_Q + P_v)$$
$$+ q_Q V_Q(P_E, I_Q - f_Q) - V_Q(P_E - s, I_Q). \tag{A.7b}$$

Now note that, for any given q_Q and P_v, $G^s_Q() = G_Q()$ (as defined in (10b)) for the equivalent voucher program (with $S = sx_v$ and x_v equal to the food demand by the poor under the price subsidy program). However, from inequality (6) (with $I'_R = I_R - P_v$ taking the place of I_R), we have

$$V_R(P_E - s, I'_R) > V_R(P_E, I'_R + S).$$

Hence, comparing $G^s_R()$ in (A.7a) to $G_R()$ in (10a), we see that $G^s_R() > G_R()$ for a given (q_R, P_v) pair and the equivalent voucher program.

Under a price subsidy policy, an efficient black-market deterrence strategy, (q^*_R, q^*_Q), will solve the analog to problem (11),

$$\min e_2(q_R, q_Q) \quad \text{s.t. } G^s_R(q_R, P_v; s) = 0 \quad \text{and} \quad G^s_Q(q_Q, P_v; s) = 0.$$

Now consider moving to the equivalent voucher program, preserving $q_Q = q^*_Q$. Because $G_R() < G^s_R() = 0$, the voucher policy permits a reduction in q_R below q^*_R (thus raising $G_R()$) that preserves black-market deterrence, $G_R() \leq 0$ and $G_Q() \leq 0$, and thereby lowers black-market enforcement costs. $\qquad\square$

PROOF OF PROPOSITION 4. (a) follows directly from (13), (14a), and $x_v > x^*_Q(P_E, I_Q + S)$. To establish (b), note that (with $s = 0$)

$$V_{QI}(P_E - s, I_Q + P_v)$$
$$= U_{Qy}\big(x^*_Q(P_E, I_Q + P_v), I_Q + P_v - P_E x^*_Q(P_E, I_Q + P_v)\big). \tag{A.8}$$

Moreover, note the following:

CLAIM.
  (i) $x_v > x^*_Q(P_E, I_Q + P_v)$,
  (ii) $I_Q + P_v - P_E x^*_Q(P_E, I_Q + P_v) > I_Q - P_E x_v + S$.

PROOF OF CLAIM. First suppose that inequality (i) is violated, $x_Q^*(P_E, I_Q + P_v) \geqslant x_v$. Then, with $P_v < S$ (by $G_R(\ ) = 0$ in (12) and the definition of $G_R(\ )$ in (10a)), we have

$$V_Q(P_E, I_Q + P_v) = U_Q(x_Q^*, I_Q + P_v - P_E x_Q^*)$$
$$< U_Q(x_Q^*, I_Q + S - P_E x_Q^*)$$
$$\leqslant U_Q(x_v, I_Q + S - P_E x_v), \qquad (A.9)$$

where $x_Q^* = x_Q^*(P_E, I_Q + P_v)$; the first inequality is due to $P_v < S$; and the second inequality is due to the following revealed preference: Given that $x_Q^* \geqslant x_v$, a voucher recipient who does not sell the vouchers can consume the food quantity x_Q^* and enjoy the full monetary value of the vouchers (S); however, with $x_v > x_Q^*(P_E, I_Q + S)$ (by premise), the voucher recipient chooses instead to consume the food quantity x_v. (A.9) implies that $G_Q(\ ) < 0$, violating condition (12) and establishing the desired contradiction.

Given inequality (i), inequality (ii) now follows directly from $G_Q(\ ) = 0$ (Equation (12)). (If (ii) were violated, $G_Q(\ )$ in (10b) is negative.) □

With $U_{Qyx} \geqslant 0$ and $U_{Qyy} < 0$, the claim implies

$$U_{Qy}(x_Q^*(\ ), I_Q + P_v - P_E x_Q^*(\ )) < U_{Qy}(x_v, I_Q - P_E x_v + S). \qquad (A.10)$$

Proposition 4(b) now follows directly from Equations (A.8), (A.10), (13), and (14b). □

A.2. *Section 3 propositions*

PROOF OF PROPOSITION 6. See Gale and Hellwig (1985, Proposition 4). □

Define $I_J^*(\varepsilon^*; \rho) = \operatorname{argmax} J(I, \varepsilon^*; \rho)$ and $I_G^*(\varepsilon^*; \rho) = \operatorname{argmax} G(I, \varepsilon^*; \rho)$.

PROPOSITION 7'. $\hat{I} < I_J^*(\varepsilon^*; \rho) \leqslant I^*$ if $\hat{\varepsilon}^* < \bar{\varepsilon}$.

PROOF OF PROPOSITION 7'. It is useful first to define $I_J^*(\varepsilon^*; \rho) = \operatorname{argmax} J(I, \varepsilon^*; \rho)$ and $I_G^*(\varepsilon^*; \rho) = \operatorname{argmax} G(I, \varepsilon^*; \rho)$, and to establish the following preliminary results:

LEMMA.
   (i) $I_J^*(0; \rho) = I^*$ and $I_J^*(\varepsilon^*; \rho)$ is non-increasing in ε^*;
   (ii) $I_G^*(\varepsilon^*; \rho) < I_J^*(\varepsilon^*; \rho)$ for all $\varepsilon^* < \bar{\varepsilon}$; and
   (iii) $\hat{I} \in [I_G^*(\varepsilon^*; \rho), I_J^*(\varepsilon^*; \rho)]$.

PROOF OF LEMMA. (i) follows from the definition and implicit differentiation of the I_J^* function. (ii) follows from (a) concavity of G and J in I and (b) comparison of the first order necessary conditions (FONC) that characterize I_G^* and I_J^* ($G_I = 0$ and $J_I = 0$, respectively). To establish (iii), consider the FONC for $\hat{I}$, Equation (A.11) below with $\lambda \geqslant 0$. If $\hat{I} < I_G^*$, then the derivative in (A.11) is positive by result (ii) and concavity of G and J. Similarly, if $\hat{I} > I_J^*$, then the derivative in (A.11) is negative.   □

The first order conditions for problem (26) are

$$J_I + \lambda G_I = 0, \tag{A.11}$$

$$J_{\varepsilon^*} + \lambda G_{\varepsilon^*} = 0, \tag{A.12}$$

with $\lambda \geqslant 0$. From (ii) of the lemma, (A.11) will be satisfied at $\hat{I} = I_J^*(\hat{\varepsilon}^*; \rho)$ if and only if $\lambda = 0$. But (A.12) cannot be satisfied if $\lambda = 0$ since $J_{\varepsilon^*} < 0$. The first inequality now follows from the lemma, part (iii), and the second from the lemma, part (i).   □

PROOF OF PROPOSITION 8. Drawing on Proposition $7'$, there are two cases to consider:
  (1) $\hat{I}(\rho - s) \leqslant \hat{I}(\rho)$, and
  (2) $\hat{I}(\rho) < \hat{I}(\rho - s) \leqslant I_J^*(\hat{\varepsilon}^*(\rho); \rho)$.
In case (1), the inequality $\hat{\varepsilon}^*(\rho - s) \leqslant \hat{\varepsilon}^*(\rho)$ holds by construction and is strict if $\hat{I}(\rho - s) = \hat{I}(\rho)$. Further, by optimality of $(\hat{I}(\rho - s), \hat{\varepsilon}^*(\rho - s)) \neq (\hat{I}(\rho), \hat{\varepsilon}^*(\rho))$ and feasibility of $(\hat{I}(\rho), \hat{\varepsilon}^*(\rho))$ under subsidized interest rates, we have

$$J\big(\hat{I}(\rho - s), \hat{\varepsilon}^*(\rho - s); \rho - s\big) > J\big(\hat{I}(\rho), \hat{\varepsilon}^*(\rho); \rho - s\big), \tag{A.13}$$

which implies

$$J\big(\hat{I}(\rho - s), \hat{\varepsilon}^*(\rho - s); \rho\big) > J\big(\hat{I}(\rho), \hat{\varepsilon}^*(\rho); \rho\big) + s\big(\hat{I}(\rho) - \hat{I}(\rho - s)\big)$$
$$\geqslant J\big(\hat{I}(\rho), \hat{\varepsilon}^*(\rho); \rho\big), \tag{A.13$'$}$$

with the second inequality following from the construction of case (1). (A.13$'$) gives the inequality required for the proposition. In case (2), $J_{\varepsilon^*} < 0$, $J_I(I, \hat{\varepsilon}^*(\rho); \rho) > 0$ for $I \in [\hat{I}(\rho), I_J^*(\hat{\varepsilon}^*(\rho); \rho)]$, and $\hat{\varepsilon}^*(\rho) \geqslant \hat{\varepsilon}^*(\rho - s)$ imply

$$J\big(\hat{I}(\rho - s), \hat{\varepsilon}^*(\rho - s); \rho\big) \geqslant J\big(\hat{I}(\rho - s), \hat{\varepsilon}^*(\rho); \rho\big) > J\big(\hat{I}(\rho), \hat{\varepsilon}^*(\rho); \rho\big). \tag{A.14}$$

Inequality (A.14) completes the proof.   □

PROOF OF PROPOSITION 9. Let $(\hat{I}_s, \hat{\varepsilon}_s^*)$ denote the entrepreneur's optimal choices with the subsidy policy. Again there are two cases to consider: (1) $\hat{I}_s > \bar{I}$, and (2) $\hat{I}_s \leqslant \bar{I}$. If $\hat{I}_s > \bar{I}$, then $(\hat{I}_s, \hat{\varepsilon}_s^*)$ solves

$$\max_{I, \varepsilon^*} J(I, \varepsilon^*; \rho) + s\bar{I} \quad \text{s.t. } G(I, \varepsilon^*; \rho) + s\bar{I} \geqslant 0. \tag{A.15}$$

By revealed preference, the solution to (A.15) yields $J(\hat{I}_s, \hat{\varepsilon}_s^*; \rho) > J(\hat{I}(\rho), \hat{\varepsilon}^*(\rho); \rho)$. If $\hat{I}_s \leqslant \bar{I}$ then by the construction of $\bar{I}$, $\hat{\varepsilon}_s^* \leqslant \hat{\varepsilon}^*(\rho)$ and the proof of Proposition 8 applies. $\qquad\square$

PROOF OF PROPOSITIONS 13–14. See Innes (1993a).

PROOF OF PROPOSITION 15. The F.O.C. defining $\hat{I}$ is

$$\frac{dV^*(I, \hat{e}(I))}{dI} = \frac{\partial V^*()}{\partial I} + \frac{\partial V^*()}{\partial e}\frac{d\hat{e}(I)}{dI} = 0.$$

From Proposition 13, $\partial V^*(I, \hat{e}(I))/\partial e > 0$. Therefore, the proposition follows from concavity of $V^*()$ in I and $\partial V^*()/\partial I = 0$ at $I^*(\hat{e})$. $\qquad\square$

PROOF OF PROPOSITION 16. The proposition is proven for the case of substitutable inputs. Results for complementary inputs follow directly from the mathematics presented in this proof. $\hat{e}(I)$ solves the following F.O.C. (after integration and simplification):

$$-\int_P P \int_{\bar{y}(P,I)}^\infty G_e(y \mid I, e, P)\,dy\,h(P)\,dP - v'(e) = 0. \tag{A.16}$$

Differentiating, we obtain:

$$\frac{d\hat{e}(I)}{dI} \overset{S}{=} -\int_P P \int_{\bar{y}(P,I)}^\infty G_{eI}(y \mid I, e, P)\,dy\,h(P)\,dP$$

$$+ \int_P P G_e(\bar{y}(P, I) \mid I, e, P)\frac{\partial \bar{y}(P, I)}{\partial I}h(P)\,dP. \tag{A.17}$$

By substitutability of (I, e), the first term in (A.17) is negative. Further, using the optimality condition for choice of $\bar{y}()$ [see Innes (1993a)], the second term in (A.17) can be written as follows:

$$\int_P P G_e(\bar{y}() \mid \cdot)\frac{\partial \bar{y}()}{\partial I}h()\,dP$$

$$= -\lambda^* \int_P P(1 - G(\bar{y}() \mid \cdot))\frac{\partial \bar{y}()}{\partial I}h(P)\,dP$$

$$= -\lambda^* E\left\{\frac{\partial B^*(\bar{y}())}{\partial \bar{y}}\frac{\partial \bar{y}^P()}{\partial I}\bigg| I, e\right\}. \tag{A.18}$$

Now note that, drawing on Propositions 13–14, the entrepreneurs' choice problem can be written as

$$\max_{I,e} \mathrm{E}\{Py \mid I, e\} - \mathrm{E}\{B^*(\bar{y}(P, I)) \mid I, e\} - v(e). \tag{A.19}$$

Thus, since $\lambda^* > 0$, if the expression in (A.18) were nonnegative, the entrepreneur would raise the value of the objective function in (A.19) by increasing I and, hence, I could not be at its optimal level. Therefore, at the optimum (i.e., at the solution to (A.19)), the expression in (A.18) is negative. □

PROOF OF PROPOSITION 17. (a) It first must be shown that $\phi(I, e^*(I))$ is increasing in I, or equivalently, that

$$-\left\{ \phi_{ee}() - \phi_{Ie}() \cdot \frac{\phi_e()}{\phi_I()} \right\} + \left[(v''(e)/\mathrm{E}(PF_\phi())] > 0. \tag{A.20}$$

The inequality in (A.20) follows from $v''(\ ) \geqslant 0$, $F_\phi > 0$, and a declining marginal product of I along the isoquants for $\phi(\ )$. Now note from Proposition 13 that $\hat{e} < e^*(\hat{I})$. Therefore, $\phi(\hat{I}, \hat{e}) < \phi(\hat{I}, e^*(\hat{I})) \leqslant \phi(I^*, e^*(I^*))$ when $\hat{I} \leqslant I^*$.

(b) Fixing the market output index y_E in the background, let $C(y)$ and $C^*(y)$ denote the "moral-hazard-constrained" and "first-best" cost functions defined in Equations (36) and (38), respectively. Further, let $(\hat{e}_c(y), \hat{I}_c(y))$ and $(e_c^*(y), I_c^*(y))$ denote solutions to the associated cost minimization problems, and let $I_o(e, y)$ solve $\phi(I, e) = y$.

CLAIM. *Either* $\hat{y} = \phi(\hat{I}, \hat{e}) < \phi(I^*, e^*) = y^*$ *or* $e_c^*(\hat{y}) > \hat{e}$.

PROOF OF CLAIM. Suppose the claim is false, so that $e_c^*(\hat{y}) \leqslant \hat{e}$ and $\hat{y} \geqslant y^*$. Then, because $e_c^*(\hat{y})$ satisfies the constraints in problem (36), $C(\hat{y}) = C^*(\hat{y})$. Therefore, since $C(y) \geqslant C^*(y)$ everywhere, $C'(\hat{y}) \geqslant C^{*\prime}(\hat{y})$, implying that $\hat{y} \leqslant y^*$. Further, since $\hat{y} \geqslant y^*$ by supposition, $\hat{y} = y^*$ and, since $C(\hat{y}) = C^*(\hat{y})$, $\hat{e} = e^*$ and $\hat{I} = I^*$. But, using Proposition 13, $\hat{e} < e^*(\hat{I}) = e^*(I^*) = e^* = e_c^*(y^*) = e_c^*(\hat{y})$, contradicting the supposition that $\hat{e} \geqslant e_c^*(\hat{y})$. □

Now suppose Proposition 17(b) is false, $\hat{y} \geqslant y^*$ and $d\hat{e}(\hat{I})/dI \leqslant 0$. To derive a contradiction, it suffices to show that $C'(\hat{y}) > C^{*\prime}(\hat{y})$, where the two cost functions are related as follows:

$$C(y) = C^*(y) - \int_{\hat{e}_c(y)}^{e_c^*(y)} \left[(1 + \rho) \frac{\partial I_o(e, y)}{\partial e} + v'(e) \right] de. \tag{A.21}$$

Using the F.O.C. from the cost minimization in problem (38) to eliminate a term, (A.21) can be differentiated to yield:

$$C'(y) = C^{*\prime}(y) + \frac{d\hat{e}_c(y)}{dy} \cdot \left[(1+\rho) \frac{\partial I_o(\hat{e}_c(y), y)}{\partial e} + v'(\hat{e}_c(y)) \right]$$

$$- \int_{\hat{e}_c(y)}^{e_c^*(y)} (1+\rho) \frac{\partial^2 I_o(e, y)}{\partial e \partial y} \, de. \qquad (A.22)$$

Now note the following:

(i) $d\hat{I}_c(\hat{y})/dy = (\phi_I + \phi_e \cdot (d\hat{e}(\,)/dI))^{-1} > 0$; if not, investment could be lowered, output raised, and the entrepreneur made better off, contradicting the definition of $\hat{y}$ as the solution to problem (37).

(ii) $\hat{e}_c(y) = \hat{e}(\hat{I}_c(y))$ and $\hat{I}_c(y)$ solves $\phi(I, \hat{e}(I)) = y$; hence, $d\hat{e}_c(\hat{y})/dy = (d\hat{e}(\hat{I})/dI) \cdot (d\hat{I}_c(\hat{y})/dy) \leqslant 0$, where the inequality follows from $d\hat{e}(\hat{I})/dI \leqslant 0$ and the inequality in (i).

(iii) From the above claim and $\hat{y} \geqslant y^*$, $e_c^*(\hat{y}) > \hat{e}_c(\hat{y}) = \hat{e}$. Therefore, drawing upon the definition of $e_c^*(y)$, the bracketed term in (A.22), $[(1+\rho)\partial I_o(\,)/\partial e + v'(\,)]$, is negative.

(iv) Finally, due to declining marginal products along isoquants,

$$\partial^2 I_o(e, y)/\partial e \partial y = \frac{\partial}{\partial I} \left(\frac{-\phi_e(I_o(\,), e)}{\phi_I(I_o(\,), e)} \right) \cdot \frac{\partial I_o(e, y)}{\partial y} < 0;$$

hence, $\hat{e}_c(\hat{y}) < e_c^*(\hat{y})$ implies that the third right-hand expression in (A.22) is positive.

Thus, we have $C'(\hat{y}) > C^{*\prime}(\hat{y})$, the desired contradiction. ☐

PROOF OF PROPOSITION 18. From (i), the policy enlarges the opportunity set for problem (33). Therefore, from condition (ii), Proposition 13, and by revealed preference, the policy elicits a higher value of the objective function in (33). ☐

PROOF OF PROPOSITION 19. (i) The F.O.C. defining $\hat{e}(I; y_E)$ (recalling note 42) is

$$- \int_\theta P(y_E, \theta) \int_{\bar{y}(\theta, y_E, I)}^\infty G_e(y; I, e, \theta) \, dy \, q(\theta) \, d\theta - v'(e) = 0. \qquad (A.23)$$

Differentiating and appealing to the second order condition,

$$\frac{\partial \hat{e}(I; y_E)}{\partial y_E} \overset{s}{=} - \int_\theta (\partial P(\,)/\partial y_E) \int_{\bar{y}(\,)}^\infty G_e(\,) \, dy \, q(\theta) \, d\theta$$

$$+ \int_\theta P(\,)G_e(\bar{y}(\,); .)(d\bar{y}(\,)/dy_E) q(\theta) \, d\theta. \qquad (A.24)$$

With $\partial P(\ )/\partial y_E < 0$ and $G_e(\ ) > 0$, the first term in (A.24) is negative. The second term can be rewritten using the optimality condition for choice of $\bar{y}(\ )$ as follows (recalling note 42):

$$-\lambda^* \int_\theta P(\ )\big(1 - G(\bar{y}(\ ); .)\big)\big(d\bar{y}(\ )/dy_E\big)q(\theta)\,d\theta, \tag{A.25}$$

where $\lambda^* > 0$. Finally, noting that $dE\{B^*(P(\ ), y, \bar{y}(\ ); I, e, y_E)\}/dy_E = 0$ in order to preserve investor expected returns, we have

$$\int_\theta P(\ )\big(1 - G(\bar{y}(\ ); .)\big)\big(d\bar{y}(\ )/dy_E\big)q(\theta)\,d\theta$$

$$= -\int_\theta \big(\partial P(\ )/\partial y_E\big)\left[\big(1 - G(\bar{y}(\ ); .)\big)\bar{y} + \int_0^{\bar{y}(\ )} yg(\ )\,dy\right]q(\theta)\,d\theta > 0. \tag{A.26}$$

(A.25) and (A.26) together imply that the second term in (A.24) is also negative, completing the proof.

(ii) Let L denote the Lagrangian function for problem (36), with λ_a and λ_b denoting the Lagrange multipliers for the constraints (36a) and (36b), respectively:

$$L = \big\{(1 + \rho)I + v(e)\big\} + \lambda_a\big(y - \phi(I, e)\big) + \lambda_b\big(e - \hat{e}(I; y_E)\big).$$

With (36b) strictly binding (by Proposition 13 and our premise that positive borrowing occurs in equilibrium), λ_b is strictly positive at the optimum. Hence, differentiating L, at the cost minimum, gives

$$\partial L(\ )/\partial y_E = -\lambda_b\big(\partial\hat{e}(I; y_E)/\partial y_E\big) > 0,$$

where the inequality follows from $\lambda_b > 0$ and Proposition 19(i).   □

PROOF OF PROPOSITION 20. First note the following:

CLAIM. If $y_E^o < y_E^1$, then $y^*(y_E^o) > y^*(y_E^1)$.

PROOF OF CLAIM. From the definition of $y^*(\ )$ in (38), the claim follows if $\partial^2 R(\hat{y}; y_E)/\partial\hat{y}\partial y_E < 0$. Expanding this derivative (using the definition of $R(\ )$ in Equation (35)) gives the desired inequality:

$$\partial^2 R(\hat{y}; y_E)/\partial\hat{y}\,\partial y_E = \int_\theta \big(\partial P(\ )/\partial y_E\big)\big[\partial E(y; \hat{y}, \theta)/\partial\hat{y}\big]q(\theta)\,d\theta < 0. \qquad □$$

Now suppose the proposition is false, $\hat{y}^* \geqslant y^{**}$. Then, from the claim, $y^*(\hat{y}^*) \leqslant y^*(y^{**})$. Further, from Proposition 17, $\hat{y}^*(\hat{y}^*) < y^*(\hat{y}^*)$, implying that $\hat{y}^*(\hat{y}^*) = \hat{y}^* < y^*(y^{**}) = y^{**}$, a contradiction.   □

A.3. Section 4 propositions

PROOF OF PROPOSITION 23. By construction, (53)–(55) ((a) or (b)) are satisfied with equality at $\{t_+, P_+^T, z_+^c\}$. Now note that the first term in (53a) and (53b) is the partial derivative of farmer expected utility with respect to expected output; if positive, production z^c is less than the farmer would choose in the absence of a control. Hence, a sufficient condition for $z_+^c < z^{**}(P_+^T, t_+)$ is that the other terms in (53) be negative at the optimum. For Case 2 (Equation (53b)), the second term is clearly negative (since $P_+^T > P_2^+ > P_1^+$ for this case). For Case 1 (Equation (53a)), the third term is negative (since $P_+^T > P_1^+$ by assumption). To sign the second term, substitute the equality version of (55a) into (54a), yielding:

$$.5\big(1 - (\alpha_2\eta_2/\gamma_2)\big)\big(\lambda V_{2Y} - U_2'\big) = 0. \tag{54a'}$$

Now note the following:

$$\big(1 - (\alpha\eta/\gamma)\big) = \gamma^H/\gamma > 0, \tag{A.27}$$

where γ^H denotes the own-price elasticity of the compensated (Hicksian) demand for food, which is positive from consumer theory. Thus, from (54a') and (A.27), the second term of (53a) is zero, completing the proof. □

PROOF OF PROPOSITION 24. Due to Proposition 23, it only needs to be shown that, with conditions (i)–(ii), the derivative in (55a) is positive at $\{t_o, P^T = P_1(t_o, 0, z_o^c), z_o^c\}$. To evaluate this derivative, substitute for l from (54a) and rewrite:

$$
\begin{aligned}
\partial W/\partial P^T = {}& \big(.5\theta_1 z^c\big)\big(.5U_1' + .5U_2'(1 - \alpha_2\eta_2/\gamma_2)\big) \\
& \cdot \big\{\big[U_1'/(.5U_1' + .5U_2'(1 - \alpha_2\eta_2/\gamma_2))\big] \\
& \quad - \big[V_{1Y}/(.5V_{1Y} + .5V_{2Y}(1 - \alpha_2\eta_2/\gamma_2))\big]\big\}.
\end{aligned}
\tag{55a'}
$$

Given the inequality in (A.27), the sign of (55a') is determined by the bracketed difference. Further, price inelastic demand ((ii)) implies that farmer profits are higher in state 2 when $P^T = P_1$. Thus, given (i), $U_1' > U_2'$. Further, from Equation (5), $\phi^* > \eta$ implies that $V_{YP} > 0$, which, with $P^T = P_1$, yields the inequality $V_{1Y} < V_{2Y}$. Using Equation (A.27), $U_1' > U_2'$, and $V_{1Y} < V_{2Y}$, we obtain:

$$
\begin{aligned}
& U_1'/\big(.5U_1' + .5U_2'(1 - \alpha_2\eta_2/\gamma_2)\big) \\
& \quad > U_1'/\big(.5U_1' + .5U_1'(1 - \alpha_2\eta_2/\gamma_2)\big) = 1/(1 - .5\alpha_2\eta_2/\gamma_2), \tag{A.28a} \\
& V_{1Y}/\big(.5V_{1Y} + .5V_{2Y}(1 - \alpha_2\eta_2/\gamma_2)\big) \\
& \quad < V_{1Y}/\big(.5V_{1Y} + .5V_{1Y}(1 - \alpha_2\eta_2/\gamma_2)\big) = 1/(1 - .5\alpha_2\eta_2/\gamma_2). \tag{A.28b}
\end{aligned}
$$

With (A.27), (A.28) implies that the derivative in (55a$'$) is positive at $P^T = P_1(t_o, 0, z_o^c)$, completing the proof. $\qquad\qquad\qquad\qquad\qquad\qquad\qquad\qquad\qquad\qquad\qquad\qquad\qquad\qquad\qquad\qquad\qquad$ □

References

Arrow, K.J. (1971), Essays in the Theory of Risk Bearing (Markham Publishing Co., Chicago).

Barry, P. (1984), Risk Management in Agriculture (Iowa State University Press, Ames).

Becker, G. (1968), "Crime and punishment: An economic approach", Journal of Political Economy 76:169–217.

Besanko, D., and A. Thakor (1987), "Collateral and rationing: Sorting equilibria in monopolistic and competitive credit markets", International Economic Review 28:671–689.

Bolton, P., and D. Scharfstein (1990), "A theory of predation based on agency problems in financial contracting", American Economic Review 80:93–106.

Borch, K. (1968), The Economics of Uncertainty (Princeton University Press, Princeton).

Brander, J., and T. Lewis (1986), "Oligopoly and financial structure: The limited liability effect", American Economic Review 76:956–970.

Brander, J., and B. Spencer (1989), "Moral hazard and limited liability: Implications for the theory of the firm", International Economic Review 30:833–849.

Butler, J., and J. Raymond (1996), "The effect of the food stamp program on nutrient intake", Economic Inquiry 34:781–798.

Campbell, R., and S. Turnovsky (1985), "An analysis of the stabilizing and welfare effects of intervention in spot and futures markets", Journal of Public Economics 28:165–209.

Chambers, R.G. (1989), "Workfare or welfare?", Journal of Public Economics 40:79–98.

Chambers, R.G. (2002), "Information incentives, and the design of agricultural policies", in: B.L. Gardner and G.C. Rausser, eds., Handbook of Agricultural Economics, Vol. 2 (Elsevier, Amsterdam) 1751–1825.

Cho, I., and D. Kreps (1987), "Signaling games and stable equilibria", Quarterly Journal of Economics 102:179–222.

Debreu, G. (1959), Theory of Value (Yale University Press, New Haven).

DeMeza, D., and C. Southey (1996), "The borrower's curse: Optimism, finance and entrepreneurship", Economic Journal 106:375–386.

DeMeza, D., and D. Webb (1987), "Too much investment: A problem of asymmetric information", Quarterly Journal of Economics 102:281–292.

DeMeza, D., and D. Webb (1988), "Credit market efficiency and tax policy in the presence of screening costs", Journal of Public Economics 36:1–22.

DeMeza, D., and D. Webb (1989), "The role of interest rate taxes in credit markets with divisible projects and asymmetric information", Journal of Public Economics 39:33–44.

Devaney, B., and R. Moffitt (1991), "Dietary effects of the food stamp program", American Journal of Agricultural Economics 73:202–211.

Diamond, D. (1984), "Financial intermediation and delegated monitoring", Review of Economic Studies 51:393–414.

Diamond, P. (1980), "Efficiency with uncertain supply", Review of Economic Studies 47:645–651.

Eswaran, M., and A. Kotwal (1989), "Why are capitalists the bosses?", Economic Journal 99:162–176.

Fullerton, D. (1991), "Reconciling recent estimates of the marginal welfare cost of taxation", American Economic Review 81:302–308.

Gale, W. (1990), "Collateral, rationing, and government intervention in credit markets", in: G. Hubbard, ed., Asymmetric Information, Corporate Finance and Investment (University of Chicago Press, Chicago) 43–61.

Gale, D., and M. Hellwig (1985), "Incentive compatible debt contracts: The one-period problem", Review of Economic Studies 52:647–664.

Gardner, B. (1983), "Redistribution through commodity markets", American Journal of Agricultural Economics 65:225–234.

Gawn, R., R. Innes, D. Zilberman and G. Rausser (1993), "Nutrient demand and the allocation of time: Evidence from Guam", Applied Economics 25:811–830.

Harris, M., and R. Townsend (1985), "Allocation mechanisms, asymmetric information and the 'Revelation principle'", in: G. Fiewal, ed., Issues in Contemporary Microeconomics and Welfare (SUNY Press, Albany).

Hart, O. (1983), "On the optimality of equilibrium when the market structure is incomplete", Journal of Economic Theory 11:418–443.

Hellwig, M. (1987), "Some recent developments in the theory of competition in markets with adverse selection", European Economic Review 31:319–325.

Helms, L.J. (1985), "Expected consumer's surplus and the welfare effects of price stabilization", International Economic Review 26:603–618.

Innes, R. (1990a), "Imperfect information and the theory of government intervention in farm credit markets", American Journal of Agricultural Economics 72:761–768.

Innes, R. (1990b), "Limited liability and incentive contracting with ex-ante action choices", Journal of Economic Theory 52:45–67.

Innes, R. (1990c), "Government target price intervention in economies with incomplete markets", Quarterly Journal of Economics 105:1035–1052.

Innes, R. (1990d), "Uncertainty, incomplete markets and government farm programs", Southern Economic Journal 57:47–65.

Innes, R. (1991), "Investment and government intervention in credit markets when there is asymmetric information", Journal of Public Economics 46:347–381.

Innes, R. (1992), "Adverse selection, investment and profit taxation", European Economic Review 36:1427–1452.

Innes, R. (1993a), "Debt, futures and options: Optimal price-linked financial contracts under moral hazard and limited liability", International Economic Review 34:271–295.

Innes, R. (1993b), "Financial contracting under risk neutrality, limited liability and ex-ante asymmetric information", Economica 60:27–40.

Innes, R., and G. Rausser (1989), "Incomplete markets and government agricultural policy", American Journal of Agricultural Economics 71:915–931.

Jewitt, I. (1988), "Justifying the first-order approach to principal-agent problems", Econometrica 56:1177–1190.

Just, R., and D. Zilberman (1986), "Does the law of supply hold under uncertainty?", Economic Journal 96:514–524.

Kaplow, L. (1997), "The optimal supply of public goods and the distortionary cost of taxation", National Tax Journal 49:513–533.

Knudsen, O., and P. Scandizzo (1982), "The demand for calories in developing countries", American Journal of Agricultural Economics 64:80–86.

Mankiw, N.G. (1986), "The allocation of credit and financial collapse", Quarterly Journal of Economics 101:229–264.

Milde, H., and J. Riley (1988), "Signaling in credit markets", Quarterly Journal of Economics 103:101–129.

Milgrom, P. (1981), "Good news and bad news: Representation theorems and applications", Bell Journal of Economics 21:380–391.

Miranda, M., and P. Helmberger (1988), "The effects of commodity price stabilization programs", American Economic Review 78:46–58.

Miyazaki, H. (1977), "The rat race and internal labor markets", Bell Journal of Economics 8:394–416.

Myers, R. (1988), "The value of ideal contingency markets in agriculture", American Journal of Agricultural Economics 70:255–267.

Myers, S. (1977), "Determinants of corporate borrowing", Journal of Financial Economics 4:147–175.

Newbery, D., and J. Stiglitz (1981), The Theory of Commodity Price Stabilization (Oxford University Press, Oxford).

Newbery, D., and J. Stiglitz (1982a), "The choice of techniques and the optimality of market equilibrium with rational expectations", Journal of Political Economy 90:222–246.

Newbery, D., and J. Stiglitz (1982b), "Risk aversion, supply response, and the optimality of random prices: A diagrammatic analysis", Quarterly Journal of Economics 97:1–26.

Olsen, E. (1971), "Some theorems in the theory of efficient transfers", Journal of Political Economy 79:166–176.

Pauly, M. (1970), "Efficiency in the provision of consumption subsidies", Kyklos 23:33–57.

Perrin, R., and G. Scobie (1981), "Market intervention policies for increasing the consumption of nutrients by low income households", American Journal of Agricultural Economics 63:73–82.

Poitevin, M. (1989), "Financial signaling and the 'Deep Pocket' argument", Rand Journal of Economics 20:26–40.

Radner, R. (1970), "Problems in the theory of markets under uncertainty", American Economic Review 60:454–460.

Ravid, S. (1988), "On the interactions of production and financial decisions", Financial Management 17:87–99.

Rodgers, J. (1973), "Distributional externalities and the optimal form of income transfers", Public Finance Quarterly 1:266–299.

Rogerson, W. (1986), "The first order approach to principal-agent problems", Econometrica 53:1357–67.

Ross, S. (1976), "Options and efficiency", Quarterly Journal of Economics 90:75–89.

Scandizzo, P., and O. Knudsen (1996), "Social supply and the evaluation of food policies", American Journal of Agricultural Economics 78:137–145.

Sexton, R.J., and N. Lavoie (2001), "Food processing and distribution: An industrial organization approach", in: B.L. Gardner and G.C. Rausser, eds., Handbook of Agricultural Economics, Vol. 1 (Elsevier, Amsterdam) 865–932.

Shavell, S. (1979), "Risk sharing and incentives in the principal and agent relationship", Bell Journal of Economics 10:55–73.

Stiglitz, J., and A. Weiss (1981), "Credit rationing in markets with imperfect information", American Economic Review 71:393–410.

Subramanian, S., and A. Deaton (1996), "The demand for food and calories", Journal of Political Economy 104:133–162.

Sumner, D. (1995), "Agricultural trade policy reform", in: D. Sumner, ed., Agricultural Policy Reform in the United States (The AEI Press, Washington, DC).

Titman, S. (1984), "The effect of capital structure on a firm's liquidation decision", Journal of Financial Economics 13:137–151.

Townsend, R. (1979), "Optimal contracts and competitive markets with costly state verification", Journal of Economic Theory 21:1–29.

Vercammen, J. (1995), "Credit bureau policy and sustainable reputation effects in credit markets", Economica 62:461–478.

Wallace, T.D. (1962), "Measures of social costs of agricultural programs", Journal of Farm Programs 44:580–594.

Webb, D. (1991), "Long term financial contracts can mitigate the adverse selection problem in project financing", International Economic Review 32:305–320.

Whitt, W. (1980), "Uniform conditional stochastic order", Journal of Applied Probability 17:112–123.

Williamson, S. (1987), "Costly monitoring, loan contracts and equilibrium credit rationing", Quarterly Journal of Economics 102:135–145.

Wilson, C. (1977), "A model of insurance markets with incomplete information", Journal of Economic Theory 16:167–87.

Wright, B. (1979), "The effects of ideal production stabilization: A welfare analysis under rational behavior", Journal of Political Economy 87:1011–1033.

Chapter 36

POLITICAL ECONOMY OF AGRICULTURAL POLICY

HARRY DE GORTER

Department of Applied Economics and Management, Cornell University, Ithaca, NY

JOHAN SWINNEN

Department of Economics, Katholieke Universiteit Leuven, Leuven, Belgium

Contents

Handbook of Agricultural Economics, Volume 2, Edited by B. Gardner and G. Rausser

Abstract

Explanations are provided for why governments do as they do in agriculture. Alternative frameworks are assessed to explain government policy including collective action and politician–voter interaction models. Several key patterns of policies are analyzed including the "developmental paradox" where the tendency for support to agriculture increases with GDP and decreases with the proportion of the population in agriculture. The chapter also assesses why governments employ inefficient policy instruments in agriculture, why there appears to be a status quo bias, and why policy is biased against trade. Particular emphasis is given on the interaction between redistributive and growth-promoting policies.

Keywords

commodity policy, collective action, politician–voter, developmental paradox, revealed preference, lobbying, instrument choice, status quo bias, trade bias, rent-seeking, public goods

JEL classification: Q18

1. Introduction

All countries implement agricultural and food policies that redistribute income (often with negative consequences for allocative efficiency) or correct market failures (inevitably also with consequences on the distribution of income). These widespread government policies in world agriculture have varied in direction, form, extent and impact [Lindert (1991)]. In terms of *direction*, it has long been recognized that farmers in industrial countries are subsidized while they are often taxed in developing countries [see Kerr (1986) and the World Bank (1986) for extensive empirical evidence].[1] Countries use many *forms* of programs such as alternative trade taxes and non-tax barriers/enhancements, and domestic subsidies/taxes and quantitative controls [World Bank (1986)]. The *extent* of intervention varies across countries and sectors [OECD (1999), World Bank (1986)], while the *impact* of government polices varies across countries and policy instruments (see Alston and James in the preceding chapter).

The active role of government in allocating resources between agriculture and the rest of the economy is undeniable. It is therefore imperative to understand why governments do what they do in agriculture. A rich literature has developed in agricultural economics on the political economy of farm policy [surveyed in several contributions including Rausser, Lichtenberg and Lattimore (1982), Carter, McCalla and Sharples (1990), Young, Marchant and McCalla (1991), Alston and Carter (1991), Swinnen and van der Zee (1993), and Binswanger and Deininger (1997)]. The purpose of this chapter is to synthesize the literature on the political economy of agricultural policy in a concise and integrated manner. We first review the extensive studies on patterns of policy interventions in Section 2, and then provide a general framework of two major alternative models (collective action and political support function approaches) in Section 3 that attempt to explain these policy patterns. We evaluate many studies that model both collective action lobby and politician (or government) behavior. The section concludes with a discussion on the politics of international trade relations as well as on the empirical studies of endogenous government (including revealed preference models). We then pose several questions on central issues in the political economy of farm policy in Section 4: Why the use of inefficient policy instruments? Why the *status quo* bias? Why is policy biased against trade? What are the conditions affecting rent-seeking? The political economy of public research expenditures in agriculture is described in Section 5 (with particular emphasis on the interaction between research and commodity policy). The final section provides some directions for future research.

2. Background on agricultural policy interventions

Central to the understanding of agricultural policy is that governments intervene to both increase social welfare (correct for market failures through research investments, for in-

---

[1] Schultz (1978) and Binswanger and Scandizzo (1983) are the first systematic studies, while Krueger, Schiff and Valdés (1988) synthesizes more recent studies.

stance) and redistribute incomes through commodity policies [Rausser (1982, 1992a)]. Significant underinvestment in research occurs in both industrial and developing country agriculture [Huffman and Evenson (1994), Ruttan (1982), Birkhaeuser, Evenson and Feder (1991)]. Protection to agriculture increases with the level of economic development (measured by the per capita GDP) and is called the "developmental paradox" [Anderson and Hayami (1986), World Bank (1986)]. This is observed in both cross-section and time series data.

There is also a protection bias for imports and against exports [Lindert (1991)]. Sectors with inelastic demands or with a small number of farms are found to have higher rates of protection. Several factors are also found to affect the level of protection in agriculture, such as the share of food in total expenditures, of agriculture in total GDP, the level of "fixed factors" in agriculture, the capital intensity of agriculture, and the level of food self-sufficiency [Anderson and Hayami (1986), Honma and Hayami (1986a, 1986b)].

Another stylized fact is that developing countries tax agriculture mostly through indirect means (e.g., overvalued exchange rates and import barriers on inputs into agriculture) versus direct means (e.g., price controls via parastatal organizations), and that sectors with comparative advantage are taxed more heavily (e.g., plantation-based export sectors vs. small-holder import-competing agriculture) [Kerr (1986) and the World Bank (1986), and later in the studies synthesized by Krueger, Schiff and Valdés (1988)]. Meanwhile, protection to manufacturing industries has declined in industrial countries but has increased in developing countries. This occurs even though large farms are found to benefit relatively more than small farms from any direct subsidies provided to agriculture in developing countries. Finally, governments everywhere typically use inefficient policy instruments (like international trade barriers) in trying to achieve their domestic policy objectives.

The stated objectives of politicians on farm policy are varied and inevitably include self-sufficiency, balance of trade (payments), farm income and employment goals, secure supplies and low prices to consumers, and stability of farm incomes, supplies, and prices [Winters (1989)]. Both entrepreneurial politicians and active lobby groups often invoke (and perpetuate) agricultural fundamentalism as their cause in encouraging farm price policies and trade interventions, especially in industrial countries, and remind citizens of past periods of hunger or supply shortfalls to push for the mercantilist self-sufficiency and "exports are good – imports are bad" decrees.

Nevertheless, governments have improved social welfare by correcting for such market failures as absence of or incomplete futures and insurance markets, and failure to attain equilibrium because of cobweb cycles and the like. These market failures have been partially corrected often as a by-product of price support and other risk insurance programs. Furthermore, governments invest in public goods (e.g., research and extension expenditures), countervail imperfect market structure in up-stream and down-stream industries (e.g., price supports and marketing orders), internalize externalities (especially in agricultural production), provide merit wants (e.g., domestic and foreign food aid), offset private versus social risk and discount rates (e.g., public information and forecasts), and provide for economies of coordination (e.g., cooperatives). However, the primary motivation for observed agricultural policy has been to *transfer income to farmers* in industrial countries [Gardner (1992)] and *provide cheap food for consumers* in developing countries [Krueger (1992)].

Central to the focus of agricultural policy has been the dramatic transformation of industrial and newly industrialized country agriculture in the past sixty years. Relative productivity of agriculture has skyrocketed, resulting in an approximate 3 percent annual reduction in the number of farms and rural population migrating to urban areas in the United States [Gardner (1993)].[2] In the meantime, agriculture became the most capital-intensive industry in industrial countries like the United States with this large decrease in agricultural employment. The total use of cropland also declined over the past sixty years. Farmers invested in purchased inputs like mechanical, chemical, and biological capital, which have been substituted for land and labor. These rapid structural adjustments occurred with significant government investments in public goods that accelerated the increase in output and hence a decline in number of farms, while improving the education and infrastructure for remaining farmers. The increase in total factor productivity of agriculture contributed to the long-term decline in agricultural prices. Indeed, in the face of inelastic demand and the "technological treadmill" [Cochrane (1965)], the relative decline in farm incomes and the ensuing hardship caused by the structural adjustment and outflow of labor was called the "farm problem" [Schultz (1953)]. The combination of growth in the non-agricultural sector and a decline in agricultural prices pulled labor from agriculture [Gopinath and Roe (1995)]. Governments have focused their attention therefore on offsetting the adverse effects of the so-called farm problem and so incomes have been central to agricultural policies.[3]

Policies have largely been ineffective because people have continued to exit farming and rural communities over the past sixty years and because most transfers were not retained in agriculture but were usurped by landowners and owners of capital. With labor mobile in the long run, returns are determined in the factor markets rather than in product markets, with benefits accruing to the incumbent farmers and not to newcomers. As in most industrial countries, a small percent of farmers now produce a majority of the output in the United States (so most of the benefits of price supports are often accruing to these larger farms). Part-time farmers with significant share of total income from off-farm sources now constitute the majority of farms. Ineffectiveness of programs is also revealed by the fact that government support was based on production and not directly on the needs of individuals (with little attention paid to education and structural

---

[2] Similar patterns have occurred in Europe and Japan and in newly industrialized countries although with different degrees and timing [see Hayami (1988) for Japan, Tracy (1989) for Europe, and Anderson and Hayami (1986) for East Asia].

[3] Although income distribution will be shown to be a major driving force of the political economy models to follow, these same models will also show that politicians have a political incentive for economic growth in providing for public goods and correcting for market failures.

adjustment programs to facilitate movement out of farming at lower costs, rather than to encourage farms to stay in production as most policies attempt to do).

Developing countries, on the other hand, have more price elastic demand curves with low consumer incomes and an increasing Engel coefficient. With low growth in agricultural production and an inelastic supply curve, these countries are faced with what has been called the "food problem". Governments therefore try to lower food prices for consumers and so tax farmers in doing so, while raising tax revenues. Much of developing agriculture too has faced a major structural adjustment as landless laborers have migrated to urban fringe areas. Developing country governments, as in industrial countries, generally have been ineffective as well in achieving their stated goals [Krueger (1992)].

2.1. Protection across countries, sectors, and over time

A large body of literature using econometric techniques has analyzed the determinants of protection to agriculture among countries, over time, and across different sectors.[4] The typical approach is to regress some measure of protection on economic and political variables, some of which are endogenous. Loose appeals to the theoretical literature are normally made. Very few successful direct tests of theory have been made, and as will be shown later, very few theories can adequately explain the empirical regularities now to be discussed.

Most studies use some measure of the rate of protection as the dependent variable for alternative commodity sectors over time and across countries. To summarize the key findings of this literature, the protection received by agriculture is hypothesized to be higher with:

- a country's per capita GDP [Lindert (1991), Alston et al. (1990), Balisacan and Roumasset (1987), Fulginiti and Shogren (1992), Beghin, Foster and Kherallah (1996), Swinnen et al. (2000), Beghin and Kherallah (1994), David and Huang (1996), López (1994), van Bastelaer (1994)];
- a smaller number of farmers [Alston et al. (1990), Swinnen et al. (2000), Sarker, Meilke and Hoy (1993), Gardner (1987), Miller (1991), de Gorter and Tsur (1991), Fulginiti and Shogren (1992), David and Huang (1996), Lindert (1991), van Bastelaer (1994)];
- a lower agricultural share of GDP [Skully (1990), Sarker, Meilke and Hoy (1993), Lindert (1991), Miller (1991), Beghin and Kherallah (1994), Fulginiti and Shogren (1992), López (1994), Swinnen et al. (2000)];[5]

---

[4] There have also been a number of case studies and descriptive anti-theoretical studies on the political economy of agricultural policies including Petit (1985), Petit et al. (1987), Moyer and Josling (1990), Orden (1994), Orden, Paarlberg and Roe (1999), Wilson (1977), Browne (1988), Rapp (1988), Michelmann, Stabler and Storey (1990), Pinstrup-Andersen (1993), and many others.

[5] Swinnen et al. (2000) and Swinnen, de Gorter and Banerjee (1999) show a positive sign on agricultural share of GDP, explained theoretically in Swinnen (1994).

- a lower share of food in total expenditures [Sarker, Meilke and Hoy (1993), Balisacan and Roumasset (1987), Fulginiti and Shogren (1992), Swinnen (1996)];
- lower farm incomes [Gardner (1987), Swinnen et al. (2000), Carter et al. (1990), de Gorter and Tsur (1991), López (1994), von Witzke and Hausner (1993), Lindert (1991)];[6]
- lower relative productivity of agriculture [Honma and Hayami (1986a), Sarker, Meilke and Hoy (1993), Fulginiti and Shogren (1992), Beghin and Kherallah (1994), van Bastelaer (1994)];[7]
- a lower factor endowment ratio in agriculture [Honma and Hayami (1986a), Sarker, Meilke and Hoy (1993), Balisican and Roumasset (1987), de Gorter and Tsur (1991), Fulginiti and Shogren (1992), David and Huang (1996)];[8]
- lower international terms of trade for agriculture [Honma and Hayami (1986a), Sarker, Meilke and Hoy (1993), Beghin, Foster and Kherallah (1996), Beghin and Kherallah (1994)];
- lower share of agriculture in trade [Fulginiti and Shogren (1992), Beghin and Kherallah (1994), Carter et al. (1990), van Bastelaer (1994)];
- importers [Gardner (1987), Lindert (1991), de Gorter and Tsur (1991), Sarker, Meilke and Hoy (1993), Alston et al. (1990), Miller (1991), Fulginiti and Shogren (1992), Swinnen et al. (2000), Carter et al. (1990), David and Huang (1996)];
- output per farm [Gardner (1987), Miller (1991)];
- geographic concentration and less geographic movement of farms [Gardner (1987), Carter et al. (1990), van Bastelaer (1994)];
- lower production growth per farm [Gardner (1987), Carter et al. (1990)];
- lower elasticities of supply or demand [Gardner (1987), Alston et al. (1990), de Gorter and Tsur (1991), Carter et al. (1990)].[9]

Several of these studies employ other variables as well, including institutional characteristics (to be explored later), regional dummies, price levels, lagged dependent variables, exchange rates, and protection in other sectors. The level of per capita GDP and farm numbers is postulated to reflect both the ease of farmers to organize and the decreasing resistance to protection as a group gets smaller because the per capita costs to the general population become smaller (and the increasing demands for protection due to per capita benefits to farmers become larger). Shares of agriculture in total GDP and food in total expenditures are also purported in general to reflect these basic phenomena. Farm incomes, agricultural productivity, factor endowments, and terms of trade all basically reflect the relative income situation for agriculture and the tendency for governments to support sectors in (relative) distress. The studies by Honma and Hayami

---

[6] De Gorter and Tsur (1991) and Carter et al. (1990) use relative incomes instead of absolute farm income levels, while López (1994) uses wage rates as an indicator.

[7] Fulginiti and Shogren (1992) use absolute level of agricultural productivity only.

[8] The last three studies use land per farm only as an indicator.

[9] Gardner (1987) uses four proxies of the lowest of supply/demand elasticities as does Alston et al. (1990) and Carter et al. (1990), while de Gorter and Tsur (1991) look at the demand elasticity only.

(1986a, 1986b) determine a strong relationship between agricultural protection in industrial countries and East Asia and the effects of economic growth, industrialization, and sectoral adjustment. Protection increases significantly with a decline in agriculture's comparative advantage (measured by the ratio of land per farmer to capital per industrial worker or the ratio of labor productivity), agriculture's share of the economy (either in labor force or GDP), and the international terms of trade of agriculture to manufactured commodities. As in many later studies, dummy variables for several institutional or political factors are also included. Honma and Hayami (1986a, 1986b) find that protection to farmers peaks when the farm population is less than 10 percent of total population, and then begins to decline after it reaches 5 percent of the population.

Gardner (1987) in a time series-cross section analysis of U.S. farm sectors found protection to be negatively related to the maximum of the supply/demand elasticity, farm numbers, geographical movement index, farm income, and the share of land in costs, while positively related to a geographical concentration index, output per farmer, and imports. It is postulated that farmers are able to organize more effectively with fewer farm numbers, less geographic movement, and more geographic concentration, thereby reducing the cost of communication and organization. Demands for protection are higher if incomes are lower, output per producer is higher, and the share of land in costs is higher. Elasticities, trade shares, trade position, and share of land in costs reflect the impact of deadweight costs on the effectiveness of farmers receiving more protection.

Skully (1990) determines a strong correlation between agricultural protection and non-agricultural share of GDP (related to a lower budget share for food, agricultural population share, and the level of economic development and market integration). Using cross country and commodity analysis as in Honma and Hayami (1986a, 1986b), Skully (1990) estimates two identical equations to explain the net policy bias and the fiscal balance (net tax or subsidy). The estimated iso-protection frontiers have net exporters subsidizing farmers when the non-agricultural proportion of GDP is greater than 80–85 percent, and net importers subsidizing farmers after non-agriculture's share of GDP is 75–80 percent (and even earlier for East Asian countries). Skully (1990) determines that the pro-farmer bias for commodity sectors is determined to be feed-grains > sugar > food-grains > milk > livestock. Feed-grains have an indirect effect on the final consumer, while milk and livestock are more direct (however, livestock farmers may be better equipped to resist protection to feed-grain producers if price supports rather than production subsidies are used).

In a very comprehensive study, Lindert (1991) confirms the correlation between agricultural protection and level of economic development and the anti-trade bias by carefully analyzing historical patterns of agricultural protection for several countries. He rejects the standard notions of protection such as the goal for food security, concerns over instability in the farm sector, sympathy for farmers as poor people, and political nostalgia for farmers. Instead, he tests a statistical model of the lobby-group model and concludes that a smaller sector size, agricultural decline (share of agriculture in GDP), lower relative farm incomes, deadweight costs, and government demand for revenue are far more important determinants of agricultural protection. Lindert (1991) concludes that sector size and income shares are related to development itself, and so regressions cannot unlock the development puzzle because so many variables are collinear with development itself. This is a problem of most empirical studies, and so will be analyzed later in the theoretical explanations for these observed patterns of agricultural protection.

However, studies using commodity-level data are less prone to collinearity problems. Swinnen, de Gorter and Banerjee (1999) include both the share of food in consumer expenditures and the share of agriculture in GDP. They find that the share of the food product in consumer expenditures has a negative impact on farm protection. A lower expenditure share means reduced opposition to increased protection. Protection increases with the share of the commodity in GDP, if one accounts for the other factors. This confirms the hypothesis that the size of the "vested interest" is positively related to protection. This result is also found by Swinnen et al. (2000) in a cross-country study on the joint determination of agricultural protection and government expenditures on public research.

2.2. Influence of political institutions

Theoretical and empirical analysis on the influence of political institutions on agricultural policy outcomes is still in its infancy. Rausser (1992b) argues that the legal, regulatory, and institutional framework has important ramifications for public policies promoting economic growth. Rausser (1992b) and Rausser and Johnson (1993) argue that sound policies cannot be sustained unless basic political and civil freedoms exist, while Ruttan (1991) argues that success in developing countries can more readily be achieved in an environment characterized by a liberal economic and political order. Bardhan (1990) argues that credible commitment of governments and enforcement of rules is equally important. The state needs to coordinate stable alliances in favor of long-run development goals, and so institutionalized networks of connections and understandings between public officials and private agents is key.

McMillan, Rausser and Johnson (1993) analyze the bi-causality problem (economic growth changes institutions or vice-versa) by decomposing annual data on growth rates into "permanent" and "transitory" components. They conclude that the economic benefits of a reform of rights are systematic and significant, and that economic benefits, in the form of increased growth, occur with a lag after the initiation of reforms in political or civil rights.[10] Mohtadi and Roe (1998) show evidence of an inverted U curve

---

[10] Levine and Renelt (1992) claim that the cross-country relationship between long-run average growth rates and almost every particular macroeconomic indicator is fragile in several empirical models, except for one robust correlation between GDP and investment. They also conclude that the relationship between institutional freedoms and economic growth is fragile. McMillan (1993), using an alternative method to deal with multicollinearity and principal components rather than the extreme bound approach, contests the latter conclusion.

with economic growth measured on the vertical axis and democracy on the horizontal axis.

Several studies have focused on the influence of political decision-making structure on patterns of agricultural policies. Beghin and Kherallah (1994) conclude that pluralistic systems are associated with higher agricultural protection levels, although in a nonlinear fashion, with further democratization partly dissipating protection to farmers. Civil liberties affect developing countries more than industrial countries. Beghin, Foster and Kherallah (1996) apply a similar approach to the international tobacco industry, and find similar robust results where the most pluralistic countries support tobacco less. Results of Swinnen et al. (2000) are consistent with Alesina and Rodrik's (1993) hypothesis that the autonomy of authoritarian regimes makes their behavior less predictable on the basis of structural economic variables and more dependent on the government's preferences. Swinnen et al. (2000) support Rausser's (1992b) argument that institutional changes leading to more political freedom and rights for citizens do not lead to more distortionary transfers (agricultural protection), nor to lower investment in public goods. Runge and von Witzke (1987) have identified the impact of the European Union's decision-making structure on the Common Agricultural Policy (CAP) by arguing that the institutional framework of the unanimity rule and financial solidarity among member countries is a key determinant of the excessive cost of the CAP, and that institutional reform is a prerequisite for CAP reform.

Lindert (1991) shows the importance of institutional reform in explaining the exceptionalism of the British Corn Laws. Lindert (1991) also determines that agriculture gets more protection under democratic regimes if its share in total GDP is declining rapidly.

3. General framework

Traditional approaches of agricultural economics in political economy have been mostly descriptive or have evaluated the level and efficiency of policy instruments against the paradigm of economic efficiency. In the past three decades, however, a literature has emerged employing the economics of politics or the "public choice" approach to study government intervention in agriculture.[11] There are four key elements that political economy models of agricultural policy have considered:
- individual preferences of the citizenry,
- collective action by lobby groups,
- preferences of politicians,
- political institutions.

---

[11] As will be shown later, economic efficiency is an important aspect of the "public choice" approaches to policy, so these literatures are indeed very complementary.

Individual preferences of the citizenry are conditioned by their economic conditions, structure, and institutions (income, endowments, contract arrangements, etc.). Atomistic citizens can demand political action directly through voting, political contributions, and other forms of political support. On the other hand, individual citizens can organize into lobby groups to demand political action. On the political supply side, politician preferences can have at one extreme significant influence on the political outcome if they have any autonomy for partisan preferences, maximizing social income, or transferring income to particular groups. At the other extreme, politician preferences are submissive to either the preference of individual citizens or to organized lobby groups, conditioned by the institutional characteristics politicians and citizens/lobbies are faced with. Subject to the structure and constraints of the economy, politicians can have several competing objective functions, such as maximizing the probability of getting re-elected if in a democracy, or maximizing their legitimacy if in a non-democratic regime. Institutions in this context include many characteristics of the political environment, including structure and motives/power of the bureaucracy, parliamentary/legislative versus executive branch power structures, alternative forms of representation (e.g., geographical versus proportional, etc.), the constitution, the structure of the judiciary branch, agenda-setting mechanisms, and all other rules on how rules are made in society.

Between these two extreme conceptualizations of autonomous and submissive states are models that allow for a combination of forces determining political outcomes. However, for ease of exposition, I categorize three major approaches found in the agricultural economics literature: lobby groups organizing for "collective action" (with politicians and voters assumed, respectively, passive and rationally ignorant) in the tradition of Olson (1971) and Becker (1983), the interaction between politicians and their citizens, in the tradition of Downs (1957), with politicians being entrepreneurs and *collective action* on the part of lobby groups being a secondary factor;[12] and the revealed preference approach that takes the weights governments give to each interest group in a social welfare function as fixed (or "revealed" in the data – hence the name). These new approaches treat the policy-making process just like any other economic activity: agents, like voters, politicians, and lobbyists, are rational, self-interested, and maximize an objective function in responding to incentives and constraints.[13]

The first studies in the agricultural economics literature to use this approach are Rausser and Freebairn (1974), Zusman (1976), Zusman and Amiad (1977), Anderson (1978), and de Janvry (1983). Understanding why governments do as they do allows one to analyze the policy formation process and alter incentive constraints through institutional reform in order to achieve desired policy outcomes.[14]

---

[12] As will be shown later, a combination of these last two approaches is also popular in the literature.

[13] The term "voters" is employed hereafter but is interchangeable with "citizens" for those countries with no democracy.

[14] Persson and Tabellini (1990) identify two major types of incentive constraints reflecting the conflict of interest between politicians and citizens: political role or economic constraints where the policymaker objective does not coincide with citizens' interests; and the economic role or credibility constraints where policy is time-inconsistent and so lacks credibility.

3.1. Collective action by lobby groups

Olson (1971, 1985, 1986, 1990) developed a new framework of analysis (and applied it extensively to farm policy) that depicts a passive government responding to lobby activities by interest groups who organize themselves for *collective action as a lobby group*. The outcome is determined by this collective action by lobby groups, which hinges critically on the ability to overcome costs of organization and free-riding. Lobbying group activities determine the outcome with geography and communication costs central to agriculture.

Olson (1990) uses his theory to explain why the United States and Europe currently subsidize farmers even though they taxed farmers before the industrial revolution, and why developing countries are currently taxing agriculture. His explanation focuses on factors affecting the ability of a group to *organize for collective action*, such as a small group size, and low costs of communication and transportation. Many economists have extended Olson's (1971) analysis, including Peltzman (1976) and Hardin (1982). Becker (1983) develops a more comprehensive game-theoretic framework, emphasizes lobby group activities in determining political outcomes, and assumes that "politicians are passive while voters are rationally ignorant". Many of the empirical studies reviewed earlier invoke the Olson/Becker hypotheses in explaining the patterns of agricultural policy interventions not only for variables like farm numbers and geographic concentration but also per capita GDP and farm share of GDP and the like.

Olson (1971) devotes a section in his watershed book on how his lobby group model *cannot* explain the passage of farm legislation that heaped large subsidies on such a large part of the population (farmers represented almost 25 percent of the total U.S. population in the early 1930s). To circumvent organization costs and the free-rider problems of large groups, both positive and negative selective incentives are used [Olson (1971), Hardin (1982)].

Moe (1980) extends Olson's (1971) model to include lobby group organizational structures and processes, including the leadership role of political entrepreneurs. Moe (1980) conducts an empirical test of his theory that includes farm lobbies and finds that political or group goals are also important in addition to economic selective incentives.

Olson (1971) also argues that farmers got together at meetings for social reasons and that political activity was a by-product that generated lobby activities and hence government action on their behalf. Farmers therefore became politically powerful through their lobbying strength as a "by-product" of their non-political functions.

Becker (1983) develops a more comprehensive game-theoretic framework, emphasizes lobby group activities in determining political outcomes, and assumes that "politicians are passive while voters are rationally ignorant". Coggins, Graham-Tomasi and Roe (1991) develop a model similar to Becker's (1983) with noncooperative lobby groups. Conditions for the existence of equilibrium in a general equilibrium Walrasian model are established with lobbying activities. In a small open economy with two goods and two agents, assumptions concerning preferences (as opposed to response functions) are needed, as well as a government able to finance trade deficits from lobbying contributions. The technical difficulty overcome in the paper is due to the fact that prices and income are simultaneously determined through the agents' lobbying contributions. While the model is fairly abstract, it provides an important underpinning to the related literature by demonstrating that an equilibrium can exist in a lobbying game.

Becker's (1983) formal analysis describes a game theoretic equilibrium among lobby groups generating political pressure through the use of expenditures on political activities. The key issue is what determines the level of political expenditure on lobbying activities and the reaction functions and the conditions governing the equilibrium of the reaction function of the lobby groups. As in Olson (1971) and Peltzman (1976), Becker's (1983) results explaining farm policy rest heavily on factors affecting organization and free-rider control costs. In particular, group size is a fundamental variable, and Becker (1983) argues that this explains why industrial countries subsidize farmers while developing countries tax them. However, Becker (1983) achieves his result that "politically successful groups tend to be small" only in terms of how an increase in the number of taxpayers reduces deadweight costs of taxation. The production of pressure by taxpayers declines as a result, and so subsidies go up, assuming a fixed transfer and number of members in the subsidized group.

Lobby group models predict the correlation between agricultural protection and per capita incomes because the richer the country, the fewer the farmers, and so there are lower organization costs/less free-riding, less space/geographical concentration, larger farm size, a less uniform size distribution, and more specialization in production. Gardner (1987) finds empirical support for these factors in explaining U.S. farm policy, Bates (1987) for African agricultural policies, and Krueger (1996) for developing countries. Import sectors and sectors with inelastic demand receive more protection because deadweight loss per unit of protection is lower, as derived in Becker (1983) [although in Gardner (1987), it is the minimum of the demand and supply elasticity that determines transfer efficiency – it will be shown later in the politician–voter model that a lower deadweight loss per unit subsidy is equally important as the unit tax in determining political outcomes].

De Gorter and Tsur (1991) and de Gorter and Swinnen (1994a) question the uniqueness of the collective action model in explaining the patterns of agricultural policy worldwide. To begin, farmers represented a large proportion of the U.S. labor force when they received substantial subsidies in the 1930s. Further, they question why Argentina and Canada, both highly urbanized economies with similar agro-climatic conditions, have diametrically opposite farm policies. It cannot be due to differences in transportation and communication costs or other factors emphasized by Olson (1971). Krueger, Schiff and Valdés (1988) synthesize several studies that found direct protection to agriculture was negative for exportables (typically non-food or cash crops) but positive (with exceptions) for importables (often food staples). Total protection averaged 7 percent for importables and −35 to −40 percent for exportables. Kerr (1986) reached similar conclusions earlier in a background study for the World Bank (1986). Exportable crops are often perennials and so taxes now do not have disincentive effects on production until well into the future, making it attractive for governments with a high discount rate to tax these sectors. What is perplexing for collective action theory is that the exportable sector in developing countries usually consists of large, cost-efficient farms (including plantations), far fewer in number relative to the many small-sized farms (including peasant holdings) that typically comprise the importable sector.

Another puzzling observation in this perspective is the past polarization between the United Kingdom (U.K.) and the Federal Republic of Germany (FRG) in the formulation of support prices in the CAP, where the U.K. preferred lower prices and the FRG higher support. De Gorter and Tsur (1991) and de Gorter and Swinnen (1994b) look at farm numbers, farm size, farm size distribution, geographic dispersion of farms, specialization of production, and per capita benefits to farmers, consumers, and taxpayers. In many cases, the Olson/Becker collective action model has different predictions. Von Witzke (1986), on the other hand, is able to explain the supranational influences of policy determination in the European Union.

3.2. Political support function approach

Another class of models focuses on the interaction of (groups of) voters or citizens with politicians and how this interaction is affected by external conditions, and changes in these conditions, independent of the costs of political organization. In the literature on explaining farm policy, these models have extended and formalized the basic political–voter interaction model of Downs (1957).[15] The political decision-making process is modeled as the interaction between rational, fully informed politicians and voters. Politicians provide transfers to their constituency in return for political support. De Gorter and Tsur (1991) specify support as a function of the change in income due to policy and relative endowment incomes. The latter captures the importance of relative incomes on political support,[16] while the former follows Peltzman (1976), but by itself has politicians always choosing a zero transfer. A combination of the two influences of political support results in transfers from rich to poor but less than an egalitarian outcome. This model was generalized by Hillman (1982), Swinnen and de Gorter (1993), and Swinnen (1994), who follow Downs' (1957, Chapter 4) specification that political support is a function of the change in utility induced by the policy. Voters increase their political support if they benefit from the policy and reduce support if the policy decreases their welfare.

Politicians are active entrepreneurs [Bates (1990)] who maximize total political support, subject to the government budget constraint. Competition between politicians

---

[15] Peltzman (1976) specifies a support function depending on the change in income from each voter which by itself implies zero transfers [de Gorter and Tsur (1991)] but later specifies support as a function of each group's income, as does Hillman (1982), Magee, Brock and Young (1989), and Rausser and de Gorter (1988). Becker (1976) shows that this framework has zero transfers if there are no deadweight costs.

[16] Krugman (1998) notes that median family income in 1950 in the United States would be below the poverty line in real terms in 1994, while DeLong (1998) argues that professors now have more real purchasing power than the super rich in the nineteenth century. Clearly, relative rather than absolute incomes affect current voter attitudes towards their expectations of society and politicians for their income status.

ensures an equilibrium. Unlike Downs (1957), however, it is assumed that both politicians and voters have perfect information and that there are no voting costs.[17]

This model provides an explanation for the negative correlation between agricultural protection and farm incomes. A decline in the relative farm (pre-policy) endowment income will induce political support maximizing politicians to compensate farmers. This is an important and fundamental result and reflects the "liberal" feature of the model.[18] However, the endogenous transfer leads to an increase in the (implicit) political weight of the taxed group in the politician's objective function, limiting the transfer to the low income group and preventing an egalitarian outcome: this is the "conservative" feature of the model. This shows "influence" of particular interest groups is endogenous (rather than fixed as in the empirical revealed preference models), and formally shows Gardner's (1987) hypothesis that "it is plausible that political power is not exogenous but changes as income is redistributed". Furthermore, it also explains why governments may give up on declining industries if transfers are high relative to endowment incomes [Hillman (1982)].

The "relative income" hypothesis as derived in these models addresses an important theoretical deficiency in the literature and provides an explanation for several inconsistencies between empirical observations and the collective action model. Relative incomes provide an explanation for why agriculture received increasing support in industrialized countries over the past 60 years, while protection declined in the manufacturing sector (and vice-versa in developing countries). Farm incomes in the 1930s in the United States dropped 50 percent more than their urban counterparts [Alston and Hatton (1991)]. Furthermore, it partially explains Honma and Hayami's (1986a, 1986b) empirical finding of a correlation between farm protection and productivity in the manufacturing sector, and Kerr's (1986) study and the studies synthesized by Krueger, Schiff and Valdés (1988) showing why exportables in developing countries get taxed far more, and the Argentina–Canada farm policy paradox. Finally, it provides an explanation for why the U.K. supported lower price supports while the opposite was the case in the FRG. The FRG had a strong industrial sector and many small farms with relatively low incomes in the post-war period. The opposite was the case in the U.K. Hayami (1988) and Gardner (1993) find post-policy relative incomes (including off-farm sources) to have equalized in Japan and the United States, respectively, possibly having implications for future farm policy changes.

---

[17] It is important not to confuse the politician–voter model with the revealed preference model. In addition to not being subject to some of the caveats of the latter model discussed earlier, the politician–voter model has an objective function and constraint structure that gives a very different basis for evaluating the behavior of politicians or governments [see Downs (1957) or Mueller (1989) for a broad overview]. The weights in a revealed preference model could be the outcome of either politician–voter interactions or lobby group activities or a combination thereof.

[18] The models of Peltzman (1976) and Magee, Brock and Young (1989), with support as a function of income levels, also have relative income effects which Magee, Brock and Young (1989) call the "compensation effect".

The relative pre-policy endowment income effect of the politician–voter model also overcomes the theoretical deficiency of many studies showing the correlation between per capita income and farm protection or what is known as the "developmental paradox". For example, Bullock (1992) argues that revealed preference models are inadequate in explaining the countercyclity of income transfer in agriculture,[19] and Gardner (1989b) concludes that "such an income effect has not been a feature of the general economic theories of politics".

In fact, the lobby group literature has an opposite sign with respect to the effects of relative incomes on political outcomes [de Gorter and Swinnen (1995)]. Gardner (1992, p. 52) summarizes the quandary by noting that "[while] intervention to assist farmers occurs when economic conditions turn against agriculture seems trivially obvious, it is conceivable that the richer an industry becomes the better placed it is to win political favors". However, there does not necessarily need to be a paradox in this argument. Empirical results from Swinnen, de Gorter and Banerjee (1999) and Swinnen et al. (2000) show that both effects can occur simultaneously: commodity protection is negatively related to (changes in) the world market price of the commodity, but positively to the economic size of the commodity sector. In other words, when economic conditions turn against agriculture, governments are more likely to protect farmers, and more so when their vested interest is larger.

Another important contribution of the relative endowment income effect in the politician–voter model as described above is that it overcomes the Dr. Jekyll and Mr. Hyde view of politics so common in the literature. Two examples are Baldwin's (1989) "social concerns" model (observing higher protection in declining industries) and Mueller's (1989) depiction of altruistic politicians and the ethical voter hypothesis to explain why low income groups receive protection. With the politician–voter model, rationality can be a part of the political market as well as the economic market [Swinnen and de Gorter (1993)] in explaining why low income groups are subsidized.

The politician–voter model also explains why small groups get higher protection. There are fewer people to subsidize so the per capita transfer increases (the economic effect), but there are fewer votes, which reduces the transfer (the political effect). It turns out that the economic effect dominates [Swinnen and de Gorter (1993)]. This reflects the fact that politicians have an incentive to choose policies that concentrate benefits and disperse the costs. Notice that this result is independent of the effect of group size on political outcomes, analyzed by Olson (1971) and Becker (1983). Indeed, Downs (1957) did not analyze the mathematical properties of his model and assumed that uncertainty and information costs were required for small groups to be subsidized. The result is observationally equivalent to Olson's (1971) result, but the politician–voter model hinges on the fundamental result that politician–voter calculus is for costs to be dispersed and benefits concentrated [Anderson (1993) emphasizes this point using

---

[19] Bullock (1994b) introduces altruism to allow Becker's (1983) model to include relative income effects of the type described in de Gorter and Tsur (1991).

empirical analysis but argues on the basis of lobbying and collective action models of Olson (1971) and Becker (1983)].

As in the Becker (1983) collective action model, the politician–voter model with active politicians and rational voters predicts farm protection will decline with deadweight costs of the transfer: the higher the deadweight cost of a tax, the higher the tax required for a given transfer, so it increases the political opposition to the tax. A higher deadweight cost of a subsidy to farmers reduces the net transfer to a subsidized group for a given transfer and so reduces support for the subsidy. In both cases, the transfer declines [de Gorter and Tsur (1990), Swinnen and de Gorter (1993), Swinnen (1994)].

Both the politician–voter and collective action models recognize formally the important effect of a change in the income transfer effects of a given policy. As in the politician–voter model, the lobby group literature explicitly acknowledges that lobbying is induced by an increase in the effect of a given policy on per capita income transfers.[20] For example, Olson (1971) argues that the higher the potential levels of income transfers, the more likely to organize lobby groups are (ceteris paribus, i.e., for a change in the endowment income, group numbers, policy level, etc.). Likewise, although groups are not organized, an exogenous change in this per capita income transfer of a given policy affects the political outcome in the politician–voter model. However, this exogenous change in the per capita income transfer of a given policy is a very different issue from the exogenous change in per capita endowment income discussed earlier. An exogenous change in endowment income has no (direct or first-round) impact on the per capita income transfer of a given policy. Because political support is a function of the policy-induced change in per capita utility, an increase in the per capita transfer to the subsidized group (or a decrease in the per capita transfer from the taxed group) for a given policy level will result in more (per capita) protection. There are several key structural variables through which this can occur in the politician–voter model: a change in either deadweight costs, group numbers (absolute numbers or with migration), share of agriculture in total GDP, share of food in total consumption expenditures, or the capital intensity in agriculture [Swinnen (1994)].

The precise mechanism through which a change in the per capita transfer for a given policy affects the political outcome in this model can be summarized as follows. Any exogenous factor that results in an increase in a per capita subsidy (or a decrease in a per capita tax) generates an increase in support for (or a decrease in opposition to) a given level of policy (through the impact of an initial change in the implicit transfer on utility). For example, a decrease in the deadweight costs of a per capita tax results in a higher level of income transfer for a given per capita deadweight cost of the subsidy, and thus opposition to the existing policy (transfer) declines. Because support is a function of the change in utility from the transfer, politicians will increase the transfer to maintain a political equilibrium. Similar reasoning applies to the other

[20] Olson (1971) writes that the likelihood of a group organizing and bearing pressure is affected by the "extent to which he will be benefited by a given level of provision of the collective good".

structural variables named above, such as the share of population in agriculture and the share of food in total household expenditures, found so important in empirical studies in agricultural protection patterns cited above.

However, "interaction" effects can also occur, whereby a change in an exogenous variable such as capital intensity has an impact on deadweight costs. Furthermore, Swinnen (1994) shows that "simultaneous" effects can also occur, rendering the causal impact of some exogenous variables even more complex. An example of a "simultaneous" effect is when an increase in capital intensity affects the per capita transfer from a group and the per capita transfer to another group at the same time. This "simultaneous" effect cannot happen with a change in the deadweight costs of a subsidy alone, so the political outcome in this case is unambiguous. Because both sides of the per-capita-income-effect-of-a-given-policy coin are affected, it is not clear *a priori* in the politician–voter model what the outcome will be. The process determining the outcome is very subtle and complex, depending on a multiplicity of factors including input substitutability, relative sectoral capital intensities, the level of transfer, and the like [Swinnen (1994)].

Roe (1995) develops a Ricardo–Viner general equilibrium model of heterogeneous households lobbying government. Traded and non-traded goods are included with both income transfer and public good policies. He shows that the government's choice of instrument depends on the household's net market surplus (deficit) and net labor market position, and explains why industrial countries subsidize farmers and developing countries tax agriculture. Roe (1995) also finds that protection increases with the level of specific factor endowments for a given level of lobbying because the household's welfare increases per unit change in the market price.

Barrett (1999) analyzes the microeconomic basis of coalitions for food policy by recognizing the heterogeneity of interests across households. The demand for food price policy is derived using a household modeling approach that incorporates uncertainty by considering simultaneously agents' preferences over the mean and variance of prices. Different characteristics such as endowments, the level of marketable surplus (deficit), and technologies help explain the microeconomic origins of coalition alignments and hence food price policy outcomes.

3.2.1. The issue of observational equivalence

Before discussing studies that combine collective action and politician–voter models, an important issue is that of observational equivalence between the two models. Recommendations for political change based on the wrong model may not obtain the desired results. An example of an element common to both the lobby group and politician–voter models is the institutional factors that may affect both the "influence function" of Becker's (1983) lobby group model and the "support function" of the politician–voter models. This commonality may not allow one to distinguish between the models. Geographic representation in the United States with two senators from each state allows wheat farmers concentrated in Kansas to have disproportionately more representation than farmers in New York or Ohio who have more competing interests in the politician–voter model. However, geographic concentration is also a factor in the Olson (1971) lobby group approach, confirmed empirically by Gardner (1987), which predicts that Kansas wheat farmers would collectively organize more easily and so generate more political lobbying intensity. No model is unique in this situation and so there is observational equivalence. Likewise, asymmetric information and differential uncertainty between farmers and consumers (for example) will affect each model in their own way but with identical outcomes, thereby leading to observational equivalence again. One example where these two models can be distinguished with respect to institutional factors is proportional representation in the FRG and geographic representation in the U.K., with a parliamentary system in the latter case. Many farmers scattered in the FRG have more influence than fewer farmers in the U.K. concentrated geographically (and so the politician–voter model provides yet another rationale for the U.K.–FRG price support preference paradox).

3.3. Strategic interaction between lobby groups and politicians

Zusman (1976) was one of the earliest contributors to the political economy literature to include both lobby group activities and a politician objective function. He modeled the policy process as a cooperative bargaining game between lobby groups (who either reward or penalize the government) and a government that minimizes subsidy costs (and so implicitly maximizes social income, subject to the rewards and punishments of the lobby groups). Zusman (1976) develops a "political efficiency" frontier once lobbying has occurred with the solution of the bargaining process involving the resolution of the non-cooperative equilibrium determining the threat points and of the cooperative equilibrium that will be adopted. He shows that endogenous government can be characterized as maximizing a policy preference function with fixed weights on the welfare of each interest group. His paper provided a rigorous analytical foundation for revealed preference models (to be discussed later) and was a precursor to other models in the literature extending the government–lobby group interaction, including Findlay and Wellisz (1982), Magee, Brock and Young (1989), Appelbaum and Katz (1987), Long and Vousden (1991), Bates and Rogerson (1980), and Grossman and Helpman (1994).

Beghin (1990) follows this approach in providing a formal structure of criterion functions by depicting policies as the equilibrium outcome of a cooperative game among lobby groups and the government. Beghin (1990) stresses the interdependence between policies and lobbies' bargaining strengths. He derives comparative static results with respect to changes in the economic structure based solely on information yielded by the estimated game. This leads to a specification of behavioral equations that links shocks of the bargaining process underlying policies to changes in these policies. The effect of shocks on price policies was estimated with the bargaining game model and with behavioral equations. The incorporation of the bargaining framework and agents' behavior and reactions into the policy process improves upon the earlier reduced form endogenous models of agricultural price policy of Abbott (1979), Lattimore and Schuh

(1979), and Zwart and Meilke (1979), all studies which do not have a theoretical explanation for why prices are endogenous.

Fafchamps, Sadoulet and de Janvry (1991) analyze endogenous tariffs in a general equilibrium framework with three sectors (one non-tradable) and two factors, one of which is fixed. The government's objective function is a weighted average of each interest group's welfare, where the weights are determined by the lobbying exerted by each group. Each group acts rationally with full information and all are Stackelberg leaders vis-à-vis the government but engage in a non-cooperative Nash game among themselves. Fafchamps, Sadoulet and de Janvry (1991) determine that groups always engage in lobbying (even if their influence is offset), the non-tradable sector benefits from lobbying of other sectors, and governments still have an incentive to promote growth despite the lobbying. Sectors with low consumption shares get more protection, as do sectors with more rigid production, and the more so the more concerned government is with equity.

Rausser and de Gorter (1988) and Rausser and Foster (1990) advance this model framework further by considering both a redistributive and public good providing policies simultaneously. Weights on the government's criterion function change with the lobby groups' cost of organization, and hence its response to changes in its collective welfare. But the observed weights are also shown to be a result of a combination of the two types of policies. If farmers lose from research, then the implied weight to farmers may not be increasing relative to that of consumers even though redistribution occurs to farmers. Rausser and Foster (1990) postulate a government maximizing political support as a function of the absolute level of income, subject to the strategic behavior of lobby groups who are sensitive to changes in their welfare affected by government policies. Each lobby behaves like a Stackelberg leader with respect to the government's choice of optimal income transfer from the policy combination. Rausser and Foster (1990) conclude that reform cannot occur unless there is a change in the political technology through institutional changes in the relative costs of political activity in order to allow compensation but at a lower cost.

Rausser and Zusman (1992) expand on both Zusman (1976) and Rausser and Foster (1990). Again, the government has some autonomy but reacts to lobbying activities by particular interest groups. Rausser and Zusman (1992) develop a relationship between the underlying constitution (or rules by which rules are made as to how governments and lobbies are allowed to interact) and the weights on the criterion function of the government. The potential impacts of constitutional rules are quantified in terms of expected transaction costs that arise in pursuing the public interest. The selection of a particular constitutional design must establish voting rules, law and order, property rights, and laws governing exchange and the like. Transaction costs include the wasteful rent-seeking by lobbies. Rausser and Zusman (1992) show that the externalization of costs and benefits by lobby groups, the internalization of lobby group goals by the government, and the power of lobbies are key in determining the degree of government failure. Therefore, any constitutional prescription must address the degree of centralization, the balance of power, access of interests to the government, which issues are negotiable, rules of consensus and the like. They conclude that the constitutional rules structure the tradeoff between public and special interests while generating testable propositions on the choice of policy instruments by the government.

Guyomard et al. (1993), Coleman and Tangermann (1997), Patterson (1997), Anania (1997), Paarlberg (1997), and Coleman et al. (1996) analyze how policy-making at the international level affected domestic policy choices during the Uruguay Round of negotiations on agriculture. Each of these papers uses some version of Putnam's (1988) concept of linked games to allow for the influence of autonomous international (supranational or intergovernmental) organizations. For European agricultural policy, Paarlberg (1997) argues that international agreements have little impact while Patterson (1997) concludes they have some influence. Coleman and Tangermann (1997), however, determine that European Union domestic policies were shaped by international policy-making. Johnson, Mahe and Roe (1993) specify political preference functions for the European Union and the United States governments with weights for each interest group and simulate policy games. Several possible policy actions by each government are modeled to predict optimal negotiating strategies. Kennedy, von Witzke and Roe (1996a, 1996b) develop a two-stage non-cooperative and cooperative game theoretic approach to analyze the U.S. and European Union's (EU) actions in the Uruguay Round on agriculture. Each country chooses policies based on a political preference function and Pareto optimal reform results in the cooperative game.

Beghin and Foster (1992) question aggregate rationality as the underlying process for policies being an outcome of a single optimization problem that balances the welfare between competing interest groups. Analyzing an aggregate criterion function makes it difficult to test for the Pareto efficiency hypothesis. They characterize this as the integrality problem to confirm or reject the existence of a criteria function. Beghin and Karp (1991) show with multiple policy instruments that the first-order condition of one rate of welfare transformation is not necessarily equal to the rate of another. If the Pareto efficiency hypothesis is rejected, then sensitivity of the transformation curve is in doubt, especially if lobbying occurs and there are many instruments [Bullock (1996b)].

Beghin and Karp (1991) investigate agricultural policies in Senegal and determine that well-behaved criterion functions cannot be recovered and so reject the efficiency hypothesis. Beghin and Foster (1992) also highlight the problem of revealed preference models of not including the objective of the government itself in the criterion function. Beghin and Foster (1992) argue that traditional revealed preference models have government as a clearing house and have no game theoretic framework like that of Zusman (1976) or Becker (1983). Beghin and Foster (1992) parameterize influence and pressure functions and a surplus transformation frontier from Becker's (1983) model to derive implications for the concavity of the real income frontier. They determine a concave frontier only when deadweight costs are small and when the taxed group is unorganized and inefficient in producing pressure. Therefore, the criterion function will not correspond to a well-defined maximization problem, even though the lobbying equilibrium is well defined. Beghin and Foster (1992) determine that a hybrid of

Zusman's (1976) and Becker's (1983) model does uniquely determine weights on the government's criterion function.

Several problems have been identified in the literature with respect to revealed preference models. Makin (1976) identifies a broad class of restrictions in which estimates of preferences can be separated out, including the number of targets and instruments and the functional form of the objective function and constraint system. Fixed weights in the political criterion function implies linear indifference curves. Von Cramon-Taubadel (1992) clarifies the relationship between the transformation frontier and the political preference function and how weights change with a shift in either function. He emphasizes how neglecting sub-interest groups, predatory government, and bureaucrats can lead to problems of misspecification. He also argues that the revealed preference framework inadequately considers the effects of the length of run on both the transformation frontier and social indifference curves. Bullock and Jeong (1994) argue that von Cramon-Taubadel (1992) incorrectly assumes a linear policy preference function question in his conclusion that the transformation frontier is not concave. Another problem with the revealed preference approach is that it relies on *ex post* measurements, but inferred actions of governments may be affected by what is intended rather than what actually happened. Additionally, the Lucas critique applies in that the structure and behavior relationships describing the economy cannot be taken as independent of the values of the instruments chosen.

Recent critiques of the revealed preference model by Bullock (1994a, 1995) show that weights are accurate only if observed policies are Pareto efficient, which may depend on the assumed number of interest groups and policy instruments. Marginal rates of transformation may not, under some conditions, reveal anything meaningful about interest group power in a policy preference function, and may indeed incorrectly measure the direction of transfers. Beghin and Karp (1991) estimate the restrictions implied by first order conditions and reject the hypothesis of efficiency for the case of agriculture in Senegal. Bullock (1996a) meanwhile finds that observed policy outcomes are not Pareto efficient in European agriculture and so deems revealed preference models unable to obtain appropriate measures of relative political power.

3.4. Empirical studies of revealed preference models

Revealed preference models have government maximizing a weighted sum of interest group welfare measures. A surplus possibility or transformation frontier reflects the economic structure facing policy-makers and constrains their choice of policy. One infers (or the data "reveals") the relative weights attached by governments to each interest group from the marginal rate of transformation of one welfare measure into another. The resulting political preference (or criterion) function describing the political outcome allows one to simulate the effects of alternative changes in the economic structure on government policy choice. Alternatively, maximizing a weighted social preference function can be used to derive a representation of government policy choices known as a reaction function, relating policy to past values and other targets [Makin

(1976)]. The endogenous policy depends on the parameters of both the preference function and structure of the economy. In many empirical studies, the objective function is typically quadratic and so the reaction and criteria (or preference) functions are linear.

Rausser and Freebairn (1974) is the path-breaking study in agricultural economics on endogenizing price policy using revealed preference of weights in the political preference or government criterion function. Their application is on the U.S. beef industry and their analysis allows one to assess the effects of different shocks to the beef economy on the choice of price policy by government and the resulting welfare levels of each interest group. Numerous studies have estimated weights in a government criterion function [e.g., Gerrard and Roe (1983), Sarris and Freebairn (1983), Paarlberg and Abbott (1986)] or estimated reaction functions resulting from the maximization problem [Riethmuller and Roe (1986), López (1989)]. Sarris and Freebairn (1983) analyzed the world wheat market with prices modeled as Cournot equilibrium interactions of national excess demands, which in turn are solutions to domestic welfare optimization problems. Sarris and Freebairn (1983) analyze the effects of unilateral trade liberalization on both price levels and instability of each interest group's welfare. Vanzetti and Kennedy (1988) reformulate Sarris and Freebairn's (1983) model by allowing for international price effects of individual country policy. This results in a different solution, and the implied weights of producers in exporting countries are higher and in importing countries lower than those reported by Sarris and Freebairn (1983). Tyers (1990) generalizes Sarris and Freebairn's (1983) model to include multiple interactive commodity markets (including inputs) and derives conjectures from an established multi-country model with endogenous governments. The approach is then applied to negotiations on agricultural trade policy with specific emphasis on reform of the EU's CAP.

Paarlberg and Abbott (1986) adapt Sarris and Freebairn's (1983) framework by adding several interest groups and policy choices, and also by allowing for oligopolistic behavior by governments in international trade. The oligopolistic nature of the international wheat sector is captured by assuming policymakers form conjectures on the slope of the excess demand function they face and use that information to determine domestic and trade policy. After solving for the weight of each interest group in the criterion function, each country's conjecture of the policy retaliation on the world market is determined. Several structures of the game can be specified, and once chosen, first order conditions are used to determine the country's conjecture of its world market influence. Paarlberg and Abbott (1986) extend the analysis of Karp and McCalla (1983), who used a dynamic game to analyze the international corn market. Karp and McCalla (1983) incorporate the dynamic nature of supply and demand and model the interactions between importers and exporters. The resulting non-cooperative Nash solution gives endogenously determined reaction functions and resulting policy prices chosen by governments.

Other empirical applications include Zusman and Amiad (1977) who augment the government criterion function to include a competitive bargaining game between interest groups and the government. The policy outcome is the equilibrium of a variable threat cooperative game, with each lobby group's welfare a function of the economic payoff due to policy and lobbying expenditures to the government. Field and Fulton (1994) specify a model of revealed preference but specify a bargaining model between the FRG and the EU's CAP determining agricultural price supports. Gallagher (1988) analyzes several alternative European policy options with endogenous transfer to farmers by specifying a government maximizing producer profits subject to no increases in existing government expenditures (where farmers have a larger welfare weight than consumers and taxpayers).[21]

In summary, many contributions on revealed preference models in studies of agriculture have been made to the literature. These include rigorous and informative critiques of the underlying assumptions and structure of such models. In addition, extensions have included a better understanding as to the interaction between the social planner (or government) and the lobby groups.

3.5. Empirical studies on lobbying and politician behavior

Many studies have examined the relationship between legislative votes by politicians and political action committee (PAC) contributions to politicians by agricultural lobby groups in the United States. The decision to contribute to an individual politician depends in part on the anticipated vote of that politician on proposed legislation, while the politician's voting decision depends in part on anticipated contributions from lobby groups. The politician's decision and the level of contributions both affect his or her re-election chances. Hence, this line of research embodies elements of both the politician–voter and the collective action lobby models [Stratmann (1992a, 1992b)]. The literature (including that on agricultural legislation) is mixed in terms of how strongly PAC monies affect individuals' votes.[22] Chappell (1982) finds little impact of PAC monies on congressional voting. This is substantiated in studies of agricultural legislation by Welch (1982), Brooks (1994), Vesenka (1989), and Abler (1991),[23] who find limited evidence of contributions on votes by legislators.

De Gorter (1983), de Gorter and Rausser (1989), Tanaka (1998), Brooks (1994), and Brooks, Cameron and Carter (1998), on the other hand, do determine highly significant effects of PAC monies on agricultural price support legislation.[24] De Gorter and Rausser (1989) specify a logit model explaining that the probability of an individual member

---

[21] As described in more detail later, the revealed preference model is also used to analyze the interaction between commodity and public research policies [Gardner (1989a), Oehmke and Yao (1990), de Gorter, Nielson and Rausser (1992, 1995b)].

[22] Several studies also question the effect of campaign spending on re-election chances [e.g., Jacobson (1987)], but Krasno and Green (1988) show a much larger influence of incumbent spending on election outcomes if challenger quality is taken into account.

[23] Abler (1991) determines statistically that lobby groups for sugar and dairy cannot influence the vote of legislators who would otherwise not support the group, but can influence a legislator who is ideologically predisposed to support the group.

[24] For details on PAC monies in agriculture, see Brooks and Carter (1994) and Tanaka (1998).

voting for the legislation is simultaneously a function of the dairy lobby contribution. They use an ideal point model following Davis et al. (1970). Any deviation of the price support from the ideal price (above or below) represents a decrease in the preference for the politician.

The probit model (simultaneous with the logit model above) explaining dairy lobby contributions has two critical determinants: the probability that the politician will favor the higher price support (determined by all other factors such as economic effects on district, party affiliation, etc.) and chances of re-election. If the probability of a congressman voting in favor of price support is close to 0.5, then it is certainly in the best interest of producers to contribute more resources to influence the outcome. However, if the propensity of a congressman to favor price support is either very high or very low, then resource contributions will have minimal effects and, subsequently, fewer resources will be expended by the pressure group. In addition, contributors are shown to also evaluate the chances of re-election for each congressman in conjunction with their preference for price supports.

Tanaka (1998) analyzed several individual sector votes on the 1996 U.S. FAIR Act in both the House and Senate and found PAC monies significant in all legislative votes. Brooks, Cameron and Carter (1998) extend the conventional analysis to include a three-equation simultaneous system in which a congressman's vote also depends on PAC monies from coalitions opposing sugar farmers. This study follows that of de Gorter and Rausser (1989) and includes both a proxy for chances of re-election and a latent variable for voting for/against in the contribution equation. All of these studies included several other variables accounting for ideology, farm numbers, party affiliates, committee membership, seniority, and the like. Other factors like presidential elections could also condition the outcome [von Witzke (1990)]. Gardner (1995) tests the determinants of contributions to agricultural committee members by various commodity PACs in single-equation regressions and concludes that such contributions are not random.

Another literature assesses the determinants of total PAC monies spent by individual agricultural lobbies. Studies like Gardner (1987) test the collective action model with protection on the left-hand side, which is really an outcome of supply and demand, not just demand by lobby groups. Hence, a good test of the collective action lobby group theory is to statistically analyze the level of PAC monies expended by group.

López and Pagoulatos (1996) found that the number of firms was a significant determinant of total campaign contributions from the U.S. food and tobacco industries in 1987–88, confirming Olson's (1971) hypothesis. Pittman (1976) also found support for the collective action lobby theory in analyzing contributions from industry in three 1972 U.S. Senate campaigns in Illinois, Michigan, and Minnesota. Pittman (1976) found that more concentrated industries give more in contributions, a result also found by Heywood (1988). Tanaka (1998) analyzes per farm PAC contributions from each commodity to federal candidates (House, Senate, and presidential candidates). Tanaka (1998) finds support for the collective action lobby model whereby the number of farms, the rate of growth in production, geographic dispersion, and levels of government support all affect the level of total contribution expenditures.

Another area of research is the effect of lobbying (instead of campaign contributions) on legislator voting decisions. Abler (1989) studied the 1985 Farm Bill and found vote trading used heavily by tobacco, sugar, peanut, and dairy farmers, and to a lesser extent by other farm groups. Wright (1985, 1990) determines that lobbying efforts from coalitions impact voting decisions by legislators. Lobby groups working together, especially at the committee level, influence voting, and so monies affect voting in an indirect fashion by influencing groups' choices of whom to lobby. Wright (1990) studies the wheat and feed grain provisions of the 1985 Farm Bill and finds little evidence of the influence of monies once lobbying was controlled for. Ellison and Mullin (1995) empirically analyze congressional roll call decisions on sugar tariff reform and find that economic concentration and wealth are relatively unimportant. The most effective pressure groups were those that had tariffs already in place, suggesting that government policy can form interest groups as well as be influenced by them.

4. Why the use of inefficient instruments?

Much of the literature surveyed thus far focuses on the political economy of *redistribution* across countries, sectors, and over time. Another question is the choice of *policy instruments* by governments. Furthermore, there is a widespread consensus that governments use *inefficient* policy instruments in achieving their objectives, including farm income goals.[25] This is all part of a broader question on why governments do not maximize social income in achieving their policy goals. The literature on the level of redistribution is more developed than that on the inefficiency of policy instruments, yet political decisions to redistribute are made simultaneously with the choice of instrument.[26] Indeed, the choice of policy instrument, level of redistribution, and under-investment in public research are all part of the same question of why governments do not reform policy by implementing Pareto improvements with compensation. Because distributional issues are at the center of politics, more research is required in understanding why institutions or political arrangements do not evolve in compensating losers from potential policy reform.

However, most political economy models, including the revealed preference models with a policy criterion function, assume governments are efficient in achieving policy goals [Bullock (1995)]. For example, both the collective action model of Becker (1983) and the politician–voter model of Swinnen and de Gorter (1993) assume full

---

[25] Sectors heavily protected by government-support programs have often reported net income lower than transfers from government, lending support to inefficiency by government in achieving their redistributive goals.

[26] Trebilcock et al. (1982) argue that there should not be a dichotomy between means and ends in political markets, so the choice of instrument should not be viewed as a neutral exercise once the policy objective has been specified.

information and certainty on policy effects by all economic agents involved. Competition between collective action lobby groups in Becker (1983) and between politicians in Swinnen and de Gorter (1993) ensures that the most efficient instrument is used. Of course, these assumptions are unrealistic and, while relaxing them does not change the basic results of group numbers, relative incomes and the like in the politician–voter model, they do alter the result that efficient policy instruments will be used.[27] Imperfect or asymmetric information on policy effects simply implies that the transformation of the change in economic welfare into political support varies across policy instrument types.[28] Entrepreneurial politicians, in choosing among alternative policy instruments, will make simultaneous choices about trade-offs among different policy objectives in maximizing support. Asymmetric information by voters and competing politicians on both the distribution and social costs of alternative instruments results in relatively inefficient instruments being chosen, just as the level of redistribution results in inefficiency (there is no such thing as a distortion-free transfer in reality). Trebilcock et al. (1982) argue that, independent of imperfect information, instruments that concentrate the benefits on marginal voters and costs on infra-marginal voters will be favored. Politicians with aid from their bureaucracies will divulge subsidized, selective information to voters and collective action groups. Therefore, inefficient instruments can be politically efficient in realizing re-election goals. For example, price supports are chosen over direct income transfers because self-sufficiency appeals to a nationalistic sentiment of voters, and because farmers fear a "welfare" stigma.

The basic politician–voter model has competitive politicians choosing the most efficient instrument because otherwise a competing politician can transfer more to one group without harming another, and hence receive more political support. However, this model can be easily augmented to include uncertainty and asymmetric information to predict inefficient policy choice. The game theoretic formulations of collective action models need to augment their equilibrium between competing collective action groups with uncertainty and asymmetric information in order to obtain the result of inefficient policy instrument choice.

There is an important literature that argues that efficient instruments are chosen if all costs of government programs are incorporated appropriately. For example, Munk (1987, 1989) argues that if one includes the cost of raising revenues from taxpayers, then the European systems of price supports are efficient policy instruments in redistributing income to farmers.[29] Following Trebilcock et al. (1982), Munk (1994) and Dixit (1996)

---

[27] For an extensive discussion on imperfect information for both voters and politicians/political parties (including incumbents), see Downs (1957).

[28] Indeed, it could be argued that full information and certainty generates instrument types that are possibly inefficient from an economic point of view also. For instance, one has school lunch programs for milk with open-ended price supports, but not for tobacco which has production quotas. Neither of these cases will necessarily pass the efficient redistribution test, depending on the relative supply and demand elasticities and the like [Gardner (1983)].

[29] Alston and Hurd (1990) and Alston, Carter and Smith (1995) make a similar argument that production quotas and export subsidies, respectively, can be efficient policy instruments in the United States.

argue further that governments adopt efficient policy instruments if one also includes transaction costs, including costs of implementation, administration, and enforcement by governments, and compliance costs for the private sector. Another venue for research is the different incentive structures alternative instruments will have on the degree of rent-seeking and the timeline involved. For example, many instruments confer benefits in the short run (e.g., base acreage limitations) that farmers can get around in the long run, and so benefits are dissipated. However, politicians have limited time horizons, while farmers seem to get utility from (and hence support) policy rules that they can take advantage of by altering their production plans.

Gardner (1987) finds empirical support for the hypothesis that government is efficient in redistributing income. For example, sectors with particular supply/demand elasticities should have production quotas for efficiency of transfers and subsidies otherwise. Bullock (1994a, 1995) critiques Gardner's approach and develops an alternative test that he [Bullock (1996a)] empirically uses in analyzing the European Union's agricultural policy, where he rejects the case for efficient instruments.

Bullock (1994a) determines that marginal rates of transformation needed for political preference functions need to be on a Pareto frontier to reflect relative political power. Tests for efficient instruments therefore become critical. Bullock (1995) uses vector optimization theory to clarify assumptions and results when the Pareto criterion is established, and bootstrap methodology to test empirically the efficient redistribution hypothesis. The statistical test is more systematic and less reliant on assumptions about unobservable aspects of political economy than previous models. However, its accuracy is dependent on the estimated Jacobian matrix of welfare vector, the underlying econometric model, parameters, number of policy instruments, and number of interest groups. Beghin and Karp (1991) also develop a methodology to test Gardner's (1987) hypothesis [based on Becker's (1983) model] and they reject efficiency of government transfers. Policies are the outcome of a cooperative bargaining process between producers, consumers, and the marketing board. Beghin and Karp (1991) empirically estimate the game and bargaining strengths of each agent and reject the efficiency axiom when testing alternative bargaining game solutions.

Support implemented in the early part of this century for farmers in both North America and Europe relied primarily on tariffs. Significant changes have been made since then, such as the introduction of import quotas and other non-tariff barriers, that would suggest a move to inefficient policy instruments. However, after antitrust exemptions, favorable treatment in tax laws, credit subsidies and the like were introduced, price supports were implemented in the depression of the 1930s. Output controls were introduced (including payments to reduce herd size and acreage), especially for exports or those sectors whose price supports were deemed expensive for taxpayers. In the United States and Europe, these took the form of production quotas, frozen program yields and average diversion base acreage, and other limits on payments (like maximum guaranteed quantities in Europe). Many sectors had multiple instruments, the combination of which resulted in less distortion and more efficient transfers [Bullock and Salhofer (1997), Gisser (1993), Bullock, Kola and Salhofer (1997)]. There is, therefore, some evidence for a tendency in the long run for governments to adopt more efficient instruments as economic conditions change. However, there is still a consensus that inefficient instruments are the norm and that government can do better in achieving its objectives. This conclusion can be made even when all costs are included and the actual objectives of the government are properly identified. Winters (1987), for example, argues that European agricultural policies have changed incrementally over time but are still inefficient. Winters (1989) convincingly argues that few of the many stated non-economic objectives of agricultural policy are achieved efficiently [including food security – see Winters (1990)]. Lindert (1991) also dispels the myth that protection in agriculture can be explained by concerns over food security, nostalgia for the farm sector, sympathy for farmers, and instability.[30]

Magee, Brock and Young (1989) argue that politicians determine the optimal point of obfuscation in their instrumental choice decision when marginal political costs of so doing in terms of support equal the marginal political costs of obfuscation. However, their framework is not grounded in an information theoretic framework with explicit incorporation of uncertainty.

One important contribution is Foster and Rausser (1993), where commodity policy involving deadweight costs is deemed superior to lump sum transfers because the effect of cost-reducing public research has differential effects across a heterogeneous group of farmers. Farmers as a group can lose from public research, but price supports forestall the farmers' blocking coalition, thus assuring the political feasibility of welfare-enhancing public research expenditures. Hence the political need to compensate a minimum blocking coalition from vetoing efficiency-enhancing government policies results in the choice of commodity policy over what appears to be more efficient instruments.

Chambers (1992) uses principles of mechanism design under asymmetric information to uncover the link between the choice of farm policy tools and the redistributional preferences of agricultural policymakers. In examining motivations underlying the choice of agricultural policy mechanisms that differ across sectors, he determines that supply control mechanisms favor high-cost producers and taxpayers, while mechanisms favoring overproduction favor low-cost producers. Farmers are assumed to have more information as to the policy effects, and Chambers (1992) shows how different government objectives (for example, budget concerns and the interests of different segments of farm sectors) are reflected in the choice of agricultural policy instruments. The government is assumed to maximize a weighted utilitarian objective function and determines the conditions under which decoupling, production diversion by high cost farmers, and buyouts are second best.

---

[30] Timmer (1989) argues that policymakers are more concerned about stability of domestic prices than their level relative to world prices, while Larue and Ker (1993) develop parametric and non-parametric causality tests of the relationship between world price variability and agricultural protectionism. Their results identified causal relationships from protectionism to price variability, but not bi-causal influences.

Rodrik (1986), Cassing and Hillman (1985), and Campos (1989) model the level of redistribution and instrument choice as a two-stage political process, with the choice of instrument chosen second. Rodrik (1986) shows that subsidies are firm-specific while tariffs are not, but tariffs have a free-rider problem, resulting in subsidies being more efficient. Wilson (1977) claims that government chooses more inefficient policy instruments because it results in a lower intervention level or distortionary transfers. Incumbent politicians play lobbies off against one another, and inefficient instruments lower the deadweight costs in total. These studies by Rodrik (1986) and Wilson (1977) show that tariffs are preferred to production subsidies because distortions that endogenously emerge in the former regime are fewer than in the latter. Indeed, their positive theory conforms to Brennan and Buchanan's (1985) normative theory of constitutional limits to force the polity to choose inefficient instruments in order to prevent excessive government intervention.

Coate and Morris (1995) explain inefficient instrument choice with a model of uncertainty in both politicians' motives and in the effects of instruments on group welfare. Uncertainty and asymmetric information between the effects of policies and the predisposition of politicians has rational governments implementing disguised transfer mechanisms with concealed costs. Policy and politician uncertainty results in a concern by politicians about reputation and so inefficient instruments are chosen. Rogoff (1990) shows how entrepreneurial politicians criticizing incumbents on the efficacy of alternative and more efficient policy instruments lack credibility. Tabellini and Alesina (1990) show how policies with time-inconsistent preferences result in the choice of inefficient policy instruments. Grossman and Helpman (1994) argue in their model that lobbies may make larger contributions with subsidies than with trade interventions because each lobby might have to contribute in equilibrium the difference between what rival lobbies and government could jointly achieve with and without intervention. Higher lobby contributions might lead organized industries to limit the available policy instruments to trade policy if they can, but Schleich and Orden (1996) show that the government efficiently chooses subsidies over trade policy if both instruments are available.

Campos (1989) presents a legislative model of instrument choice where a two-stage voting procedure results in a sub-game equilibrium, and then introduces a lobby and establishes the existence of Stackelberg equilibrium. Just as a lobby cares primarily about maximizing the gains to its members, legislators are equally narrow in caring mostly about re-election. The net result of their interaction produces a choice that often fails to maximize social welfare. Political institutions are shown to decisively influence the policy process and define the nature of the equilibrium. Integrating the legislative process with lobbying and the economic structure results in political institutions having a significant impact on the choice of inefficient policy instruments.

Dixit and Londregan (1995) show that the political process compensates losers from technical change or international competition in an economically inefficient way. The political process redistributes income on the basis of political characteristics that do not coincide with economic characteristics. Politicians are unable to commit themselves to ignoring the political characteristics and to making long-term promises to reward economically efficient choices. The political dynamics of redistribution interacts with the economic dynamics of occupational choice of agents in a declining industry. The political process makes the decision after constituents have decided to adjust or not to economic conditions. Therefore economic gains and losses occur over a period longer than the electoral cycle, and so compensation policies cannot be credibly committed to in advance. Constituents fear the political process will be free to renege on promises and produce new schemes and perhaps lower transfers.

Stiglitz (1998) argues Olson's (1971) theory is incomplete because it does not explain why potential Pareto improvements fail to be adopted by the political process. Government is unable to make credible commitments in a dynamic policy process because groups losing from reform anticipate that they will be worse off in the long run even though compensation is promised now. Direct payments to farmers are more visible than price fixing and hence more vulnerable to political pressure for reductions in transfers later. The absence of a commitment mechanism can be overcome partially by affecting the transactions costs of reversing the policies,[31] but these can impede Pareto improvements by making change difficult and represent obstacles to reform later.

Hartle (1983) shows how Coasian bargaining breaks down for efficient solutions in the political marketplace [for an opposite view, see Wittman (1989)]. Comprehensive bargaining is impossible for all voters who are inadequately represented in a multi-party system. Political bargaining transaction costs are very high, while damages of policy and the rules of the game are not well known by all. Stiglitz (1998) also argues that Coasian bargaining does not lead to efficient bargaining in political markets because of imperfect information where politicians and pressure groups are solving a dynamic program problem with uncertainty and imperfect information. Groups hold out, and so the current legislation is the fall-back position when politicians support trading and forming coalitions.

The implication of this literature is that reforms of existing political constraints are needed, such as electoral rules, legislation governing political resource contribution, subsidization of information and organization costs of less influential groups, constitutional constraints on government activities like the budgetary process, and other similar institutional reforms that overcome credibility and time-inconsistency problems of public decision-making.

4.1. Discrete policy changes and the status quo bias

An important observation is that there is inertia in the political system with respect to changing farm policy, with changes made often only incrementally over long periods of time. This reflects a bias for the status quo. Otherwise, the introduction and removal of

---

[31] For example, deliberately giving U.S. grain farmers higher subsidies under the new FAIR Act of 1996 than what would have occurred under the old regime may create a constituency that will resist going back to the old legislation.

policy measures can be abrupt and major, and infrequent, often in response to a "crisis". There is a dearth of research on why discrete policy changes such as the 1933 Agricultural Adjustment Act in the United States occur. Orden, Paarlberg and Roe (1999) describe the "process establishment" such as producer associations and legislative committees represents fixed institutional capital that is most likely to be overcome only by some exogenous event. However, many studies have advanced theories to explain inertia in the political system where at best only incremental change occurs.

In the politician–voter model of Swinnen and de Gorter (1993), for example, an increase in the endowment income of the subsidized group has the "conservative" feature of putting a brake on the decrease in subsidies, and so contributes to the status quo bias. An important augmentation of the political support function for voter resistance to change is to incorporate Thaler's (1991) theory of the endowment income effect. Another possibility would be to include prospect theory [Kahneman and Tversky (1979)] for politicians, support from voters, and voters' economic welfare. This would imply that the slope of the political support function is much steeper for losses. Losses loom larger than gains, independent of endowment incomes. A loss is forced on agents when the constraint set is changed but that does not occur with an economic gain. This may be an important priority for future research to explain the status quo bias of agricultural policies.

Fernandez and Rodrik (1991) develop a theory of status quo bias whereby a future gain from an institutional reform is uncertain, and the distribution among various social groups is difficult to predict relative to the obvious loss of the specific group. Opposition to reform tends to be strongly organized while support is only weakly so. Their paper shows that some gainers or losers from reform cannot be identified *ex ante*. Many policy reforms that are politically sustainable *ex post* will not be adopted *ex ante* even though agents are risk-neutral, rational, and forward-looking. Uncertainty prevents reform and so large reform is needed to overcome the status quo bias. Basu, Jones, and Schlicht (1987) argue that developing countries continue to be trapped in economic stagnation and poverty under a dysfunctional system because of "structural" and "inertial" institutions or policies. The former are institutions bound and demanded by competing forces in response to transaction costs while the latter are institutions as products of history or origin (the importance of policy path dependency). Roe (1995) and Bates (1981, 1987), among others, argue that food is a wage good in developing countries so there is a natural coalition between urban labor and urban capitalists because the former wants higher real wages and the latter gain from lower nominal wages. Thus, there is a vested interest in maintaining taxes on agriculture. Krueger (1990b) develops a theory of identity bias whereby losers in society are well known relative to beneficiaries and so protection is perpetuated. If both imports and exports increase, the gains to the export sector are relatively unknown and so protection is maintained.

An interesting study on the politics of American farm policy by Orden, Paarlberg and Roe (1999) posits several theories of why it is difficult to reform agricultural policies. They cite Sachs and Warner (1995) on the importance of intellectual beliefs and state-building that gives rise to policy instruments that perpetuate the equilibrating interest group forces. They also cite Hall (1993), who argues that there are three degrees of policy reform. The first involves small changes in the settings of policy instruments, the second has instruments modified slightly, and finally, cases where a new policy is introduced. The third choice occurs only when major problems have occurred with existing policies and after distortions are so large that a threshold has been reached. Orden, Paarlberg and Roe (1999) give detailed examples of how this has affected American farm policy in the past decades, and explain the shift toward decoupled payments in the United States in 1996 by a combination of changed party control of Congress and unusually high commodity prices. This created an opportunity to provide a payments windfall to farmers by changing policy instruments.

Goldstein and Keohane (1993) argue that even rational actors maximizing a utility function rooted in material interests will be independently influenced by ideas. Applying this ideas-based approach to the problem of policy durability, ideas will retain power over time partly because they tend to become embedded in political institutions. Goldstein (1993) argues that ideas can influence policy even after the interests of the creators have changed. Bonnen and Browne (1989) argue that ideas can be influential for a long time because of the potency of the mythology of agrarian values. Pierson (1994) goes further and argues that policies endure in part because the organizations that want these programs will actually be strengthened by the programs themselves. A feedback effect occurs where bureaucracy and congressional committees will share lobby groups' defense of policy. This results in a nexus of program-preserving institutions as an agricultural policy establishment and so helps explain the durability or status quo bias of farm policy.

Winters (1987) emphasizes the role of bureaucracies and bureaucrats in the United States in administering protection because it is more difficult to make changes to redistributive policies in the political arena. Winters (1993) shows that bureaucrats have relatively more autonomy in Europe and so make decisions on behalf of untenured politicians. Hence, bureaucrats attempt to maximize their own power and influence.

Dewatripont and Roland (1992) show that the unanimity rule requires equal per capita compensation for a declining industry being harmed by policy reform. The implication of a dynamic version of their model is that gradualism is optimal: each partial reform induces the least profitable firm to exit and so the distorting costs of the reform are alleviated compared to "shock therapy".

De Janvry and Sadoulet (1989) offer an explanation for the limited success of land reforms, which fail to be redistributive because governments first modernize large farms, which allows landlords to reinforce their political power. This allows them to receive credible commitments of nonexpropriation if they modernize or lobby to externalize the cost of modernization such that expropriation with compensation becomes no longer feasible. De Janvry and Sadoulet (1989) use a game-theoretic framework between landlords and government by integrating lobbying with government behavior to show that policy change is a path-dependent sequence of events. Governments have a short-term political horizon and high discount rate for economic gains such that future losers block policy change.

4.2. Why is policy biased against trade?

Lindert (1991) best summarizes the overwhelming evidence of the anti-trade bias in agricultural support programs. There is more evidence of political pressure against trade liberalization than for it. The tendency is to contract trade (especially imports but exports too), although export/import subsidies (direct and indirect through production/consumption subsidies, respectively) are common in agriculture.

In either case, overall, imports are protected more than exports are subsidized. This means that relatively more protection to imports necessarily taxes the export sector. Various theories have been put forward to explain this phenomenon. The politician–voter models of de Gorter and Tsur (1991), Swinnen (1994), and Swinnen and de Gorter (1993) explain anti-trade bias with two results of their models: deadweight costs per unit of transfer are higher for exportables, and relative incomes of sectors with comparative advantage (i.e., the export sector) are higher and so the latter demand and receive less protection.

Rodrik (1995) notes that Findlay and Wellisz (1982) simply assume groups lobby for tariffs but not for export subsidies, while Hillman (1982) assumes politicians want support from import-competing interest groups and not from export-competing groups. Corden (1986) appeals to the conservative social welfare function as an explanation of why society is adverse to negative income shocks (but this begs the question of why there are more negative income shocks for the import sector). Mayer (1984) and Mayer and Riezman (1987) posit a median voter rule that is neutral as to whether import or export sectors get more protection, while Grossman and Helpman's (1994) model predicts that sectors with a high level of production relative to trade will receive more protection. However, sectors with comparative advantage are in the export sector and so Grossman and Helpman's (1994) model predicts that the export sector will receive more protection, which contradicts observed phenomenon [Rodrik (1995)].

Krueger (1990b) notes that Cave's "adding machine" model has elected officials more sympathetic to the claims of import-competing industries, in which there are a large number of voters. However, this model is in contradiction to the political support model of de Gorter and Tsur (1991), Swinnen and de Gorter (1993), and Swinnen (1994), whereby politicians favor smaller groups, *ceteris paribus*. Krueger (1990a) goes on to argue that import tariffs are a revenue motive for government which automatically favors imports and discriminates against exports. However, many countries use non-tariff barriers and export targets that involve no budget expenditures. Another argument is that the transparency of export subsidies makes it a less favorable political form of intervention than import tariffs.

4.3. Instrument type and the degree of rent-seeking

Different instruments will generate different incentive structures to "rent seek" and hence will have differential impacts on social costs. One can delineate two categories of, or stages in, rent-seeking, defined as an investment (or transaction cost) to

(1) increase (or avoid a decrease in) income as a result of securing (blocking) a change in public policy (or institutional arrangement); or

(2) maximize the benefits (or minimize the costs) once these policy changes have created non-exclusive rights.

The first category has policy endogenous if rent seeking has an impact (and so has implications for political economy) while the second has policy as exogenous. Rent-seeking therefore occurs when agents try to change the structure of entitlements and/or is in response to the involuntary change in entitlements by trying to change the agent's share of the aggregate transfer in the sector. There are two issues here: gains from political investments in lobbying for policy changes, and gains from economic investments in taking advantage of the policy once in place. The issue in political economy is the former, even though both are called "rent-seeking" and have normative implications, while the latter is purely normative and analyzed by Alston and James in the preceding chapter.

From a mechanism design perspective, the issue of what political and institutional conditions affect the amount of resources wasted in vying for transfer levels and the particular policy instruments used is critically important. In other words, how do alternative institutional settings or governance rules (including economic conditions) induce a variety of incentive distortions to be chosen in the form of alternative (inefficient) policy instruments? The implication is that not only should there be legislation on how to regulate lobbying and the like, but emphasis should also be on institutional arrangements resulting in policy instruments that are less prone to rent-seeking and welfare-reducing incentive structures. The research on agricultural policy in this respect is sparse and so is a priority for future research. Once the institutional and economic characteristics are identified in the outcome of a policy choice, the degree of social waste induced by agents maximizing benefits or minimizing losses from the policy may have feedback effects on the incentives for lobbies, voters, and politicians to augment the policy instrument choice later. Under these circumstances, both categories of rent-seeking identified above are endogenous.

Brooks and Heijdra (1989) offer a comprehensive survey of the normative implications of alternative policy instruments and economic environments on the degree of rent-seeking[32] [a theoretical generalization by Bhagwati (1982) shows that not all rent-seeking is wasteful]. Olson (1982) sees collective action by lobby groups as a vicious circle of ever-increasing rents and waste. De Gorter and Swinnen (1995), Rausser and Foster (1990), and Zusman and Rausser (1990), on the other hand, view the politician–interest group interaction as a tendency towards growth-promoting policies and cooperative solutions rather than non-cooperating "wars". Hillman and Riley (1989) analyze the strategic (nature of bargaining games) and political (institutional rules) elements that determine the outcome of lobbying by different groups. Conditions for when rents are

---

[32] Brooks and Heijdra (1989) review Varian's (1983) path-breaking study and several other studies that show under what conditions all rents (or more) can be wasted in rent-seeking by interest groups.

fully dissipated by lobbying are determined and depend critically on asymmetric valuations of potential benefits. Hillman and Riley (1989) determine that the equilibrium number of participants (and non-participants) is critically dependent on the rival's evaluation of the potential rents from policy (for both a pre-existing policy-contrived rent and for contestable income transfer policies).

Coggins (1995) extends the work of Hillman and Riley (1989) and others by positing a model of opposing lobbies spending resources to influence government choice of a price policy determined from the Nash equilibrium of a non-cooperative game. This potentially results in waste beyond the rents available as the lobbying efforts of equally matched opponents offset each other and no rent-creating change in the price policy is achieved. The more similar are the incomes and influence of opposing groups, the more likely waste exceeds available rents from price policy. Coggins (1995) also shows that if the opposing groups are unequally matched, then lobbying or waste can be much smaller than the rents obtained from a price policy. This is the situation we observe in agriculture, where producer groups are active lobbyists but consumer groups are not.

5. Explaining public investments in agricultural research

The first studies that systematically explain public good research expenditures in agriculture include Guttman (1978), Huffman and Miranowski (1981), and Rose-Ackerman and Evenson (1985). Each of these studies uses cross-section data focusing on state research funding only in the United States. Guttman (1978) finds empirical support for the lobby group model by showing that research is related to size distribution of farmers, cooperative memberships, firms producing inputs, and proportion of farmers as owner-operators. Huffman and Miranowski (1981) relate research as a function of the importance of farming in the state, the state's budget, and measures of the benefits of research to farmers and their ability to organize for political action. Rose-Ackerman and Evenson (1985) build on these two studies by including the important influence of federal government research expenditures on state funding and the effect of reapportionment (a one-time change in the institutional structure).

Guttman (1978) determines that the number of farms is positively related to the level of research expenditures (when farmers benefit from research), thereby rejecting the lobby group and politician–voter model results earlier on the relationship between group size and political influence. Huffman and Miranowski (1981) argue that the importance of farming causes more research expenditures, again contrary to the predictions of small groups getting more political favors. Rose-Ackerman and Evenson (1985) find that research is positively related to non-farm income, a result that may confirm the politician–voter model's prediction that lower income groups receive more support if farmers gain relatively less (lose) from research. All studies argue that farmers favor more research expenditures and therefore technological change.

Khanna (1993) and Khanna, Huffman and Sandler (1994) analyze the demand for state public research expenditures in the United States using time series data. Systems of simultaneous demand equations are estimated in each study analyzing two polar equilibria: Nash–Cournot and Lindahl (optimal) behavior. Expenditure by an individual state provides benefits to other states as well. States are grouped by geoclimatic conditions so as to identify the boundaries associated with spillovers. Results indicate that demand for public research is price elastic and income inelastic. Their results lend support to the joint public/private hypothesis of research provision whereby each state's private benefits reduce the degree of free-riding and hence underinvestment that otherwise would occur.

5.1.   Research expenditures and commodity policy

Analytical frameworks of Alston, Edwards and Freebairn (1988), Murphy, Furtan and Schmitz (1993), Chambers and López (1993) and Alston and Martin (1995) have price supports exogenous, resulting in sectors with more support from commodity policy demanding (and receiving) higher levels of research funding. De Gorter, Nielson and Rausser (1995b) and de Gorter and Zilberman (1990) show that the ratio of public goods expenditures to price supports is lowest for sectors with high levels of support. They also find that under-funding in public research is higher in sectors with high levels of commodity price support, and that research financed privately by farmers is higher in sectors with less public research funding.

Gardner (1989a), Oehmke and Yao (1990), and de Gorter, Nielson and Rausser (1992, 1995b) develop formal revealed preference models with both endogenous price supports and research to explain how governments react to the relative gains from research by farmers and taxpayers/consumers. Gardner (1989a) and Oehmke and Yao (1990) determine that underinvestment occurs if farmers gain relatively less from research. Rausser (1982) hypothesized that commodity policy allows governments to increase research by compensating farmers for any income losses. The first formal analysis of this hypothesis was undertaken by Rausser and de Gorter (1988) and by Gardner (1989a), who showed that commodity policy can induce more research expenditures. Rausser and Foster (1990) came to a similar conclusion using a lobby group model with reaction functions and a game-theoretic solution. Each political organization representing the interest group acts as a Stackelberg leader with respect to the optimal combination of transfer chosen by the government.

Murphy, Furtan and Schmitz (1993), Anania and McCalla (1995), Chambers and López (1993), and Alston and Martin (1995) emphasize the change in deadweight costs of commodity policy with a change in research funding. These studies conclude that research may have negative effects on aggregate social welfare as it increases the distortions caused by existing commodity price supports. Alston and Pardey (1994) provide empirical evidence for this on a world scale. The first study to determine analytically the conditions under which commodity and research policy is complementary was de Gorter, Nielson and Rausser (1992, 1995b). "Complementarity" [as in Gardner (1989a) and Rausser and Foster (1990)] depends on the structure of the economy but is shown to be likely under the conditions characterizing U.S. agriculture. De Gorter, Nielson and Rausser (1995a) provide an empirical example for the U.S. dairy sector and find complementarity: an increase in commodity price supports leads to more research than otherwise would have been the case.

Roe (1995) determines the bias in public good provision to depend on the level of a household's expenditures on home goods, on wage income, and on the level of market price distortion. He finds that price and public good policy are substitutes under particular circumstances where taxation of agriculture is substituted for public good provision to the urban sector (the result may differ between the traded and non-traded goods markets). He finds tendencies to bias the provision of public goods to urban households when rural households are labor surplus and urban households are labor deficit.

Extending the analysis to the politician–voter model, Swinnen and de Gorter (1998), de Gorter and Swinnen (1998), and Swinnen et al. (2000) analyze the aspects of research and commodity policy together. Because each policy has a differential impact on income distribution, preferences for the public good investment and commodity policy differ between sectors. The policy combination chosen by the government will depend on the preferences of the government, and on the constraints facing it.[33]

These studies distinguish between an "economic interaction effect" and a "political interaction effect" between research and commodity policy. The political interaction effect occurs when the introduction of the commodity policy to reduce income inequality generated by the original research expenditure results in a further increase in research towards the social optimum research level (the latter with no political constraints and no commodity policy, or the political optimum can coincide with the social optimum if there are no deadweight costs associated with the commodity policy).[34] There are two directions to the political interaction effect:

- the level of the price support to reduce income inequality generated by research;
- reduction in inequality with commodity policy induces more research.

The political interaction effect is determined to be positive for conditions facing agriculture:

- Commodity policies increase welfare by inducing an increase in research but not always. A positive aggregate effect is more likely if research benefits are distributed very unequally.
- The choice of commodity policy instrument is very important. The lower the deadweight costs and the larger the economic interaction effect, the more likely the overall effect is positive.

This means social welfare decreases with the deadweight costs associated with the introduction of a commodity policy, but this decrease in social welfare can be offset by social welfare increases due to [see Swinnen and de Gorter (1998)]:

---

[33] Swinnen and de Gorter (1999) emphasize the importance of dynamics and the time inconsistency problem with research and commodity policy.

[34] Social optimum also occurs if the income distribution effects of research are identical between groups with deadweight costs, and assuming no endowment income differentials between groups.

- more research now than otherwise would have been the case without commodity policy (remember that there is always underinvestment in research provided unequal distribution of benefits to research); and
- the deadweight cost per unit transfer declines as research increases (the economic interaction effect).

Therefore, the change in total deadweight costs can be positive or negative.

Economic interaction effects increase the level of research because the deadweight costs per unit of transfer decline. Instead of deadweight costs of a given price support increasing with research, transfers go up automatically with research. With endogenous policies, both research and commodity policy adjust in the presence of political and economic interaction effects. The use of commodity policy to offset relative income effects of research results in a decrease in the opposition to increased research expenditures. This increase in research results in an increase in social income, but the deadweight costs of the commodity policy can offset this [Swinnen and de Gorter (1998)]. The analysis shows in a politician–voter model that commodity policy does not necessarily reduce social welfare and that social welfare is higher if one includes the effects of economic interaction effects in the analysis. A further implication is that governments always underinvest in research except when research benefits are equal between groups or when deadweight costs of commodity policy are zero.

Swinnen et al. (2000) use an econometric model with data on protection levels and research expenditures for industrial and developing countries as dependent variables. These are explained by proxies for pre-policy endowment incomes and income distribution effects of research for each of the rural and urban sectors across time, countries, and sectors. The study shows further that each policy is affected by the structure of economic and political preferences, deadweight costs associated with redistribution, relative numbers in each group, and the level of political and civil liberties. The effect of endowment incomes, distribution of research benefits, and relative group numbers depend critically on who benefits relatively more from research and whether farmers are being taxed or subsidized.

This study provides support for the endogenous research/commodity policy approach that predicts underinvestment in agriculture everywhere, with farmers benefiting relatively less from research in industrial countries (inelastic demand, elastic supply) and relatively more in developing countries (elastic demand, inelastic supply).[35] There exists high productivity of research in both situations. With commodity policy subsidizing farmers in industrial countries for the "farm problem" of the past and taxing farmers in developing countries for the so-called "food problem", there not only is under-investment in research, but the distribution of research benefits provides another explanation for why farmers are taxed in developing countries and subsidized in industrial countries.

---

[35] Baland and Kotwal (1998) specify a social welfare function with weights determined by lobbying and determine that farmers lose from research in India because of inelastic demand, and so there is underinvestment in research.

6. Implications and an agenda for future research

A distinguished literature has emerged in explaining the patterns of agricultural policies, including instrument policy choice and underinvestment in public research expenditures. The instrument policy choice literature is, however, far less advanced than that
of redistribution in terms of theory and particularly the empirical analysis. The empirical literature dealing with the determinants of protection levels across countries, sectors,
and over time needs to be better integrated with the corresponding theoretical models
and vice-versa. More analysis is required on discrete policy changes and the status quo
bias as well as on the institutional and economic factors affecting rent-seeking and policy instrument choice.

There is a wealth of descriptive studies on the agricultural policy process that
needs to be better integrated into existing theory, including studies on various
rules and institutions like agenda control, legislative practices, constitutions, electoral
political structures, regulations on lobbying, bureaucratic behavior, different layers of
government, principal-agent problems for political parties and lobby groups, and the
like. Further work is required in integrating collective action lobby group theory with
that of the politician–voter model and in unraveling observational equivalence. Current
models need to be augmented to include uncertainty and imperfect information, and the
role of credibility commitments and time inconsistency problems. The implications of
the political economy literature for normative analysis also need to be better understood
[see *Economics and Politics* (1997)]. Because distributional issues are at the center of
agricultural policies, we need to determine why institutions do not form to compensate
the affected groups in order for Pareto improvements to be made in terms of policy
instrument choice.

Acknowledgements

We are particularly indebted to Gordon Rausser for his considerable input and help on
this chapter, and as a mentor, for his many insights on the political economy of agriculture. We would also like to thank Christopher Barrett, David Bullock, Jay Coggins,
Bruce Gardner, David Orden, Terry Roe, C. Ford Runge, Vernon Ruttan, Erik Thorbecke and an anonymous referee for their very helpful comments.

References

Abbott, P.C. (1979), "Modeling international grain trade with government-controlled markets", American
    Journal of Agricultural Economics 61:22–31.
Abler, D.G. (1989), "Vote trading on farm legislation in the U.S. House", American Journal of Agricultural
    Economics 71:583–591.
Abler, D.G. (1991), "Campaign contributions and house voting on sugar and dairy legislation", American
    Journal of Agricultural Economics 73:11–17.
Alesina, A., and D. Rodrik (1993), "Distributive politics and economic growth", NBER Working Paper 3668.
Alston, J.M., and C. Carter (1991), "Causes and consequences of farm policy", Contemporary Policy Issues
    9:107–121.

Alston, J.M., C. Carter, J. Chalfant and S. Schonberger (1990), "Redistribution through farm programs: instrument choice and transfer levels", Invited paper presented at the 34th Annual Conference of the Australian Economics Society, Brisbane.

Alston, J.M., C. Carter and V.H. Smith (1995), "Rationalizing agricultural export subsidies", American Journal of Agricultural Economics 77:209–213.

Alston, J.M., G.W. Edwards and J.W. Freebairn (1988), "Market distortions and benefits from research", American Journal of Agricultural Economics 70:281–288.

Alston, J.M., and B.H. Hurd (1990), "Some neglected social costs of government spending in farm programs", American Journal of Agricultural Economics 72:149–156.

Alston, J.M., and W. Martin (1995), "Reversal of fortune: immiserizing technical change in agriculture", American Journal of Agricultural Economics 77:225–259.

Alston, J.M., and P.G. Pardey (1994), "Distortions in prices and agricultural research investments", in: J.R. Anderson, ed., Agricultural Technology: Policy Issues for the International Community (CAB International, Wallingford, CT) 59–84.

Alston, L.J., and T.J. Hatton (1991), "The earnings gap between agricultural and manufacturing laborers, 1925–1941", The Journal of Economic History 51:83–100.

Anania, G. (1997), "Policy choices and interdependence of country decisions in the implementation of the 1994 GATT Agreement on Agriculture", European Review of Agricultural Economics 24:161–181.

Anania, G., and A.F. McCalla (1995), "Assessing the impact of agricultural technology improvements in developing countries in the presence of policy distortions", European Review of Agricultural Economics 22:5–24.

Anderson, K. (1978), "On why rates of assistance differ between Australia's rural industries", Australian Journal of Agricultural Economics 22:99–114.

Anderson, K. (1993), "Lobbying incentives and the pattern of protection in rich and poor countries", Economic Development and Cultural Change 41:401–423.

Anderson, K., and Y. Hayami (eds.) (1986), The Political Economy of Agricultural Protection: East Asia in International Perspective (Allen and Unwin, Sydney).

Appelbaum, E., and E. Katz (1987), "Seeking rents by setting rents: the political economy of rent seeking", The Economic Journal 97:685–699.

Baland, J.-M., and A. Kotwal (1998), "The political economy of underinvestment in agriculture", Journal of Development Economics 55:233–247.

Baldwin, R.E. (1989), "The political economy of trade policy", Journal of Economic Perspectives 3:119–135.

Bale, M., and E. Lutz (1981), "Price distortions in agriculture and their effects: an international comparison", American Journal of Agricultural Economics 63:8–22.

Balisacan, A.M., and J.A. Roumasset (1987), "Public choice of economic policy: the growth of agricultural protection", Weltwirtschaftliches Archiv 123:232–248.

Bardhan, P. (1990), "Symposium on the state and economic development", Journal of Economic Perspectives 4:3–7.

Barrett, C. (1999), "The microeconomics of the developmental paradox: on the political economy of food price policy", Agricultural Economics 20:159–172.

Basu, K., E. Jones and E. Schlicht (1987), "The growth and decay of custom: the role of the new institutional economics in economic history", Exploration in Economic History 24:1–21.

Bates, R.H. (1981), Markets and States in Tropical Africa, California Series on Social Choice and Political Economy (University of California Press, Berkeley, CA).

Bates, R.H. (1983), "Patterns of market intervention in agrarian Africa", Food Policy.

Bates, R.H. (1987), Essays on the Political Economy of Rural Africa, California Series on Social Choice and Political Economy (University of California Press, Berkeley, CA).

Bates, R.H. (1988), "Governments and agricultural markets in Africa", in: R. Bates, ed., Toward a Political Economy of Development: A Rational Choice Perspective, California Series on Social Change and Political Economy, No. 14 (University of California Press, Berkeley, CA) 331–358.

Bates, R.H. (1989), "Discussion of de Janvry–Sadoulet paper", in: A. Maunder and A. Valdés, eds., Proceedings of the 20th ICAE (Dartmouth) 253–258.

Bates, R.H. (1990), "The political framework for agricultural policy decisions", in: C. Eichner and J. Staatz, eds., Agricultural Development in the Third World, 2nd edn., Johns Hopkins Studies in Development (Johns Hopkins University Press, Baltimore, MD) 154–159.

Bates, R.H., and W.P. Rogerson (1980), "Agriculture in development: a coalition analysis", Public Choice 35:513–527.

Becker, G. (1976), "Comment", Journal of Law and Economics 19:245–248.

Becker, G. (1983), "A theory of competition among pressure groups for political influence", Quarterly Journal of Economics 98:371–400.

Beghin, J.C. (1990), "A game theoretic model of endogenous public policies", American Journal of Agricultural Economics 72:138–148.

Beghin, J.C., and W.E. Foster (1992), "Political criterion functions and the analysis of wealth transfers", American Journal of Agricultural Economics 74:787–793.

Beghin, J.C., W.E. Foster and M. Kherallah (1996), "Institutions and market distortions: international evidence for tobacco", Journal of Agricultural Economics 47:355–365.

Beghin, J.C., and L.S. Karp (1991), "Estimation of price policies in Senegal: an empirical test of cooperative game theory", Journal of Development Economics 35:49–67.

Beghin, J.C., and M. Kherallah (1994), "Political institutions and international patterns of agricultural protection", The Review of Economics and Statistics 76:482–489.

Bhagwati, J.N. (1982), "Directly unproductive profit seeking activities: a welfare theoretic synthesis and generalization", Journal of Political Economy 90:988–1002.

Binswanger, H.P., and K. Deininger (1997), "Explaining agricultural and agrarian policies in developing countries", Journal of Economic Literature 35:1958–2005.

Binswanger, H.P., and P.L. Scandizzo (1983), "Patterns of agricultural protection", Report No. ARU 15 (World Bank, Washington, DC).

Birkhaeuser, D., R.E. Evenson and G. Feder (1991), "The economic impact of agricultural extension: a review", Economic Development and Cultural Change 39:607–650.

Bonnen, J.T., and W.P. Browne (1989), "Why is agricultural policy so difficult to reform?", in: C.S. Kramer, ed., The Political Economy of U.S. Agriculture: Challenges for the 1990s (Resources for the Future, National Center for Food and Agricultural Policy, Washington, DC).

Brennan, G., and J. Buchanan (1985), The Reason of Rules: Constitutional Political Economy (Cambridge University Press, Cambridge, MA).

Brooks, J.C. (1994), "Bringing U.S. sugar policy into the GATT", in: G. Anania, C. Carter and A. McCalla, eds., Agricultural Trade Conflicts and GATT (Westview Press, Boulder, CO) 471–492.

Brooks, J.C., A.C. Cameron and C.A. Carter (1998), "Political action committee contributions and U.S. congressional voting on sugar legislation", American Journal of Agricultural Economics 80:441–454.

Brooks, J.C., and C.A. Carter (1994), "The political economy of U.S. agriculture", ABARE Research Report 94.8, Canberra.

Brooks, M.A., and B.J. Heijdra (1989), "An exploration of rent seeking", The Economic Record 188:32–50.

Browne, W.P. (1988), Private Interests, Public Policy, and American Agriculture (University Press of Kansas, Lawrence, KS).

Bullock, D.S. (1992), "Objectives and constraints of government policies: the countercyclicity of transfers to agriculture", American Journal of Agricultural Economics 74:617–629.

Bullock, D.S. (1994a), "In search of rational government: what political preference function studies measure and assume", American Journal of Agricultural Economics 76:347–361.

Bullock, D.S. (1994b), "The countercyclicity of government transfers: a political pressure group approach", Review of Agricultural Economics 16:93–102.

Bullock, D.S. (1995), "Are government transfers efficient? An alternative test of the efficient redistribution hypothesis", Journal of Political Economy 103:1236–1274.

Bullock, D.S. (1996a), "Pareto optimal income redistribution, political preference functions, and the European Community's common agricultural policy", in: J. Antle, D. Sumner and B. Gardner, eds., Essays on Agricultural Policy in Honor of D. Gale Johnson (University of Chicago Press, Chicago, IL) 244–262.

Bullock, D.S. (1996b), "Cooperative game theory and the measurement of political power", American Journal of Agricultural Economics 78:745–752.

Bullock, D.S., and K.-S. Jeong (1994), "A critical assessment of the political preference function approach in agricultural economics: comment", Agricultural Economics 10:201–206.

Bullock, D.S., J. Kola and K. Salhofer (1997), "Transfer efficiency of agricultural policies – a review", Contributed paper, 22nd International Conference of Agricultural Economics, Sacramento, CA.

Bullock, D.S., and K. Salhofer (1997), "Measuring the social costs of suboptimal combination of policy instruments: a general framework and an example", Agricultural Economics 18:233–247.

Campos, J.E.L. (1989), "Legislative institutions, lobbying, and the endogenous choice of regulatory instruments: a political economy approach to instrument choice", Journal of Law, Economic and Organization 5:333–353.

Carter, C., M.D. Faminow, R.M.A. Loyns and E. Peters (1990), "Causes of intervention in Canadian agriculture", Canadian Journal of Agricultural Economics 38:785–795.

Carter, C., A.F. McCalla and J.A. Sharples (eds.) (1990), Imperfect Competition and Political Economy: The New Trade Theory in Agricultural Trade Research (Westview Press, Boulder, CO).

Cassing, J.H., and A.L. Hillman (1985), "Political influence motives and the choice between tariffs and quotas", Journal of International Economics 19:279–290.

Chambers, R.G. (1992), "On the design of agricultural policy mechanisms", American Journal of Agricultural Economics 74:646–654.

Chambers, R.G., and R. López (1993), "Public investment and real-price supports", Journal of Public Economics 52:73–82.

Chappell, H.W. (1982), "Campaign contributions and congressional voting: a simultaneous probit-tobit model", Review of Economics and Statistics 64:77–83.

Coate, S., and S. Morris (1995), "On the form of transfers to special interests", Journal of Political Economy 103:1210–1235.

Cochrane, W. (1965), The City Man's Guide to Farm Problems (University of Minnesota Press, Minneapolis, MN).

Coggins, J.S. (1995), "Rent dissipation and the social cost of price policy", Economics and Politics 7:147–166.

Coggins, J.S., T. Graham-Tomasi and T.L. Roe (1991), "Existence of equilibrium in a lobbying economy", International Economic Review 32:533–550.

Coleman, W.D., G. Skogstad and M. Atkinson (1996), "Paradigm shifts and policy networks: cumulative change in agriculture", Journal of Public Policy 16:273–301.

Coleman, W.D., and S. Tangermann (1997), "Linked games, international mediators, and agricultural trade", Paper presented at the International Agricultural Trade Research Consortium Annual Meeting, December 14–16, San Diego, CA.

Corden, W.M. (1986), "Policies towards market disturbance", in: R.H. Snape, ed., Issues in World Trade Policy (St. Martin's Press, New York) 121–139.

Coughlin, P.J. (1992), Probabilistic Voting Theory (Cambridge University Press, Cambridge, MA).

David, C.C., and J. Huang (1996), "Political economy of rice protection in Asia", Economic Development and Cultural Change 44:463–483.

Davis, O.A., M.J. Hinich and P.C. Ordeshook (1970), "An expository development of a mathematical model of the electoral process", American Political Science Review 64:426–448.

de Gorter, H. (1983), "Agricultural policies: a study in political economy", Ph.D. thesis (University of California, Berkeley, CA).

de Gorter, H., D.J. Nielson and G.C. Rausser (1992), "Productive and predatory public policies: research expenditures and producer subsidies in agriculture", American Journal of Agricultural Economics 74:27–37.

de Gorter, H., D.J. Nielson and G.C. Rausser (1995a), "The determination of technology and commodity policy in the U.S. dairy industry", in: G.C. Rausser, ed., GATT Negotiations and the Political Economy of Policy Reform (Springer-Verlag, Berlin) 253–274.

de Gorter, H., D.J. Nielson and G.C. Rausser (1995b), "The political economy of redistributive policies and the provision of public goods in agriculture", in: G.C. Rausser, ed., GATT Negotiations and the Political Economy of Policy Reform (Springer-Verlag, Berlin) 85–106.

de Gorter, H., and G.C. Rausser (1989), "Endogenizing U.S. milk price supports", Working Paper No. 504 (Department of Agricultural and Resource Economics (CUDARE), University of California at Berkeley).

de Gorter, H., and J. Swinnen (1994a), "Can price supports negate the social gains from public research expenditures in agriculture?", Working Paper 94-06 (Department of Agricultural, Resource and Managerial Economics, Cornell University, Ithaca, NY).

de Gorter, H., and J. Swinnen (1994b), "The economic polity of farm policy", Journal of Agricultural Economics 45:312–326.

de Gorter, H., and J. Swinnen (1995), "The economic polity of farm policy: reply", Journal of Agricultural Economics 46:403–414.

de Gorter, H., and J. Swinnen (1998), "Impact of economic development on commodity and public research policies in agriculture", Review of Development Economics 2:41–60.

de Gorter, H., and Y. Tsur (1990), "The political economy of price policy preferences in European agriculture", Paper presented at the Sixth Congress of the European Association of Agricultural Economists (The Hague, The Netherlands) 3–7.

de Gorter, H., and Y. Tsur (1991), "Explaining price policy bias in agriculture: the calculus of support-maximizing politicians", American Journal of Agricultural Economics 73:1244–1254.

de Gorter, H., and D. Zilberman (1990), "On the political economy of public goods inputs in agriculture", American Journal of Agricultural Economics 72:131–137.

de Janvry, A. (1983), "Why do governments do what they do? The case of food price policy", in: D.G. Johnson and G.E. Schuh, eds., The Role of Markets in the World Food Economy (Westview Press, Boulder, CO) 185–212.

de Janvry, A., A. Fargeix and E. Sadoulet (1991), "The political feasibility of rural poverty reduction", Journal of Development Economics 37:351–367.

de Janvry, A., and E. Sadoulet (1989), "A study in resistance to institutional change: the lost game of Latin American land reform", World Development 17:1397–1407.

DeLong, J.B. (1998), "How fast is modern economic growth?", B. DeLong's website, http://econ161. berkeley.edu.

Dewatripont, M., and G. Roland (1992), "Economic reform and dynamic political constraints", Review of Economic Studies 59:703–30.

Dixit, A. (1996), The Making of Economic Policy (MIT Press, Cambridge, MA).

Dixit, A., and J. Londregan (1995), "Redistributive politics and economic efficiency", American Political Science Review 89:856–866.

Downs, A. (1957), An Economic Theory of Democracy (Harper and Row, New York).

Economics and Politics (1997), Special Issue on the "Determining Paradox" 9(3):205–280.

Ellison, S.F., and W.P. Mullin (1995), "Economics and politics: the case of sugar tariff reform", Journal of Law and Economics 38:335–366.

Fafchamps, M., E. Sadoulet and A. de Janvry (1991), Optimal Tariff Seeking in a General Equilibrium Framework (University of California, Berkeley, CA).

Fernandez, R., and D. Rodrik (1991), "Resistance to reform: status-quo bias in the presence of individual-specific uncertainty", American Economic Review 81:1146–1155.

Field, H., and M. Fulton (1994), "Germany and the CAP: a bargaining model of EC agricultural policy formation", American Journal of Agricultural Economics 76:15–25.

Findlay, R.J., and S. Wellisz (1982), "Endogenous tariffs, the political economy of trade restrictions and welfare", in: J.N. Bhagwati, ed., Import Competition and Response (University of Chicago Press, Chicago, IL) 223–238.

Foster, W.E., and G.C. Rausser (1993), "Price-distorting compensation serving the consumer and taxpayer interest", Public Choice 80:173–289.

Fulginiti, L.E., and J.F. Shogren (1992), "Agricultural protection in developing countries", American Journal of Agricultural Economics 74:795–801.

Gallagher, P. (1988), "The grain sector of the European Community: policy formation, price determination, and implications for trade", American Journal of Agricultural Economics 70:767–778.

Gardner, B.D. (1995), Plowing Ground in Washington: The Political Economy of U.S. Agriculture (Pacific Research Institute for Public Policy, San Francisco, CA).

Gardner, B.L. (1983), "Efficient redistribution through commodity markets", American Journal of Agricultural Economics 65:225–334.

Gardner, B.L. (1987), "Causes of U.S. farm commodity programs", Journal of Political Economy 95:290–310.

Gardner, B.L. (1989a), "Price supports and optimal spending on agricultural research", Working Paper (Department of Agricultural and Resource Economics, University of Maryland).

Gardner, B.L. (1989b), "Economic theory and farm politics", American Journal of Agricultural Economics 71:1165–1171.

Gardner, B.L. (1992), "Changing economic perspectives on the farm problem", Journal of Economic Literature 30:62–101.

Gardner, B.L. (1993), "Demythologizing farm income", Choices 8:22–32.

Gerrard, C., and T. Roe (1983), "Government intervention in food grain markets", Journal of Development Economics 12:109–132.

Gisser, M. (1993), "Price support, acreage controls, and efficient redistribution", Journal of Political Economy 101:584–611.

Goldstein, J. (1993), Ideas, Interests, and American Trade Policy (Cornell University Press, Ithaca, NY).

Goldstein, J., and R.O. Keohane (eds.) (1993), Ideas and Foreign Policy: Beliefs, Institutions and Political Change (Cornell University Press, Ithaca, NY).

Gopinath, M., and T. Roe (1995), "Sources of sectoral growth in an economy wide context: the case of U.S. agriculture", Bulletin No. 95-7 (Economic Development Center, Department of Economics and Department of Applied Economics, University of Minnesota).

Grossman, G.M., and E. Helpman (1994), "Protection for sale", The American Economic Review 84:833–850.

Grossman, G.M., and E. Helpman (1995), "Trade wars and trade talks", Journal of Political Economy 103:675–708.

Guttman, J.M. (1978), "Interest groups and the demand for agricultural research", Journal of Political Economy 86:467–484.

Guyomard, H., L.-P. Mahe, K.J. Munk and T.L. Roe (1993), "Agriculture in the Uruguay Round: ambitions and realities", Journal of Agricultural Economics 44:245–263.

Hall, P.A. (1993), "Policy paradigms, social learning and the state: the case of economic policy making in Britain", Comparative Politics 25:275–297.

Hardin, R. (1982), Collective Action (Resources for the Future, Washington, DC).

Hartle, D.G. (1983), "The theory of 'rent seeking': some reflections", Canadian Journal of Economics 16:539–554.

Hayami, Y. (1988), Japanese Agriculture under Siege (St. Martin's Press, New York).

Heywood, J.S. (1988), "The structural determinants of corporate campaign activity", Quarterly Review of Economics and Business 28:39–48.

Hillman, A.L. (1982), "Declining industries and political-support protectionist motives", American Economic Review 72:1180–1187.

Hillman, A.L., and J. Riley (1989), "Politically contestable rents and transfers", Economics and Politics 1:17–39.

Honma, M., and Y. Hayami (1986a), "The determinants of agricultural protection levels: an econometric analysis", in: K. Anderson and Y. Hayami, eds., The Political Economy of Agricultural Protection (Allen and Unwin, Boston, MA) 39–49.

Honma, M., and Y. Hayami (1986b), "Structure of agricultural protection in industrial countries", Journal of International Economics 20:115–129.

Huffman, W.E., and R.E. Evenson (1994), Science for Agriculture (Iowa State University Press, Ames, IA).

Huffman, W.E., and J.A. Miranowski (1981), "An economic analysis of expenditures on agricultural experiment station research", American Journal of Agriculture Economics 63:104–118.

Jacobson, G.C. (1987), The Politics of Congressional Elections, 2nd edn. (Little and Brown, Boston, MA).

Johnson, M., L. Mahe and T. Roe (1993), "Trade compromises between the European Community and the United States: an interest group – game theory approach", Journal of Policy Making 15:199–222.

Kahneman, D., and A. Tversky (1979), "Prospect theory: an analysis of decision under risk", Econometrica 47:263–291.

Karp, L.S., and A. McCalla (1983), "Dynamic games and international trade: an application to the world corn market", American Journal of Agricultural Economics 65:641–650.

Kennedy, P.L., H. von Witzke and T.L. Roe (1996a), "Strategic agricultural trade policy interdependence and the exchange rate: a game theoretic analysis", Public Choice 88:43–56.

Kennedy, P.L., H. von Witzke and T.L. Roe (1996b), "Multilateral agricultural trade negotiations: a non-cooperative and cooperative game approach", European Review of Agricultural Economics 23:381–399.

Kerr, T.C. (1986), "Trends in agricultural protection", Special Background Report prepared for the World Bank.

Khanna, J. (1993), "Cooperative versus noncooperative behavior: the case of agricultural research", The Review of Economics and Statistics 75:346–352.

Khanna, J., W.E. Huffman and T. Sandler (1994), "Agricultural research expenditures in the United States: a public goods perspective", The Review of Economics and Statistics 76:267–277.

Krasno, J.S., and D.P. Green (1988), "Preempting quality challengers in House elections", Journal of Politics 50:920–936.

Krueger, A. (1990a), "Government failures in development", NBER Working Paper No. 3340.

Krueger, A. (1990b), "Asymmetries in policy between exportables and import-competing goods", in: R. Jones and A. Krueger, eds., Essays in Honor of Robert E. Baldwin (Blackwell, Oxford) 161–178.

Krueger, A. (1992), The Political Economy of Agricultural Pricing Policy: A Synthesis of the Political Economy in Developing Countries (Johns Hopkins University Press, Baltimore, MD).

Krueger, A. (1996), "Political economy of agricultural policy", Public Choice 87:173–175.

Krueger, A., M. Schiff and A. Valdés (1988), "Agricultural incentives in developing countries: measuring the effects of sectoral and economy wide policies", World Bank Economic Review 2:255–272.

Krugman, P. (1998), The Accidental Theorist and Other Dispatches from the Dismal Science (W.W. Norton and Co., New York).

Larue, B., and A. Ker (1993), "World price variability versus protectionism in agriculture: a causality analysis", The Review of Economics and Statistics 342–346.

Lattimore, R.G., and G.E. Schuh (1979), "Endogenous policy determination: the case of Brazilian beef sector", Canadian Journal of Agricultural Economics 27:1–16.

Levine, R., and D. Renelt (1992), "A sensitivity analysis of cross-country growth regressions", American Economic Review 942–963.

Lewis, T., R. Ware and R. Feenstra (1989), "Eliminating price supports: a political-economy perspective", Journal of Public Economics 140:159–185.

Lianos, T.P., and G. Rizopoulos (1988), "Estimation of social welfare weights in agricultural policy: the case of Greek cotton", Journal of Agricultural Economics 39:61–68.

Lindert, P.H. (1991), "Historical patterns of agricultural policy", in: C.P Timmer, ed., Agriculture and the State: Growth, Employment and Poverty in Developing Countries, Food Systems and Agrarian Change Series (Cornell University Press, Ithaca, NY) 29–83.

Long, N.V., and N. Vousden (1991), "Protectionist responses and declining industries", Journal of International Economics 30:87–103.

López, R.A. (1989), "Political economy of U.S. sugar policies", American Journal of Agricultural Economics 71:20–31.

López, R.A. (1994), "Political economy of pricing policies: the case of Philippine sugar", The Developing Economies 22:155–166.

López, R.A., and E. Pagoulatos (1996), "Trade protection and the role of campaign contributions in U.S. food and tobacco industries", Economic Inquiry 34:237–248.

Magee, S.P., W.A. Brock and L. Young (1989), Black Hole Tariffs and Endogenous Policy Theory: Political Economy in General Equilibrium (Cambridge University Press, Cambridge, MA).

Makin, J.H. (1976), "Constraints on formulation of models for measuring revealed preference of policy makers", Kyklos 29:709–732.

Marchant, M.A. (1993), Political Economic Analysis of U.S. Dairy Policies and European Community Dairy Policy Comparisons (Garland, New York) 13, 258.

Mayer, W. (1984), "Endogenous tariff formation", American Economic Review 74:970–985.

Mayer, W., and R. Riezman (1987), "Endogenous choice of trade policy instruments", Journal of International Economics 23:337–381.

McMillan, J. (1993), "A principal components analysis of cross-country growth regressions", Working Paper (Institute for Policy Reform, Washington, DC).

McMillan, J., G. Rausser and S.R. Johnson (1993), "Freedoms and economic growth: transitional and permanent components", WP 93-WP 115 (CARD, Iowa State University).

Michelmann, H.J., J.C. Stabler and G.C. Storey (eds.) (1990), The Political Economy of Agricultural Trade and Policy: Toward a New Order for Europe and North America (Westview Press, Boulder, CO).

Miller, T.C. (1991), "Agricultural price policies and political interest group competition", Journal of Policy Modeling 13:489–513.

Moe, T.M. (1980), The Organization of Interests: Incentives and the Internal Dynamics of Political Interest Groups (University of Chicago Press, Chicago, IL).

Moe, T.M. (1990), "Political institutions: the neglected side of the story", Journal of Law, Economics, and Organization 6:213–253.

Mohtadi, H., and T. Roe (1998), "Growth, lobbying and public goods", European Journal of Political Economy, 14:453–473.

Moyer, H.W., and T.E. Josling (1990), Agricultural Policy Reform: Politics and Process in the EC and the USA (Iowa State University Press, Ames, IA).

Mueller, D.C. (1989), Public Choice II (Cambridge University Press, Cambridge, MA).

Munk, K.J. (1987), "The introduction of the co-responsibility levy for cereals on surplus production", Paper presented in the EC Grain Policy Workshop at the 5th European Congress of Agricultural Economists, Balatonzeplak, Hungary, 31 August–4 September.

Munk, K.J. (1989), "Price support to the EC agricultural sector: an optimal policy?", Oxford Review of Economic Policy 5(2):76–89.

Munk, K.J. (1994), "Explaining agricultural policy, agricultural policy for the 21st century", European Economy, Reports and Studies 4(annex):93–119.

Murphy, J.A., W.H. Furtan and A. Schmitz (1993), "The gains from agricultural research under distorted trade", Journal of Public Economics 51:161–172.

Neville-Rolfe, E. (1984), The Politics of Agriculture in the European Community (European Center for Policy Studies, London).

OECD (1999) (annual), "Agricultural policies, markets and trade in OCED countries", Main Report, Paris.

Oehmke, J.F., and X. Yao (1990), "A policy preference function for government intervention in the U.S. wheat market", American Journal of Agricultural Economics 72:631–640.

Olson, M., Jr. (1971), The Logic of Collective Action: Public Goods and the Theory of Groups (Harvard University Press, Cambridge, MA).

Olson, M., Jr. (1982), The Rise and Decline of Nations: Economic Growth, Stagflation and Social Rigidities (Yale University Press, New Haven, CT).

Olson, M., Jr. (1985), "Space, agriculture, and organization", American Journal of Agricultural Economics 67:928–937.

Olson, M., Jr. (1986), "The exploitation and subsidization of agriculture in developing and developed countries", in: A. Maunde and U. Renborg, eds., Agriculture in a Turbulent World Economy (Aldershot, Gower, UK) 49–59.

Olson, M., Jr. (1990), "Agricultural exploitation and subsidization: there is an explanation", Choices 4:8–11.

Orden, D. (1994), "Agricultural interest groups and the North American Free Trade Agreement", Working Paper No. 4790 (National Bureau of Economic Research, Cambridge, MA).

Orden, D., R. Paarlberg and T. Roe (1999), Policy Reform in American Farm Agriculture (University of Chicago Press, Chicago, IL).

Paarlberg, R. (1997), "Agricultural policy reform and the Uruguay round: synergistic linkage in a two-level game?", International Organization 51:413–444.

Paarlberg, P.L., and P.C. Abbott (1986), "Oligopolistic behavior by public agencies in international trade: the world wheat market", American Journal of Agricultural Economics 68:528–542.

Patterson, L. (1997), "Agricultural policy reform in the European Community: a three-level game analysis", International Organization 51:135–166.

Peltzman, S. (1976), "Toward a more general theory of regulation", Journal of Law and Economics 19:211–240.

Persson, T., and G. Tabellini (1990), Economic Policy, Credibility and Politics (Harwood Academic Publishers, Reading, MA).

Persson, T., and G. Tabellini (1992), "Growth, distribution and politics", European Economic Review 36:593–602.

Persson, T., and G. Tabellini (1994), "Is inequality harmful for growth?", American Economic Review 84:600–621.

Petit, M. (1985), "Determinants of agricultural policy in the United States and the European Community", Research Report 51 (International Food Policy Research Institute, Washington, DC).

Petit, M., M. de Benedictis, D. Britton, M. de Groot, W. Henrichsmeyer and F. Lechi (1987), Agricultural Policy Formation in the European Community: The Birth of Milk Quotas and CAP Reform (Elsevier, Amsterdam).

Pierson, P. (1994), Dismantling the Welfare State? Reagan, Thatcher, and the Politics of Retrenchment (Cambridge University Press, Cambridge, MA).

Pinstrup-Andersen, P. (ed.) (1993), The Political Economy of Food and Nutrition Policies (Johns Hopkins University Press, Baltimore, MD).

Pittman, R. (1976), "The effects of industry concentration and regulation on contributions in three 1972 U.S. senate campaigns", Public Choice 27:71–80.

Putnam, R. (1988), "Diplomacy and domestic politics: the logic of two-level games", International Organization 42:427–460.

Rapp, D. (1988), How the U.S. Got into Agriculture and Why It Can't Get out (Congressional Quarterly, Washington, DC).

Rausser, G.C. (1982), "Political economic markets: PERTs and PESTs in food and agriculture", American Journal of Agricultural Economics 64:821–833.

Rausser, G.C. (1992a), "Predatory versus productive government: the case of U.S. agricultural policies", Journal of Economic Perspectives 6:133–158.

Rausser, G.C. (1992b), "An emerging framework for economic development: an LDC perspective", Working Paper (Institute for Policy Reform, Washington, DC).

Rausser, G.C., and H. de Gorter (1988), "Endogenizing policy in models of agricultural markets", Working Paper No. 482 (Department of Agricultural and Resource Economics (CUDARE), University of California at Berkeley), in: A. Maunder and A. Valdés, eds. (1989), Proceedings of the 20th ICAE (Dartmouth) 253–258.

Rausser, G.C., and W.E. Foster (1990), "Political preference functions and public policy reform", American Journal of Agricultural Economics 72:641–652.

Rausser, G.C., and J.W. Freebairn (1974), "Estimation of policy preference functions: an application to U.S. beef import quotas", Review of Economics and Statistics 56:437–449.

Rausser, G.C., and S.R. Johnson (1993), "State-market-civil institutions: the case of Eastern Europe and the Soviet Republics", World Development 21:675–689.

Rausser, G.C., E. Lichtenberg and R. Lattimore (1982), "Developments in theory and empirical applications of endogenous governmental behavior", in: G.C. Rausser, ed., New Directions in Econometric Modeling and Forecasting in U.S. Agriculture (North-Holland, New York) 547–614.

Rausser, G.C., and P. Zusman (1992), "Public policy and constitutional prescription", American Journal of Agricultural Economics 74:247–257.

Riethmuller, P., and T.L. Roe (1986), "Government behavior in commodity markets: the case of Japanese rice and wheat policy", Journal of Policy Modeling 8:327–349.

Rodrik, D. (1986), "Tariffs, subsidies, and welfare with endogenous policy", Journal of International Economics 21:285–296.

Rodrik, D. (1995), "Political economy of trade policy", in: G. Grossman and K. Rogoff, eds., Handbook of International Economics, Vol. 3 (Elsevier, Amsterdam) 1458–1494.

Rodrik, D. (1996), "Understanding economic policy reform", Journal of Economic Literature 34:9–41.

Roe, T. (1995), "Political economy of structural adjustment: a general equilibrium – interest group perspective", in: A. de Janvry, S. Radwan, E. Sadoulet and E. Thorbecke, eds., State, Market and Civil Organizations (Macmillan Press, London).

Rogoff, K. (1990), "Equilibrium political budget cycles", American Economic Review 80:21–36.

Rose-Ackerman, S., and R.E. Evenson (1985), "The political economy of agricultural research and extension grants, votes, and reapportionment", American Journal of Agricultural Economics 67:1–14.

Runge, C.F., and H. von Witzke (1987), "Institutional change in the common agricultural policy of the European Community", American Journal of Agricultural Economics 69:213–222.

Ruttan, V. (1982), Agricultural Research Policy (University of Minnesota Press, Minneapolis, MN).

Ruttan, V. (1991), "What happened to political development?", Economics Development and Cultural Change 265–292.

Sachs, J.D., and A. Warner (1995), "Economic reform and the process of global integration", Brookings Papers on Economic Activity 1–118.

Sarker, R., K. Meilke and M. Hoy (1993), "The political economy of systematic government intervention in agriculture", Canadian Journal of Agricultural Economics 41:289–309.

Sarris, A.H., and J. Freebairn (1983), "Endogenous price policies and international wheat prices", American Journal of Agricultural Economics 65:214–224.

Schleich, J., and D. Orden (1996), "Efficient choice among domestic and trade policies in Grossman–Helpman Interest-Group Model", Center for Political Economy Bulletin 96-3 (University of Minnesota, Minneapolis, MN).

Schultz, T.W. (1953), The Economic Organization of Agriculture (McGraw-Hill, New York).

Schultz, T.W. (1978), "On economics and politics of agriculture", in: T.W. Schultz, ed., Distortions of Agricultural Incentives (Indiana University Press, Bloomington, IN).

Skully, D.W. (1990), "Government intervention in agriculture: a regulatory approach", Staff Report AGES 9039 (Agriculture and Trade Analysis Division, Economic Research Service, U.S. Department of Agriculture).

Stiglitz, J. (1998), "Distinguished lecture on economics in government – the private uses of public interests: incentives and institutions", Journal of Economic Perspectives 12:3–22.

Stratmann, T. (1992a), "Are contributors rational? Untangling strategies of political action committees", Journal of Political Economics 100:647–664.

Stratmann, T. (1992b), "The effects of logrolling on congressional voting", American Economic Review 82:1162–1176.

Swinnen, J. (1994), "A positive theory of agricultural protection", American Journal of Agricultural Economics 76:1–14.

Swinnen, J. (1996), "Endogenous price and trade policy developments in Central European agriculture", European Review of Agricultural Economics 23:133–160.

Swinnen, J., and H. de Gorter (1993), "Why small groups and low income sectors obtain subsidies: the 'altruistic' side of a 'self-interested' government", Economics and Politics 5:285–293.

Swinnen, J., and H. de Gorter (1998), "Endogenous commodity policies and the social benefits from public research expenditures", American Journal of Agricultural Economics 80:107–115.

Swinnen, J., and H. de Gorter (1999), "On government credibility, compensation, and underinvestment in public agricultural research", Working Paper #22 (KU Leuven Policy Research Group, Department of Agricultural Economics).

Swinnen, J., H. de Gorter and A. Banerjee (1999), "Agricultural protection and economic development: an econometric study of the determinants of agricultural protection in Belgium since the 19th century", Working Paper #8 (revised) (KU Leuven Policy Research Group, Department of Agricultural Economics).

Swinnen, J., H. de Gorter, G. Rausser and A. Banerjee (2000), "The political economy of public research investment and commodity policies in agriculture: an empirical study", Agricultural Economics 22:111–122.

Swinnen, J., and F.A. van der Zee (1993), "The political economy of agricultural policies: a survey", European Review of Agricultural Economics 20:261–290.

Tabellini, G., and A. Alesina (1990), "Voting on the budget deficit", American Economic Review 80:37–49.

Tanaka, S. (1998), "An empirical analysis of political demand and supply in U.S. agriculture: PACS contributions and farm bill votes", Masters Thesis (Department of Agricultural, Resource and Managerial Economics, Cornell University, Ithaca, NY).

Temel, T., and T. Roe (1996), "Endogenous technological change via industry lobbying: closed versus open economy models", Journal of Economic Development 21:81–119.

Thaler, R.H. (1991), Quasi Rational Economics (Russell Sage Foundation, New York) 11–22.

Timmer, C.P. (1989), "Food price policy, the rationale for government intervention", Food Policy 17–27.

Tracy, M. (1989), Governments and Agriculture in Western Europe 1880–1980 (Granada, London).

Trebilcock, M.J., D.G. Hartle, R.S. Prichard and D.N. Dewees (1982), "The choice of governing instruments", Study prepared for the Economic Council of Canada.

Tyers, R. (1990), "Implicit policy preferences and the assessment of negotiable trade policy reforms", European Economic Review 34:1399–1426.

van Bastelaer, T. (1994), "A collective action approach to food pricing distortions", Ph.D. Dissertation (University of Maryland).

Vanzetti, D., and J. Kennedy (1988), "Endogenous price policies and international wheat prices: comment", American Journal of Agricultural Economics 70:743–746.

Varian, H. (1983), "Models of rent seeking", Discussion Paper No. 40 (Centre of Policy Studies, Monash University, Australia).

Vesenka, M.H. (1989), "Economic interests and ideological conviction, a note on PACS and agricultural acts", Journal of Economic Behavior and Organization 12:259–263.

von Cramon-Taubadel, S. (1992), "A critical assessment of the political preference function approach in agricultural economics", Agricultural Economics 7:371–394.

von Witzke, H. (1986), "Endogenous supranational policy decisions: the common agricultural policy of the European Community", Public Choice 48:157–174.

von Witzke, H. (1990), "Determinants of the U.S. wheat producer support price: do presidential elections matter?", Public Choice 64:155–165.

von Witzke, H., and U. Hausner (1993), "A public choice analysis of U.S. producer price support in wheat and corn: implications for agricultural trade and policy", Staff Paper P93-18 (Department of Agricultural and Applied Economics, University of Minnesota).

Welch, W.P. (1982), "Campaign contributions and legislative voting: milk money and dairy price supports", Western Political Quarterly 35:478–495.

Wilson, G.K. (1977), Special Interests and Policymaking: Agricultural Policies and Politics in Britain and the United States of America, 1956–70 (John Wiley and Sons, London).

Winters, L.A. (1987), "The political economy of the agricultural policy of industrial countries", European Review of Agricultural Economics 14:285–304.

Winters, L.A. (1989), "The so-called non-economic objectives of agricultural policy", OECD Economic Studies 13:237–266.

Winters, L.A. (1990), "The national security argument for agricultural protection", The World Economy 13:170–190.

Winters, L.A. (1993), "The political economy of industrial countries' agricultural policies", in: A.J. Rayner and D. Colman, eds., Current Issues in Agricultural Economics (St. Martin's Press, New York) 11–31.

Wittman, D. (1989), "Why democracies produce efficient results", Journal of Political Economy 97:1395–1424.

World Bank (1986), World Development Report (Oxford University Press, New York).

Wright, J.R. (1985), "PACs, contributions, and roll calls, an organization perspective", American Political Science Review 79:400–414.

Wright, J.R. (1990), "Contributions, lobbying, and committee voting in the U.S. House of Representatives", American Political Science Review 84:417–438.

Yeldan, A.E., and T. Roe (1991), "Political economy of rent-seeking under alternative trade regimes", Weltwirtschaftliches Archiv 127:563–583.

Young, L., M. Marchant and A. McCalla (1991), "The political economy of agricultural trade, a review of the literature on domestic policy behavior and international price formation", Staff Report No. AGES 9103 (Agriculture and Trade Analysis Division, Economic Research Service, U.S. Department of Agriculture).

Zusman, P. (1976), "The incorporation and measurement of social power in economic models", International Economic Review 17:447–462.

Zusman, P., and A. Amiad (1977), "A quantitative investigation of political economy: the Israeli dairy program", American Journal of Agricultural Economics 59:88–98.

Zusman, P., and G.C. Rausser (1990), "Organization equilibrium and the optimality of collective action", Working Paper No. 528 (Giannini Foundation of Agricultural Economics, Berkeley, CA).

Zwart, A.C., and K.D. Meilke (1979), "The influence of domestic pricing policies and buffer stocks on price stability in the world wheat industry", American Journal of Agricultural Economics 61:434–447.

Chapter 37

A SYNTHESIS OF AGRICULTURAL TRADE ECONOMICS

LARRY S. KARP and JEFFREY M. PERLOFF

Department of Agricultural and Resource Economics, University of California, Berkeley, CA

Contents

Handbook of Agricultural Economics, Volume 2, Edited by B. Gardner and G. Rausser
© 2002 Elsevier Science B.V. All rights reserved

Abstract

Government intervention in agricultural sectors in both developed and developing countries has resulted in huge distortions in international markets. We describe the types of policies used in the agricultural sector and summarize quantitative measures that suggest their importance. Agricultural trade economists have tried to measure these distortions, to explain their causes, and to recommend policy reform. The discipline has been primarily empirical, relying chiefly on econometric and synthetic models and to a lesser extent on historical analysis and case studies.

A review of attempts to measure trade elasticities, exchange rate effects, and market power illustrates the empirical questions that agricultural trade economists have studied and their results. A summary of empirical political economy models shows how these have been used to explain the types and the levels of government intervention. We then use U.S. grain trade policy in the 1970s and 1980s to illustrate in more detail the kinds of policies that agricultural economists have studied, and their assessments of these policies.

In a theoretical section we outline several important ideas that underpin the empirical work in the discipline: the theory of comparative advantage, the theory of the second best, and the Principle of Targeting. We review the theory of trade policy for a country large enough to alter its terms of trade, and assess its relevance to agricultural trade. We also discuss the extent to which uncertainty and missing insurance markets might justify trade policy. In a concluding section we comment on the contribution that agricultural economists have made to trade reform and the manner in which changes in markets are likely to cause a change in the focus of the discipline.

Keywords

trade, government policies (or "intervention"), distortions, tariffs, politics

JEL classification: Q17

1. Introduction

This chapter provides an overview and synthesis of the discipline of agricultural trade economics, with an emphasis on the role of government policy. The study of agricultural trade, as of trade in general, concerns how decisions in one part of the world affect producers and consumers in another. Most agricultural trade studies present institutional descriptions or empirical analyses of the effects of government policies rather than new theoretical models. The central questions in this research are:

- How does domestic government intervention affect agricultural trade?
- Why do governments choose the types of polices, and the policy levels, that we observe?
- How should the policies be reformed, and how can this reform be achieved?

Most nonagricultural economists view agricultural markets as textbook examples of competition because of the large number of price-taking producers. However, a Byzantine system of government intervention has made agricultural markets among the most distorted in the world. Frequently this intervention has taken the form of direct trade restrictions, but even ostensibly domestic policies have important trade effects.

Agricultural trade restrictions have a long history. The English Corn Laws, which lasted for nearly two centuries until they were dismantled in 1843, restricted imports of grain. By increasing domestic grain prices, these laws increased the rents obtained by domestic landowners. The laws were discarded when it became apparent that they hurt the manufacturing sector (by increasing the cost of labor due to increased food costs), and when that sector achieved political dominance.

In many ways, the modern history of agricultural intervention, especially in developed countries, recapitulates the Corn Laws. Government intervention has sought to protect the owners of quasi-fixed factors in agriculture. As the cost, to other elements of society, of this protection has become more apparent, political forces have gathered to force policy changes. D. Gale Johnson's (1973) influential *World Agriculture in Disarray* describes modern agricultural policies through the mid-1970s. Twenty years later, Tyers and Anderson's (1992) *Disarray in World Food Markets: A Quantitative Assessment* reviews continued government intervention and provides a quantitative assessment of its costs. The completion of the Uruguay Round of GATT negotiations, the continued pressure for reform of the Common Agricultural Policy, successive reforms in the last several U.S. Farm Bills, and major reforms in Australia and New Zealand are the most visible expressions of efforts to liberalize agricultural markets.

While developed countries have typically subsidized their agricultural sectors, non-industrialized countries have taxed them in pursuing the post-World War II development strategy of import substitution. This strategy has been largely abandoned in favor of export promotion during the past fifteen years. To the extent that export promotion favors open international markets, and encourages countries to exercise their comparative advantage, it contributes to liberalized agricultural trade. The last decade has also seen the demise or withering of International Commodity Agreements, institutions favored by developing nations as a means of regulating commodity trade.

The fall of the Soviet system and the substantial agricultural reforms in China have also eroded the old system of government-regulated agricultural production and trade. Thus, during the last ten or fifteen years the interventionist policies that have characterized agricultural trade have come under attack from all quarters.

In the early history of international trade, agricultural goods were among the most important traded commodities. It was natural that classical economists such as Ricardo chose agricultural commodities to illustrate the theory of comparative advantage. The size of the agricultural sector, relative to other parts of the economy, and the importance of agriculture in trade have both diminished over time. However, international agricultural trade is more significant than the size of the agricultural sector would suggest. In many developed countries agriculture is important in the trade balance, and international trade is important to the agricultural sector. World trade in agricultural commodities as a percentage of agricultural production has risen in this century for both developed and developing countries, despite high levels of protectionism.

Whether measured as a percentage of gross national product (GNP) or of the labor force, agriculture's share is 6.2 percent or less in most developed economies (Table 1). However, agricultural trade is a larger component of total trade in many of these countries. Agriculture's share of exports exceeds 50 percent for New Zealand and 20 percent for Australia and Turkey. International trade accounts for a significant share of both domestic consumption and production. For the U.S., exports have accounted for 55 percent of wheat production and 40 percent of rice and cotton production over the last several years. According to recent U.S. Department of Agriculture (USDA)

Table 1
The importance of agriculture in GNP and trade

	Percent of agriculture in GDP			Percent of agricultural exports in total exports (Percent of agricultural imports in total imports)		
	1980–82	1990–92	1993	1980–82	1990–92	1993
Australia	4.1	2.8	2.7	41.1 (4.4)	26.0 (4.5)	21.7 (4.4)
Austria	4.1	2.8	2.3	4.6 (7.6)	3.5 (5.7)	3.7 (6.0)
Canada	2.8	1.2	1.4	11.5 (7.8)	8.2 (6.2)	7.6 (6.1)
EC	3.6	2.3	–	11.9 (13.5)	11.1 (11.2)	–
Finland	3.6	2.1	3.3	5.4 (7.6)	2.9 (5.8)	3.6 (6.8)
Iceland	3.4	2	2.5	3.0 (10.5)	1.9 (8.9)	1.3 (10.3)
Japan	2.5	1.7	–	0.7 (12.7)	0.4 (12.8)	0.4 (13.4)
New Zealand	7.8	5.7	6.2	66.7 (6.5)	53.2 (7.4)	50.4 (8.0)
Norway	2.5	1.7	1.5	1.9 (7.2)	1.2 (5.7)	1.3 (5.4)
Sweden	1.5	0.7	0.6	2.7 (7.0)	2.1 (6.8)	2.0 (7.6)
Switzerland	2.7	2.9	2.6	3.7 (9.3)	3.1 (6.9)	3.1 (7.6)
Turkey	16.8	15.9	14.4	52.2 (3.9)	24.9 (8.7)	23.7 (7.8)
United States	2.8	1.7	1.4	19.3 (7.5)	11.4 (5.2)	–

Source: Agricultural policies, markets and trade in OECD countries [OECD (1995), Tables II.1 through II.13].

estimates, exports have accounted for approximately 25 percent of U.S. producers' gross cash receipts over the past decade. Imports account for approximately 8 percent of food consumed in the U.S. Thus, agricultural trade is important to the national trade balance and to the agricultural sector, even where that sector is a small fraction of the economy. The prominent role of agricultural issues during the GATT negotiations in the early 1990s is another indication of the importance both of agricultural trade and of government intervention in agricultural markets.

Policies that affect agricultural trade include domestic policies such as producer subsidies; explicit trade intervention such as tariffs, quotas, and export subsidies; nontariff barriers; and state trading. Hereafter, when we speak of "government policies" we mean the entire web of government intervention. Many agricultural trade economists have studied the effects of such policies on trade and have encouraged policy reform. There is broad agreement that a general liberalization of trade improves welfare. Beyond that limited and unremarkable agreement, controversy exists about the distribution of benefits and about the effects of piecemeal reforms.

There are at least three fundamental reasons for this controversy. First, even if policies elsewhere remain constant, a policy change in one country has uncertain effects because of uncertain supply and demand elasticities in the "rest of the world" (ROW). Second, government policies are endogenous, and these may change in response to policy changes elsewhere. Third, the effects of policy reform are unclear according to the theory of the second best, which holds that an apparent move toward free markets may reduce welfare in the presence of other distortions. Since there are many sometimes offsetting and sometimes reinforcing distortions in agricultural markets, the theory of the second best has to be taken seriously.

The rest of this chapter discusses how the policy environment (with its attendant uncertainties) has influenced the direction of the agricultural trade economics profession. Section 2 summarizes the history of government involvement in agricultural trade. Section 3 discusses important empirical issues in agricultural trade. Section 4 examines the application of political economy models in the study of agricultural policy and trade. Section 5 focuses on two U.S. policies that affect the international grains market. These policies, and the manner in which the agricultural economics profession analyzes them, illustrate the issues and the methods in the profession. Section 6 discusses some of the theoretical ideas central to agricultural trade economics, and Section 7 concludes.

2. Review of policy intervention[1]

Changes in the discipline of agricultural trade economics have largely been determined by changing agricultural policies, rather than by developments in mainstream economic

---

[1] This section is based extensively on Anania et al. (1994), Josling (1990), Kamp and Runge (1994), Meilke and Sarker (1997), Salvatore (1992), and International Agricultural Trade Research Consortium (1994). See also Sumner and Tangermann (2002) in this Handbook.

Table 2
Measures of government intervention: PSEs and CSEs (in percentages)

	1979–81[a]	1986–88[a]	1989–91[a]	1992	1993[b]	1994e[b]	1995p[b]
Australia	8 (−2)	10 (−9)	10 (−8)	11 (−8)	9 (−6)	10 (−7)	9 (−6)
Austria	27 (−24)	46 (−48)	48 (−47)	57 (−52)	59 (−52)	61 (−53)	*
Canada	20 (−12)	43 (−24)	42 (−23)	38 (−23)	31 (−21)	26 (−19)	27 (−15)
European Union[c]	36 (−28)	48 (−44)	45 (−39)	47 (−39)	49 (−39)	49 (−38)	49 (−34)
Finland	51 (−44)	68 (−69)	70 (−71)	66 (−68)	64 (−65)	69 (−65)	*
Iceland	68 (−33)	82 (−48)	84 (−33)	83 (−24)	76 (−37)	72 (−40)	75 (−41)
Japan	60 (−36)	73 (−57)	66 (−49)	73 (−53)	73 (−51)	74 (−50)	77 (−51)
New Zealand	18 (−5)	18 (−8)	5 (−5)	3 (−3)	3 (−4)	3 (−5)	4 (−8)
Norway	70 (−26)	74 (−62)	74 (−61)	76 (−63)	75 (−60)	47 (−57)	74 (−54)
Sweden	42 (−23)	55 (−57)	57 (−57)	57 (−52)	53 (−42)	51 (−41)	*
Switzerland	64 (−48)	78 (−64)	76 (−56)	77 (−52)	80 (−56)	81 (−59)	81 (−56)
Turkey	17 (−10)	26 (−18)	33 (−27)	36 (−32)	35 (−31)	34 (−24)	23 (−14)
United States	15 (−9)	30 (−13)	22 (−10)	22 (−11)	23 (−11)	20 (−10)	15 (−8)
OECD	29 (−22)	45 (−37)	40 (−33)	42 (−34)	43 (−33)	42 (−33)	41 (−30)

[a]Source: Agricultural policies, markets and trade in OECD countries [OECD (1995), Annex Table III.29 p. 256–257].

[b]Source: Agricultural policies, markets and trade in OECD countries [OECD (1995), Annex Table III.23, 24 p. 187–188].

[c]EU-10 for 1979–81, EU-12 for 1986–1994, EU-15 for 1995 and EU includes ex-GDR from 1990.

Notes: e = estimates; p = provisional; * = included in EU-15.

theory. Understanding the field requires some knowledge of the nature and extent of these policies, which we review in this section. We first discuss summary statistics of aggregate levels of government intervention. Then, we review the evolution of international negotiations and describe important agricultural policies. We conclude the section with a discussion of nontariff barriers.

2.1. Aggregate measures of policy intervention

Traditionally, agricultural production in developed countries has been subsidized and protected against imports. The share of producers' revenue provided by government transfers and subsidies, called the producer subsidy equivalent (PSE), is one measure of government involvement (Table 2). From the late 1970s to the mid 1990s, government intervention accounted for over 70 percent of producer revenue in Japan, approximately 20 percent in the U.S., and nearly half of revenue in the European Union (EU).[2] The PSEs for many other developed countries, excluding Australia and New Zealand, were

[2] For brevity we refer to the countries that collectively maintain the Common Agricultural Policy (CAP) as the European Union (EU), even though the name has changed several times and the number of members has doubled since the CAP began in the 1960s.

of similar orders of magnitude. Major reforms in the 1970s and 1980s resulted in significantly lower levels of government intervention in Australia and New Zealand. The OECD estimates that in 1994 government support of agriculture, in U.S. dollars, amounted to $81.64 billion in the EU, $39.02 billion in Japan, and $25.73 billion in the U.S.

Proponents of PSEs [such as Tangermann, Josling and Pearson (1987)] thought that they would be useful in GATT negotiations. By providing a broad measure of government intervention, PSEs enable negotiators to focus on the extent and general nature of government policy without becoming bogged down in the minutiae of a large number of specific policies. Some parties to the negotiations, principally the EU, initially resisted the idea of calculating these measures and were reluctant to make public the early estimates. However, the PSEs were eventually estimated for all parties and played an important role in negotiations.

Government policies in most developed countries raise consumer prices above world prices, thus effectively taxing consumers. The consumer subsidy equivalent (CSE) is the difference between world prices and domestic consumer prices divided by world prices. For most countries, the consumer tax (measured by the CSE) is slightly smaller than the PSE, but it is a similar order of magnitude. The U.S., where consumer taxes are significantly lower than producer subsidies, is an exception.

In calculating PSEs and CSEs, analysts aggregate a broad spectrum of policies that have different effects on supply and demand. Therefore, we cannot tell which countries' policies most distort trade by comparing PSEs and CSEs unless we have detailed information on the underlying policies. The magnitude of PSEs and CSEs shows that there is considerable government intervention in agricultural markets, but the ranking of PSEs does not necessarily imply a ranking of degree of distortion. Similarly, a reduction in a particular PSE can have widely different effects on agents in the agricultural sector, depending on the nature of the policies and how the reduction is made. For example, Hertel (1989) points out that by increasing subsidies for inputs that are complementary to labor, and reducing other subsidies, the PSE can be reduced without decreasing the demand for agricultural labor.

In most cases, government intervention distorts trade. Some policies, such as export subsidies, drive a wedge between domestic and world prices and have direct trade effects. Other policies (e.g., deficiency payments) drive a wedge between domestic producer prices and world prices. Since these policies affect domestic supply, they also distort trade.

2.2. Evolution of agricultural trade negotiations

We now sketch the evolution of trade negotiations. A great irony of these negotiations is that the U.S. has struggled for the past thirty years to dismantle a system of agricultural trade that it initially promoted. At the formation of GATT, the U.S., which used import quotas to regulate domestic prices, insisted that agriculture receive special treatment. Following a challenge from the Netherlands in the early 1950s, GATT granted a waiver that exempted most agricultural policies from the rules that bound trade in other commodities. This waiver permitted quantitative import restrictions taken in conjunction with domestic supply controls.

The U.S. reversed its position and began to promote liberalization of agricultural trade in the Dillon and Kennedy Rounds of GATT negotiations in the 1960s. In the Dillon Round, the EU accepted a zero tariff for cotton and oilseeds, and agreed not to raise ("bound") tariffs on several other commodities. In the Kennedy Round, the U.S. proposed a complete "tariffication" of the EU's variable levies, but achieved only modest concessions. The U.S. continued to promote liberal agricultural markets and the EU continued to favor managed markets during the Tokyo Round in the 1970s. The compromise reached in the Tokyo Round did not achieve a principal U.S. objective, the reduction of export subsidies.

Agriculture moved to the front of trade negotiations during the Uruguay Round, which began in the late 1980s. A group of exporting countries, the Cairns Group, which includes Canada, Australia, and New Zealand, advocated substantial liberalization, while the U.S. supported more moderate reform and the EU resisted both reform proposals. However, even within the EU, there was support for reform because of the enormous cost of existing programs. The eventual compromise of the Uruguay Round required developed countries to reduce intervention by an amount sufficient to achieve a 20 percent reduction in an index known as the Aggregate Measure of Support (AMS). This index, like the PSE, measures government support for producers. However, the AMS excludes "decoupled" or "Green Box" policies, which supposedly do not distort producer and consumer decisions. Such policies include conservation measures, crop insurance, disaster payments, and income payments not based on production. Payments based on a fixed area and yield or on a fixed number of livestock are also viewed as nondistortionary. Because of previous domestic reforms, U.S. policies for most commodities were already "decoupled" by the time agreement in the Uruguay Round was reached.

The agreement requires conversion of the EU's variable levies into "equivalent" tariffs,[3] as the U.S. had requested thirty years earlier during the Kennedy Round. Tariffication of these and other policies (such as quotas and import licenses) makes government intervention more transparent, and thus may make it easier to negotiate reductions and monitor existing agreements. In some cases the resulting tariffs restrict imports more than the quotas they replaced (so-called "dirty tariffication"). The agreement sets minimum average tariff reductions as well as minimum reductions for each commodity. These reductions are greater for developed than for less-developed

---

[3] The equivalence of tariffs and other policies such as quotas requires very restrictive (and implausible) conditions. See Moschini (1991) for an overview and Moschini and Meilke (1991) for an example based on the U.S.–Canada chicken trade. This nonequivalence complicates the negotiated replacement of policy instruments and introduces error to numerical models in which complicated policies are incorporated by using "tariff-equivalents".

countries. The agreement also requires the volume of subsidized exports be reduced by over 20 percent and the value of export subsidies reduced by 36 percent.

The Uruguay Round was a step toward dismantling nations' complex domestic agricultural support programs. This agreement reflects the belief that government intervention in agriculture should be made more transparent and less distortionary. Greater transparency would be achieved by converting quotas and other nontariff barriers into "equivalent" tariffs. Smaller distortions would result by reducing tariffs and replacing policies that affected production and consumption decisions (virtually all existing policies) with policies that would approximate pure income transfers (the so-called decoupled policies). While the extent to which the agreement results in freer agricultural trade in the short run has been debated, it does increase the transparency of domestic policies and offers the hope of long-term liberalization.

2.3. Trade and domestic agricultural policies

Producer subsidies, tariffs, quotas, voluntary export restraints, and export subsidies are the most important domestic and trade policies to distort international agricultural markets. The key domestic policies in developed countries include deficiency payments and other direct producer subsidies. These account for up to two-thirds of producer support in the U.S., Canada, New Zealand, and Australia prior to the Uruguay Round.

The U.S. deficiency payments system began in the 1960s as a means to make direct payments from the U.S. Treasury to producers. In the early 1970s the Agricultural and Consumer Protection Act codified the two-price system based on target prices and loan rates. The 1985 Farm Bill reduced target prices by approximately 10 percent. Further reductions occurred in the 1995 Farm Bill, as a result of both domestic and international political pressure to cut farm subsidies. This farm bill reduced support for some commodities (such as milk), but others (such as sugar and peanuts) escaped substantial reform.

The variable levy was the cornerstone of the EU Common Agricultural Policy (CAP). This levy is a tariff that is adjusted to reflect changes in world prices in order to maintain a domestic target price. The levy insulates the domestic market from price fluctuations in the ROW, thereby increasing ROW price instability. Variable levies have been used since the 1960s to limit imports of rice, olive oil, milk, and other products that competed with EU production.

Most countries have used tariffs. U.S. tariffs in recent periods have ranged from 2 to 4 percent for poultry and grains and up to almost 200 percent for peanuts. Japan, a net importer of agricultural goods, has used much higher tariffs than either the U.S. or the EU.

Typically, however, tariffs have been less important for agricultural trade than nontariff barriers (NTBs). NTBs also distort agricultural trade [Hillman (1978, 1997)]. Most countries have imposed quotas on agricultural trade. Quotas were an important policy instrument in the U.S. from the 1930s to the 1950s. During the 1990s, U.S. quotas restricted imports of beef and veal, cotton, peanuts, sugar, and cheese. Prior to the Uruguay Round agreement, Japanese agricultural trade policies relied on quotas. The number of Japanese commodities protected by quotas declined in the 1960s, but protection for the most important ones (rice, citrus and dairy products, beef, and lamb) continued.

Voluntary export restraints (VERs) have been used in agricultural trade, but are less important than in car and steel manufacturing. A VER controlled New Zealand's exports of milk products to the Australian market prior to 1990. France had a VER agreement with Argentina in 1988 for sheep and goat meat.

Both the U.S. and EU have used export subsidies extensively. Prior to the 1960s, most U.S. agricultural exports other than wheat were subsidized. These subsidies were eliminated as the U.S. became a net exporter of agricultural products, but they reappeared in 1985 with the Export Enhancement Program. In the 1970s, the EU began using export subsidies routinely, causing friction with other exporters. The EU subsidy is based on restitution payments; exporters receive the difference between the internal EU price (including the cost of transport) and the world price. The EU budget finances the program for most commodities. The sugar export subsidy is an exception. It is self-financed, and uses a tax levied on sugar producers for above-quota production. The Canadian government has also implicitly subsidized wheat exports using a freight subsidy.

Other nontariff barriers include economy-wide policies (i.e., exchange rates and antitrust laws) that affect all sectors and not just agriculture. While many government interventions affect agricultural trade, some are more likely candidates for reform than others. Countervailing duties and quality and health restrictions are two prominent examples. Their importance to trade is likely to grow; however, it is difficult to quantify their effects.

Countervailing duties and anti-dumping laws are a disguised means of protection in the U.S., Canada, EU, and Australia. How much these measures distort agricultural trade is disputed. Kherallah and Beghin (1998) report that half of U.S. trade complaints against Canada are for agricultural products, and a large percentage of total U.S. anti-dumping cases also involve agriculture. In France, however, only 1.2 percent of the anti-dumping cases in the 1980s involved agricultural products [Salvatore (1992), p. 164, Table 8.2].

Countries are able to protest anti-dumping rulings against their exports by appealing to a GATT panel. During the last twenty years, 19 of the 32 complaints brought before this panel involved agricultural trade. Twelve of these complaints were against EU policies.

Trade restrictions ostensibly based on health concerns may also be disguised protection [e.g., Peterson, Paggi and Henry (1988), and Roberts (1998)]. International trade in beef products is a frequently cited example. The EU has restricted beef imports from Central Europe and the U.S., and continental Europe has restricted beef imports from the U.K. on the basis of alleged health concerns.

The success of the Uruguay Round in making agricultural policies more transparent may increase governments' incentives to find more subtle means of intervention. An unintended consequence of the agreement may be increased use of NTBs. GATT negotiators attempted to guard against this danger by establishing a dispute resolution mechanism under the World Trade Organization (WTO). For example, health and quality standards are covered by the Sanitary and Phytosanitary Agreement of the Uruguay Round. This agreement allows countries that view the international standard as inadequate to adopt more stringent standards based on scientific evidence. These standards must meet health and safety goals in a manner that minimizes trade distortions. It remains to be seen whether the WTO will permit countries to impose more stringent standards. For example, it ruled in favor of the U.S. in a 1997 case involving EU restrictions on beef imports on the grounds that the restrictions had an insufficient scientific basis.

Marketing orders, which exist for many commodities and frequently set minimum quality standards, may be another means of disguised protection. Since domestic producers control marketing orders, they are able to set the standard in a manner that discriminates against foreign producers [Chambers and Pick (1994)]. Greater differentiation between domestic and foreign products increases the potential for this kind of disguised protection.

2.4. Summary

Historically, governments in developed countries have given large subsidies to agriculture. Although many of the policies were nominally domestic, they affected producers and consumers in other countries through international trade. Agricultural policies have been a major obstacle to trade liberalization over the past four decades. The agreement negotiated in the Uruguay Round promotes liberalization, but the magnitude of its effects, especially in the short run, is unclear. NTBs are likely to be among the most important trade policies and the source of the most contentious disputes in the future.

3. Empirical issues in agricultural trade

Most policy debates in agricultural trade turn on empirical issues. For example, the effect of export subsidies or supply restrictions in one country or region depends on supply and demand responses elsewhere. The magnitude (and sometimes even the direction) of price and quantity effects and the welfare effects of these policies depend on parameters that we cannot measure precisely. Agricultural trade economists have devoted much of their research efforts to obtaining better parameter estimates and making better use of current estimates. This section describes three of the most important empirical questions and the approaches taken to answer them.

The first question involves the magnitudes of the excess demand elasticity facing exporters and the excess supply elasticity facing importers. These elasticities summarize the aggregate effect of commodity-specific or sector-specific policies. To properly predict the effects of a variety of trade policies, we need to know the size of these elasticities.

The second question concerns the effects of exchange rates on agricultural trade. Macro policies affect agricultural trade through their effects on exchange rates. We discuss reasons why the exchange rate may be important to agricultural trade and review empirical findings.

The third empirical question concerns the degree of market power in international agricultural markets. The extent and distribution of market power are important determinants of agricultural trade, and of the trade effects of government policies. We briefly review the empirical literature on market power, and we close the section with a discussion of how the empirical models have been applied to policy issues.

3.1. Trade elasticity estimates

Two approaches – the *direct* and the *synthetic* methods – are used to estimate excess supply and demand elasticities [Gardiner and Dixit (1986)]. A researcher taking the direct approach typically estimates the elasticity of export demand by regressing exports on border prices and variables that determine supply and demand in importing countries. These variables include other commodity prices, government policies, and weather in the importing countries. If one believes that these explanatory variables are exogenous, such equations can be viewed as reduced-form specifications.

A researcher using the synthetic method constructs estimates of export demand elasticity by combining estimates of supply and demand elasticities with estimates of the price-transmission elasticity. The price-transmission elasticity measures the percentage change in the domestic price caused by a percentage change in the world price, and thus captures endogenous changes in sector- or commodity-specific policies. If the ratio of the domestic and the world price is constant (due to free trade or a fixed ad valorem tariff), the price-transmission elasticity is one, its upper bound. If the country uses a (binding) quota or a variable levy, domestic price is completely insulated from world price, and the price-transmission elasticity is zero, its lower bound. The import-demand elasticity is the product of the price-transmission elasticity and the (weighted) difference between the domestic demand and supply elasticities. Thus, the synthetic method decomposes a trade elasticity into the product of two terms, where one summarizes endogenous government policy responses, and the other summarizes aggregate producer and consumer behavior.

Abbott (1988) reviews a number of econometric problems common to both methods. With either approach it is difficult to determine which variables to include and what functional form to use. Thursby and Thursby (1988) discuss these specification problems in detail and show by example how they can be resolved.

Multicollinearity is a common problem. More serious, if the importing country has a sufficiently large part of the market, its net supply and demand affect world price, causing that variable to be endogenous. Unless the endogeneity problem is corrected, it leads to biased and inconsistent estimates. Aggregation problems further reduce the usefulness of these estimates for policy analysis, which sometimes requires isolating excess demand elasticities for narrowly defined commodities and regions (as with targeted-export subsidies).

Much empirical work has been done to estimate excess supply and demand elasticities. Stern, Francis and Schumacher (1976), and Goldstein and Khan (1985) review over 200 empirical studies, including agricultural and nonagricultural commodities. Gardiner and Dixit (1986) review over 40 empirical studies for five crops (wheat, coarse grains, soybeans, rice, and cotton). Karp et al. (1994) review nearly 40 studies for coffee, sugar, and cotton.

Although tremendous effort has been devoted to this research, no consensus has been reached. Researchers using different models draw different conclusions about issues as basic as whether the U.S. faces an elastic or inelastic demand for its agricultural exports. A government's policy choice depends on the size of this elasticity. If demand for U.S. exports is inelastic, export earnings will increase as exports decrease, so supply controls would increase income to the agricultural sector. Gardiner and Dixit (1986) report varying estimates of long-run export demand elasticities facing the U.S. (0.23 to 5 for wheat, 0.4 to 10 for coarse grains, and 0.3 to 2.8 for soybeans). In an earlier review of the literature, Schmitz et al. (1981) found similar variation.

Estimates of short-run elasticities are more consistent. For example, according to most estimates for grains, cotton, and soybeans, the U.S. faces an inelastic ROW demand in the short run.

Tyers and Anderson's (1988) multicommodity trade model incorporates estimated price-transmission elasticities obtained using a partial adjustment model. The dynamic nature of this model makes it possible to distinguish short- and long-run price-transmission elasticities. However, few models use econometrically estimated price-transmission elasticities [Sullivan (1990)].

To decide which current estimates to use for future simulation models, it would help to know whether the direct or synthetic approach gives more reliable estimates. Unfortunately, there are no convincing answers to this question, although some writers have strong opinions. The synthetic approach imposes more structure. It decomposes a total effect into two partial effects, one comprised of endogenous policy changes and the other consisting of net changes by producers and consumers. It is not obvious, however, that adding more structure provides a better estimate of the export response to changes in world price. Greater efficiency is gained if the structure is correctly specified, but additional errors are introduced if the structure is misspecified.

The direct approach usually produces lower elasticity estimates than the synthetic. Researchers who use the estimates in policy models frequently choose an intermediate value. There is no systematic means of selecting one estimate over another.

Often the preferred approach depends on the policy question rather than on econometric considerations. For example, to determine the effects of the Uruguay Round's tariffication of quotas (and the subsequent tariff reductions), elasticity estimates obtained using the direct method are of little use. Tariffication of quotas alters the elasticity of price-transmission but does not necessarily affect domestic supply and demand relations. A reliable synthetic elasticity is more useful because it decomposes the two effects. Thus, the appropriate choice between synthetic and estimated elasticities may depend on whether we are interested in studying a marginal or a structural change, such as tariffication.

3.2. Exchange rate effects

Policies designed to influence macroeconomic variables, such as unemployment and interest rates, affect the agricultural sector. Often such policies impact agricultural trade only indirectly, and these are unlikely to be altered because of effects in the agricultural sector. However, the exchange rate is a macro variable that has a direct and important effect on agricultural trade. This link is especially clear in developing countries, where agricultural (or other natural-resource-intensive) goods comprise a large fraction of exports. In these countries, government influence on the exchange rate is an important agricultural policy issue [Bautista and Valdés (1993)].

A static, two-commodity model illustrates the effects of a devaluation. "Home" is a small (price-taking) country that produces and imports machines, and produces and exports food. There are no transportation costs, and domestic and foreign goods are homogeneous. We choose units of goods so that the world price of each is one dollar, and we choose units of Home currency so that the initial exchange rate is one (e.g., the price of a dollar is one unit of the Home currency). At the initial Home prices, a 10 percent devaluation of the domestic currency means that the ROW can import a Home unit of food for only 90 cents, but it costs Home 1.1 units of its currency to import a machine. The demand for Home's exports increases because their dollar price has fallen, while Home's demand for imports decreases because their domestic price has risen. A 10 percent devaluation has the same effect on domestic prices as a 10 percent tariff or export subsidy. One possible conclusion is that a devaluation increases a country's exports and "improves" its balance of trade much as a 10 percent tariff or export subsidy would. A corollary is that if the country maintains too high an exchange rate, its exports suffer.

This logic forms the basis for the view that an overvalued dollar during the 1960s inhibited U.S. agricultural exports [Schuh (1974)], and that the boom in exports during the early 1970s was due to the dollar's devaluation. This claim spurred a series of empirical studies, some of which [e.g., Konandreas, Bushnell and Green (1978)] supported the hypothesis, while others [e.g., Greenshields (1974), Bessler and Babula (1987), Johnson, Grennes and Thursby (1977)] challenged it.[4]

There is an important difference between a devaluation and the combined tariff/export subsidy. A government chooses a tariff/export subsidy and enforces it at the border. If

---

[4] Most of the empirical work in agricultural economics on exchange rates is partial equilibrium. Adelman and Robinson (1992) provide one of the early general equilibrium analyses of effects of exchange rates on exports.

the government rationed foreign currency, control of the nominal exchange rate would give it the same leverage over domestic prices, and thus over trade. When currencies are freely traded, changes in nominal exchange rates reflect changes in fiscal and trade policy. These fundamental policies can affect agricultural trade, and the exchange rate may be the mechanism through which the effect is felt. However, it is a mistake to view changes in the exchange rate as the cause of changes in agricultural trade.[5]

In order to see this point, imagine there was a change in the nominal exchange rate without any associated change in fundamental policy. At constant domestic prices, this change promotes exports and reduces imports, and causes an increase in the balance of trade. However, the possibility of arbitrage causes the domestic price of both goods to increase. Equilibrium is restored when domestic prices have risen by the amount of the devaluation, cancelling its effect.

The model described above, which ignores transportation costs and treats goods as homogeneous, assumes that the "law of one price" holds. For example, a ton of wheat sells for the same price at Home as in the ROW. This "law" is unlikely to hold exactly because its underlying assumptions are false. It is straightforward to modify the model (and the predicted relation between prices) by including transportation costs or tariffs. Data for these variables can be obtained. However, even when prices are adjusted by these costs, the price of wheat may differ across countries because of differences in quality.[6] Whatever the explanation for the price difference, it is unlikely to be caused by nominal exchange rates. Therefore, changes in the exchange rate should have no long-run effect on this price difference under perfect competition. Under imperfect competition, changes in the exchange rate may lead to changes in price differentials, for reasons discussed in Section 3.3.

A large empirical literature tests whether some form of the law of one price holds. Goodwin, Grennes and Wohlgenant (1990a, 1990b)] find that the law is more likely to hold for expected prices than contemporaneous prices. Thus, the law is more likely to describe a long-run tendency than to hold at any point in time. Dutton and Grennes (1988) provide a general description of the role of the exchange rate in trade models.

Although devaluation has no long-run effect when other policies are held constant, it can certainly have a short-run effect. Countries typically do not have zero balance of

---

[5] Bautista and Valdés (1993, p. 11) make this point in describing the effect of government policies on agriculture in developing countries: "This price bias against agriculture cannot be eliminated simply by adjusting the nominal exchange rate. It can be corrected only at its source, that is, by lowering the import barriers that unduly protect domestic industry and restoring the balance of payments equilibrium".

[6] An increase in the level of aggregation of commodities increases the likelihood that commodities with the same name are actually different: Canadian wheat is not identical to U.S. wheat. It is usually impractical to use a sufficiently fine level of disaggregation to ensure that commodities with the same name are actually the same. A commonly used alternative, known as the "Armington assumption", identifies commodities by their national origin. For example, U.S. wheat and Canadian wheat are treated as imperfect substitutes which combine to form a single commodity called wheat. This assumption, or something like it, is needed to explain the fact that the U.S. both exports and imports wheat. See Alston et al. (1990) for a discussion of the Armington assumption in trade models.

trade in the short run, and the balance changes from year to year. A nominal devaluation can affect exports and trade balances in the short run, even in the absence of other policy changes; however, the direction of the change is ambiguous. If Home prices of domestically produced goods are sticky in the short run, the devaluation increases exports as described above. However, import demand at Home and in the ROW may be inelastic in the short run, as the review in Section 3.1 suggests. If price is more flexible than quantity in the short run, devaluation increases the value of imports, decreases the value of exports, and causes a deterioration in the balance of trade, which is exactly the opposite of the previous hypothesis. A devaluation may cause an initial deterioration in the balance of trade, followed by an improvement (the so-called "J curve"), but have no effect in the long run. The pattern of effects over time depends on the magnitude of short- and long-run elasticities, about which, as we have seen, there is no consensus.

Changes in the exchange rate in the short run can substantially alter measures of protection. For example, in the mid-1980s the dollar was strong relative to the ecu (a basket of European currencies), and the EU support price for wheat was approximately equal to the world price. The EU support price declined 30 percent by 1992. However, depreciation of the dollar relative to the ECU meant that the support price was substantially above the world price. Here, a change in the exchange rate caused a policy to become more protectionist. There is nothing peculiar about exchange rates in this regard. The target price, coupled with the variable levy, is similar to a quota. Any change in supply or demand external to the EU, which results in cheaper imports, makes a given quota or target price more restrictive. Variations in exchange rates are like other sources of instability.

The variability of exchange rates is sometimes cited as an argument for government protection of agriculture. One hypothesis is that the risk associated with variable exchange rates tends to decrease production and, therefore, decrease exports. Anderson and Garcia (1989) and Pick (1990) find that exchange rate risk is not an important factor in trade for countries where producers have access to futures markets or other forms of insurance.

Chambers and Just (1979) demonstrate the importance of cross-price effects. They use a multicommodity model to show that the domestic price elasticity of some goods, with respect to the exchange rate, can exceed one. Chambers and Just's (1981) study of wheat, corn, and soybean exports provides empirical evidence of short-run and long-run elasticities in excess of one. Their emphasis on the importance of choosing the appropriate price indices was confirmed by subsequent empirical work by Henneberry et al. (1987) and Belongia (1986).

Various authors [e.g., Orden (1986)] attempt to estimate the dynamic effects of a devaluation. Carter and Pick (1989) estimate a structural model and find evidence of a J curve. Coleman and Meilke (1988) include inputs in a structural model of Canada–U.S. red meats trade. The increase in domestic input price caused by a devaluation dampens the increase in final goods exports. Pieri, Meilke and Macaulay (1977) calibrate a dynamic world trade model for pork, which they use to analyze the effect of exchange rate variations on U.S.–Japanese pork trade. Martin and Shaw (1986) estimate a structural model for Australian agricultural exports and find a significant lagged response to exchange rate changes. Bessler and Babula (1987) and Bradshaw and Orden (1990) estimate time-series models. The former authors find only a weak causal relation from exchange rates to wheat exports, but a stronger relation to prices. The latter present evidence that exchange rates "Granger cause" export volumes.

These empirical results suggest that exchange rates can affect agricultural exports in the short- and medium-run. The static model outlined at the beginning of this subsection helps to explain why exchange rates have ambiguous effects on exports outside of a steady state equilibrium. However, the static model has no predictive power outside the steady state. A dynamic model is required to understand the economic forces that determine the trajectory of the effects of an exchange rate change.

3.3. Estimates of market power

It is useful to distinguish between two broad types of market power in agricultural trade: power exercised by governments and power exercised by private firms. Governments of large trading nations can affect market outcomes indirectly, using the kinds of trade and domestic policies discussed in Section 2.3. They can also affect international markets directly, by state trading (as in the former Soviet Union or Japan) or by state-sanctioned trading boards (such as the Canadian Wheat Board). Usually governments exercise market power unilaterally, but they sometimes act in concert, as with some of the International Commodity Agreements. Private firms, if they are sufficiently large, can exercise power in international agricultural markets, just as in domestic markets.

Agricultural trade economists have focused on market power exercised by governments rather than private firms. The potential for market power is more obvious for governments than for private firms because a small number of countries account for a large percentage of world trade in several commodities. These high national concentration ratios suggest that some countries have the ability to exercise market power. Those governments that intervene in markets (by state trading and support for marketing boards) may actually take advantage of this potential.

Some countries follow policies that are consistent with the exercise of market power, even if that is not the rationale for the policies. For example in the 1970s, when the EU imported wheat, the variable levy may have improved their terms of trade. In the Philippines, which supplies four-fifths of the world's coconut oil exports, the government used taxes and a centralized agency to restrict exports. This increased market power from the competitive level to near that of a Cournot-duopoly market [Buschena and Perloff (1991)].

Even if governments do not actually exercise market power, policy changes might enable them to do so. The possibility of a grain exporters' cartel, inspired by the success of OPEC, was debated during the 1970s and early 1980s. See Carter, Gallini and Schmitz (1980) and Schmitz et al. (1981) for early discussions and McGarry and Schmitz (1992) for a recent review of grain markets.

For other commodities, quasi-cartels were actually established in the form of International Commodity Agreements (ICAs). A (rarely explicit) objective of ICAs was to increase producer prices. The practicality of ICAs and other proposed cartels depends on the ability of governments or international groups to manage markets. The virtual disappearance of ICAs, the weakening of OPEC, and the fact that no new international cartels were formed, have decreased interest in this form of market power.

Production of basic commodities is widely dispersed across firms within any country, so it is unlikely that even the largest firms could exercise market power. On the other hand, industry concentration ratios for the *distribution* of basic commodities and for the production of some *processed* commodities are high, so it would be reasonable to look for market power there.

Private market power may be important in a number of markets. For example, after large subsidized U.S. grain sales to the USSR in the early 1970s (and subsequent price rises), there were accusations that multinational trading firms had conspired in a "great grain robbery". Such a conspiracy would have been possible only if these firms had market power. In 1996, Archer Daniels Midland (ADM) Company pleaded guilty to federal antitrust charges of price-fixing for lysine (a livestock feed supplement) and citric acid (a food additive). ADM agreed to pay $100 million, the largest criminal antitrust fine to date, and the U.S. government agreed to drop its investigation of price-fixing of high fructose corn syrup (HFCS, a sugar substitute). Later that year Bayer AG agreed to pay a fine of $50 million to settle criminal price-fixing charges involving worldwide sales of citric acid.

Agricultural economists have estimated market power in many agricultural markets, usually at the level of the processors (see Sexton and Lavoie, this Handbook). Markets examined include bananas, beef, beer, cigarettes and tobacco, coffee, fruit cocktail, rice, tomato harvesting, pears, pork, rice, textiles, and others. The majority of these studies have focused on domestic rather than export markets.

Just and Chern (1980), in their study of tomato harvesters, were among the first econometricians to show how to identify the market structure. A monopoly (or oligopoly) and competitive firms respond differently to exogenous changes in demand or costs. Observing actual responses to exogenous changes allows the econometrician to determine the market structure.

A number of papers [Love and Murniningtyas (1992), Park and Pick (1996), Pick and Carter (1994), Pompelli and Pick (1990)] test whether exporters exercise market power in the sale of wheat, other grains, soybeans, cotton, chicken, beef, and tobacco. The model they use is known as "Pricing to Market" (PTM). The studies investigate whether exporters charge different prices in different markets. This behavior would be evidence that exporters are noncompetitive, since competitive exporters are price-takers and would not sell the same good at different prices. These models rely on measures of "exchange rate pass through": the extent to which an import price is affected by a change in exchange rates. If, for example, exporters are selling competitively to a small country, a 10 percent devaluation of that country's currency would result in a 10 percent increase in its domestic price. In that case, the "pass through" is 100 percent. However, if exporters are behaving as monopolists or oligopolists in the country, it is typically optimal for them to increase price by less than 10 percent following the devaluation. The econometric model regresses the exporters' price (say, in dollars) against the importing country's exchange rate and variables designed to measure the exporters' costs of sales (such as transport costs). The hypothesis that the coefficient on exchange rate is zero is consistent with perfect competition, whereas a negative value is consistent with some degree of market power (imperfect pass through). The econometric evidence is mixed, but most of the PTM models are unable to reject the hypothesis of competition, or find only weak evidence of market power.

The importance of grain in world trade, the high country concentration rates in the market, and the prevalence of government intervention (frequently in the form of state trading) have led to many attempts to determine whether countries are exercising market power. Early evidence of market power relied on informal analysis. McCalla (1966), one of the first agricultural economists to study imperfect competition in the world wheat market, claimed that the U.S. behaved as a price leader and Canada as a follower. Many subsequent papers revisit this issue using a combination of econometric and simulation techniques. Kolstad and Burris (1986) use a spatial-equilibrium model and conclude that observed outcomes are consistent with the U.S. and Canada behaving as Cournot duopolists in the early 1970s. Paarlberg and Abbott (1986) estimate a model of the wheat market and find that some countries' public policies are endogenous. Mitchell and Duncan (1987) model grains (coarse grains, wheat, and rice) markets, and show the U.S. as a dominant firm facing residual sellers. Schmitz et al. (1997) assemble data that suggest the Canadian Wheat Board obtains a premium through the exercise of market power.

Most of the empirical literature is based on static oligopoly models. However, the dynamic aspect of market power may be important for storable commodities, for commodities that require a long investment period (such as orchards and vineyards), or where there is a nonlinear cost of changing production or sales. Karp and Perloff (1989, 1993a) estimate dynamic models in which producing nations incur convex costs of adjusting exports. Their results indicate that coffee and rice markets are imperfectly competitive, but less collusive than the Nash–Cournot equilibrium. An advantage of this model is its ability to capture dynamics explicitly; a disadvantage is that it imposes a linear-quadratic structure (linear demand curves and quadratic adjustment costs), which may be too restrictive.

Under the International Coffee Agreement, the coffee market was organized as a quasi-cartel. Bates (1997) argues that this was effective in raising prices, but the evidence he reviews is mixed. In the last few decades, there have been many unsuccessful attempts by countries to form OPEC-like cartels for agricultural products and natural resources [Gilbert (1996)], including potash, lead, zinc, copper, nickel, sugar, cotton, timber, jute, nutmeg, and pepper. As with coffee, the tin, cocoa, and natural rubber cartels were joined by some industrialized countries that were customers.[7]

3.4. Policy applications of estimates

Policy analysis relies on the description of institutions, theoretical modeling, and econometric estimation. The analysis provides estimates of the effects of specific reforms. These estimates are an important product of research in agricultural trade economics. Among the two most intensively studied policy questions in agricultural trade during the last ten years are the effect of multilateral liberalization under the Uruguay Round and the effect of liberalization in North America under NAFTA. Martin and Winters (1995) survey the literature that estimates the likely welfare effects of the trade liberalization achieved by the Uruguay Round of GATT. These estimates suggest that the agreement would result in an increase of world GDP of 0.2 percent to 0.9 percent. Other policy questions that generate a great deal of empirical research include the effects of unilateral policy reform within the U.S. (e.g., to prepare the periodic Farm Bills) and in the EU (e.g., to study the McSharry proposals), and effects of regional liberalization, e.g., between Central and Eastern Europe and the EU [Tangermann (1996)] and Western Hemisphere agreements outside of NAFTA.

For all of these potential reforms, researchers produced estimates of the effects on endogenous variables such as prices, trade flows, surplus measures, farm income, and program costs. The range of models used to generate these estimates is extensive, and includes static and dynamic, single- and multi-commodity, partial and general equilibrium, rational versus static or adaptive expectations, and synthetic versus econometric models.

The simplest and probably still the most popular approach to studying policy questions uses multicommodity partial equilibrium supply and demand models. The USDA's simulation model, SWOPSIM [Roningen, Sullivan and Dixit (1991)], is a good example of this approach. This method is relatively easy to understand, and it uses data that are readily available (prices, policy instruments, and trade flows) and parameters (supply and demand elasticities) that can be estimated or synthesized. However, partial equilibrium models cannot account for factor mobility between agricultural and nonagricultural sectors. In practice, these models typically do not take into account marketing margins or substitutability within the agricultural sector [Peterson, Hertel and Stout (1994)], although these limitations are not inherent in the partial equilibrium approach.

Computable general equilibrium (CGE) models emerged in the 1980s as a viable alternative to partial equilibrium models. Hertel (1993) contrasts the predictions of partial and general equilibrium analyses of trade reforms. He finds that the partial and general equilibrium models make substantially different predictions of the changes in

---

[7] Farnsworth (1988). See Teece, Sunding and Mosakowski (1993) for a survey of natural resource cartels.

production and trade flows when the policy change is economy-wide. In contrast, the two types of models provide similar results when the policy change is sector-specific. If, as Hertel assumes, a CGE model is more accurate than a partial equilibrium model, then partial equilibrium models are inappropriate for the analysis of economy-wide changes.

Of course this conclusion does not follow if CGE models are less accurate. CGE models are an elegant and internally consistent description of the economy. However, they require more data (or assumptions) than partial equilibrium models. CGE models that emphasize the linkages between agriculture and nonagriculture typically treat the agricultural sector at an aggregated level. This change of focus may lead to less rather than more accuracy in answering some policy questions. Due to their greater complexity, CGE models are more of a black box, making the results harder to understand (and thus to explain to policymakers). Nevertheless, these models have been used in many policy analyses [e.g., Kilkenny and Robinson (1990), Robinson, Kilkenny and Adelman (1989), Piggot and Whalley (1991), Francois and Shields (1994), Lewis, Robinson and Wang (1995), Sadoulet and de Janvry (1992)].

Advances in computing have made it possible to extend CGE models to dynamic environments with rational expectations [Keuschnigg and Kohler (1995)], although these models are not yet widely used in agricultural economics. Most dynamic analyses still rely on partial equilibrium models. Tyers and Anderson's book (1992) represents one of the most sophisticated applications of dynamic modeling. Their models show, for example, that the effects of rich countries' food policies in the 1980s almost exactly offset the effects of poor countries' policies. If this result is correct, generalized liberalization of agricultural policies will not cause large price increases for less-developed agricultural importers.

When different models lead to qualitatively different predictions of the effects of policy changes, they may be of limited use for policymakers. The extent to which the numerical estimates arrive at a consensus depends on the generality of the question the models address. For example, most models show that there are global gains from liberalization, but this is the sort of issue that one might argue does not require an empirical model. For more specific questions, such as the division of gains or the change in exports, the models frequently produce quite different results. Given the disagreement about such fundamental matters as the magnitude of trade elasticities and the different assumptions built into models, it would be surprising if the models did agree.

Interest in the extent of agreement among models is usually secondary to the models' results, but occasionally it is paramount. For example in 1985, the International Agricultural Trade Research Consortium met to compare the predictions of five prominent models with regard to two scenarios: (i) a 5 percent shortfall of U.S. crop production and (ii) the effect of full trade liberalization. Agricultural trade modelers and their clients recognized that important policy reforms were in the air. Comparing models would help to determine how useful they and their successors would be in studying reforms. The conference report [Liu and Seeley (1987)] summarizes the extent of (dis)agreement among the results, but is unable to rank the plausibility of the results.

It proved as difficult then as it does now to evaluate and synthesize the predictions of competing models with regard to specific policy questions.

Even though the models are unlikely to arrive at consensus – and even less likely to approach an objective truth – they are useful in exploring the implications of a set of assumptions. The results of such exploration are intrinsically interesting, especially when the policy reform involves highly political issues, such as the employment effect of NAFTA. The implications can also be useful in testing the plausibility of assumptions, such as the extent of market power. In addition, agreement on even such a noncontroversial issue as the global gains from trade liberalization can have pedagogic value.

3.5. Summary

Policy debates in agricultural trade usually turn on empirical issues. The bulk of research in the discipline has attempted to improve econometric estimates and use them in more sophisticated models. Fundamental empirical questions include the magnitude of excess supply (demand) elasticities, the effect of exchange rates on agricultural trade, and the degree to which nations or firms might or do exercise power in agricultural markets. Although agricultural economics research has not led to a consensus on these issues, it has at least provided a basis for discussion.

4. Political economy models

A basic lesson of trade theory is that free trade tends to maximize real domestic income. An important exception is that large countries can increase their welfare by using trade restrictions to improve their terms of trade (Section 6.1). Agricultural policies of very few nations (except perhaps New Zealand and Australia in recent years) are consistent with the normative conclusions of neoclassical economics. Large exporters typically pursue policies that worsen their terms of trade, and most countries are willing to liberalize agricultural trade only as a quid pro quo for others' liberalization. Thus, it is difficult to explain agricultural policies as the result of governments' maximizing domestic welfare. Agricultural economists have therefore turned to political economy explanations [see de Gorter (2002), this Handbook].

Much of the empirical work in agricultural political economy focuses on domestic policies [e.g., Gardner (1983, 1987)]. Often these policies have direct, albeit unintended, effects on trade. In political economy as in other branches of the discipline, it is not possible to isolate research in domestic and trade issues. Most of the effort in agricultural political economies involves measuring and explaining the success that different groups have had in obtaining rents. The bulk of this research is statistical, although institutional analyses have made important contributions. Less effort has been devoted to understanding the choice, as opposed to the level, of policies.

4.1. Measuring political power

Political economy models view existing policy as an outcome of the interaction of agents with competing interests. Most empirical political economy models replace the problem of determining an equilibrium with that of optimizing a function. Researchers proceed as if a social planner were maximizing the weighted sum of the welfare of different groups (e.g., producers, consumers, and taxpayers). This weighted objective function is known as the "political preference function" (PPF). The empirical task is to estimate the values (and possibly the determinants) of the weights on the different interest groups. Swinnen and van der Zee (1993) and Swinnen (1994) review both the empirical and theoretical literature.

Empirical analysis typically begins with a PPF, or maximization problem of the fictitious social planner. Rausser and Freebairn's paper (1974), the earliest agricultural example of this approach, motivates the PPF as a representation of a political economy equilibrium. The weights in the PPF are the reduced-form parameters of that equilibrium. These weights measure the policymaker's willingness to sacrifice one group's welfare for another's gain (the policymaker's "revealed preference"). Most papers that use the PPF estimate the weights without imposing an explicit game-theoretic structure. A few [Zusman and Amiad (1977), Beghin (1990), Beghin and Karp (1991)] attempt to estimate the structural parameters of a cooperative game: the threat points and bargaining weights. The structural parameters may be important for policy analysis if they are invariant to exogenous changes in other countries' policies.

The PPF approach is consistent with the interpretation that a policymaker maximizes the weighted sum of his own and of interest groups' welfare. For example, a cynical policymaker may care only about the probability of election. With this interpretation of the PPF, agents affect the policy choice indirectly by some combination of voting, lobbying, or political contributions. Whether the PPF is viewed as representing an equilibrium to a cooperative game or as a literal description of a policymaker's preference, agents other than the policymaker affect the outcome.

The primary objective of many papers is to estimate the weights on the different interest groups. These estimates provide a summary statistic of agricultural policies, and they measure the inefficiency of policies relative to some ideal. For example, Oehmke and Yao (1990) estimate that U.S. wheat policies in the late 1970s implied that the government was willing to spend $1 of tax revenue to increase producer surplus by 70 cents, and it was willing to tax consumers over $2 to save $1 of government revenue. Thus, marginal producer welfare was valued at three times the marginal consumer welfare. If a pure income transfer were possible, it would transfer income at a rate of $1 of producer gain for $1 of consumer loss. Of course, pure income transfers are generally infeasible, since all tax systems involve deadweight losses. However, the deadweight loss of raising government revenue is probably small relative to estimates of the costs of agricultural policies. Thus, it is unlikely that public finance arguments rationalize agricultural policies as a way to achieve income transfers.

For example, suppose that the actual social cost of public finance was 15 percent, so that every dollar of government revenue raised by general taxes costs consumers $1.15 worth of utility. Suppose also that the ratio of producer to consumer weights in the government preference function is 3/1, as in the Oehmke and Yao study. This ratio means that marginal excess cost or deadweight loss of using agricultural policy to transfer a dollar to producers is $1.85 (= $2–$0.15). Since the marginal excess costs exceed the average cost, multiplying the total amount of revenue (that the policy transfers to producers) by 1.85 exaggerates the deadweight loss of the policy. However, this back-of-the-envelope calculation suggests that the deadweight loss is likely to be large. Other things equal, a larger ratio of producer to consumer welfare weights implies a larger deadweight loss. If the ratio is 1, nonintervention is optimal, and the deadweight cost is zero by definition.

The PPF weights are also useful for models that endogenize policy, and are particularly important for international trade models. By treating policy as endogenous, researchers can construct a coherent model of how agricultural policy in a large country (or a group of small countries) affects policy elsewhere. For example, the level of the target price in the U.S. may affect the ROW excess-supply function facing EU policymakers. This supply function enters as a constraint in determining the political economy equilibrium within the EU. A change in this U.S. target price can affect the equilibrium policy levels in the EU.

The papers by Sarris and Freebairn (1983) and Paarlberg and Abbott (1986) are among the earliest and most ambitious attempts to endogenize policy in an international trade model. Recent contributions, including Kennedy, von Witzke and Roe (1996a, 1996b), incorporate exchange rate policy. These papers assume that producers and consumers in all countries are competitive and that governments choose agricultural policies to maximize a standard PPF. Sarris and Freebairn (1983) model the international wheat market and assume that each government acts as if policy elsewhere is fixed. Their estimates indicate that U.S. and Canadian policymakers place the same weight on the welfare of different groups, and that EU policymakers favor producers slightly. These results are difficult to reconcile with the substantial policy intervention in the wheat market.

Paarlberg and Abbott (1986) use a conjectural variations model to estimate the strategic interaction among governments. They find that U.S., Japanese, and EU policies are insensitive to policy in other countries, while Canadian and Australian policies are responsive to policy elsewhere. The estimated welfare weights imply that policymakers are willing to incur a substantial deadweight loss to transfer income to producers. Kennedy, von Witzke and Roe (1996a, 1996b) estimate PPF weights that also show a substantial preference for producers' groups. For example, their estimates show that EU policymakers are willing to tax consumers $1.60 to transfer $1 to sugar producers. The authors use these estimates in a simulation model to study trade reform in both noncooperative and cooperative games. In a noncooperative setting, they show how the availability of pure income transfers facilitates trade liberalization.

4.2. Explaining political power

One set of empirical political economy studies estimates the revealed preferences of policymakers (the weights in the PPF). A closely related research objective seeks to explain these preferences. There is a large body of literature that tries to explain why developed countries tend to subsidize their agricultural sectors whereas developing countries tend to tax those sectors [e.g., Olson (1985), Balisacan and Roumasset (1987), Anderson and Tyers (1989), Anderson (1995), Honma and Hayami (1986)]. The explanations turn on differences in costs of collective action (lobbying) for different groups and on the different effects of protection on factor returns. Anderson uses a specific factors model to show that the effects of agricultural policy on factor returns is closely related to the size of the agricultural sector. He argues that these effects are strong enough to explain policy differences across stages of development, even ignoring differences in the costs of collective action.

Several papers use political and demographic as well as economic variables to explain agricultural policies. For example, von Witzke (1990) examines whether agricultural support changes in election years. Beghin, Foster and Kherallah (1996) study protection in the tobacco market. Beghin and Kherallah's (1994) analysis of multicommodity data for 25 countries confirms that agricultural protection tends to increase with economic development, but their results do not support the hypothesis that protection depends on the costs of collective action. The study by de Gorter and Tsur (1991) finds that increases in rural income (relative to urban income) and decreases in rural population (relative to urban population) tend to decrease agricultural protection. Sarker et al. (1993) find that labor productivity ratios, agriculture's international terms of trade, and the share of food expenditures in disposable income are important determinants of wheat subsidy levels in developed countries. Factor endowment ratios, agriculture's international terms of trade, and the share of imports financed by agricultural exports are important determinants of developing countries' taxation levels of wheat exporters.

These empirical papers attempt to measure or explain the relative power of different interest groups for a given set of policies. A different kind of puzzle concerns the *choice* of policies, rather than their level. If policymakers want to transfer income from the general public to a specific group, why do they use apparently inefficient methods? For example, Babcock, Carter and Schmitz (1990) show that U.S. wheat programs during the mid-1980s caused large deadweight losses to taxpayers. They claim that mandatory production controls could have made wheat producers as well off without imposing costs on taxpayers.

The "Principle of Targeting" states that a policy objective should be achieved by intervening in the market most closely associated with the objective (see Section 6.1). This principle assures us that there are few situations in which trade policy is the appropriate remedy. Nevertheless, trade or other similarly distortionary policies are frequently used. There are four types of explanation for this apparent paradox. The first is simply that policymakers "prefer" to pay for the transfer by taxing consumers, perhaps by using a tariff, rather than by taxing the general public. This response takes policymakers' preferences as exogenous, and really provides no explanation at all.

The second explanation is that some groups benefit from obfuscation [Magee, Brock and Young (1989)]. For example, because consumers are more aware of taxes than tariffs, governments have more political difficulty raising taxes. It may be easier for policymakers to balance competing interests when they use indirect policies such as tariffs. Also, producers may feel that direct payments are uncomfortably close to welfare. An indirect transfer makes it easier for them to preserve cherished illusions.

The third explanation, already alluded to, is that indirect transfers may not lower efficiency substantially. If domestic supply and demand elasticities are low, the deadweight loss from indirect policies (such as tariffs) may be small. These costs need to be compared to the deadweight losses associated with other methods of raising government revenue to pay for a direct transfer. This public finance argument for agricultural policies is well known as a theoretical possibility. It may be relevant for less-developed countries with inefficient tax systems. It is less plausible for developed countries, where the tax system is relatively efficient and where the deadweight losses from trade policies are relatively large.

A fourth approach provides theoretical models that explain the choice of policy instrument as a political-economy equilibrium. Cassing and Hillman (1986), Rodrik (1986), and Hillman and Ursprung (1988) study the endogenous choice between different trade policies (such as tariffs versus quotas) under different assumptions about market structure and lobbying. Since these models compare different trade policies, rather than trade versus nontrade policies, they cannot explain why a less distortionary way to support producers is not chosen. Recent papers by Grossman and Helpman (1994, 1995) provide a game theoretic foundation for the type of political economy models reviewed above. The papers by Schleich and Orden (1996) and Schleich (1997) use the Grossman and Helpman formulation to explain when trade restrictions may emerge as equilibrium policies.

4.3. Institutionalist political economy

The empirical research described above relies on econometrics and simulations. An alternative approach uses historical analysis of specific policies. This case-study approach seldom leads to broad hypotheses or conclusions, such as the relation between the level of development and the level of support for the agricultural sector, but it does provide insight into specific policies, and it may help to frame broader empirical questions. Recent papers by Gardner (1996) on the Export Enhancement Program, Orden (1996) on the passage of NAFTA, and Sumner (1995) on general U.S. farm policy, are good examples of political economy of agricultural policy case studies.

Robert Bates's *Open-Economy Politics* (1997), a historical study of national and international coffee policies, is an ambitious application of institutionalist political economy. Bates explains the evolution of domestic policies in Brazil and Colombia as the outcome of conflict among coffee producers, other agricultural producers, and government officials. The international agreements on coffee marketing that operated in the 1970s and 1980s required a resolution of conflict among groups within and across nations.

The large coffee producers were unable to force their small competitors to restrict supply. A successful international coffee cartel therefore required the U.S. (and other large consumer nations) to enforce supply quotas by restricting imports. Since the International Coffee Organization (ICO) sought to raise coffee prices, support from consuming nations would appear irrational on narrow economic grounds. The principal source of U.S. support came from foreign policy circles, where it was argued that higher producer prices would promote development in Latin America and discourage revolution. Many believe that leading U.S. coffee-processing firms supported the ICO in the belief that a higher input price gave them a competitive advantage over smaller processors.[8]

Coffee provides one of the (presumably few) cases where importing firms lobbied for policies that apparently hurt them because their strategic interests coincided with those of exporters. With coffee, the pursuit of a foreign policy objective generated domestic rents. The desire to capture these rents generated domestic support from interests that would have been expected to oppose the policy. For other agricultural policies, the causality is reversed. For example, U.S. sugar policy rewards U.S. sugar producers by maintaining a high domestic price through limiting imports. Countries that have quota rights to export sugar to the U.S. earn rents. The distribution of these quotas is viewed as a significant foreign policy instrument (e.g., as part of the Caribbean Initiative). In this case, a domestic policy generates rents, and the control of these rents generates support for the policy from foreign policy sources.

The examples of coffee and sugar suggest an important explanation for the use of inefficient policies. These policies are often politically attractive *because* they fail the Principle of Targeting. The policies generate rents, a major portion of which go to their intended beneficiaries. However, some of the rents are captured by other groups, which then have a reason to support the policy. A structure of coalitions, rather than a monolithic special interest group, is responsible for this form of agricultural policy.

Although coalitions can be responsible for policies that restrict trade, in other cases political competition can lead to liberal trade. Bredahl, Schmitz and Hillman (1987) study a model of international rent-seeking in winter vegetable trade between the U.S. and Mexico. They explain reasons for failures to form export/import coalitions. These failures led to (approximately) free trade in winter vegetables between the two countries.

---

[8] An industry-wide cost increase tends to cause rival firms to supply less, thus shifting out the residual demand curve facing a particular firm. The increase in profits caused by this increase in the residual demand curve may more than offset the direct effect of the cost increase for the particular firm. This possibility is especially likely if firms are heterogeneous and the direct effect of the cost increase is felt most strongly by rivals.

4.4. Summary

Political economy has become an important part of the study of the economics of international agricultural trade. This subdiscipline arose because of the failure of traditional trade theory to explain observed policies. Most empirical researchers model the political economy equilibrium in reduced form and estimate weights of a political preference function. These weights are summary statistics of the deadweight cost of policies. For example, they may measure the marginal number of dollars taken from consumers for each marginal dollar given to producers. Researchers have also attempted to relate observed policy levels and estimated preference weights to demographic, political, and exogenous economic variables. A growing body of political-economy research replaces formal modeling and econometrics with detailed analysis of institutions.

The emphasis in the political economy of agriculture has been to explain why one group wins the political battle and to measure how great a victory it achieves. An equally important but less studied empirical puzzle concerns society's reasons for using inefficient trade policies rather than less distorting transfers.

5. U.S. trade policy and the grains market

International agricultural policies are sometimes designed to achieve political ends while ignoring economic constraints. As a consequence, such policies are often ineffective or harmful. Agricultural trade economists dedicate much of their research effort to studying such policies. During the early 1980s the U.S. attempted to influence the world grains market by using an embargo on U.S. exports to the Soviet Union. In the mid-1980s the U.S. began the Export Enhancement Program (EEP) in an attempt to influence the grains market by subsidizing exports to certain countries. Economic analysis played a minor or negligible role in the formulation of both polices, but it has been used to good effect in their evaluation. These analyses are interesting for the light they shed on the policies, and they are good examples of how economics has been used to study agricultural trade.

In some respects the two policies were similar. Both were intended to punish past actions and discourage their continuation. The purpose of the embargo was to punish the USSR (in the form of higher import prices for grains) for invading Afghanistan and to encourage it to withdraw. A major purpose of the EEP was to punish the EU for its use of export subsidies to enter markets deemed important to the U.S. The 1990 Congressional authorization of EEP, for example, listed "discouraging unfair trade practices" as the only rationale of the act [Gardner (1996), p. 321].

Both policies required the ability to "target" specific markets. To the extent that the policy spilled over into other markets, punishment of the intended victim (the USSR in one case, and the EU in the other) would be diluted, and there would be unintended injuries and benefits to other agents. If the study of economics provides us with any clear lesson, it is that markets link actions in one place and time with consequences elsewhere. Markets make it virtually impossible to carry out the sort of tactical strike that policymakers probably envisioned when they designed the embargo and EEP. The substantial failures of both policies were due to the ability of markets to distribute policy effects over space and time.

Although the two policies shared a similar motivation (punishment and dissuasion) and required similar conditions for success (segmentation of markets and the inability to re-export imports), in other respects they differed. The embargo tried to restrain exports, while the EEP tried to increase them. As a large grain exporter, the U.S. might benefit from an increase in world price caused by a reduction in its exports. The first-order effect of a subsidy, on the other hand, causes a decrease in a large exporter's welfare via a decrease in world price.

5.1. The grain embargo

The agricultural economics profession carried out an extensive post mortem on the U.S. grain embargo policy, which was summarized in "Embargoes, Surplus Disposal, and U.S. Agriculture", United States Department of Agriculture, Economic Research Service (ERS) (1986). A subsequent study by Anania and McCalla (1991) uses a single commodity spatial equilibrium model to show how arbitrage weakened the embargo. The authors consider several policy scenarios, reflecting different degrees of cooperation from importers and competing exporters. Lack of cooperation by a large exporter such as Argentina would defeat the embargo. Even if other exporters refrained from increasing their sales to the USSR, importers (chiefly in Eastern Europe) could undermine the embargo by re-exporting their purchases to the USSR.

The directions of change in price and volume under the various scenarios can (at least for competitive markets) be determined by simple economic reasoning. However, obtaining even a rough idea of the magnitude of changes requires a numerical model using plausible supply and demand estimates. As we noted in Section 3.1, there is little consensus about these estimates, and therefore the model results can only be considered suggestive. Subject to this caveat, the main policy implication of the simulation model is that success of the embargo (i.e., imposing a large cost on the USSR) would have required an unlikely degree of cooperation by other importers and exporters. In adopting the policy, U.S. decision-makers exaggerated the degree of market segmentation, and thus were over-optimistic about the effectiveness of a U.S. embargo.

5.2. The Export Enhancement Program

The EEP was more complicated than the grain embargo but was vulnerable to the same forces of market arbitrage. The policy was supposed to satisfy four goals: (i) budget neutrality, (ii) targeting, (iii) additionality, and (iv) cost effectiveness. "Targeting" meant that the policy should promote exports to countries that the EU heavily subsidized. Friendly rivals, such as Canada and Australia, should not be hurt by the policy.

"Additionality" meant that EEP sales should supplement rather than replace commercial sales. "Cost effectiveness" was not defined. Exporting firms that received the subsidies, and producers who benefited indirectly, formed the main constituency for the EEP.

During the early years of the program, the subsidy took the form of credits for government-owned stocks. When these stocks were run down in the early 1990s, the in-kind subsidy was replaced by cash payments. In-kind and cash subsidies have different effects on the four goals [Chambers and Paarlberg (1991)]. By assigning a value of zero to government stocks, the direct cost of the program was small with in-kind subsidies, and it appeared to achieve budget neutrality. The real value of these stocks, although not zero, might have been low due to high government storage costs. However, in-kind subsidies increase U.S. supply by releasing government stocks. To the extent that these stocks increase domestic availability, U.S. domestic price falls. This decrease benefits U.S. consumers but increases the deficiency payment to farmers, raising government costs. Cash subsidies, on the other hand, represent a direct cost to the U.S. treasury, and thus automatically fail the budget neutrality criterion. However, these subsidies divert sales from the domestic to the export market. The resulting increase in domestic price hurts domestic consumers but reduces the deficiency payment to farmers. The lower deficiency payment offsets, to some extent, the direct cost of the subsidy.

There is mixed empirical evidence about the EEP's success in increasing U.S. exports. However, the design of the program made success unlikely. In most markets, EEP-subsidized sales occurred concurrently with nonsubsidized sales. In such situations, inframarginal units are subsidized, but the price of marginal imports is the world price. If the subsidy does not lower the marginal price, it has little effect on the level of imports. A standard subsidy, on the other hand, reduces the import price of every unit imported, thereby reducing the marginal price. Since sales occur at a lower point on the import demand curve, exports to that market increase. An inframarginal subsidy is a pure income transfer, and therefore may affect income. Inframarginal subsidies can relax a foreign reserve constraint, leading to increased imports of a commodity. However, these kinds of effects would be spread over all imported commodities, making the effect on import levels of a single commodity small.

The distinction between marginal and inframarginal subsidies may have been overlooked in the design of the EEP. Economic modelers frequently make the same kind of mistake when they summarize complicated government policies using price wedges. [The paper by Anania, Bohman and Carter (1992) is an exception; it takes into account that the subsidy was inframarginal.] The distinction between marginal and inframarginal subsidies is less important if the market within a country is segmented. If aggregate exports to a market are the sum of independently negotiated contracts, then what appears to be a subsidy on an inframarginal unit may actually be a subsidy on the marginal unit for an individual deal. However, it is unlikely that these various deals are really independent. Within a single country, especially small countries that were the original targets of EEP, deal-makers would probably have a good idea of what other buyers and sellers were doing, so the result would be much as if there were a single auction.

Even if each deal is the outcome of a bargaining problem in which both the buyer and seller have strategic power, the distinction between a marginal and inframarginal subsidy is crucial. Consider the situation where a large exporting firm confronts a state importer and the two bargain over price and quantity. The exporter receives EEP subsidies for some sales, but pays the world price for its marginal supply. The EEP subsidy does not change the exporter's marginal cost, and thus does not change its incentives to supply a marginal unit. If the two agents bargain efficiently, then the quantity of sales equates the seller's marginal cost and the importer's marginal utility of consumption, and is independent of the (inframarginal) subsidy. The subsidy does change the unit cost that the importer pays. In the Nash equilibrium to a cooperative game, for example, the bargain splits the surplus between parties. Since the subsidy does not alter the efficient quantity of sales, but increases the sum of buyer and seller surplus, the subsidy decreases the price the buyer pays.

Informational problems may prevent an efficient outcome to the bargain. For example, agents may misjudge their opponents' reservation values, leading to a positive probability that no bargain is reached. The subsidy, by increasing the amount of surplus, may decrease the probability of a bargaining failure that results in no sales. In that case, the subsidy would increase the expected level of sales. In order for an inframarginal subsidy to have a significant effect on the level of sales, the market within an importing country must be highly segmented and/or there must be substantial inefficiencies in bargaining.

The EEP had no greater success in achieving the goal of targeting. This objective required that the effects of the policy be contained in markets the EU had entered using subsidies. The intent was to make life difficult for the EU without hurting exporters who did not use subsidies. The objective was not achieved for two reasons. First, even if the program had been applied as originally intended, with subsidies available only for specific markets, arbitrage would have ensured that the effects were widely felt. Displacing EU sales in one market would have driven them elsewhere, lowering the price in those markets.

Second, the terms of the policy were changed, allowing more countries to receive the subsidy. This change was motivated by domestic political reasons rather than to make the policy more effective. The USSR and China were originally ineligible for subsidies, but later became major recipients. In 1988, for example, the bulk of U.S. sales to the USSR were subsidized by EEP. Within the space of a few years the U.S. switched from prohibiting to subsidizing exports to the USSR, an eloquent testimony to its flexibility. Subsidies to China, an important market for Australia but not for the EU, hurt Australian exporters.

Decision-makers in the U.S. hoped the EEP would make it too costly for the EU to subsidize exports, and would thereby contribute to CAP reform. Various factors made this outcome unlikely. First, the policy created substantial unanticipated costs to the U.S. in terms of the opportunity cost of CCC stocks, increased deficiency payments, and later, direct costs to the treasury. Second, the inframarginal nature of the subsidy meant that the increase in sales was probably small. Third, to the extent that there was an increase in sales in targeted markets, arbitrage caused a fall in price in other importing countries. The cost of the U.S. policy was borne by most or all exporters, diluting the cost to the EU. Fourth, the limits of the policy were soon exceeded, resulting in subsidies to previously ineligible importers. This change increased the cost both to the U.S. treasury and to "friendly" exporters. Fifth, the increased costs that the EU had to bear as a result of the program were probably small and the susceptibility of the EU to this kind of pressure was probably greatly exaggerated.

5.3. Summary

Two important and highly publicized recent U.S. grain policies received substantial attention from agricultural trade economists. Motivation for the embargo originated outside the agricultural sector; agriculture was merely a lever. The EEP was promoted as a means to achieve an agricultural-related foreign policy goal (decreased EU subsidies), but domestic U.S. interests were its chief beneficiaries. These two policies are intrinsically interesting examples both of international agricultural policy and of the response they elicited from the agricultural economics profession. The study of these policies involved the full range of economic tools: institutional political economy, econometrics, numerical simulation models, and applied theory. Policymakers underestimated the resilience of international markets and exaggerated their ability to influence market outcomes. Because of the uncertainty of other nations' responses and of exogenous economic parameters, it was not possible to forecast with assurance the effect of the policies. Even with the benefit of hindsight there is room for disagreement about their exact effect. However, the evidence suggests they did not achieve their stated goals in either case. The reasons for their failure could have been (and in some cases were) anticipated based on economic theory.

6. Theory and agricultural trade policy

Research in agricultural trade economics has addressed specific policy issues rather than general theoretical questions. The discipline has therefore contributed primarily to the applied, rather than the theoretical literature. However, the theory of international trade has been essential in understanding the policy questions. This section reviews several aspects of trade theory that are important to agricultural trade economics. The theory can be grouped around three important ideas, which we discuss in the next subsection. We then discuss the application of these ideas in situations where a country is large enough to exert market power or where insurance markets are missing.

6.1. Three ideas central to agricultural trade theory

The first idea is that liberal markets in general, and free trade in particular, promote social welfare. This idea rests on the two fundamental theorems of welfare economics, which provide conditions under which a competitive equilibrium and a socially optimal allocation are equivalent. The theory of comparative advantage provides substance to the argument for free trade. This theory explains why nations have the potential to gain from trade, even if they have absolute disadvantages such as high labor costs, old technology, or a poor resource base. The potential gains from trade arise because, in general, nations have different *opportunity costs*. The cost of producing one good, in terms of foregone production of other goods, differs across nations. Opportunity costs depend on relative rather than absolute production costs. Even if a nation is "less efficient" at producing every good relative to its trading partner, its relative disadvantage is (typically) less severe in some sectors. The nation has a comparative advantage in those sectors, and this provides a basis for it to gain from trade.

Many participants in the free trade debate conclude either that neoclassical theory presents an unassailable case for free trade or that neoclassical theory is so remote from reality that it has little to say about the real world. In fact, neoclassical theory has a more equivocal view of trade liberalization. The assumptions required for the two fundamental welfare theorems, which form the core of the neoclassical preference for free trade, are unlikely to be satisfied. Rather than predict outcomes, these theorems only suggest tendencies of market economies.

The theory of the second best, the second of the three important ideas that guide agricultural trade economics, explains why market reform may have perverse effects. If there is a single market imperfection, then correcting that imperfection increases economic efficiency. For example, if the only distortion (or market failure) in the economy is a tariff on a particular agricultural commodity, then reducing or eliminating this tariff increases efficiency. Policymakers, however, sometimes consider changing the level of a particular policy instrument, or set of instruments, in isolation from other possible policy reforms. For example, they might consider changing the target price of a commodity or group of commodities, without changing the policies for other commodities or other sectors. Political constraints frequently require this kind of piecemeal policy reform. However, treating other government policies (or other market failures) as fixed can be confused with treating them as nonexistent. The uncritical conclusion that trade liberalization necessarily increases efficiency is sometimes based on exactly this confusion. It makes sense to regard a tariff as a distortion, something that keeps the economy from achieving an efficient outcome, *if there are no other distortions in the economy*. When there are other distortions, a particular tariff may improve efficiency.

The theory of the second best states that, if there are two or more market imperfections, correcting one of them may either increase or decrease welfare.[9] For example, if there are two tariffs, eliminating one may not increase welfare. This conclusion is "negative" in that it tells us what we cannot say, rather than what we can

---

[9] Baumol (1977) states the theorem of the second best: It is not necessarily worse for society if a large number of optimality conditions are violated than if a few are violated.

say. The most pessimistic interpretation is that it implies that economic theory allows us to reach no conclusions about real world markets, since we know they are subject to many imperfections. A more moderate interpretation is that we cannot use economic theory *uncritically* to conclude that a particular reform, such as trade liberalization, necessarily improves efficiency. Understanding the theory of the second best is essential to assess the relevance of economic arguments for trade liberalization. We first provide a simple example of the theory, which illustrates the basic argument behind it. We then present a graphical treatment which shows the generality of the argument.

Imagine an economy in which there are only two market failures, both in a particular sector. The first market failure is that production of the commodity damages the environment, but the producer does not pay for this damage (there is a negative environmental externality). The second market failure is that the producer is a monopolist rather than a price taker. These two imperfections tend to offset each other. The first causes the market outcome to result in excessive production, from the standpoint of society. The second causes the market outcome to result in too little production, since the monopolist reduces output to increase price. At this level of generality, we do not know whether there is too little or too much production on balance. We cannot conclude that welfare would be higher if we removed one of the imperfections (e.g., by forcing the monopolist to produce where price equals marginal cost in order to mimic the competitive outcome). The salient feature of this example is that each distortion affects the welfare cost of the other distortion.

Figure 1 illustrates the theory in a more abstract setting, showing its generality. The figure's two panels illustrate two possibilities. In each panel, the axes d_1 and d_2 represent two distortions. A larger (absolute) value of d_i is a larger distortion. For the example in the previous paragraph, we can think of d_1 as the gap between price and marginal cost (the monopoly distortion) and d_2 as the amount of environmental damage not internalized by the firm. In another setting, we can think of d_1 and d_2 as the tariffs in two sectors. If $d_i < 0$, Sector i imports are subsidized. Both d_1 and d_2 are *distortions*: policies or market failures that cause a competitive equilibrium to differ from an efficient outcome.

The curves in Figure 1 are iso-welfare curves, with higher welfare on curves closer to the origin. The maximum welfare is achieved when both distortions are completely removed: $d_1 = d_2 = 0$. In both panels of Figure 1, welfare increases as we move along either axis toward the origin. We pass through higher iso-welfare curves on this trajectory. If we are on the d_1 axis, for example, the other distortion (d_2) is constant at 0. In that case, we are in a world with only one distortion, and decreasing that distortion raises welfare.

We represent a world with two distortions by a point off the axes, such as point α. Once again, removing both distortions (moving to the origin) increases welfare. Suppose, however, that we hold d_1 fixed at d_1^* and consider the piecemeal reform of removing only the second distortion. The geometric representation is that we move north along the dotted vertical line beginning at α, until $d_2 = 0$.

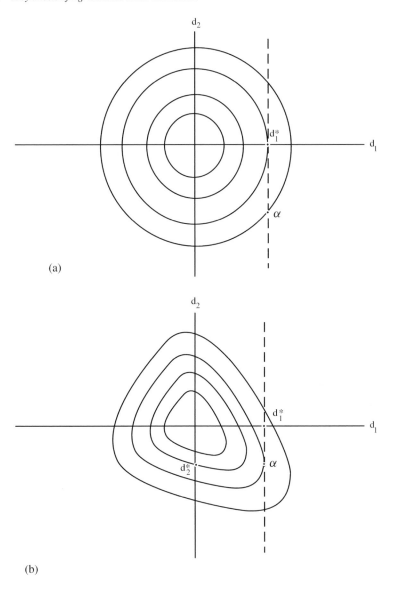

Figure 1. Illustration of the theory of the second best.

In panel a of Figure 1, this piecemeal reform improves welfare, because as we move along the dotted line away from α toward the horizontal axis, we pass through higher iso-welfare curves. In panel b, the corresponding trajectory takes us through lower iso-welfare curves. Decreasing the absolute value of d_2 lowers welfare: removing the "distortion" d_2 decreases efficiency. In panel b, the original point α gives the optimal level of d_2, given that d_1 is fixed at d_1^* . Any movement along the vertical dotted line away from α decreases welfare. In general, there is no reason to think that panel a is more plausible than panel b.

There is nothing odd about these two examples, which show the reduction of one "distortion" lowers welfare. Thus, the theory of the second best may appear to make economic theory powerless to prescribe reform, since in the real world there are always other distortions that policymakers reasonably regard as fixed. For example, proponents of existing agricultural policies might argue that distortionary policies in the nonagricultural sector are fixed and justify offsetting agricultural policies. In order to address this type of objection, economists have investigated sufficient conditions under which piecemeal reform improves welfare [Fukushima and Kim (1989)].

In many circumstances these sufficient conditions are not met, in which case the welfare effect of piecemeal reform is an empirical issue, which requires an empirical model. For example, Beghin and Karp's (1991) CGE model suggests that second-best arguments based on nonagricultural distortions did not justify U.S. agricultural policies in the early 1980s. Arndt et al. (1997) use a general equilibrium model to decompose second-best effects. They apply these methods to study how growth in China affects other Southeast Asian nations. Moschini and Sckokai (1994) demonstrate that decoupled payments to farmers are superior to trade restrictions even in the presence of distortionary taxes. Most empirical agricultural models are based on assumptions that *imply* that reform increases welfare. These models are used to measure the welfare effects of reform, but because of their assumptions they do not address second-best questions.

Another application of the theory of the second best concerns the welfare effect of growth under distorted trade. In the 1950s and 1960s economists showed that growth could lower welfare (i.e., be "immiserising") when it occurred in the presence of trade distortions. The term "distortions" was interpreted broadly to include the failure to exercise monopoly power or to satisfy exogenous constraints (so-called "noneconomic objectives") in an optimal manner. Alston and Martin (1995) apply the idea of immiserising growth to the agricultural sector, where distortions are rife. Murphy, Furtan and Schmitz (1993) show empirically that trade distortions can greatly reduce the benefits of agricultural research that leads to technological improvements. Clarete and Whalley (1994) use a CGE model to illustrate the possibility of immiserising growth.

Despite theoretical ambiguity, most economists are broadly united in favor of liberal trade and skeptical of second-best arguments for trade restrictions. This position is based on a set of theoretical results known as the "Principle of Targeting" [Bhagwati and Srinivasan (1992)], rather than on a wealth of empirical evidence.[10]

---

[10] Political judgment is an additional reason for economists' skepticism of second-best arguments for government intervention. Such intervention *might* improve a market outcome, but the possibility of political capture by lobbyists creates the danger that the government will promote narrow interests at the cost of social welfare. In this case, it might be better to tie the hands of politicians and bureaucrats, removing the possibility that they will do good as well as the danger that they will misbehave.

The Principle of Targeting is the third important idea for agricultural trade economics. It states that distortions, or market failures, should be "targeted" as directly as possible. For example, suppose that policymakers believe that domestic agricultural production provides security, which benefits society. Consumers do not pay, nor are producers compensated, for this security. The security conferred by domestic production is a positive externality. The unregulated competitive equilibrium results in too little domestic production, from the standpoint of society, because producers do not internalize this benefit. In this situation, an agricultural import tariff (or export subsidy) raises welfare over that of the competitive equilibrium. Such a tariff or subsidy is a second-best policy: it ameliorates the distortion caused by producers' failure to internalize the positive production externality, but in the process it creates a consumption distortion. On balance, the second-best tariff improves welfare, but it does so at a cost. The first-best policy in this example is an agricultural *production subsidy*. The target, after all, involves the level of production. A production subsidy achieves this target without generating other distortions.[11] Trade restrictions are seldom a first-best policy. For most plausible scenarios, other policies can correct the fixed distortion or achieve the target at lower cost.

It is worth emphasizing that *first-best policies might affect the level of trade*, as with the example of the production subsidy used to achieve food security. This subsidy reduces imports or increases exports. In general, the first-best policy might be trade-distorting (i.e., it is not necessarily decoupled). If the social goal is to maintain producers' *income*, then the Principle of Targeting implies that the optimal policy is decoupled. However, the first-best policy is seldom a direct trade restriction, such as a tariff or quota.

An important qualification to the Principle of Targeting is the assumption that distortions are independent of the type of policy used [Rodrik (1987)]. To continue the food security example, suppose policymakers decide that security implies a target of a certain quantity of domestic food production. Further suppose that there is no distortionary cost associated with raising government revenue, so that the production subsidy is the first-best means to achieve the target. The level of the production target deemed necessary to achieve security may be influenced by lobbying of domestic producer groups. The resources these groups are willing to devote to lobbying may depend on the degree of success they expect to obtain.

Producers do not care whether a price increase is due to a production subsidy or a tariff. The distinction matters to the government, however. If the government uses the first-best policy, it can achieve the target without creating the consumption distortion. If it is forced to use the second-best tariff, meeting the target creates a real cost. Therefore, if the government has to use a tariff, it may modify its security target. When producers

---

[11] We might argue that the target is really food security rather than domestic production. There may be cheaper ways to achieve this security than promoting domestic production. When invoking the Principle of Targeting, one must be careful to select the correct target.

anticipate that the government will use a tariff, they recognize that their lobbying will be less effective and they therefore devote fewer resources to it. This reduced lobbying results in a lower target (or less pressure to reach the target). In this example, the target is endogenous. Here, government commitment to use an apparently second-best policy instrument, and producers' belief that the government will honor that commitment, changes the equilibrium level of the target. The change may be great enough that welfare is higher than under an apparently first-best policy.

To summarize, the theory of the second best is an antidote to the uncritical acceptance of the fundamental welfare theorems of neoclassical economics. The real world is unlikely to satisfy the assumptions of these theorems. Most economists nevertheless support liberal trade, largely because of the belief that policies *other than trade restrictions* are more likely to increase welfare. Other policies can correct market failures while imposing fewer additional distortions. If the theory of the second best is a remedy for the adage that "a little learning is a dangerous thing", the Principle of Targeting is the proper response to the wholesale rejection of economic theory.

6.2. Optimal trade policies for a "large country"

One of the few situations where a trade policy is actually a first-best means to intervene occurs where a country is large enough to alter its terms of trade. A large country can use export taxes or import tariffs to increase the price of its exports or reduce the price of its imports. In a static model, the optimal *ad valorem* tariff for a large importer equals the inverse of the elasticity of the ROW excess supply. In Section 3.1 we reviewed the empirical uncertainty regarding these elasticities, and in Section 3.3 we discussed whether countries actually attempt to exert monopoly/monopsony power. During the 1980s, there was considerable academic interest in the possibility of a grain-export cartel, but such a cartel was never formed. In the recent past, there have been several (usually unsuccessful) attempts to form cartels in nutmeg, peppers, rubber, tea, coffee, and other agricultural products.

There are a number of interesting theoretical extensions of the optimal tariff/subsidy literature. Here we mention three: (i) the role of dynamics, (ii) the use of second-best tariffs or subsidies, and (iii) the effect of oligopolies.

If the short- and long-run elasticities of the ROW supply are different, how should a large importer set the tariff? If we use the inverse-elasticity formula with the (relatively small) short-run elasticity, we conclude that the importer should use a relatively large tariff; if we use the formula with the (relatively large) long-run elasticity, we conclude that the tariff should be lower. In fact, the importer would like to announce a tariff trajectory rather than a constant tariff. The equilibrium tariff trajectory depends on the importer's ability to make commitments and on the reason for the difference between short- and long-run elasticities.

Suppose, for example, that increased production of the commodity in the ROW requires investment (such as coffee trees) involving nonlinear adjustment costs. It is cheaper to increase capacity slowly. Here, farmers in the ROW have a dynamic-decision problem: their choice of investment today depends on prices they expect to obtain in the future, and those prices depend on the large country's future tariffs. Thus, farmers' current investments depend on their anticipation of future tariffs.

If the importer is able to make commitments (use an "open loop" strategy) the optimal trajectory begins with a high tariff (to take advantage of the low short-run elasticity of supply). The tariff is gradually reduced, giving farmers incentives to invest, and thus shifting out the supply curve in the future. However, this trajectory is "time inconsistent". In the future, the importer would like to renege on the trajectory of tariffs that he announces today. In the future, "tomorrow" (when the tariff is supposed to be low) becomes "today" (when the importer would like to use a large tariff). If the importer is unable to make binding commitments, his equilibrium level of welfare may be lower than under perfect competition [Karp (1987)].

Maskin and Newbery (1990) provide another example where the possession of market power, without the ability to promise not to use this power, can lower a country's welfare. A simple version of their model illustrates the reason for this possibility. Suppose that the world lasts for two periods, and competitive, price-taking firms own a resource (such as oil) that they can extract costlessly. Once extracted, the resource cannot be stored. When the one-period interest rate is r, firms are only willing to save some of the resource to sell in the second period if $P_2 \geqslant (1 + r)P_1$, where P_i is the price in period i. By assumption, the monopsonistic importer has low demand for the resource in the first period and a high demand in the second. Conversely, oil importers in ROW have a relatively high demand in the first period and no use for the resource in the second.

In the second period the monopsonistic importer is a pure monopsonist and faces no competing demand. If there is any of the resource left, the monopsonist faces a perfectly inelastic supply and imposes a (nearly) infinite tariff rate, thus essentially expropriating the resource. Because competitive resource owners anticipate this action, they choose to sell all of their oil in the first period, when it does the monopsonist very little good (because of the assumption about its demand). In this case, the monopsonist buys almost no oil and has almost no gains from trade in the equilibrium without commitment. If the monopsonist had been able to commit to a tariff of zero (to behave like a price taker), the exporter would have wanted to save some of the oil to sell in the second period, and the large importer would have received the usual (positive) gains from trade. The possession of market power can be disadvantageous when agents cannot make commitments about future behavior.

These two examples of a disadvantageous equilibrium tariff illustrate that large countries may have incentives to enter international agreements that prohibit them from exercising market power. By entering such agreements, the large countries sacrifice short-run gains but change the incentives of their trading partners in ways that ultimately benefit them.

Another variation of the optimal tariff argument considers the case where the large country is unable to use the first-best policy [Abbott, Paarlberg and Sharples (1987), Itoh and Kiyono (1987)]. A second-best policy may have the opposite sign (i.e., be a subsidy rather than a tax). For example, the first-best policy for a large exporter is an export tax, which decreases exports and raises prices. The export tax induces competitive producers to behave as if they were a cartel and restrict supply.

Suppose, however, that the government is prohibited from using an export tax, but is allowed to use an export subsidy. If the country exports to market A, where demand is very elastic, and market B, where demand is very inelastic, then the country may benefit from a targeted export subsidy to A. This subsidy results in a transfer of welfare to market A, at a cost to the exporter. However, by diverting sales from B to A, the price in B increases, raising revenue in that market and possibly raising total welfare in the exporting country. This possibility requires segmented markets.

Paarlberg (1995, 1996) discusses the effect of export subsidies on intermediate goods. Alston, Carter and Smith (1993) show that, when raising government revenue requires distortionary taxes, it may be efficient to use export subsides to support domestic producers. In Section 4.2 we described a similar public finance argument that has been used to rationalize apparently inefficient policies. These arguments are applications of the theory of the second best; they are theoretically coherent, but their practical significance is questionable.

A third variation of the optimal tariff/subsidy model involves oligopolistic sellers. There has been an explosion in the theoretical literature on this subject, which Brander (1995) and Karp (1997) survey. When domestic sellers are noncompetitive, the optimal trade policy may be an export subsidy or an export tax, depending on the nature of the oligopoly. Governments may use an export tax to induce domestic firms to behave more like a cartel, or they may choose a subsidy to "shift rents" from foreign competitors. These models have been very important for mainstream trade theory, but have made a smaller impact in agricultural economics. Agricultural economists' contributions to the literature on strategic trade policy include McCorriston and Sheldon (1991, 1996) and Thursby and Thursby (1990). In addition, Thursby (1988) and Krishna and Thursby (1992) explain how the presence of government marketing boards (which are important in many commodity markets) may give rise to strategic incentives.

The increased importance of processed commodities in international trade, and the high degree of concentration in the processing sector, may cause oligopoly trade models to become more important in future agricultural research. These same factors may make another strand of mainstream economic trade theory, the role of increasing returns to scale and monopolistic competition, important in agricultural trade economics in the future. Lanclos and Hertel (1995) compare the effects of both input and output tariffs for U.S. food processing industries, under the assumption that these exhibit monopolistic competition. Karp and Perloff (1993b, 1995) study government intervention in dynamic oligopoly models.

6.3. Insurance arguments for trade restrictions

The claim that incomplete insurance markets provide a second-best justification for trade restrictions is centuries old. Ricardo (1975, p. 266) endorses an insurance argument that promotes temporary protection in the case of an external supply shock. He describes a scenario in which tariffs should restrain a surge in agricultural imports following the end of a war that has disrupted trade. The failure to protect agriculture would lead to losses to farmers who had invested in the sector during the war, making them reluctant to undertake similar investments should war recur. By developing a reputation of protecting farmers against losses when external supply is high, the government encourages farmers to make investments when external supply is low. In this way, agricultural protection transfers risk from farmers to society.

The inherent randomness of agricultural production is often given as a rationale for trade restrictions. The instability of world price generated from foreign supply shocks can cause fluctuations in domestic price under free trade, resulting in costs to domestic producers and consumers. Developing countries that are heavily dependent on export earning of commodities for which world demand is very inelastic may be particularly vulnerable to price (and foreign revenue) instability. Attempts to control these price fluctuations led to the International Commodity Agreements in the 1960s and 1970s. By the 1990s most of these ICAs had become minor forces or were defunct [Gilbert (1993, 1996)].

Policies that insulate domestic consumers from price instability frequently increase instability elsewhere in the world [Zwart and Meilke (1979)]. The desire to transfer instability abroad (much like the desire to transfer rents to domestic producers) can create strategic incentives to use trade policies [Bigman and Karp (1993)]. We first illustrate the manner in which trade transfers price instability from one country to another, and then describe a model in which trade can reduce welfare *for every agent in every country* because of price instability.

Figure 2 shows a partial-equilibrium model for trade with random supply. Panel a shows demand and random supply in the foreign country. Half the time supply is S_1, otherwise it is S_2. Thus, half the time the autarkic price in the foreign country is P_1, and half the time it is P_2. The supply and demand in the home country (panel b) are nonstochastic, so that the autarkic price in the home country is constant at P^*. Panel

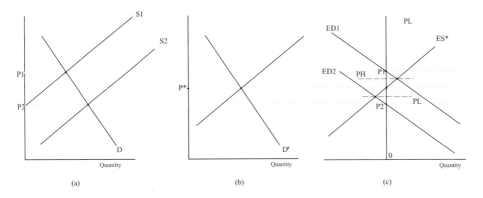

Figure 2. A trade model with random supply.

c shows the (stochastic) free-trade equilibrium. The horizontal difference between the home country's supply and demand – its excess supply function – is the curve labeled $ES*$.[12] The horizontal differences between the foreign country's demand and supply curves (its excess demand functions) are labeled ED_1 and ED_2. The relevant excess demand function depends on whether the foreign supply is high or low. The equilibrium world price is P_H half the time and P_L half the time.

In this example, trade transfers price instability from the foreign to the home country. Trade increases the price variability in the home country and decreases the price variability in the foreign country. (To see this result, compare the two equilibrium world prices, P_H and P_L, with the two autarkic equilibrium prices in the foreign country.) Trade reallocates risk much as it reallocates goods and services. If producers are sufficiently risk-averse with respect to fluctuations in profits, and consumers sufficiently risk-averse with respect to fluctuations in real income, they both dislike price risk.[13] When consumers dislike price risk, price instability erodes the usual gains from trade for the home country, and increases those gains for the foreign country. It would appear that the home country may want to restrict trade.

This example with countries that have asymmetric price instability may be misleading. One country may import price instability for some commodities and export price instability for others. The increased price instability for some commodities may then be worth the decreased instability for others. In order to use a single commodity model to illustrate this situation, we treat the home and foreign countries symmetrically, so that each has random supply. In such a model, each country's *average* exports (and imports) are zero, but in most states of nature they trade. Trade reduces price instability in each country; the amount of the reduction is negatively related to the correlation between supply shocks.

The elaboration of the simple model, making supply stochastic in both countries, may appear to imply that, in the symmetric case at least, price variability does not alter the standard argument for trade. That conclusion is incorrect because it is based on the assumption that the supply functions are exogenous. If trade changes the distribution of prices, it can change producers' supply decisions, and thus change the supply function in every state of nature. Newbery and Stiglitz (1984) explain how this situation can arise. They show that producers and consumers in both (symmetric) countries *might* be worse off under free trade than under autarky. Their model has a representative producer and

---

[12] The excess supply function is the horizontal difference between the domestic supply and demand functions. The excess demand function (the negative of the excess supply function) is the horizontal difference between the domestic demand and supply functions. In the region to the left of the vertical line labeled "0" in panel c, quantities are negative. Thus, for prices below P^*, where the home country's excess supply is negative, the home country wants to import. Since the equilibrium can occur to the left or the right of the vertical line labeled "0", it does not matter whether we associate an excess supply or demand function with a country. In other words, in drawing the excess demand function for the foreign country, we do not prejudge whether that country imports the commodity in equilibrium.

[13] If individuals can make their decisions after they observe price, they may benefit from price variation. For simplicity we do not discuss the possibility that agents have higher expected utility under price variability.

consumer in each country. The risk-averse producer allocates his land (the only input) between a "safe" crop and a "risky" crop. After the farmer makes his land allocation decision, a random weather shock occurs, determining the output of the risky crop. The output of the safe crop is deterministic, and depends only on the amount of land devoted to its cultivation. The consumer is risk-neutral, and her preferences are such that her elasticity of demand for the risky crop equals 1.

First, consider the equilibrium under autarky. The assumption of unitary elasticity of demand for the risky crop means that a 10 percent decrease in supply causes a 10 percent increase in equilibrium price. Consequently, the farmer's revenue from the risky crop is nonstochastic under autarky. The harm to the farmer from a decrease in supply is exactly offset by an increase in price. As long as the consumer's demand is downward-sloping, the quantity supplied and the equilibrium price are negatively correlated, so a reduction in quantity tends to be balanced by an increase in price. Thus, in general, markets implicitly give the farmer some degree of *revenue insurance* to offset fluctuations in supply; with unitary elasticity of demand, the implicit insurance provided by the market is "complete" in the sense that the farmer's revenue is certain. Given that the farmer faces no revenue uncertainty from producing the risky crop, he behaves as if he has full insurance. He allocates the socially optimal amount of land to the risky crop.

Now consider the free-trade equilibrium. Suppose that two countries are exactly the same, except that the random shock to supply is perfectly negatively correlated. When there is good weather in one country, there is bad weather in the other. Because the two countries are identical in each period, prior to the realization of their respective random variables, the farmers in each country make the same land allocation decision (before the weather shock is realized). However, given the negative correlation in the supply shock, when output is high in one country, it is low in the other. Thus, *aggregate output* of the risky crop is nonstochastic, so under free trade the price of the risky crop is also nonstochastic.

Under autarky the farmer faces price uncertainty but no income uncertainty. With trade, the farmer faces no price uncertainty but substantial income uncertainty. Of course, the farmer cares about his income, not the price *per se*. Given his risk aversion, he allocates less than the socially optimal amount of land to the risky crop under free trade. Trade provides the consumer with price stability, but this is unimportant to her in view of her assumed risk neutrality. The consumer is worse off with trade because it reduces the average supply of the risky crop below the socially optimal (perfect insurance) level. The farmer is worse off because he faces income risk with trade. Thus, the agents in both of the countries have lower expected welfare with trade than under autarky.

The unrealistic assumptions in this model serve to make the result (relatively) clear. Any of the assumptions can be weakened. The intuition for this result is that there is no insurance market: markets are incomplete. This missing market is unimportant under autarky, since the spot market provides a perfect substitute. With trade and nonstochastic aggregate supply, the spot market no longer serves this function. Trade opens up one market (international sales) but effectively closes down the (implicit) insurance market.

In Figure 1, we can view one distortion as the missing insurance market and the other distortion as a prohibitive tariff. Reducing the tariff to zero can make all agents worse off, which decreases social welfare in both countries.

The example of Pareto-inferior trade (like the example of the disadvantageous tariff) is primarily useful to sharpen our intuition about second-best settings. However, in order to determine whether missing insurance markets provide a plausible argument for trade policy, it is important to ask why the markets are incomplete [Dixit (1987)]. If the reasons have to do with informational problems, such as adverse selection or moral hazard, and if the government has no better information than private agents, trade policy may be powerless to improve upon a competitive equilibrium. The theory of the second best tells us that insurance arguments *might* provide a justification for trade policy. However, the fact that these markets are incomplete certainly does not provide a *presumption* that trade restrictions are welfare-improving.

6.4. Summary

Most agricultural trade economists, like neoclassical trade economists in general, think trade liberalization will lead to global welfare gains. Most members of the profession enthusiastically support efforts to liberalize agricultural markets further. The fundamental theorems of welfare economics, together with the theory of comparative advantage, provide the intellectual basis for this support. The widespread endorsement of trade liberalization by agricultural trade economists probably also owes something to the culture of the profession. An individual who presumed that liberal trade decreases welfare would not be taken seriously in the world of academic economists.

However, trade theory does not provide unambiguous support for liberalized trade. The theory of the second best recognizes that reducing some distortions, while holding others fixed, may decrease welfare. This qualification does not really challenge the presumption in favor of liberal trade. Although trade restrictions *might* improve welfare, the Principle of Targeting assures us that other policies are likely to be much more effective.

One of the few situations when trade restrictions are actually the first-best policy for a single country occurs where a large country can change its terms of trade. However, even in that situation, reasonable changes in assumptions (such as the introduction of dynamics without an ability to commit to future policies, or the introduction of oligopolistic producers) can dramatically change policy prescriptions. For most policy issues, trade intervention would create secondary distortions even if it were applied optimally. For example, arguments in favor of trade restrictions based on missing insurance markets have a long and distinguished pedigree. These arguments are often interesting and sometimes intellectually coherent. However, it is unlikely that trade restrictions are the appropriate means to deal with insurance problems.

Some economists are reluctant to consider second-best arguments for trade restrictions because these may open the door to disguised protectionism. This problem is an important concern, for example, in the controversy surrounding health and phytosanitary standards or more general environmental problems. Economists appeal to the Principle of Targeting and argue that trade may be associated with, but does not cause, these health and environmental problems, so trade restrictions should not be used to remedy them. In some cases this response is appropriate, but in others it represents a failure to engage in the debate and decreases the possibility of economic contributions.

7. Conclusions and conjectures

Governments are key agents in international agricultural trade due to their massive intervention in their domestic agricultural sectors. For the past thirty years, since trade emerged as a distinct field within agricultural economics, government policy has been the *raison d'être* for the discipline. As international trade in agriculture became increasingly important, domestic policies such as price supports and input subsidies acquired international significance. These policies affect domestic supply and demand and therefore affect imports, exports, and world prices. International trade causes (nominally) domestic policies in one country to affect producers and consumers in other countries. In addition, the growth of agricultural trade has increased the available policy menu. Governments use trade policy, such as tariffs and export subsidies, to protect domestic agriculture.

Although international trade is a recognizably distinct field within agricultural economics, agricultural trade economists are aware that there is not a sharp distinction between domestic and trade policy. The profession studies both the international effects of domestic policy and the domestic effects of trade policy.

A large part of the research effort is devoted to describing government policies and measuring their effects. Thus, agricultural trade economics is primarily an empirical and institutional discipline. The empirical work attempts to determine the magnitudes of excess supply and demand elasticities, the effects of currency devaluations and other macro-economic changes, and the extent of market power in international markets. Summary statistics such as PSEs provide a useful, but limited means to describe policies. Partial equilibrium and CGE models also are widely used to estimate the trade and welfare effects of existing policies and of policy reform. Political economy models measure the welfare trade-offs among different groups of existing policies. Other political economy models attempt to explain policies on the basis of demographic, social, and political variables.

There is disagreement on many technical issues, including the proper way to measure elasticities, the effects of currency devaluations, and the weights in political preference functions. However, the belief that liberalization of markets leads to greater efficiency is virtually unchallenged. Most empirical models are based on the assumption that liberal reform increases welfare. These models are used to measure the magnitude of welfare gains under maintained assumptions, but few models are sufficiently general to test those assumptions.

The profession's endorsement of liberal trade is based on neoclassical theory, which creates a strong presumption in favor of free trade. However, neoclassical theory qualifies this endorsement, recognizing that reducing some distortions in the presence of other fixed distortions can lower welfare. Agricultural trade economists are aware of this qualification, which is formalized in the theory of the second best. Most trade economists are skeptical of second-best arguments for trade restrictions. The theory states that trade restrictions *might* increase welfare, but provides no basis to presume that they *do* increase welfare. Economists are also wary of second-best arguments being co-opted by crypto-protectionists. Finally, and most important, the Principle of Targeting assures us that policies other than trade restrictions can more efficiently improve welfare in most circumstances.

There is a widespread popular belief that intrinsic differences between agriculture and other sectors justify government intervention. This belief amounts to a second-best argument for government policy because it assumes that market failures create a role for government. The usual problems cited include the inherent randomness of agricultural production due to weather and the fact that "food is a basic necessity". However, it is not clear that weather (rather than, for example, input prices) is the most important source of randomness in agriculture, nor that agriculture is subject to more randomness than other sectors, nor that private (futures and insurance) markets are not a more efficient way to deal with risk than government intervention. While food is certainly one of our basic needs, it is not our only one. It also is not clear that production is the most vulnerable stage in the provision of food, nor the most in need of government supervision. Thus, the argument that agriculture is intrinsically different than other sectors is simply not convincing. Agricultural trade economists have devoted a great deal of research effort to debunking these arguments.

The profession has not, however, clearly explained why these arguments are so widely accepted by the public, nor why the agricultural sectors of developed countries are so highly protected. Perhaps the explanations have more to do with political inertia and social sentiment than with economics.

Some fields (such as macroeconomics) have been enlivened by debates concerning appropriate policies. Agricultural trade economics (and to some extent agricultural economics in general) provides a striking contrast. There is broad agreement within the profession that government policies over the last several decades have been tremendously wasteful. The profession has taken a political role by developing and disseminating the intellectual arguments for policy reform.

For decades governments resisted attempts to liberalize agricultural trade, while domestic policies became more entrenched and inefficient. During the 1980s, several developed countries, including Australia, New Zealand, and to a lesser extent the U.S., moved toward more liberal domestic agricultural policies. This movement was reinforced by the worldwide trend towards adoption of market economies, notably in the former Soviet bloc and in developing countries in Latin America. The completion of the Uruguay Round of GATT negotiations changed the basic premise of agricultural trade. Trade-distorting government policies were recognized as a legitimate concern of international negotiations, and liberal trade in agriculture became a realistic goal. Of course, trade-distorting policies have not been abandoned, and liberal trade has not been achieved. However, the rhetoric of agricultural policy, and probably the mood that determines this policy, has fundamentally changed.

A possible measure of the success of the discipline of agricultural (trade) economics is the extent to which it loses its sector-specific character and comes to resemble other specialties within economics. The high degree of consensus within the discipline is largely due to the egregious nature of government policies. The general direction of welfare-improving reform is so obvious that differences of opinion about specifics have seemed like hair-splitting.

If the current movement toward more liberal trade persists, the consensus within the discipline is likely to diminish. Differences in opinion will emerge regarding the proper role for government in addressing health and environmental concerns. Government involvement in these areas will sometimes have trade effects, as have past policies. In addition, the structure of agricultural trade is changing, as processed goods become increasingly important. This change is associated with increased vertical integration and the likelihood of increasing returns to scale and monopolistic competition or oligopoly. Together with heightened concern for health and the environment, these structural changes could lead to a fundamental change in the field of agricultural trade economics.

Acknowledgements

We thank the two editors of this volume and two anonymous referees for their comments on an earlier draft. While planning this paper we received suggestions from over twenty International Agricultural Trade Research Consortium (IATRC) members. We thank them for their help. We also thank Melanie Raymond for her outstanding research assistance.

References

Abbott, P.C. (1988), "Estimating U.S. agricultural export demand elasticities: Econometric and economic issues", in: C.A. Carter and W.H. Gardiner, eds., Elasticities in International Agricultural Trade (Westview Press, Boulder, CO and London) 53–85.

Abbott, P.C., P. Paarlberg and J.A. Sharples (1987), "Targeted agricultural export subsidies and social welfare", American Journal of Agricultural Economics 69:723–732.

Adelman, I., and S. Robinson (1992), "U.S. competitiveness and the exchange rate: A general equilibrium analysis of the U.S. economy, 1982–86", in: B.G. Hickman, ed., International Productivity and Competitiveness (Oxford University Press) 276–298.

Alston, J., C.A. Carter, R. Green and D. Pick (1990), "Whither Armington trade models?", American Journal of Agricultural Economics 72:455–467.

Alston, J., C.A. Carter and V.H. Smith (1993), "Rationalizing agricultural export subsidies", American Journal of Agricultural Economics 75:1000–1009.

Alston, J., and W.J. Martin (1995), "Reversal of fortune: Immiserizing technical change in agriculture", American Journal of Agricultural Economics 77:251–259.

Anania, G., M. Bohman and C.A. Carter (1992), "U.S. export subsidies in wheat", American Journal of Agricultural Economics 74:534–545.

Anania, G., C.A. Carter and A.F. McCalla (1994), "Agricultural policy changes, GATT negotiations, and the United States–EC agricultural trade conflict", in: G. Anania et al., eds., Agricultural Trade Conflicts and GATT: New Dimensions in United States–European Agricultural Trade Relations (Westview Press, Boulder, CO) 1–31.

Anania, G., and A.F. McCalla (1991), "Does arbitraging matter? Spatial trade models and discriminatory trade policies", American Journal of Agricultural Economics 73:103–117.

Anderson, K. (1995), "Lobbying incentives and the pattern of protection in rich and poor countries", Economic Development and Cultural Change 43:401–423.

Anderson, K., and R. Tyers (1989), "The pattern of distortions to agricultural incentives", in: A. Maunder and A. Valdes, eds., Agriculture and Governments in an Interdependent World, Proceedings of the 20th International Conference of Agricultural Economists, Buenos Aires, Argentina, 1988 (Aldershot, Dartmouth) 175–186.

Anderson, M., and P. Garcia (1989), "Exchange rate uncertainty and demand for U.S. soybeans", American Journal of Agricultural Economics 71:721–729.

Arndt, C., T. Hertel, B. Dimaranan, K. Huff and R. McDougall (1997), "China in 2005: Implications for the rest of the world", Journal of Economic Integration 12:505–547.

Babcock, B.A., C.A. Carter and A. Schmitz (1990), "The political economy of U.S. wheat legislation", Economic Inquiry 28:335–353.

Balisacan, A.M., and J.A. Roumasset (1987), "Public choice of economic policy: The growth of agricultural protection", Weltwirtschaftliches Archives 123:232–248.

Bates, R. (1997), Open-Economy Politics: The Political Economy of the World Coffee Trade (Princeton University Press, Princeton, NJ).

Baumol, W. (1977), Economic Theory and Operations Analysis, 4th edn. (Prentice Hall, Englewood Cliffs, NJ).

Bautista R., and A. Valdés (eds.) (1993), The Bias Against Agriculture: Trade and Macroeconomic Policies in Developing Countries (Institute for Contemporary Studies, San Francisco, CA).

Beghin, J.C. (1990), "A game-theoretic model of endogenous public policies", American Journal of Agricultural Economics 72:138–148.

Beghin, J.C., W.E. Foster and M. Kherallah (1996), "Institutions and market distortions: International evidence for tobacco", Journal of Agricultural Economics 47:355–365.

Beghin, J.C., and L.S. Karp (1991), "Estimation of price policies in Senegal: An empirical test of cooperative game theory", Journal of Development Economics 35:49–67.

Beghin, J.C., and L.S. Karp (1992), "Tariff reform in the presence of sector specific distortions", Canadian Journal of Economics 25:294–309.

Beghin, J.C., and M. Kherallah (1994), "Political institutions and international patterns of agricultural protection", The Review of Economics and Statistics 76:482–489.

Belongia, M.T. (1986), "Estimating exchange rate effects on exports: A cautionary note", Federal Reserve of St. Louis Review 68:5–16.

Bessler, D.A., and R.A. Babula (1987), "Forecasting wheat exports: Do exchange rates matter?", Journal of Business and Economics Statistics 5:397–406.

Bhagwati, J., and T.N. Srinivasan (1992), Lectures in International Trade (MIT Press, Cambridge, MA).

Bigman, D., and L. Karp (1993), "Strategic trade policies under instability", International Review of Economics and Finance 2:163–180.

Bradshaw, G.W., and D. Orden (1990), "Granger causality from the exchange rate to agricultural prices and export sales", Western Journal of Agricultural Economics 15:100–110.

Brander, J.A. (1995), "Strategic trade policy", in: G.M. Grossman and K. Rogoff, eds., Handbook of International Economics, Vol. 3 (Elsevier, Amsterdam) 1395–1456.

Bredahl, M.E., A. Schmitz and J.S. Hillman (1987), "Rent seeking in international trade: The great tomato war", American Journal of Agricultural Economics 69:1–10.

Buschena, D.E., and J.M. Perloff (1991), "The creation of dominant firm market power in the coconut oil export market", American Journal of Agricultural Economics 73:1000–1008.

Carter, C.A., N. Gallini and A. Schmitz (1980), "Producer consumer trade-offs in export cartels: The Wheat cartel case", American Journal of Agricultural Economics 62:812–818.

Carter, C.A., and D.H. Pick (1989), "The J-curve effect and the U.S. agricultural trade balance", American Journal of Agricultural Economics 71:712–720.

Cassing, J.H., and A.L. Hillman (1986), "Shifting comparative advantage and senescent industry collapse", American Economic Review 76:516–523.

Chambers, R.G., and R.E. Just (1979), "A critique of exchange rate treatment in agricultural trade models", American Journal of Agricultural Economics 61:249–257.

Chambers, R.G., and R.E. Just (1981), "Effects of exchange rate changes on U.S. agriculture: A dynamic analysis", American Journal of Agricultural Economics 63:32–46.

Chambers, R.G., and P.L. Paarlberg (1991), "Are more exports always better? Comparing cash and in-kind export subsidies", American Journal of Agricultural Economics 73:142–154.

Chambers, R.G., and D.H. Pick (1994), "Marketing orders as nontariff trade barriers", American Journal of Agricultural Economics 76:47–54.

Clarete, R.L., and J. Whalley (1994), "Immiserizing growth and endogenous protection", Journal of Development Economics 45:121–133.

Coleman, J.R., and K.D. Meilke (1988), "The influence of exchange rates on red meat trade between Canada and the United States", Canadian Journal of Agricultural Economics 36:401–424.

de Gorter, H. (2002), "Political economy of agricultural policy", in: B.L. Gardner and G.C. Rausser, eds., Handbook of Agricultural Economics, Vol. 2 (Elsevier, Amsterdam) 1893–1943.

de Gorter, H., and Y. Tsur (1991), "Explaining price policy bias in agriculture: The calculus of support-maximizing politicians", American Journal of Agricultural Economics 73:1244–1254.

Dixit, A. (1987), "Trade and insurance with moral hazard", Journal of International Economics 23:201–220.

Dutton, J., and T. Grennes (1988), "The role of exchange rates in trade models", in: C. Carter and W. Gardiner, eds., Elasticities in International Agricultural Trade (Westview Press, Boulder, CO, London) 87–135.

Farnsworth, C.H. (1988), "OPEC isn't the only cartel that couldn't", New York Times, April 24, 3.

Francois, J.F., and C.R. Shields (1994), Modeling Trade Policy: Applied General Equilibrium Assessments of North American Free Trade (Cambridge University Press, Cambridge and New York).

Fukushima, T., and N. Kim (1989), "Welfare improving tariff changes", Journal of International Economics 26:383–388.

Gardner, W.H., and P.M. Dixit (1986), "Price elasticity of export demand", ERS Staff Report AGES860408 (U.S. Department of Agriculture, Washington, DC).

Gardner, B.L. (1983), "Efficient redistribution through commodity markets", American Journal of Agricultural Economics 65:225–334.

Gardner, B.L. (1987), "Causes of U.S. farm commodity programs", Journal of Political Economy 95:290–310.

Gardner, B.L. (1996), "The political economy of U.S. export subsidies for wheat", in: A.O. Kreuger, ed., The Political Economy of American Trade Policy (University of Chicago Press, Chicago and London) 291–331.

Gilbert, C. (1993), "Domestic price stabilization schemes for developing countries", in: S. Claessens and R.C. Duncan, eds., Managing Commodity Price Risk in Developing Countries (Johns Hopkins University Press for the World Bank, Baltimore and London) 30–67.

Gilbert, C. (1996), "International commodity agreements: An obituary notice", World Development 24:1–19.

Goldstein, M., and M.S. Khan (1985), "Income and price effects in foreign trade", in: R.W. Jones and P.B. Kennen, eds., Handbook of International Economics (North Holland, Amsterdam) 1041–1105.

Goodwin, B., T. Grennes and M. Wohlgenant (1990a), "Testing the law of one price when trade takes time", Journal of International Money and Finance 9:21–40.

Goodwin, B., T. Grennes and M. Wohlgenant (1990b), "A revised test of the law of one price using rational expectations", American Journal of Agricultural Economics 72:682–693.

Greenshields, B.L. (1974), "Changes in exchange rates: Impact on U.S. grain and soybean exports to Japan", ERS Report FAER No. 364 (U.S. Department of Agriculture, Washington, DC).

Grossman, G.M., and E. Helpman (1994), "Protection for sale", American Economic Review 84(4):833-850.

Grossman, G.M., and E. Helpman (1995), "Trade wars and trade talks", Journal of Political Economy, 103(4):675-708.

Henneberry, D., S. Henneberry and L. Tweeten (1987), "The strengths of the dollar: An analysis of trade weighted foreign exchange rate indices with implications for agricultural trade", Agribusiness 3:189–206.

Hertel, T.W. (1989), "Negotiating reductions in agricultural support: Implications of technology and factor mobility", American Journal of Agricultural Economics 3:559–573.

Hertel, T.W. (1993), "Partial vs. general equilibrium analysis of trade policy reform", Journal of Agricultural Economics Research 44:3–15.

Hillman, A.L., and H.W. Ursprung (1988), "Domestic politics, foreign interests and international trade policy", American Economic Review 78:729–745.

Hillman, J. (1978), Nontariff Agricultural Trade Barriers (University of Nebraska Press, Lincoln, NE).

Hillman, J. (1997), "Nontariff agricultural trade barriers revisited", in: D. Orden and D. Roberts, eds., Understanding Technical Barriers to International Trade, Proceedings of a Conference of the International Agricultural Trade Research Consortium (University of Minnesota, Dept. of Applied Economics, IATRC, St. Paul, MN) 1–32.

Honma, M., and Y. Hayami (1986), "Structure of agricultural protection in industrial countries", Journal of International Economics 20:115–129.

International Agricultural Trade Research Consortium (1994), "The Uruguay Round agreement on agriculture: An evaluation", IRATRC Commissioned Paper 9 (University of Minnesota, Dept. of Applied Economics, IATRC, St. Paul, MN).

Itoh, M., and K. Kiyono (1987), "Welfare enhancing export subsidies", Journal of Political Economy 95:115–137.

Johnson, D.G. (1973), World Agriculture in Disarray (Macmillan St. Martin's Press, London).

Johnson, P.R., T. Grennes and M. Thursby (1977), "Devaluation, foreign trade controls, and domestic wheat prices", American Journal of Agricultural Economics 59:619–627.

Josling, T. (1990), "The GATT: Its historical role and importance to agricultural policy and trade", in: H.J. Michelmann, J.C. Stabler and G.G. Storey, eds., The Political Economy of Agricultural Trade and Policy (Westview Press, Boulder, CO and London) 155–171.

Just, R.E., and W.S. Chern (1980), "Tomatoes, technology, and oligopsony", The Bell Journal of Economics 11:584–602.

Kamp, P.V., and C.F. Runge (1994), "Trends and developments in United States agricultural policy: 1993–1995", Review of Marketing and Agricultural Economics 62:317–335.

Karp, L. (1987), "Consistent tariffs with dynamic supply response", Journal of International Economics 23:369–376.

Karp, L. (1997), "Is strategic trade policy practical?", in: D. Pick, D. Henderson, J. Kinsey and I. Sheldon, eds., Global Markets for Processed Foods (Westview Press, Boulder, CO and London) 55–74.

Karp, L., C. Dumas, B.W. Koo and S. Sacheti (1994), "International trade and the internalization of environmental damages", Working Paper 746 (University of California, Dept. of Agricultural and Resource Economics, Berkeley, CA).

Karp, L.S., and J.M. Perloff (1989), "Dynamic oligopoly in the rice export market", Review of Economics and Statistics 71:462–470.

Karp, L.S., and J.M. Perloff (1993a), "A dynamic model of oligopoly in the coffee export market", American Journal of Agricultural Economics 75:448–457.

Karp, L.S., and J.M. Perloff (1993b), "Industrial policy as an alternative to trade policy: Helping by hurting", Review of International Economics 1:253–262.

Karp, L.S., and J.M. Perloff (1995), "Why industrial policies fail: Limited commitment", International Economic Review 36:887–905.

Kennedy, P.L., H. von Witzke and T.L. Roe (1996a), "Strategic agricultural trade policy interdependence and the exchange rate: A game theoretic analysis", Public Choice 88:43–56.

Kennedy, P.L., H. von Witzke and T.L. Roe (1996b), "Multilateral agricultural trade negotiations: A non-cooperative and cooperative game approach", European Review of Agricultural Economics 23:381–400.

Keuschnigg, C., and W. Kohler (1995), "Dynamic effects of tariff liberalization: An intertemporal CGE approach", Review of International Economics 3:20–35.

Kherallah, M., and J. Beghin (1998), "U.S. trade threats: Rhetoric or war?", American Journal of Agricultural Economics 80:15–29.

Kilkenny, M., and S. Robinson (1990), "CGE analysis of agricultural liberalization: Factor mobility and macro closure", Journal of Policy Modeling 12:527–556.

Kolstad, C.D., and A.E. Burris (1986), "Imperfectly competitive equilibria in international commodity markets", American Journal of Agricultural Economics 68:25–36.

Konandreas, P., P. Bushnell and R. Green (1978), "Estimation of export demand functions for U.S. wheat", Western Journal of Agricultural Economics 3:39–49.

Krishna, K., and M. Thursby (1992), "Optimal policies and marketing board objectives", Journal of Development Economics 38:1–15.

Lanclos, D.K., and T.W. Hertel (1995), "Endogenous product differentiation and trade policy: Implications for the United States food industry", American Journal of Agricultural Economics 77:591–601.

Lewis, J.D., S. Robinson and Z. Wang (1995), "Beyond the Uruguay Round: The implications of an Asian free trade area", China Economic Review 6:35–90.

Liu, K., and R. Seeley (eds.) (1987), "The international agricultural trade research consortium: Agricultural trade modeling, the state of practice and research issues", ERS Staff Report AGES861215 (United States Department of Agriculture, Washington, DC).

Love, H.A., and E. Murniningtyas (1992), "Measuring the degree of market power exerted by government trade agencies", American Journal of Agricultural Economics 74:546–555.

Magee, S.P., W.A. Brock and L. Young (1989), Black Hole Tariffs and Endogenous Policy Theory: Political Economy in General Equilibrium (Cambridge University Press, Cambridge and New York).

Martin, W., and I. Shaw (1986), "The effect of exchange rate changes on the value of Australia's major agricultural exports", Economic Record Supplement, 101–107.

Martin, W., and L.A. Winters (1995), The Uruguay Round: Widening and Deepening the World Trading System (The World Bank, Washington, DC).

Maskin, E., and D. Newbery (1990), "Disadvantageous oil tariffs and dynamic consistency", American Economic Review 80:143–156.

McCalla, A. (1966), "A duopoly model of world wheat pricing", Journal of Farm Economics 48:711–727.

McCorriston, S., and I.M. Sheldon (1991), "Government intervention in imperfectly competitive agricultural input markets", American Journal of Agricultural Economics 73:621–632.

McCorriston, S., and I.M. Sheldon (1996), "Incorporating industrial organization into agricultural trade modelling", in: D. Martimort, ed., Agricultural Markets: Mechanisms, Failures, Regulations (North-Holland, Amsterdam) 313–330.

McGarry, M.J., and A. Schmitz (eds.) (1992), The World Grain Trade: Grain Marketing, Institutions, and Policies (Westview Press, Boulder, CO and London).

Meilke, K.D., and R. Sarker (1997), "National administered protection agencies: Their role in the Post-Uruguay Round world", in: D. Orden and D. Roberts, eds., Understanding Technical Barriers to International Trade, Proceedings of a Conference of the International Agricultural Trade Research Consortium (University of Minnesota, Dept. of Applied Economics, IATRC, St. Paul, MN) 195–225.

Mitchell, D.O., and R.C. Duncan (1987), "Market behavior of grains exporters", The World Bank Research Observer 2:3–21.

Moschini, G. (1991), "Economic issues in tariffication: An overview", Agricultural Economics 5:101–120.

Moschini, G., and K.D. Meilke (1991), "Tariffication with supply management: The case of the U.S.–Canada chicken trade", Canadian Journal of Agricultural Economics 39:35–68.

Moschini, G., and P. Sckokai (1994), "Efficiency of decoupled farm programs under distortionary taxation", American Journal of Agricultural Economics 76:362–370.

Murphy, J.A., W.H. Furtan and A. Schmitz (1993), "The gains from agricultural research under distorted trade", Journal of Political Economy 51:161–172.

Newbery, D.M., and J.E. Stiglitz (1984), "Pareto inferior trade", Review of Economic Studies 51:1–12.

Oehmke, J.F., and X. Yao (1990), "A policy preference function for government intervention in the U.S. wheat market", American Journal of Agricultural Economics 72:631–640.

Olson, M. Jr. (1985), "Space, agriculture and organization", American Journal of Agricultural Economics 67:928–937.

Organisation for Economic Co-Operation and Development (1995), Agricultural Policies, Markets and Trade in OECD Countries (OECD, Paris).

Orden, D. (1986), "Agriculture, trade and macroeconomics: The U.S. case", Journal of Policy Modeling 8:27–51.

Orden, D. (1996), "Agricultural interest groups and the North American Free Trade Agreement", in: A.O. Kreuger, ed., The Political Economy of American Trade Policy (University of Chicago Press, Chicago and London) 335–382.

Paarlberg, P.L. (1995), "Agricultural export subsidies and intermediate goods trade", American Journal of Agricultural Economics 77:119–128.

Paarlberg, P.L. (1996), "In-kind export subsidies for processed and bulk goods", American Journal of Agricultural Economics 78:670–676.

Paarlberg, P.L., and P.C. Abbott (1986), "Oligopolistic behavior by public agencies in international trade: The world wheat market", American Journal of Agricultural Economics 68:528–542.

Park, T.A., and D.H. Pick (1996), "Imperfect competition and exchange rate pass-through in U.S. wheat exports", in: I.M. Sheldon and P.C. Abbott, eds., Industrial Organization and Trade in the Food Industries (Westview Press and Harper Collins, Boulder, CO and Oxford) 53–64.

Peterson, E.B., T.W. Hertel and J. Stout (1994), "A critical assessment of supply-demand models of agricultural trade", American Journal of Agricultural Economics 76:709–721.

Peterson, E.W., M. Paggi and G. Henry (1988), "Quality restrictions as barriers to trade: The case of European Community regulations on the use of hormones", Western Journal of Agricultural Economics 13:82–91.

Pick, D.H. (1990), "Exchange rate risks and U.S. agricultural trade flows", American Journal of Agricultural Economics 72:694–700.

Pick, D.H., and C.A. Carter (1994), "Pricing to market with transactions denominated in a common currency", American Journal of Agricultural Economics 76:55–60.

Pieri, R.G., K.D. Meilke and T.G. Macaulay (1977), "North American–Japanese pork trade: An application of quadratic programming", Canadian Journal of Agricultural Economics 25:61–79.

Piggot, J., and J. Whalley (eds.) (1991), Applied General Equilibrium (Physica-Verlag, Heidelberg).

Pompelli, G.K., and D.H. Pick (1990), "Pass-through of exchange rates and tariffs in Brazil–U.S. tobacco trade", American Journal of Agricultural Economics 72:676–681.

Rausser, G.C., and J.W. Freebairn (1974), "Estimation of policy preference functions: An application to U.S. beef import quotas", Review of Economics and Statistics 56:437–449.

Ricardo, D. (1975), On the Principles of Political Economy and Taxation, Vol. 1, The Works and Correspondence of David Ricardo, P. Sraffa, ed. (Cambridge University Press, Cambridge and New York).

Roberts, D. (1998), "Implementation of the WTO agreements on the application of sanitary and phytosanitary measures: The first two years", International Agricultural Trade Research Consortium Working Paper 98-4 (University of Minnesota, Dept. of Applied Economics, IATRC, St. Paul, MN).

Robinson, S., M. Kilkenny and I. Adelman (1989), "The effects of trade liberalization in agriculture on the U.S. economy", in: A.B. Stoeckel, D. Vincent and S. Cuthbertson, eds., Macroeconomic Consequences of Farm Support Policies (Duke University Press, Durham, NC) 222–259.

Rodrik, D. (1986), "Tariffs, subsidies, and welfare with endogenous policy", Journal of International Economics 21:285–299.

Rodrik, D. (1987), "Policy targeting with endogenous distortions: Theory of optimum subsidy revisited", Quarterly Journal of Economics 94:903–911.

Roningen, V., J. Sullivan and P. Dixit (1991), "Documentation of the Static World Policy Simulation (SWOPSIM) Modeling Framework", ERS Staff Report AGES9151 (U.S. Department of Agriculture, Washington, DC).

Sadoulet, E., and A. de Janvry (1992), "Agricultural trade liberalization and low income countries – a general equilibrium-multimarket approach", American Journal of Agricultural Economics 74:268–280.

Salvatore, D. (ed.) (1992), National Trade Policies (Greenwood Press, New York).

Sarker, R., K. Mielke and M. Hoy (1993), "The political economy of systematic government intervention in agriculture", Canadian Journal of Agricultural Economics 41:289–309.

Sarris, A.H., and J. Freebairn (1983), "Endogenous price policies and international wheat prices", American Journal of Agricultural Economics 65:214–224.

Schleich, J. (1997), "Environmental protection with policies for sale", International Agricultural Trade Research Consortium Working Paper 97-2 (University of Minnesota, Dept. of Applied Economics, IATRC, St. Paul, MN).

Schleich, J., and D. Orden (1996), "Efficient choice among domestic and trade policy in the Grossman-Helpman interest-group model", The Center for Political Economy Bulletin 96-3 (University of Minnesota, St. Paul, MN).

Schmitz, A., R. Gray, T. Schmitz and G. Storey (1997), The CWB and Barley Marketing: Price Pooling and Single Desk Selling (Dept. of Agricultural Economics, University of Saskatchewan, Saskatoon).

Schmitz A., A.F. McCalla, D.O. Mitchell and C.A. Carter (1981), Grain Export Cartels (Ballenger Publishing, Cambridge, MA).

Schuh, G.E. (1974), "The exchange rate and U.S. agriculture", American Journal of Agricultural Economics 56:1–13.

Sexton, R.J., and N. Lavoie (2001), "Food processing and distribution: An industrial organization approach, in: B.L. Gardner and G.C. Rausser, eds., Handbook of Agricultural Economics, Vol. 1 (Elsevier, Amsterdam) 863–932.

Stern, R.M., J. Francis and B. Schumacher (1976), Price Elasticities in International Trade: An Annotated Bibliography (Macmillan, London).

Sullivan, J. (1990), "Price-transmission elasticities in the trade liberalization database", ERS Staff Report AGES 9034 (U.S. Department of Agriculture, Washington, DC).

Sumner, D.A. (1995), Agricultural Trade Policy: Letting Markets Work (American Enterprise Institute Press, Washington, DC).

Sumner, D.A., and S. Tangermann (2002), "International trade policy and negotiations", in: B.L. Gardner and G.C. Rausser, eds., Handbook of Agricultural Economics, Vol. 2 (Elsevier, Amsterdam) 1999–2055.

Swinnen, J. (1994), "A positive theory of agricultural protection", American Journal of Agricultural Economics 76:1–14.

Swinnen, J., and F. van der Zee (1993), "The political economy of agricultural policies: A survey", European Review of Agricultural Economics 20:261–290.

Tangermann, S. (1996), "Implications of alternative options for future levels of support for agriculture in Central and Eastern Europe", American Journal of Agricultural Economics 78:786–791.

Tangermann, S., T.E. Josling and S. Pearson (1987), "Multilateral negotiations on farm-support levels", World Economy 10:265–281.

Teece, D.J., D. Sunding and E. Mosakowski (1993), "Natural resource Cartels", in: A.V. Kneese and J.L. Sweeney, eds., Handbook of Natural Resource and Energy Economics, Vol. 3 (North-Holland, Amsterdam) 1131–1136.

Thursby, M. (1988), "Strategic models, market structure and state trading: An application to agriculture", in: R.E. Baldwin, ed., Trade Policy Issues and Empirical Analysis (University of Chicago Press).

Thursby, J.G., and M.C. Thursby (1988), "Elasticities in international trade: Theoretical and methodological issues", in: C.A. Carter and W.H. Gardiner, eds., Elasticities in International Agricultural Trade (Westview Press, Boulder, CO and London) 17–52.

Thursby, M.C., and J.G. Thursby (1990), "Strategic trade theory and agricultural markets: An application to Canadian and U.S. wheat exports to Japan", in: C.A. Carter, A.F. McCalla and J.A. Sharples, eds., Imperfect Competition and Political Economy: The New Trade Theory in Agricultural Trade Research (Westview Press, Boulder, CO and London) 87–106.

Tyers, R., and K. Anderson (1988), "Imperfect price-transmission elasticities in a multi-commodity world", in: C.A. Carter and W.H. Gardiner, eds., Elasticities in International Agricultural Trade (Westview Press, Boulder, CO and London) 255–295.

Tyers, R., and K. Anderson (1992), Disarray in World Food Markets: A Quantitative Assessment (Cambridge University Press, Cambridge and New York).

United States Department of Agriculture, Economic Research Service (ERS) (1986), "Embargoes, surplus disposal, and U.S. agriculture", Economic Research Service Report 564 (Washington, DC).

von Witzke, H. (1990), "Determinants of the U.S. wheat producer support price: Do presidential elections matter?", Public Choice 64:155–165.

Zusman, P., and A. Amiad (1977), "A quantitative investigation of political economy: The Israeli dairy program", American Journal of Agricultural Economics 59:88–98.

Zwart, A.C., and K.D. Meilke (1979), "The influence of domestic pricing policies and buffer stocks on price stability in the world wheat industry", American Journal of Agricultural Economics 61:434–447.

Chapter 38

INTERNATIONAL TRADE POLICY AND NEGOTIATIONS

DANIEL A. SUMNER

Department of Agricultural and Resource Economics, University of California, Davis

STEFAN TANGERMANN

Directorate of Food, Agriculture and Fisheries, Organization for Economic Cooperation and Development, Paris, France

Contents

Handbook of Agricultural Economics, Volume 2, Edited by B. Gardner and G. Rausser

Abstract

Trade policy has been one of the most important issues in agricultural economics for more than 200 years. Our focus here is on evaluating relatively recent contributions to the understanding of agricultural trade policy and trade agreements. We present some background concerning trade policies and agreements and then consider the economic analysis of these agreements and policies. We concentrate on recent trade agreements, especially the Uruguay Round Agreement of 1994, and on recent analyses of this agreement and other trade policies in agriculture. We conclude by discussing current issues facing trade negotiations.

Keywords

WTO, GATT, trade policy, trade liberalization, Uruguay Round

JEL classification: Q17

1. Introduction

Trade and trade policy have been important in the world economy, and in the evolution of economics, since before the British Corn Law debates of the first half of the nineteenth century. The historical reach of this chapter is not that long, but the substantive importance of the topic has not diminished over time. Indeed, the agricultural trade policy debate remains one of the most important and discussed issues in agricultural economics. Our focus is on evaluating contributions to the understanding of agricultural trade policy and trade agreements. To this end, we present some of the necessary factual background about agricultural trade agreements and the policies they have attempted to cover, as well as economic analysis of trade policies.

Section 2 begins with a review of the role of agriculture in international trade agreements, especially the General Agreement on Tariffs and Trade. The recent Uruguay Round Agreement and the negotiations that led to it have a prominent place in the recent literature and are a major part of this first section. After describing the necessary policy background, we turn in Section 3 to an analysis of each of the major issue areas that are considered in trade policy analysis and in trade agreements. This section considers economic analysis of agricultural import barriers, export subsidies, and internal subsidies, and how these policies relate to trade negotiations. Section 4 of the chapter reviews the quantitative projections used to evaluate prospective and actual trade agreements. The primary focus is on economic analysis of issues surrounding the Uruguay Round Agreement on Agriculture. We consider research conducted in the period prior to an agreement as well as more recent studies that attempt to project the consequences of the actual agreement. We consider projections from a variety of models and approaches. Finally, Section 5 deals with a variety of topics that surround future agricultural trade negotiations.

2. Agriculture in the GATT negotiations

In agricultural trade, the gap is particularly large between the free trade philosophy of economic textbooks and the reality of pervasive government intervention. Economists have continued to preach the efficiency benefits derived from full use of comparative advantage, free consumer choice, and uninhibited international trade flows. In agriculture, strongly divergent natural conditions across the globe create ideal conditions for making use of comparative advantage, and differentiated consumer tastes for food call for free access to the wide variability of foods available in different parts of the world. It would therefore seem that free trade should be particularly attractive and relevant in agriculture. However, as in a small number of other sectors (such as textiles), agriculture has traditionally been an area where governments in most parts of the world have been strongly reluctant to open up domestic markets to international trade [Johnson (1991)]. Indeed, as noted by McCalla (1969), agricultural protectionism has prevailed since at least the fifteenth century. The typical pattern this century is that developing countries tend to keep domestic food prices below prices in international trade in the interest of food consumers, while industrialized countries tend to maintain high domestic farm prices in order to protect farmers' incomes [Anderson and Hayami (1986), Honma and Hayami (1986), Tyers and Anderson (1992)]. Moreover, in agriculture and food, the tendency to insulate domestic markets from the wide price fluctuations in international trade has been strong [Tyers and Anderson (1992)]. The welfare losses resulting from these trade interventions are large. Some authors have estimated that even the limited liberalization of agricultural trade agreed to in the Uruguay Round negotiations will add some U.S.$60 billion to world income (see below, Section 4.2).

Free international trade may be considered a global public good [Kindleberger (1986)]. In the absence of a global government, international agreements between national governments may have to provide this public good. The General Agreement on Tariffs and Trade (GATT) can be seen as an attempt to act in this sense. Indeed, in the framework of the GATT, participating countries have tried to establish the delicate balance between their domestic economic interests and their desire to create conditions for liberalizing international trade. In agriculture, the attempt to liberalize trade in this institutional framework largely failed for a long time. National interests to control domestic markets have prevailed over attempts to establish international discipline (Section 2.1). It was not until the Uruguay Round of GATT negotiations that more determined progress was made towards integrating agriculture more fully into the liberal international economic order (Section 2.2). The new commitments for agricultural policies accepted by all participating countries in the Uruguay Round are manifold, and go a significant step beyond the "old" GATT rules for agriculture (Section 2.3). However, the real effects for international agricultural trade will depend a great deal on the practical implementation of these new commitments (Section 2.4).

2.1. The traditional treatment of agriculture in the GATT

In the Western world, particularly in the United States and the United Kingdom, planning for postwar reconstruction and economic cooperation began in the early years of the Second World War. This planning led to the establishment of the International Monetary Fund (IMF) and the International Bank for Reconstruction and Development (later the World Bank) in 1944. In the area of international trade, plans were to establish an International Trade Organization (ITO), and in March 1948, at a conference in Havana, Cuba, representatives of 54 nations signed a charter establishing the ITO. The overall charter and the ITO eventually failed to be approved by the U.S. Congress and never became law, but the trade provisions of the Havana Charter and the tariff reductions negotiated in parallel were signed by 23 countries (including the United States). These trade provisions formed the GATT, which became the legal basis for the conduct of trade policies of all countries which were and later became contracting parties of that agreement.[1] However, it was not until the establishment of the World Trade Organization (WTO), through an agreement signed after the Uruguay Round of GATT negotiations in Marrakesh, Morocco, in April 1994, that an official international organization was added to what before had remained an intergovernmental agreement.

As stated in the preamble to the agreement, the GATT aims at "raising standards of living, ensuring full employment and a large and steadily growing volume of real income and effective demand, developing the full use of the resources of the world, and expanding the production and exchange of goods". Its most important principles are (i) most-favored-nation treatment (trade benefits conferred on one country should be extended unconditionally to all other suppliers); (ii) national treatment (imports should be treated no less favorably than domestic products); (iii) elimination of quantitative restrictions on imports and exports; (iv) tariffs, bound in member-country Schedules, as the only means of protection; and (v) reciprocity (negotiations should be conducted on a reciprocal and mutually advantageous basis). These principles take a concrete form in the detailed provisions and rules contained in the 38 Articles of the GATT.[2] Another important element of the GATT are the country Schedules annexed to the Agreement, which specify the concessions and commitments the individual member countries have made under the GATT. In the periodical rounds of formal multilateral trade negotiations, countries agree on tariff bindings and reductions, other commitments, codes of conduct, and rule improvements. The Uruguay Round (1986–94) was the eighth round of such negotiations.

It has often been said that until the early 1990s, agriculture was largely outside the GATT.[3] Well to the point as this phrase may be in a more general sense, it is not really appropriate as a technical description of the status agriculture had in the GATT before the Uruguay Round. Agriculture has always been fully in the GATT, in the sense that all the provisions of the General Agreement have applied to agricultural products. Indeed, contrary to trade in textiles and clothing, which was effectively taken out of the GATT through the Multi-Fiber Arrangement and its rather specific provisions, there had never been a separate GATT agreement on agriculture which exempted agricultural trade from any rules of the General Agreement. Hence, agriculture has always been in the GATT in that formal sense, and it has played a prominent role in the various rounds of GATT negotiations as well as in the day-to-day business of the GATT.

[1] For accounts of the history of the GATT, see the standard texts on the GATT by Curzon (1965), Jackson (1969), Kock (1969), Dam (1970), and Hudec (1975).

[2] In legal terms, after the Uruguay Round, one has to distinguish between the "old" text of the General Agreement, now called GATT 1947, and the "new" GATT 1994, agreed to at Marrakesh. GATT 1994 consists of the (unchanged Articles of) GATT 1947, a number of protocols and decisions agreed to before 1994, and a number of understandings on the interpretation of GATT Articles agreed to at Marrakesh.

[3] For early analyses of the treatment of agriculture in the GATT, see Curzon (1965, Chapter VII) and Dam (1970, Chapter 15). The situation on the eve of the Uruguay Round is discussed in Hathaway (1987). A complete history and analysis of the role of agriculture in the GATT, from the beginning to the Uruguay Round, is provided in Josling, Tangermann and Warley (1996).

On the other hand, it is true that the actual conduct of policies in agriculture was significantly less disciplined under the GATT than was the case in the sector of manufactures. Non-tariff barriers to imports played a large role in agriculture, as many countries used quantitative restrictions, restrictive state trading, variable levies, minimum import prices, and similar measures to provide protection to their farmers. In many industrialized countries, these import barriers were complements to administered domestic support prices which had been established to keep domestic market prices insulated from, and generally above, international prices. As a consequence of domestic price support or other programs, many countries began to have, or continued to produce, commodity supplies that could not be sold on world markets without the help of export subsidies. Many of these policies were not in conformity with the fundamental spirit of the GATT, but in most cases the letter of the General Agreement did not provide the means for the GATT to discipline them. This was only partly due to the fact that the text of the GATT contained some special provisions for agriculture. As a matter of fact, there are only a very few places in the text of the General Agreement where agricultural products (or rather primary products) are specifically mentioned.[4] The single most important of these special provisions, as far as the actual conduct of trade policies is concerned, was the exemption of agriculture from the general prohibition of export subsidies in Article XVI:3.[5] This exemption was not unconditional, but required countries to respect their "equitable share of world trade" in the product concerned. Naturally, what exactly these equitable shares were proved very difficult to define in practice. Hence, there were nearly no cases in which countries were found to be in violation of their GATT obligations regarding agricultural export subsidies, in spite of a considerable number of disputes brought before the GATT. As a consequence, before the Uruguay Round, countries could feel largely free to subsidize their agricultural exports as appeared necessary from the point of view of managing domestic markets. The result was a situation in which large shares of world exports of agricultural products were sold with the help of export subsidies. For example, in 1992–93, the subsidized share of world exports was 60 percent in the case of wheat and 64 percent in the case of cheese (see below, Table 3, where some other products are also listed).

There was also a special exemption in the General Agreement for agricultural market access. This was the much-debated Article XI:2(c) which allowed quantitative restrictions on agricultural imports. Again, this exemption was not unconditional. In particular, countries wanting to invoke it had to impose effective constraints on the

---

[4] For an excellent legal analysis of the GATT rules for agriculture before the Uruguay Round Agreement, see Davey (1993). Shorter treatments are found in Hathaway (1987, Chapter 5) and Josling, Tangermann and Warley (1996, Chapter 6). Hudec (1997) provides an excellent comparison of the legal treatment of agriculture under the "old" GATT with the new conditions created in the Uruguay Round.

[5] The GATT rules described in the rest of this section were those relevant before the close of the Uruguay Round. In purely formal terms they still exist as the Uruguay Round has left the text of the GATT 1947 intact. However, both agricultural exceptions discussed in this section have effectively been superseded by the new rules and commitments agreed under the Agreement on Agriculture concluded in the Uruguay Round.

domestic volume of production. However, contrary to the case of export subsidies, this agricultural GATT exemption on the import side did not have a major impact in practice, essentially because the conditions to be fulfilled were so demanding that they were met in rather few cases. Indeed, in the many GATT disputes brought to bear on this agricultural exception, not one single case was found where a quantitative import restriction was justified by this agricultural exception. Nonetheless, many governments found other loopholes that allowed them to impose non-tariff barriers on agricultural imports, and consequently did not feel much of a need to invoke Article XI:2(c). Many different justifications were used to impose non-tariff measures. In some cases, "grandfather" clauses and protocols of accession allowed the continued use of non-tariff barriers. Other countries had refused to bind tariffs on many agricultural items, and under this legal cover they applied gray area measures such as variable levies and minimum import prices. When none of these options appeared sufficiently convenient, waivers were sought and obtained which allowed the implementation of non-tariff measures. The result was that the "tariffs only" principle of the GATT was not adhered to in agriculture. Before the Uruguay Round, developed countries had refused to bind tariffs on 42 percent of all tariff lines in agriculture, while only 22 percent of all tariff lines remained unbound in industry [GATT Secretariat (1993, pp. 22, 34)]. In the mid-1980s, 30 percent of all tariff lines for agricultural products in major developed countries were covered by such barriers as tariff quotas, seasonal tariffs, quantitative restrictions, and minimum price policies such as variable levies; the equivalent ratio for manufactures was only 9 percent [World Bank (1986, p. 117)].

Not only did many border policies in agriculture escape effective GATT disciplines in these various ways, but there was also little restraint in the provision of domestic subsidies. This situation was not due to any specific weakness of the GATT rules for agriculture. Indeed, in a number of cases, countervailing duties were brought to bear on other countries' domestic subsidies in agriculture, and there were also notable cases in which GATT panels found that domestic subsidies had impaired earlier tariff concessions for agricultural products. However, there was no direct constraint on a government's power to grant domestic subsidies to its farmers.

Another area where agriculture was treated specifically was in the establishment of regional trading arrangements. Under general GATT rules, customs unions and free trade areas were required not to erect higher protection against third countries, and to eliminate all trade barriers on "substantially all the trade" on intra-regional trade (GATT Article XXIV). In agriculture, the latter requirement regularly created difficulties because agricultural policies, and in particular, levels of protection, often differed significantly among the founding member countries of regional trading arrangements. In customs unions, the decision on the common level of external protection was therefore politically difficult, as evidenced by the heated debate about the appropriate level of common agricultural prices in the emerging European Economic Community in the early 1960s [Tracy (1982)]. However, once the common level of protection had been decided, elimination of trade barriers among the members of a customs union was not a major issue. Yet in the more frequent cases of free trade areas, elimination of trade barriers in agriculture among the member countries has been a significant problem.

In principle, rules of origin can prevent arbitrage trade between member countries with significantly different levels of external tariffs, and this device was successfully (though at high administrative expense) used for industrial products. In agriculture, though, where many products are relatively homogeneous, domestic produce can easily substitute for imported goods and thereby effectively undermine the functioning of rules of origin [Josling (1993)]. Hence, elimination of all agricultural trade barriers within a free trade area would tend to reduce the level of protection in all member countries to the lowest common denominator, and would constrain the ability of member country governments to pursue their national agricultural policies [Josling (1993)]. Member countries of free trade areas have been, therefore, typically reluctant to include agriculture in the free trade arrangement. It was for this reason that exclusion of agriculture from free trade within the regional arrangement was a customary practice for a long time. The European Free Trade Association (EFTA), and its later free trade arrangement with the European Economic Community under the auspices of the European Economic Area (EEA), are prominent cases in point. The practice of excluding agriculture completely from free trade areas was definitely not in line with the letter of the GATT, but it was tacitly accepted for a long time.

In summary, though agriculture was always fully in the GATT in a formal sense, in practice, agricultural policies were not greatly constrained by GATT disciplines before the Uruguay Round. The damage resulting from this situation, both in agricultural trade and for the functioning of the world trade order, was always strongly felt. In all previous GATT rounds, determined attempts were made to rectify the state of affairs in agriculture, largely without success. In addition, the GATT dispute settlement machinery was kept busy with a far larger than proportional number of agricultural cases.[6] However, little progress was made; on the eve of the Uruguay Round, the discipline in agricultural trade had not improved, and probably was worse than at the time the GATT was established.

2.2. The Uruguay Round negotiations on agriculture

The seven GATT rounds that had been conducted by the end of the 1970s did not achieve much improvement in agricultural trade [see Josling, Tangermann and Warley (1996) and the literature cited there]. How much change was needed became particularly obvious in the 1980s when international market conditions again deteriorated notably and agricultural commodity prices collapsed. In this environment, financial and economic costs of agricultural policies rose sharply in many industrialized countries,

---

[6] According to a count by Hudec (1993, p. 327), 43 percent of all complaints brought before the GATT between 1948 and 1989 dealt with agricultural issues. This percentage contrasts rather unfavorably with the much smaller share of agricultural products in total world trade. Hudec also provides an interesting analysis of the outcome of GATT disputes, including those on agriculture.

triggering an agricultural policy crisis. At the international level, one of the responses was agreement in the Organization for Economic Cooperation and Development (OECD) to embark, in 1982, on a study of agricultural trade issues under what became known as the Ministerial Trade Mandate (MTM). The analytical methodology of the MTM was based on two approaches: the extent of support provided to agriculture in individual countries was measured by the Producer Subsidy Equivalent (PSE) and the Consumer Subsidy Equivalent (CSE). The quantitative impact of policies on trade was estimated in a multi-commodity trade model that was used to analyze the effects of reducing support in all countries for all agricultural products by 10 percent. Results were published by OECD (1987). After that original publication, OECD continued to publish PSE/CSE estimates on an annual basis, in the series whose title now is "Agricultural Policies in OECD Countries". The study created a new dimension of transparency in agricultural policies at the international level, and served to demonstrate that a gradual and balanced reduction in support across all countries would have less dramatic consequences on domestic markets and prices than sometimes feared and always asserted by domestic farm lobbies. This work was an important intellectual preparation for the agricultural negotiations of the Uruguay Round.

In the GATT, the 1982 Ministerial Session established a new body, the Committee on Trade in Agriculture (CTA), which effectively (though not formally) prepared the ground for the Uruguay Round negotiations on agriculture.[7] The mandate of the CTA was to examine all policies affecting agricultural trade, and to make recommendations for improvements of GATT provisions for agriculture. All participating countries were requested to notify all measures affecting agricultural exports and imports. The result of these notifications, however, remained largely inconsequential. The CTA also discussed how the GATT should deal with agricultural policies in the future, and considered alternative approaches to bring policies under more operationally effective GATT rules and disciplines. Though no consensus was reached in the CTA, the approaches considered include some of those later adopted in the Uruguay Round, such as gradual reduction of export subsidies, conversion of all non-tariff measures into tariffs, and minimum access commitments.

The eighth round of GATT negotiations was launched in Punta del Este, Uruguay, in September 1986. It had a broader agenda than any preceding GATT round, and included services, a sector that had previously not been covered by the GATT. An overall assessment of the Uruguay Round is provided by Schott (1994), OECD (1994), Senti (1994), Croome (1995), and Hauser and Schanz (1995). To a large extent, agriculture determined the pace and progress of the negotiations. Ingersent, Rayner and Hine (1994), Josling, Tangermann and Warley (1996, Chapter 7), and Swinbank and Tanner (1997) have described the agricultural negotiations of the Uruguay Round in detail.

In the first phase of the agricultural talks, the initial proposals tabled by major countries in 1987 indicated how far apart their positions were. The United States

---

[7] The Chairman of the CTA, Aart de Zeeuw from the Netherlands, later was to become the Chairman of the Uruguay Round Negotiating Group on Agriculture.

suggested a complete phaseout over 10 years of all agricultural subsidies and import barriers. The Cairns Group of 14 "non-subsidizing" countries played an important role in the negotiations; they proposed an approach which would have come close to that of the United States. The EU, on the other hand, preferred to deal with short-term issues through more traditional measures of market management before embarking, at a later stage, on support reductions. Japan could not see a point in reducing internal support, but argued for a prohibition of export subsidies. No significant progress was made before the mid-term ministerial meeting at Montreal in December 1988; during the meeting, the gap between U.S. insistence on "elimination" and EU unwillingness to go beyond "reduction" of support could not be bridged. However, in April 1989, the deadlock was resolved by an agreement to engage in "substantial progressive reductions in agricultural support and protection sustained over an agreed period of time" [GATT (1989)], and to freeze support levels for the remainder of the negotiations.

In the second phase of negotiations, countries were requested to table comprehensive proposals by the end of 1989. The U.S. proposal still envisaged an eventual elimination of export subsidies and trade-distorting domestic subsidies. On market access, though, the U.S. introduced the concept of "tariffication", i.e., conversion of all non-tariff barriers to trade into bound tariffs which would then be reduced, though not necessarily completely eliminated. The EU reluctantly said it was prepared to consider tariffication, provided it was allowed to engage in "re-balancing" the commodity structure of protection, i.e., raising protection for oilseeds and non-grain feeds so as to make it similar to that for cereals. The EU stated a preference for reducing support and protection in terms of an aggregate measure of support (AMS), an indicator closely related to the PSE, though based on fixed external reference prices.

In an attempt to close the still rather wide gap between the negotiating parties, the Chairman of the Negotiating Group for Agriculture tabled a draft agreement in July 1990 calling for final quantified offers by October 1990. The offers submitted by the major countries turned out to be much closer than were their starting positions. However, the gaps between these offers were still too wide; in particular, the EU was not prepared to accept significant reduction commitments on export subsidies. The ministerial meeting at Brussels, in December 1990, therefore ended in stalemate.

The third and final phase of the negotiations started in 1991 with proposals for a fundamental CAP reform by the EU Commission, which allowed the EU to accept reduction commitments on export subsidies. Based on essential agreement between the United States, the EU, and other major players on all the key elements, in December 1991, GATT Director General Arthur Dunkel submitted a Draft Final Act. However, submission and verification of draft Schedules with all detailed quantified commitments, product by product, by all participating countries was still needed. Also, disagreement over a number of details between the U.S. and the EU still needed to be settled; this was eventually achieved in two sets of bilateral negotiations, in November 1992 (at Blair House, Washington) and, shortly before the final deadline, in December 1993 (sometimes called Blair House II). The agreement on agriculture then freed the way to the overall conclusion of the negotiations. The Final Act of the Uruguay Round, as well

Table 1

Structure of the Agreement on Agriculture and the country commitments*

Type of rule	Market access Base: 1986–1988	Export competition Base: 1986–1990	Domestic support Base: 1986–1988
Price	Tariffication of non-tariff measures	Reduction of outlays on export subsidies by 36% (product-specific)	
	Reduction of all bound tariffs by 36% on average (minimum of 15%)		Reduction of total AMS by 20%, except for "green box" measures
Quantity	Minimum access commitments: 3% of domestic consumption, growing to 5%	Reduction of subsidized exports by 21% (product-specific)	
	Current access maintained		
Other	Safeguard provision	Peace clause	

*Reduction rates in this table are those for industrialized countries. Reduction rates for developing countries are two-thirds of these rates. Least developed countries are exempt from reduction commitments.

as the agreement establishing the World Trade Organization, incorporating all detailed results of the negotiations, was signed at Marrakesh, Morocco, in April 1994.

The Uruguay Round Agreement on Agriculture (the Agreement) establishes new rules for domestic and trade policies; it effectively overwrites the respective provisions of the "old" GATT. The Agreement can only be briefly summarized here. For more detail, see Josling, Tangermann and Warley (1996, Chapter 8). Contrary to the situation under the "old" GATT, the definition of what countries are expected to do was not simply left to general rules, but was determined in country Schedules of legally binding commitments. These quantitative commitments were derived from policies that existed in a historic base period and from agreed-upon rates of reduction, to be implemented in the period 1995 to 2000.[8] The Agreement and the country Schedules cover the three areas of market access, export competition, and domestic support, as summarized in Table 1.

Regarding *market access*: all WTO members agreed to bind all tariffs in agriculture, to convert all existing non-tariff barriers (with very few exceptions) into bound duties,

[8] The methods according to which countries were expected to derive their quantitative commitments from past policies and agreed-upon rates of reduction had earlier been specified in a document entitled "Modalities for the Establishment of Specific Binding Commitments under the Reform Programme". After the Marrakesh meeting, this document no longer had legal power, and whatever had been put into the Schedules became legally binding. For developing countries, the implementation period for reductions is 1995 to 2003.

and not to introduce new non-tariff measures. During the implementation period, tariffs have to be reduced by 36 percent, on a simple (unweighted) average basis, with a minimum rate of reduction of 15 percent for each tariff line. The tariffs and reduction rates are specified in the country Schedules. Because of political difficulties, Japan and Korea had (with the notion of opening up their rice markets) a Special Treatment clause included in the Agreement which, under rather specific conditions, allowed them to delay tariffication.[9] Moreover, Safeguard Provisions were introduced for products that had undergone tariffication, which allowed importers to guard against import surges and low world prices.

Where past imports were small or nil, importers had to establish "minimum access" opportunities, usually rising from 3 percent to 5 percent of base period domestic consumption. Moreover, access opportunities existing in the past ("current access") had to be maintained. Both minimum and current access commitments have been implemented mainly through tariff rate quotas with tariffs below "ordinary" tariffs, but do not require countries to import the quantities concerned.

Based on past levels of *export subsidization* for individual product groups, countries have accepted legally binding commitments leading to a reduction in expenditure on export subsidies by 36 percent, as well as a reduction in the quantity of subsidized exports by 21 percent during the implementation period. In addition, export subsidies cannot be extended to commodities that were not subsidized in the base period. The Agreement contains a list of export subsidies falling under Schedule commitments, provisions against circumvention of commitments, and includes rules on food aid. Developed countries and net-food exporting developing countries now have to observe somewhat more restrictive rules regarding export restrictions and prohibitions in cases of critical shortages. However, export taxes are not banned by the Agreement.

In the area of *domestic support*, the variable constrained is not expenditure on domestic subsidies, but the level of sector-wide (rather than product-specific) total support provided by policies covered under the Agreement (the Aggregate Measurement of Support, or AMS). The AMS includes support provided through administered prices, measured against fixed external reference prices, in domestic currency, of the base period. The AMS has to be reduced by 20 percent during the implementation period. However, measures with minimal or no trade distortion effects, or effects on production, are exempted from reduction commitments. This "green box" of exempt policies is defined in both general form and in terms of an illustrative list of eligible policies.

As a result of the Blair House Accord between the United States and the EU, another exemption (called the "blue box") was agreed to for certain "direct payments under production-limiting programs". The result is that both U.S. deficiency payments and compensation payments under the reformed CAP of the EU need not be included in the AMS calculation and the reduction commitment. Though this provision targeted the

---

[9] In addition to Japan and Korea for rice, the Special Treatment clause has also been invoked by the Philippines for rice, and by Israel for pig meat, cheese, and milk powder.

two country-specific cases mentioned, it is general and can be invoked by any country for any policy that meets the criteria specified.

As an incentive for countries to accept the new disciplines and commitments on domestic support and export subsidies, it was agreed that policies conforming to the new rules be sheltered from international challenge under the GATT. This "peace clause" remains in force three years beyond the implementation period of the Agreement, i.e., until the year 2003.

Implementation of the Agreement is monitored by a newly established Committee on Agriculture that receives and discusses notifications which countries are required to submit regularly. In these notifications, countries have to report how they are implementing their commitments. In the Agreement, countries also committed themselves to another round of negotiations on the continuation of the reform process in agriculture, to be initiated in 1999.

Along with the provisions on domestic and trade policies in the Agreement, the Uruguay Round also resulted in an Agreement on Sanitary and Phytosanitary Measures. The objective was to improve on the rules for technical trade barriers under the "old" GATT by making it easier to distinguish between disguised protection and genuine health and safety issues. The right of countries to set their own safety and health standards was reaffirmed with the proviso that such standards should be based on scientific evidence and an appropriate risk assessment.

Another area where some progress was made in the Uruguay Round was in the treatment of regional trading arrangements. One of the many arrangements agreed upon at Marrakesh was the Understanding on the Interpretation of Article XXIV of the GATT, which deals with customs unions and free trade areas. This Understanding does not fundamentally alter the old GATT rules in this area, but largely confirms them and adds a few procedural requirements hoped to result in more stringent application of the rules. In particular, the Understanding does not drop the requirement that "substantially all the trade" between the member countries of a regional trade arrangement should be included in intra-regional trade liberalization. It appears that this requirement is now taken more seriously by the countries forming or extending the rapidly growing number of regional trading arrangements around the world. In particular, the traditional tendency to exclude most of agriculture from regional trade liberalization appears to have faded. The Canada–U.S. Free Trade Agreement (CUSTA), and the subsequent North American Free Trade Agreement (NAFTA), which included Mexico, were prominent early examples of regional arrangements that included agriculture (though not fully). Both agreements were concluded while the Uruguay Round negotiations were underway. Under the complex trilateral arrangements of NAFTA (plus the remaining parts of CUSTA), most agricultural tariffs will eventually be eliminated in trade among the three countries, but some non-tariff barriers remain in place, in particular between Canada and the other parties [USDA/Economic Analysis Staff (1993)]. Another example of a regional trade arrangement fully including agriculture is MERCOSUR, the common market among Argentina, Brazil, Paraguay, and Uruguay, also concluded while the Uruguay Round was going on.

The rapid spread of regional trade arrangements in recent times raises a number of important questions. In particular, are regional trade pacts a threat to the process of multilateral trade liberalization? Or are they, on the contrary, a useful step in the direction of more liberal global trade? Is there a chance that regional trade liberalization is achieved simultaneously with a reduction of trade barriers in external trade of the regional associates, in what could be called "open regionalism" [Bergsten (1997)]? In agriculture, will growing liberalization of regional trade impose constraints on protectionist agricultural policies of the constituent countries, and thereby trigger agricultural policy reforms, as argued by Josling (1993, 1997)? Is the GATT requirement to include agriculture fully in regional trading arrangements, coupled with the political desire to strengthen international cooperation through more liberal trade in regional groupings, bound to undermine inward-looking forces in agriculture? Or is liberalization of intra-regional trade more likely to consume all political capital which governments need in their dealings with domestic farmers, and thereby block progress towards further multilateral agricultural trade liberalization under the auspices of the WTO? The Uruguay Round negotiations have not provided immediate answers to such questions, but have at least made sure that the spread of regional trading arrangements cannot result in higher protection for agriculture.

In summary, the Uruguay Round Agreement on Agriculture has fundamentally changed the nature of GATT provisions for agriculture. In particular, reasonably well-defined quantitative commitments have replaced qualitative rules. Under the "old" GATT, the widespread lack of tariff bindings and the existence of a large "gray area" allowed many countries to maintain non-tariff barriers for their agricultural imports. After the Uruguay Round, nearly all agricultural imports are covered by tariff bindings. In the past, the "equitable share" rule was too vague to define quantifiable constraints on export subsidies; after the Uruguay Round there are numerically specified limits to the extent each country can subsidize agricultural exports. In the area of domestic support, quantitative commitments now define the scope for policies that earlier were only vaguely circumscribed by the general GATT rules on domestic subsidies. The actual practice of trade policies for agriculture in the period immediately following the Uruguay Round has not yet changed noticeably in many countries. However, the new legal framework created in the Uruguay Round will make it easier in future to negotiate further reductions; as commitments become tighter in quantitative terms, policies are likely to be increasingly constrained. To the extent that this materializes, the Uruguay Round will have finally created the basis for liberalizing worldwide agricultural trade.

2.3. Commitments accepted in the Uruguay Round

Among the specific quantitative commitments participating countries accepted in the Uruguay Round, some directly bind policies (i.e., tariffs), while others bind the effects of policies (i.e., quantities of subsidized exports, expenditure on export subsidies, and levels of domestic support). The practical outcome of the Uruguay Round negotiations for international agricultural trade in the second half of the 1990s was bound to depend on the extent to which these commitments constrained policies. Largely qualitative analyses of the commitments accepted in the Uruguay Round have been provided by Josling et al. (1994), Hathaway and Ingco (1995), OECD (1995), Tangermann (1996), and Josling, Tangermann and Warley (1996). More quantitative assessments are reviewed below in Section 4.

Because country-specific quantitative commitments did not exist before (under the "old" GATT), a starting point had to be agreed upon in the negotiations. In general, actual policies pursued in the past served as that starting point, and the base period chosen was the beginning of the Uruguay Round negotiations, i.e., the years 1986–88 for market access and domestic support, and 1986–90 for export subsidies. Since both market conditions and policies keep changing over time, this choice may have been either more or less "generous", in the sense of allowing countries wide or little scope for future policies, depending on the specific conditions prevailing in the base period.

Many countries in various parts of the world engaged in agricultural policy reforms after the mid-1980s; this resulted in declining levels of price support and protection [Josling (1997)]. In many cases, the levels of protection and support prevailing in the base period, which became the starting levels for reduction commitments, were higher than the levels actually prevailing in 1995 when implementation of the Uruguay Round agreements began. Wherever that was the case, the outcome of the Uruguay Round could not be expected to result in immediate policy adjustments and corresponding improvements in agricultural trade. It also is true that the commitments differ in their direct trade implications.

After the base period, many OECD countries had significantly reduced their levels of domestic support, and it was estimated that before the implementation period began, several had reached AMS levels below their commitments for 2000 [OECD (1995, p. 39 ff); similar estimates are provided by Tangermann (1996)]. This was confirmed when countries officially began notification of their 1995 domestic support levels to the WTO Committee on Agriculture; it turned out that in many cases they were already lower than required at the end of the implementation period. In such cases, policy adjustments (as required by the reduction commitments) had already been made before the implementation period, and the new domestic support commitments, which do not require further policy changes, can be said to contain "policy water" [Tangermann (1996)]. A similar example is the element of "policy water" in EU tariffs for cereals and cereal-based livestock which resulted from the large reductions of support prices the EU made after 1992, such that the tariff bindings derived from the domestic–external price gap prevailing in the base period are no longer necessary to defend the new, much lower, EU prices. However, that "policy water" was largely taken out of EU cereal tariffs, as the EU agreed, in the Blair House II negotiations, not to charge tariffs higher than necessary to defend its new lower support price.

The base period chosen also was relatively "generous" for tariffication because of the pattern of prevailing world prices for major commodities. World market prices were depressed in the mid-1980s, and rose only slightly until 1988. Hence, the gap between domestic prices and international prices, which determined the tariffs to be bound under the tariffication process, was relatively large in that base period compared to the gap that prevailed in the mid-1990s in many cases [Tangermann (1996)]. For the same reason, that base period also was "generous" for the market support element of the AMS commitments.

For export subsidies, the base period chosen was more neutral, as the quantities exported with subsidies kept growing during the 1980s and the early 1990s [Tangermann (1996)]. This was a key feature of the Uruguay Round negotiations because most observers agreed that whereas the other elements were important in principle and for the long term, immediate gains in farm trade benefits would most likely be realized in the context of the quantity commitments for subsidized exports. This was the view in the United States as early as the end of 1990 [Sumner (1992)].

Another important factor in implementation was the way in which data were collected and processed to establish the base period policy situation from which the starting levels for reduction commitments were derived. Rather than appoint an independent body for this purpose (which probably would have been very difficult), each country provided the analysis for its own policies. The results then had to be presented to all participants in the negotiations in the form of draft Schedules (and supporting tables), so that other countries could check them during the "verification" process in the last months before the Marrakesh meeting. For example, for tariffication, it was agreed to start from the tariff equivalents of the non-tariff measures existing in the past, measured as the gap between domestic prices and international prices during the base period.[10] Countries were expected to collect their own data on their relevant domestic and external prices, and to calculate tariff equivalents on that basis. Naturally, in this process, countries that typically resisted reductions in their own protectionist policies had a tendency to use "favorable" data showing that their levels of protection and support during the base period were high. This meant that their bindings and reduction commitments started at a high level and left as much scope as possible for future policies or negotiations. Though other countries could and did spot such cases during the process of verification, it appears that the base period data originally presented has rarely been officially challenged. In this context, it is important to remember that whatever was in the Schedules at Marrakesh, whether justified or not, became legally binding, and could not later be legally disputed.

Use of "favorable" data was prominent in the establishment of tariff equivalents, and the term "dirty" tariffication is often used in this context. For example, Hathaway and Ingco (1995, p. 36) have estimated that the "true" tariff equivalent for sugar in the EU during the base period 1986–88 would have been 234 percent, while the tariff actually bound by the EU was equivalent to 297 percent. Similarly, the OECD (1995, p. 27) has estimated that the *ad valorem* equivalent of the domestic–external price gap (the market price support element in OECD terms) of the EU for white sugar in 1986–88

---

[10] Developing countries were instead allowed to offer "ceiling bindings", not resulting from such calculations.

Table 2

Tariffs resulting from the Uruguay Round Agreement on Agriculture, *ad valorem* equivalents, selected countries and products

	Common wheat		White sugar		Beef carcasses, fresh or chilled		Butter	
	Initial tariff (%)	Reduc-tion (%)	Initial tariff (%)	Reduc-tion (%)	Initial tariff (%)	Reduc-tion (%)	Initial tariff (%)	Reduc-tion (%)
Australia	0.0	–	31.7	50	0.0	–	4.6	78
Canada	90.0	15	10.7	15	37.9	30	351.4	15
EC	142.3	36	207.1	20	96.9	36	235.3	36
Hungary	50.0	36	80.0	15	112.0	36	159.0	36
South Korea	10	82	94.6	10	44.5	10	99.0	10
Japan	422.9	15	326.7	15	93.0	46	97.7	15
New Zealand	0.0	–	0.0	–	0.0	–	10.0	36
Poland	143.2	36	120.0	20	162.0	36	160.0	36
Switzerland	477.6	15	159.9	15	139.7	15	862.2	15
USA	6.0	55	134.7	15	31.1	15	116.7	15

Adopted from Josling, Tangermann and Warley (1996, p. 187).

was 235 percent, while the EU base tariff on white sugar was equivalent to 274 percent. It is difficult to produce accurate independent estimates of the amount of "dirt" in the newly bound tariffs, but there is little doubt that some tariff bindings resulting from the Uruguay Round are higher than a reasonable equivalent of the non-tariff measures existing in the base period. On the other hand, cases have also been reported [for example, by Hathaway and Ingco (1995)] where bound tariffs appear to be lower than the estimated tariff equivalents would have suggested.

Probably more important is the fact that many of the newly bound tariffs are extremely high, as would be expected if they are designed to be "equivalent" to a prohibitive quota, and for all practical purposes, prohibitive. Table 2 shows initial ad valorem tariffs or calculated ad valorem tariff equivalents in those cases for which the actual tariff was specified on a per unit basis. We converted the specific tariffs to ad valorem equivalents using 1994 data in order to facilitate comparison across commodities and countries and to provide meaningful numbers to readers who may not be familiar with market conditions for each commodity. However, with this standard procedure the resulting ad valorem equivalents of specific tariffs should be interpreted with care. In particular, the market effects of ad valorem and specific tariffs may differ as domestic and world prices change over time. When world prices rise, the ad valorem equivalent of the specific tariff falls and vice versa. For example, the tariff on sugar is stated in the U.S. tariff schedule as falling from about 40 cents per kg in 1995 to about 33 cents per kg in 2001. In 1994 the world price of sugar was about 30 cents per kg, and Table 2 shows the ad valorem equivalent was 134.7 percent. This U.S. policy was designed to insure that the internal U.S. sugar price could remain above about 45 cents per kg. In 1999, the world price fell to about 11 cents per kg. As a result, given the current 1999 tariff of about 35 cents per kg, the tariff-included import price fell to about 46 cents per kg and the U.S. price remained secure behind the tariff wall. This would not have been the case had the tariff actually been bound as an ad valorem tariff, in which case it would have been reduced to about 118 percent in 1999, yielding a tariff-included price of only about 24 cents per kg. As this example shows, the specific per unit tariff can be an effective device to protect a given internal price against international price declines – in times of declining world market prices more effective than an ad valorem tariff.

There were also many cases of tariff-only products where the tariff reductions agreed to in the Uruguay Round promised welcome access improvements; in exporting countries this result of the negotiations has helped to create political support for the agreement. However, many of the new tariffs resulting from tariffication may well continue to be prohibitive even after the reductions agreed to in the Uruguay Round have been made. Hence, improvement of market access in many cases was expected to result mainly from the new minimum access commitments implemented through tariff rate quotas (TRQ) at reduced tariffs. In the negotiations, these access commitments appear to have attracted more attention than the tariffs resulting from tariffication, and rather than resulting only from mechanical calculations (based on the agreed-upon percentages of domestic consumption), many TRQs were agreed to in bilateral request-and-offer negotiations. Overall, the volume of minimum access commitments is not very large. A politically important result was that Japan and Korea, though not engaging in tariffication for rice, at least agreed to open up their rice markets under minimum access commitments. Whereas in these two cases import quotas have been readily filled, countries are not required by the Uruguay Round to guarantee that tariff rate quotas will be filled. If there is no import demand at the within-quota tariffs, the minimum access commitments will not result in increased trade.

Avoidance procedures seem not to have been important in the case of export commitments. Given the fact that this was the element expected to be most important in terms of practical trade implications, it can be assumed that cross-country verification of the draft schedules was particularly meticulous in the case of export subsidies. However, not only did the base period chosen for export subsidies extend to a more recent year (1986–90), a "front-loading" provision allowed countries to start their reduction commitments for quantities at a higher level if subsidized exports in 1991–92 were larger than in the base. This provision did not affect allowable subsidized exports in the last year of the implementation period or thereafter. It did however raise significantly the quantities of allowable subsidized exports over the whole of the Uruguay Round implementation period. Such "front-loading" was particularly important in percentage terms in cases where export subsidies are a small part of total exports. For example, front-loading raised the quantity commitment by 262 percent in the case of rice exports from the U.S. However, inclusion of this provision in the agreement was driven by EU fears that it might otherwise be forced to cut total exports of wheat by a very large percentage in the first year of the implementation period. For some important commodities, a large part of world trade in major agricultural products had been

Table 3
Subsidized exports and aggregate reduction commitments, selected commodities

	Total volume of subsidized exports in the base period*		Reduction of subsidized exports between base period and 2000	
	Mil. metric tons	Proportion of world exports[†] 1992/93 (%)	Mil. metric tons	Proportion of world exports 1992/93 (%)
Wheat	61.45	59.7	21.09	20.5
Coarse grains	21.24	23.0	4.98	5.4
Rice	0.87	6.0	0.37	2.5
Beef	1.75	38.4	0.48	10.6
Butter	0.64	90.1	0.15	21.6
Cheese	0.60	64.4	0.17	18.4
Milk powder	0.61	59.0	0.15	14.7

*Base period is 1986–90 or 1991–92, whichever is higher (because of "front-loading").
[†]World trade excludes intra-EC trade.
Source: Adopted from Josling, Tangermann and Warley (1996).

subsidized in the base period. The reduction commitments accepted are often significant relative to the size of world markets, e.g., between 10 and 20 percent in the cases of wheat, butter, and cheese (see Table 3). Exceptions are rice and coarse grains, where subsidized exports are only a small fraction of world trade.

Overall, the quantitative commitments accepted in the Uruguay Round negotiations on agriculture are not expected to result in a big step towards liberalizing agricultural trade.[11] However, this is not to say that the Uruguay Round did not make a major contribution to improving the situation in agricultural trade in a number of regards. First, the negotiations may already have triggered agricultural policy reform in some cases. For example, it has been argued that the EU reform of the CAP, as decided in 1992, might not have occurred had the EU not felt it needed to make a contribution to a successful conclusion of the negotiations [Coleman and Tangermann (1997)]. Second, some policies were adjusted during the implementation period, such as elimination in Canada of the rail subsidies under the Western Grain Transportation Act, and in Japan access of private companies to the importation of some agricultural products which was previously completely controlled by state agencies [Tangermann et al. (1997)]. Third, policy adjustments already made were locked in through the new commitments, thus guarding against backsliding. Fourth, with further reductions to be made during the Uruguay Round implementation period, more and more water will be squeezed out of existing commitments, and constraints may become increasingly binding. Fifth, the new bindings accepted during the Uruguay Round have created a better basis for future

---

[11] A quantitative analysis of projections of the impacts of the liberalization effort is provided in Section 4 below.

negotiations; the next round of agricultural talks as agreed to in the Uruguay Round therefore have a chance of making further progress.

2.4. Implementation of the Uruguay Round Agreement on Agriculture

Overall implementation of the Uruguay Round Agreement on Agriculture has so far (by early 1999) occurred reasonably smoothly and without major surprises, though a number of concerns have arisen, some resulting in formal WTO disputes. Hathaway and Ingco (1995), Tangermann (1996), Cordeu, Valdés and Silva (1997), Tangermann et al. (1997), and Osorio Londoño (1997) have surveyed the implementation process. In that process, the newly established Committee on Agriculture plays an important role, not the least by gathering information through extensive country policy notifications. The notification process generates an enormous wealth of information on countries' policies. Fortunately, the decision was taken to make the notifications available to the general public, and this will also provide useful information for research.[12] Based on these notifications and other information, countries discuss each other's policies in the Committee, creating a new degree of transparency. Work in the Committee is also expected to generate an important basis for the next round of agricultural negotiations. A process of "analysis and information exchange" was started in the Committee in mid-1997 based on "non-papers" on selected issues considered important for future negotiations.

Tariffication has required major technical adjustments of border regimes in many countries. For example, the U.S. had to eliminate its "Section 22" import quotas for WTO members, and the EU had to convert its variable levies into tariffs. However, as expected, tariffication has not so far resulted in a significant growth of imports in most cases. In some cases (e.g., in the EU, for cereals, fruit, and vegetables; in Japan for pork) and for different reasons, tariffication has not fundamentally changed the nature of the previously existing non-tariff measures [Tangermann et al. (1997)]. Developed countries have generally tended to make full use of their bound tariffs (New Zealand is an exception). Developing countries, with their often high ceiling bindings, have in many cases applied tariffs below bound levels. They have a tendency, particularly in Latin America, to adjust tariff levels inversely to fluctuations in world market prices in order to stabilize landed prices of imports. In South Asia, residual quantitative restrictions based on the balance of payments exception (GATT Article XVIII) still play a major role. The Safeguard Provisions have occasionally been used, mainly by the EU and Japan. However, except for the case of pork in Japan and lamb in the United States, no major controversies have so far arisen out of these provisions.

The full binding power of the new export subsidy commitments, expected by most observers to be the most constraining element in the new WTO framework for

---

[12] The WTO Secretariat, commendably, makes the notifications accessible through the internet on the WTO Web site.

agriculture, has already been felt in some cases (e.g., cheese in the EU). High world market prices for cereals in the first years of the implementation period meant that policies in this important product sector were not much constrained. However, with lower prices after 1997, the subsidy committee will bind EU exports of grain towards that of the Uruguay Round implementation period. In two cases (Australia and Canada), previous dairy policies have been re-instrumented without much harm to domestic producers, such that they, arguably, no longer involve export subsidies as defined under the Agreement. However, in the case of Canada's new dairy regime, the WTO ruled that Canada's policies violated the agreement. In order to ease its already binding constraint on export subsidies for cheese, the EU has introduced a regime whereby processed cheese can be produced outside the EU customs territory, thus benefiting from export subsidies on butter and skim milk powder (two products where constraints were not yet binding). This case, too, has led to a WTO dispute. In a much publicized case, Hungary claimed that its export subsidy commitments were based on wrong data and were therefore too restrictive; it was subsequently granted subsidies beyond the original commitments. This resulted in a formal WTO dispute, and in the end, a waiver was granted allowing Hungary to define extra amounts of export subsidies until the year 2001 (but not thereafter).

Another not unexpected outcome of the implementation so far is that many agricultural state trading enterprises have not fundamentally changed their operations. For example, in Japan, private traders are now (in principle) allowed to import products that have undergone tariffication. However, in practice, the volumes imported by them have remained small compared to imports of the same products effected by the Agriculture and Livestock Industries Corporation. In South Asia too, state trading enterprises still play a major role in agricultural imports. On the export side, the Canadian Wheat Board and the various state trading enterprises in Australia and New Zealand were not expected to, and did not, change their operations as a result of the Agreement.

In the new dispute settlement procedures agreed to in the Uruguay Round, agriculture has continued to play a significant role, though somewhat less than before. Under the "old" GATT, according to a count by Hudec (1993, p. 327), out of a total of 207 GATT complaints between 1948 and 1990, 89 complaints (i.e., 43 percent) were related to agricultural products. In the first roughly three years after the Uruguay Round (by October 20, 1997), among a total of 73 distinct cases, 17 complaints (i.e., 23 percent) dealt with agriculture [Hudec (1997)]. However, only a minority of these disputes related to core elements of the Agreement on Agriculture. This was also true for the two most prominent cases, both of which were directed against the EU. One of them was related to quota administration under the EU banana market regime. The other one, against the EU ban on the importation of beef produced with hormones, dealt with provisions under the new Uruguay Round Agreement on Sanitary and Phytosanitary Measures. Implementation of this Agreement so far, and of the beef hormones case, is surveyed by Roberts (1997). The EU has lost in both cases (after both cases had gone to the WTO Appellate Body), and is expected to adjust the policies concerned.

Overall, experience with agricultural disputes following the Uruguay Round can be said to have been reassuring in three regards. First, the new agricultural provisions and commitments established in the Uruguay Round have not (so far) resulted in a sudden upsurge of complaints. Indeed, a number of complaints had remained in the waiting line until the Uruguay Round was finished. In that sense, the number of complaints which had to be dealt with immediately after the Round may not be representative of the longer run amount of agricultural disputes in the WTO. Second, the new SPS Agreement has allowed some cases to be brought before the WTO that might have been very difficult to resolve bilaterally. Third, the new rules on dispute settlement agreed to in the Uruguay Round have been successful in the sense of reducing the time required to reach conclusions, and of not allowing countries found in violation of their obligations to block the adoption of panel reports. The improved effectiveness of the new dispute settlement process in the WTO may also have helped to avoid some formal disputes as well as settle differences bilaterally through consultations. However, the real test for the validity of the new regime will come only when countries have to adjust those measures found to be inconsistent with their obligations.

3. Major agricultural issues negotiated in the Uruguay Round

The Uruguay Round was supported by an unprecedented amount of economic analysis and discussion. Section 4 provides a brief survey of some of the quantitative studies that contributed to the Uruguay Round negotiations. This section discusses the economic issues and reasoning that surrounds the three major policy elements dealt with in the Uruguay Round and in other trade agreements.

Trade agreements have traditionally dealt mainly with tariff reductions, and as noted previously, this was indeed a major element of the Uruguay Round. However, given the variety of non-tariff import barriers used in agriculture, it was clear that tariff cuts alone would be unsatisfactory. The concept of tariffication was proposed and implemented to deal with this complicated issue. Tariffication, minimum access, tariff cuts, and the maintenance of current access comprised the package of import access tools that were used in the Uruguay Round negotiations and subsequently in NAFTA. Market access is discussed next, in Section 3.1.

As noted in Section 2, the immediate trade effects of tariffication were expected to be rather small in most cases. In fact, throughout the Uruguay Round negotiations, it was export subsidy programs that were perceived to be the most disruptive policy practiced by the major trading nations of temperate zone products. Economic analysis of agricultural export subsidies has been extensive over the past decade, but most of this research has dealt with the domestic welfare consequences of such policies. Our review, in Section 3.2, deals with only some of these issues and focuses mainly on trade consequences and the role of the export subsidy battle in trade negotiations.

The third leg of the Uruguay Round was an attempt to use the multilateral negotiations to limit directly the use of trade-distorting domestic programs. Section 3.3 discusses the economic logic of this attempt and how the Uruguay Round dealt with the complexity of underlying policies and programs.

3.1. *Economic issues of market access policy and tariffication*

Agricultural trade barriers proliferated in the decades leading to the Uruguay Round. Non-tariff barriers were generally not accepted for trade between GATT members in other goods, and tariff rates fell steadily through successive GATT negotiation rounds. In agriculture, many tariffs were also bound in the GATT, though less than for industrial goods. Among wealthy countries and GATT members, new or increased import barriers in agriculture mainly took forms other than simple import tariffs (see above, Section 2.1). Nations applied non-tariff barriers either to exploit the gray areas of the GATT, or in the context of explicit exceptions from broad GATT commitments. The use of variable levies by the EU and the use of Section 22 quotas by the United States are examples of these two cases.

Tariffs and non-tariff barriers have much in common. Import tariffs directly raise the price of potential imports and allow larger quantities of domestic import substitutes to be sold at higher prices than would otherwise occur. Agricultural non-tariff barriers also can further the interests of domestic producers by directly limiting the quantity of imports of competing goods. An equivalence of tariffs and import quotas (as well as other non-tariff barriers) under certain simple market conditions is well known, and used for quantitative measurement of protection rates already in the famous Haberler Report [GATT (1958)]. However, the "equivalence" between tariffs and import quotas applies only under limited conditions. For example, when there is potential monopoly power in the domestic market, equivalence breaks down because a tariff continues to limit prices charged in the domestic market, whereas a quantitative import barrier allows the domestic supply more scope for monopoly pricing [Bhagwati (1970)]. In agriculture, we may often assume competition applies, but nonetheless, differences in consumer or seller consequences remain. For example, tariffs may provide less protection to the domestic industry than "equivalent" quantitative limits under variable domestic or world prices [Vousden (1990)].

Tariffs and non-tariff barriers also differ in broader effects that are important in many applications. For example, government revenues received from tariffs and quotas are likely to differ. The variety and complexity of non-tariff barriers mean they are less transparent in their effects than tariffs. Publication of tariff schedules allows easy comparison across tariff lines. This transparency was a key argument for tariffication applied in the Uruguay Round Agreement, even though these tariff rates do not necessarily provide accurate assessments of rates of protection, domestic price effects, or broader consequences for consumers.

Directly limiting the quantity that may be imported is a simple and straightforward border barrier. However, quantitative import restrictions may be less transparent than tariffs. Import quotas may be sold, in which case they may provide government revenue, or they may be given away to importing firms or exporters. A variety of mechanisms have been used to ration access in the case of quotas or quota-like programs (for tariff rate quotas, see below, Section 5.4). This rationing means that, under quotas, the government in the importing country continues to control sources or other characteristics of imports to a large degree.

Other agricultural import measures include variable levies, as practiced most prominently by the European Union, and the so-called "voluntary export restraint" (VER). VER was used, for example, by the United States and Canada to limit beef imports, and by the EU to constrain manioc imports from Thailand. Under a pure variable levy scheme, the import duty varies inversely with the border price such that the imported price inclusive of the levy is held constant. The EU variable levy policy restricted imports to allow the domestic price support policies of the EU to operate without interference from international market conditions. A variable levy uses an adjustable tariff to achieve domestic price objectives that would not be possible with a pure tariff or import quota. A domestic price-band policy is similar to a variable levy. In this case, a variable import tariff is added to the border price in order to keep the inclusive price within a proscribed range. Chile has used a price band policy for wheat, and other countries in Latin America continue to use price bands after the Uruguay Round.

Under a VER, an importing nation uses various trade or other pressures to encourage trading partners to "voluntarily" limit shipments to the import market. Sometimes these import barriers are informal, or ad hoc, such as when Canada agreed to a VER for wheat sales to the Unites States in 1994 [Alston, Gray and Sumner (1994)]. In other cases, the VER policy is a permanent feature of law. For example, the U.S. meat import law, which was in force for more than two decades, stated that if imports were projected to exceed a trigger quantity, then an import quota would be imposed that was 10 percent below the trigger. Major importers were then offered the opportunity to negotiate an import amount that was above the quota quantity, but below the trigger. With this policy in place, the quota itself was used as a threat, and major exporters (Australia and New Zealand) often "voluntarily" restrained their exports to the U.S. market [Sumner (1995)].

Faced with a variety of border barriers, the Uruguay Round negotiations focused on the standardization of import regulations such that all barriers were converted to ad valorem or specific tariffs at a rate calculated to provide "equivalent" domestic protection to the non-tariff barrier that was replaced. The rationale behind tariffication was to provide transparency in border measures and a basis for further tariff reductions in the next rounds of multilateral trade negotiations.

In a world with variable prices and a large array of product qualities and other characteristics that fall within tariff lines, the tariff equivalent concept is difficult to apply. The result of the URA tariffication requirement has been a set of new tariffs that were quite high by objective standards, and may in some cases have provided more protection than the non-tariff barriers they replaced (see above, Section 2.3). Recognizing this tendency, the Agreement also provided for minimum access quantities that would expand gradually over time, for gradual reductions in all tariffs, including the newly created ones, and for a broad principle that access could not be lower following the agreement than it was before the agreement.

Most observers agree that tariffication was a major accomplishment of the URA. Even starting from high and inflated initial points, if tariff reductions are maintained at the URA average rate of 6 percent per year from the initial base beyond the current implementation period, most agricultural border barriers would be zero by 2013, and free trade in agriculture would follow a few years later [Josling et al. (1994)]. As with any phased-in reform, staying on the reform path is key to success.

3.2. *The role of export subsidies in trade negotiations*

To a significant extent, the Uruguay Round negotiations on agriculture were driven by the grain trade war between the United States and the European Union. Increased price support, export subsidies, and other developments in Europe caused the EU to shift from being a major grain importer to becoming a major export competitor of the United States. This, plus the residual from a 1980 embargo, exchange rate movements, high U.S. price supports, and large acreage set-asides, caused a drop in U.S. exports [USDA/ERS (1986)]. The result was a renewal of U.S. export subsidies targeted specifically at markets important to the EU. The United States explicitly tied its use of export subsidies to EU subsidies and discussed trade agreements in the context of multilateral "disarmament" in a trade war.

Often, export subsidies have been used as a complement to other trade-distorting farm programs as a mechanism to shift production surpluses off the domestic market while maintaining high producer prices. That is, in agriculture at least, export subsidies have been used mainly because other policies created domestic production that could not be sold at high policy-created domestic prices. Examples include the CAP of the European Union. Further, programs to shift out the demand curve by subsidizing, or otherwise promoting, exports can substitute for programs that shift back the supply curve by requiring land to be idled. Examples include wheat policy of the United States from 1985 to 1995.

For some countries, explicit export price subsidies are the most important part of a package of export assistance that includes credit guarantee programs, subsidy for international promotion, and food aid. Each of these policies uses government assistance to attempt to increase exports; they differ in the form of the aid, the international market they target, and their effectiveness. They are also treated differently in international agreements [Sumner (1995), USGAO (1993), Ackerman, Smith and Suarez (1995), Smith and Lee (1994), Trostle, Meilke and Sanders (1994)].

Export subsidies were a part of modern farm policy that began in the 1930s. In the United States, the Agricultural Adjustment Act (AAA) of 1933 applied export subsidies to wheat and wheat flour. Then, under Section 32 of the AAA Amendments of 1935, 30 percent of tariff receipts were used to encourage the export or domestic consumption of agricultural commodities [Johnson (1950)]. Export subsidies have also been authorized under various *ad hoc* schemes and agreements such as the International

Wheat Agreement of 1949. In that case, the domestic price support for wheat was above the maximum export price allowed under the agreement. The government provided the difference between the domestic price and the agreed international maximum export price [Benedict and Stine (1956), Ackerman and Smith (1990)].

With its CAP, the EU has been the most inveterate recent user of export subsidies. Throughout the period of negotiation of the URA, the CAP maintained domestic prices above world prices and protected domestic producers with variable levies or other import barriers. EU exporters were given a rebate on exports that was adjusted to world market conditions on a regular basis. The EU set high prices for domestic consumers and producers alike, while it expanded exports. These basic policies were used for meats, dairy products, grains, and many other products such as fruits and vegetables. Export subsidy policy also included programs to compensate food manufacturers for high-priced domestic ingredients [Gerken (1997)].

Canada's major export subsidy scheme, under the Western Grain Transportation Act, provided shipping subsidies conditional on export until these were eliminated in response to budget pressure and URA requirements [Barichello (1995)]. These Canadian subsidies were a part of the context, but the main trade battle motivating Uruguay Round negotiations was between the United States and the EU.

In response to low farm incomes, EU programs, and a loss in export market share in the early 1980s, the United States introduced a new round of export subsidies under the Export Enhancement Program (EEP) and related programs (each with euphonious acronyms). The EEP began under the continuing charter authority of the Commodity Credit Corporation (CCC). It was subsequently authorized under the 1985 Farm Security Act (FSA). At first, the EEP provided export subsidies in the form of commodities from CCC inventory, but as these inventories became depleted, the program continued by providing cash subsidies. The Dairy Export Incentive Program (DEIP) was also authorized under the 1985 FSA; the Sunflowerseed Oil Assistance Program (SOAP) was authorized in 1988; and the Cottonseed Oil Assistance Program (COAP) began in 1989. The importance of export subsidies varies widely even among the commodities to which they have been applied [Ackerman and Smith (1990), Ackerman, Smith and Suarez (1995), Trostle, Meilke and Sanders (1994), Gardner (1996)].

As noted, a key target for the EEP was the EU export subsidy program. (For an early discussion, see de Gorter and Meilke (1987).) Because the EU provided subsidies on the total amount of its wheat exports, anything that lowered export prices in the markets in which they participated caused the EU to make higher outlays to maintain exports. There is some evidence that the budget costs of EU export subsidies were higher because of U.S. export subsidies. Note, however, lower export prices also reduce the direct benefit of export subsidies for the United States wheat industry.

Policy pressure on the other subsidizing exporters is created by a fall in quantities exported, not in export price. In this case, losses for the foreign government may co-exist with large export gains by the United States if the expansion of U.S. exports replaces foreign exports, and the export price declines little. In this case, the missed export sales by foreigners are reflected mainly in increased stocks or reduced production in the foreign country (EU), but not so much in increased budget outlays for subsidies in other exporting countries. There is some evidence that this occurred in Europe in the early 1990s.

Using export subsidies as a negotiating tool makes sense only if the degree of pressure placed on foreign governments from the export subsidy is intense enough to significantly affect the path of policy reform. The intensity of the pressure depends on how much the foreign decision makers perceive that the competitor's subsidy reduces prices in international markets or reduces the size of the export market. There was substantial discussion in the late 1980s and early 1990s about the extent to which the EU felt the pressure of the U.S. EEP program. Anania, Bohman and Carter (1992) were skeptical about the EEP success and argued that, at least in the early years, EEP hurt exporters other than the EU, and provided little help to the United States wheat industry. Their argument was, in essence, that by dumping stocks on the market, the EEP simply drove down all wheat prices, including U.S. domestic prices. This argument could have been true only until the wheat stocks were depleted in the first two years of EEP operation, and then only if one assumes that government stocks would not have been released on the market without the EEP. Paarlberg (1985) argued that the extra cost to the EU caused by EEP was too small to trigger policy reform in the EU. Moyer and Josling (1990), however, have shown that rising budgetary expenditure on the CAP, resulting from U.S. export subsidies among other things, was a central factor in decision making on CAP reform. Vahl (1996) claimed that pressure on the CAP exerted by the United States was strongly instrumental in driving the EU to the negotiating table in the Uruguay Round.

Goldberg and Knetter (1997) use some relatively simple time-series regressions in an attempt to measure the contribution of the EEP to U.S. wheat prices, supplies, and export quantities. Their results suggest that the impacts of the EEP on U.S. prices and U.S. market share were both small, and that exchange rate movements were behind world wheat market dynamics in the 1980s. Their results also do not support the idea that EU export subsidies for wheat played a major role in lowering the U.S. export share. The approach is based on time-series behavior over a relatively short period and may miss complex structural changes induced by policy shifts. And, of course, these results do not counter the idea that perceived EU budget costs or export quantities were affected by U.S. export subsidies.

As the EEP matured, the explicit trade policy objectives were refined. The 1990 Food, Agriculture, Conservation, and Trade Act (FACT), which was passed as the Uruguay Round seemed stuck at an impasse over agriculture, explicitly required the use of the EEP and related programs to counter "unfair" trade practices. Further, the 1990 Omnibus Budget Reconciliation Act (OBRA) tied spending for export programs directly to progress in the Uruguay Round. The Act required that spending on export programs increase if the Round was not successfully concluded by June 1992 [USDA/ERS (1991)]. This threat did not succeed, and the required additional budget allocations were made. In its implementation of the URA, the United States government pledged to use the EEP program to the fullest allowable extent as a tool to continue subsidizing politically powerful industries and to continue pressuring the EU and other subsidizing exporters [U.S. Congress (1994)].

Any evaluation of a complex commodity policy hinges on what other policies and market conditions are expected to hold independently of the policy evaluated. In order to evaluate export subsidies, one must first consider which income and price support programs are in place so that second-best considerations may be included in the analysis [Gardner (1983), Alston and Hurd (1990), Alston, Carter and Smith (1993)]. One must also consider whether other policies are exogenous or are likely to respond to adjustments in the export program. In the United States, the EU, and other countries, domestic policies changed several times during the life of the ongoing export subsidy programs. In addition to alternative policy responses, evaluation of the effects of export subsidies depends on key supply and demand parameters. It is well accepted that some subsidy will always be paid on export sales that would have occurred even without the subsidy. In these cases, the subsidy was unnecessary, and a pure gain to the foreign buyers. Reasonable estimates of the additional export value per unit of subsidized export for United States export subsidies have ranged from as high as 40 percent to almost zero. [See Abbott, Paarlberg and Sharples (1987), Anania, Bohman and Carter (1992), Alston, Carter and Smith (1993), Dutton (1990), Gardner (1996), and especially USGAO (1994), for empirical literature and simulations on these topics.]

The literature supports the conclusion that export subsidies generally reduce national welfare, at least as social costs and benefits are conventionally measured. Export subsidy programs, as they are currently operated, provide benefits to specific farm interests, but they do so at significant cost to the national and world economy. Further, in most cases, larger benefits could be delivered to farmers at smaller budget and economic costs if export subsidies were not used. In practice, the conceptual possibility that export subsidies could be one part of a policy mix that maximized benefits to farmers for a fixed economic cost, does not seem to apply [Hanson, Vogel and Robinson (1995), Sumner (1995), Alston et al. (1997)].

As with import barriers, the basic tools available to deal with export subsidies were relatively clear; the questions for negotiators related to definitions, modalities, and time schedules. The Uruguay Round disciplines require a phasedown in both the quantities subsidized and the value of direct export price subsidies on a commodity-by-commodity basis (sometimes commodity groups), but not on a tariff-line basis. These disciplines were chosen based on considerable economic analysis, which included a review of international markets in the 1980s and early 1990s, and projections of the commodity price impacts of required policy reforms [Sumner (1992)]. Under normal supply and demand conditions, the disciplines were expected to limit EU exports and thus encourage policy reform by the EU. This, in turn, would allow export expansion and higher prices for other exporters, including the United States and members of the Cairns Group. Much of the academic literature on export subsidies dealt with how these policies affected domestic welfare and was therefore less directly relevant to how export subsidies affected trading partners.

3.3. Reform of domestic subsidies in a trade context

In the run-up to the Uruguay Round, trade rhetoric included not only trade policy and trade effects, but also accusations about the whole scheme of farm subsidy policy pursued by developed countries [Miller (1986)]. Particularly, with the widespread use of the PSE concept, agricultural or trade ministers and other farm leaders emphasized that by stimulating domestic output, domestic subsidies would reduce imports or expand exports, even without border measures [USDA/ERS (1989), OECD (1987)].

The economic logic of the focus on domestic subsidies was straightforward. Domestic production subsides can and sometimes do substitute for border measures to some degree. The GATT and individual country trade laws had long recognized the trade effects of domestic subsidy policy. Provisions related to nullification and impairment (of tariff bindings) limited a country's use of indirect measures that reduce the trade benefits legitimately expected from a trade policy concession. In the GATT, a Subsidies Code had also been agreed upon during the Tokyo Round, and antidumping and countervail law also applied to trade effects of domestic subsidies [International Agricultural Trade Research Consortium (1990)]. For one specific case study, see Moschini and Meilke (1992).

The linkage between border measures and domestic policies was also explicit in waivers and exceptions from broad GATT principles. For example, the famous Section 22 waiver of the United States explicitly acknowledged the primacy of domestic support policy and allowed the United States to apply quantitative import restrictions in cases in which imports threatened the effective operation of internal farm support programs. GATT Article XI:2(c) allowed members to use import quotas to limit imports if domestic production was effectively restricted through internal programs (see above, Section 2.1). Both of these GATT provisions acknowledged the close interaction between internal and border measures.

The two-way connection between internal policies and border measures was acknowledged, and even incorporated in trade policy debate and law, well before the Uruguay Round. However, as the Uruguay Round progressed, there was a widespread sense that the failure to include the full set of farm policy instruments directly within GATT limits had allowed conflict between border measures and internal support to minimize the accomplishments of previous GATT rounds. The idea was to use multilateral negotiations to reduce all support for agriculture and thus directly limit the trade effects of internal subsidies. Failing better measures, outlays for farm programs were sometimes taken as a proxy for subsidy impact; for example, the United States would point to the size of the EU agricultural budget as evidence of trade distortion. When Producer Subsidy Equivalent (PSE) and Consumer Subsidy Equivalent (CSE) data became available from the OECD and the USDA, these figures were used despite regular warnings that the PSE concept did not apply directly to trade-distorting policies [USDA/ERS (1989), and see references to the empirical literature below in Section 4].

Some trade policy participants, a number of advisors, and others had an additional rationale for including domestic support measures in agricultural trade negotiations.

These observers emphasized the negative welfare effects of farm programs generally, and were discouraged by the political success of program supporters. This group reasoned that if domestic farm programs could not be dealt with directly in the domestic political realm, perhaps they could be dealt with indirectly in the context of trade policy reform. In Europe, the farm interest opposed both trade liberalization and limits to domestic subsidy; most farm subsidy was tied to trade measures anyway. The idea was to include internal supports to limit the extent to which governments could substitute domestic subsidy for export subsidy and import barriers [Josling, Tangermann and Warley (1996)].

Domestic support programs mostly conform to a few basic policy types, but they have a withering variety of specific forms. This variety was one of the problems that plagued the GATT negotiators in devising effective modalities for constraining domestic support. It was clearly impossible to specify particular policies to be reformed in enough detail to capture all the various ways domestic programs subsidize agriculture. One idea was to apply an index that summarized the trade consequences of the whole mix of agricultural policies for a commodity. However, the construction of an indicator to aggregate the trade effects of internal programs proved elusive in practice. It is not trivial to summarize trade or even production subsidy effects of commodity policies without detailed knowledge of supply and demand parameters, and these are known as at best only rough approximations.

Various aggregate measures of policy-induced distortions have been defined and analyzed. Recently, one of the most widely discussed is the "Trade Restrictiveness Index" (TRI) of Anderson and Neary (1992, 1994, 1996). Anderson, Bannister and Neary (1995), Draaisma and Fulponi (1996), and Salvatici, Carter and Sumner (1997) discuss the TRI in an agricultural policy context. The idea of the TRI is to aggregate policies, using a uniform tariff index, according to their effect on a measure of domestic welfare of the country imposing the policy. Two sets of policies will have the same TRI if they impose the same aggregate welfare loss on the consumers, producers, and taxpayers in a country. The TRI weighs individual policies according to their welfare consequences and includes both border measures and distorting domestic programs, giving no weight to pure transfers that do not distort markets. As a welfare distortion index, the TRI is built on relatively simple foundations (though it is expressed in complex ways), and the analysis would be much more complex if national market power, market failures, and public goods were added to the mix.

The TRI has appealing properties, but it does not seem to be suited for use as a negotiating tool or modality for international agreements. Besides its operational complexity, the TRI has a more fundamental characteristic that limits its use in an international context. Despite its name, the TRI seems to have little to do with trade per se, and it clearly is not an index of how much trade is restricted [Salvatici, Carter and Sumner (1997)]. Two sets of policies with the same TRI can have quite different consequences for trade flows or market prices. Further, because the TRI is oriented to the home country's welfare, it does not provide a guide to the degree which policies affect a country's trading partners. One can consider the "mercantilistic TRI" which aggregates policies based on the impact on import flows. In this context, one can also conceive of something like a Trade Partners Welfare Index (TPWI), built on the same conceptual foundation as the TRI, that focuses instead on the welfare consequences of policies for a nation's trade partners. Using the TPWI, negotiators could agree to reform policies to lower the welfare consequences imposed on other countries on a non-discriminatory basis. Of course, to be operational, such an index would need to be transparent and accepted as a reliable measure of externally imposed costs. Because the TRI depends on a complex model and parameter estimates about which there is little consensus, we are a long way from implementing such an index in trade policy negotiations.

The most important practical problem of applying aggregate measures is that the trade or subsidy element of policy measures depends on world and domestic market prices, and these vary in accordance with climate-driven crop conditions and policies in other countries. For example, the PSE, which aggregates budget outlays and differences between domestic prices and world prices, varies widely from year to year even when domestic support prices do not change. No country can make serious, credible commitments with respect to an index which it could control only if it were prepared to adjust domestic support prices to continuously changing conditions on domestic and international markets.

Under the Uruguay Round Agreement, the total of those domestic support policies labeled as "trade-distorting", in the sense that they tend to increase exports or reduce imports, must be reduced gradually from a base period. Total support in this category is measured by a single Aggregate Measurement of Support (AMS). The AMS is a relative, though a rather distant one, of the PSE measure as originally developed by Josling for FAO [FAO (1973, 1975)] and later adopted by OECD in its Ministerial Trade Mandate (see above, Section 2.2). Differences between the two types of measurement, and the potential for and history of their use in the Uruguay Round, have been discussed by Tangermann, Josling and Pearson (1987), International Agricultural Trade Research Consortium (1990), van der Hamsvoort (1994), Josling, Tangermann and Warley (1996), and Silvis and van der Hamsvoort (1996). Design of quantitative measures of protection and support has a long history in modern economics and is one of the prime examples where economics has made a direct contribution to international negotiations and agreements. Relationships between and comparative advantages of the various protection measures, including the PSE, are discussed by (among others) Scandizzo (1989), Josling and Tangermann (1989), and Laird (1996).

The AMS as agreed in the URA includes, in addition to direct payments, market price support provided through administered domestic prices calculated against fixed external reference prices. One of the differences between the AMS and the PSE is that the AMS is not influenced by movements in international commodity prices because it is calculated on the basis of fixed external reference prices. Another important difference is the fact that the AMS includes the gap between domestic and international prices only if there is an administered domestic support price, while the PSE includes the price gap also if it is implemented through border measures like tariffs and export subsidies.

Though the AMS (like the PSE) is calculated on a commodity-specific basis, the constraint agreed to in the URA applies only to its sector-wide aggregate. Hence, unlike for border measures, the internal support disciplines were applied to the aggregate of all commodities. Support for some commodities could be increased so long as support was reduced enough for other commodities.

Two sets of internal support policies are not in the AMS, and they are referred to as "green box" and "blue box" measures. The "permitted" policies in the green box are many and varied. Conservation programs, research and extension, direct payments meeting strict criteria, and certain crop insurance and disaster aid programs are among those policies likely to qualify for the green box. These policies are also exempt from countervailing duty actions and such GATT challenges as nullification and impairment actions, and serious prejudice actions. The blue box exempts from the requirement for reduction in total support for the implementation period certain direct payments that are made on a fixed quantity and on less than base period production.

There are several reasons why internal support disciplines were less restrictive than those devised for border measures. First, the practical effects on trade of most internal support programs are relatively small compared to direct trade barriers or subsidies [Sumner and Hallstrom (1997)]. Second, it seems nearly impossible to devise schemes to actually restrict indirect subsidies that have tangential trade effects. Third, the national political support of programs such as crop insurance and environmental subsidies is much larger than the international support for restricting them. Therefore, these programs were accepted in the green box, even though the supply effects of some of the policies may be as large as those of some direct income and price subsidies. However, it should be noted that all policies for which green box status is claimed must also meet, in addition to the specific characteristics of the green box measures listed in the URA, some general criteria "that they have no, or at most minimal, trade distortion effects or effects on production" (Agreement on Agriculture, Annex 2:1). It will be interesting to see how strictly these general criteria are applied when and if it comes to WTO disputes over the green box status of some of the more questionable measures. Interestingly, there have been no countries reporting income insurance in the green box, and both the United States and Canada report crop insurance subsidies under the AMS.

Buckwell (1997) suggests that farm program payments may evolve as payments from the government to rural landowners for provision of some environmental amenities or other services. This "multi-functionality" idea has been gaining currency especially in Europe in recent years. If indeed direct payments were set and adjusted based on some non-commodity service provided by growers, then these payments would naturally be assigned to the Uruguay Round Agreement green box. Complications arise when the services the government claims to buy on behalf of its citizens are the production of wheat on land that would otherwise be left to pasture or reindeer habitat. Further, if the degree of service is measured in tons of wheat, and the payment is made in dollars per ton, then it becomes difficult indeed to see how this differs from a simple production subsidy. Environmental amenities provided by farmland may be public goods for which a solution is service payments to farmers. Disciplining domestic support becomes complicated when there is a strong positive relationship between the public good and the agricultural production.

The so-called "peace clause" places restraints on increasing commodity-specific subsidy rates. In particular, if direct payments conform with the agreement, and if the level of support is not raised above the level that applied in the 1992 marketing year for a specific commodity, then these measures are exempt from GATT actions against subsidies (Article XVI) or nullification and impairment. Direct payments exempt from reduction, and other internal supports subject to reduction, are not exempt from countervailing duty actions. The "non-distorting" permitted (green) policies are exempt from countervailing duty actions and other GATT challenges (for example, nullification and impairment actions, serious prejudice actions).

The specific language in the Uruguay Round on "peace" was among the most contentious elements. A key issue in interpreting the peace clause is to consider whether it can be used to protect trade practices that would have been subject to GATT disciplines before the Uruguay Round. Does the peace clause allow trade to be more distorted under the Uruguay Round rules than before? The distinction between green internal support policies and the category of non-reduced subsidies may become important in this regard.

The result of this approach to internal support has been that reduction commitments for internal support have been largely irrelevant for the major agricultural nations of Europe, North America, and even Japan. [For documentation for the United States and other rich countries, see OECD (1995), USDA/ERS (1996), Young and Westcott (1996), and Nelson (1997).] Consistent with findings for developed countries, Konandreas and Greenfield (1996) find that the domestic support disciplines of the URA have little impact in developing countries. They argue that even though the URA provisions constrain developing countries from exceeding the low amounts of trade-distorting domestic support that they have provided in the past, these limits are unlikely to be binding. The basic argument is that budget pressure, and an effort to meet economic efficiency goals, would temper trade-distorting domestic support for agriculture even without the URA. The financial turmoil in East Asia in 1997 makes the prospects for large subsidies even less likely.

Silvis and van der Hamsvoort (1996) argue that the AMS played a relatively minor role in the URA. They note that the PSE concept was inapplicable in trade negotiations, so the AMS idea was only used in the internal support disciplines, most of which were designed to be non-binding. The OECD, which championed the use of an AMS in trade negotiations, disagrees and argues that inclusion of these disciplines limits the choice set of potential policies and will thus "profoundly influence future policy developments ..." [OECD (1995, p. 45)]. The OECD work, though, does not document that the "limits on the choice set" were in a feasible range, and so it does not show that the URA limits have more than a theoretical effect.

4. Quantitative analysis of agricultural trade liberalization

In the period leading up to serious negotiations in the Uruguay Round, agricultural economists invested significant resources into projecting likely effects of trade liberalization in agriculture. Studies vary in degree of policy detail, commodity detail, international coverage, economy-wide coverage, and specific questions posed, as well as in many details of specification. Nonetheless, it is useful to compare modeling approaches and results. One of the early published attempts to do this was Gardner (1989), whose review was met with expressions of frustration from the model builders.

The general approach of quantitative studies in this arena has been to (1) specify a set of supply and demand equations (or their equivalent) and an equilibrium point or path; (2) include in this initial specification a set of current policies or policy "wedges" between domestic and international prices; (3) perturb the initial equilibrium by removing (or modifying) the policies or wedges; and (4) observe the new set of equilibrium quantities, prices, and other variables of interest. Results may be presented as deviations from base period reality or base period model results. The results of such liberalization experiments are in the form of counter-factual economic history. To apply these counter-factual historical results to the questions about the impact of future trade liberalization, one must use them to inform conjectures about what the alternative futures are likely to bring. An alternative approach is to incorporate the applied questions more fully into the modeling. The base case may be projected forward and compared to an equilibrium in which the policy wedges are removed at some specified future date. In this way, the practical question is posed: How would the future be different if the policies were changed?

4.1. Issues for studies projecting effects of trade reforms

The studies that were most influential in motivating and setting the terms for the Uruguay Round generally dealt with several interrelated commodity markets with explicit linkages across commodity supplies and demands. Among the best known and influential studies was that of Tyers and Anderson (1986, 1988), which was expanded and refined in Tyers and Anderson (1992). Tyers and Anderson found, for example, if major trading countries had liberalized trade policy for major temperate-zone farm products, substantially higher world prices would have held during the period 1980 to 1982.

Simulation studies reported in Rausser (1995), though published after the conclusion of the Uruguay Round, were based on research completed before specific proposals became available for analysis. Thus, this work considered stylized reforms of farm policy, especially in the United States. A major focus of Rausser (1995) was how economic forces may exert pressure on political institutions to lead to unilateral or multilateral agricultural policy reform. This is pursued in a framework under which policies are classified as either contributing to additions to national or global welfare (as conventionally defined), or contributing to redistribution, with a loss of national or global welfare. Agricultural commodity trade barriers generally fall into the redistribution class.

Income distribution often plays a large role in the political economy of the trade negotiations. Levy and Wijnbergen (1994, 1995) concentrate on the distributional impacts of trade policy reform in a general equilibrium model, with the economy divided into urban and rural sectors. In their results, the main beneficiaries of the trade policy reform are the wealthy in both urban and rural areas. This particular result is specific to the specific way these authors model the reduction in support in maize production in Mexico. In particular, they do not fully incorporate the fact that the remote and very poor maize producers maintained self sufficiency and did not gain from price supports, but were scheduled to benefit from direct payments. It is true, however, that if low endowment farmers have less flexibility across crops, they may find it more difficult to shift production patterns in response to the changes in incentives created by liberalization.

Because of the expense and effort involved in model building and data management, major empirical trade liberalization studies have often been conducted by international or governmental organizations or research centers, or with substantial grants of government funding. Relatively early work by OECD and USDA fits this description. The work by OECD helped set the stage for Uruguay Round negotiations by helping provide internationally credible support for the notion that trade liberalization would have global benefits [OECD (1987)] (see above, Section 2.2). The USDA modeling and analysis helped to inform decision makers in the United States [Roningen and Dixit (1989)]. Both these studies and the organizations that sponsored them aided further research by providing data, ready access to parameter estimates, and a basic model structure that was used by others [for example, Vanzetti et al. (1994)].

Neoclassical trade theory within the Hecksher–Ohlin framework is usually developed in a 2-country, 2-good, 2-factor of production general equilibrium model. Obviously, real trade policy applications do not fit neatly into the strong version of this theory. Empirical trade models therefore must deviate from the simplest of theoretical structures. In this context, applied general equilibrium models attempt to provide a complete and explicit representation of the relevant economies, while abstracting from much sectoral detail. These models facilitate analysis of (1) effects of non-agricultural economy-wide policies on the agricultural sector, (2) linkages between agriculture and the rest of the economy, and (3) factor market linkages [Hertel (2002)]. As Hazledine and MacDonald (1992) point out, there is often a trade-off between making the model general and making the model more representative in the sector of interest. A partial equilibrium modeler has the advantage of being able to concentrate exclusively on a particular sector of interest. By striving for an exhaustive accounting of economic interrelationships, general equilibrium modelers forego sectoral detail. The result may be a complete model composed of questionable parts. Improvements depend upon refining the partial equilibrium specifications of the various sectors, and an ongoing dialogue between partial and general equilibrium modelers.

Differences between sector-specific and economy-wide models depend on the application or question posed for the models. Hertel (1992) obtains quite different partial and general equilibrium projections of the response in agriculture to a liberalization of all non-CAP farm and food policies. However, when he simulated the equilibrium response of a reform in the CAP starting from a position in which all non-agricultural distortions had already been removed, the partial equilibrium and general equilibrium results were similar. If agricultural policy is being reformed within a wider setting, such as the GATT, and the policy analyst wishes to calculate the total effect on agriculture of the trade policy reform, there may be sizeable errors unless economy-wide effects are incorporated. Of course, one may include effects of non-agricultural policy reform without using a full general equilibrium model. For example, the informal agricultural sector projections of URA effects that are cited below all include (exogenous) macroeconomic impacts of the overall URA on agriculture along with endogenous effects of agricultural policy reform.

In reviewing trade liberalization results that had been reported by 1988, Gardner (1989) expressed concern that projected impacts of reform differed widely. He was right that the array of "results" was quite wide. Although it is never clear precisely why model results differ, that they do differ is not surprising. The studies that Gardner considered were completed before serious negotiations were underway, and individual researchers had little guidance from the negotiations about how to frame policy-relevant questions. Thus the "answers" they reported responded to quite different research questions. The results are most naturally reported as percentage differences from some actual or simulated base, and if the simulation experiment differs, and the base differs, the reported "results" would differ even if models were identical. Of course, results also differ because models differ, but given the complexity of the models and the data, it is just about impossible to understand the source of differences in model results. The task of reconciling these models was also of limited practical interest, because none of these results were directly relevant to the eventual policy changes implied by the URA itself. Thus, there is no "reality check" on the model results either. The value of these early models was in suggesting, in broad outline, the likely direction and orders of magnitude of the impacts of trade liberalization.

Implicit in partial equilibrium modeling is the assumption that inter-industry linkages are either small enough to be disregarded, or may be specified as exogenous and unidirectional. Kilkenny and Robinson (1990) demonstrate the implications of this type of inter-industry linkage by examining a general equilibrium model under various factor mobility assumptions. They find that the impact of trade liberalization on the agricultural sector in the United States depends strongly on the degree of factor mobility, both within agriculture and out of agriculture, into the rest of the economy. This result says that rents accrue to inelastic factors of production, and reminds us that assumptions about factor markets are crucial [Robinson et al. (1993)].

4.2. Projections of specific trade policy options and agreements

As the Uruguay Round negotiations progressed, economic analysis played a role in informing the negotiators about the projected consequences of specific proposed reform alternatives. Little of that work was released publicly; rather it was used by the various negotiating teams and in discussions with interest groups in building support for the negotiations. Projections that were released were tailored to particular proposals and were based on a relatively informal mix of partial models and expert knowledge. The USDA work focused particularly on effects of multilateral reform for agricultural interests in the United States [USDA, Office of Economics (1992)]. Similar work was done with respect to NAFTA [USDA, Economic Analysis Staff (1993)]. The directions of impacts found in these studies were generally consistent with those in the earlier studies. At the conclusion of the Uruguay Round, the informal studies were updated and applied to the final Uruguay Round Agreement [USDA, Office of Economics (1994)]. These studies all considered real proposals in detail. To do that, they relied on an ad hoc combination of formal models and specific industry knowledge. They also included exogenous economy-wide projections that were used to provide input on income growth in the agricultural models [see also Helmar et al. (1994), Rosson, Runge and Hathaway (1994), and Ingco (1995)].

Projections of the effects of the Uruguay Round on individual commodities markets could apply detailed knowledge of specific policies and provide reasonable estimates, even if the scope of the analysis was limited. Such research represents a sound approach for commodities that were, in some sense, insulated from broader effects that are important in integrated grain, feed, and livestock markets. Rucker, Thurman and Borges (1996) consider the effects of the Uruguay Round for peanut markets and capitalize on their detailed specification of the policies involved.

After the completion of the Uruguay Round Agreement, there were a number of simulation studies that assessed its impacts on global agriculture. Sharma, Konandreas and Greenfield (1996) presented a synthesis of the results from five models that were used to assess the impacts of the URA. As in the studies conducted prior to the Uruguay Round, results vary from model to model. This is no longer due to differences in the reality to which they are applied. It turns out, however, that the modelers chose to specify the URA in quite different terms and, of course, the models also differ in closure, breadth, specificity, levels of aggregation, and parameter specification.

Of the models considered by Sharma, Konandreas and Greenfield (1996), the Agriculture Trade Policy Simulation Model (ATPSM) from UNCTAD, and the World Food Model (WFM) from FAO (1995) are multi-commodity partial equilibrium models. The Rural–Urban North–South (RUNS) model from Goldin and van der Mensbrugghe (1995), the FMN model, done for the World Trade Organization by Francois, McDonald and Nordstrom (1995), and the Multi-Regional Trade Model (MRT) by Harrison, Rutherford and Tarr (1995) are general equilibrium models.

The partial equilibrium models include results for many countries that have small global effects. ATPSM includes 145 countries, while WFM covers over 130 countries and 10 country aggregates. The general equilibrium models are more aggregated across countries. The models also differ in how they handle tariff reduction, market access quantity requirements, export subsidies, and domestic support. Tariff reduction is incorporated into the WFM, RUNS, and MRT models by using PSEs. Tariff reduction is then achieved by reducing the market price support component of the PSE. All of the models incorporate export subsidy restrictions, but two of the models used quite rough approximations to these commitments. In the RUNS model, per unit export subsidies were first translated into *ad valorem* rates; in the MRT model, export subsidy restrictions were treated as reductions in expenditures on export subsidies. Domestic support disciplines are incorporated in ATPSM, RUNS, and MRT, while the remaining two models assume they are non-binding. Minimum access requirements are ignored in the RUNS model and MRT.

Table 4 summarizes the projected changes in world market prices for several commodities included in various models that examined trade liberalization. All the results except Tyers and Anderson (1992) were specified to relate to the results of the Uruguay Round agreement. Models summarized include the WFM, ATPSM, and RUNS models that are reviewed in Sharma, Konandreas and Greenfield (1996). Table 4 also includes results from Vanzetti et al. (1994), Tyers and Anderson (1992), and the less formal projections by the USDA, Office of Economics (1994). Almost all the price changes are positive; those for the most protected or subsidized sectors tend to rise most as some of the protection is removed. Of course, that statement could have been made with no model, and any model that produced a contrary result would likely be considered suspect.

The most striking feature of these results is that the projected percentage price effects differ widely from model to model. The models differ in which price series they project, the exact time period, and other characteristics. The differences in price projections must be due to a complex mix of model specification and empirical experiment. These differences do not seem to be due to model type (CGE or partial equilibrium) or any other easily identified characteristic. Each model's results are defensible within the context of that model, and a detailed analysis of each model and associated results could probably account for differences across models. Nonetheless, without specialized knowledge of model particulars, or prior knowledge about which model to trust most for which specific question, readers are left without any real guidance about the projected effects of Uruguay Round trade liberalization on commodity prices.

Table 5 summarizes projections on income or net welfare effects of Uruguay Round trade liberalization. The projections from the two general equilibrium models, MRT and FMN, are taken from Table 4 in Sharma, Konandreas and Greenfield (1996). These models provide results for agricultural liberalization alone and for the economy-wide liberalization accomplished in the Uruguay Round. Projection results from the agricultural sector models of Vanzetti et al. (1994) (ABARE) and Tyers and Anderson (1992) (T&A) are also presented. Gains in global income for economy-wide liberalization are U.S.$39.6 billion in the FMN model and U.S.$92.9 billion in the MRT model. Total gains from agricultural reform are about $5 billion in the FMN model and $58 billion in the MRT model. For both these models (FMN and MRT), the aggregate benefits of agricultural reform are far larger for the developed than for developing countries. The Tyers and Anderson (1992) results are provided for the developed industrialized countries. Gains from agricultural liberalization projected by MRT and T&A are large, especially in the protectionist importers. The gains from agricultural liberalization are quite small for both the FMN and ABARE models.

Table 4
International market price effects of Uruguay Round partial trade liberalization: a summary of projections

Commodity	Model projections* (percentage changes)						
	T&A	WFM	ATPSM	RUNS	ABARE	USDA	FAPRI
Wheat	2.6	6.9	1.0	6.3	6	4.5	18[†]
Course grains	−4.3	4.4	3.2	3.2	6	2.5	9[†]
Rice	4.1	7.3	0.7	0.8	7	12.5	3[†]
Cotton	na	na	na	−0.3	3	1.5	na
Sugar	12.3	na	4.5	2.5	3	3.5	na
Beef[‡]	18.3	8.0	5.3	1.4	4	3	1
Dairy products	39.7	7.6	4.5	2.3	12[§]	na	17[§]

*T&A: Tyers and Anderson (1992). Based on a 50 percent phased reduction in agricultural protection in industrial countries as reported in their Table 7.1 for year 2000. Alternative estimates for full liberalization are in their Table 6.3. WFM: World Food Model, FAO (1995). Entries are from Table 2, Sharma, Konandreas and Greenfield (1996). Percentage changes are from a year 2000 base. ATPSM: Agricultural Trade Policy Simulation Model. Entries are from Table 2, Sharma, Konandreas and Greenfield (1996). Percentage changes are from a year 2000 base with assumed policy response in non-OECD counties. Impacts are large in the scenario with no policy response to world market prices in these countries. RUNS: Rural–Urban North–South model, Goldin and van der Mensbrugghe (1995). Percentage changes are from a year 2002 base, with adjustments in policies from the 1991–1993 average levels. The price changes using a 1982–1993 average policy base were all between +1.2 (wheat) and −1.5 (rice), but showed no clear direction of difference compared to those reported here. ABARE: Australian Bureau of Agricultural and Resource Economics, Vanzetti et al. (1994). Based results reported in their Table 13.2 for percentage changes from a 1989 base for the Uruguay Round Agricultural Agreement as represented in the Blair House Accord using the SWOPSIM Model [Roningen and Dixit (1989)]. USDA: United States Department of Agriculture, USDA, Office of Economics (1994). Projections include both agricultural sector impacts and economic growth impacts from the overall Uruguay Round Agreement. Projected changes refer to percentage changes from baseline projections for the year 2000. They represent explicit or implied world price changes. FAPRI: Food and Agricultural Policy Research Institute, Helmar, Meyers and Hayes (1994). Based on projections of the Uruguay Round Agreement, including CAP reform as part of the overall package as reported in their Table 12.8.
[†] Based on the change in CIF Rotterdam prices, except rice, which is FOB Bangkok.
[‡] Tyers and Anderson (1992) aggregate ruminant meal. For the RUNS model, this includes bovine and sheep meat. ABARE provides estimates for FMD-free and FMD-affected markets. This figure is a weighted average based on an estimated 60 percent of trade in the FMD-free market. For FAPRI, this is the Nebraska Direct Fed Steer price.
[§] For ABARE, Dairy includes a single average of butter, milk powder (both 10 percent), and cheese (17 percent). For FAPRI, this is the average FOB Northern Europe price change where the cheese price rose by 40 percent, butter price rose by 10 percent, and nonfat dry milk price fell by 1.5 percent.

The modeling completed after the URA is troublesome in that, even with the reform commitments spelled out in detail, modelers have not been able to incorporate the implied policy changes into their models in any real detail. For example, the use of a PSE to capture trade effects of policy change will always be suspect and even model builders know this is a very rough approximation at best. Further, researchers seem to have found no standard way to report projections in ways that allow for convenient

Table 5
Effects of Uruguay Round trade liberalization on incomes (U.S.$ billion)

	Model*					
	T&A	MRT		FMN		ABARE
	Agricultural reform	Agricultural reform	Economy-wide reform	Agricultural reform	Economy-wide reform	Agricultural reform
United States	0.4	1.7	12.8	0.1	10.1	0.2
EU-12	14.1	28.5	38.9	4.8	14.6	0.7
Japan	17.9	15.2	16.7	−0.5	1.3	1.1
Australia/New Zealand/Canada	1.6	1.4	2.7	0.6	0.3	1.2[†]
Developed	35.6	49.1	75.2	4.3	26.9	na
Developing	na	9.2	17.7	−0.2	10.3	na
World	na	58.3	92.9	4.6	39.6	3.5

*Tyers and Anderson (1992). Table entries based on a year 2000 net economic welfare effects of a phased 50 percent reduction in agricultural protection in industrial market economies. Changes reported in 1985 U.S. dollars in Table 7.7. MRT: Multi-Regional Trade Model, Harrison, Rutherford and Tarr (1995). Reported in 1992 U.S. dollars in Sharma, Konandreas and Greenfield (1996), Table 4.

FMN: Prepared for the World Trade Organization, Francois, McDonald and Nordstrom (1995). Reported in 1992 U.S. dollars in Sharma, Konandreas and Greenfield (1996), Table 4. ABARE: Australian Bureau of Agricultural and Resource Economics, Vanzetti et al. (1994), Table 1.3.

[†] Includes entire Cairns Group except Fiji.

cross-mode comparisons. It is not helpful for researchers to point out that differences in results are due to different policy specifications, if each of the models purports to analyze the same policy.

Given the range of projected effects, and the general inability of these models to specify fully the policy reforms imposed by the Uruguay Round, it seems reasonable to treat these efforts as contributions to model building rather than contributions to reliable knowledge about the Uruguay Round. Nonetheless, more recent research has begun to build upon both the models and the results just reviewed. This second generation of analysis of the impacts of the URA is represented by recent work by Anderson (1997). Anderson uses a small CGE model to examine the welfare impacts of the URA on several developing countries, basing his analysis on output from the larger CGE results from the RUNS model by Goldin and van der Mensbrugghe (1995). Anderson notes that the international price increases implied by the URA have two broad impacts on national welfare. The first, labeled the terms of trade effect, indicates the gains or losses experienced from changing import and export prices. The magnitude of the terms of trade effect is approximated by the quantity of net trade times the size of the price change. The second effect, labeled the "distortion effect", measures the degree by which changes in international prices offset or reinforce distortions created by domestic agricultural policies. In this CGE connection, see also Martin (1997). Anderson and Tyers (1993) provide similar quantitative analysis using their sector-specific multi-commodity model.

Most developing countries are net importers of agricultural products, but these same countries have often biased internal prices against agriculture. Thus, if world prices are allowed to penetrate the domestic markets, the higher world prices caused by the URA may partially offset the low prices experienced by developing country farmers and consumers. Anderson estimates that the distortion effects dominate the terms of trade effects for most of the 15 commodities and 9 countries he examines. As Anderson notes, his results depend crucially on the (for him) exogenous estimates of the world price impacts and internal price policies. For a measure of price distortion, Anderson uses USDA calculations of the PSE and CSE by commodity for each country. Of course the PSE and CSE estimates provide only a very rough guide to price distortions. This problem is compounded in this application because missing observations are assigned zero values, and because the PSE and CSE data are seriously out of date for a forward-looking analysis of the impact of price increases likely to occur mainly in the period after 1999.

In summary, the ex post quantitative analysis of the Uruguay Round seems sadly limited in providing a solid basis for understanding the likely impacts of the agreement. The models economists use are, on the one hand, complex enough to defy comprehension of what drives the results, and on the other hand, so simple that they cannot incorporate crucial features of a complex policy reform.

Further, these quantitative models are built on parameters that seems based on evidence or estimation that is inappropriate to the specific questions being posed. Sumner (1993), Just, Rausser and Zilberman (1995), and McDonald and Sumner (1998) discuss such parameter problems in more detail in the context of agricultural supply functions. They suggest paying much more attention to defining and devising parameter estimates that are tailored to each application. Standard econometric estimates from historical data are simply not appropriate for most policy analysis questions because they are based on a set of ceteris paribus conditions that no longer apply. Researchers must devote much more attention to the empirical basis of simulation models before projections can be treated as reliable evaluations of trade agreements or other policy shifts [Gardiner and Carter (1988)]. This means that parameters must be tailored to the specific policy question, not simply taken off the shelf and assumed to fit any question that presents itself.

5. Issues for future research and policy reform

In spite of the progress made in the Uruguay Round, international agricultural trade is still far from being truly liberalized. Indeed, some of the new rules and commitments agreed to in the Uruguay Round have opened up new questions, as discussed in the preceding sections. Moreover, economic research and political debate have indicated a number of new issues that need to be dealt with in the future. Another multilateral round of negotiations on agricultural trade will have to be initiated in 1999, as stipulated in the Uruguay Round Agreement on Agriculture. In this next round of agricultural negotiations, the unfinished business of the Uruguay Round, as well as some of the new issues, will have to be tackled. Josling (1996a, 1997), Tangermann (1996), and Tangermann et al. (1997) have discussed issues for the next round in detail. Some of the more pressing items include future treatment of state trading (Section 5.1), further development of rules on sanitary and phytosanitary measures (Section 5.2), reduction of tariff dispersion (Section 5.3), and improvements in the administration of tariff rate quotas (Section 5.4).

5.1. State trading

State trading was not much dealt with during the Uruguay Round, except for the negotiations which finally led to the Understanding on the Interpretation of Article XVII of the GATT 1994. However, this Understanding does not change or strengthen GATT rules for state trading.[13] Hence, a number of important issues still remain to be settled. As rules for agricultural trade are tightened in the WTO and state trading becomes increasingly an anomaly, the next round of negotiations should deal in more detail with the issues arising out of this anomaly. In agriculture, state trading enterprises (STEs) still play a large role,[14] and there are a number of issues where state trading in agriculture is different from state trading in other areas. Moreover, the importance of tightening rules on state trading in agriculture has grown as countries such as China and Russia become closer to joining the WTO.

One fundamental requirement of better rules on state trading is a proper definition of what constitutes an STE. The Uruguay Round Understanding came up with an institutionalist definition, though it leaves a number of key questions unresolved [Dixit and Josling (1997)]. More important, however, are decisions on what STEs can and what they must not do. Josling (1996b), Dixit (1996), and Dixit and Josling (1997) have discussed approaches that could be used.

On the import side, the major issues involved in state trading are that import volumes are likely to be lower than those that would be achieved under competition and an equivalent tariff barrier. Also, STEs are more likely to discriminate between different national sources of imports. In theory, no such problems should arise after the Uruguay Round. After all, tariffication has included those cases where state enterprises conduct imports (with the exception of the "rice clause"). Hence, tariffs are now bound; where state enterprises sell imports domestically at a price higher than the world market price plus tariff, such mark-ups have also been bound. Article II:4 of the GATT 1994 requires state trading enterprises not to provide more protection than bound in the Schedule of the country concerned. Therefore, importing STEs should now be operating under tightly defined rules. In theory, this should result in a situation where the domestic price

---

[13] However, as stipulated by the Understanding, a WTO Working Party on State Trading was established, and WTO members are required to notify the WTO about their state trading enterprises.

[14] On international wheat markets, for example, 40 percent of total wheat trade in 1996 was imported by countries identified as relying on STEs [Abbott and Young (1997)]. In 1995 and 1996, 30 countries notified the WTO of more than 100 STEs involved in agricultural trade [Dixit and Josling (1997)].

of the product concerned is no higher than the lowest available international price plus tariff and mark-up. If this were the case, then discrimination between sources would also not occur, as the supplier offering the lowest price would determine the domestic price in the importing country.

In practice, however, the operations of STEs often lack transparency, and it is therefore not clear whether they actually honor these fundamental rules. This, however, would not need to be the case if the outcome of the operations of state trading enterprises were monitored more closely with regard to two basic criteria. First, domestic prices in the importing country should, indeed, not be higher than international prices plus bound tariffs and mark-ups. Second, the quantities imported should be fully sufficient to satisfy domestic demand at those prices. Neither of these concepts is new. Hence, it may be sufficient to reconfirm their applicability, and to agree on practical modalities for monitoring consistency of state trading operations with these rules.

Among the issues relating to exporting state trading enterprises, discrimination among destinations ("pricing-to-market") and price pooling between domestic and export sales are probably the most controversial potential problems. Pricing-to-market is a very difficult issue to deal with. To an extent, it is a normal commercial practice related to transport costs, quality differences, and other similar factors. However, pricing-to-market can also be used as predatory pricing. Even then it can be a "normal" commercial practice, also used by private trading companies. Price discrimination among different destinations is not prohibited by the Agreement on Agriculture, or by the GATT 1994, as long as no subsidies are involved. STEs, though, have to honor Article XVII:1(a) of the GATT 1994, which requires them to "act in a manner consistent with the general principles of non-discriminatory treatment prescribed ... for governmental measures affecting imports or exports by private traders". Whether this provision also prohibits price discriminating state agency exports where no subsidies are involved (and hence no "governmental measure affecting exports" is used) is a question to be answered by lawyers.

In general, one should not forget that in practice it is difficult to determine price discriminating export subsidies. The Tokyo Round Subsidies Code (now defunct) had provisions against agricultural export subsidies displacing other countries' exports or resulting in "prices materially below those of other suppliers". However, panels had major difficulties finding such practices, and in no single case has it been ruled that a country violated these provisions. It should also be noted that price discrimination on export markets is not limited to cases where state agencies operate. It can also occur where governments grant export subsidies to private traders in a differential manner, depending on the destination. Of course, remaining export subsidies must be notified and are being reduced.

Price pooling between domestic and export markets, as often done by exporting STEs (or resulting from domestic state agencies with similar powers), should be easier to deal with. After all, the issue in this case is essentially one of export subsidies and falls under the export subsidy provisions of the Agreement on Agriculture. Where a state agency sells domestically at a price above the price charged for exports, while domestic producers are paid the average price, exports are implicitly subsidized. In this case, both domestic consumers and domestic producers have prices above the export price. In some cases, the subsidy element is even more than would be achieved through direct export subsidy programs [Alston and Gray (1998)]. Countries should not be allowed therefore to escape their export subsidy commitments by using price pooling. It should be clear that an effective constraint on the extent of price pooling is established through the commitments on export subsidies. It may be useful to confirm the applicability of the export subsidy provisions to these cases explicitly in the next round of negotiations.

Indeed, price pooling is much broader than state trading, and appears often in the context of internal price regulation schemes. For example, cooperatives (which may have some government backing or tax advantages) apply price pooling across markets without any direct government regulations. Many countries regulate dairy prices to facilitate price discrimination across end-uses of milk and use price pooling to distribute the returns of the rents from price discrimination. Where they contribute to export price discrimination, such schemes are a substitute for export subsidies and are quite similar in trade effect to price discrimination with price pooling as practiced by some STE exporters [Sumner (1996)].

5.2. Analysis of sanitary and phytosanitary trade barriers

The Uruguay Round Agreement on the Application of Sanitary and Phytosanitary Measures (SPS) was negotiated to clarify the rights of governments to take protective actions, and to clarify the conditions that must be met to ensure that these actions are not unjustified barriers to trade. The key provision in this agreement is that all measures must be scientifically based. To meet this condition, countries have two options. They can either use international standards, or set their own standard if there is scientific justification based upon an assessment of risk [Stanton (1997)]. In either case, the commitment to a given level of protection must be reflected domestically. Equivalent regulations are to be applied to both domestically produced products and imports. Also, the measures are not to be more restrictive to trade than necessary to provide the desired level of protection.

Analysis of the impacts of SPS trade barriers remains a difficult subject, both theoretically and empirically. Analysis requires the tools of traditional trade policy analysis and risk assessment. If the effects of agricultural imports on human, animal, and plant health were known with certainty, policy analysis of SPS measures could be performed using standard trade models. The sheer number and variety of regulations adds to the complexity of the analysis. However, the problems in this case are ones with which economists are relatively comfortable. [Sumner and Lee (1997) discuss how SPS regulations may be incorporated into a multi-commodity model.] SPS effects are not known with certainty, and this raises the complexity of the analysis. The empirical challenge is to quantify the tradeoffs between the risks and benefits of allowing agricultural imports. Higher degrees of protection are typically associated with lower import levels. This means that any gain in health-related benefits from an SPS policy must be balanced against the costs imposed on consumers of the imported commodity.

The first step in an analysis of this type is to determine the range and probabilities over this range of possible health-related consequences associated with trade in the commodity. Protection offered by an SPS measure is then characterized by the conditional probabilities over the range of consequences, given that measure is in place. Tradeoffs between a higher degree of health certainty and the costs associated with trade-restricting regulations can then be quantified by simulating how the distributions of consequences (both health-related and economic) change in response to proposed regulatory actions. Performing such an analysis requires a large amount of detailed and site-specific information on the physical and economic characteristics of the region of interest. However, analysis of this type has been used in other contexts to examine trade, health, and environmental linkages [see, for example, Antle et al. (1996)], and is feasible if sufficient time and resources are available.

Powell (1997) and Hillman (1997) review the role of science in SPS trade disputes. They note that the scientific risk assessment needed for effective dispute resolution is not generally available and may not be unbiased. Powell examines two "headline" cases where scientific evidence has been strongly supportive of relaxing trade barriers. Based on scientific evidence that U.S. industry supporters continue to question, the U.S. government agreed to allow Mexican fresh avocados a small and geographically limited market in the United States. The WTO panel and appeal process has now ruled that the EU ban on beef from cattle fed growth hormones is not supported by science, but the ban continues pending additional risk analysis in the EU. Powell goes on to provide lessons about how future disputes in this area are likely to proceed and how scientific evidence is likely to be used.

Roberts (1997) also reviews the progress of a number of SPS disputes that have appeared before the WTO. She concludes that disputes are likely to continue in this area as new products, such as genetically modified organisms, are released into international markets. The cases to date have yet to settle issues of law or evidence that would allow traders to predict the outcome of disputes and respond with preventative policy change. Thus we may expect to see disputes in this area until issues are clarified. We also do not yet know if large and powerful traders will actually allow internal SPS rules to be dictated from Geneva.

A standard concern is that the use of SPS regulations will increase as other means of restricting trade are reduced under the Uruguay Round. One reason for this concern is the difficulty in distinguishing disguised trade barriers from trade restrictions due to legitimate health concerns. Because the comparison is between a distribution of consequences with and without the regulation, it is not possible to draw conclusive results from past experiences, as any such experience is only one realization from the distribution of possible outcomes. Also, the causes and mechanisms of the health risks associated with trade in agricultural commodities are often poorly understood and hard to quantify. This makes it difficult to come up with a scientific consensus on the nature and probabilities of the risks involved. There are a number of public choice studies in this area trying to understand the complex web of economic and political factors that determine a final regulatory decision [see, for example, Roberts and Orden (1997)].

Table 6
Average tariff reductions agreed to in the Uruguay Round

	EU	Japan	USA
(1) Base period average tariff level (%)	26.2	52.3	11.3
(2) Final period average tariff level (%)	17.7	40.2	7.9
(3) Average of reduction rates (%)	37.7	36.8	38.8
(4) Difference (1) − (2) (in % of (1))	32.4	23.2	30.0
(5) Coefficient of variation of base tariffs (%)	163.7	399.8	213.6
(6) Coefficient of variation of final tariffs (%)	169.6	426.4	259.0

All averages are unweighted.
Source: Tangermann (1995).

However, there is still much to be learned about the conditions under which international trade agreements can discipline the use of SPS measures as disguised trade barriers.

5.3. Tariff dispersion

In the Uruguay Round, it was agreed that agricultural tariffs had to be reduced by a simple unweighted average rate of 36 percent (in developed countries), with a minimum rate of reduction of 15 percent for each tariff line. This provision opened up the possibility of spreading the reduction requirement rather unevenly across products. For example, it was possible for a country to reduce tariffs on three items with an initial tariff of more than 100 percent by only 15 percent each, and still meet the overall 36 percent unweighted average reduction by eliminating (i.e., reducing by 100 percent) the 4 percent initial tariff of one other product. As a result, countries continue providing particularly high protection to their "sensitive" products. Countries have used this flexibility differently, but in many cases, with a tendency to reduce high tariffs less than low ones. The result is that after the implementation period of the Uruguay Round, many tariff peaks will remain, and tariff dispersion will in many cases be even more pronounced than it was at the beginning of the implementation period. For example, as shown in Table 6, in major industrialized countries (EU, Japan, United States) the unweighted average of tariff rates will, at the end of the Uruguay Round implementation period, be reduced by less than 36 percent compared to the base level (row 4), and dispersion of final tariff rates, indicated by the coefficient of variation, will be higher than dispersion of the base rates (compare rows 5 and 6).

The detrimental implications of the approach to tariff-cutting adopted in the Uruguay Round may be significant. Economic theory and quantitative analysis suggest that uneven rates of protection among products closely related in production or use can distort the use of resources in world agriculture even more than a slightly higher, but more uniform level of protection [Corden (1971), Koester et al. (1988)].

An issue related to tariff dispersion, though of a more specific nature, is tariff escalation along given processing chains. Depending on the share of value added through processing in a given product, even slight increases in tariff rates along the processing chain can afford very significant protection to the processing activity involved.[15] Exporting countries then find it difficult to access the market for the processed product concerned, and may have to export the unprocessed raw material, even though their domestic processing industries could be competitive. This is a particular problem for developing countries in their efforts to diversify their traditional commodity exports into higher value-added products. Recent empirical results show that tariff escalation has at least not become more pronounced as a result of the Uruguay Round reductions in agricultural tariffs [Lindland (1997)].

It seems clear, though it has not been studied in great detail, that a serious effort to reduce tariff dispersion and tariff escalation would provide substantial welfare gains. This is an area in which additional empirical analysis would be helpful. A flat-rate uniform reduction of all tariffs would yield some gains. Of course, an agreement to reduce higher tariffs by more than lower tariffs would reduce dispersion even more. This is exactly what was achieved for industrial tariffs during the Tokyo Round, through use of the so-called Swiss formula for tariff reductions.[16] However, there is good reason to believe that higher tariffs are more likely to be prohibitive and perhaps higher than required to continue to limit imports severely. This means that dropping these tariffs most would expand trade less in the short run, but allow more to be achieved later. An interesting variation on this theme may be an approach by which countries are allowed to choose among (a) a flat-rate reduction of all tariffs, and (b) a formula cut which yields an agreed-upon somewhat smaller average reduction of tariffs, but attenuates tariff dispersion.

5.4. Tariff rate quotas

The host of new tariff rate quotas (TRQs) in agriculture which have resulted from the Uruguay Round Agreements for Agriculture, mainly under the minimum access and current access provisions, constitute one of the most strongly criticized elements of the current WTO regime for agriculture [Hathaway and Ingco (1995)]. Under TRQs, there is a strong flavor of managed trade. TRQs are considered to be a tool of tariffication because they may be viewed as simply two (or more) tariffs applied to the same product and are conditional on the quantity of prior imports. Where above-quota tariffs are prohibitive (which often was the case after the Uruguay Round), TRQs function

---

[15] Even constant rates of tariffs along a processing chain provide protection to processing, at the rate of those tariffs. Thus, in order to avoid effective protection of processing activities, tariffs would actually need to de-escalate along processing chains. See Tangermann (1989).

[16] The Swiss formula is $y = 100 - (100a)/(a + x)$, where y is the percentage tariff reduction, x is the original *ad valorem* (equivalent of the) tariff rate, and a is an agreed-upon number determining the average size of tariff reductions. In the Tokyo Round, a was set at 14. See Senti (1986, p. 85). For results which would have been obtained had that formula been used for agricultural tariff cuts in the Uruguay Round, see Tangermann (1995).

similarly to quantitative trade barriers. Governments get heavily involved in trade as they are allocating licenses under TRQs. Major monetary gains may be derived from such licenses. Where the difference between the domestic price and the world price exceeds the within-quota tariff, a quota rent accrues to the holder of the license. In these cases, interest in obtaining licenses is high among the agents concerned, and some form of allocation mechanism has to be established. The mechanism used has direct implications for the income distribution resulting from quota rents, but it may also affect trade flows. For example, in some cases, administration of TRQs is left to parties directly interested in the outcome, with the expected questionable results for quota fill.[17] Many TRQs are administered openly or silently on a bilateral basis, thereby undermining the MFN principle. On the other hand, in many cases TRQ commitments were the only tangible improvement of market access achieved in the Uruguay Round. For the next round of negotiations, the objective should be to preserve the trade expansion features of this instrument, and to minimize its trade-distorting effects.

The trade-expanding features of the TRQs which have resulted from minimum access provisions can be preserved if the respective quantities are further increased. At the same time, it could be agreed that the lower within-quota tariffs must not exceed a given percentage of the base tariffs. In the Uruguay Round it was essentially left to countries to decide by how much they wanted to reduce their "normal" tariffs within minimum-access TRQs. As a result, the ratio between within-quota and above-quota tariffs now differs very much from case to case [for some evidence, see Tangermann (1996)]. In the longer run, the issue of TRQs could gradually fade away as "normal" (i.e., above-quota) tariffs are reduced more and more and the gap between within-quota and above-quota tariffs is reduced and finally eliminated.

Minimization of the trade-distorting implications of TRQs requires that transparent and impartial methods are used to allocate import licenses. Indeed, there is one clear and simple, neutral approach – the auctioning of licenses. The advantages of auctioning import quotas have been discussed in detail by Bergsten et al. (1987), who also suggest approaches to overcoming potential drawbacks of this approach. Some countries (for example, Iceland, Korea, and Norway) have already begun to auction some of their agricultural TRQs after the Uruguay Round. However, exporting countries have raised doubts as to whether the resulting auctioning fees do not constitute (GATT illegal) extra duties, over and above the bound tariffs. Economic reasoning clearly suggests that auctioning fees do not add to the costs of imports. In an auction, an importer would not offer (and pay) fees that are higher than the rent he can expect to gain from the import activity concerned. For the exporter, it is irrelevant whether a rent flows to the importing company or an equivalent fee is paid to the government of the importing country. As a corollary, fees paid in an auction do not reduce the volume of trade and do not impair incentives to use quotas fully.

---

[17] For example, licenses for butter imports may be given to processors (rather than retailers); licenses for broiler chicks may be given to domestic hatcheries, in proportion to the number of chicks hatched in the preceding year.

As a matter of fact, under an auctioning system there is competition among trading companies, and the most efficient company will get access to the licenses. That company, being efficient, is also likely to pay the exporter the highest possible price. This price may well turn out to be higher than the price paid by an inefficient trading company which received a license just because it used to be in the business in the past, or because it was the first to apply for licenses, or because it had particularly good relations with the agency responsible for allocating a license. Moreover, as an auctioning system fosters competition, the most competitive exporting country is bound to get the best access to the market of the importing country concerned. This is exactly what the MFN principle requires. Hence, the requirement to implement quantitative government measures such that the MFN principle is honored, as laid down in GATT Article XIII, is best (if not only) met if licenses are auctioned. Competition as fostered through auctions also means that trading companies cannot simply rely on past performance. Sometimes it is argued that this can disrupt established trading relations among companies and countries [Bergsten et al. (1987)], and some exporting countries have taken this as an argument against auctioning (and in favor of quota allocation on the basis of past performance). However, an auctioning system need not disrupt established trade relations because provisions can be introduced which allow for "correcting" the immediate outcome of an auction. In particular, licenses can be made tradable after auctions. Moreover, exporters' rights could be improved by giving them full access to auctions.

Another objection occasionally raised against auctioning is that individual importing companies can try to buy up all licenses and then monopolize the import market. Monopoly rents may be earned by "short shipping" the product concerned by not actually using the whole amount of licenses. (This also allows the monopolist to outbid other participants in the auction.) If this were to occur, it would disadvantage not only domestic consumers in the importing country, but also the other exporters concerned. However, antitrust provisions could be used to mitigate this threat, and specific regulations (such as "use-it-or-lose-it" requirements) can also be introduced [see Bergsten et al. (1987, pp. 53–54)].

It would, therefore, be advisable to agree generally in the WTO that auctioning is an appropriate (if not the only appropriate) approach to the administration of TRQ. Possible legal concerns regarding the consistency of license auctioning with various GATT provisions [see Bergsten et al. (1987, pp. 125–133)] should be openly discussed, and if necessary, the legal framework should be adjusted such that auctions can replace the many questionable approaches which are so far being used to allocate TRQ licenses.

6. Conclusions

This chapter has looked at the history, results, and analysis of international negotiations on agricultural trade, with an emphasis on the GATT and in particular on the Uruguay Round. For a long time, international negotiations as pursued in the framework of the GATT had done little to discipline national agricultural policies or liberalize agricultural trade. Moreover, because of the predominance of protectionist tendencies in so many countries, the international rules for agricultural trade as embedded in the GATT were formulated such that they remained largely ineffective. The Uruguay Round can be described as the first serious attempt to overcome this situation. New and more stringent disciplines have been established for market access, export competition, and domestic support in agriculture. This chapter has looked into the issues dealt with in each of these three areas covered in the Uruguay Round negotiations, and highlighted their specific characteristics. It concludes that progress has been made, but also that the effects on national policies and the liberalization of agricultural trade achieved remain limited for the time being. Much unfinished business remains in the area of international negotiations on agricultural trade.

Agricultural economics has made important contributions towards analysis of issues that have plagued agricultural trade for a long time. This chapter has highlighted these contributions. Academic analysis has helped negotiators to better understand the implications of policies and the potential effects of alternative negotiating approaches. Much progress has been made in this regard too. Some of the solutions adopted in the Uruguay Round directly reflect the results of research done by agricultural economists over the years. However, this chapter also concludes that there is much to do in the analysis of international trade issues in agriculture. For example, further progress is needed in the design of distortion measures and in the quantitative analysis of the trade impacts of policy changes as agreed at the international level.

The next round of WTO talks will provide an opportunity to settle some of the unfinished business, and to make further progress towards international agricultural policy reform. However, it will probably require a number of further negotiating rounds before agricultural trade is truly liberalized. In agricultural economics, major efforts are required to keep up with the growing demand for sound analytical results that can foster and underpin these negotiations.

Acknowledgements

We thank Bruce Gardner, three reviewers, and Daniel Hallstrom for helpful comments and assistance.

References

Abbott, P.C., P.L. Paarlberg and J.A. Sharples (1987), "Targeted agricultural export subsidies and social welfare", American Journal of Agricultural Economics 69:723–732.

Abbott, P.C., and L.M. Young (1997), "Wheat importing state trading enterprises: impacts on world wheat market", Paper presented to the International Agricultural Trade Research Consortium Annual Meeting, San Diego, December 15–16, 1997.

Ackerman, K.Z., and M.E. Smith (1990), "Agricultural export programs", Staff Report No. AGES 9033 (USDA/ERS, Washington, DC).

Ackerman, K.Z., M.E. Smith and N.R. Suarez (1995), "Agricultural export programs: background to the 1995 farm legislation", Agricultural Economic Report No. 716 (U.S. Department of Agriculture, Washington, DC).

Alston, J.M., C.A. Carter, R. Gray and D.A. Sumner (1997), "Third country effects and second-best trade policies: export subsidies and bilateral liberalization", American Journal of Agricultural Economics 79:1300–1310.

Alston, J.M., C.A. Carter and V.H. Smith (1993), "Rationalizing agricultural export subsidies", American Journal of Agricultural Economics 75:1000–1009.

Alston, J.M., and R.S. Gray (1998), "Export subsidies and state trading: theory and application to Canadian wheat", in: A. Schmitz, ed., Proceedings of the Conference on World Agricultural Trade: Implications for Turkey, Ankara, Turkey, September 18–20, 1997.

Alston, J.M., R.S. Gray and D.A. Sumner (1994), "The wheat war of 1994", Canadian Journal of Agricultural Economics 42:231–251.

Alston, J.M., and B.H. Hurd (1990), "Some neglected social costs of government spending in farm programs", American Journal of Agricultural Economics 72:149–156.

Anania, G., M. Bohman and C. Carter (1992), "United States export subsidies in wheat: strategic trade policy or expensive beggar-thy-neighbor tactic", American Journal of Agricultural Economics 74:534–545.

Anderson, J.E. (1997), "The Uruguay Round and welfare in some distorted agricultural economies", Journal of Development Economics 56:393–410.

Anderson, J.E., G.J. Bannister and J.P. Neary (1995), "Domestic distortions and international trade", International Economic Review 36:139–156.

Anderson, J.E., and P.J. Neary (1992), "Trade reform with quotas, partial rent retention and tariffs", Econometrica 60:57–66.

Anderson, J.E., and P.J. Neary (1994), "Measuring restrictiveness of trade policy", World Bank Economic Review 8:151–170.

Anderson, J.E., and P.J. Neary (1996), "Measuring restrictiveness of trade policy", Review of Economic Studies 63:107–125.

Anderson, K., and Y. Hayami (1986), The Political Economy of Agricultural Protection: East Asia in International Perspective (Allen and Unwin, London).

Anderson, K., and R. Tyers (1993), "More on welfare gains to developing countries from liberalizing world food trade", Journal of Agricultural Economics 44:198–204.

Antle, J.M., C.C. Crissman, R.J. Wagenet and J.L. Hutson (1996), "Empirical foundations for environmental–trade linkages: implications of an Andean study", in: M.E. Bredahl, N. Ballenger, J.C. Dunmore and T.L. Roe, eds., Agriculture, Trade, and the Environment: Discovering and Measuring the Critical Linkages (Westview Press, Boulder, CO) 173–197.

Barichello, R.R. (1995), "Overview of Canadian agricultural policy systems", in: R.M.A. Loyns, R. Knutson and K. Meilke, eds., Understanding Canada/United States Grain Disputes (University of Manitoba) 37–60.

Benedict, M.R., and O. Stine (1956), The Agricultural Commodity Programs: Two Decades of Experience (Twentieth Century Fund, New York).

Bergsten, C.F. (1997), "Open regionalism", APEC Working Paper 97-3 (Institute of International Economics, Washington, DC).

Bergsten, C.F., K.A. Elliott, J.J. Schott and W.E. Takacs (1987), Auction Quotas and United States Trade Policy, Policy Analyses in International Economics No. 19 (Institute of International Economics, Washington, DC).

Bhagwati, J. (1970), "On the equivalence of tariffs and quotas", in: Trade, Tariffs, and Growth; Essays in International Economics (MIT Press, Cambridge, MA) 248–265.

Buckwell, A. (1997), "If … agricultural economics in a brave liberal world", European Review of Agricultural Economics 24:339–358.

Coleman, W.D., and S. Tangermann (1997), "Linked games, international mediators and agricultural trade", Paper presented to the Theme Day of the International Agricultural Trade Research Consortium, San Diego, December 14, 1997.

Corden, W.M. (1971), The Theory of Protection (Oxford University Press, Oxford).

Cordeu, J.L., A. Valdés and F. Silva (eds.) (1997), "Implementing the Uruguay Round agreement in Latin America: the case of agriculture", FAO/World Bank Workshop (FAO Regional Office for Latin America and the Caribbean, Santiago, Chile).

Croome, J. (1995), Reshaping the World Trade System: A History of the Uruguay Round (World Trade Organization, Geneva).

Curzon, G. (1965), Multilateral Commercial Diplomacy: The General Agreement on Tariffs and Trade and Its Impact on National Commercial Policies and Techniques (Joseph, London).

Dam, K.W. (1970), The GATT – Law and International Economic Organization (University of Chicago Press, Chicago, IL).

Davey, W.J. (1993), "The rules for agricultural trade in GATT", in: M. Honma, A. Shimizu and H. Funatsu, eds., GATT and Trade Liberalization in Agriculture (Otaru University of Commerce, Otaru, Japan).

de Gorter, H., and K.D. Meilke (1987), "The EEC's wheat price policies and international trade in differentiated products", American Journal of Agricultural Economics 69:223–229.

Dixit, P.M. (1996), "State trading enterprises: will it be the next big issue in the WTO?", Paper presented at the Agricultural Trade Policy Workshop, Taipei, Taiwan, June 3–4, 1996.

Dixit, P.M., and T. Josling (1997), "State trading in agriculture: an analytical framework", Working Paper No. 97-4 (International Agricultural Trade Research Consortium).

Draaisma, T., and L. Fulponi (1996), "Measuring the aggregate trade effects of the change in domestic policies: an application of the trade restrictiveness index", Paper presented at the VII Meeting of the European Agricultural Economic Association, Edinburgh.

Dutton, J. (1990), "Targeted export subsidies as an exercise of monopoly power", Canadian Journal of Economics 23:705–710.

FAO (1973), "Agricultural protection: domestic policy and international trade", Document C 73/LIM/9 (FAO, Rome).

FAO (1975), "Agricultural protection and stabilisation policies: a framework for measurement in the context of agricultural adjustment", Document C 75/LIM/2 (FAO, Rome).

FAO (1995), "Impact of the Uruguay Round on agriculture" and "Impact of the Uruguay Round on agriculture: methodological approach and assumptions", Document ESC/M/95/1 (FAO, Rome).

Francois, J.F., B. McDonald and H. Nordstrom (1995), "Assessing the Uruguay Round", in: W. Martin and L.A. Winters, eds., The Uruguay Round and the Developing Economies, The World Bank Discussion Paper No. 307 (The World Bank, Washington, DC) 117–214.

Gardiner, W.H., and C.A. Carter (1988), "Issues associated with elasticities in international agricultural trade", in: C.A. Carter and W.H. Gardiner, eds., Elasticities in International Agricultural Trade (Westview Press, Boulder, CO) Chapter 1, 1–16.

Gardner, B.L. (1983), "Efficient redistribution through commodity markets", American Journal of Agricultural Economics 65:225–234.

Gardner, B.L. (1989), "Recent studies of agricultural trade liberalization", in: A. Maunder and A. Valdés, eds., Agriculture and Government in an Interdependent World (Dartmouth Publishing, Andershot, England) 361–371.

Gardner, B.L. (1996), "The political economy of U.S. export subsidies for wheat", in: A. Krueger, ed., The Political Economy of American Trade Policy (University of Chicago Press, Chicago, IL) 291–331.

GATT (1958), Trends in International Trade. A Report by a Panel of Experts (Haberler Report) (GATT, Geneva).

GATT (1989), "Trade negotiations committee: mid term meeting", MTN.TNC/11, April 21.

GATT Secretariat (1993), "An analysis of the proposed Uruguay Round agreement, with particular emphasis on aspects of interest to developing countries", Document MTN.TNC/W/122, MTN.GNG/W/30 (Geneva).

Gerken, A. (1997), Die Außenhandelspolitik der Europäischen Union bei landwirtschaftlichen Verarbeitungs-produkten. Ausgestaltung, Auswirkungen und Anpassungen an die GATT-Bestimmungen (Vauk Verlag, Kiel).

Goldberg, P.K., and M.M. Knetter (1997), "Causes and consequences of the export enhancement program for wheat", in: R.C. Feenstra, ed., The Effects of U.S. Trade Protection and Promotion Programs (University of Chicago Press, Chicago, IL) 273–296.

Goldin, I., and D. van der Mensbrugghe (1995), "The Uruguay Round: an assessment of economy-wide and agricultural reforms", in: W. Martin and L.A. Winters, eds., The Uruguay Round and the Developing Economies, The World Bank Discussion Paper No. 307 (The World Bank, Washington, DC) 25–52.

Hanson, K., S. Vogel and S. Robinson (1995), "Sectoral and economywide impacts of eliminating the export enhancement program", Staff Paper No. AGES-9929 (Rural Economy Division, Economic Research Service, USDA).

Harrison, G., T. Rutherford and D. Tarr (1995), "Quantifying the Uruguay Round", in: W. Martin and L.A. Winters, eds., The Uruguay Round and the Developing Economies, The World Bank Discussion Paper No. 307 (The World Bank, Washington, DC).

Hathaway, D.E. (1987), Agriculture and the GATT: Rewriting the Rules, Policy Analyses in International Economics No. 20 (Institute for International Economics, Washington, DC).

Hathaway, D.E., and M.D. Ingco (1995), "Agricultural liberalization and the Uruguay Round", Paper presented at the World Bank Conference on The Uruguay Round and the Developing Economies, Washington, January 26–27, 1995.

Hauser, H., and K.-U. Schanz (1995), Das neue GATT. Die Welthandelsordnung nach Abschluß der Uruguay-Runde (Oldenbourg, Munich).

Hazledine, T., and T.D. MacDonald (1992), "A critique of computable general equilibrium models for trade policy analysis", IATRC Working Paper #92-4.

Helmar, M.D., W.H. Meyers and D.J. Hayes (1994), "GATT and CAP reform: different, similar, or redundant?", in: G. Anania, C. Carter and A. McCalla, eds., Agricultural Trade Conflicts and the GATT: New Dimensions in U.S.–European Agricultural Trade Relations (Westview Press, Oxford) 313–339.

Helmar, M.D., V. Premakumar, K. Oerter, J. Kruse, D.B. Smith and W.H. Meyers (1994), "Impacts of the Uruguay Round on agricultural commodity markets", GATT Research Paper 94-GATT 21 (Center for Agricultural and Rural Development, Iowa State University).

Hertel, T.W. (1992), "Partial vs. general equilibrium analysis of trade policy reform", The Journal of Agricultural Economics Research 44(3):3–15.

Hertel, T.W. (2002), "Applied general equilibrium analysis of agricultural policies", in: B.L. Gardner and G.C. Rausser, eds., Handbook of Agricultural Economics, Vol. 2 (Elsevier, Amsterdam) 1379–1419.

Hillman, J.S. (1997), "Non-tariff agricultural trade barriers revisited", in: D. Orden and D. Roberts, eds., Understanding Technical Barriers to Agricultural Trade (International Agricultural Trade Research Consortium, Department of Applied Economics, University of Minnesota, St. Paul, MN) 1–32.

Honma, M., and Y. Hayami (1986), "The structure of agricultural protection in industrial countries", Journal of International Economics 20(1/2):115–129.

Hudec, R.E. (1975), The GATT Legal System and World Trade Diplomacy (Praeger, New York).

Hudec, R.E. (1993), Enforcing International Trade Law: The Evolution of the Modern GATT Legal System (Butterworth Legal Publishers, Salem, NH).

Hudec, R.E. (1997), "Does the agreement on agriculture work? Agricultural disputes after the Uruguay Round", Paper presented to the Theme Day of the International Agricultural Trade Research Consortium, San Diego, December 14, 1997.

Ingco, M.D. (1995), "Agricultural trade liberalization in the Uruguay Round – one step forward, one step back?", Policy Research Working Paper #1500 (The World Bank, Washington, DC).

Ingco, M.D., and D.E. Hathaway (1996), "Implementation of the Uruguay Round commitments in agriculture: issues and practice", Paper for the Roundtable Discussion of the Uruguay Round Agreement on Agriculture, "Rural Well-Being: From Vision to Action" (The World Bank, Washington, DC).

Ingersent, K.A., A.J. Rayner and R.C. Hine (eds.) (1994), Agriculture in the Uruguay Round (Macmillan, London).

International Agricultural Trade Research Consortium (1990), "Bringing agriculture into the GATT: potential use of an aggregate measure of support", Commissioned Paper No. 5 (University of Missouri).

Jackson, J.H. (1969), World Trade and the Law of GATT (The Michie Company, Charlottesville, VA).

Johnson, D.G. (1950), Trade and Agriculture: A Study of Inconsistent Policies (John Wiley & Sons, New York).

Johnson, D.G. (1991), World Agriculture in Disarray, 2nd edn. (Macmillan, London).

Josling, T. (1993), "Agriculture in a world of trading blocs", Australian Journal of Agricultural Economics 37(3):155–179.

Josling, T. (1996a), "Emerging issues for the 1999 round: options for agricultural policy reform", Paper presented to the Fourth World Bank Conference on Environmentally Sustainable Development: Rural Well-Being – From Vision to Action, Washington, DC, September 25–27, 1996.

Josling, T. (1996b), "The WTO, the Uruguay Round and state trading in agricultural products", Paper presented to the International Agricultural Trade Research Consortium Annual Meeting, Washington, DC, December 15, 1996.

Josling, T. (1997). Agricultural Trade Policy: Completing the Reform (Institute for International Economics, Washington, DC).

Josling, T.E., M. Honma, J. Lee, D. MacLaren, B. Miner, D.A. Sumner, S. Tangermann and A. Valdés (1994), "The Uruguay Round agreement on agriculture: an evaluation", Commissioned Paper No. 9 (International Agricultural Trade Research Consortium, St. Paul, MN).

Josling, T., and S. Tangermann (1989), "Measuring levels of protection in agriculture: a survey of approaches and result", in: A. Maunder and A. Valdés, eds., Agriculture and Governments in an Interdependent World, Proceedings of the XX International Conference of Agricultural Economists (Dartmouth, Aldershot, England) 343–360.

Josling, T.E., S. Tangermann and T.K. Warley (1996), Agriculture in the GATT (Macmillan, Houndmills).

Just, R.E., G.C. Rausser and D. Zilberman (1995), "Modeling policy reform in the U.S. wheat and feed grain sectors", in: G.C. Rausser, ed., GATT Negotiations and the Political Economy of Policy Reform (Springer-Verlag, Berlin) Chapter 8, 175–252.

Kilkenny, M., and S. Robinson (1990), "Computable general equilibrium analysis of agricultural liberalization: factor mobility and macro closure", Journal of Policy Modeling 12(3):527–556.

Kindleberger, C.P. (1986), "International public goods without international government", American Economic Review 76(1):1–13.

Kock, K. (1969), International Trade Policy and the GATT 1947–1967 (Almqvist and Wiksell, Stockholm).

Koester, U., M. Petit, A. Buckwell, T. Josling, L. Mahe, W. Meyers, K. Munk, A. Oskam, G.E. Rossmiller, S. Tangermann, S. Tarditi and K. Thomson (1988), "Disharmonies in EC and US agricultural policy measures", Study prepared for the Commission of the European Communities (EC Commission, Luxembourg).

Konandreas, P., and J. Greenfield (1996), "Uruguay Round commitments on domestic support: their implications for developing countries", Food Policy 21(4&5):433–445.

Laird, S. (1996), "Quantifying commercial policies", Staff Working Paper TPRD-96-001 (Trade Policies Review Division, World Trade Organization, Geneva).

Levy, S., and S. Wijnbergen (1994), "Agriculture in the Mexico–U.S. free trade agreement: a general equilibrium analysis", in: J.F. Francois and C.R. Shells, eds., Modeling Trade Policy: Applied General Equilibrium Assessments of North American Free Trade (Cambridge University Press, Cambridge, MA) 151–195.

Levy, S., and S. Wijnbergen (1995), "Transition problems in economic reform: agriculture in the North American free trade agreement", American Economic Review 85(4):738–754.

Lindland, J. (1997), "The impact of the Uruguay Round on tariff escalation in agricultural products", Food Policy 22(6):487–500.

Martin, W.J. (1997), "Measuring welfare changes with distortions", in: J.F. Francois and K.A. Reinert, eds., Applied Methods for Trade Policy Analysis (Cambridge University Press, Cambridge, MA) 76–94.

McCalla, A.F. (1969), "Protectionism in international agricultural trade, 1850–1968", Agricultural History 43(3):329–344.

McDonald, J., and D.A. Sumner (1998), "The influence of commodity programs on supply response: the case of rice in the United States", Draft paper presented at the Rice Technical Workers Conference, Reno, NV, March.

Miller, G. (1986), The Political Economy of International Agricultural Policy Reform (Department of Primary Industry Australia, Canberra).

Moschini, G., and K.D. Meilke (1992), "Production subsidy and countervailing duty in vertically related markets: the hog-pork case between Canada and the United States", American Journal of Agricultural Economics 74:951–961.

Moyer, H.W., and T. Josling (1990), Agricultural Policy Reform – Politics and Process in the EC and the USA (Harvester Wheatsheaf, New York).

Nelson, F. (1997), "U.S. ag. policy – well below WTO ceilings on domestic support", in: Agricultural Outlook (USDA/ERS).

Organization for Economic Co-operation and Development (1987), National Policies and Agricultural Trade (OECD, Paris).

Organization for Economic Co-operation and Development (1994), The New World Trading System: Readings, OECD Documents (OECD, Paris).

Organization for Economic Co-operation and Development (1995), The Uruguay Round – A Preliminary Evaluation of the Impacts of the Agreement on Agriculture in the OECD countries (OECD, Paris).

Osorio Londoño, N. (1997), "Implementation of the agreement on agriculture and the work of the WTO committee on agriculture", Paper presented to the Theme Day of the International Agricultural Trade Research Consortium, San Diego, December 14, 1997.

Paarlberg, R.L. (1985), "United States agricultural objectives and policy options", in: C.E. Curry, W.P. Nichols and R.B. Purcell, eds., Confrontation or Negotiation: United States Policy and European Agriculture (Associated Faculty Press, Millwood, New York) 227–262.

Powell, M. (1997), "Science in sanitary and phytosanitary dispute resolution", Discussion Paper 97-50 (Resources for the Future, Washington, DC).

Rausser, G.C. (1995), GATT Negotiations and the Political Economy of Policy Reform (Springer-Verlag, Berlin).

Roberts, D. (1997), "Implementation of the WTO agreement on the application of sanitary and phytosanitary measures: the first two years", Paper presented to the Theme Day of the International Agricultural Trade Research Consortium, San Diego, December 14, 1997.

Roberts, D., and D. Orden (1997), "Determinants of technical barriers to trade: the case of US phytosanitary restrictions on Mexican avocados, 1972–1995", in: D. Orden and D. Roberts, eds., Understanding Technical Barriers to Agricultural Trade (International Agricultural Trade Research Consortium, Department of Applied Economics, University of Minnesota, St. Paul, MN) 117–160.

Robinson, S., M.E. Burfisher, R. Hinojosa-Ojeda and K.E. Thierfelder (1993), "Agricultural policies and migration in a U.S.–Mexico free trade area: a computable general equilibrium analysis", Journal of Policy Modeling 15(5&6):673–701.

Roningen, V.O., and P.M. Dixit (1989), "Economic implications of agricultural policy reforms in the industrial market economies", Staff Report AGES 89-36 (Economic Research Service, USDA).

Rosson, C.P., III, C.F. Runge and D.E. Hathaway (1994), "International trade agreements", in: M. Hallberg, R. Spitze and D. Ray, eds., Food, Agriculture and Rural Policy into the Twenty First Century: Issues and Tradeoffs (Westview Press, Boulder, CO) 187–198.

Rucker, R.R., W.N. Thurman and R.B. Borges (1996), "GATT and the peanut market", in: A. Schmitz, G. Coffin and K.A. Rosaasen, eds., Regulation and Protectionism under GATT: Case Studies in North American Agriculture (Westview Press, Boulder, CO) 160–179.

Salvatici, L., C.A. Carter and D.A. Sumner (1997), "The trade restrictiveness index: the potential contribution to agricultural policy analysis", Paper presented at the Conference of the International Association of Agricultural Economists, Sacramento, 1997.

Scandizzo, P.L. (1989), "Measures of protection: methodology, economic interpretation and policy relevance", FAO Economic and Social Development Paper 84 (FAO, Rome).

Schott, J. (1994), The Uruguay Round. An Assessment (Institute for International Economics, Washington, DC).

Senti, R. (1986), GATT – Allgemeines Zoll – und Handelsabkommen als System der Welthandelsordnung (Schulthess Polygraphischer Verlag, Zürich).

Senti, R. (1994), GATT–WTO. Die neue Welthandelsordnung nach der Uruguay-Runde (Institut für Wirtschaftsforschung der ETH Zürich, Zürich).

Sharma, R., P. Konandreas and J. Greenfield (1996), "An overview of assessments of the impact of the Uruguay Round on agricultural prices and incomes", Food Policy 21(4&5):351–363.

Silvis, H.J., and C.P.C.M. van der Hamsvoort (1996), "The AMS in agricultural trade negotiations: a review", Food Policy 21(4&5):527–539.

Smith, M.E., and D.R. Lee (1994), "Overseas food aid programs", in: M. Hallberg et al., eds., Food, Agriculture and Rural Policy into the Twenty First Century: Issues and Tradeoffs (Westview Press, Boulder, CO) 153–166.

Stanton, G.H. (1997), "Implications of the WTO agreement on sanitary and phytosanitary measures", in: D. Orden and D. Roberts, eds., Understanding Technical Barriers to Agricultural Trade (International Agricultural Trade Research Consortium, Department of Applied Economics, University of Minnesota, St. Paul, MN) 75–78.

Sumner, D.A. (1992), "The economic underpinnings of Uruguay Round proposals", in: T. Becker, R. Gray and A. Schmitz, eds., Improving Agricultural Trade Performance under the GATT (Wissenschaftsverlag Vauk, Kiel) 239–250.

Sumner, D.A. (1993), "Economic analysis for better agricultural trade policy", The James N. Snyder Memorial Lecture (Department of Agricultural Economics, Purdue University, West Lafayette, IN).

Sumner, D.A. (1995), Agricultural Trade Policy: Letting Markets Work (American Enterprise Institute Press, Washington, DC).

Sumner, D.A. (1996), "Export subsidy by adjustments in domestic price policy: U.S. dairy schemes after the Uruguay Round", Paper presented at the ASSA meeting, San Francisco, North American Economics and Finance Association Session, "State Trading, Export Subsidies, and Trade Disputes", January 7, 1996.

Sumner, D.A., and D.G. Hallstrom (1997), "Commodity policy compatibility with free trade agreements", in: R. Loyns, R. Knutson, K. Meilke and D.A. Sumner, eds., Harmonization/Convergence/Compatibility in Agriculture and Agri-Food Policy: Canada, United States and Mexico, a Conference Proceedings (University of Manitoba, Winnipeg) 47–61.

Sumner, D.A., and H. Lee (1997), "Sanitary and phytosanitary trade barriers and empirical trade modelling", Understanding Technical Barriers to Agricultural Trade (International Agricultural Trade Research Consortium, St. Paul, MN) 273–285.

Swinbank, A., and C. Tanner (1997), Farm Policy and Trade Conflict: The Uruguay Round and Common Agricultural Policy Reform (The University of Michigan Press, Ann Arbor, MI).

Tangermann, S. (1989), Tariff Escalation in Agricultural Trade, Forum No. 19 (Wissenschaftsverlag Vauk, Kiel).

Tangermann, S. (1995), "Implementation of the Uruguay Round agreement on agriculture by major developed countries", Report prepared for the United Nations Conference on Trade and Development, Document UNCTAD/ITD/16 (UNCTAD, Geneva).

Tangermann, S. (1996), "Implementation of the Uruguay Round agreement on agriculture: issues and prospects", Journal of Agricultural Economics 47:315–337.

Tangermann, S., M. Honma, T. Josling, J. Lee, D. MacLaren, D. McClatchy, B. Miner, G. Pursell, D.A. Sumner and A. Valdés (1997), "Implementation of the Uruguay Round agreement on agriculture and issues for the next round of agricultural negotiations", Commissioned Paper No. 12 (International Agricultural Trade Research Consortium, St. Paul, MN).

Tangermann, S., T. Josling and S.R. Pearson (1987), "Multilateral negotiations on farm support levels", World Economy 10(3):265–281.

Tanner, C. (1996), "Agricultural trade liberalisation and the Uruguay Round", The Australian Journal of Agricultural Economics 40:1–35.

Tracy, M. (1982), Agriculture in Western Europe. Challenge and Response. 1880–1980, 2nd edn. (Granada, London).

Trostle, R.G., K.D. Meilke and L.D. Sanders (1994), "U.S. agricultural trade policy", in: M. Hallberg et al., eds., Food, Agriculture and Rural Policy into the Twenty First Century: Issues and Tradeoffs (Westview Press, Boulder, CO) 199–219.

Tyers, R., and K. Anderson (1986), "Background paper", World Development Report 1986 (World Bank/Oxford University Press, New York) Chapter 6.

Tyers, R., and K. Anderson (1988), "Liberalizing OECD agricultural policies in the Uruguay Round: effects on trade and welfare", Journal of Agricultural Economics 30:197–216.

Tyers, R., and K. Anderson (1992), Disarray in World Food Markets: A Quantitative Assessment (Cambridge University Press, Cambridge, MA).

UNCTAD (1995), "Report on evaluating the outcome of the Uruguay Round agricultural agreement using the agricultural trade policy simulation model", Consultancy Report to ITP by O. Gulbrandsen (Geneva).

United States Congress, House of Representatives (1994), "Uruguay Round agreements act", Bill H.R. 5110.

United States Department of Agriculture, Economic Analysis Staff (1993), Effects of the North American Free Trade Agreement on U.S. Agricultural Commodities.

United States Department of Agriculture, Economic Research Service (1986), "Embargoes, surplus disposal, and U.S agriculture", Agricultural Economic Report No. 564.

United States Department of Agriculture, Economic Research Service (1989), "GATT and agriculture: the concepts of PSEs and CSEs", Miscellaneous Publication No. 1468.

United States Department of Agriculture, Economic Research Service (1991), "Provisions of the food, agriculture, conservation, and trade act of 1990", Information Bulletin No. 624.

United States Department of Agriculture, Economic Research Service (1996), "Provisions of the 1996 farm bill", Agricultural Outlook, Special Supplement, AGO-961.

United States Department of Agriculture, Office of Economics (1992), Preliminary Analysis of the Economic Implications of the Dunkel Text for American Agriculture.

United States Department of Agriculture, Office of Economics (1994), Effects of the Uruguay Round Agreement on U.S. Agricultural Commodities.

United States General Accounting Office (1993), International Trade: Effectiveness of the Market Promotion Program Remains Unclear, GAO/GGD-93-103.

United States General Accounting Office (1994), Wheat Support: The Impact of Target Prices Versus Export Subsidies, GAO/RCED-94-79.

Vahl, R. (1996), "Leadership in disguise: the role of the European Commission in EC decision-making on agriculture in the Uruguay Round", Ph.D. Thesis (Leiden University).

Valdés, A., and A.F. McCalla (1996), "The Uruguay Round and agricultural policies in developing countries and economies in transition", Food Policy 21(4&5):419–431.

van der Hamsvoort, C.P.C.M. (1994), PSE as an Aggregate Measure of Support in the Uruguay Round (Agricultural Economics Research Institute (LEI-DLO), The Hague).

Vanzetti, D., N. Andrews, S. Hester and B.S. Fisher (1994), "US–EC agricultural trade relations and the Uruguay Round: a cairns group perspective", in: G. Anania, C. Carter and A. McCalla, eds., Agricultural Trade Conflicts and the GATT: New Dimensions in U.S.–European Agricultural Trade Relations (Westview Press, Oxford) 341–364.

Vousden, N. (1990), The Economics of Trade Protection (Cambridge University Press, New York).

World Bank (1986), World Development Report 1986 (Oxford University Press, New York).

World Trade Organization (1996), Report of the Committee on Agriculture, adopted on 6 November 1996, WTO Document G/L/131 (WTO, Geneva).

Young, E., and P. Westcott (1996), "The 1996 U.S. farm act increases market orientation", Agriculture Information Bulletin No. 726 (USDA, ERS).

Chapter 39

PUBLIC POLICY: ITS MANY ANALYTICAL DIMENSIONS

GORDON C. RAUSSER

Department of Agricultural and Resource Economics, University of California, Berkeley

RACHAEL E. GOODHUE

Department of Agricultural and Resource Economics, University of California, Davis

Contents

Handbook of Agricultural Economics, Volume 2, Edited by B. Gardner and G. Rausser

1. Introduction

Agricultural policy is a complex web of interventions covering output markets, input markets, trade, public good investments, renewable and exhaustible natural resources, regulation of externalities, education and the marketing and distribution of food products. At the level of the U.S. federal government, these interventions have resulted in enormous budgetary costs; huge surpluses of farm products; major disputes with other countries; distorted international markets; and benefits to special interests that are often highly concentrated. The same programs, however, have been part of a U.S. agricultural sector whose productivity increases over much of the last century have been spectacular.

Do these massive governmental interventions correct for market imperfections, lower transaction costs, effectively regulate externalities and enhance productivity [Rausser (1982)]? Or are these programs the result of manipulation by powerful commodity or agricultural interest groups actively engaged in rent-seeking or directly unproductive activities [Buchanan and Tullock (1962), Krueger (1974), Bhagwati (1982)]?

In the design and implementation of governmental policy in agriculture, conflicts naturally emerge between public and special interests. A conceptual formulation that attempts to explain or prescribe public policy emphasizing only one of these interests is doomed to fail. Frameworks that neglect political forces and the role of special interest groups will have little explanatory power. Models that presume the government has no autonomy nor any interest in the size of the economic pie will also face serious limitations as explanatory, predictive, or prescriptive frameworks [Rausser and Zusman (1992)].

As demonstrated by the six chapters on agricultural policy [Alston and James (2002), Chambers (2002), Innes (2002), de Gorter and Swinnen (2002), Karp and Perloff (2002), Sumner and Tangermann (2002)] *analytical* frameworks typically focus on only one of four dimensions: *incidence, mechanism design, political economy* and *governance structures*. Few attempts have been made to integrate these four critical dimensions. The major theme and fundamental message of this chapter is that only by formally recognizing each of these dimensions is it possible to design and implement public policies that are sustainable and robust to an evolving economy and society.

As the chapters in this section reveal, there is a long and rich history regarding the *incidence* dimension of public policy analysis. Beginning in the 1950s, concrete empirical analyses analyzing policy incidence were widely performed and accepted. Serious theoretical and empirical investigations of *mechanism design* and modern *political economy* began to emerge in the 1970s and early 1980s. If anything, modern political economy analysis preceded professionally recognized studies of the mechanism design analytical dimension. Only very recently, in the 1990s, has some progress been made on the governance structures analytical dimension. This is due, in part, to a number of serious challenges involved in formally analyzing collective decision-making and coalition formation. Accordingly, the adoption rate by professional economists of this particular dimension has been dramatically less rapid than the other analytical dimensions.

The four analytical dimensions can be distinguished in accordance with their *imposed maintained hypotheses*, or assumptions, and the type of *failures* that arise. The incidence analytical dimension focuses on impact of existing policies and/or on the selection among various policy instruments. For this dimension, as revealed in the chapters by Alston and James as well as in Karp and Perloff, perfect implementation (PI), no feedback effects from interest group formation (NF) and a given governance structure (GG) assumptions are imposed. Since the benchmark for any governmental intervention is typically perfectly competitive partial or general market equilibrium, *government failure is a natural consequence*. The business of government is presumed to be only the redistribution of income and wealth. Strategic behavior on the part of agents affected by the policies is typically hidden from view. It is only after the fact of actual policy implementation that strategic behavior on the part of individual agents is formally recognized.

The PI assumption of the incidence analytical dimension is relaxed when we turn to mechanism design. Typically, however, the NF and GG assumptions are maintained. In the chapters by Chambers and Innes, the focus turns to market or institutional failures. Modern economics is used to isolate the consequences of asymmetric information, moral hazard, adverse selection, misalignment of incentives and the structured interpretation of signals. In essence, the analytical dimension has highlighted incentive effects, potential strategic behavior on the part of agents, and the credibility of many commonly proposed public policies.

Modern political economy has come in many shapes and forms. For example, the public choice literature emphasizes *government failure* and the unproductive consequences of rent seeking behavior on the part of interest groups. Social waste occurs and governmental intervention detracts from a Pareto optimum. Regardless, all of these formulations relax the assumption of NF, and typically impose GG. The inherent value of this analytical dimension is that it formally recognizes the groups and agents affected by public policies are not passive and can pursue strategies to influence and alter the selection and incidences of policies. As noted in the chapter by de Gorter and Swinnen, the nature of the failure identified by the positive economic analytical dimension depends on the form and shape of the government intervention. If government intervention occurs as *PESTS* or *Predatory Governmental Intervention* government failures result, and if it comes in the form of *PERTSs* or *Productive Interventions* market failures are emphasized [Rausser (1982, 1992)]. Many political economic frameworks generate a mix of both predatory and productive policies, as discussed in Section 4, in such frameworks the focus is on balancing government with market failures.

For the analytical dimension of constitutional structures, the inherent collective decision making processes of public policy are formally recognized. The governance structures delineate the boundaries on negotiations among stakeholders that take place. In its most general form, this analytical dimension relaxes the restrictive assumptions of PI and NF, as well as GG. This paradigm emphasizes the level and distribution of political power; the distribution of power determines the balance and tradeoffs between public and special interests. The fundamental failure that arises from this analytical dimension is an *organizational* failure. This failure results from a maldistribution of power, inadequate enforcement of economic and political freedoms or an absence of *the rule of law* [Rausser (1992, 1992)]. The resulting constitutional analytical framework is the basis for conceptualizing the bargains and compromises that are undertaken to shape policies that are acceptable, not only to those who have the greatest capacity to obstruct the policy but also to others who have stakes in the outcome. Formally, this analytical dimension evaluates alternative collective choice or constitutional rules that underlie the policy making process, namely (i) who has access to the negotiation process, (ii) how are admissible coalitions formed, (iii) what is the space of issues over which various stakeholders negotiate and (iv) the specification of a default option.

In the balance of this chapter we synthesize and extend the chapters on incidence by Alston and James (Chapter 33) as well as portions of Karp and Perloff (Chapter 37) that pertain to this analytical dimension; the mechanism design chapters of Chambers (Chapter 34) as well as Innes (Chapter 35); the political economic analytical dimension chapter by de Gorter and Swinnen (Chapter 36); and the chapter by Sumner and Tangermann (Chapter 38) that relate to the constitutional structures for international trade agreements. Section 2 focuses on the selection of policy instruments and the dimension of incidence; Section 3 on policy implementation or the mechanism design dimension; Section 4 on the political economy analytical dimension; and finally Section 5 turns to recent advancements in the constitutional structure analytical dimension.

2. Instrument design: The dimension of incidence

Early evaluations of U.S. commodity programs saw the use of partial equilibrium frameworks for policy analysis. Economists evaluated the effect of such tools as acreage restrictions on the price of a commodity using a ceteris paribus, myopic approach. The effect of policies was analyzed in terms of functional groups such as consumers, landowners, farm operators, and taxpayers.

Over time, the analyses became more sophisticated as additional factors affecting program outcomes were identified. For example, the voluntary nature of commodity programs mean that participation was less than complete. Farmers faced a discrete/continuous choice problem: for example, whether to participate in an acreage retirement program, and, once choosing to participate, which acres to retire. Heterogeneity in land quality allowed the least productive acres to be idled, so that the decrease in total production resulting from acreage reductions was smaller than expected. Further, as shown by Rausser, Zilberman and Just (1984), when land and production technologies are heterogeneous and capital markets are imperfect, land diversion programs tend to benefit landowners and harm farm operators. The programs increase the separation of ownership and operation, and increase the concentration of operators.

Policy incidence analysis is based on a number of simplifying assumptions. In the simplest case, discussed in Alston and James, assumptions include static supply and demand, perfect and costless information and policy enforcement, and perfect competition. These assumptions imply that changes in consumer and producer surplus may be used to evaluate changes in welfare due to government policy. In Chapter 33, Alston and James consider some cases where one or more of these restrictions must be relaxed, in order to evaluate a specific policy.

Perhaps the most influential assumption in policy incidence analysis is that markets are perfect in the absence of government intervention; accordingly, imposing government policies creates market distortions. In other words, any introduction of policy is a *government failure*. The perfect markets assumption provides a powerful basis for arguing for free trade and other eliminations of government interventions. However, it neglects to include market power, imperfect information and other market failures that may be mitigated by government policies. Second-best theory demonstrates that removing one policy-induced distortion does not guarantee a welfare improvement in the presence of other distortions. The theory of the second-best applies to most, if not all, empirical policy analyses. Chambers illustrates this concept in his discussion of policy design when agricultural production is risky and a risk-increasing agricultural input produces a negative externality. In this case, if (risk-averse) farmers were not initially insured against production risk, introducing insurance would reduce distortions in their production decisions due to risk aversion, but will increase use of the risky, polluting input, which will lower welfare.

Another gap in the policy incidence literature is the lack of explicit analysis of implementation and enforcement costs, noted by Alston and James. These costs can prove significant, even insurmountable, particularly in developing countries where the necessary infrastructure is often inadequate. Most of the *ex ante* policy incidence literature assumes *perfect implementation* (PI). Under perfect implementation, economic agents respond to government policies by, for example, increasing their production by moving along their supply curve, rather than structurally altering their behavior in response to incentives embedded in the policy design and as a result shifting their supply curve. In addition to these direct costs, some policies are more costly to change than others, due to the resistance of interest groups benefiting from the policy. Most of the policy incidence literature ignores these considerations, implicitly imposing the assumption of *no feedback effects from interest groups* (NF). Alston and James illustrate the importance of this assumption in their discussion of tradable versus nontradeable quotas. While tradable quotas are best from a pure economic efficiency point of view, they may prove to be more costly to remove or adjust than nontradeable quotas due to greater resistance from quota holders. More generally, the policy incidence literature evaluates only the economic desirability of policies. Underlying political-economic considerations are not included in the evaluation. Furthermore, policy incidence analysis imposes a given *governance structure* (GG). Interactions between which interest groups have access to the policymaking process and the resulting selection of policy instruments are not considered. This omission limits the usefulness of policy incidence analysis to understand the selection of particular policy instruments.

The essential insights and problems associated with using partial equilibrium frameworks for commodity program analysis can be seen in the analysis by Floyd (1965): the incidence of agricultural policies which seek to increase farm-level prices depends on the exact nature of the instruments used, and on the relative supply elasticities of the different factors of production. Floyd emphasized another important point: A common goal of agricultural policies in developed nations is to increase farmers' incomes. In some cases, the functional distribution of income may not clearly reflect the distributional impacts on the target group. If farmers do not own a factor of production, they will not obtain the returns accruing to it. This has a dynamic implication: to the extent that a farm program increases returns to land, which has a relatively inelastic supply, it will provide current landowners with a windfall gain, while increasing the price of this factor of production for all future entrants.

Floyd's analysis considered two competitively supplied inputs, land and labor. He found that land values will increase by at least as much under an output quota tied to land as under a price support achieving the same output price with no restrictions on output. Further, land values increase less when a quota is placed on land (to achieve the same output price) than under a price support with no restrictions. Under reasonable restrictions on parameter values, returns to labor increase less under an acreage reduction program than under the other two policy alternatives.

Floyd's interpretation of his results was that landowners and current farmers benefited from the federal farm programs at the expense of tenants and prospective entrants. While the observation is not incorrect, it does not explain the historical bias toward acreage reduction policies for major crops in the federal farm programs. Generally, incidence analysis cannot explain the factors motivating policy design and implementation choices.[1]

While a partial equilibrium approach does yield important insights, it ignores the effects of a policy on other markets. Intermarket effects are important in agriculture, where products may be substitutes in production, substitutes in consumption, or inputs into other products. Brandow's (1961) pioneering work "Interrelations among demand for farm products and implications for control of market supply", empirically introduced the concept of relevant markets to the analysis of agricultural policy. Brandow estimated the extent to which substitutability among food products and increasing elasticities along the agrofood chain makes farm-level incomes extremely sensitive to small changes in retail-level demand. Without understanding the relevant markets, it is impossible to evaluate policies accurately.

---

[1] Any ahistorical analysis of a policy program is by definition incomplete. Major commodity programs have evolved over time, often in response to unanticipated producer responses to program provisions. For example, unexpectedly high output levels in response to per unit subsidies led to program modifications that limited the amount of output eligible for subsidization. Recognizing this incompleteness, we focus our attention on questions of policy implementation rather than design.

Since Brandow, many of the debates in agricultural policy analysis have been centered around appropriately defining the scope of analysis and its relevance for the identified question. Often, the debate is over the measurement of the relevant policy parameter(s), such as the elasticity of residual demand (Karp and Perloff, Alston and James). On the supply side, elasticities of substitution among factors and the importance of different factors in production affect policy incidence, as do elasticities of factor supply. In Volume 1 of this Handbook, Mundlak (2001) addresses agricultural production and supply. The empirical problems and concerns he elucidates must be addressed when undertaking any policy incidence analysis.

3. Policy implementation: The mechanism design dimension

The policy incidence literature largely views agriculture as a passive recipient of policy instruments. This view was reflected in the design of agricultural policy instruments such as target prices and the use of historical yields as a basis for payments. Alston and James identify the consequences of "cheating", as producers respond to the incentives embedded in policies, as an area where further research is essential. As the Lucas critique predicts, farmers' responses to government programs intended to control production and support prices dampened the desired effects on production and prices. This "slippage", which occurred in a number of forms, illustrated the importance of incentive compatibility. As we previously noted, when faced with acreage retirement programs, farmers retired their least productive land. When acreage retirements were combined with output price supports, farmers increased their use of variable inputs per acre. These decisions meant that a less than proportionate decrease in output occurred as a result of the retirement program.

Literature emphasizing the mechanism design of policy analysis explicitly recognizes the possibility of market failure, unlike much of the incidence analysis literature. In Chapter 35, Innes explores the design of government policies intended to correct market failures. Nonetheless, the possibility of government failure still exists; a policy may be implemented in an inefficient manner. Institutions, if incorrectly designed, may fail as part of the implementation process. The most important contribution of the mechanism design approach to the policy analysis literature has been its relaxation of the PI assumption. When this assumption is relaxed, the ordering of policy instruments obtained from simple incidence analysis often change. In order to relax this assumption and ensure analytical tractability, however, the literature has made a number of other simplifying assumptions, which in some cases may limit the usefulness of the resulting analysis.

3.1. Conceptual and empirical issues

Concepts including asymmetric information, incentive compatibility and participation constraints allow economists to conduct policy analyses that allow farmers to actively respond to the incentives embodied in specific policy regimes. Asymmetric information problems are commonly divided into problems of hidden actions, and hidden information [Salanie (1997)]. Hidden action problems are also known as moral hazard problems. Hidden information problems may be divided into two types: adverse selection problems, and signaling problems.

In a moral hazard problem, the actions of one player, known as the agent, affect the payoffs to another player, the principal. If it is not in the agent's self-interest to act in the manner that maximizes the principal's payoff, the principal must design an incentive contract that will induce the agent to do so. Commonly, the second-best solution to this sort of information problem involves a tradeoff between inducing the profit-maximizing amount of effort and another consideration, such as insuring a risk averse agent against income risk. In the absence of moral hazard, or the first-best solution, the agent would be fully insured.

There are two types of hidden information problems. In a signaling problem, the informed player moves first. In an adverse selection problem, the uninformed player moves first. In a two-type signaling problem, the second-best solution generally involves the higher quality, lower cost, or otherwise superior type incurring additional costs *relative to the costs he would incur in the first-best solution* in order to distinguish himself from the inferior type. For the typical theoretical constructs, the inferior types cannot afford to sustain these costs.

In a two-type adverse selection problem, the second-best solution generally involves the uninformed party adjusting the inferior type's contract requirement relative to the first-best case. The level of the effort or production specified in the contract is adjusted downward, in order to reduce the information rents obtained by the high ability type. In this type of problem, the superior agent type produces his first-best output, and receives information rents. The inferior agent produces less than his first-best output, and receives his reservation utility.

Of course, many real world problems involve more than one information asymmetry, which complicates the modeling process. Further, many problems involve repeated interactions between the same set of two or more players. Repetition may reduce the importance of initial information asymmetries, or, at a minimum, will complicate players' strategies. To date, increasingly complex theoretical asymmetric information models have not translated into an increase in well-articulated, testable hypotheses. In fact, the paucity of testable hypotheses is, to date, one of the greatest shortcomings of the mechanism design literature. In many cases, findings are driven by assumptions regarding government preferences. To draw conclusions regarding the form of government preferences by consistency between observed programs and policy designs generated by specific preferences ignores the historical, political-economic processes underlying all existing programs.

To some extent, it may be argued that this failing is less important in this context than in other economic contexts, since one value of the mechanism design approach lies in ex ante policy analysis. Provided policy is correctly designed and implemented, the insights of ex ante modeling can be effectively validated by the effectiveness of executed policy. Prescriptive policy analysis, properly approached, is the most challenging type of policy analysis, with the largest scope for errors. More basic levels of policy analysis include descriptive analysis, which simply addresses existing policies and institutions; explanatory analysis, which develops explanations consistent with existing policies and institutions; and predictive analysis, which predicts policy outcomes given existing institutions [Rausser and Just (1982)].

To what extent should economists rely on prescriptions based on mechanism design, a theoretical approach that has been relatively unsuccessful in providing testable predictions? Second, what is the price of being wrong? If policy prescriptions are based on an incorrect assessment of the underlying problems, how socially inefficient will the resulting policies be? Economists have paid some attention to these concerns. For example, James (2000) focuses on the costs of policies that assume a homogeneous product when the product is actually heterogeneous. Much more of this type of analysis should be undertaken in a variety of policy contexts.

3.2. Key insights

In spite of its shortcomings, mechanism design analysis has proved to be valuable for investigating agricultural policies. In particular, it highlights the effects of many commonly proposed agricultural policies, such as food subsidies via vouchers, agricultural land control programs, and the decoupling of farm production from farm program payments. For voucher programs, determining which individuals are eligible for subsidies can prove to be extremely costly, to the extent that a uniform price subsidy may be a more desirable policy option (Innes). Two chapters in this section of the Handbook, the Chambers chapter on the design of agricultural policy and the Innes chapter on market failures and policy, focus on designing and evaluating food and agricultural policy in the presence of asymmetric information when the uninformed party moves first. The policymaker or government, referred to as the principal, wishes to optimize her objective function, such as maximizing social welfare. The level achieved, however, is conditional on information known only to other economic actors, referred to as agents. The existence of this asymmetric information, commonly an action taken by the agent (moral hazard) or information known only to the agent (adverse selection) makes it costlier for the policymaker to achieve a given objective, such as a target price.

This framework may be used as a means of linking and interpreting existing mechanism design analyses of agricultural policy. Chambers uses a model with two farmer types, and interprets three standard game-theoretic outcomes in terms of the government's relative policy preferences. He allows for the possibility of policies that encourage overproduction. (He maintains policy comparability by assuming output demand is perfectly elastic.) When the government weights transfers to low cost farmers more heavily than the budget, which in turn it weights more heavily than transfers to high cost farmers, it adopts policies which result in overproduction by all farmers. This outcome corresponds to the standard signaling game equilibrium. When the government weights the budget more heavily than transfers to low cost farmers, the standard adverse selection solution results. This solution minimizes rents obtained by the low cost farmers. When the government weights transfers to low cost farmers and the budget equally, then the policy outcome corresponds to the perfect information equilibrium output levels. Since the government is indifferent between paying and not paying information rents to low cost farmers, it chooses the policy instruments that results in the first best production level by low cost and high cost farmers. He generalizes this approach in Chapter 34.

For the analysis of food vouchers developed in Chapter 35 by Innes, a major finding was that if it is sufficiently costly to determine voucher eligibility it may be more desirable to implement a uniform food price subsidy in order to help the poor. In that case, the cost of determining eligibility was a monitoring cost, rather than the information rents agents must be paid in order to truthfully reveal their type. Converting this finding into the context of the simple model developed above, if the cost difference between efficient and inefficient farmers is sufficiently large (given their relative shares of the population), then it will be less costly for the government to implement a price support than an output restriction. In some modeling frameworks, this cost difference would be reflected in the probabilities of high and low output for each effort level for farmers of each type.

Lewis, Ware and Feenstra (1989) evaluate the optimal design of policies intended to eliminate price supports. In addition to information constraints, they include a political feasibility constraint. This constraint requires that a specified share of the affected industry members must approve the policy change. The political feasibility constraint may be interpreted as a weaker version of a participation constraint, which requires all industry members to obtain their reservation utility.

Johnson (1998) examines the complementarity of mechanism design and more general game theoretic approaches to the design and evaluation of agricultural policies. Mechanism design is a useful tool for normative analysis, since it allows the evaluation of the effects of the principal altering parameters facing the agent. Game theory facilitates the analysis of strategic interactions among players, given the parameters that they face. Johnson discusses potential applications, including university research policies, the incentives for mergers among biotechnology firms, and market timing and policy consistency in commodity market interventions.

In this Handbook, Chambers develops the use of hidden action models for analyzing the agricultural insurance problem. He demonstrates that it is the combination of hidden actions by producers with unobservable states of nature that results in the failure of multi-peril crop insurance. Better observability of the relevant states of nature, even in conjunction with hidden actions by producers, results in the relative success of hail insurance and other single-peril insurance.

3.3. Modeling participation

Private agents' rational expectations are explicitly recognized in the mechanism design literature. For U.S. agricultural policy, perhaps the most important constraint this imposes is that the analysis must recognize that farmer participation is voluntary. Farmers must benefit from joining the program and meeting its requirements.[2] We illustrate the importance of this constraint using a simple sector model in Appendix A to this chapter. The government's objective is to minimize its budgetary costs under each policy instrument, while guaranteeing a specified increase in farm income from its equilibrium level. We compare the government's choice of policy variables under a mandatory and a voluntary program for each of three policy instruments: a price support, an output restriction, and a land restriction.[3]

We analyze the effect of the participation constraint on the government's choice of price support, output restriction, and land restriction policy instruments. Simple incidence analysis often assumes implicitly that program participation is *mandatory*: if a policy restricts output in order to increase the market price, the effect on the returns to non-participants is not considered. Such an assumption is implicit, for example, in specifying a participation constraint that requires each producer to receive a positive (or nonnegative) return from the government program. Lewis, Ware and Feenstra (1989) consider a weaker version of a participation constraint in the general form we use in the context of policy reform; in their case, only a majority of producers must receive an equal or higher return under the proposed reform as under the current policy in order for the policy to be implementable.

Our focus here differs from that of much of the existing agricultural policy literature discussed above, which focuses on questions of design and incentive compatibility. We emphasize the impact of participation constraints on implementable policy choices. Even in the absence of producer heterogeneity (adverse selection), and modeling incentive compatibility as simple profit maximization under government program parameters, we demonstrate that the need to induce voluntary participation affects the set of policies achievable by the government. Specifically, we obtain the following three results derived in the Appendix:

RESULT ONE. *The budget cost minimizing voluntary price support policy will be characterized by the same price and output as the budget cost minimizing mandatory price support policy.*

---

[2] Historically, meeting farmers' participation constraints has conflicted with the social objective of transferring income to poor small farmers. Agricultural programs transferred the most benefits to larger farmers, who were better off, since payments were done on a per acre or per unit output basis. In order to limit the socially undesirable transfers to relatively prosperous farmers, policymakers enacted total payment limitations that applied to every farming entity. Of course, farmers responded rationally to this economic incentive, and strategically reconstituted their operations into multiple entities that were legally separable, and thus each eligible for government payments up to the maximum allowed.

[3] We do not consider the efficacy of a simple fixed transfer as a policy option for two reasons. First, it does not minimize direct budgetary costs. In our analysis, a lump sum payment is not optimal in the presence of information problems. Second, as noted previously, history is an essential dimension of any complete policy analysis. In the United States, there has been a tradition of a quid pro quo in the design of agricultural support policies: producers must undertake certain activities in exchange for payments. Arguably, unconditional lump sum payments to agricultural producers have not been *politically feasible*.

RESULT TWO. *The budget cost-minimizing voluntary output quota program results in a smaller decrease in output than does the budget cost minimizing mandatory output quota program for a given farm income objective.*

RESULT THREE. *The budget cost-minimizing voluntary acreage reduction program results in a smaller decrease in acreage and output than does the budget cost minimizing mandatory acreage reduction program for a given farm income objective.*

These results suggest that it is essential to include the voluntary nature of many U.S. farm programs when evaluating their efficacy, since the need to induce participation will affect program provisions. A policy outcome that appears to result in inefficiently high output levels, given the stated farm income goal and fixed transfers, may be due to the need to induce voluntary participation.

3.4. Major implementation lessons

Policy analysis is an iterative process. Economists provide input into policy formation, and evaluate the outcomes of the policy process. The feedback that results is a procedural illustration of an analytical lesson: proper policy design is not enough. The details of implementation are often critical to policy success. As discussed in the Chambers chapter, the mechanism design framework identifies and highlights conditions under which different government policy goals, such as insuring farmers against production risk and reducing non-point source pollution from agricultural chemicals, are mutually reinforcing. The mechanism design framework is most likely to be useful for policy analysis when the government's objective and the set of agents who are eligible to participate are both clearly defined, since these components are exogenous to the analysis.

The realities of policy implementation provide other lessons regarding policy design and analysis. Whenever there are differences between the unit of measurement for the policy goal, and the unit of measurement for the policy tool, socially costly distortions will result. For example, policies intended to protect the welfare of individual producers are often paid on a per acre basis. Payment limitations were enacted in part to reduce the costliness of the distortion due to the difference between the instrument and the goal, as mentioned in footnote 2. Once in place, however, such policies can also be costly to correct. One of the main findings of Lewis, Feenstra and Ware was that complete decoupling of farm program payments from farm production is an excessively costly means of reducing overproduction and government expenditures in a previously supported sector, relative to the second-best solution in the presence of concealed information. Further, the second-best policy reform path is dependent upon the existing composition of the sector in terms of this concealed information so that history matters.

There are many margins for adjusting behavior. Since the 1930s, attempts to address these adjustments have resulted in a piecemeal proliferation of policy instruments.

On the supply side, this includes the land controls and land conservation mentioned earlier, along with production quotas; and on the demand side, it includes export subsidies and enhancements, concessional foreign sales and food grants, and food stamps. Unfortunately, each additional policy instrument brought its own unanticipated side effects, requiring still additional mechanisms. Sometimes the side effects seems so obvious that policy-makers can only have missed them through sheer myopia. For example, the initial voluntary acreage-reduction programs focused on compliance requirements for a particular commodity, neglecting the fact that farmers might substitute and grow other crops like soybeans, rather than corn. In fact, it was sometimes possible for the party that had demanded the original crop to substitute and use the new crop the farmer was growing [Brandow (1961)]. Of course, if too many restrictions on substitute crops are placed on farmers, relative to the payments they receive, they will choose not to participate.

Most frameworks assume that the group of agents affected by the policy is fixed and well-defined. Most analysis assumes that all members of the target population have the same outside option or reservation utility. In actual policymaking situations, this is unlikely. Producers and other economic actors will respond to the incentives present in policies. They will strategically reconstitute themselves and otherwise seek to obtain more rents. In cases where policies were intended to provide rents to a specified interest group, if the policy does not explicitly define group members and prevent entry, then agents can be expected to enter the favored group until the rents from the enacted policy are driven to zero. Historically, one of the major barriers to entry in program crop production had been land bases on which acreage restrictions are imposed.

Two classic examples of agricultural regulations that encouraged agent reconstitutions are the payment limitations for federal commodity programs and acreage limitations for irrigation rights in federal reclamation irrigation projects. Limits on overall payments that could be received by a single farming entity led to the creation of 'Christmas trees' of related farm organizations, generally managed in common but legally owned by different individuals or groups. For example, until the criteria were adjusted, siblings could each collect payments on their own account, and a family corporation that they wholly owned could also collect payments. Similarly, the Reclamation Act of 1902 initially limited single owners to irrigating no more than 160 acres with federal project water. Further, absentee ownership was prohibited, in order to further discourage speculation. Leases and ownership arrangements similar to the commodity program Christmas trees were used successfully to evade this restriction. In 1983, the Reclamation Reform Act attempted to address these abuses by increasing the acreage limit to 960 acres, and placing a total limit on owned and leased land of 2080 acres [Getches (1997)].

A second example of the costliness of limiting distortions regards entry by farming entities. While successful redistribution requires limiting entry, restrictions on entry can, over time, threaten the continued viability of an agricultural sector that has historically been dependent on innovation and entrepreneurship. Hence, the very success of farm programs designed to increase farm incomes explains the need for the introduction of other government programs to assist young farmers through preferential credit and other provisions for new entrants. A third example is entry of new land into the agricultural land base. Government payments increased the profitability of marginal acreage. Sodbuster and swampbuster provisions, that prohibited payments on production from new acres, were implemented in order to prevent producers from responding to this incentive.

Each of these instances illustrates the importance of the historical development of agricultural policy. The lesson for policymakers and analysts is that implementation questions are essential for the evaluation of agricultural policies. The piecemeal historical development of agricultural policy can be characterized by a series of policy corrections necessitated by strategic producer responses to previous policy implementations. These corrections are themselves subject to strategic behavior.

Such examples suggest that the tools of game theory should be brought to bear on the problem of designing "strategy-proof" policies. Strategy-proof policies would be ones that fully recognize and control for distortionary incentives. Due to problems of entry, exit and capitalization, however, no interventionist policy can be truly non-distortionary. Attempts to limit such distortions can themselves be costly: at the most basic level, any attempt to reduce 'gaming' of the policy framework by fixing production patterns reduces the flexibility of the sector to respond to changes in market conditions. However, an appropriate goal may be to focus on reducing the strategic response costs of policies, as well as direct and implementation costs. At a minimum, the mechanism design dimension of agricultural policy analysis demonstrates that the relative desirability of different policy instruments may change when implementation costs and incidence are both used as criteria.

Another concern of policy implementation is the problem of structuring dynamically consistent government interventions. Kydland and Prescott (1977) were the first to clearly demonstrate that public policies could be dynamically inconsistent.[4] A policy that requires a series of government actions over time is dynamically inconsistent if a government action at some point in the future that is part of an optimal policy path today will never be the government's optimal decision at that future point, even in the absence of new information. Since private actors know this is the case, the government will be unable to induce them to respond as desired. However, the government can induce the desired response if it can credibly precommit today regarding all its future actions.

Karp and Perloff discuss an example where precommitting to an otherwise dynamically inconsistent trade policy improves a country's welfare. If a country is designing its tariffs for an agricultural good over time, its first-best tariff trajectory begins

---

[4] Earlier, Hicks (1969) presents an interesting perspective on why kings had such difficulty securing debt. Having absolute power, they could never credibly precommit to full repayment. Hence, it was predictable that the King would face significant incentives not to honor such obligations. The authors are indebted to Bruce Gardner for this example.

at a high level (to exploit the low short-run elasticity of supply) and declines over time. However, in the absence of a precommitment, the country will never find it optimal to reduce tariffs in period t to the level announced initially. International trade agreements can provide a means for a country to credibly commit to such a policy trajectory.

The Reagan administration's approach to the Uruguay Round of international trade negotiations can be interpreted as an attempt to achieve dynamic consistency through precommiting to a specified policy trajectory. The commitment to move agricultural supports to "green box" policies in this international agreement limited the ability of future administrations to move away from this administration's efforts to decouple farm supports from marginal production levels.

The need for dynamic consistency limits the set of implementable policies. Economic analysis of dynamic consistency has focused on two main lines of inquiry. The first has explored optimal policy design, given the need for dynamic consistency. Much of this literature uses a mechanism design approach. Essentially, this literature examines the implementability of policies when economic actors have rational expectations. The Lucas critique observed that private actors will adjust before actual government policy is implemented. Implicitly, this argument presumes that the policy in question is credible. When a policy is not credible, private actors will anticipate that the government will in fact not implement the policy as announced.

When a government's preferences are known, an announced policy must be dynamically consistent or backed by a credible precommitment in order for private agents to respond to the policy in the desired fashion. When a policymaker's preferences are unknown to other actors, the set of implementable policies may be further limited by this asymmetric information. Essentially, this occurs because whether or not a policy is dynamically consistent depends on the policymaker's preferences. Private actors base their response to an announced policy or policy trajectory on their beliefs regarding the policymaker's preferences. A policymaker may have to adjust his policy choice from his optimal choice under symmetric information in order to signal his true preferences, and differentiate himself from policymaker types with different preferences [Rodrik (1989)]. Along similar lines, Morris (2001) has structured an analysis of incentives for policy advisers to truthfully reveal information.

Dynamic consistency and credibility are important concerns in agricultural policy. For example, water markets have been proposed as a way of increasing the efficiency of water use throughout much of the world. One obstacle to their implementation and use has been uncertainty regarding the security of water rights. Rights holders are concerned that if they sell their water use rights today, they will increase the chance that their rights will be confiscated at some later time. Population and demand for water are projected to increase dramatically over the next fifty years, so such a prospect is not out of the realm of possibility. Policymakers have yet to find a means of credibly committing that this will not occur.

4. Political economic dimension

For this dimension, the no feedback effects from interest group formation (NF) assumption is relaxed. The use of this analytical dimension as a basis for explaining agricultural policies, as in Rausser and Freebairn, was a natural progression from the incidence and mechanism design analytical dimensions. The latter dimensions treat policy instruments as exogenous in model representations of agricultural markets. The political economic dimension seeks to explain the selection and implementation of actual public policies by endogenizing the instrument choice as a function of the actions of stakeholders. Interest groups as agents representing stakeholders, rather than individuals, are the unit of analysis. In the formation of public policies, interest groups compete by spending time, energy and money on the production of pressure to influence both the design and tactical implementation of policies.

As noted by de Gorter and Swinnen (Chapter 36), attempts to explain public policies using this analytical dimension requires the recognition of both political and economic forces. As a result, this analytical dimension squarely confronts empirical evidence on both market and governmental failures. Extensions of this analytical dimension have also focused on prescriptive analysis [Rausser and Zusman (1992)] and policy reform [Rausser (1990), Rausser and Irwin (1989)]. The core argument for both of these extensions is that public policies superior to the status quo cannot be sustainable unless the political and economic forces that form the causal basis for existing policies are understood. For example, in Rausser and Irwin existing political and economic forces only allow superior policies to emerge through the design of partial compensation schemes and new institutional rules. For prescriptive purposes, the political economic analytical dimension attempts to "identify policy rules that are robust and are important not only economically but, in a fundamental sense, politically" [Aaron (1989, p. 13)].

Even though the application of this dimension to agricultural policies did not begin in earnest until the 1970's, the historical origins of political economic analysis can be traced back to the original architects of the economic discipline, namely Adam Smith, Mill, Wicksell, and Marshall. None of these original architects were strangers to political economic analysis. In fact, the foundation of the economics discipline emerged from an integration of political science, economics and philosophy. With the introduction of the Walrasian framework, however, mainstream economics swept aside our political economic origins. This process was accelerated by the remarkable elegance and clarity of the Arrow–Debreu extensions of the basic Walrasian model. Essentially, many features of reality were discarded by mainstream economists in order to facilitate theorizing.

Although some of us might bemoan the distortions of reality emanating from separating our discipline from political science, it certainly had the value of allowing mainstream economics to proceed unencumbered. The separation of economics from other disciplines resulted in the formulation of an abstraction that might not otherwise have been delineated, and it permitted the development of the most significant of social theories, classical microeconomics [Alt and Shepsle (1990)]. However, the separation of politics and other social relationships from mainstream economics has meant that no conceptual frameworks existed for explaining the formation of public policies. Over the last three decades, this circumstance has changed dramatically with the emergence of the political economic analytical dimension. To varying degrees, the frameworks representing this policy dimension have allowed political forces to be integrated with economic influences.

4.1. Political economic theory

There are at least six alternative political economic frameworks that have emerged over the last three decades. While the conclusions of the frameworks often overlap, the genesis of each framework is a distinct school of thought. In our presentation, we order these six frameworks in terms of their degree of departure from mainstream economics. With the exception of the Marxian frameworks and its derivatives, all of these schools of thought are indebted to the pathbreaking work of Downs (1957).

The first framework can be characterized as the University of Chicago framework of political economy. This framework emerged with Stigler's (1971) theory of economic regulation; Peltzman's (1976) corrections and extensions of Stigler's theory; and Becker's (1983, 1985) perspective that governmental intervention can be conceptualized as rational and efficient. In each of these models, the government acts as a broker for redistribution among interests groups. The government has no autonomy, and the public interest is hidden from view.[5] The Stigler model results in interest groups totally capturing the government; the Peltzman formulation corrects this result which leads to only partial capture; and the Becker model isolates the price of redistribution as the per unit dead weight losses that result. For each of these models, public policy emerges from the competition among private self-interested stakeholders and easily manipulated governments.

Peltzman specifies a number of reasonable assumptions including (a) opposition is enhanced by increasing tax rates and mitigated by voter per capita educational expenditures; (b) the probability of the members of the beneficiary group members granting support is subject to decreasing returns with respect to per capita net transfers; (c) the probability of opposition exhibits similar properties with respect to per capita educational expenditures; and (d) there are increasing political costs of taxation. The most critical assumption imposed by Peltzman is that the wealth of each member of the potential opposing group is a decreasing function of the transfer tax. This assumption rules out a "pure" transfer, i.e., one which has no allocative effects. The general proposition that wealth is not totally inelastic with respect to taxes has important implications for the evaluation of the whole range of government redistributive policies.

---

[5] A second paper by Becker (1985) admits both envy and altruism on the part of interest groups. Accordingly, for this formulation it is possible for governmental intervention to supply public goods that serve the collective interest.

The second school highlights the rent-seeking perspective. This school of thought emerged with a classic paper by Tullock (1967). This work extended the dead weight losses which were measured as Harberger "triangles" to larger rent dissipations associated with "rectangle" losses. The original Tullock formulation was extended by Krueger (1974), whose model presumes that all rents are dissipated through competition among interest groups; Brock and Magee (1979), whose model results in all competition in political economic markets being wasteful, providing the basis for a number of "black hole" theorems; and Bhagwati (1982), whose model focuses on directly unproductive political activities that form the basis for social waste. Once again, as in the first school of thought, governments have no autonomy and all special interests engage in lobbying, which is a "bad" from a public interest perspective.[6] In contrast to the first school, especially as represented by the Becker formulations, redistributions resulting from governmental intervention may not be efficient. Both schools consider only government failures, or "predatory" government behavior. Under this approach, interest group activity can only reduce overall social welfare.

An illustrative example of the rent-seeking formulation is represented by Brock and Magee's (1979) specification of competing politicians, each attempting to maximize their probabilities of election. These probabilities are functions of campaign contributions from lobbies and the politicians' tariff positions. The political market equilibria that are obtained from this formulation, regardless of whether information is perfect or imperfect, have the following properties: (a) at any equilibrium point, the reaction function of one politician is always positively sloped while that of another is negatively sloped (he counteracts his political opponent); (b) inconsistent politicians make large changes in their tariff positions for a given change by their opponent, which results in unstable political markets; (c) wide differences among consistent politicians in terms of their respective campaign contribution responses to tariff changes lead to stable political market equilibria; (d) increased political power by a tariff lobby always causes one politician to increase while the other politician decreases his tariff position; (e) the average tariff position of two politicians may either rise or fall with increased power by the tariff lobby; and (f) increased lobbying power will augment the range between the tariff positions of two politicians when the high tariff politician increases his position and vice versa when the high tariff politician decreases his position.

The third framework is the public choice school. Here, some government autonomy begins to emerge, as well as some integration of political science and economics. In fact, political scientists such as Black (1958) and Riker (1962) are members of the founding group of this school of thought. Buchanan and Tullock (1962) are also early contributors. The political process specified in these models formally recognizes voting behavior and thus political candidates. As with the second school of thought, rent

---

[6] In much of political science, lobbying is "good" while in the rent-seeking formulations it is "bad". Ball (1995) introduces into a conventional political economic model asymmetric information that admits the possibility of social gains, not waste, from lobbying efforts. His key results depend critically upon whether lobbying is "information-revealing" or "information-concealing".

dissipation is one of the key results of these models. In many of these formulations, the median voter determines not only who is elected, but what policies are selected by democratic representatives.

Related to this school of thought are the so-called liberal-pluralist frameworks that appeared originally in the public finance literature [Rausser, Lichtenberg and Lattimore (1982)]. These frameworks concentrate on forces shaping the distribution of income and wealth in the private-sector. Examples include the "self-interested coalition"; the "self-interested median voter"; the "private insurance"; the "social insurance"; the "Pareto-optimal income redistribution"; and the "relative income" specifications. The purpose of each of these formulations is to account for observed changes in the distribution of income (Rausser, Lichtenberg and Lattimore).

The analytical value of integrating political and economic forces is not confined to the explanation of government or state policies. In fact, such forces play a role in all organizations and thus the focal point of the political-economic analytical dimension could quite simply be collective decision making. Based on this observation, the advances in new institutional economics can be identified as a fourth school of thought. The intellectual architects of this school are Coase (1937), North (1981), and Williamson (1975, 1993). This framework extends transaction cost economics to the theory of organizations, and the design of governance structures. As noted by Williamson (1993), the transaction cost economics perspective "...examines alternative forms of organization that differ in kind (that is, in discrete structural rather than marginal respects)... and examines only feasible forms of organization, the efficacy of which forms are assessed comparatively".

Rausser (1982) united the rent-seeking school and the new institutional economics school in a model that considered both productive and predatory government actions. The new institutional economics school is the foundation for his PERTs or productive governmental policies. Such policies are intended to correct for institutional or market failures by reducing by reducing transaction costs of the private economic system. The net effect of such policies is to increase the "size of the pie". The rent-seeking school was his foundation for PESTS, or predatory government behavior which decreases the "size of the pie" via dead weight losses and wasteful lobbying activities.

Another framework that has enjoyed a long history is the "theory of the state", or the radical political economy formulation. Here, political power plays a crucial role. In this framework, the interest groups of the other formulations are replaced by two classes: the dominant capitalist class and the working class. In its simplest versions, the dominant class, or owners of capital, make use of their political power to control or direct resources of the state. The dominant class transfers wealth to itself via the government through a number of institutional mechanisms [Jessop (1977), O'Conner (1973), Roemer (1978)]. As the observed distribution of income and wealth becomes very unequal, the legitimacy of government is maintained by the state providing a range of social services and income supplements for the non-dominant classes (working class, unemployed, impoverished, farmers, etc.).

A number of internal inconsistencies have been identified for the theory of state formulations, e.g., no attempt is made to explain the formation and maintenance of the dominant class; product demand is ignored; monopoly power in political-economic markets is assumed, never explained; and asymmetric knowledge between the dominant and non-dominant classes is imposed with the empirically unjustified result that working classes remain ignorant and never learn [Rausser, Lichtenberg and Lattimore (1982)]. This formulation has been creatively reconstructed by Bowles and Gintis (1993), who introduced the concept of a "contested exchange" where the benefit parties derive from a transaction depends on their respective capacities to enforce competing claims. In this reconstructed formulation, *power* continues to play a critical, but empirically non-testable role.

The sixth framework, the political-economic bargaining paradigm, brings the role of power front and center. In contrast to the "clearing-house" perspective of the first two political-economic frameworks (Chicago school, rent seeking) the government is presumed to have some, but not complete, autonomy. This framework recognizes that power is distributed between the various interest groups and government and that maldistribution of power can blunt any and all efforts at improved efficiency.[7] As argued by Williamson (1975), all collective action organizations, government or otherwise, consist of a "center" which directs group actions and peripheral participants. The center's choices affect individual well-being so that objective functions of the peripheral participants are, to some extent, expressed in terms of the center's choices. Individual peripheral participants will naturally strive to influence the center's choices. The center also consists of individuals with their own private interests; and while it is not unreasonable to expect central decision makers to fully internalize the group's goals, it would be unrealistic to ignore their personal interests. As a result, the center is exposed to potential influence attempts by peripheral participants who are in a position to award or penalize members of the center. In this setting, the concept of price is not well defined, and unlike the non-personal Walrasian exchange, agents' identities do matter in "political markets".

The foundation of this political-economic framework emerged from the early Nobel prize-winning work of Nash (1950, 1953) and Harsanyi (1963, 1977) on bargaining. Early theoretical and empirical applications of the bargaining framework to agricultural policy may be found in Rausser and Freebairn (1974) and Zusman (1976). For applications where the Nash (1950, 1953) axioms are too restrictive, Rausser and Simon (1999) have developed a non-cooperative multilateral bargaining framework for political-economic investigations.

A core concept in all of these formulations is bargaining power. As Russell (1938) argued long ago "the fundamental concept in social science is power in the same sense in which energy is the fundamental concept in physics". As Dahl (1957) has noted

---

[7] In this framework, governments can have some separate autonomy and can seek "leadership surplus" [Froelich, Oppenheimer and Young (1971)].

A has power over B to the extent to which "he can get B to do something that B would not otherwise do". [8] However, as Harsanyi (1963, 1977) has emphasized, power relationships need not be unilateral; bilateral or reciprocal power relationships also exist.

When a center's choices further the interests of particular peripheral participants, these interests may reward the center by extending material benefits and material support. Conversely, peripheral participants may penalize the center – for example, by withholding material benefits or by supporting the center's appointments when such choices are contrary to their interest. For the case of n peripheral participants, an $n + 1$ bargaining game is created whose cooperative solution constitutes an organizational equilibrium. [9] Cooperative equilibrium group choice is, in fact, a compromise among stakeholder or participant interest and the center's interests, reflecting the relative power of each group.

In the context of governmental behavior, the center consists of policy makers constitutionally authorized to make policy choices. As we shall see in the following section, this specification facilitates the constitutional analytical dimension. Constitutionally, in some instances, a polycentric structure comprising several centers (federal, state, local) is required. Regardless, a hierarchy structures the relationship between the authoritative center and the subordinate peripheral participants or interest groups. These interest groups can be organized, i.e., structures capable of rallying group members into coordinated joint action [de Gorter and Swinnen (2002), Olson (1965)]; unorganized but responsive interest groups: groups that share common interests but are unable to evolve any machinery for deliberate political action; politically inert interest groups: groups which not only lack any mechanism for coordinated policy action but their members are also unresponsive to policy choices.

The relationship between organized interest groups and policy-making centers defines a reciprocal power structure in which each party employs its means of power in the bargaining process. For this process and a presumed cooperative outcome defined by group rationality, Zusman has derived a political-economic equilibrium. For applications involving g policy making centers and n organized interest groups,

---

[8] More recently, Hirshleifer (1991) has offered the following definition "power is the ability to achieve one's ends in the presence of rivals". Bowles and Gintis (1993) offer a sufficient condition for the exercise of power, namely the ability of furthering one's interest by imposing (or credibly threaten to impose) sanctions on another agent when the converse is not also true.

[9] There has been an active debate about cooperative versus non-cooperative outcomes of multilateral bargaining frameworks (Rausser and Simon). In the political-economic context, even though politics appears to be conflict-ridden, it is essentially also a process of conflict resolution. In the Nash–Harsanyi world, when bargaining parties share similar perceptions on their respective disagreement payoffs, it is rational for each party to seek an agreement which will benefit all interests compared to the disagreement outcome. Essentially if the bargaining parties can improve their lot by shifting from a non-cooperative to a cooperative solution, the former solution cannot be a long-run equilibrium. Accordingly, the tendency will be for the bargaining parties to move from a non-cooperative short-run equilibrium to a cooperative outcome. As a result, Zusman (1976) presumes a cooperative solution or "group rationality" in characterizing his political economic equilibrium. A contrary perspective is reflected in the work of Hillman and Riley and Coggins.

political-economic equilibrium corresponds to a cooperative solution of a $(g+n)$ person bargaining game.[10]

Allowing for some government autonomy and agency representation of organized interest groups there is not one political economic equilibrium but many. Agent representation of organized interest groups as principals results in the second best world [Karp and Perloff (2002)], where there is not one Pareto frontier but many. Accordingly, the political economic equilibrium is a local concept, not a global concept of the type emerging from Becker's efficient redistribution hypothesis. Armed with this perspective, Rausser and Freebairn (1974) suggest that construction of a functional set rather than a unique function. These functions reflect the extreme viewpoints and preferences of different central decision makers actively involved in the bargaining process as well as preference sets lying between these extremes.[11]

4.2. Empirical issues

For each of the six conceptual frameworks, there are at least four alternative empirical formulations for investigating endogenous government behavior. The first is a structural form that specifies the objective function for the center or government, the objective functions for each of the agents representing the organized interest groups, lobbying expenditures and effective political support. The second empirical form is the constraint structure. In these studies, the constraint structure is often represented by the performance measure transformation frontier, i.e., typically the tradeoff between consumer and producer surplus resulting from various policy selections. Gardner (1983, 1987, 1989) has extensively analyzed the Becker theoretical model in the context of U.S. agricultural policy using the constraint structure empirical form. A third empirical formulation is the instrument behavioral equation form or policy reaction functions (Rausser, Lichtenberg and Lattimore). The final empirical form is the governing criterion function, or what has been frequently referred to in the literature as the political preference function [Rausser (1982)].

The policy preference function is a weighted sum of the central policy-maker's policy objectives and the organized interest groups' policy objectives. The weight of each group's objective function reflects its relative political power (Zusman). This function is simply a reduced form representation of the political economic equilibrium of the Nash–Harsanyi multilateral bargaining process. The political preference function allows

---

[10] When in addition to the g policy making centers and n organized interest groups, the group configuration comprises k unorganized but unresponsive interest groups, the ensuing political-economic equilibrium consists of a solution to a $(g+n)$ person bargaining game, where each of the $(g+n)$ organized parties takes into account the effects of the reactions of the k unorganized but unresponsive interest groups on its own policy objective function. Under these circumstances, a bargaining game emerges between $(g+n)$ Stackelbergian leaders in the presence of k Stackelbergian followers.

[11] One of the purposes of their analysis is to generate information that might contribute to the efficiency of the bargaining process in reaching a consensus.

the performance of empirical tests that distinguish among alternative political economic frameworks. For the Chicago school, leadership does not matter. Equivalently, the center has no autonomy. This theoretical hypothesis can be tested empirically using the null hypothesis that the weight on the policy-maker's objective function is zero. Similarly, to examine whether the government has total autonomy, the joint null hypothesis to be tested is that the weights on all organized interest group objective functions are zero.

For each of the empirical forms: structural, constraints, policy reaction functions, and reduced forms representations, de Gorter has outlined and synthesized the major empirical insights. One major insight relates to interest group size and the distribution of benefits versus cost of any redistribution policy. From a voting standpoint, the greater the relative membership of a group, the greater the potential political support it has to offer. However, as a group increases in size, diseconomies set in with respect to cohesiveness and free-riding. Furthermore, the "power of the few" is diluted, namely the benefits are distributed over an increasing number of group members and with free entry to the interest group, the rents are dissipated. On the contrary, as the group increases in size that is taxed to finance the policy, the per capita burden falls with the result that the redistribution policy is more sustainable.

Other empirical insights relate to the government's preference structure reflecting the socio-political characteristics of the politicians (seniority, ideology, party affiliation) and the governance structure of the political process (branches of the government, role of bureaucracy, interest group access, admissible coalitions). Another set of causal relationships focus on the economic performance experienced by each interest group, their corresponding lobbying expenditures and the resulting effective political pressure or influence. Influence or pressure has been shown to be causally connected to spatial versus proportional representation as well as the distribution of burden and benefits across various interest groups (de Gorter). A rural bias often develops with pluralism because the geographic distribution of cost and benefits corresponds to the distribution of influence [Ferejohn and Rundquist (1975), Weingast et al. (1981)]. Geographic representation in some non-democratic, developing societies results in an urban bias. Lipton (1977) has argued that the urban population is often strategically located to provide political support for authoritative regimes.

Surplus transformation frontiers link redistribution to the underlying market structure [Wallace (1962), Gardner (1983, 1987, 1989)]. For example, in the context of rising producer prices, a more elastic supply function will result in larger redistribution transfers. A lower food share in consumers' aggregate expenditures has the same qualitative effect. Similarly, an increase in input costs increases the level of redistributive transfers, the degree depending on the input substitution policies and the share of the fixed cost.

Several factors affecting the redistribution's dead weight loss have been identified. A more elastic demand or supply results in a larger dead weight loss per unit of income transferred. Accordingly, products with inelastic demands, such as wheat and fluid milk, experience more active governmental intervention than more elastic products, such as beef or fruits and vegetables. The dead weight losses associated with transfers have been empirically verified to be higher for exporters than for importers. This differential is magnified if a country is "large" on world markets because subsidizing exporters' production reduces world prices and thus expands the transfer costs. Larger importers on the other hand may even improve their terms of trade. Empirical evidence thus supports the claims that endogenous policy will vary according to import versus export status of a commodity and according to whether the country is large or small in markets for a particular commodity.

One of the key empirical insights emerging from the political-economic analytical dimension is that it is not possible to fundamentally understand, explain or reform current policies without integrating both redistributive (PEST) and public good (PERT) policies [Rausser (1982)]. Integrative empirical frameworks have been used to explain the significant underinvestment in public research in a number of industrial and developing countries [de Gorter, Rausser and Nielson (1992)]. This integrative framework has been widely applied to explain and measure the rate of protection for alternative commodities sectors over time and across countries (de Gorter and Swinnen, Chapter 36). It has been shown that empirical investigations of these two types of policy instruments can lead to results which are both puzzling and subject to misinterpretation if the joint determination of the policies is not explicitly recognized.

In most political economic models, members of the interest groups are presumed to be predetermined, with no entry or exit from one interest group to another. Empirical evidence demonstrates, however, that the extent of heterogeneity among members of a particular interest group can form the basis for policy reform through creative mixes of policies or the introduction of new political technology to split interest groups as well as to form new coalitions [Foster and Rausser (1993)]. Effectively, a potentially winning group may tax itself in order to mitigate the losses suffered by another group whose political strength lies in the ability to veto a move from the status quo. In a prescriptive sense, a political-economic robust mix of policies may manage special interests whose influence might otherwise obstruct the public interest.

The political economic analytical dimension has also been applied to land reform and to the analysis of water resource systems. Land reform consists of major changes in the structure of property rights in land and stringent restriction of tenurial contracts. It has been shown that the efficiency of the land reform program depends on both legislation and implementation, the latter generally is the responsibility of local bureaucrats. Rausser and Zusman (forthcoming) have shown that the ensuing political-economic equilibrium is the result of a solution to a two-level nested bargaining game.

In applications to water resources, two policy-making centers are specified: (a central water supply district and a government fiscal authority) along with a large number of water districts, each acting as an organized interest group, whose policy objective is the maximization of the districts' net incomes. They demonstrate that due to the narrow rationality of water districts the resulting political-economic equilibrium is inefficient. Politically set water prices are too low and water utilization quotas are too liberal so that either an excessive amount of land is lost through water logging or ground water aquifers are over-utilized (Rausser and Zusman, Rausser).

The political-economic analytical dimension has also been widely applied to trade liberalization and to transition economies. In the former category, liberalization has been shown to harm some groups. If these groups are sufficiently powerful they can block moves from the status quo. Using this dimension, Pareto-fulfilling compensation schemes have been advanced to assess the likelihood of reform taking place [Foster, Gray and Rausser (1995)]. In the case of transition economies, displacing the old order or status quo often leads to widespread social disruption which may ultimately threaten the very viability of the reform process. Lyons has used the political-economic analytical dimension to identify conditions and empirical evidence under which closed economies outperform, or underperform, open economies in terms of social welfare for the public interest.

Among the various empirical forms, the most widely used in investigating the political-economic analytical dimension is the reduced form political preference function, or the governing criterion function [Rausser and de Gorter (1989)]. As Steiner has emphasized, some solution to the "preference weighting" problem is implicit or explicit in any public action that might be taken. Specifically, Steiner (1969, p. 31) has argued:

> If objectives were genuinely multidimensional and not immediately comparable, some solution to the weighting problem is implicit in any choice and that solution reflects someone's value judgment. Formally, we now accept in principle that the choice of weights is itself an important dimension of the public interest. This choice is sometimes treated as a prior decision which controls public expenditure decisions (or at least should) and sometimes is a concurrent or joint decision that is an inseparable part of the process of choice.

Since much confusion has arisen in the literature on the empirical estimation of PPFs the following subsection is devoted to clarifying and interpreting this literature.

4.3. Political preference function: Reduced form

The political preference function (PPF) approach, first introduced by Rausser and Freebairn (1974), has been frequently used in agricultural economics. The estimated function is simply an "*as if*" outcome originating from the strategic interactions of the inherent bargaining process among individual agents representing both the public interest and specialized interests. It is a reduced form specification, rather than a structural one. Reduced form models are common in other areas of empirical analysis, including price determination, and production. Recent papers, including [Bullock (1996, 1995, 1994, 1992), von Cramon-Taubadel and Gardner (1989)], have critiqued the PPF approach. Many of these critiques fail to realize that, as a reduced form empirical model, literal interpretations of the PPF approach should be avoided.

As previously noted, political economic processes may be viewed as ones of accommodation among conflicting interests. A bargaining game among organized groups with conflicting interests is a way to explicitly model the process of accommodation among policy makers and interest groups. If Nash's (1950) axioms or the axioms of its non-symmetric variant hold, then the equilibrium of the economic system with government intervention is identified with the solution of the corresponding bargaining game, and the PPF approach internally consistent. In order for the PPF approach to be valid, there must be an exact correspondence between the solution map of the bargaining model and the maximization map of the PPF. A necessary condition for this to occur is that the independence of irrelevant alternatives (IIA) axiom must be satisfied. If the IIA axiom is not satisfied, the Nash–Harsanyi bargaining framework is not applicable.

In the PPF approach to modeling political economic decision-making, a policy maker chooses levels of policy instruments to maximize a function of special interests' welfare (sometimes including his own utility) subject to a feasibility constraint. Therefore, it is valid to use the PPF framework as a proxy for a bargaining model of the political economic process when there is a correspondence of the PPF maxima to the solution of the corresponding bargaining model. Empirical PPF studies use the PPF approach to estimate the relative power of organized interest groups (Rausser and Freebairn). Such support relies crucially on the validity of the axioms on which these models are founded.

Nash, in his axiomatic approach to bargaining in a two-person bargaining game, showed that there is only one solution to a two-person bargaining game which satisfies the following: (1) the Pareto optimality (PO) axiom, (2) the symmetry axiom, (3) the scale invariance axiom, and (4) the independence of irrelevant alternatives (IIA) axiom. The PO axiom requires that the solution lie on the Pareto frontier. The symmetry axiom requires that the solution lie on the 45-degree line if the feasibility set is symmetric about this line. If the scale invariance axiom holds, the solution is invariant to equivalent utility representations. Finally, if the IIA axiom holds, feasible alternatives (other than the original bargaining solution or the disagreement point) can be taken away from the original feasible set of a bargaining problem, and the solution to the reduced bargaining problem will be equivalent to the solution of the original bargaining problem. Harsanyi (1963) showed that Nash's solution can be generalized to n-person games. In particular, the solution can be computed as the point in the feasibility set that maximizes a function equal to the product of the players' utility gains from cooperation, measured relative to the exogenous disagreement point.

Nash's model exactly satisfies the condition for determining when it is appropriate to substitute a PPF framework or a reduced form (shown by Zusman) for a bargaining model. Nash's central result is to construct a function whose associated maximization map coincides with the solution map implied by his four axioms. Nash's function is not very realistic as a PPF because it sets equal weights on the policy maker's and all interests' relative influence on policy decisions. A variant of Nash's model that does allow for differences (that is, the symmetry axiom can be dropped) is obtained if the strong individual rationality axiom holds. The strong individual rationality axiom requires that all players strictly gain from cooperation if one player does. The resulting set of axioms implies a family of solution maps, each of which again coincides with the maximization map of a function equal to the product of the players' utility gains, except that these utility gains are now weighted by a set of non-zero exponents that sum to unity.[12]

One of Nash's axioms that may be violated in PPF studies is the Pareto-optimality (PO) axiom. Like the IIA axiom, the PO axiom is a necessary condition not just for the Nash bargaining solution but also more generally: for the maximization map of any strongly monotonic PPF to coincide with the solution map of a bargaining model, the solution map must satisfy the PO axiom. This raises the question of whether it is reasonable to expect bargaining outcomes to be Pareto optimal. Note, however, that the bargaining outcome must be Pareto optimal only with respect to the parties represented at the bargaining table. Hence, even if the PO axiom holds, it does not mean that the bargaining solution is Pareto efficient in the sense that it maximizes social surplus.

Gardner (1989) suggests that the PPF may change over time even if the feasible set is stable. This would happen if the weight given to interest groups in the PPF depends on the resources they spend on lobbying, and if in turn, the amount of resources allocated to interest groups depends on the PPF. That could then set in motion a spiral where a slightly higher weight given to a particular interest group results in the government allocating more resources to it, which in turn results in the government allocating even more resources to the interest group, and so forth.

Implicit in Gardner's story is that the government, on the one hand, and the interest groups, on the other, act alternatively as Stackelberg leaders and Stackelberg followers. When the government allocates resources, it is in the position of Stackelberg leader relative to the interest groups: it knows how interest-group support will depend on its allocation, in the manner of the Peltzman model. When the interest groups lobby, they are in the position of Stackelberg leader relative to the government (they perhaps play Nash–Cournot amongst themselves): the interest groups know how the PPF weights, and thereby the outcome of the government's maximization of the PPF over the feasible set, will depend on their lobbying expenditures, in the manner of the Becker model. Such flip-flopping between information conditions seems a bit implausible. The more natural way of analyzing the interaction between the government and the interest groups is via a bargaining framework.

Bullock (1994, 1992) takes a literal interpretation of the PPF approach. Bullock (1994) incorrectly argues that PPF's are, or are equivalent to, social welfare functions. Ignoring that use of the PPF framework as a proxy for a bargaining model of the political economic process results in an "*as if*" outcome originating from the strategic interactions among individual actors, he criticizes empirical applications for ignoring the implications of the interpretation that PPF's are really social welfare functions. Bullock (1994) does question Pareto efficiency by testing whether government is rational. However, Pareto efficiency may be violated for reasons other than a non-rational government. For example, an outcome may not be Pareto efficient because of the presence of asymmetric information or agency issues. The political preference

---

[12] See Peters (1992) for a proof of this result.

function approach is a reduced form representation for a bargaining model of the political economic process. In addition, for the PPF approach to be valid, the underlying bargaining outcome must only be Pareto optimal with respect to the parties represented at the bargaining table. It may well be the case that in the policy-making arena, certain groups may not have any access to the bargaining process.

Bullock (1994, 1996) argues that in empirical PPF studies, the real world is complicated and, accordingly, some feasible policy instruments are often ignored. This criticism is not an issue if the IIA axiom holds. Pareto efficiency with respect to the participants at the bargaining table is necessary to use the PPF framework, but Bullock fails to represent the fundamental structure of political bargaining. Researchers specify m policy instruments and n groups. Bullock (1994) shows as others have before him that a necessary condition for a unique solution, is $n - 1 = m$.[13] However, if Nash's Independence of Irrelevant Alternatives (IIA) axiom is satisfied, this is not a critical issue. If $n - 1 < m$, we can eliminate feasible policy instrument alternatives other than the original solution and the disagreement point until $n - 1 = m$. Similarly, if $n - 1 > m$, we can add feasible policy instrument alternatives until $n - 1 = m$. If the Independence of Irrelevant Alternatives (IIA) axiom is not satisfied, then it is inappropriate to use the PPF framework. Therefore, given the $n \geqslant 2$ interest groups, we can choose any set of $n - 1$ policy instruments that include the original solution and the disagreement point. Second, the outcome must only be Pareto optimal with respect to the parties at the bargaining table, which is a weaker criterion than Bullock's (1994) effective criterion of being Pareto optimal with respect to all of society.

Bullock (1994) is also concerned about the aggregation or omission of interest groups. Aggregation of interest groups means that the strong axiom of revealed preference may no longer be satisfied, but the weak axiom will still hold. However, there should not be a need to aggregate because the number of groups that are actually lobbying in a particular policy situation will not be large. We are not considering the bargaining problem with reference to *all the groups in society as a whole*, but only with reference to either the constituencies represented *at the bargaining table* or their representative agents.

Zusman and Amiad (1977) highlight the potential importance of the existence of agency issues in empirical work with a PPF study of government intervention in the Israeli dairy market. Observed levels of policy instruments are highly inefficient – again, in the special sense used here – when the utility of farmers' groups, consumers, and the government are identified as producer surplus, consumer surplus, and net cost of the dairy program, respectively. If, however, the size of the production quotas enter the bargaining representatives' utility functions, then the observed outcome of the political process may well be efficient for those with negotiation access. Pareto efficiency in this space is obviously not equivalent to Pareto efficiency among the underlying interest groups or "principals". To explain their results, Zusman and Amiad suggest farm *leaders*

---

[13] This result was presented earlier by Love, Rausser and Burton (1990).

feel pressured to bargain for higher production quotas in particular, rather than just for higher net farm income. A very plausible source of such pressure might be the simple fact that percentage increases in production quotas are easy to *communicate* as concrete bargaining achievements; much more so than the changes in net farm incomes, which are influenced by a number of other causal factors.

Bullock (1995) notes that "since the PPF is not directly observable, relative political power or social welfare weights cannot be directly measured".[14] Lobbying efforts, threats, and rewards move the political power coefficients and are generally non-observable. However, there are many economic applications in which non-observables are crucial and whose influences have been quantified. One response to the PPF problem of non-observables has been the use of reduced forms and another has been to propose non-traditional estimation techniques, such as Generalized Maximum Entropy [Golan, Judge and Karp (1996)].

A legitimate criticism of empirical PPF studies is that changes in welfare with respect to changes in policy instrument are assumed to be known and nonstochastic [Love, Rausser and Burton (unpublished)]. For a given point in time this assumption allows reasonable approximations of the PPF weights. For general inferences, such revealed preference weights are functions of stochastic variables and thus the underlying sampling distributors must be estimated. These distributions have been quantified and statistical inference tests on the estimated weights have constructed using bootstrapping methods [see Love, Rausser and Burton (unpublished), Jeong, Bullock and Garcia (1999)].

5. Constitutional analytical dimension

For this dimension, the given governance structure assumption (GG) is relaxed. As a result, it is possible to evaluate the causal connection between policy instrument selection and implementation, and the underlying collective choice, or constitutional rules. A particular constitutional design establishes voting rules, the rule of law, property rights, laws governing exchange and more generally, *the rules by which rules are made.* The constitutional space structures the constitutional rules that determine the nature and scope of the political feedback mechanisms from groups effected by public policies (NF). In its most expansive representation, the constitutional analytical dimension investigates the implications of alternative legal regulatory and institutional frameworks as well as alternative degrees of political, civil and economic freedoms [Rausser (1992), Rausser and Johnson (1993)].

Constitutional rules set the boundaries for economic, political and civil freedoms. In the case of legal institutions, the constitutional space is concerned with more than simply the rule of law, but the choice of law and the extent of liberty as well. This includes a selection from among the legal institutions that rule mankind: civil law,

---

[14] [Bullock (1995, p. 1240)].

common law, religious law and Socialist law. As is true for all constitutional space selections, such choices affect the political economic landscape, the culture and the customs of a particular society.

From one country to another, there is large variation in the selection of constitutional rules. Over the course of the last decade, many public agencies, including the Agency for International Development, the International Monetary Fund and the World Bank have formally recognized that the "right" constitutional selection is a crucial underpinning for economic growth. These agencies have begun to equate the "right" constitutional framework with good governance and have slowly recognized that making assistance conditional on outcomes is a mistake. Both the IMF and the World Bank have moved away from the "get the prices right" prescription of the 1980's to promoting good governance structures in all its aspects "including insuring the role of law, improving the efficiency and accountability of the public sector and tackling corruption" (IMF Declaration) as essential for sustained economic growth. Only by appropriate constitutional design is it possible to establish governance structures that promote productive policies (PERTs) while controlling or minimizing predatory policies (PESTs).

Insights from this analytical dimension illuminate the relationship between constitutions and the distribution of political power and influence. The resulting distribution of political power and influence creates a tradeoff between public and special interest in the selection of particular policies. The relevant questions posed by this analytical dimension include: Does the constitutional order provide free entry into the economic and political system? Does the constitutional order provide sufficient self-correcting mechanisms to limit excessive predatory governmental policies? Does the determined constitutional order motivate agreement on basic values and processes for conflict resolution? As de Gorter and Swinnen (Chapter 36) have correctly noted, the theoretical and empirical applications of this analytical dimension are still in their infancy.

5.1. Conceptual frameworks

The constitutional analytical dimension extends the political economic analytical dimension by viewing current policies as a rational outcome of the collective decision-making process conditional on the constitutional rules. For any outcomes that might arise, the public sector is naturally exposed to attempts by various interest groups to exert their influence. Constitutional rules determine, in part, the degree of success that will be achieved by interest groups pursuing their self-interest. If power is unevenly distributed among the special interests and societal interests, organizational failures naturally arise [Rausser and Zusman (1992)].

Under the Nash–Harsanyi axioms, the weights estimated from the political preference function are conditional on the specified constitutional rules. Such rules come in many shapes and forms. For example, Nitzan and Paroush (1965) discuss a host of rules including expert rule, almost expert rule, tie-breaking chairman rule, rule of the chairman and two aids, restricted simple majority rule, multiple majority rule, simple majority rule. Rules that have been examined in the literature range from those in which one member of the organization has sole authority on all policies and issues to those in which referendum over policy alternatives are decided by simple majority and to those in which policy selections require unanimity of all members. In this context, the impact of rules on the political preference function define the benefits, but obviously the associated decision costs must also be taken into account [Rausser and Zusman (1992)].

The relationship between constitutional rules and political power allows prescriptive analysis to be performed. The most important conditioning elements of the political power coefficients developed in Section 4 are the underlying collective choice rules. These underlying rules comprise the constitutional space that sets boundaries on the policy formation process. Prescriptive selection across alternative constitutional rules entails evaluating their associated expected utility and their bargaining cost. Bargaining and organizing costs increase as constitutional rules go from the sole decision maker rule to a unanimity rule. Formally, constitutional choices can be determined by balancing the expected transaction costs of implementation with the expected benefits reflected by the governing criterion function.

The constitutional rules determine who has access to the policy making process, and thus what performance measures appear in the governing criterion function. The length of the policy center's planning horizon is also specified by the governing criterion function. The length of time that a policy maker serves is a constitutional rule. Assessments of appropriate lengths of time must balance the value of longer planning horizons with the possible pursuit of a policy-maker's self-interest rather than public interest. Specifically, the constitutional democratic processes can remove elected officials who pursue their self interest with significant dead weight losses to the public interest.

Constitutional rules are critical in determining the formation of interest groups who exercise influence over the political economic process. For developing countries, De Soto (1989) has detailed the enormous political and institutional hurdles that must be overcome by individual businesses which have little access to the political economic process. His prescription is to mobilize these alternative factions in order to enable them to represent their self-interest. However, as shown by Foster, Gray and Rausser (1995), public sectors seeking sustainable reductions in wasteful rent seeking activities should select constitutional principles that foster resource mobility and ownership diversification. Under these circumstances, there are no benefits to interest groups acquiring and exercising political power. Along similar lines, governments wishing to compensate groups losing from trade liberalization should design compensation schemes that promote mobility and/or ownership diversification of immobile resources. Trade reform is more likely to be sustained in this fashion since future rent seeking behavior will be mitigated.[15]

An open polity may be the single most important underpinning for productive public policies. Diffusion of political power, ease of entry and representation in the political

---

[15] Of course, this comes at an economic cost of some forgone gains from diminished specialization.

arena by alternative economic factions, the fair rule of law, and clear limitations of access to governmental officials all facilitate productivity and economic growth. The economic success of authoritarian regimes, such as Singapore, has led to arguments that political repression may facilitate rapid economic development. The irony of this position, based on evidence from a relatively short time period and limited geographic area, is that dictatorship, far from being necessary for economic growth, may be its antithesis. Under such regimes, corrupt and inept policy makers cannot be changed by the will of the citizens. Sustainable movements toward productive public policies and away from predatory public policies are more likely in a climate of freedom and diffuse political power. Diffuse political power is alive and well in countries with ample resource mobility and widely diversified asset portfolios.

As implied by Section 4.3, when the Nash–Harsanyi axioms are not satisfied, a causal connection between constitutional rules and the distribution of political power becomes more complex. For public policy making processes which violate the independence of irrelevant alternatives axiom [Rausser, Simon and van't Veld (1995)], the multilateral bargaining framework developed by Rausser and Simon (1999) is applicable. As with Harsanyi's generalization of Nash, this framework incorporates multiple players and multiple dimensional issue spaces. From the standpoint of the constitutional analytical dimension, political power is contingent on a number of collective choice rules. First, the interest groups with access to the political bargaining process are predetermined. Their relative power is determined in accordance with an exogenously specified vector of access probabilities. A default option or a distinguished disagreement policy is determined by the initial conditions for the policy making process. Admissible coalition rules determine the subset of interest groups or agents that can impose a policy decision on the group as a whole. For example, for majority rule, a coalition is defined to be admissible if and only if it contains a majority of the group. For many policy-making processes, some representatives of the public sector can be viewed as a "central coordinator" or, in the parlance of game theory, an *essential player*. For unanimity admissible coalitions, all interest groups are essential players.

Formally, the Rausser and Simon multilateral bargaining framework considers a sequence of games with finite bargaining horizons, and examines the limit points of the equilibrium outcomes as the horizon is extended without bounds. These limit points are interpreted as a proxy for the equilibria of a bargaining game in which the number of negotiation rounds is finite, but arbitrarily large. There is a simple characterization of the set of equilibrium strategy profiles – in each response round, a player will accept a proposed policy if and only if it generates at least as much utility as his reservation utility in that round; that is the utility he expects to receive if no agreement is reached and the play continues into the following round.[16] For each admissible coalition, players maximize their utility over the set of policies that provide each coalition member with at

---

[16] More precisely, the Rausser–Simon model consists of a sequence of finite round bargaining games, with the number of rounds increasing without bound as the sequence progresses. For each of these games, there is a unique equilibrium outcome. Under certain conditions, this sequence of equilibria will converge as the

least his reservation utility in the following round. Rausser and Simon prove uniqueness and existence of an equilibrium solution so long as one of these groups that has access to the policy making process is an essential player.

5.2. Empirical issues

For the constitutional analytical dimension, de Gorter and Swinnen (Chapter 36) have summarized what empirical evidence has appeared in the literature on the causal connection between political institutions and agricultural policy outcomes. Much of this literature turns on the impact of political freedoms and civil liberties. Some of the more interesting results examine the tradeoff between productive (PERT) and predatory policies (PEST). As political freedoms and civil liberties increase, productive policies are augmented while predatory policies are diminished. de Gorter also presents a number of descriptive studies that have investigated the causal connection between admissible coalitions and public policy outcomes, particularly the common agricultural policy of the European Union.

Other descriptive studies have focused on the Uruguay Round of the GATT negotiations and the WTO as a vehicle to change the constitutional rules that underlie the public policy process [Rausser (1995), Sumner and Tangermann (2002), Chapter 38]. For example, the internal constitutional rules within the United States, and the resulting distribution of political power during the 1980's did not allow the emergence of a new political economic equilibrium supporting agricultural policy reform. Global, and even regional trade agreements alter the rules under which rules are made by explicitly placing limits on the issue space, as well as who has access to the bargaining process.

In the 1980's, the Reagan administration in the United States made two serious attempts (1981, 1985–86) to reform U.S. agricultural policy. Because of the distribution of political power among various interest groups, the center represented by Reagan's administration was unsuccessful. Having failed under internal constitutional rules and the resulting distribution of political power, the administration turned to international negotiations and as a result, an alternative set of constitutional rules. The U.S. government also shifted the burden of redistributive agricultural policies from consumers to taxpayers. This shift increased the transparency of societal costs, and the degree of effective opposition to the subsidized agricultural interest groups [Rausser (1995), Rausser and Irwin (1989)]. The successful conclusion of the Uruguay Round of the GATT negotiations and the signing of the NAFTA regional trade agreement altered the rules by which rules are made.

The "central coordinators" of the sixth political economic formulation (see Section 4.1), especially those seeking significant policy reforms, recognize the importance

number of rounds increases. A solution to the bargaining model is the limit of the sequence of equilibria for the finite games. The resulting outcome is the equilibrium of a negotiating process with a large but unspecified number of negotiating rounds.

of strategically expanding the policy space to alter the distribution of political power of affected interest groups. Under the current WTO constitutional rules, this is often what precisely happens in the resolution of trade disputes. Hence it is surprising that many governments have not more actively pursued the institution of such rules in the WTO or GATT forums, where agriculture has been treated as a *separable* negotiation issue. As a result, many interests (e.g., manufacturing, intellectual property, services) who are harmed by redistributive agricultural policies do not have access to the GATT or WTO agriculture bargaining process. Given both the limited issue space and the lack of access, many interests that are harmed by redistributive agricultural policies play no direct role in conceptualizing the bargains, pacts, compromises and efforts that are undertaken to shape the rules by which agricultural policies are designed and implemented.

One of the more interesting applications of the constitutional analytical dimension is the work of McCubbins, Noll and Weingast (1989). These authors advance a multilateral bargaining framework to evaluate the negotiations between the executive branch, and the U.S. Congress. Each of these parties has distinctly different policy preferences. Once a conclusion to the legislative negotiation process is reached, the supporting coalition becomes the principal with the bureaucratic agency assuming the role of an agent. The authors find that the standard agency solution of relying on rewards, punishment and oversight is costly and runs contrary to the risk aversion of members of the principal coalition. As a result, the principal coalition seeks constraints on the flexibility of the agents, and in the case of U.S. environmental policy, relies heavily on third party interest groups to monitor and report agency non-compliance.

In effect, the three policy-making bodies (President, Senate and House) bargain over the outcome they wish the agency to administer. If the agency engages in policy drift, as long as it stays within the Pareto optimal set of outcomes for the three principal parties, there is no coalition that can be formed to return the agency to the original solution in the multilateral bargaining framework. If the agency however, moves away from the Pareto optimal set, the principal parties can achieve a cooperative solution to redefine guidelines for the agency. One of the more interesting implications, however, is that the point of drift will define a new Pareto optimal set and that the new point agreed upon is unlikely to be the initial one from which the agency drifted. Since the principal coalition relies upon effective third party monitoring a second source of policy drift arises if the set of interest groups shift. Under these circumstances the structural and procedural safeguards that limit the flexibility of bureaucratic agencies may no longer be effective. In this context, rules that set the access of interest groups to the agency decision-making process become critical.

There have been a number of empirical applications of the constitutional analytical dimension to water policies in agricultural systems [Adams, Rausser, and Simon (1996), Rausser (2000), Goodhue et al. (2001)]. In the case of California water policy Adams et al. find that rules on access and issues space can have dramatic implications for the policy making process. For example, for the case of three essential interest groups: agriculture, urban and environmental, restrictions on the issue space can be counterproductive to achieving a Pareto optimal outcome. In this empirical application, environmental interests argued that new infrastructure development should be excluded from the issue space. The two other interest groups strongly supported investments in water transportation infrastructure. While environmental groups can block new infrastructure projects, agricultural and urban groups have the power to block many of the water policy goals of the environmental interests. Accordingly, environmental interests are potentially better off by relaxing their opposition to negotiating over infrastructure development. Since their level of utility can be enhanced through "gains from trade", environmental groups can exchange augmentations in infrastructure for more environmental protection and thus achieve gains to trade for all three interest groups.

In the context of a national water law passed in France, Goodhue et al. investigate the multilateral bargaining among stakeholders assigned responsibility for designing the regulations governing water use. In the Adour basin in southwestern France, stakeholders were charged with determining the amount of water that should be allocated to irrigation, how this water should be allocated among agricultural users, and the price that users should be charged for this water. The constitutional rule that is investigated is interest group or stakeholder access to the negotiation process. Experiments are conducted where bargaining power is reallocated from the river/aquatic environmental group to the landscape environmental group. Adjusting the relative bargaining power of the two environmentalists affects not only the returns to their respective natural allies, but also the returns to their mutual natural opposing interests, the farmers. An increase in the access of the river/aquatic environmentalist at the expense of the landscape environmentalist increases the manager's utility and reduces the taxpayer's utility. Farmers' utility is affected by the relative bargaining strength of the two environmentalists. Further, not all farmers are affected in the same way. Farmers with a relatively low marginal revenue product of water are always made worse off by an increase in access for the river/aquatic environmentalist.

6. Conclusion

Public policy in agriculture and natural resources has proved to be fertile ground for theoretical and empirical analysis. As the chapters in this section (Alston and James, Chambers, Innes, deGorter, Karp and Perloff, and Sumner and Tangermann) have demonstrated, public policy evaluated by agricultural economists is a complex set of interconnected interventions. These interventions are pervasive throughout developing and developed economies. As a result, it is not possible to investigate descriptive, explanatory, predictive or prescriptive models of agriculture and natural resource systems without accounting for the formation and impact of public policy.

Given its complexity, it is understandable that economists have employed a number of analytical frameworks to evaluate the formation and impacts of agricultural policy. We have represented these analytical frameworks in terms of four dimensions: incidence, mechanism design, political economic and governance structures. These four analytical dimensions can be distinguished in accordance with their *imposed maintained hypotheses*, or assumptions, and the type of *failures* that arise. The incidence analytical dimension focuses on impact of existing policies and/or on the selection among various policy instruments. For this dimension, as revealed in the chapters by Alston and James as well as in Karp and Perloff, perfect implementation (PI) , no feedback effects from interest group formation (NF) and a given governance structure (GG) assumptions are imposed. Since the benchmark for any governmental intervention is typically perfectly competitive partial or general market equilibrium, *government failure is a natural consequence*. The PI assumption of the incidence analytical dimension is relaxed when we turn to mechanism design. Typically, however, the NF and GG assumptions are maintained. In the chapters by Chambers and Innes, the focus turns to market or institutional failures. All of the political economic formulations relax the assumption of NF, and typically impose GG. The inherent value of this analytical dimension is that it formally recognizes the groups and agents affected by public policies are not passive and can pursue strategies to influence and alter the selection and incidences of policies. As noted in the chapter by de Gorter and Swinnen, the nature of the failure identified by the positive economic analytical dimension depends on the form of the government intervention. For the constitutional structures analytical dimension, the inherent collective decision making processes of public policy are formally recognized. The governance structures delineate the boundaries on negotiations among stakeholders that take place. In its most general form, this analytical dimension relaxes the restrictive assumptions of PI and NF, as well as GG. This paradigm emphasizes the level and distribution of political power; the distribution of power determines the balance and tradeoffs between public and special interests. The fundamental failure that arises from this analytical dimension is an *organizational* failure.

Much of the literature treats the four dimensions as separable investigative pursuits. From the perspective of communicating with professional colleagues, such separability is unsurprising. However, to fundamentally understand, explain or reform current policies, all four dimensions must be integrated. In the final analysis, the message of this chapter is that only by formally recognizing each of the four dimensions is it possible to design and implement public policies that are sustainable and robust to uncontrollable economic and political forces.

Appendix A. Mandatory and voluntary programs

In this appendix, we develop a simple, stylized agricultural sector model in order to compare mandatory and voluntary producer participation for a set of policy instruments. As in Floyd (1965), we compare three policies: a price support, a price support paired with an output restriction, and a price support paired with a land restriction. Unlike Floyd, we do not focus on returns to factors. Instead, we focus on the values of policy parameters, including the necessary price support, acreage reduction, or output quota necessary to achieve a specified increase in farm income.

Our results illustrate the importance of considering participation constraints. Commonly, more emphasis is placed on incentive compatibility constraints in the policy design literature.

The need to induce participation in voluntary programs alters the values of second-best program parameters relative to the values in the corresponding mandatory case. Further, when participation is voluntary, some programs such as a paired output restriction and price support are not implementable that were implementable under mandatory participation.

The appendix is organized as follows: we first report the elasticities of the relevant policy variables with respect to a change in the desired ratio of farm income under the policy to its equilibrium level, denoted Ω, for mandatory government programs. We then report the corresponding elasticities for these policy variables for voluntary government programs, and compare the mandatory and voluntary elasticities.

A.1. Mandatory programs

The government's objective is to minimize its budgetary costs under each policy instrument, while guaranteeing a specified increase in farm income from its equilibrium level:

$$P^* X(P^*) \geqslant \Omega P_e X_e, \tag{A.1}$$

where P_e is the original equilibrium output price and X_e is the original equilibrium output quantity,

$\Omega > 1$ is the ratio of the desired farm sector income relative to its equilibrium level, and P^* is the price such that the quantity demanded $X(P^*)$ at that price results in the desired farm income. To illustrate incidence analysis, we evaluate three policy options specified above that can aid policymakers in achieving a specified increase in farm income. We assume that output quotas are transferable. For the cases of output and land restrictions, mandatory programs have an interesting implication: the desired increase in farm incomes can be achieved through restricting supply and raising the price for agricultural output. The net effect on government expenditures and taxpayers is zero.

We assume that the demand for output takes the following form: $X = P^\eta$, where η is the elasticity of demand. Individual producers are subject to decreasing returns to scale in land, L and capital K, perhaps due to the presence of a fixed factor, such as management. When management is treated as variable, A, production is constant returns to scale. The resulting sector-level production function is $X = I^{1-s} A L^\alpha K^\varphi$, where A reflects the contribution of management, I is the number of producers, and $s = \varphi + \alpha$. All I producers are assumed to be identical in every respect. Land and capital have constant elasticities of supply, with supply curves of $L = w_L^{\beta_L}$ and $K = w_k^{\beta_K}$, respectively, where w_L is the price of land and w_k is the price of capital.

A.1.1. Case I: Price support program

For the simple price support, we are interested in analyzing the necessary change in output price for a specified increase in sector income, relative to the initial equilibrium. The formula for this elasticity is

$$\varepsilon_{P^*,\Omega} = \left(1 - \frac{\alpha}{\frac{1}{\beta_L}+1} - \frac{\varphi}{\frac{1}{\beta_K}+1}\right) > 0. \tag{A.2}$$

A.1.2. Case II: Output restriction

For the output restriction case, we determine the necessary decrease $(1 - \theta)$ in output from its initial level to obtain the desired increase in farm income. Since participation is mandatory, the associated output price can be calculated using the equation describing market demand, viz.

$$\varepsilon_{\theta,\Omega} = \frac{\eta}{1+\eta} < 0 \tag{A.3}$$

$$\varepsilon_{P^*,\Omega} = \frac{1}{1+\eta} > 0. \tag{A.4}$$

A.1.3. Case III: Land restriction

For the land restriction case, we determine the necessary decrease $(1-\phi)$ in output from its initial level in order to obtain the desired increase in farm income. Since participation is mandatory, the associated output price can be calculated using the equation describing market demand.

$$\varepsilon_{\phi,\Omega} = \frac{\Omega P_e X_e}{\alpha(1+\eta)(P^*)^{1+\eta}} \left(\frac{\frac{\eta}{K}\left(\frac{1}{\beta_K}+1-\varphi\right) - \frac{\varphi}{K^\varphi}}{\frac{1}{K}\left(\frac{1}{\beta_K}+1-\varphi\right)+\varphi}\right) \tag{A.5}$$

$$= \frac{1}{\alpha(1+\eta)} \left(\frac{\eta\left(\frac{1}{\beta_K}+1-\varphi\right) - \varphi K^{1-\varphi}}{\left(\frac{1}{\beta_K}+1-\varphi\right)+\varphi K}\right), \tag{A.6}$$

$$\varepsilon_{P^*,\Omega} = \frac{1}{1+\eta}. \tag{A.7}$$

A.2. Voluntary programs

Now, we consider the question of policy design when government programs are voluntary. In most cases, policy design analysis focus on incentive compatibility within a program rather than on the relative desirability of participation or non-participation. This is certainly true when homogeneous producers are considered. For farm income support policies, however, the market-level effects of the chosen policy instruments affect the desirability of producer participation in these programs. As we will show, taking the need for participation to be more profitable than non-participation into account may alter the optimal policy instrument.

We evaluate the same three policy options as in the analysis of mandatory programs. However, in order to account for the participation constraint and the profit-maximizing choices made by non-participants we allow P^* to be a choice variable for the government, rather than being defined by demand, as in the output restriction and land restriction cases. We allow for a fixed transfer T, so that the government can transfer no more than its desired level to producers. Formally, the government's objective is

$$\min(P^* - \tilde{p})x(P^*) + IT \tag{A.8}$$

$$\text{s.t. } P^*x(P^*) \geqslant \Omega P_e X_e, \tag{A.9}$$

where $\Omega > 1$, $\tilde{p} = p(x(P^*))$, and T is the lump-sum transfer to each producer. Output demand and input supply relationships remain the same.

For the two policies, an output restriction or a land restriction, there are two mechanisms for implementation. In the case of an output restriction, the government can either impose an output restriction on participants and allow producers to sell output at the market price, or impose a quota and pay producers the difference between the target price and the market price (a deficiency payment) on their quota production. When participation is mandatory, the two processes are equivalent. When participation is voluntary, only the second mechanism may potentially result in a Nash equilibrium where producers choose to participate in the program.

Similarly, for the case of a land use restriction, the government can either impose a land use restriction on participants and allow them to sell all resulting output at the market price, or can impose a land use restriction and compensate participants above their market returns. Again, only the second mechanism may potentially result in a Nash equilibrium where producers choose to participate in the program. Intuitively, it is impossible to meet producers' participation constraints through a combination of production restrictions for participants and market returns. The individual incentives facing producers will induce them to not participate.

We formally evaluate the effect of including voluntary participation for each of the three policy instruments.

A.2.1. Case I: Price support only

Case I does not have a binding participation constraint, because participating is always more profitable than not participating. The results and elasticities are the same as for the mandatory program.

RESULT ONE. *The budget cost minimizing voluntary price support policy will be characterized by the same price and output as the budget cost minimizing mandatory price support policy.*

A.2.2. Case II: Output quotas

We wish to compare the voluntary output reduction program that achieves the same farm income objective, defined by Ω, as the mandatory output reduction program. To do so, we compare the elasticities of θ with respect to Ω. For the voluntary participation case, the elasticity has the following value:

$$
\varepsilon_{\sigma,\Omega} = (P^* X_e/I)\left[\left(\left(\frac{1}{s}+s-M\right)s\theta^{1/s+s-M-1}\frac{(P^*)^{s-M}}{(IA)^{1/s}Z}X_e^{1/s+s-M}\right.\right.
$$

$$
\left.\left. + \left(\frac{1}{\eta}+M-s\right)\theta^{\frac{1/\eta+M-1}{1-s}}(AZ)^{1/(1-s)}(P^*)^{\frac{M-s}{1-s}}(X_e)^{\frac{1/\eta+M-s}{1-s}}\right)\right]^{-1}, \quad (A.10)
$$

where

$$
Z = \alpha^{\frac{\alpha\beta_L}{1+\beta_K}}\varphi^{\frac{\varphi\beta_K}{1+\beta_L}} \quad \text{and} \quad M = \frac{\alpha\beta_L}{1+\beta_K}+\frac{\varphi\beta_K}{1+\beta_L}.
$$

Reducing θ decreases production by program participants. Intuitively, this reduction has two effects: it decreases the program output, for which the government must pay P^* per unit, and it raises the market price, $\tilde{p}$, which increases the utility of non-participation. When participation is voluntary, the choice of θ reflects both of these considerations, while when participation is mandatory only the first effect is considered. Comparing the two elasticities, we find the following:

RESULT TWO. *The budget cost minimizing voluntary output quota program results in a smaller decrease in output than does the mandatory output quota program, for a given farm income objective.*

Using Case II voluntary program first order necessary condition with respect to θ, we can demonstrate that the acreage reduction is larger in magnitude under the mandatory program provided that $\lambda > I\frac{\tilde{p}\theta}{\Omega P_e}$. Since the shadow value of relaxing the participation constraint is at least I, the value of reducing the fixed transfer for each producer by \$1, the expression will hold if $1 > \frac{\tilde{p}\theta}{\Omega P_e}$. If this expression does not hold, then either the solution will not induce participation, or it is not cost-minimizing.

When $1 < \frac{\tilde{p}\theta}{\Omega P_e}$, then the revenue obtained from selling the restricted amount of output on the market is greater than the desired increase in producer income: $\tilde{p}\theta X_e > \Omega P_e X_e$. Each individual producer has an incentive to defect and increase his individual production, so producers will not voluntarily join the government program unless the government increases P^* or T enough to increase the profits from participating above those from not participating. The government can reduce its direct expenditures by increasing θ. This increases the total quantity supplied by participants, and lowers $\tilde{p}$.

Consider the special case where $\tilde{p}\theta X_e = \Omega P_e X_e$. This is the mandatory program solution. Here, the government spends zero in direct expenditures. Again, however, producers will not voluntarily participate in this program, unless the government raises P^* or T enough to increase the profits from participating above those from not participating. The resulting solution will induce participation, but will not be cost-minimizing. The government can reduce its direct expenditures by increasing θ. This increases the total quantity supplied by participants, and lowers $\tilde{p}$. We conclude that $\lambda > I \frac{\tilde{p}\theta}{\Omega P_e}$, and therefore, the reduction in output is larger in magnitude under the mandatory program than under the voluntary program.

The other difference between our analysis for the voluntary and the mandatory output restriction programs is the introduction of a fixed transfer, T. Conventionally, a simple fixed transfer is the first-best means of raising farm incomes, since it does not distort production choices for profit-maximizing firms. When would the government desire to transfer income entirely through a fixed payment? If the government is concerned with all the distortions induced by payments tied to output production or input use, then a non-distortionary fixed payment dominates. In our analysis, however, the government wishes to minimize its direct costs, subject to raising farm incomes to some target level. When participation is voluntary, output and acreage controls have two potential advantages in this framework. First, the separation of market and program prices for output affects the relative desirability of program participation. Non-participants must compete in the land and capital markets for inputs with participants who are receiving higher output prices. This reduces the relative profitability of non-participation.

Second, influencing the market outcome may in some cases reduce the government's direct costs. At the initial equilibrium, participation would be costless. On the other hand, the entire desired farm income increase must come directly from the government's budget, increasing its costs. By reducing the amount of land in production, or the amount of output produced, the government can increase the returns to producers from the market, providing that demand for agricultural output is sufficiently inelastic ($\eta > -\frac{1}{2}$). Since the government cares only about farm revenues, the cost of the resulting input allocation distortions are not reflected in this decision, *except* to the extent that they lower the cost of inducing participation, as noted previously.

A.2.3. Case III: Land restriction

The analysis for the land restriction policy is similar to the analysis for the output restriction policy. Intuitively, the argument may be summarized as follows: The government wishes to minimize its direct costs, while providing producers with a larger gross revenue than their free market gross revenue. Consider the equilibrium acreage reduction for a mandatory program. If all producers chose to participate in a voluntary program with the same acreage reduction, and no additional transfer, they would obtain all of the desired revenue increase through the market. However, such a program would never induce participation, since returns would be higher for an individual non-participating producer.

Consider now a voluntary program with the mandatory program's acreage reduction level, plus a large enough increase in payments to producers to make participation profitable. This program would induce participation, but would increase government costs and result in a larger increase in producer income than desired. Clearly, the government could do better if it could reduce the additional payment needed to induce producers to participate. A larger acreage reduction, resulting in anticipated higher prices, would increase the additional required payment. A smaller acreage reduction would lower anticipated market prices, and the additional payment required to induce participation. For some set of potential acreage reductions, the government could reduce its direct costs and still maintain producer income at or above the target level.

RESULT THREE. *The budget cost-minimizing voluntary acreage reduction program results in a smaller decrease in acreage and output than does the budget cost minimizing mandatory acreage reduction program for a given farm income objective.*

References

Aaron, H.J. (1989), "Politics and the professors revisited", American Economic Review 79:1–15.
Adams, G.D., G.C. Rausser and L.K. Simon (1996), "Modelling multilateral negotitations: An application to California water policy", Journal of Economic Behavior and Organization 30(1):97–111.
Alston, J.M., and J.S. James (2002), "The incidence of agricultural policy", in: B.L. Gardner and G.C. Rausser, eds., Handbook of Agricultural Economics, Vol. 2 (Elsevier, Amsterdam) Chapter 33, 1689–1749.
Alt, J.E., and K.A. Shepsle (1990), Perspectives on Positive Political-Economy (Cambridge University Press, Cambridge).
Ball, R. (1995), "Interest groups, influence and welfare", Economics and Politics 7:119–146.
Becker, G.S. (1983), "A theory of competition among pressure groups for political influence", Quarterly Journal of Economics 98(3):371–400.
Becker, G.S. (1985), "Public policies, pressure groups, and dead weight costs", Journal of Public Economics 28(3):329–347.
Bhagwati, J.N. (1982), "Directly unproductive profit seeking activities: A welfare theoretic synthesis and generalization", Journal of Political Economy 90:988–1002.
Black, D. (1958), The Theory of Committees and Elections (Cambridge University Press, Cambridge).
Bowles, S., and H. Gintis (1993), "Power and wealth in a competitive capitalist economy", Philosophy and Public Affairs 21(4):334–353.
Brandow, G.E. (1961), "Interrelations among demands for farm products and implication for control of market supply", Bulletin 680 (Pennsylvania Agricultural Experiment Station).
Brock, W.A., and S.P. Magee (1979), "Tariff formation in a democracy", in: J. Black and B. Hindley, eds., Current Issues in International Commercial Policy and Economic Diplomacy (MacMillan Press, London).
Buchanan, J.M., and G. Tullock (1962), The Calculus of Consent (University of Michigan Press, Ann Arbor).
Bullock, D.S. (1992), "Objectives and constraints of government policy: The countercyclicity of transfers to agriculture", American Journal of Agricultural Economics 74:617–629.
Bullock, D.S. (1994), "In search of rational government: What political preference function studies measure and assume", American Journal of Agricultural Economics 76:347–361.

Bullock, D.S. (1995), "Are government transfers efficient? An alternative test of the efficient redistribution hypothesis", Journal of Political Economy 103:1236–1275.

Bullock, D.S. (1996), "Cooperative game theory and the measurement of political power", American Journal of Agricultural Economics 78:745–752.

Chambers, R.G. (1992), "On the design of agricultural policy mechanisms", American Journal of Agricultural Economics 74(3):646–652.

Chambers, R.G. (2002), "Information, incentives and the design of agricultural policies", in: B.L. Gardner and G.C. Rausser, eds., Handbook of Agricultural Economics, Vol. 2 (Elsevier, Amsterdam) Chapter 34, 1751–1825.

Coase, R.H. (1937), "The nature of the firm", Economica N.S. 4:386–405.

Dahl, R.A. (1957), "The concept of power", Behavioral Science 2:201–215.

de Gorter, H., G.C. Rausser and D.J. Nielson (1992), "Productive and predatory public policies: Research expenditures and producer subsidies in agriculture", American Journal of Agricultural Economics 74(1):27–37.

de Gorter, H., and J. Swinnen (2002), "Political economy of agricultural policy", in: B.L. Gardner and G.C. Rausser, eds., Handbook of Agricultural Economics, Vol. 2 (Elsevier, Amsterdam) Chapter 36, 1893–1943.

De Soto, H. (1989), The Other Path: The Invisible Revolution in the Third World (Harper & Rowe, New York).

Downs, A. (1957), The Economic Theory of Democracy (Harper, New York).

Ferejohn, J.A., and B.S. Rundquist (1975), "Observations on a distributive theory of policy making", in: C. Liske, W. Loehr and J. McCannant, eds., Comparative Public Policy (John Wiley and Sons, New York).

Floyd, J.E. (1965), "The effects of farm price supports on the returns to land and labor in agriculture", Journal of Political Economy 73:148–158.

Foster, W.E., and G.C. Rausser (1993), "Price distorting compensation serving the consumer and taxpayer interest", Public Choice 77(2):275–291.

Foster, W.E., R. Gray and G.C. Rausser (1995), "Mobility, diversification, and sustainability of trade reform", in: G.C. Rausser, ed., GATT Negotiations and the Political Economy of Policy Reform (Springer-Verlag, Berlin, Heidelberg, New York) Chapter 7, 145–164.

Froelich, N.J., A. Oppenheimer and J. Young (1971), Political Leadership and Collective Goods (Princeton University Press, Princeton, NJ).

Gardner, B.L. (1983), "Efficient redistribution through commodity markets", American Journal of Agricultural Economics 225–234.

Gardner, B.L. (1987), "Causes of U.S. farm commodity programs", Journal of Political Economy 95:290–310.

Gardner, B.L. (1989), "Economic theory and farm politics", American Journal of Agricultural Economics 71:1165–1171.

Getches, D.H. (1997), Water Law in a Nutshell (West Publishing, St. Paul).

Golan, A.A., G.G. Judge and L.S. Karp (1996), "A maximum entropy approach to estimation and inference in dynamic models or counting fish in the sea using maximum entropy", Journal of Economic Dynamic and Control 20:559–582.

Golan, A.A., G.G. Judge and D. Miller (1996), Maximum Entropy Econometrics (John Wiley and Sons, New York).

Goodhue, R., S. Mordadet, G. Rausser, P. Rio, L. Simon and S.Thoyer (2001), "Implications of the structure of power in multilateral negotiations: An application to French water policy", Working paper (University of California, Davis).

Harsanyi, J.C. (1963), "A simplified bargaining model for the N-person cooperative game", International Economic Review 4:193–220.

Harsanyi, J.C. (1977), Rational Behavior and Bargaining Equilibrium in Games and Social Situations (Cambridge University Press, Cambridge).

Hicks, J.R. (1969), A Theory of Economic History (Claredon Press, Oxford).

Hirshleifer, J. (1991), "The paradox of power", Economics and Politics 3(3):177–200.

Innes, R. (2002), "Market failures and second-best analysis, with a focus on nutrition, credit and incomplete markets", in: B.L. Gardner and G.C. Rausser, eds., Handbook of Agricultural Economics, Vol. 2 (Elsevier, Amsterdam) Chapter 35, 1827–1892.

International Monetary Fund (1997), "Partnership for sustainable growth", IMF Declaration.

James, J. (2000), "Quality responses to commodity policies", Ph.D. thesis (University of California, Davis).

Jeong, K.-S., D.S. Bullock and P. Garcia (1999), "Testing and the efficient redistribution hypothesis: An application to Japanese beef policy", American Journal of Agricultural Economics 81(2):408–423.

Jessop, B. (1977), "Recent theories of the capitalist state", Cambridge Journal of Economics 1:353–373.

Johnson, S.R. (1998), "Strategic behavior, institutional change and the future of agriculture", American Journal of Agricultural Economics 80(5):898–915.

Karp, L.S., and J.M. Perloff (2002), "Agricultural trade economics", in: B.L. Gardner and G.C. Rausser, eds., Handbook of Agricultural Economics, Vol. 2 (Elsevier, Amsterdam) Chapter 37, 1945–1998.

Krueger, A.O. (1974), "The political economy of the rent-seeking society", American Economic Review 64:291–303.

Kydland, F.E., and E.C. Prescott (1977), "Rules rather than discretion: The inconsistency of optimal plans", Journal of Political Economy 85:473–492.

Lewis, T., R. Ware and R. Feenstra (1989), "Eliminating price supports: A political-economy perspective", Journal of Public Economics 140:159–185.

Lipton, M. (1977), Why Poor People Stay Poor: Urban Bias in World Development (Harvard University Press, Cambridge, MA).

Love, H.A., G.C. Rausser and D.M. Burton (1990), "Policy preference functions: grand themes and new directions", Paper presented at the Advances in Public Choice Modeling invited paper session at the Joint meetings of the American and Western Agricultural Economics Association meetings, Vancouver, BC, August 1990, Working Paper No. 571 (California Agricultural Experiment Station, Department of Agricultural and Resource Economics, University of California, Berkeley).

Love, H.A., G.C. Rausser and D.M. Burton (unpublished), "Estimating statistical properties of political economic decisions", Unpublished manuscript.

Lyons, R.F. (1999), "Essays on dynamic game theory and policy analysis", Ph.D. Dissertation (Department of Agricultural and Resource Economics, University of California, Berkeley).

McCluskey, J.J., and G.C. Rausser (2001), "Estimation of perceived risk and its effect on property values", Land Economics 77(1).

McCubbins, M.D., R.G. Noll and B.R. Weingast (1989), "Structure and process, politics and policy: Administrative arrangement and the political control of agencies", Virginia Law Review 75:431–482.

Morris, S. (2001), "Political correctness", Journal of Political Economy 109(2):231–265.

Mundlak, Y. (2001), "Production and supply", in: B.L. Gardner and G.C. Rausser, eds., Handbook of Agricultural Economics, Vol. 1 (Elsevier, Amsterdam) Chapter 1, 3–85.

Myerson, R.B., and M.A. Satterthwaite (1983), "Efficient mechanisms for bilateral trading", Journal of Economic Theory 29:265–281.

Nash, J.F. (1950), "The bargaining problem", Econometrica 18:155–162.

Nash, J.F. (1953), "Two person cooperative games", Econometrica 21:128–140.

Nitzan, S., and J. Paroush (1965), Collective Decision Making: An Economic Outlook (Harvard University Press, Cambridge).

North, D.C. (1981), Structure and Change in American History (Norton, New York).

O'Conner, J. (1973), The Fiscal Crisis of the State (St. Martin's Press, New York).

Olson, M., Jr. (1965), The Logic of Collective Action (Harvard University Press, Cambridge, MA).

Peltzman, S. (1976), "Toward a general theory of regulation", Journal of Law and Economics 211:211–240.

Peters, H.J.M. (1992), Axiomatic Bargaining Game Theory (Kluwer Academic Publishers, Dordrecht).

Rausser, G.C. (1982), "Political economic markets: PESTs and PERTs in food and agriculture", American Journal of Agricultural Economics 64(3):821–833.

Rausser, G.C. (1990), "A new paradigm for policy reform and economic development", American Journal of Agricultural Economics 72(3):821–826.

Rausser, G.C. (1990), "Implications of structural adjustment: Experience in developing world for Eastern Europe", American Journal of Agricultural Economics 72(5):1252–1256.

Rausser, G.C. (1992), "Predatory versus productive government: The case of U.S. agricultural policies", Journal of Economic Perspectives 6:133–158.

Rausser, G.C. (1993), "An emerging framework for economic development: An LDC perspective", in: S.R. Johnson and S.A. Martin, eds., Industrial Policy for Agriculture in the Global Economy (Iowa State University Press, Ames) Chapter 11, 229–245.

Rausser, G.C. (1995), GATT Negotiations and the Political Economy of Policy Reform (Springer-Verlag, Berlin, Heidelberg, New York).

Rausser, G.C. (2000), "Collective choice in water resource systems", in: A. Dinar, ed., The Political Economy of Water Pricing Implementation (The World Bank, Washington, DC; Oxford University Press, New York, NY).

Rausser, G.C., and H. de Gorter (1989), "Endogenizing policy in models of agricultural markets", in: A. Maunder and A. Valdes, eds., Agriculture and Governments in an Interdependent World, Proceedings of the 20th International Conference of Agriculture Economists, Buenos Aires, August 1988 (International Association of Agricultural Economists, University of Oxford, Dartmouth) 259–274.

Rausser, G.C., and J.W. Freebairn (1974), "Estimation of policy preference functions: An application to U.S. beef import quotas", Review of Economics and Statistics 56:437–449.

Rausser, G.C., and D. Irwin (1989), "The political economy of agricultural policy reform", European Review of Agricultural Economics 349–366.

Rausser, G.C., and S.R. Johnson (1993), "State-market-civil institutions: The case of Eastern Europe", World Development 21(4):675–689.

Rausser, G.C., and R. Just (1982), "Principles of policy modeling in agriculture", in: Modeling Agriculture for Policy Analysis in the 1980s, September 1981 (Federal Reserve Bank of Kansas City, Kansas City) 139–174. Also in: New Directions in Econometric Modeling and Forecasting in U.S. Agriculture (Elsevier, North-Holland, New York) 1982, pp. 763–800.

Rausser, G.C., E. Lichtenberg and R. Lattimore (1982), "Developments in theory and empirical applications of endogenous governmental behavior", in: G.C. Rausser, ed., New Directions in Econometric Modeling and Forecasting in U.S. Agriculture (Elsevier, New York) Chapter 18.

Rausser, G.C., and L.K. Simon (1999), "A non-cooperative model of collective decision making: A multilateral bargaining approach", Working Paper (Department of Agricultural and Resource Economics, University of California at Berkeley).

Rausser, G.C., L.K. Simon and K. van't Veld (1995), "Political economic processes and collective decision making", in: G.H. Peters and D.D. Hedley, eds., Agricultural Competitiveness: Market Forces and Policy (Aldershot, Hants, England; Brookfield, Dartmouth, VT) 261–273.

Rausser, G.C., D. Zilberman and R.E. Just (1984), "The distributional effects of land controls in agriculture", Western Journal of Agricultural Economics 9(2):215–232.

Rausser, G.C., and P. Zusman (1992), "Public policy and constitutional prescription", American Journal of Agricultural Economics 74(2):247–257.

Rausser, G.C., and P. Zusman (forthcoming), Political Power and Endogenous Policy Formation (Cambridge University Press).

Riker, W. (1962), The Theory of Political Coalitions (Yale University Press, New Haven, CT).

Rodrik, D. (1989), "Promises, promises: Credible policy reform via signalling", Economic Journal 99:756–772.

Roemer, J.E. (1978), "Neoclassicism, marxism, and collective action", Journal of Economic Issues 12(1):147–161.

Rubinstein, A. (1982), "Perfect equilibrium in a bargaining model", Econometrica 50.

Russell, B. (1938), Power: A New Social Analysis (George Allen & Unwin, London; W.W. Norton, New York).

Salanie, B. (1997), The Economics of Contracts: A Primer (MIT Press, Cambridge, MA).

Steiner, P.O. (1969), "The public sector and the public interest", in: An Analysis and Evaluation of Public Expenditures: The PPB System, Commendium of papers submitted to the Subcommittee on Economy and Government of the Joint Economic Committee, Vol. 1 (Congress of the United States) 14–65.

Stigler, G. (1971), "The theory of economic regulation", Bell Journal of Economics 2:3–21.

Sumner, D.A., and S. Tangermann (2002), "International trade and policy negotiations", in: B.L. Gardner and G.C. Rausser, eds., Handbook of Agricultural Economics, Vol. 2 (Elsevier, Amsterdam) Chapter 38, 1999–2055.

Tullock, G. (1967), "The welfare costs of tariffs, monopolies and theft", Western Economics Journal 5:224–232.

von Cramon-Taubadel, S. (1992), "A critical assessment of the political preference function approach in agricultural economics", Agricultural Economics 7:371–394.

Wallace, T.D. (1962), "Measures of social costs of agricultural programs", Journal of Farm Economics 44:580–594.

Weingast, B.R., K.A. Shepsle and C. Johnson (1981), "The political economy of benefits and costs: A neoclassical approach to distributive politics", Journal of Political Economy 89(4):642–664.

Williamson, O.E. (1975), Markets and Hierarchies: Analysis and Antitrust Implications (The Free Press, MacMillan, New York).

Williamson, O.E. (1993), "Contested exchange versus the governance of contractual relations", Journal of Economic Perspectives.

Zusman, P. (1976), "The incorporation and measurement of social power in economic models", International Economic Review 17:447–462.

Zusman, P., and A. Amiad (1977), "A quantitative investigation of a political economy – The Israeli dairy program", American Journal of Agricultural Economics 59:88–98.

Chapter 40

FOOD SECURITY AND FOOD ASSISTANCE PROGRAMS

CHRISTOPHER B. BARRETT

Department of Applied Economics and Management, Cornell University, Ithaca, NY

Contents

Handbook of Agricultural Economics, Volume 2, Edited by B. Gardner and G. Rausser

Abstract

Widespread hunger and malnutrition persist today despite considerable growth in per capita food availability. This has prompted an evolving conceptualization of food security and of mechanisms to attain and maintain food security. This chapter discusses both food security and food assistance programs designed to respond to the threat of food insecurity.

Keywords

food security, food aid, hunger, malnutrition, undernutrition

JEL classification: Q18, I12, O12

1. Introduction

Although aggregate food security has improved markedly over the past half century, thanks to increasing global food availability per capita and decreasing real food prices, hunger, malnutrition, and food insecurity remain widespread. Estimates range widely, centering on roughly one billion people suffering undernourishment today, while probably at least one-third of the world's population bears nutritional risk. In an era of ample food availability to provide for sufficient nutrient intake for everyone on earth, the continued suffering of a substantial part of humanity is seen by many as morally repugnant, thus finding appropriate distribution mechanisms to resolve the problem is considered a political imperative. The impulse to action is strong but does not guarantee success. Most nations have implemented food assistance programs of some sort, but many of these have proved expensive, ineffective, or both.

For these reasons, food security remains a prominent concern for economists. This chapter discusses both food security and food assistance programs. The latter are a response to threats to the former, so the topics are best treated jointly. Section 2 reviews the concept of food security, then presents a basic analytical model of food security, approached as a subtopic of the economics of health. The discussion then turns to the multiple threats to food security, available empirical indicators of food security, and various mechanisms for reducing vulnerability. Food security is linked to the consumption, production, and marketing of food, the functioning of factor markets – especially for labor – social safety nets, governmental and nongovernmental assistance agencies, initial asset and income distributions, and a myriad of other subjects across several disciplines. The aim of this chapter is therefore not to plumb each subtopic in depth so much as to identify the key issues and the relevant literatures to which readers interested in greater detail should turn. Section 3 reviews the literature on government food assistance programs, the suite of distributive and regulatory interventions through which states try to ensure citizens' food security. A range of domestic food assistance programs are considered first, emphasizing in particular the United States' relatively well-studied programs. Then attention turns to international assistance programs, especially food aid. The next and largest subsection considers issues common to both domestic and international food assistance programs: additionality, targeting, intertemporal variability, direct and indirect costs, and incentives. Section 4 briefly concludes.

Several interrelated themes repeatedly appear. First, food security is inherently an individual phenomenon, and thus a subject with its roots in microeconomics. Second, food security is a dynamic problem subject to uncertainty and thus best conceptualized as an *ex ante* status rather than an *ex post* outcome. Third, the unobservability of food security makes data collection and analysis challenging. A variety of indicators are available, but we have only preliminary, not conclusive, answers to many key issues about food security and food assistance programs. Fourth, although both policy and research have focused on macronutrient (i.e., calorie and protein) sufficiency, micronutrient deprivation is just as serious an issue. Fifth, the incentive effects of nutritional vulnerability and of food assistance programs, as well as the moral hazard and selectivity problems associated with the latter, may be significant. Sixth, the impulse to action often motivates government interventions without careful consideration of the effectiveness of their targeting and financing, much less the broader question of whether the state has a comparative advantage in the particular method of food assistance undertaken. Markets and civil society are crucial complements to governments in ensuring food security at all levels of analysis, individual through national. As yet, we have only a vague understanding of the appropriate blend of private, public, and state institutions and interventions.

2. Food security

Food security is an inherently unobservable concept that has largely eluded a precise and operational definition. Thinking about food security has advanced from a first generation focus on aggregate food availability – the supply side – through a second generation emphasizing individual- and household-level access to food – the demand side – toward a nascent third generation conceptualization that places food security in a broader framework of individual behavior in the face of uncertainty, irreversibilities, and binding constraints on choice. This section offers a simple, formal framework for understanding this third generation, microeconomic view of food security and the multiple threats thereto. A range of indicators exist for measuring the concepts closely related to food security, but we do not yet have good, direct measures of food security of the third generation sort. Nonetheless, the available indicators generally show that the past forty years have brought noteworthy improvement in per capita food availability, nutrient intake, and nutritional outcomes. But huge numbers of people – one to four billion, depending on how one estimates – continue to suffer food insecurity. The continuing, large-scale problem of food insecurity is primarily a distributional issue, a matter of getting available food to people who need it, when they need it, and of ensuring their regular, appropriate, affordable access to food. An array of sometimes complementary, sometimes competing public and private mechanisms have been deployed in an attempt to enhance food security locally and globally. Section 3 will discuss one subset of mechanisms: state-sponsored food assistance programs.

2.1. Concepts and definitions

The most common definition of "food security" is "access by all people at all times to enough and appropriate food to provide the energy and nutrients needed to maintain an active and healthy life". If food security involves access at all times to enough and appropriate foods, then "food insecurity" reflects uncertain access to enough and appropriate foods. Food security is thus an inherently *ex ante* status with respect to nutrition and health. There are a number of closely related, *ex post* concepts, i.e., concepts related to realized outcomes. "Hunger" is a physiological sensation associated with insufficient food intake [American Dietetic Association (1990)], closely related to the concept of "food insufficiency", meaning that an individual or household sometimes or often goes without food. Until recently, food insufficiency was the primary variable collected in USDA domestic research on food security. While hunger and food insufficiency imply food insecurity, the converse does not hold. Significant shortfalls in the consumption of macronutrients (calories, protein, fats) subsequently become manifest in "undernutrition" or "protein energy malnutrition" (PEM). I will use these terms interchangeably. These too are potential but not necessary consequences of food insecurity [Campbell (1991)]. "Malnutrition" is an outcome with a complex relationship to hunger, because it is influenced by many other variables as well (e.g., health status, energy expenditure in work, caregiver education levels, community infrastructure, micronutrient intake) [Scrimshaw et al. (1968), Behrman and Deolalikar (1988), Strauss and Thomas (1995, 1998)]. Malnutrition is another potential but not necessary consequence of food insecurity. Food security is sufficient but not necessary for freedom from hunger but neither necessary nor sufficient for adequate nutrition. Furthermore, malnutrition can reflect insufficient intake and absorption of micronutrients (vitamins and minerals), even if protein and energy intake are satisfactory. Micronutrient deficiencies – particularly of iodine, iron, and vitamin A – are increasingly recognized as serious and widespread food security issues, primarily but not exclusively in low-income countries [Behrman (1995), Calloway (1995), Bouis and Novenario-Reese (1997), Oldham et al. (1998)]. The concept of food security thus concerns the risk of macronutrient or micronutrient deficiency, which may threaten one's physical well-being.

There are five key elements to an analytically and operationally useful model of food security. First, it must work from the physiological need of individuals for nutrients supplied by food, but it must also be aggregable, i.e., useful in assessing food security at units of analysis larger than individuals (e.g., households, communities, occupational groups, provinces, nations, and international regions). The concept of food security is most precise at the individual level because its foundation is the individual-specific nutrient requirements for maintaining an active and healthy life. For this reason, nutritionists tend to approach food security issues from the individual level. However, until recently – at least until the pathbreaking work of Sen (1981) – most economic analysis of food security focused on more aggregate levels of analysis: households containing multiple persons, districts or income or wealth classes containing multiple households, nation states containing multiple districts or classes, or international regions. Aggregation inevitably suppresses within-group variability and has thereby probably led to substantial downward bias in estimates of the food-insecure proportion of studied populations. As a consequence, more disaggregated data consistently reveal greater prevalence and severity of food insecurity [Popkin (1981), McLean (1987)]. More disaggregated analysis also improves understanding of the correlates and causality of food insecurity, which does not arise exclusively – even predominantly – because of covariate shocks to an entire population.

Along these lines, an important, recent literature probes intrahousehold allocation issues, including the potentially differential food security status of different members of the same household [Pitt and Rosenzweig (1985), Rosenzweig (1986), Behrman (1988), Haddad and Kanbur (1990), Pitt, Rosenzweig and Hassan (1990), Rogers and Schlossman (1990), Haddad and Kanbur (1992), Haddad and Reardon (1993), Haddad and Hoddinott (1994), Kanbur and Haddad (1994), Doss (1996), Behrman (1997), Haddad et al. (1997)]. Given that the literature overwhelmingly rejects the hypothesis of full risk pooling between households [Townsend (1995)], there is no compelling reason to expect full risk pooling to exist within the household [Doss (1996)]. The implication is that there may be significant intrahousehold variation in food security. Since children typically depend entirely on others (parents or adult relatives, charities, or the state) for access to food, it is widely believed that food-insecure children in apparently food-secure households are those most commonly overlooked in aggregate analysis.

Second, a useful model of food security must recognize the complementarities and trade-offs between food and other variables, notably education, care-giving, and health. One reason it is difficult to estimate precisely the number of undernourished people in the world is that macro- and micronutrient requirements vary intra- and inter-personally with body mass, occupation, environment, activity level, and health status. Observers are sometimes puzzled when obviously hungry people consciously limit food intake in order to conserve shelter, durable assets, health expenditures, etc. But people struggling to survive sometimes need (and are able) to sacrifice food intake to protect future income-earning potential. Likewise, even hungry people are unlikely to spend windfall gains on food alone. Hence the widespread empirical evidence of very low income elasticity of demand for calories, even among very poor populations [Behrman and Deolalikar (1987), Bouis and Haddad (1992), Alderman (1993), Strauss and Thomas (1995)].

Third, a useful model of food security must capture behavioral dynamics. The biological necessity of high frequency nutrient intake means that food security status may be time-varying, and that current behavior and circumstances may be a function of both past experience and expected future patterns. Moreover, because an individual's optimal nutrient intake range is relatively narrow, people concerned about their physical well-being seek stable intake patterns, i.e., food consumption smoothing. This places a premium on continuous access to factor and product markets that facilitate trade across space and time according to comparative advantage, and on safety nets to stitch up holes left by incomplete markets.

Fourth, a useful food security model must be built upon an understanding of uncertainty and risk. The biological lags inherent to food production, and the intertemporal variability of market prices, employment, transfers, etc., subject food consumption decisions to temporal uncertainty. The term "security" implies freedom from risk. Food security therefore relates to the risk of insufficient nutrient access to ensure physical well-being, i.e., not only to deprivation but also to exposure to risk of adverse nutrient intake shocks.[1] Most of the literature nevertheless fails to address issues

---

[1] Others use the terms "nutritional risk" and "vulnerability" in much the same sense [Beaton (1987), McLean (1987), Chambers (1989), Morduch (1994, 1995), Davies (1996), S. Maxwell (1996)].

of risk and uncertainty, perhaps due to a lack of longitudinal data necessary to address these issues empirically. This matters because (i) individuals have preferences with respect to risk, in particular, empirical research suggests most people are risk averse, and (ii) irrespective of risk preferences, temporal risk induces behavioral changes that affect consumption, production, marketing, savings, and investment patterns with long-term consequences for food security. Risk may thus be both intrinsically and instrumentally detrimental. The basic aim of food assistance programs (FAPs) is to reduce food insecurity, i.e., to avert rather than to reverse nutritional problems. This subtle but crucial distinction is often overlooked and complicates evaluation of FAP effectiveness, as Section 3 discusses. Food insecurity is perhaps best understood as the probability of falling below some threshold level of nutrient access, a point developed more fully in the next subsection.

Fifth, a useful model of food security must capture irreversibilities and associated threshold effects that make the threat of an adverse nutritional state so worrisome. Much recent research has explored the implications of the joint existence of sunk costs and uncertainty for investment behavior [Dixit and Pindyck (1994)]. If food is a source of nutrients that are an input into the production of physical well-being – a type of human capital – the literature on investment under uncertainty applies to issues of food security as well. The key irreversibilities to be considered relate to death and permanent cognitive or physical impairment. Behaviors may change radically as one approaches the threshold of adverse, irreversible states, thereby introducing important nonlinearities into many economic and nutritional relationships, and helping provide an explanation for anomalous observations such as Giffen goods.

2.2. A microeconomic modeling approach

The above five elements are not commonly synthesized in the literature on food security, particularly not in a formal model. This section sketches out a microeconomic model of individual behavior that incorporates uncertainty, dynamics, irreversibilities, and the interactions of food with other variables in producing physical well-being. The model builds on Becker's (1965) household model, in which physical well-being is a good produced by the household, and on important contributions by Dasgupta (1993), Glomm and Palumbo (1993), and Chavas (1995), each of whom addresses technical issues omitted here in the interest of accessibility and brevity. Food security falls out of the model as an indicator of risk exposure. This model formally captures the complex interactions among many different variables endogenous and exogenous to the individual, including various mechanisms through which society can attempt to enhance food security. It therefore provides the analytical framework for the rest of the chapter.

Assume an individual maximizes the discounted stream of expected utility derived from the consumption of various goods and services $(x)^2$ and from his or her

---

[2] In this notation, bold type denotes vectors, capitals denote matrices, subscripts index time, superscripts index elements of vectors and matrices, and uppercase and lowercase Greek letters reflect unobservable, estimable functions, and parameters or shocks, respectively.

physical well-being (w). Consumption quantities (x), asset stockbuilding (s), and activity levels (l) are chosen directly, i.e., they are control variables in the stochastic dynamic optimization problem. Physical well-being, however, is a state variable that is influenced both by the control variables and by stochastic, exogenous variables (z) according to imperfectly known laws of motion. Utility is strictly increasing in x and w. Without loss of generality, utility and physical well-being are both nonnegative, with $U(x, w|_{w=0}) = 0$, i.e., minimal physical well-being yields minimal utility no matter the level of contemporaneous material consumption. Individual choice can be understood as if it were the solution to the following problem.

$$\text{Max}_{x_t, l_t, s_t} E_0 \sum_{t=0}^{\infty} \beta^t U(w_t, x_t) \tag{1}$$

$$\text{s.t. } w_{t+1} = \Theta\left(w_t, n_t, l_t, x_t^{nf}, z_t, \phi_t^h\right), \tag{2}$$

$$n_t = \gamma\left(x_t^{f'} N, \phi_t^h, I_t\right), \tag{3}$$

$$a_{t+1} = \delta a_t + s_t + \phi_t^a, \tag{4}$$

$$p_t^{x'}(x_t + s_t) = p_t^{q'}(q_t) + b_t + g_t, \quad \forall x, s, q \in T, \tag{5}$$

$$x_t + s_t = q_t + k_t, \quad \forall x, s, q \in NT, \tag{6}$$

$$\Lambda\left(q_t, l_t, a_t, w_t \mid \phi_t^q\right) = 0, \tag{7}$$

$$b_t \leqslant \Omega(a_t), \tag{8}$$

$$e' l_t \leqslant l_0, \tag{9}$$

$$a_t, l_t, x_t \geqslant \mathbf{0}. \tag{10}$$

In this formulation, $\beta \in [0, 1]$ is the time discount factor used to capture individual intertemporal preferences and thereby to permit calculation of the net present value of choices with implications for future behaviors. Now suppressing time subscripts for the sake of clarity, Equation (2) is the law of motion for physical well-being, which captures the complex, joint influence of preexisting conditions, current nutrient intake, n,[3] current activity patterns, l, current nonfood consumption (e.g., of medicine, shelter, clothing, etc.) patterns, x^{nf}, exogenous variables (potentially including others' activity patterns and well-being, or available infrastructure), z, and stochastic shocks to health, ϕ^h.[4] The function $\Theta(\bullet)$ is arbitrarily censored at a minimum value of zero, beyond which it is strictly increasing in n, x^{nf}, and z over a considerable range – the one

---

[3] The distinction between nutrient intake and nutrient absorption is ignored for the sake of brevity. See Strauss and Thomas (1998) for a good discussion of some of the methodological issues involved.

[4] The large literature on household production of health and nutrition is meticulously reviewed in Behrman and Deolalikar (1988), Strauss and Thomas (1995, 1998).

relevant to the present analysis – before reaching a maximum at w^* and then potentially decreasing in at least some arguments as gluttony, overmedication, etc., degrade well-being.

Food consumption enters into the utility function directly insofar as people enjoy nonnutritional attributes such as taste, texture, color, etc., and indirectly through the provision of bioavailable nutrients (Equation (3)) that help produce physical well-being (Equation (2)). Equation (3) establishes that current nutrient intake is a function, $\gamma(\bullet)$, of nutrient availability – the product of food consumption volumes, x^f, and the nutrient content of those foods, reflected in a nonnegative matrix, N – health shocks, ϕ^h, and the consumer's nutritional understanding (e.g., how to make best use of given foods), as reflected in the information set I. N can be disaggregated to any level of micronutrient detail. This formulation emphasizes that nutrient intake is not solely a function of food intake, nor does good health reduce to good nutrition. Individuals with extremely unsanitary living conditions and little access to health care are likely to be malnourished, even at relatively high levels of food intake [Alderman (1993), Strauss and Thomas (1998)].

Equation (4) represents the law of motion for asset stocks, capturing physical depreciation $\delta \in [0, 1]$, stockbuilding (s), and shocks to property rights (ϕ^a) that might cause extraordinary gains or losses (e.g., theft, destruction). Equation (5) is an intertemporal budget constraint for tradable goods and services (the set T includes tradable consumption goods, assets, and outputs); the monetary value of current consumption cannot exceed the sum of the value of output, net cash borrowing, b, and net gifts or unrequited transfers, g. Where in-kind transfers of a tradable occur, $g = p^{x'}k$, where k represents a vector of in-kind transfer flow volumes. Equation (6) represents the corresponding intertemporal budget constraint for nontradables (the set NT includes nontradable consumption goods, assets, and outputs).

Equation (7) is a stochastic production technology that maps the netput, labor activity, and asset stock vectors, q, l, and a, respectively, physical well-being, and stochastic production shocks, ϕ^q, into output quantities. This includes not only food production, but also production of goods and services, including wage labor (i.e., ϕ^q includes market unemployment risk). The borrowing constraint potentially imposed by one's asset holdings is reflected in (8), with the function $\Omega(a)$ weakly increasing in each asset. Relation (9) reflects a time constraint on the individual's activity patterns, where e is simply a vector of ones.

This model captures how improved nutrition today contributes to health, thereby generating utility not only directly, through individuals' valuation of current physical well-being, but also indirectly through (1) the persistence of physical condition, (2) the functional consequences of ill health on productivity, (3) the effects of productivity on asset holdings and access to credit, and (4) the effects of these latter two on consumption patterns. If the indirect effects of good nutrition are considerable, then individuals, households, communities, and governments should invest more in health than would be implied by its pure utility [Strauss and Thomas (1998)]. The literature on nutrition and labor productivity suggests that a well-fed population exhibits greater productivity, thereby contributing to economic growth and development [Leibenstein (1957), Stiglitz (1976), Bliss and Stern (1978a, 1978b), Strauss (1986), Sahn and Alderman (1988), Behrman (1993), Strauss and Thomas (1998)]. Protein-energy malnutrition and some forms of micronutrient deficiency (e.g., anemia caused by insufficient iron absorption) directly reduce cognitive and physical activity, and hence labor productivity. Undernutrition also has indirect impacts on labor productivity, by increasing vulnerability to infection and injury, which cause lost labor time and unnecessary health expenditures, and by decreasing cognitive achievement in and outside of school [American Dietetic Association (1990)].[5] There are important feedback effects: higher incomes not only foster good health and nutrition, but good health and nutrition also contribute to greater well-being. Entering into this virtuous cycle – and avoiding the corresponding vicious one of low incomes and poor health and nutrition – is the aim of all FAPs.

Irreversibilities and threshold effects are crucial to health dynamics. Individuals are finitely lived but of unknown duration *ex ante*. This is captured in this model by an absorbing state representing death. When $w_t = \Theta(\bullet) = 0$ at some time t^D, thereafter, $w_t = 0$, $\forall t > t^D$. This is a survival constraint. There is likewise an intermediate absorbing state, m, representing permanent impairment, as with blindness brought on by vitamin A deficiency or cretinism caused by iodine deficiency. So, once $w_t = \Theta(\bullet) \leqslant m$ at some time t^M, then $w_t \in [0, m]$, $\forall t > t^M$. These absorbing states capture the irreversibility of the damage done by severe malnutrition, illness, and injury, while still permitting use of the dynamic optimization techniques associated with infinite horizon problems. In general, there will not be an analytical solution to problems so posed, but numerical methods can be used to simulate alternative behavioral patterns. Moreover, as a conceptual tool, the irreversibilities of the model focus attention appropriately on potentially catastrophic conditions and on mechanisms by which individuals can be pulled away from the precipice of permanent impairment or death.

Proximity to adverse irreversible states is problematic because people face temporal uncertainty regarding future prices, transfers, and shocks to health (ϕ^h), asset stocks (ϕ^a), and production yields (ϕ^q). Consequently, all decisions are made subject to risk, defined as exposure to potentially adverse states of nature [Hardaker et al. (1997)]. Assuming these risks can be quantified, each individual thus makes decisions conditional on a subjective joint density function, $\Phi(\bullet)$, over exogenous variables. This density function and the control variables – l, s, and x – together establish the endogenous probability of (i) maintenance of near-optimal physical well-being ($w \approx w^*$),[6] (ii) avoidance of permanent impairment ($w > m$), and (iii) survival ($w > 0$). Food security can thus be defined as the marginal probability at time t of any or all of those three states in time $t + s$ (where $s \geqslant 0$), as a function of current nutrient intake, $\mathbf{n}$,

---

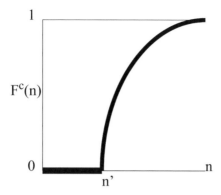

Figure 1. The relation between food security and nutrient intake, $F^c(n)$, in one dimension.

and conditional on a host of other variables, which we suppress for the sake of clarity. Three ordered, formal definitions of food security thus emerge:

- Class one (or "survival") food security:

$$F_t^1(\boldsymbol{n}) = \text{Prob}(w_{t+s} > 0), \tag{11}$$

- Class two (or "nonimpairment") food security:

$$F_t^2(\boldsymbol{n}) = \text{Prob}(w_{t+s} > m), \tag{12}$$

- Class three (or "healthy") food security:

$$F_t^3(\boldsymbol{n}) = \text{Prob}(w_{t+s} \approx w^*). \tag{13}$$

At time t (i.e., when $s = 0$), all variables are (directly or indirectly) observable, so the time series functional F_t^c (where c denotes the particular class of food security considered) starts with a binary variable equal to zero or one in the current period. An individual is either currently food secure or not. A non-binary definition identifying whether or not someone is food secure at any given future time (i.e., $s > 0$) can be generated by establishing a threshold probability – p^1 for F^1, p^2 for F^2, and p^3 for F^3 – at or above which one is considered food secure and below which one is considered food insecure. As with the setting of poverty lines, determination of such thresholds is necessarily somewhat arbitrary. Given the relative severity of the underlying conditions associated with each class of food security, however, it should be axiomatic that $p^1 > p^2 > p^3$.

Recall that $\Theta(\bullet)$ is censored at zero and then strictly increasing in $\boldsymbol{n}$ through the point of maximal physical well-being, w^*. $F^c(\boldsymbol{n})$ will therefore likewise be censored at zero each period and then increase to the maximal value of one.[7] Figure 1 depicts

---

[7] The positive monotonicity of $F^c(\boldsymbol{n})$ helps distinguish food security status, an *ex ante* concept related to downside risk, from nutritional status, an *ex post* concept that must incorporate overconsumption outcomes.

this relation graphically for a single nutrient, n (an element of $\boldsymbol{n}$), e.g., calories or protein. The kink in $F^c(\boldsymbol{n})$ at n' depicts the subsistence or nonimpairment constraints for $F^1(\boldsymbol{n})$ and $F^2(\boldsymbol{n})$, respectively. This corner can significantly affect food demand patterns, yielding low or negative income or expenditure elasticities of nutrient intake, as we discuss in Section 3.3. $F^c(\boldsymbol{n})$ reflects the change in marginal probabilities with respect to $\boldsymbol{n}$, holding constant the other arguments of $\Theta(\bullet)$: $w_t, l_t, x_t^{nf}, z_t, \phi_t^h$. Shifts in these variables induce shifts in $F^c(\boldsymbol{n})$, moving the upward-sloping portion left, right, up, down, or some combination of these. For example, medicines or oral rehydration salts (in x^{nf}) to help control diarrheal diseases and thereby improve the bioavailability of nutrients given constant intake volumes would shift $F^c(\boldsymbol{n})$ upward since the same food would now generate a greater level of physical well-being. The F^c measures are thus indicators of risk of suboptimal health, conditional on current nutrient intake and other variables. Food security reflects not only ensured access to sufficient quantities and quality of food, but also secure access to complementary inputs (e.g., education, health, sanitation, water) that affect the efficiency of conversion of consumed food into physical well-being.

This framework provides a convenient, graphic way to capture the effects of various interventions, especially FAPs, aimed at reducing individuals' nutritional vulnerability, i.e., moving out along the $F^c(\boldsymbol{n})$ functional. Such shifts can occur at the extensive margin, by improving food availability and consumption (e.g., via food stamps or supplementary feeding programs). Section 3 will refer to these as "Type I" FAPs. Or they can occur at the intensive margin, by improving the physical well-being produced by existing food availability and consumption patterns (e.g., via micronutrient fortification or nutrition education). Section 3 labels these "Type 2" FAPs.

Food security thus defined comprises an intertemporal sequence of probabilities. Considerable attention has been given in the literature to the degree and nature of temporal variation in food security. While transitory food insecurity – especially extreme forms manifest in famines – captures the attention of the general public, chronic food insecurity is a far more intractable problem. Chronic food insecurity occurs when the subject is continuously unable to ensure access to sufficient appropriate foods, i.e., $F_t^c < p^c$ for all time periods. As Section 2.3 develops, chronic food insecurity is closely related to structural factors associated with poverty, as people with few productive assets and low expected incomes persistently struggle to access adequate food to remain healthy and active. The poor are nevertheless not always chronically food insecure, nor are the chronically food insecure necessarily poor.

It is worthwhile to distinguish between three distinct categories of transitory food insecurity: periodic, regular, and conjunctural. Perhaps the best example of periodic food insecurity is the seasonal cycling typical of low-income agriculture. Food availability and prices, and peasant incomes and nutritional status go through a predictable intraannual cycle, with high food availability and incomes per capita and low food prices during the harvest period, and low food availability and incomes and high prices prior to the main (or only) harvest period, often known as the "hungry" season [Chambers et al. (1981), Sahn (1989)]. At lower frequency, there is also periodic food insecurity associated with the human life cycle. Children and the elderly are more dependent than working age adults on transfers from others to ensure food access, they evince lower labor productivity, and they are more susceptible to illness and injury. For these reasons, there is a life cycle component within the $F^c(n)$ functional. It shifts upwards as infants grow to adulthood, then reverses direction as adults become elderly and food security deteriorates.

Regular food insecurity is associated with repeated but a- or quasi-periodic events. Climatic extremes (e.g., drought, flood), disease epidemics, and business or electoral cycles are the four principal sources of regular food insecurity at aggregate levels. Climate variability repeatedly causes crop failures, livestock die-offs, and natural disasters that expose otherwise food-secure subpopulations to extraordinary risk of nutrient shortfall, particularly in rural areas where people depend heavily on agriculture and natural resources to generate income as well as food. Disease epidemics – among crops, livestock, or humans – cause sharp falls in income and asset values and increased expenditures to combat disease, which together degrade affected individuals' command over commodity bundles, including the nutrients necessary for an active and healthy life. Business cycle troughs routinely cause increased unemployment that cripples workers' purchasing power, thereby causing transitory food insecurity, particularly among unskilled rural and urban laborers. Elections commonly induce episodic state spending in some places, violence in others, each of which may affect food security.

Finally, conjunctural food insecurity is associated with the conjuncture of periodic or regular food insecurity with irregular disasters, most importantly and commonly, civil unrest and war.[8] The number of refugees and internally displaced people is large and has increased substantially in recent years, from 22 million worldwide in 1985 to 37 million in 1995 [International Federation of Red Cross and Red Crescent Societies (1996)]. The same (generally sociopolitical) disruptions that drive such a large number of people from their homes surely leave huge numbers of people who did not flee conjuncturally food insecure. Bosnia, Cambodia, Haiti, Rwanda, and Somalia have presented vivid images in recent years of masses of people suffering conjunctural food insecurity caused by conflict. Even peaceful but dramatic transitions in market and state institutions, as in much of the former Soviet Union or many countries undertaking structural adjustment programs, can cause significant conjunctural food insecurity [Cornia et al. (1987)]. Likewise, oppressive state control, whether by colonial masters (e.g., Bengal in 1943) or a sovereign state (e.g., North Korea in the latter half of the 1990s) too often leads to conjunctural food insecurity when natural disaster strikes.

The distinction between chronic and transitory food security has become popular among both researchers and policymakers. This framework offers a convenient, consistent way to represent this taxonomy as relating food security status, $F^c(n)$, to

---

[8] Famines, the worst realization of transitory food insecurity, commonly stem from conjunctural food insecurity, especially that associated with severe sociopolitical disruptions [Sen (1981), Foster (1992), Devereux (1993), Webb and von Braun (1994)].

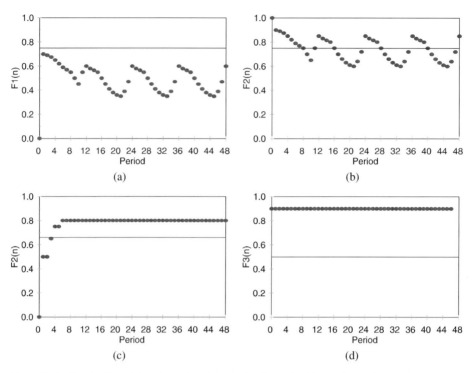

Figure 2. (a) Chronic Class 1 food insecurity. (b) Periodic Class 2 food insecurity. (c) Regular Class 2 food insecurity. (d) Class 3 food security.

chosen thresholds, p^c. The degree and temporal variation in food security status, $F^c(\boldsymbol{n})$, can be depicted easily, as in Figures 2(a)–2(d). Arbitrarily setting $p^1 = 0.75$, $p^2 = 0.67$, and $p^3 = 0.50$, Figure 2(a) depicts chronic (albeit time-varying) class 1 food insecurity – $F^1(\boldsymbol{n}) < p^1$ at all time horizons – of the sort perhaps experienced by the child of landless rural laborers. Figure 2(b) shows a stylized case of periodic class 2 food insecurity – $F^2(\boldsymbol{n}) < p^2$ with regular periodicity, but not continuously – that might represent a small farmer in rainfed, semi-arid agriculture. Figure 2(c) reflects regular class 2 food insecurity – $F^2(\boldsymbol{n}) < p^2$ with irregular periodicity, but not always – as might face pastoralists in time of drought. Finally, Figure 2(d) represents the case of constant class 3 food security – $F^3(\boldsymbol{n}) > p^3$ at all time horizons – as might describe tenured faculty at North American universities.

The above model highlights an important feature of food consumption insufficiently appreciated by economists.[9] Although key exogenous stochastic variables (e.g., rainfall, real food prices, crop yields, wages, employment rates) are commonly covariance or

---

[9] Rosenzweig and Wolpin (1993), Glomm and Palumbo (1993), and Morduch (1994) discuss the persistence of vulnerability.

trend stationary, they may have nonstationary indirect effects by inducing distress sale of productive assets like land or livestock, or reduced nutrient intake, or interruption of education that permanently reduces human capital. In the standard life cycle model, consumption is stable and pegged to permanent income; consequently, independent and identically distributed shocks to prices or production have no effect on consumption. In this model, however, constrained intertemporal redistribution – through borrowing constraints and nonnegativity constraints on commodity stockholdings (relations 6 and 10, respectively), and the survival and impairment constraints represented by the absorbing states – causes consumption, productive asset holdings, or both to vary with transitory shocks. Moreover, food security status can therefore be nonstationary even if all the exogenous driving variables are stationary. As Morduch (1994, p. 223) puts it in discussing stochastic poverty, "[g]ood shocks will ease ... constraints and lead to more risk-taking and higher expected income [and food security] in the future. Bad shocks can lead to a poverty [or food insecurity] trap". Individuals' vulnerability to shocks, especially to shocks' persistence due to loss of human or nonhuman productive capital through coping strategies, is a function of resource endowments. The structural and stochastic determinants of food insecurity are inextricably related.

2.3. Threats to food security

Understanding of the threats to food security (i.e., the sources of food insecurity) has become steadily more refined as thinking about food security has advanced from a first generation focus on aggregate food availability, through a second generation emphasizing individual- and household-level access to food, toward a third generation conceptualization that places food security in a broader framework of individual behavior in the face of uncertainty, irreversibilities, and binding constraints on choice. Food insecurity has multiple causes which coexist at the individual, household, community, and national levels. A solid understanding of the individual level causes of food insecurity is essential to successful targeting of FAPs and other interventions, while an understanding of the covariate causes of food insecurity (e.g., crop yields, food prices, wages, civil unrest) is essential to generalized interventions (e.g., food aid, famine early warning systems) and to long-term, aggregate improvement in food security.

At the time of the World Food Conference of 1974, food security was widely viewed as a problem of insufficient and unstable production [FAO (Food and Agriculture Organization of the United Nations) (1974), United Nations (1974), Weiss and Jordan (1976)]. Variability in domestic food production significantly increases national-level cereals consumption instability [Diakosavvas (1989), Sahn and von Braun (1989), Barrett (2001)]. Food availability is a necessary but not a sufficient condition for food security. There must be ample food for all, but distributional problems commonly lead to food insecurity despite sufficient aggregate food availability. This is true at the national level as well as the individual level. Although food is plentiful at the global level, food availability is insufficient in some poor countries, especially without significant external assistance. International trade is helpful, but of limited use in relieving aggregate food insecurity in low-income, food-deficit (LIFD) countries because limited export earning and international borrowing capacity constrain current account deficits. Barrett (2001) finds that the standard deviation of nonconcessional (i.e., domestic production plus trade) cereals availability per capita among U.S. Public Law 480 recipients of 15.6 percent, is more than three times the world standard deviation around trend of 4.7 percent. The LIFD countries as a group suffer transitory food availability problems due to binding foreign exchange constraints and rudimentary marketing (especially transportation) infrastructure that renders foods internationally nontradable across large, interior regions.[10] So food availability is an issue at the national level in LIFD economies and, perhaps, can be enhanced by food deliveries or balance of payments assistance to support the import of food, as discussed in Section 3.2.

Sen's (1981) seminal work helped shift the focus from supply side issues associated with aggregate food availability toward the levels of individual and household access to food, and thus to the role of (perhaps idiosyncratic) demand failure brought about by lost employment, adverse movement in the terms of trade, production failure, termination of transfers, or other forms of "entitlement failure". Sen's concept of "entitlements" represents the commodity bundles that a person can rightfully make her own, through production, trade, or transfers. Sen (1981) explains hunger as the failure of an individual's entitlements to provide a commodity bundle offering sufficient nutrients, and famine as the result of widespread entitlement failures.

The third generation view of food security builds on food availability and entitlements as a summary of food access. Chambers (1989, p. 1) identifies two dimensions of food insecurity: "an external side of risks, shocks and stress to which an individual or household is subject; and an internal side which is defenselessness, meaning a lack of means to cope without damaging loss". Individuals with excessive risk exposure and without access to noninjurious coping mechanisms are the most food insecure [Chambers (1989), Watts and Bohle (1993)]. Both risk exposure and the availability of noninjurious coping mechanisms depend heavily on structural patterns of control of (financial, human, and natural) resources and on access to markets, technologies, and finance. Food security is thus closely related to poverty and to social, economic, and political disenfranchisement [Sen (1981), Drèze and Sen (1989)].

This section therefore emphasizes the interaction of structural and stochastic factors – *ex ante* risk exposure and *ex post* coping mechanisms – to produce predictable patterns of food insecurity. Adverse shocks to an economy rarely affect all persons equally. Nature may not discriminate among people, but intermediating social and economic institutions certainly do.

---

[10] For example, Barrett and Carter (1999) estimate that 53 percent of sub-Saharan Africa's 1979–81 calorie supply came from nationally nontradable foods.

2.3.1. Structural factors

The model of Section 2.2 highlights the six interrelated structural mechanisms by which an individual may suffer entitlements failure: low labor productivity, adverse terms of trade, limited market access, asset poverty, restricted borrowing capacity, and the absence of a reliable safety net to provide (perhaps state-dependent) transfers. Individuals have an asset endowment, a_0, and a production technology, $\Lambda(\bullet)$, with which they produce food or goods and services, q, they consume directly or trade for food. A quarter of the world's population – and a far larger proportion of the food insecure – produces food, most using rudimentary technologies and little physical capital. Under such conditions, and given a time constraint on labor, low labor productivity caused by poor technologies, meager productive asset endowments, or weak physical condition can condemn one to an unsatisfactory diet. Because all able-bodied people are endowed with labor power, labor is a primary factor in production-based entitlements and the most important item exchanged for trade-based entitlements. The proximate cause of food insecurity is therefore relatively low and unstable labor productivity.

A large majority of the world's population depends on markets for access to food. Adverse movements in the terms of trade between purchased food and the goods or services they produce and sell (including wage labor) can cause entitlements failures. On the other hand, many net food sellers are poor themselves, and declining relative food prices hurt them. This is the essence of the "food price dilemma" [Timmer et al. (1983)]: higher food prices are necessary to induce increased local food production and to increase the incomes of poor, net seller food producers, yet high food prices threaten the food security of low-income consumers. The dilemma is complicated further by the observation that a large proportion of small-holder food producers are net food buyers [Mellor (1978), Weber et al. (1988), Barrett and Dorosh (1996)].

At the global level, increases in food productivity have far outstripped demand expansion this century, leading to declining real food prices, i.e., favorable changes in the terms of trade for most net food purchasers. But episodically relative food prices increase sharply, especially where markets are (partially) segmented or noncompetitive due to frictions in the marketing chain. Most at risk are those without reliable access to markets, for the nonfungibility of their assets and produce impairs their ability to smooth consumption. Market access is impeded primarily by excessive transactions costs, including the absence of good market information, hence the disproportionate concentration of the food insecure in areas with rudimentary communications, storage, and transport infrastructure.

When current production fails and markets are inaccessible, those with sufficient stocks of liquid assets or directly consumable foods can persevere; the asset poor cannot. Rapid asset depreciation (reflected by a high δ parameter in Equation (4)) (i.e., whether grain stored interseasonally by peasants, shelters that deteriorate rapidly in city slums, or cash that loses value in a hyperinflationary economy) effectively renders people asset poor unless their net savings rates, s, are high. Consumable or liquid assets offer individuals the ability to smooth consumption over time, thus guarding against both life cycle changes in productivity and transitory shocks to real income or food availability. This is also true at the aggregate level – where a nation's grain stocks and foreign exchange reserves play a central role in maintaining food availability and stable domestic food prices.

Asset holdings also have instrumental importance in maintaining food security insofar as access to credit commonly depends on one's (physical or social) capital, as reflected in constraint (8). Access to food and credit markets enables purchase of tradable foods. Binding credit constraints facing rural and urban poor populations, as well as low income nations generally, contribute significantly to food consumption volatility and thus to food insecurity.

Those who routinely suffer shortfalls in purchasing power or nontradable food availability regularly depend on transfers. But unrequited transfers are generally not enforceable rights, so transfer-dependent populations constantly face the threat of inadvertent or intentional disruption of entitlements. Transfer-dependence is the principal reason why food insecurity is disproportionately concentrated among children and the elderly, especially children. Because labor productivity is low at either end of the life cycle, and because children's asset holdings are typically negligible, these groups commonly lack capacity to self-provision in food. Social security systems that guarantee entitlements – whether formal, state-sponsored ones, or informal familial and social reciprocity arrangements – may affect remedies to food insecurity among the transfer-dependent. But few if any schemes provide full insurance against food insecurity.

These six structural threats to food security – low labor productivity, adverse terms of trade, limited market access, asset poverty, restricted borrowing capacity, and the absence of a reliable safety net to provide transfers – point to four stylized groups that are extraordinarily food insecure (chronically or transitorily). The first group is workers (urban and rural), who suffer when food prices increase or money wages or employment rates decrease precipitously. The second group is small-holder farmers, particularly in rainfed agriculture, who face the threat of harvest failure or of adverse movements in the terms of trade between those commodities they sell and those they purchase. The third is pastoralists in arid and semiarid regions, whose livestock are not only their primary sources of food and income but also their main store of wealth in an environment of thin or missing financial markets. Livestock productivity and value both fall precipitously in times of disease, drought or flood, leading to considerable seasonal and regular food insecurity among almost all pastoralists, even those not chronically food insecure. The fourth group is children and pensioners threatened by the simultaneous dismantling of preexisting safety nets and food subsidies, as in the former Soviet Union.

2.3.2. Risk exposure

Certain individuals are more vulnerable than others to stochastic economic, environmental, and social variables. There are three basic reasons for this: (1) their poverty places them nearer the subsistence constraint, (2) adverse fluctuations are more frequent and pronounced in their occupation or home region, and (3) they lack access to first-best financial and social insurance mechanisms to allay these risks. The first of these reasons relates to the structural causes of food insecurity discussed above, especially asset poverty and low labor productivity. The poor typically devote a large share of income to food expenditures and thus are highly vulnerable to adverse production or terms of trade shocks [Webb and von Braun (1994), Strauss and Thomas (1995)].

Food buyers face greater adverse food price risk than do food sellers because the nonnegativity constraint to commodity storage, constraint (10), causes food price distributions to be positively skewed, with regular upward spikes.[11] Risk exposure in low-income rural areas generally exceeds that in urban middle- or high-income settings, because agriculture is more dominant and subject to environmental variability, because marketing infrastructure is more rudimentary, thereby generating greater price variability, because the work can be physically hazardous, and because financial and social security institutions that provide insurance and facilitate intertemporal budget transfers, and thereby consumption smoothing, are less well developed [Morduch (1994, 1995), Barrett (1996b)].

Risk exposure is also inversely related to sociopolitical stability. The security of property rights against confiscation or theft is an important determinant of the stochastic distribution of the value of one's assets. Poverty is often associated with weak states, and civil disruption that creates added risks, including greater market risk since weak markets commonly accompany weak states. In the Greater Horn of Africa, for instance, a large proportion of the food insecure are affected by war and violent banditry. The same principle too often applies to inner city residents in OECD economies. Dramatic political economy transitions are also particularly difficult, leaving many people vulnerable [Cornia et al. (1987), Stewart (1998)]. Transitions often lead to devastating disruption of marketing channels, production systems, and traditional social security systems, particularly when accompanied by civil strife.

As portfolio theory emphasizes, the net risk exposure faced by individuals depends on the sign and magnitude of the covariance among the multiple stochastic variables. For instance, for net seller food producers, covariate yield shocks – due perhaps to common climate or disease patterns – covary negatively with price shocks in closed or large economies, thereby generating self-stabilizing income (the product of price and output). However, for net food buyer farmers – who comprise a sizeable proportion of food producers in low-income agriculture [Mellor (1978), Weber et al. (1988), Barrett and Dorosh (1996)] – price shocks and yield shocks have compounding effects, so net buyer farmers tend to have more variable real farm incomes than do net sellers [Fafchamps (1992a), Barrett (1996b), Barrett and Dorosh (1996)].

Observed risk exposure is endogenous. Individuals make allocative (production, labor, consumption, savings and investment) choices to mitigate perceived risks (i.e., to

---

[11] Williams and Wright (1990) and Deaton and Laroque (1992, 1996) discuss the effects of storage on food price dynamics.

compress or truncate exogenous stochastic (joint) distributions before the state of nature is realized) by selecting diversified (i.e., low covariance) activity portfolios, low variance alternatives, or both.[12] If credit and insurance markets were complete and competitive, households could better smooth consumption *ex post*. Asymmetric information problems render financial markets incomplete virtually everywhere, especially in the inner cities and rural backwaters of wealthy industrial countries, and in the hinterland and city slums of poor nations. People therefore employ second-best approaches, choosing cropping patterns conditional on weather and price distributions in order to reduce downside yield risk, choosing employment and migration patterns conditional on the joint distribution of employment and earnings patterns so as to reduce downside income risk, and choosing investments conditional on the security of property rights in particular sorts of assets [Rosenzweig (1988b), Reardon et al. (1988), Fafchamps (1992a), Binswanger and Rosenzweig (1993), Platteau (1994a, 1994b), Morduch (1995), Reardon and Taylor (1996), Reardon (1997)].

Strategies promising lower risk, however, also tend to offer lower expected returns. Thus poorer and more food insecure households tend to sacrifice expected returns and to intentionally undertake socially inefficient resource allocations in order to reduce risk exposure [Alderman and Paxson (1992), Morduch (1995), Barrett (1996a, 1996b)]. The allocative efficiency losses resulting from vulnerable peoples' struggle to self-insure against risk can be substantial, potentially impeding longer-run food security. One manifestation of this is the overexploitation of renewable natural resources by poor populations unusually dependent on the natural environment for future survival [Perrings (1989), World Bank (1992), Dasgupta (1993), Barrett et al. (1999)]. This pattern may engender a sort of low-level equilibrium trap in which risk exposure induces activity patterns that reproduce individuals' vulnerability to shocks. Moreover, limited available empirical evidence suggests that access to income diversification opportunities may be positively related to wealth, with richer households exhibiting more diversified incomes than poorer households [Reardon et al. (1988), Webb and Reardon (1992)]. This appears to be because poorer households have fewer skills to sell on the labor market, less capital to invest in microenterprise activities (e.g., artisanal work, petty trading), and less access to land and livestock with which to cultivate multiple plots in different crops.

2.3.3. Available coping mechanisms

No one can fully mitigate risk *ex ante*, so one must have effective means of coping with adverse shocks *ex post*. Given limited food security and income covariance across individuals or households, opportunities arise for community-based, *ex post*

---

[12] As Morduch (1994) points out, this endogeneity leads to an upward bias in the estimated importance of structural, rather than stochastic, sources of poverty and food insecurity. It also causes analysts to underestimate the importance of borrowing constraints, which are usually identified using income variability.

risk-sharing – including reciprocity and patronage networks, and formal or informal consumption credit arrangements [Ravallion and Dearden (1988), Platteau (1991), Alderman and Paxson (1992), Fafchamps (1992b), Coate and Ravallion (1993), Webb and von Braun (1994), Townsend (1995), Carter (1997)]. Idiosyncratic variability is more significant among households than is commonly recognized and this creates the principal opportunity for local-level risk pooling to reduce food insecurity. But covariate risks, moral hazard, contracting and monitoring costs, and unenforceable contracts lead to incomplete credit and insurance markets. The degree of incompleteness appears closely related to the extent and intensity of the risks faced. The most vulnerable generally have the least access to financial markets and social reciprocity networks, the first-best mechanisms to smooth food consumption over time. So individuals, households, and communities employ a wide array of alternative coping strategies to reduce *ex post* consumption variability, i.e., to minimize the impact of their risk exposure [Corbett (1988), Rosenzweig (1988b), Alderman and Paxson (1992), Payne and Lipton (1994), Townsend (1994, 1995), Morduch (1995), Deaton (1997)]. Food insecurity is in part a function of the range of available coping mechanisms, both because this influences the immediate impact of adverse shocks and because some coping mechanisms threaten future food security.

Coping strategies are highly context-dependent, with a continuum of responses observable within each of seven general classes of coping mechanisms: (1) transfers and loans, (2) foraging and increased reliance on wild foods, (3) disposal of nonproductive assets, (4) reduced consumption and energy expenditure, (5) selling off productive assets, (6) expropriation of others' resources through theft or refusal to meet normal social obligations, and (7) migration. There is a continuum within each of these classes, from relatively nonthreatening approaches to potentially injurious ones, e.g., from a small, short-term consumption loan to indentured servitude. Within-class variation can be important to long-term food security. Taking out interest-free loans or credit with state-dependent repayment terms is far less risky than taking out a loan at a usurious rate from a moneylender. Similarly, modest reductions in food intake may have no significant effect, while sharp reductions (in the limit, starvation) can have dire consequences. In very general terms, the latter four classes of coping strategies adversely affect future periods' production capability and physical well-being – via the relations in Equations (2), (4), and (7) – more so than do the former three. Even if they improve current food security, it is too often at a cost of diminished long-term food security. Those who depend frequently or heavily on these sorts of coping strategies commonly suffer chronic food insecurity.

Temporal risk exposure and the potential irreversibility of certain decisions (e.g., distress sale of one's land) together put a premium on the maintenance of flexibility.[13]

---

[13] The literature on resource management under temporal uncertainty and irreversibility [Arrow and Fisher (1974), Henry (1974), Miller and Lad (1984)] and the more recent literature on investment under uncertainty [Dixit and Pindyck (1994)] offer considerable insights of relevance to issues of food security, although these analytical tools have yet to be widely employed.

Most food-insecure individuals therefore consciously adopt a graduated sequence of coping strategies that are successively less flexible and potentially more injurious [Corbett (1988), Maxwell and Frankenberger (1992), Maxwell (1996)]. Up to a point, people willingly sacrifice nutrient intake in order to preserve productive assets (e.g., land, livestock) or to make other current expenditures (e.g., on medicine, shelter, or education) necessary to secure future livelihoods, and thereby future food security. For instance, households may call on family, friends, and neighbors for gifts or loans, then begin foraging for food, then use up cash savings and sell jewelry, followed sequentially by selling household effects, then livestock, land or other productive assets, then resorting to stealing or abrogating responsibilities to support dependents, or to distress migration. Simultaneously, there will be a steady reduction in the frequency, quality, and variety of meals, leading to ever more serious nutrient deprivation.

Private transfers through kinship and community reciprocity networks often serve to cushion blows, but these transfers are commonly modest in quantity, offering incomplete restitution in the wake of an adverse shock to the recipient's food security [Fafchamps (1992b), Webb and Reardon (1992), Townsend (1995)]. Short-term consumption credit and state-dependent credit contracts are likewise important to food consumption smoothing, but most households (especially poor ones) tend to be consumption credit constrained [Udry (1994), Zeller et al. (1997)].

When loans or transfers on reasonable terms will not suffice, households generally turn to disposal of nonproductive assets (e.g., jewelry, cash). All assets serve as a store of value and thus as a form of insurance. Again, this strategy is unequally available. Higher-income individuals, households, and nations often receive more than do lower-income ones from sale of identical assets because the former's greater wealth offers more self-insurance and enables them to wait until market conditions are relatively more favorable to sell [Webb and Reardon (1992)].

The range of coping mechanisms available to a given individual, household, region or nation is closely related to wealth and market access, not least of which because asset management is a critical element of most coping strategies. This is as true at the macro level as it is for households or individuals. For example, climatic shocks are more likely to lead to serious food insecurity, even famine, in poor countries largely isolated from the international trading network. Analogously, at the micro level it is common to find that wealthier households and individuals are better able than poorer ones to self-insure through savings or to access consumption credit to weather adverse exogenous shocks [Reardon et al. (1988), Webb and Reardon (1992)].

As a result, the poor rely more heavily on prospectively injurious coping strategies, especially disposal of productive assets, reduced consumption, and long-term migration. Productive assets such as land, livestock, farming implements, and human capital also have an insurance function in low-income areas where financial markets or social safety nets provide incomplete *ex post* consumption-smoothing opportunities. Livestock distress sales are common in low-income agriculture but degrade the seller's future capacity to produce and to self-insure, often trapping distress sellers in a vicious cycle of pauperization [Watts (1983), Corbett (1988), Fafchamps et al. (1998)]. A particularly noxious form of asset sale is indentured servitude and slavery, wherein one transfers rights to one's future labor power in exchange for present food or income. This is especially true because distress sales of productive assets typically occur only once all noninjurious coping mechanisms have been exhausted, so the seller has little flexibility with respect to the timing and therefore the terms of sale. Timing matters because the narrower the range of coping mechanisms available to a given group, the greater the likelihood that a large number will choose the same coping strategy in the wake of covariate shocks, thereby inducing adverse terms of trade movements. For example, while a single individual selling livestock to cope with the costs of a serious illness in the family will probably not influence livestock-grain terms of trade, a local drought that causes many pastoralists to sell livestock will probably drive down relative livestock/grain prices, exacerbating their food insecurity. The intensity of these adverse general equilibrium effects varies inversely with the range of coping mechanisms available. Such phenomena are observed not only in livestock sales in peasant communities of poor nations, but also in pawn shop deals in urban slums of wealthy ones. For these reasons, common shocks may not "level the playing field", but may instead lead to greater wealth concentration through distress sales of productive assets by the poor to the rich.

Among the most common, immediate, and graduated responses of low-income populations to an adverse shock are to eat less and worse, and to reduce energy expenditures [Payne and Lipton (1994)]. The literature extensively documents the prevalence of "famine foods" in most cultures, including leaves, roots, bushmeat and other wild nutrient sources for which desperate people forage [Corbett (1988)]. Rationed food consumption typically occurs early in the process of coping with adversity, both at individual and national levels (consider the wartime food rationing that occurred in the United States and European countries during World War II). Rationing at household level and above is often inequitable, favoring privileged classes and ethnic groups (e.g., the Ukraine famine of the 1930s) or adult males in a household [Caldwell et al. (1986), Payne and Lipton (1994)]. When destitution looms, a sort of lifeboat ethics may prevail, with especially serious consequences for the weak and powerless.

The principle of precautionary savings suggests that the mere risk of future food insecurity – in advance of any experience of adversity – induces reduced current consumption of food in favor of savings. There is some empirical evidence of such behavior among a variety of populations [Carroll (1992), Hubbard et al. (1995), Barrett and Dorosh (1996), Merrigan and Normandin (1996)]. Modest current reduction in food intake may be less injurious over the long term than disposal of productive assets or migration, but severely reduced intake risks permanent cognitive or physical impairment. A similar argument holds with respect to reduced energy expenditure, in that some labor is necessary to maintain productivity.

Once households have exhausted all local channels of credit and transfer, foraged for food, disposed of their assets, and trimmed current consumption, distress migration in search of relief is often the only remaining option [Corbett (1988)]. Given that distress migrants are typically weakened by hunger or hunger-related disease, employment is often not a reasonable aim. Rather, the search is for an effective safety net, in rural camps for refugees and internally displaced persons, urban homeless shelters, and the like. Distress migration is one of the last in a sequence of responses to food insecurity, as it often implies abandonment of access to local informal (partial) insurance arrangements and risks loss of access to land or employment left behind [Corbett (1988)].

The availability of coping mechanisms is itself time-varying and stochastic. Social obligations involved in reciprocity networks may or may not be honored, legal enforcement of contracts may be uneven, and the coverage and timeliness of safety nets provided by either the state or by charitable institutions is also uncertain [Platteau (1994a, 1994b), Sethi and Somanathan (1996)]. Furthermore, it is likely that the availability of coping mechanisms diminishes with the intensity and covariance of local shocks as social structures break down in time of widespread stress, and people are forced to renege on commitments [Carter (1997)]. We understand little, empirically or analytically, about how the feasible portfolio of coping mechanisms evolves over time.

2.4. Indicators, data, and trends

Food security is an unobservable variable with complex, multifactorial causality. As such, it is effectively impossible to measure food security precisely, and there are considerable conceptual and measurement problems associated with even estimating the incidence – much less the intensity – of food insecurity. Policymakers nevertheless need to know how many people are at risk, who they are, and how best to reach them. So considerable investments have been made in developing useful indicators and data to serve this purpose. While the available indicators remain far from perfect, they have proved operationally useful, as Section 3.3 will discuss further with relation to targeting.

The data on food security and related nutritional phenomena, and the indicators used to generate those data, have evolved along with the concept of food security. Until roughly the early 1980s, the first generation view equating food security with food availability stimulated reliance primarily on crop cutting, satellite images, and other methods of forecasting production volumes. The second generation, post-Sen view of food security as a function of incomes, prices, social safety nets, and other ingredients of entitlements, led to increasingly complex, multidimensional indicators using price, income, and anthropometric data. The emerging third generation perspective of food security as vulnerability or nutritional risk is increasingly incorporating indicators of peoples' coping behaviors as reflecting perhaps unrealized food insecurity that might be missed by better-established indicators.

There are four essential aspects of food insecurity, at all levels of analysis: (i) the quantitative availability of food, (ii) qualitative aspects concerning the types and diversity of food, (iii) psychological dimensions relating to feelings of deprivation, restricted choice, or anxiety related to the quality or quantity of available food, and (iv) the social acceptability of consumption patterns, in terms of both meal frequency and composition and the methods of food acquisition: growing or purchasing rather than begging, scrounging or stealing [Campbell (1991)]. A wealth of indicators reflect information on one or more aspect, although data have been gathered primarily on (i), with far less attention paid until recent years to (ii)–(iv).[14] Different indicators commonly identify different households as food (in)secure and yield different measures of the incidence and intensity of food insecurity in an area. So there is merit to employing multiple indicators on the principle of complementary redundancy. Cost, data collection capacity, and policymaker interest, however, often sharply limit the scale and continuity of coverage [Drèze and Sen (1989), Babu and Pinstrup-Andersen (1994), Eele (1994)].

The most commonly used indicators rely on direct observation of food insufficiency, hunger, or malnutrition, which are sufficient (but not necessary) conditions for food insecurity. These measurement techniques involve looking for physiological symptoms of deprivation, most commonly manifest in anthropometric measures of height/age, weight/height, upper arm circumference, or body mass index, in respondents' assessments of the adequacy of their diet, in nutrient intake data, or in data on nutrition-related illness and injury (e.g., anemia, goiter, rickets). There exist a wide range of methods for gathering these data – from recall to direct measurement,[15] from random sampling to either nonrandom or stratified oversampling, etc. – with considerable variation in cost, timeliness, intrusiveness, and reliability [Habicht and Meyers (1991), Babu and Pinstrup-Andersen (1994), Bouis (1994), Eele (1994), Strauss and Thomas (1998)]. Within agricultural economics, one of the most common but least reliable methods uses estimated nutrient intake volumes derived from constructed data on "food disappearances", i.e., the residual remaining from production plus purchases less sales less stockbuilding. As with any residual measure, measurement error is compounded across terms in the computation, yielding nutrient intake data of questionable reliability.

The available aggregate data are usually based on related national food availability data, i.e., based on a first generation conceptualization of food security. Estimated per capita dietary energy supplies, based on national level food balance sheets and assumptions about dietary energy distribution among countries' populations, tell us little about whether people have effective, continuous access to those supplies [Smith (1998)]. These measures are therefore quite noisy and likely biased downward in estimating the prevalence of food insecurity.

Some recent, advanced aggregate figures are extrapolations derived from survey data. The reliability of these estimates varies widely, depending on the representatives of the sample, extrapolation methods used, etc. The increasing availability of household food consumption and expenditure surveys and improved computational capabilities

---

[14] A notable exception is Guthrie and Scheer's (1981) dietary adequacy indicator, a semiquantitative measure based on food variety intake that considers both macro- and micronutrients.

[15] There is often considerable disagreement about the reliability of self-reported data on food and nutrition. The little available evidence shows the measures yield reasonably similar results, which many take as validating the use of self-reported data, which are less expensive to collect [Rose and Oliveira (1997), Strauss and Thomas (1998)].

make this method increasingly feasible and attractive. Overreliance on food consumption or expenditure data may introduce other problems, however, since these commonly have significant, systematic measurement error and incredibly fat-tailed distributions [Srinivasan (1981, 1992), Bouis (1994), Strauss and Thomas (1995, 1998)]. Inter- and intra-individual variation in macro- and micronutrient requirements – based on genetics, activity levels, health status, etc. – also complicates definition of appropriate intake thresholds and thus estimation of the incidence of hunger and undernutrition [Srinivasan (1981, 1992), Kakwani (1989), Payne and Lipton (1994), Higgins and Alderman (1997)].

Economists increasingly use anthropometric data, which is relatively easy to collect in the field and appears less subject to systematic measurement error, especially that correlated with respondents' characteristics such as gender or income [Strauss and Thomas (1998)]. The chief – and significant – weakness of anthropometric measures as indicators of food security status is that health is the product of many factors, not just nutrient intake. Anthropometric indicators may therefore yield upwardly biased estimates of the prevalence of hunger or food insecurity. This by no means denies the importance of measures of nutritional status; it merely emphasizes that *ex post* nutritional outcomes should not be conflated with food security, an *ex ante* status. Moreover, almost half the world's developing countries have not undertaken nationwide surveys of malnutrition in the past decade, and most industrialized countries collect and publish only incomplete statistics on indicators of food security [United Nations Children's Fund (1995)].[16] Out-of-sample extrapolation to generate current, much less global, estimates therefore becomes a suspect cross-national and cross-cultural exercise.

There are several reasons to believe the most common indicators may underestimate the prevalence of food insecurity. First, despite increasing recognition that household measures of consumption may be poor proxies for intake by individuals, most surveys continue to be fielded at household level, although this is known to miss a nontrivial population of food-insecure persons living in apparently food-secure households. Second, because food insecurity need not lead to food insufficiency, hunger, or malnutrition, food insecurity is likely more widespread than are these three by-products of food insecurity. The best available estimates of the incidence or intensity of food insecurity or the identity of the food insecure remain highly imprecise [Select Committee on Hunger (1989), Habicht and Meyers (1991)]. Improving the ongoing collection of good national and international data on hunger and malnutrition remains a high priority for researchers in the field.

The benchmark nutrient intake, food consumption and expenditure, and anthropometric data are also relatively expensive and cumbersome to collect and analyze. This drawback is especially germane to project managers concerned about concentrating scarce

---

[16] Indeed, some wealthy countries (e.g., Canada) have neither current nor historical data on the prevalence of hunger or food insecurity [Davis and Tarasuk (1994)].

resources on the truly needy. Shrinking domestic and international food assistance budgets around the world have focused increasing attention on issues of targeting – discussed in Section 3.3 – and thus on accurate, inexpensive, timely indicators available with which we can identify the food insecure. There has been much recent experimentation with the use of alternative correlates of food insecurity, including asset and income poverty, number of unique foods consumed, food prices, wage rates, dependency ratios, and morbidity patterns. Many of these data are routinely available, even in poor communities, or inexpensive and easy to collect, and perform reasonably well in locating the food insecure [Haddad et al. (1994), Chung et al. (1997)].

Consistent with the emerging third generation focus on risk, a recent literature attempts to infer food security status from observed coping behaviors. Because people employ a graduated sequence of responses to risk and adversity – they are not mere passive victims of inadequate food access [DeGarine (1972)] – and given the practical difficulties of measuring nutrient intake or estimating the unobservable and subjective risks individuals face, their observable behaviors may reveal a good deal about their current well-being and food security. The study of coping strategies has the added advantage of being able to capture the psychological and social acceptability dimensions of food insecurity (aspects (iii) and (iv) above) that traditional measures miss. Moreover, coping behaviors not only locate the food insecure, they also reflect the intensity of their insecurity. D. Maxwell (1996) demonstrates how one can identify a range of coping strategies, and establish severity weights and frequency scales to develop a reasonably reliable cumulative food security index. This is a promising approach to studying food security following the microeconomic principle of revealed preference. The key cautions are that coping strategies and their severity are highly context-sensitive. Certainly distress migration is a more serious response than selling an animal or eating seed stocks, but it is difficult if not impossible, even in a limited area, to generalize a hierarchy of responses *ex ante* that might be operationally useful [Davies (1996)].

Keeping in mind these cautions about the available indicators and data, two broad patterns nonetheless emerge clearly.[17] First, unprecedented improvements have been made in food availability and food security worldwide over the past two generations. While prior to this century there was not always ample food available in the world to provide everyone with an adequate diet, in most places food supply has not been a constraining factor on food security since World War II. Global per capita food production has increased 15 percent in the past twenty years despite a 45 percent increase in the world's population over the same period, demonstrating both the strength of technological improvements in agriculture and their importance to food security. This also highlights the weakness of neo-Malthusian arguments that posit an inverse relationship between population and food security. Global food trade has likewise grown rapidly, making food relatively available to those regions not well endowed with

---

[17] Fogel (1991, 1994), Johnson (1997), and Duncan (2002), this Handbook, offer lucid reviews of the global indicators that are far more comprehensive than is offered here.

cultivable land. Real food prices in the world market have generally declined sharply over the past fifty years [Grilli and Yang (1988), Cuddington (1992)].

While it is difficult to estimate intake and intake requirements accurately across broad populations, there has been steady progress in reducing the prevalence of chronically undernourished persons in most of the world over the past fifty years, with the rates of PEM falling from 40 percent in 1969–71 to 19 percent in 1988–90 in Asia, from 22 percent to 12 percent in the Near East, and from 19 percent to 13 percent in Latin America (International Conference on Nutrition 1992). This marked improvement is largely attributable to a 27 percent increase in per capita calorie consumption in developing countries since the early 1960s [Duncan (2002), this Handbook]. This is remarkable progress by any standard. Only in Africa has the percentage of the population estimated to be protein-energy malnourished remained steady over the past generation, at about one-third.

The second broad pattern is that, despite indisputable progress, hunger and food insecurity remain distressingly widespread. The absolute number of people suffering food insecurity has not fallen appreciably, as widespread poverty and increasingly unequal asset and income distributions conspire to counteract increased per capita food availability and falling food prices [International Conference on Nutrition (1992), Bread for the World Institute (1995)]. A large plurality of the world's hungry and food insecure reside in South Asia; despite a falling rate of prevalence, absolute numbers of malnourished people have risen there. The best available estimates suggest that 800–1300 million people in the world – about the same number as are classified as "poor" – suffer chronic PEM [International Conference on Nutrition (1992), Bread for the World Institute (1995)]. Another 2 billion people are affected by micronutrient deficiencies related to insufficient intake of iodine, iron, or vitamin A [International Conference on Nutrition (1992)]. The distributional challenge is highlighted by the fact that a large proportion of these people – indeed, the great majority of food-insecure children – live in homes where others have enough to eat [United Nations Children's Fund (1995)]. The distressing prevalence of macronutrient and micronutrient deficiency despite ample food availability highlights the now widely accepted fact that food availability is not the primary cause of food insecurity, the problem is in the distribution of available food.

More sobering still, these estimates reflect only head counts of those who suffer hunger or malnutrition, and not those who are threatened by those prospects. Relatedly, these estimates are all cross-sectional estimates at a particular point in time, and there appears to be considerable intertemporal mobility into and out of the ranks of the poor or the food insecure [Grootaert and Kanbur (1995), Grootaert et al. (1995)]. The cross-sectional snapshots used to estimate the undernourished population therefore capture only those suffering at any given time, not the potentially larger group that suffers some times (but not all the time), nor those who are uncertain about their access to food, irrespective of whether they ever suffer insufficient nutrient intake.[18] For instance,

---

[18] Because height/age measures capture long-run undernourishment, this issue of temporal variability in food security status would be less of a concern to the task of estimating head counts of the hungry or food insecure if such estimates relied on stunting rates. Few global estimates are derived this way.

approximately 1 billion people are identified as "at risk" of but not affected by iodine or vitamin A deficiency [International Conference on Nutrition (1992)]. Despite the centrality of dynamics and uncertainty to a solid understanding of food security, data collection and empirical work have yet to incorporate satisfactorily these dimensions. As a result, available estimates are likely lower bounds on the true incidence of food insecurity. We can only speculate as to the true numbers, but it seems safe to say that at least one out of three people on earth today – and perhaps more than half – suffers from at least transitory food insecurity. No nation and very few communities on earth lack food-insecure citizens, and women and children comprise a disproportionately large share of this subpopulation.

While it is clear that huge, albeit imprecisely known, numbers of people face food insecurity, we know less about the intensity of food insecurity [Kakwani (1989)]. Using Section 2.2's definition of three levels of food security, one can construct a measure of the nutrient shortfall of a food-insecure individual as follows. Letting n^* represent the nutrient intake vector necessary to achieve food security, such that $F_t^c(n^*) = p^c$, then one can define a nutrient shortfall equivalent to the difference between n^* and actual current intake: $n^- = n^* - n$. This vector measure may be unwieldy for policy purposes, but it can be converted to monetary terms by establishing the minimum cost food bundle, g^f, necessary to provide n^-, based on the nutrient composition of available foods, established by Equation (3).

$$g^f = \min_{x^f} p^{xf'} x^f, \quad \text{s.t. } x^{f'} N \geq n^-. \tag{14}$$

For tradable foods, the cash transfer g^f suffices to describe the nutrient intake shortfall of a food-insecure person.[19]

The key challenge in measuring both the incidence and intensity of food insecurity is the identification of the appropriate thresholds of well-being, w, the nutrients required to attain that threshold (conditional on health inputs, care, activity levels, environmental variables, etc.), n^*, and the cut-off probabilities for future food security, p^c. As Beaton (1987) and McLean (1987) highlight, there is a spectrum of categorical risk definitions, ranging from the risk of physical malfunction – including death ($w = 0$), or permanent impairment by illness or injury caused by nutrient deficiency ($w = m$) – to the risk of less than acceptable achievement ($w < w^*$). Is the objective to guard against serious physical malfunctionings (in the limit, hunger-related death), or to ensure full achievement? Similarly, there is no clear answer to the normative question of what level of food security risk, p^c, is acceptable. The appropriate extent of safety nets created by FAPs depends crucially on the answer to those normative questions. Furthermore, analogous to the problem of defining poverty lines and measures, and for reasons of intra- and interpersonal variability, discussed above, there is no unambiguously correct

---

[19] A generalized measure of food security could be built using g^f, akin to the generalized poverty measure of Foster et al. (1984).

way to define appropriate threshold levels of nutrient intake, nor of risk exposure. Arbitrary choices must necessarily be made.[20] Food security is the product of several interrelated events and is thus rarely constant across time, space, or individuals. The key, therefore, is measurement consistency to permit reliable intertemporal or cross-sectional comparison.

2.5. Mechanisms to promote food security

The model of Section 2.2 highlights the multidimensionality of food security. There exist many complementary mechanisms to promote food security, of which government-sponsored FAPs are but one. In the long run there are three key elements to a successful, food security strategy: (i) stable employment and high labor productivity to provide a regular means of sufficient income to subsist; (ii) access to finance, food markets, and storage technologies that permit consumption smoothing in the face of shocks to purchasing power or food supplies; and (iii) safety nets to provide transfers to those who suffer adverse shocks that the economic system cannot allay itself. At an aggregate level, there is also a need for continuous technological and institutional progress in food production, processing, and distribution, so as to ensure nondeclining per capita food availability and declining, stable real prices. Government policy heavily influences each of those elements. State FAPs principally serve the third, and if designed or executed poorly, may work at cross-purposes with the first two.

Broad-based income growth is central to achieving food security. This is not because income elasticities of demand for food (or nutrients) are remarkably high – they are not, as Section 3.3 reports – but rather because consumption of not only food but also (and perhaps especially) complementary inputs to the production of physical well-being (e.g., health care, education, sanitation, occupational safety) increase with income.[21] The income elasticity of health status appears positive and significant [Behrman and Deolalikar (1988), Strauss and Thomas (1995, 1998)]. This is evident empirically in a simple cross-sectional scatter plot of child stunting or wasting against 1995 per capita gross national product (in purchasing power parity terms), as seen in Figures 3(a) and 3(b). As the scatter plots and quadratic regression lines in both figures indicate, rates of child malnutrition fall with increases in per capita income. The unparalleled growth performance of the developing economies over the past two generations deserves much of the credit for the significant simultaneous improvement in global food security and nutrition indicators.

---

[20] Lipton and Ravallion (1995) offer an excellent discussion of the issues involved in establishing poverty lines and subsequently deriving poverty measures.

[21] Income growth is not strictly necessary. Remarkable reductions in stunting and wasting have been achieved in places (e.g., Cuba, Kerala, Sri Lanka) that have improved availability of these complementary inputs, even without significant growth in either food availability or incomes. But these are exceptional cases. Most improvement in physical well-being have been associated with – as distinct from directly caused by – income growth.

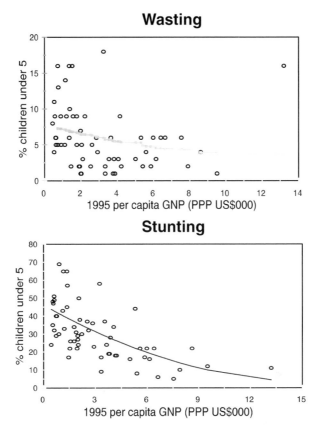

Figure 3. Data source: World Resources Institute.

The key ingredients to sustained income growth with equity remain hotly disputed in academic and policymaking circles, yet there seems to be noteworthy consensus on several points. Macroeconomic and sociopolitical stability are necessary to maintain high and stable rates of employment and investment and to avoid conjunctural catastrophes. Widespread access to productive assets – notably land, machinery, and human capital fostered by education and health – is required to achieve and maintain high labor productivity. Private financial markets offering an array of credit, insurance, and savings services to all people can play a major role in facilitating consumption smoothing and investment, and thereby in enhancing food security [Zeller et al. (1997)]. Competitive food markets supported by appropriate physical and institutional infrastructure foster consumption stabilization through storage and trade patterns that respond to opportunities for profitable arbitrage. Moreover, price incentives – combined with well-financed national and international agricultural research institutions – induce food production and technological and institutional innovation of the sort that have led to steady increases in per capita food production worldwide and in most countries over the past forty years [Duncan (2002), this Handbook].

Nonetheless, while greater prosperity is undeniably an aid toward food security, food security risks remain because people face considerable uncertainty. As has been emphasized already, food insecurity has both structural and stochastic causes. Markets in low-income settings are often unusually complex, typically involving more linkages, personalized relationships, higher transactions costs, asymmetric information, etc., than the more-nearly textbook markets of rich communities, and therefore often proving less accessible to the vulnerable and more subject to shocks to those with access.[22] The food insecure are disproportionately concentrated in areas – in both low and high income countries – where both governments and markets are weak and exogenous risks are considerable.[23] Safety nets are thus required to keep people from suffering chronic or transitory food insecurity due to bad fortune, bad choices, or both.

Humans have always provided informal safety nets for suffering family, friends, and neighbors. And an extensive private emergency food network responds to chronic and transitory food insecurity throughout most of the world. Many nonprofit, nongovernmental organizations (NGOs) were established in response to temporary crises (e.g., during the 1981–82 recession in the United States) but have become more or less permanent institutions. Now, both at the wholesale level (food banks, food rescue programs) and at the retail level (food pantries and soup kitchens), NGOs – especially those associated with religious organizations – have become the cornerstone of emergency feeding programs worldwide. It is difficult to estimate the number of NGO food assistance providers worldwide or nationwide, much less the number of clients served, but as just one indication of the breadth of the private NGO food assistance network operating today, Bread for the World Institute (1995) estimates there are now more than 150,000 emergency food programs in the United States alone. Charitable groups often receive significant support from government agencies, but they also depend heavily on the private sector, both for cash donations from businesses and individuals, and for commodities from food producers, processors, wholesalers, and retailers. While they satisfy donors' charitable impulse, there remains relatively little evidence as to whether the NGO emergency food network is a socially efficient mechanism for reducing food wastage, or improving the efficiency, targeting, and timeliness of food assistance to food-insecure people.

Private (commercial and charitable) food distribution systems are generally uneven in coverage, often leaving substantial subpopulations without sufficient access to privately provided safety nets. Beginning with the Great Depression of the 1930s and especially with the rise of the welfare state in the 1960s, the state came to play a major, even dominant role in the provision of social safety nets in the OECD economies, particularly

---

[22] The May 1997 issue of *World Development* offers a selection of papers on this theme.

[23] Even markets that work well may exacerbate food insecurity problems under certain circumstances. For example, in "slump famines" during which a collapse in purchasing power leads to falling prices locally, traders may move food out of a region suffering acute conjunctural food insecurity [Sen (1981)].

in the United States. While the international record with respect to direct state support programs is mixed, there have been clear successes under many different circumstances [Drèze and Sen (1989), Blank (1996)]. Still, debate continues as to whether countries can afford extensive public programs while average incomes remain low [Drèze and Sen (1989)], and, more generally, whether the state holds comparative advantage in the provision of food assistance, and if so, at which level(s) of government.

3. Food assistance programs

Food insecurity is a complex problem not given to simple, technical solutions [Campbell (1991), Barrett and Csete (1994)]. The partial insurance provided by private (market and nonmarket) arrangements and by charitable institutions both leaves and limits space for state-sponsored food assistance programs (FAPs). Without supplementary FAPs there are commonly large gaps in the social safety net, yet interventions must not crowd out partial private insurance and thereby inadvertently aggravate food insecurity. In other words, there must be additionality in the food security provided by FAPs. Unfortunately, there remains much we do not know, analytically or empirically, about the additionality of government FAPs. Some policies appear effective in combating food insecurity at low relative cost. Sometimes, however, they reach few of the truly vulnerable, consume inordinate resources, and significantly distort consumer or producer behavior. This section tries to summarize lessons learned in this arena.

In the context of the model of Section 2.2, FAPs are designed to move beneficiaries rightward along the $F^c(n)$ functional, either by increasing food (and thus nutrient) availability by expanding food entitlements, or by improving the utilization of existing entitlements. Micronutrient fortification, nutrition education, and early warning systems are examples of the latter; consumer food subsidies, food price stabilization, food stamps, food aid, supplementary feeding programs, etc., are examples of the former. These are discussed in Section 3.1. Section 3.2 then discusses the cross-border extension of FAPs through food aid and food security related international finance. Section 3.3 reviews core issues surrounding domestic and international FAPs: additionality, targeting, participation and leakage, program costs, and incentive effects.

Before launching into discussion of particular programs or cross-program issues, some brief discussion of the political economy of FAPs is needed.[24] In most countries, FAPs are a product of the emergence of two phenomena over the twentieth century: farm support programs that generated food surpluses and the welfare state. Governments appeal to many different, complementary rationales – economic, commercial, political, and moral – to legitimize FAPs, both domestically and internationally, and to secure political support for these programs. As a consequence, the Tinbergen principle – that there should be an equal number of policy instruments as independent economic

---

[24] Political economy questions are covered in detail by de Gorter and Swinnen (2002), this Handbook.

objectives – is routinely violated and FAPs commonly have multiple, sometimes conflicting objectives [Ruttan (1995)]. For example, the effectiveness of food aid in improving food security has suffered because the quantity and type of food available has historically been driven primarily by the patterns of surpluses generated by farm support programs, not by recipient need, and because allocation patterns have commonly followed geostrategic, not economic or humanitarian criteria. The political economy of FAPs remains an under-researched topic.[25]

Political considerations figure heavily in the existence, design, and implementation of FAPs. Domestic politics help define FAP budgets and operating procedures, not least of which the targeting of beneficiaries. Although generalized food subsidies are expensive and provide relatively little assistance to the needy per dollar spent, food riots in the capital cities of low- and middle-income countries that tried to end nontargeted food subsidies have threatened, even toppled governments. The persistence of food subsidy schemes in the face of considerable economic and nutritional evidence that these are relatively cost ineffective means of enhancing food security seems almost entirely attributable to domestic politics [Pinstrup-Andersen (1988, 1993)]. Similarly, the provision of transfers in kind has traditionally received far greater political support than cash assistance because ostensibly this supports only particular expenditures deemed worthy of support.[26]

The multiple motives for FAPs have created durable and powerful political constituencies supporting their continuation. Ironically, because these multiple motives sometimes work at cross-purposes, they may also degrade the effectiveness of some FAPs, stimulating opposition and sowing the seeds of their own failure. Nevertheless, many FAPs have proved demonstrably effective in improving the food security of vulnerable subpopulations at a modest cost. The ongoing challenge for economists is to help identify how governments might improve the additionality, targeting, intertemporal stability, efficiency, and incentives of these programs.

3.1. Domestic food assistance programs

Domestic FAPs can be separated into those that increase individuals' access to food – let us call these Type 1 FAPs – and those that improve individuals' food choices or the nutritional impact of their choices – or Type 2 FAPs. Type 1 FAPs are meant to improve food availability to vulnerable persons and have received disproportionate attention and resources worldwide. Type 2 programs are meant to improve food utilization, and while they are often overlooked in discussions of food assistance, these interventions are widespread in high-income countries and have been demonstrably effective. While

---

[25] Excellent, more in-depth treatments of the political economy issues can be found in [Drèze and Sen (1989), Timmer (1991), Pinstrup-Andersen (1993), Drèze et al. (1995), Ruttan (1995), de Gorter and Swinnen (2002), this Handbook].

[26] For example, in the United States, the federal government spent three times more on in-kind programs in 1995 than on cash transfers [Blank (1996)].

this section treats domestic FAPs in a general fashion, most of the empirical evidence relates to U.S. programs because these are the most thoroughly researched.

FAPs affect more people than is commonly appreciated. In the United States, about one in eight to one in twelve citizens receive food stamps any given year – depending on the strength of employment and the economy – approximately 83 percent of schools (and 99 percent of public schools) participate in the National School Lunch Program (NSLP), more than 7 million people participate in the Special Supplemental Program for Women, Infants and Children (WIC), and an array of other, smaller programs serve several million more. In total, Type 1 FAPs served about 1 in 6 Americans, and a far higher proportion of infants and children, in fiscal year 1996.[27] Add the vast, uncounted numbers – likely a sizeable majority of the population – that consume prepared foods manditorily fortified with essential micronutrients (e.g., iodized salt, iron-fortified flour, milk fortified with vitamins A and D),[28] or that are reached by government nutrition education programs or food labeling requirements, and it seems likely that FAPs of both types combined assist a large majority of the population in wealthy, relatively food secure nations like the United States. Because markets and states are generally more effective in reaching a broader cross-section of the population in higher-income economies, it is likely that FAPs reach a larger proportion of the population in wealthy nations than in poor ones, although need is surely proportionally greater in low-income countries.

The complementarity of private and public distribution systems raises a serious issue for economies in transition. In many low- and middle-income transition economies, former state controls severely limited the reach and efficiency of private food distribution systems. Rapid, radical reductions in the state's share of food production, processing, storage, and distribution and in the breadth of FAPs has therefore sometimes left a large (perhaps transitory) gap in coverage, with severe consequences for vulnerable subpopulations [Cornia et al. (1987), Singer (1989), Graham (1994), Bezuneh and Deaton (1997)].

Just as the range of FAP coverage seems to vary significantly across countries of different income levels, so too do the modalities of Type 1 food assistance. As a rule of thumb, poorer economies have tended to rely more heavily on generalized food subsidies and food price stabilization schemes, while wealthier ones have tended to use more means-tested food stamp and supplementary feeding programs, the latter often supplied with food surpluses generated by farm support policies. In the remainder of this section, we consider the main forms of Types 1 and 2 FAPs. Section 3.3 will address the key issues surrounding the effectiveness of these programs in increasing food expenditures, nutrient intake, and food security, in reaching vulnerable subpopulations

---

[27] These and all other data on current expenditures or participation rates for U.S. FAPs come from [Oliveira (1997)] unless otherwise indicated.

[28] Micronutrient fortification is not always mandatory. Where states invest in nutrition education campaigns, profit-maximizing can be induced to invest voluntarily in micronutrient fortification (e.g., of juices or cereals) as a form of product differentiation. Proper program evaluation must capture such "crowding-in" externalities.

with minimal leakage to unintended beneficiaries, in fostering perhaps undesirable incentives, and in the direct and indirect costs of FAPs.

Food stamps: In the United States, food stamps are coupons given to eligible persons to use as cash in order to acquire food in regular retail outlets, which then redeem the coupons, like checks, through the banking system.[29] Many other countries field similar schemes. Eligibility is based on both income and asset ceilings and, as of 1997, on citizenship status. Food stamps are the single largest Type 1 FAP in the U.S., accounting for 64 percent of all USDA FAP expenditures in fiscal 1996, and the largest public assistance program of any sort by participation, covering 1 in 10 citizens, including 1 in 7 children. Food stamps were begun in 1939 as a part of the New Deal to substitute distribution through commercial channels for more costly direct distribution of surplus foods to the poor. This program was terminated in 1943 as a part of wartime budget reductions, but annual Congressional proposals to reauthorize food stamps were approved in pilot form in 1958 and on a full, national basis in 1961. As shown in Figures 4(a) and 4(b), real expenditures on food stamps accelerated rapidly for a decade from the late 1960s, but continue to represent less than 2 percent of real annual spending by the federal government, or about $80 per U.S. citizen per year at 1992 prices. Since achieving nationwide coverage in 1974, real food stamp expenditures have essentially followed the prevailing business cycles of the U.S. economy, tracking changes in employment rates that move inversely with program participation, which stood at about 25.5 million persons per month in fiscal 1996. Recent changes to eligibility and administrative rules associated with the welfare reforms of 1996, such as time limits and citizenship restrictions, caused a sharp decline in participation rates in 1998.

Supplementary feeding programs: Throughout the world governments make special attempts to address the food security needs of infants, children, pregnant and lactating women, the elderly, and people suffering emergencies. These can be crudely divided into take-home or supervised feeding programs and can be supplied either through surplus stocks donations or through government food purchases. In low- and middle-income countries, many supplementary feeding programs have been supplied by food surpluses in wealthy countries, via domestic food distribution programs and international food aid. However, recent farm policy reforms have reduced government food stocks, particularly in the U.S., with significant effects on the food surpluses available to supply domestic and international supplemental feeding programs.

In the United States there are a suite of Child Nutrition Programs (CNPs). Most prominent among them are the school breakfast and lunch supervised feeding programs. School feeding programs were begun in 1939, at the same time as the food stamp

---

[29] A growing number of beneficiaries receive an Electronic Benefits Transfer (EBT) card that operates like a bank debit card. The impact of this innovation is not yet clearly known.

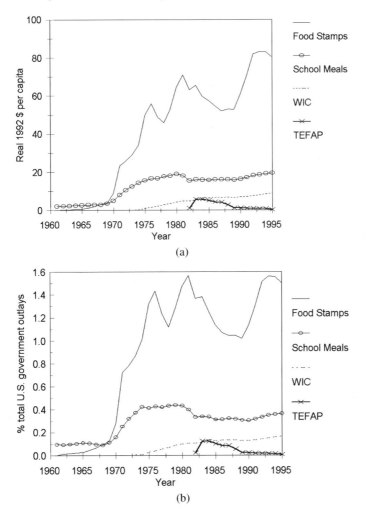

Figure 4. Data sources: Statistical Abstract of the United States, United States Budget for Fiscal Year 1998. (a) Real annual federal spending on Type 1 FAPs in the United States. (b) Percent federal government outlays on Type 1 FAPs in the United States.

program, and were likewise temporarily suspended during World War II. The National School Lunch Program (NSLP) is the second largest Type 1 FAP in the United States in terms of federal expenditures. The USDA also offers a smaller, parallel School Breakfast Program (SBP). Unlike food stamps, free or subsidized school meals, lunches in particular, have fairly steady participation and real per capita expenditure rates (Figure 4(a)) since nearly all schools now participate in NSLP. Changes in participation rates now come primarily from changing school enrollment figures and from expansion in the less widely subscribed SBP, not from program expansion in NSLP. Each school day, about 26 million children participate in the NSLP, or more than half the nation's school-age children, and about a third of those also participate in the SBP.

In the OECD economies, supplemental feeding programs have traditionally been supplied principally with surplus food generated by farm programs. In the U.S., CNPs, particularly school meals, and a suite of smaller Food Donation Programs (FDPs) have been the primary outlets for government stocks accumulated through producer price stabilization and surplus-removal programs. The FDPs primarily support food security interventions by private, nonprofit agencies running food banks, soup kitchens, and the like, and thereby support many eligible individuals who do not participate in the food stamp program or WIC, although the extent of this complementary coverage is not known precisely. The added costs of food procurement, storage, and distribution, however, make FDPs relatively expensive. With the reduction in farm support and, in particular, the uncoupling of farmer payments from the level and composition of their production, U.S. government-held surplus stocks have fallen sharply over the past decade and are unlikely to recover significantly. As a consequence, supplemental feeding programs are now funded increasingly by budget appropriations used to purchase food on the open market rather than by surplus food donated by the CCC, and food donation programs like The Emergency Food Assistance Program (TEFAP) have experienced sharp decreases in real outlays over the past decade (Figures 4(a), 4(b)). Similar patterns have emerged in other major food exporting nations, except the European Union.

A wide array of supplementary feeding programs exist in developing countries, particularly for children and for pregnant and lactating women. These interventions disproportionately employ imported foods (usually food aid) and are commonly operated in conjunction with NGOs [Beaton and Ghassemi (1982)]. Foods are served on site at feeding centers that beneficiaries must travel to regularly, or they are distributed in "take-home" packages. Participation rates among eligible beneficiaries tend to be higher and costs per beneficiary lower under take-home programs. Nevertheless, the additional nutrient intake per participant is generally higher and leakage rates lower in on-site feeding schemes.[30] Given these trade-offs, the appropriate design of a supplementary feeding program must take into consideration local circumstances, available resources, and program objectives [Underwood (1983)]. Schools and hospitals have been highly successful locations for on-site supplementary feeding programs [Beaton and Ghassemi (1982), Underwood (1983)].

WIC: WIC may be the most successful supplemental feeding program in the United States. WIC provides free supplemental foods, nutrition education, and health care referrals to low-income pregnant, breastfeeding, and postpartum women, infants, and

---

[30] These issues of additionality, participation rates, targeting, leakage, and costs are explored in more detail in Section 3.3.

children up to age five who are considered to be at nutritional risk. The food provided by WIC – primarily through vouchers redeemable at retail food outlets and restricted to particular products – is targeted to meet micronutrient needs of special importance early in childhood: calcium, iron, protein, and vitamins A and C. As a package of highly targeted, complementary interventions, WIC appears to be a cost-effective means of improving beneficiaries' physical well-being, although it does not necessarily increase food or calorie availability appreciably for beneficiaries. A national WIC evaluation found that the program's impact was felt mainly through improvements in the composition rather than the volume of food expenditures, i.e., by the combination of selective commodity eligibility and nutrition education [Rush (1987)]. In particular, WIC has been shown to significantly increase recipient women's dietary intake of protein, iron, calcium, and vitamin C, the key nutrients targeted by the program [Rush (1987)]. A 1990 study found that each dollar spent on WIC for pregnant women also participating in Medicaid saved the federal government between $1.77 and $4.75 in Medicaid costs on the woman or her newborn child(ren), with half those costs coming in the first year of a baby's life [Devaney et al. (1990)]. The apparent effectiveness of WIC – and its political popularity as a program targeted at vulnerable children – has led to rapid program expansion, from 88,000 beneficiaries when it began in 1974 to more than 7 million recipients today, although it continues to account for less than one five-hundredth of federal government outlays (Figure 4(b)). Nonetheless, and unlike food stamps or school meals, WIC is not an entitlement program; program participation is limited by available funds. As a result, there is interstate variation in participation as each jurisdiction has established its own nutritional risk criteria to ration eligibility. So, while virtually all eligible infants participate, coverage of children and women is much less comprehensive. About 45 percent of children born in the U.S. are eligible for WIC. Roughly three-quarters of program participants are infants or children.

Food-for-work schemes: Many targeted transfer programs, including most FAPs in the U.S., include a stipulation that able-bodied recipients must seek and accept private employment. By contrast, many developing country FAPs require that participants work in public employment programs. Particularly where unemployment rates run high, governments and NGOs use labor-intensive public works programs offering low wages, often paid in kind, as a means to combat food insecurity. Access to (self or market) employment offering sufficient wages to maintain entitlements over a nutritionally minimum market basket of food is the single most important determinant of food security worldwide. Sustainable employment growth is a slow process, so developing country governments often try to reduce poverty and enhance food security by employing unskilled labor through public works jobs offering low wages. Because low-wage public employment will not benefit those already able to secure jobs offering good wages, food-for-work schemes are self-targeting (see Section 3.3); only those who really need the assistance will take it. This is an important feature that distinguishes food-for-work programs from the generalized food subsidies that often preceded them in low-income economies before the 1980s. The mass of the available evidence suggests food-for-work schemes have significant potential for reaching the able-bodied vulnerable, particularly where they develop infrastructure that enhances productivity in production and marketing systems – and hence later periods' private sector employment and wages – and where food-for-work programs actively involve women [Clay (1986), Gaude et al. (1987), Ravallion (1990), Shaw and Clay (1993), von Braun (1995)].

Sen (1989) argues that India's public employment schemes to compensate those suffering misfortune due to environmental shocks (e.g., drought, flood) are a principal reason India has eliminated famine in the post-independence period despite low food availability and per capita income indicators. But our understanding remains incomplete as to how participation in food-for-work schemes affects food availability, nutrient intake or food security for either participating laborers or their families. Due to political pressures or poor administration, including insufficient availability of complementary materials and equipment to carry out public works effectively, some programs have failed to generate sustainable infrastructure, to set appropriate wage rates (either too low or, more commonly, too high, thereby leading to employment rationing and low participation rates), or to provide employment on a timely or sustainable basis [Clay (1986), Gaude et al. (1987), Ravallion (1990), von Braun (1995)].

Food subsidies and food price stabilization: Food subsidies and food price stabilization schemes have been implemented in most nations of the world at some time. These programs change the food price distributions faced by consumers (and often producers) and thereby influence food security. Such schemes have come under increasingly intense criticism over the past twenty years because most food subsidy programs are regressive – higher-income individuals purchase more food and thereby benefit more from generalized subsidies – and are therefore extraordinarily expensive if they are to have substantial impact on the most vulnerable segments of the population [Pinstrup-Andersen (1988)]. Similarly, food price stabilization is often seen as an expensive, ineffective intervention that generates little or no net benefit [Newbery and Stiglitz (1981)]. Proponents argue that there are important exceptions to this rule, for instance where subsidized foods are provided only through "fair price shops" to which only the poor have access or via inframarginal quantity-rationing through ration shops, or when the government subsidizes low-quality or inferior goods consumed only by the poor. Moreover, proponents of food subsidies and food price stabilization frequently remind analysts that removal of food subsidies sometimes leads to riots and even to the fall of ruling governments. Political expediency often trumps efficiency and equity.

Governments can combat transitory food insecurity through price stabilization schemes effectuated through variable trade duties, direct state trading (domestically, internationally, or both), or buffer stock management. Trade and storage are complementary methods for maintaining stable food consumption patterns in the face of unstable production patterns. Steady reduction in tariffs, communications, and transport costs has gradually reduced the real cost of trade relative to storage. Consequently, international trade (including properly timed food aid) is increasingly preferable to interannual food storage as a means of preempting or mitigating transitory food insecurity, at all levels, individual through multinational.[31] Where the government can credibly commit to food price stabilization, it may effectively reduce the risk experienced by individuals and thereby influence consumption, savings, and investment behaviors. Given that the non-negativity constraints on commodity storage (relation (10) in the model of Section 2.2) induce positive skewness in commodity price series, as manifest by regular spikes in time series of prices [Williams and Wright (1990), Deaton and Laroque (1992, 1996)], price stabilization schemes that can effectively cap price rises may have a favorable food security impact on vulnerable food consumers that the variance-oriented literature on food price stabilization schemes has thus far ignored.

Where Type 1 FAPs attempt to increase beneficiaries' entitlements, Type 2 FAPs aim to improve the effectiveness of a given food entitlement, either by enhancing the nutrient content of a bundle of food through micronutrient fortification, or by changing food procurement, storage, preparation, or consumption behaviors and thereby improving the utilization of entitlements in promoting appropriate nutrient intake levels and mixes. These programs are too often ignored in assessments of FAPs, although they are important, often cost-effective complements to Type 1 programs.

Micronutrient fortification: Micronutrient malnutrition is a problem underresearched in the economic literature on food security [World Bank (1994), UNICEF (1995)]. Deficiencies of iodine, iron, and vitamins A, C, and D are widespread despite simple, available technologies for solving these intake shortfalls. Vitamin A deficiency currently blinds approximately 250,000 children each year [UNICEF (1995)]. Meanwhile, roughly 1.6 billion people are at risk of iodine deficiency disorder (IDD), the world's leading cause of preventable mental retardation [UNICEF (1995)]. More than 2 billion people globally are iron-deficient, with 1.2 billion of those experiencing serious enough shortfalls to suffer anemia, which can impair physical growth and mental development. Almost half the world's women suffer anemia, especially those who are pregnant or lactating. Like macronutrient (protein and energy) deficiencies, the populations most vulnerable to micronutrient deficiencies are the poor, those living in remote areas, and monoculturalists. Medical interventions are often feasible (e.g., through supplementation by injections or capsules), but food-based approaches have generally proved the most effective means to address micronutrient deficiencies [International Conference on Nutrition (1992), Phillips et al. (1996)].

Micronutrient deficiencies occur where key micronutrients are not available naturally or in sufficient quantities in local foods, or unbalanced diets or illness interferes with nutrient availability or absorption. Nonetheless, micronutrient deficiencies are rare in industrialized countries like the United States because of mandatory fortification programs backed up by government inspection and certification procedures (in the

---

[31] One needs only modest local storage to bridge between the onset of a local supply shortfall and the arrival of imported food. The necessary storage volumes are a function of both the quality of the available transport infrastructure and the lead and accuracy of early warning systems, a topic addressed below.

United States, by the Federal Grain Inspection Service of the USDA). In low- and middle-income countries, necessary legislation and effective monitoring and enforcement mechanisms are commonly lacking, so large numbers of individuals remain at risk. But many prepared foods can be effectively and inexpensively fortified with nutrients lacking in the diets of a given population. The appeal of micronutrient fortification is that it can increase intake of key nutrients without having to improve the target population's access to food (i.e., its entitlements) or change its consumption behavior.[32] Among the feasible interventions to combat micronutrient deficiencies, "a well-designed fortification program has the lowest initial and maintenance cost and will reach the largest number of people" [Cook (1983, p. 285)].

The key challenge in most fortification programs lies in identifying a suitable fortificant, given consumption quantities, consumer preferences (for taste, color, texture, etc.), product prices, and food preparation and storage patterns. For example, iron-fortified wheat flour is widely available and effective in most high-income economies, but does not seem to be an equally effective fortificant for low-income countries, where efforts to fortify milk, salt, sugar, and staple grains with iron have met with success in some locations [Underwood (1983)]. Similarly, vitamin A fortification of milk has been effective in high-income settings, but less so among poor populations in the developing world, where efforts to fortify monosodium glutamate (MSG), sugar, and vegetable oil have met with mixed success. By contrast, salt iodization is easy, inexpensive (about five cents/person per year), and effective almost everywhere because virtually everyone consumes salt purchased through retail markets and only a thimbleful of iodine is necessary to satisfy an individual's lifetime iodine needs. In some (mainly high-income) countries, regulatory requirements and voluntary producer standards have been effective in replacing uniodized salt with the iodized variety, but elsewhere regulation has proved infeasible and governments have had to offer tax incentives to producers who iodize salt [UNICEF (1994)]. There has been rapid progress worldwide in moving toward complete iodization of salt supplies as it has become plain that iodized salt can be an effective intervention against IDD, even in remote areas where residents consume little seafood [Oldham et al. (1998)].

There has been some recent controversy surrounding the micronutrient content of food aid rations, particularly blended foods (e.g., corn-soybean meal) used at emergency feeding centers in low-income countries. With the rapid increase – to more than 40 percent today – of emergency food aid flows (see Section 3.2), micronutrient problems have become more apparent among refugees and internally displaced persons heavily dependent on supplementary feeding programs providing minimal dietary variety. Preventable micronutrient deficiencies have appeared on an epidemic scale in several refugee feeding programs, including scurvy and pellagra caused by insufficient

---

[32] In terms of the model of Section 2.2, fortification introduces an updated food nutrient matrix, N^*, that increases aggregate nutrient bioavailability from a given quantity and variety of food consumed. In mathematical terms, $(N^* - N)$ is a positive semidefinite matrix.

vitamin C and niacin intake, respectively [Toole (1993)]. It is therefore essential that rations contain a full complement of essential vitamins and minerals [International Conference on Nutrition (1992)]. The absence of international standards for fortification (including for quality assurance), and the reticence of some donors to incur the modest additional cost of fortifying donated foodstuffs (particularly blended foods), have been obstacles to achieving satisfactory micronutrient fortification of food aid to date [FAO (Food and Agriculture Organization of the United Nations) (1996)].

Nutrition education: An alternative to micronutrient fortification, particularly in addressing iron and vitamin deficiencies, is better dietary diversity through improved food consumption patterns. Nutrition education takes many forms, including the issuance of dietary guidelines (e.g., recommended dietary allowances and food goals), food and nutritional labeling, and counseling programs for targeted beneficiaries (e.g., women enrolled in WIC in the United States). Nutrition education programs aim to improve individuals' selection and preparation of foods so as to maximize the nutrient intake per unit expenditure. If people do not understand proper nutrition or the nutrient content of different foods (the information variable, I, in Equation (3) of Section 2.2), then they will be prone to make allocatively inefficient consumption choices. Nutrition education programs – and related food labeling, quality, and safety programs – can significantly improve food choice. Throughout the world, Ministries of Agriculture, Health, and Nutrition have some responsibility for nutrition education, often as a component of Type 1 FAPs. Insofar as nutrition education influences food consumption patterns, this can increase beneficiaries' marginal propensity to consume appropriate nutrients out of the Type 1 transfer, thereby improving FAP additionality [Behrman and Wolfe (1984)]. Yet evaluation of nutrition education programs has been relatively uncommon and informal, with the existing evaluations generally finding these programs worldwide to be quite effective, but able to reach only a small proportion of target populations [International Conference on Nutrition (1992), Rose and Weimer (1995), Food and Consumer Service (1997)].

Information and early warning systems: The well-being irreversibilities in the model introduced in Section 2.2 dictate rapid response to serious adverse shocks. Hence the importance of early warning systems. Food security involves anticipation, prevention, and relief of proximate threats. The independent press sometimes fulfills this need [Sen (1981, 1983), Ram (1995)]. For example, the impact of media coverage of the mid-1980s famine in the Horn of Africa ignited an unprecedented outpouring of humanitarian assistance from all corners of the globe.[33] But the public-good nature of information often causes it to be undersupplied by the market, providing a justification for government early warning systems (EWS) with respect to key variables that impact on most or all of the population (e.g., climate, food production and prices, disease epidemiology).

---

[33] Famine in North Korea in the mid- to late-1990s offers the opposite example, of the difficulty of identifying the scale of a problem and of mobilizing assistance in the absence of a relatively free press.

Over the past decade, bilateral, multilateral, and NGO development agencies have invested heavily in early warning systems, but have yet to demonstrate widespread effectiveness [Drèze and Sen (1989), Tucker et al. (1989), Babu and Pinstrup-Andersen (1994), Eele (1994)]. The essential ingredients of effective EWS are timely and accurate forecasts of prospective shocks and assessments of developing situations, communicated clearly and convincingly to decision makers having the capacity to respond. Timeliness is essential because of high frequency nutrient intake requirements. Sluggish response to an adverse shock can be deadly. The value of the information generated by EWS obviously turns on the predictive accuracy of the models used to generate warnings. Given the difficulty of making and evaluating forecasts [Fair (1986)], it is unsurprising that EWS have generally disappointed with respect to the accuracy and timeliness of weather, crop yield, or food price forecasts [Drèze and Sen (1989)]. Recent forecasting innovations nonetheless show some promise [Cane et al. (1994), Barrett (1997, 1998c), Thornton et al. (1997)]. As Section 3.3 discusses further, reliable and prompt information on the location, nature, and timing of adverse shocks and on the characteristics of threatened subpopulations is necessary to ensure effective targeting of interventions and to monitor outcomes [Eele (1994)].

Given the dynamic and stochastic nature of food consumption patterns, ensuring food security requires continuous and bidirectional information flow. Poor information can lead to biased expectations, with sometimes disastrous consequences. For example, exaggeratedly negative reports of crop failure in Bangladesh ignited excessive stockbuilding in anticipation of seasonal food shortages. Combined with temporary unemployment in flood-affected regions and bungled international relief efforts, this resulted in a sharp, transitory spike in rice prices and famine in 1974 [Ravallion (1987)]. Sen (1981) points to similar storage and price behavior caused by biased information on food availability as a contributing factor to the 1943 Bengal famine. Where market access is limited, food availability is key to maintaining food security. Since climate fluctuations are a primary driver of supply variability and forecasting methods of reasonable accuracy at multiseasonal leads have recently emerged, climate forecasting has a central role in effective early warning systems [Glantz (1987), Barrett (1998c)]. Similarly, (local and global) food price forecasting is essential to inform consumers, producers, governments, and NGOs of likely market conditions [Barrett (1997)]. EWS, particularly those focused on variables closely correlated across contiguous nations (e.g., climate or crop yields), have become increasingly internationalized since the late 1970s, with foreign aid donors and multilateral agencies (e.g., FAO) playing a major role in generating, analyzing, and disseminating information.

3.2. International food assistance

Two forms of FAPs exist at the international level: food aid and food-related international finance. These are merely cross-border extensions of domestic FAPs, involving the transfer of resources into a country for subsequent distribution by the recipient government or NGOs to individual beneficiaries therein via the sorts of schemes discussed in Section 3.1. Food aid is analogous to food distribution programs – donors provide in-kind assistance, most commonly out of their own surpluses – while food-related international finance is an analog to food stamps – recipients are given additional purchasing power with which to enter international food markets. Like domestic FAPs, international FAPs have long been driven by geopolitical interests [Ruttan (1995)]. The United States, in particular, has long used food aid to reward loyal allies [Shapouri and Missiaen (1990)]. The international character of the transfer nonetheless adds a few unique issues to international food assistance. So after reviewing the history of food aid and food-related financial assistance, this section concentrates on issues unique to international FAPs, before Section 3.3 turns to more general issues surrounding FAPs of both sorts.

Food aid: Food aid is the international provision of food commodities, usually surplus from the donor, for free or on highly concessional terms. Traditionally, half to three-quarters of the value of food aid has been free. The U.S. is by far the largest source of concessional food aid exports (through Public Law 480 Title I). Food aid is divided into three categories: program, project, or emergency (humanitarian). Program food aid has traditionally swamped the other two forms, although the 1990s have brought a dramatic transition, with program food aid flows falling sharply with the reduction in donor country farm programs and resulting food surpluses. Humanitarian aid now represents the bulk of flows, up sharply from the 10 to 15 percent pre-1990 average (Figure 5(a)). Program aid is generally an untargeted distribution sold on recipient country markets to raise general local currency revenue ("counterpart funds") used to support recipient country FAPs or other development interventions approved by the donor. Whether through managed schemes or simply by increasing local market supply, food aid subsidizes recipient-country consumers, although food aid accounts for relatively little cross-country variation in food subsidies [Hoffman et al. (1994)]. Project food aid, by contrast, is targeted at clearly defined beneficiary groups within the recipient country, often through supplementary feeding programs or food-for-work schemes. Humanitarian or emergency assistance is directed at unanticipated man-made and natural disasters, and is thus commonly used for supplementary feeding programs for refugees and internally displaced persons.

Modern food aid began with massive commodity shipments from the U.S. to Europe under the Marshall Plan, later formalized in the U.S. in 1954 under Public Law 480, the Agricultural Trade Development and Assistance Act (later renamed Food for Peace by President Kennedy). PL 480 food aid grew rapidly, accounting for more than half of U.S. food exports and most of the total overseas aid budget by the early 1960s. Today, however, food aid accounts for a much lower share of world food production and trade than it did in the 1960s or 1970s, as food aid volumes have been declining while production and trade volumes have expanded (see Figure 6 in Section 3.3). Food aid dominated all other components of foreign aid in the U.S. and Canada in the mid-1960s, but has fallen back to less than 10 percent of total overseas development assistance

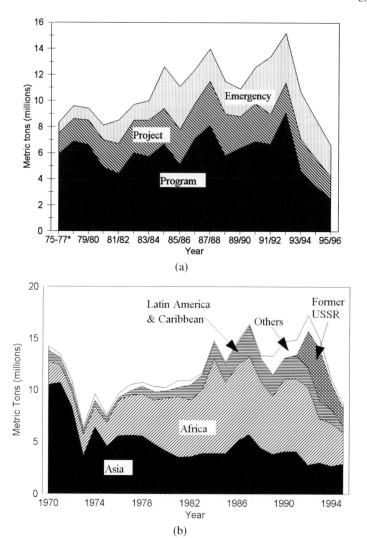

Figure 5. *1975–77 annual average. Source: World Food Programme annual reports, and FAO, Food Aid in
Figures, various issues. (a) Total cereals food aid by category. (b) Total cereals food aid by recipient.

in the 1990s [Charlton (1992), Ruttan (1995)].[34] Food aid has long been inextricable
from North American (and more recently, European Union) trade promotion and surplus
disposal objectives. The U.S. and Canada (which launched its food aid program in 1951)

[34] Food aid's proportion of total overseas development assistance has always been much lower among other
donors.

dominated not only food aid flows but also commercial food exports into the 1980s and were burdened with sizable domestic food inventories. These multiple motives provided a strong domestic constituency for food aid, but many of food aid's problems can be traced back to competing objectives.[35]

By weight, cereals comprise the vast majority of food aid, at least 90 percent most years. Wheat and wheat flour are the principal commodities, although massive dairy surpluses in the U.S. and the EU have occasionally sparked significant dairy shipments. The same has been the case for vegetable oils from the U.S. Generally, the commodity composition of donor countries' food aid reflects those items currently in surplus in the donor economy. As a consequence, while food aid represents a small share of total agricultural exports from donors, there are a few commodities (notably U.S. soybean oil and EU skimmed milk powder in the 1990s) for which food aid accounts for half or more of all shipments overseas. With the rapid increase in humanitarian food aid flows and the reduction of program aid flows, there has been a parallel expansion in noncereals food aid, notably "blended foods" – usually cereals fortified with milk powder and micronutrients for use in supplementary feeding programs.

Food aid has become increasingly multilateral over the past twenty years. Although most food aid continues to be provided bilaterally (i.e., on a government-to-government basis) the World Food Programme (WFP), established in 1963 by the Food and Agriculture Organization (FAO) of the United Nations, has accounted for a rapidly increasing share of world food aid flows since the World Food Conference of 1974. Since the late 1980s, one-quarter to one-third of global food aid has been channeled through the WFP, and the U.S. is the only donor that continues to disburse a majority of its food aid on a bilateral basis. In large measure, the rapid growth of the WFP reflects the (partial) disengagement of food aid from (declining) surpluses generated by donor country farm programs. More than half the WFP's budget now comes from cash contributions, giving it greater flexibility in delivery modalities than many bilateral donors. As Charlton (1992, p. 46) notes, "although the WFP has frequently not received much publicity, it has emerged as the second largest source [globally] of development funds after the World Bank".

Because the WFP, as an international organization, has no other diplomatic agenda, no farm surpluses to liquidate and no food exporters to promote, its rise has led to greater focus on the food security promotion objective of food aid.[36] The WFP has pushed the use of local purchases and triangular transactions as innovative means of sourcing distributed food. Local purchase schemes use donated funds to purchase food in surplus

---

[35] Ruttan (1993, 1995) and Charlton (1992) offer excellent, detailed studies of food aid programs, their histories and motivations in the United States and Canada, respectively. U.S. maritime interests are an oft-overlooked but powerful constituency in favor of U.S. food aid. The cargo preference law creates significant market power in ocean freight of concessional food grains exports, at considerable social cost [Ruttan (1995)].

[36] This is consistent with the more general finding that recipient need tends to play a larger role in multilateral assistance, while donor self-interest plays a relatively large role in bilateral assistance [Maizels and Nissanke (1984), Ruttan (1995)].

areas of the recipient country for distribution in deficit areas. This helps stimulate local production while circumventing market impediments – often weaknesses in the marketing infrastructure, sometimes simply insufficient purchasing power in deficit regions – that impede the free domestic flow of foodstuffs in the recipient country and saving on ocean transport costs. Triangular transactions work the same way, except that foods are purchased or traded for in a country other than the recipient or donor countries. Triangular transactions are commonly used when a national-level shock (e.g., drought, floods, or cyclones) that destroyed much of a nation's crop did not affect a neighboring country's harvest. In the mid-1980s, maize surpluses in Zimbabwe were purchased or obtained in exchange for wheat donated by Australia, Japan, and the U.S. for delivery in other southern African nations, particularly Mozambique. While local purchases and triangular transactions hold considerable appeal and have grown rapidly,[37] the scope for using these means of sourcing food aid is limited by the food surpluses generated in low-income economies.

Donor country surplus commodity stocks have shrunk markedly since the mid-1980s in the wake of domestic agricultural market liberalization in most OECD countries, particularly the U.S., the European Union, and New Zealand. Along with weakened geopolitical motivations for food aid following the end of the Cold War, and with limitations on subsidized exports under the Uruguay Round of the GATT, there has been a corresponding fall in global food aid flows. Moreover, foreign aid in general, and food aid in particular, evinced diminishing effectiveness, increasing politicization, and loss of focus over the years, spawning significant aid fatigue manifest in falling real aid budgets worldwide [Ruttan (1993, 1995)].

As a consequence, food aid is increasingly targeted to address emergencies, where it clearly has played a role in stemming food security and mitigating human suffering on many occasions [Maxwell and Singer (1979), Riddell (1987), Ruttan (1993, 1995)]. A spate of complex emergencies in the 1990s have intensified interest in early warning systems, improved international coordination of emergency food aid deliveries, and by some accounts improved the timeliness and coverage of humanitarian food aid distribution [Chen and Kates (1994)], although these claimed improvements are not yet apparent in the aggregate data [Barrett (2001)]. More frequent use of local purchase arrangements and triangular transactions, strategic stockpiling of emergency stocks by the WFP nearer places where they will likely be needed, and logistical and institutional lessons learned from past failures have all contributed to an apparent improvement in the record with respect to humanitarian food aid effectiveness as a safety net [Clay et al. (1996)].

The percent of general OECD country overseas aid budgets devoted to humanitarian assistance has increased more than fivefold since 1982, and this trend is mirrored in the

---

[37] Since 1990, more than half the food aid disbursed by the WFP has been sourced from developing countries. EU food aid programs have likewise sharply expanded the use of local purchases and triangular transactions, from 16 percent of total shipments in 1989–91 to 24 percent in 1992–94, with countries like Ireland, the Netherlands, and the U.K. now using these modalities for most of their food aid donations [Clay et al. (1996)].

food aid flows data (Figure 5(a)). Where program food aid comprised better than three-quarters of food aid flows as recently as a decade ago, it is now less than half and falling sharply. In 1993, U.S. Title II PL 480 (humanitarian grants) distributions surpassed Title I (concessional exports) flows for the first time. Clay et al. (1996, p. 3) note "this drift away from programme food aid is in marked contrast to the higher priority accorded more generally to giving programme support to developing countries in the form of balance-of-payments and budgetary support for stabilisation, adjustment and economic reform". The contrary trend in food aid comes in part from a (belated) recognition that program food aid has almost no comparative advantage over cash assistance to recipient governments. Where once food aid was primarily seen as a lever to be used for diplomatic ends, as a vent for farm surpluses, and as a trade promotion tool, the dominant view of food aid since the early 1990s has been that of a safety net used to guarantee access to food for the poorest populations and countries [Barrett (1998b)].

Increased emphasis on targeted interventions to enhance food security has accompanied a sharp shift in the geography of food aid (Figure 5(b)). Where the primary beneficiaries were in Europe and east Asia in the 1950s and in India and South Asia in the 1960s, sub-Saharan Africa now receives the bulk of international food aid, and low-income economies generally have received an increasing proportion of food aid flows over the past twenty years. Similarly, where the U.S. accounted for more than 90 percent of global food aid flows every year from 1955–70, due to its unparalleled food surpluses and global political interests, the EU and the WFP now account for almost half of all food aid flows. The pattern of distribution reveals how the emphasis of PL 480 distribution has shifted from Cold War and trade promotion objectives to humanitarian ones for which the Europeans especially are champions.[38]

These changes notwithstanding, food aid continues to play an important role in export market development for the United States. PL 480 Titles I and III, administered by USDA (Title II is administered by USAID), comprise a major share (about 20 percent) of global food aid flows. Farm lobby advocates for food aid commonly note that 43 of the top 50 importers of U.S. farm products once received PL 480 food aid, and that the major U.S. food aid recipients of the 1950s and 1960s (e.g., India, Israel, Italy, Korea, Spain) are now major commercial customers for U.S. food exporters. The claim is thus that while in the short run food aid significantly substitutes for commercial food imports (see the discussion of "additionality" in Section 3.3), in the longer run it appears to stimulate demand for food exports from the donor, by stimulating recipient income growth, developing a taste for American foodstuffs, or both. Although food aid may have important medium- to long-term effects, the dynamics of the relationship between food aid and commercial trade flows have received little scholarly attention, so it is impossible to either accept or reject the popular wisdom conclusively. Barrett et al.

---

[38] The increased prominence of European donors and widespread concern for vulnerable subpopulations in the transition economies of Eastern and Central Europe and the former Soviet Union has triggered substantial food aid flows to those regions in the 1990s, some of which appear to have been additional to and some of which seem to have been diverted from low-income countries [Figure 5(b), Benson and Clay (1998)].

(1999) find empirical support for this hypothesis of a J-curve relation between food aid and commercial food trade, but also find that U.S. program food aid primarily stimulates commercial imports from non.-U.S. producers, largely because there is significant food aid dependency, as manifest by high rates of persistence to shocks to food aid volumes [Barrett (1998b)]. Internal rates of return on U.S. program food aid (PL 480 Titles I and III) shipments are found to be negative at all meaningful horizons. Moreover, even if food aid stimulates growth in purchasing power and thereby in commercial food imports from the donor, then there still remains the question of whether food aid is a more effective instrument than other (nonfood) aid in promoting export markets. The key to the commercial trade response is less likely the modality of aid than the characteristics of the recipient, in particular a high income elasticity of food demand and the use of counterpart funds to stimulate demand rather than supply.

Food-related international finance: The absence of financial markets through which one can insure against adverse shocks threatens food security, no less at the macro-economic level than at the microeconomic. Poor countries commonly suffer aggregate food insufficiency but also face significant international borrowing constraints, especially since the debt crisis of the 1980s. Many therefore built up substantial food buffer stocks, although these have often proved relatively costly and ineffective. Consequently, in recent years some attention has been given to the creation of mechanisms to help improve food-deficit countries' food security without recourse to local stockbuilding or further borrowing.

In the wake of the food crisis of the mid-1970s and subsequent terms-of-trade shocks faced by low-income food importers, the International Monetary Fund established facilities specially designed to help food-deficit developing countries finance unanticipated food import requirements: the Compensatory Financing Facility, the Compensatory and Contingency Financing Facility, and the Food Financing Facility. Each has slightly different terms and eligibility, but they have in common the objective of providing medium-term credit on favorable terms to support extraordinary food import requirements caused by price shocks or crop failures. The European Community similarly established its STABEX facility to help African, Caribbean, and Pacific countries (i.e., Lomé Convention signatories) weather swings in commodity terms of trade. Simulation modeling suggests that national-level food security is enhanced by access to food-related international finance, although such access is by no means sufficient to assure food security [Huddleston et al. (1984)]. Ultimately, however, it seems relatively little use has been made of these facilities [Alamgir and Arora (1991)] and little publicly available empirical work studies their effects on the food security of borrowing nations.

3.3. General issues of effectiveness

The preceding subsections have described the motivations and various modalities of domestic and international FAPs. This section tackles the suite of issues surrounding the effectiveness of FAPs, including their additionality, targeting, intertemporal variability, direct and indirect costs, and incentive effects. Contrary to much current criticism, FAPs have not been failures, although there is considerable variation in effectiveness across modalities. This review is necessarily selective among the much good research done on FAP effectiveness issues. The main gap in the research is comparative. While one would ideally like to be able to compare among alternative FAPs, and between FAPs and other mechanisms for advancing food security (e.g., improved primary education or health services, rural financial systems development, etc.), relatively little such work has been undertaken to date. This is an area where research can clearly help policymakers make wise allocation choices among competing and complementary uses of scarce resources.

FAP evaluation is methodologically problematic for six reasons. First, food security, the target variable of all FAPs, is inherently unobservable. So one looks instead at correlated outcomes such as food expenditures, nutrient intake, morbidity, nutritional status, etc. Second, since all indicators have shortcomings (see Section 2.4), and most studies are ultimately used by a variety of readers with differing interests, it is preferable to study a range of indicators, but the necessary data have too rarely been collected (or studied) together. In some cases an indicator may overstate the effectiveness of FAPs. For example, DeWaal (1989) carefully documents how food aid limited hunger during famine in Sudan but ultimately did not save lives, as excess mortality occurred due to sickness rather than starvation. Conversely, the usual indicators may understate effectiveness. As Beaton and Ghassemi's (1982) meticulous review of supplementary feeding programs in developing countries emphasizes, "physical growth and development is only one, and not necessarily the most important one, of many potential benefits. Unfortunately, most of the studies reviewed in the present report have provided information on only one type of response – anthropometric change" (p. 879). Studies such as Beaton and Ghassemi (1982), Rush (1987), and Fraker (1990) stand out because they review a wealth of indicators and subjects.

The third problem is that outcomes are influenced by myriad uncontrollable factors,[39] only some of which are typically observed. Estimated effects are thus susceptible to omitted relevant variables bias. Econometricians commonly assume relevant omitted characteristics are fixed over time, within a household, etc., but it is impossible to test the veracity of that assumption. Fourth, given that multiple program participation is widespread in both developed and developing countries, efficient program evaluation requires studying the impact of different programs simultaneously. Fifth, many observed control variables are themselves endogenous, and while failing to account for endogeneity may yield biased estimates, instrumenting for endogenous variables generates inefficient estimates. So applied researchers always face a dilemma in how

---

[39] There has been considerable recent debate over the use of social experiments in program evaluation, wherein program participants are randomly assigned to control and treatment groups in order to distribute unobserved characteristics evenly between the two groups. Quite aside from the contestable value of quasi-experimental evidence [Heckman and Smith (1995), Heckman et al. (1997)], such studies are relatively uncommon in the FAP literature. Most research to date uses nonexperimental data with statistical controls and behavioral models to derive estimates of program effects.

to properly estimate FAPs' effects. Finally, despite the centrality of dynamics and uncertainty to the project of improving humans' physical well-being and food security, too little use has been made of longitudinal data in conjunction with estimation methods that account for dynamics, uncertainty, or both. As a consequence, there remains a great deal to learn about FAP effectiveness. That said, some broad patterns clearly emerge from the literature.

3.3.1. Additionality

The concept of additionality refers to the program's effect in adding to a participant's food security. Because food security is unobservable, researchers typically measure additionality with respect to food expenditures, nutrient intake, or anthropometric indicators. This raises an issue fundamental to FAP evaluation: Must improvement in food security be manifest in a one-for-one increase in food expenditures, nutrient intake, or some other indicator? Since Engel's Law implies the marginal propensity to consume food out of income (expenditures) is less than the average propensity to consume, one should not expect the marginal effects to be one-for-one. The model in Section 2.2 emphasizes that food is one among several complementary inputs to the production of good health, so one should reasonably expect any (de facto) income transfer to be divided between food and complementary, nonfood expenditures (e.g., shelter, health care, education, transport). And since health is but one source of pleasure, one should likewise expect individuals to use gains partly on other sources of pleasure, including the non-nutrient characteristics of food (e.g., taste, variety, preparation outside the home).[40]

A substantial recent literature has debated the range of plausible estimates of income or expenditure elasticities of food or nutrients. The emerging consensus is that plausible elasticity estimates are positive but well below one – generally between 0.2 and 0.6 – throughout the income distribution, with estimation complicated considerably by nonlinearities apparent in the relationship between nutrients and income or expenditures and by unobserved individual heterogeneity [Deaton (1986), Behrman and Deolalikar (1987, 1988), Bouis and Haddad (1992), Alderman (1993), Bouis (1994), Strauss and Thomas (1995), Huang (1996), Subramanian and Deaton (1996), Higgins and Alderman (1997)]. As Glomm and Palumbo (1993) and Davies (1994) point out, the survival constraint of the model in Section 2.2 can yield even negative income or expenditure elasticities for basic nutrition and staple goods, because near the constraint people substitute away all attributes other than the most essential nutrient bioavailability (generally calories at high frequency). A relatively low income elasticity of food consumption or nutrient intake does not imply, however, low income elasticity of nutritional status or health, more generally, since these latter outcomes are crucially influenced by nonfood variables [Strauss and Thomas (1998)].

---

[40] A positive association is commonly found between income and both implicit nutrient prices (e.g., food quality) and food variety [Silberberg (1985), Behrman and Deolalikar (1987, 1989), Davies (1994), Subramanian and Deaton (1996)].

This general discussion of elasticity estimates is germane to program evaluation because it is necessary to have reasonable expectations. Overall, the weight of the evidence suggests that FAPs have significant additionality effects by almost any outcome indicator. A 1977 USDA study found that the diets of low-income individuals improved markedly over the decade since 1965–66, and the Field Foundation similarly reported finding fewer malnourished persons in the U.S. than prior to the rapid growth of federal Type 1 FAPs [ADA (1990)]. Evaluations of specific supplementary feeding programs, in the U.S. and elsewhere, generally find positive and statistically significant increases in food availability, nutrient intake, anthropometric indicators, or some combination of these among target populations [Beaton and Ghassemi (1982), Rush (1987)].

The purpose of Type 1 domestic FAPs and of international FAPs is to improve food availability and access so as to enhance food security. If programs achieve this aim, then the quality, quantity, or both of food consumed by Type 1 FAP participants should exceed that of comparable nonparticipants. This might be achieved by lowering market prices through consumer subsidies or open market sales, by augmenting participants' purchasing power through the provision of coupons or cash, or by directly providing food. In the first case, the additionality of FAPs is manifest in reduced consumer prices and negative own price elasticities of demand for food. There is widespread evidence that subsidies lower consumer food prices [Pinstrup-Andersen (1988)] and that open market liquidation of food aid can likewise reduce consumer prices (see the section on disincentives, below). And the vast literature on applied demand analysis generally supports the negative own price elasticity implication of the theory of the consumer [Deaton (1986)].

The bigger issue among economists has been to establish the marginal increase in food consumption or nutrient intake resulting from FAP-related transfers. Not all food provided by FAPs is additional to the food that would have otherwise been consumed; both displacement and substitution occur. As such, it is important to estimate the additionality of FAPs by comparing the food consumption and nutrient intake patterns of participants with those of nonparticipants. But estimation of income and expenditure elasticities and of labor disincentives (see below) raises a host of important econometric issues. In very brief summary, since preferences, technologies, endowments, and the subjective probability distributions of exogenous variables may vary across individuals, and because these differences are known by individuals themselves but not by the econometrician, estimates may be biased by unobserved (cross-sectional or time series) heterogeneity. Moreover, program participation is itself endogenous, so reliable estimation must take into account the selection bias problem. Finally, nutritional status, expenditures, income, and food allocations among household members are determined simultaneously due to the existence of risk and incomplete markets. While it is essential to call attention to these methodological concerns, they go well beyond the scope of this chapter. Deaton (1986, 1997), Heckman and Macurdy (1986), and Strauss and Thomas (1995) address these issues in appropriate detail.

Southworth (1945) introduced a simple model that has provided the theoretical foundation for most econometric work on the additionality of FAPs. Southworth's model recognizes that food transfers (whether in the form of coupons or food distributed at either feeding centers or in take-home packages) expand the beneficiaries' budget set by the amount of the transfer, but generate a kink in the budget set since the volume of the transfer is the minimal feasible food consumption volume (ignoring the option of disposal).

This model leads to three simple, testable hypotheses. First, if both food and nonfood items are normal goods, the transfer stimulates an increase in the consumption of both through an income effect, so some of the transfer will substitute for food that would otherwise have been purchased, i.e., the marginal propensity to consume food is less than one. Second, some people would prefer to consume less food than is provided by the transfer and thus optimally choose the kinked point on the budget set for their consumption bundle. These individuals' choices are constrained by the form of the transfer. Their welfare would increase and their food consumption would decrease were the transfer converted to fungible cash. Third, those who purchase (or produce) food in addition to using their full FAP allotment are operating along the smooth part of the budget surface. Their choices are not constrained by the form of the transfer and would employ a cash transfer in the same manner as an in-kind transfer. The determinant of the additionality effect for this latter group is simply the income elasticity of food demand. Because the vast majority of participants in any FAP are inframarginal (i.e., purchase or produce food in excess of their transfer receipts), theory suggests income elasticity should be the chief determinant of FAP additionality and that the form of the transfer (cash or kind) should be immaterial.

The literature on the U.S. food stamp program – more than on other FAPs in the U.S. or elsewhere – extensively explores the additionality of FAPs in terms of elasticities of nutrient intake or food availability. Most elasticity estimates suggest that the marginal impact of food stamp benefits on nutrient or food availability is 5 to 44 percent, i.e., squarely within the consensus income elasticity estimates for food generally [Ranney and Kushman (1987), Fraker (1990), Devaney and Moffitt (1991), Levedahl (1991, 1995b), Fraker et al. (1995)]. Similar results emerge from studies of ration systems in low- and middle-income countries [Gavan and Chandrasekera (1979), Alderman and von Braun (1984), Edirisinghe (1987), Kennedy and Alderman (1987), Alderman et al. (1988), Alderman (1991)].[41]

An empirical regularity of the literature on FAP additionality is rejection of the Southworth hypothesis that the marginal propensity to consume food out of real income derived from FAPs and out of cash income should be the same for inframarginal beneficiaries. Virtually every study finds food stamps increase household nutrient availability at two to ten times the rate of a like value of cash income [Basiotis et al. (1983), Senauer and Young (1986), Devaney and Fraker (1989a), Fraker (1990), Devaney and Moffitt (1991), Fraker et al. (1995), Rose et al. (1997)]. Since food stamp benefits are relatively modest, the marginal subpopulation tends to be quite small[42] and

---

[41] Ration systems are conceptually similar to food stamps, the principal difference being whether the state is involved in food distribution or leaves that entirely to the private sector.

[42] Fraker (1990) presents estimates from the U.S. food stamps literature that vary from 11 to 14 percent.

cannot account for the magnitude of the difference between the estimated effects of food stamp benefits and cash income on food availability. Our understanding of the reasons for this remains incomplete. It may be that food obtained through FAP transfers and with cash are not perfect substitutes, perhaps due to social stigma associated with use of the former, and that virtually all FAP participants are thus marginal in that they face a binding in-kind transfer availability constraint [Ranney and Kushman (1987), Levedahl (1995b)].[43] Rejection of the Southworth hypothesis may also be due to intrahousehold differences in preferences and in control over alternative types of resource flows [Senauer and Young (1986), Haddad et al. (1997)].

This finding is germane to the debate over "cashing out" food stamps in the United States. In-kind distributions tend to yield greater additional food and nutrient intake, and better targeting, but cash transfers reduce administrative costs per unit transfer and grant beneficiaries more choice over how best to use the transfer. The heterogeneity of beneficiaries' needs in order to protect physical well-being may favor cash transfers. On the other hand, related information asymmetries that make it hard to distinguish the food secure from the food insecure may favor in-kind distribution [Blackorby and Donaldson (1988)]. Both nonexperimental studies and more recent evidence from food stamp cash-out trials suggest that there is a significant reduction in beneficiary food expenditures and availability, with only very modest savings in administrative costs [Senauer and Young (1986), Devaney and Moffitt (1991), United States Department of Agriculture, Economic Research Service (ERS) (1995), Fraker et al. (1995)]. Moreover, in most places, the political support for monetization has been weak; taxpayers and politicians prefer to know that transfers are being used for approved purchases (i.e., food rather than alcohol). Where the root problem is insufficient food supply, in-kind transfers are often best; where the problem causing food insecurity is insufficient purchasing power, cash transfers may be best.

One important implication of the relatively modest income elasticity of food is that price policies may be more effective than income policies in stimulating additional food demand, if indeed that is an objective. While food subsidy schemes substantially predated the emergence of this finding in the literature, it has been seized upon in recent years as a justification for targeted subsidy schemes, particularly on inferior foods or grades of foods (see Section 3.3.2). However, using price policy to try to enhance the food security runs the risk of either (a) creating significant production disincentives that may ultimately hurt vulnerable subpopulations more than subsidies help them (see the discussion of disincentives, below), or (b) pursuing fiscally unsustainable state subsidies, a common outcome of generalized subsidies for staple foods [Pinstrup-Andersen (1988)]. Moreover, food subsidies tend to benefit urban populations more than rural ones [Lipton (1977), Alderman (1991)].

While economists generally approach the issue of FAP additionality by studying income and expenditure elasticities, nutritionists tend to look instead at anthropometric

---

[43] This is analogous to the in-kind transfer entering into the nontradables availability constraint rather than the tradables budget constraint in the model of Section 2.2.

indicators. In their thorough review of supplementary feeding programs in developing countries, Beaton and Ghassemi (1982, p. 882) conclude that "most studies have demonstrated some degree of benefit measured in anthropometric terms in association with either take-home food distribution or supervised feeding. The benefit is not always large for the group as a whole. ... Generally speaking, the extent of benefits seems to be influenced by such matters as management quality, extent of nutritional deprivation and ration size." The effectiveness of supplementary feeding programs is sharply limited by the health of participants. Appropriate control for health factors generally increases both the magnitude and statistical significance of supplementary feeding programs' positive effects on nutritional status [Behrman (1993)].

The additionality of supplementary feeding programs has been less well studied in the U.S. and other high-income countries. The popular perception is that WIC contributes considerably to participant food security and nutrition, and there is limited econometric evidence of this [Chavas and Keplinger (1983)] to complement clinical nutritional and medical evidence suggesting very favorable returns to the program [Hicks et al. (1982), Rush (1987)]. The hypothesized reasons why WIC may do better than food stamps at improving beneficiary nutrition relate to precise targeting, both of beneficiaries and of eligible commodities rich in key macro and micronutrients, provision of complementary nutrition education and medical referrals, intertemporally more stable real coverage, and a higher level of participant motivation since beneficiaries receive benefits on behalf of their children.

Other high-income country supplementary feeding programs are even less well studied than WIC. There is some evidence of significant additionality, but it is uneven across programs and still relatively incomplete, in large measure because few studies have satisfactorily attended to the econometric issues (selectivity, endogeneity, unobserved heterogeneity) raised earlier. For example, participants in the U.S. Nutritional Program for the Elderly consume 4 to 10 percent more calories and 24 to 25 percent more calcium than a nonrecipient control group of elderly Americans [Chavas and Keplinger (1983), Ponza et al. (1996)]. School meals programs in the U.S. have generally been found to increase participants' nutrient intake and cognitive outcomes [West and Price (1976), Hoagland (1982), Chavas and Keplinger (1983), Hanes et al. (1984), Devaney and Fraker (1989b), Gordon et al. (1995)]. TEFAP and other food distribution programs have yet to be evaluated carefully with respect to the additionality effects they have on participants' food consumption or nutrient intake. Limited available evidence also suggests significant additionality from food-for-work schemes in developing countries [Athanasios et al. (1994), von Braun (1995), Bezuneh and Deaton (1997)].

Where the objective of Type 1 FAPs and international food aid is to improve food access, the purpose of Type 2 FAPs is to improve the utilization of food to which individuals already have access. Unfortunately, little effort has been made to evaluate the additionality effects of nutrition education, micronutrient fortification, or early warning systems interventions. This is an area ripe for research.

Micronutrients are unevenly distributed across different foods. Consequently, shifting food consumption patterns induced by changing incomes, prices, or tastes influence micronutrient intake patterns. Income and expenditure elasticities therefore vary markedly across micronutrients, are in general quite different from aggregate food expenditure or calorie availability elasticities, and in some cases may even be negative because consumers are often unaware of the impact of dietary choices on micronutrient intake [Bouis (1991), Behrman (1995), Huang (1997)]. Greater calorie intake does not imply better nutrition since more expensive or higher "quality" food is not always more nutritious.

Consequently, micronutrient fortification is important not only when people are poor – for instance iodized salt and iron-fortified wheat flour help prevent goiter and anemia among those too poor to consume seafood or meat regularly – but also as they become richer and change dietary habits – for example, by ensuring that children get vitamin A from milk when their families begin replacing vegetable products with dairy products in their diet. Nonetheless, there have been relatively few studies of the returns to micronutrient fortification [World Bank (1994), Phillips et al. (1996)]. There is considerable evidence that salt iodization is inexpensive and highly effective in combating iodine deficiency disorder [Underwood (1983), International Conference on Nutrition (1992), United Nations Children's Fund (1995), Oldham et al. (1998)]. But for other micronutrients, fortification's benefits are less clearly established. In one of the few such studies, Levin (1986) estimated benefit/cost ratios of 7 to 71 for iron fortification in Indonesia, Kenya, and Mexico.

There is widespread belief that nutrition education programs can induce significant behavioral changes that enhance the food security and physical well-being of participants. The nutritional literature widely reports significant, positive effects of women's general schooling on household demand for both food in aggregate and for key micronutrients, as well as on child anthropometric measures [Behrman and Deolalikar (1988), Strauss and Thomas (1995, 1998)]. The little empirical evidence available about the effectiveness of programs directed specifically at improving people's understanding of good dietary habits suggests they can generate measurable nutritional improvements when designed carefully [Achterberg (1992)]. Because micronutrients are not directly and immediately observable in food the same way as energy (calories), the returns to nutrition education are likely greatest with respect to relieving micronutrient deficiencies. This hypothesis has shaped many nutrition education programs worldwide, but it has not yet been indisputably verified empirically. Moreover, nutrition education programs may either substitute for or complement micronutrient fortification programs. For example, in low-income communities where vegetables are routinely and inexpensively available but meat is expensive, education programs to encourage vegetable consumption may be more cost-effective in preventing vitamin A deficiency, while fortification may be a better means to prevent anemia [Bouis and Novenario-Reese (1997)]. We know relatively little about these prospective trade-offs.

To this point, the discussion has focused entirely on additionality measurable at the microeconomic level of individuals or households. Additionality is also an issue at the macro level, particularly as it concerns food aid. Under the international Food Aid Convention (FAC), food aid recipients are obliged to maintain "normal" volumes of commercial food imports (the "usual marketing requirements", or UMR) so as to ensure the additionality of food aid.[44] Acker (1989, p. 165) observes that if the trade additionality principle is honored, "food aid programs provide an opportunity to empty granaries and warehouses, build up taste preferences for U.S. commodities, and through the economic development consequences of our PL 480 programs, build purchasing power for future commercial sales of U.S. agricultural commodities".

The FAC definition of additionality ignores Engel's Law – that the marginal propensity to consumer food is less than one. And so, as one would expect, the empirical evidence suggests overwhelmingly that food aid partly substitutes for commercial food imports contemporaneously, thereby providing a net foreign exchange transfer, generally of 40 to 70 percent of the value of the food aid delivered [Abbott and McCarthy (1982), von Braun and Huddleston (1988), Saran and Konandreas (1991), Barrett et al. (1999)]. So the macroeconomic marginal propensity to consume food out of food aid transfers is roughly in line with the microeconometric evidence discussed earlier. A portion of food aid flows has always been monetized to pay for transport, storage and handling charges involved in moving commodities to individual recipients, and donors have been mandating higher rates of monetization in recent years.[45] Furthermore, food aid has long provided funds for other, unrelated projects [Maxwell and Templer (1993)].

The emphasis placed by the FAC on unit-valued additionality of food aid underlines that the objective of food aid often is not food security, but rather surplus disposal and promotion of food exports. Given that food aid distributions have historically been driven by criteria other than need and that food aid flows are quite small relative to production and trade volumes, it is not surprising that there is little evidence of food aid enhancing recipient country food security [Clay et al. (1996), Barrett (2001)].

3.3.2. Targeting

The (partial) additionality of FAPs, as commonly measured by marginal propensities to consume food or micronutrients out of in-kind transfers or by improvements in nutritional status associated with program participation, implies increased food availability and consumption among beneficiaries. But are FAPs benefitting those who would be food insecure in the absence of program participation, or are they benefitting the already food secure? FAPs are effective in enhancing food security only to the extent that they reach vulnerable subpopulations. Therefore, effective targeting is fundamental to FAP design and evaluation, particularly in today's era of shrinking FAP budgets as a proportion of government spending or gross domestic product.

---

[44] Adherence to UMRs is "enforced" by the FAO's Committee on Surplus Disposal (CSD).

[45] Project and emergency food aid monetization has increased rapidly, especially U.S. Title II PL 480, 25 to 40 percent of which was monetized in fiscal years 1993–95, versus an average of less than 15 percent in the 1980s.

Targeting directs FAP benefits toward an identifiable pool of intended beneficiaries. It is disturbingly common for FAPs, like other social services, to benefit primarily those whose needs are lesser but who have the political influence to safeguard their privileges, no matter how socially costly. While there is strong and widespread support for targeting, in practice targeting is not always feasible or desirable, as the literature on food subsidies demonstrates [Pinstrup-Andersen (1988, 1993), Alderman (1991)]. When it is difficult to prevent leakage, when the additionality of the transfer is likely low, when the funds to finance food assistance are substantially raised (explicitly or implicitly) through taxes on the poor, when there is not political support for redistributive safety net interventions, when administrative capacity is weak, or when the target group is a large or spatially dispersed proportion of the general population, targeting may not be cost-effective. Moreover, narrowly targeted programs often fail for lack of political support; sometimes only imperfectly targeted programs are politically feasible [Pinstrup-Andersen (1993)].

The aims of targeting are to minimize leakage to unintended beneficiaries and to maximize participation of intended beneficiaries. There are several different targeting methods, which vary across jurisdictions and time in their effectiveness in cost-effectively meeting leakage minimization and participation maximization goals. As a crude taxonomy, one can distinguish between (i) indicator-contingent, administrative targeting (ICAT) and (ii) self-targeting programs.

ICAT FAPs rely on administrative screening, based on any of several food security indicators (e.g., income, nutritional status), to determine program eligibility and thereby concentrate benefits in the hands of the needy. In ICAT programs, administrative and delivery costs per participant and the risk of excluding intended beneficiaries due to imperfect information generally increase rapidly as targeting criteria become more narrow.

Self-targeting occurs when the benefits of the FAP are ostensibly universally available, but the program is designed so that only intended beneficiaries will voluntarily participate. Self-targeting works by resolving the problem of asymmetric information about individual attributes (e.g., income) by making participation incentive compatible only for the food insecure and then relying on self-selection based on preferences revealed by behavior. By imposing a cost (e.g., foregone income) on beneficiaries or minimizing the desirability of the attributes of the benefit (e.g., provide inferior goods or service), the non-needy may self-select out of the program. If information is held asymmetrically and leisure and goods quality are normal goods, such techniques may prove effective [Alderman (1987), Besley and Coate (1991)].

Targeting does not assure FAP effectiveness. For example, program food aid is multiply targeted, first to a recipient country with a particular bundle of commodities, and then to a subpopulation within the recipient country through a FAP vehicle. However, food aid allocation patterns bear little resemblance to the criteria (e.g., per capita income or food availability, balance of payments weakness) commonly identified by donors as influencing their allocations [Ruttan (1993, 1995), Clay et al. (1996), Barrett (2001)]. Allocations have traditionally been made largely on the basis of political criteria, and there has been only modest movement toward targeting food aid to low-income, food-deficit countries over the past decade [Ball and Johnson (1996), Clay et al. (1996)]. Moreover, once in the recipient economy, food aid disproportionately facilitates explicit or implicit consumer food subsidies [Pinstrup-Andersen (1988), Hoffman et al. (1994)], few of which are well-targeted. As prices approach zero, quantity rationing becomes necessary, whether explicitly or implicitly through queuing or patronage. Upper income households and more food secure regions or household members commonly receive at least as much food aid as needier beneficiaries [Webb and Reardon (1992)]. The frequency of regressive forms of quantity rationing and of generalized (i.e., untargeted) subsidies supporting higher quality products in relatively greater demand among urban middle and upper wealth classes (i.e., among relatively food secure subpopulations) often combine to make food subsidies supported by food aid expensive and distributionally regressive, and thus of questionable effectiveness in advancing food security.

Most FAPs in wealthy countries are ICAT programs based on means testing, wherein program staff establish applicants' need for the transfer based on assets, income, and number and status (i.e., gender, age) of dependents.[46] Collecting accurate data on these variables, however, can be costly, slow, and intrusive, sometimes outweighing the cost savings of leakage reduction and reducing the participation of eligibles by increasing the transaction costs and social stigma of program participation. Means testing based on income is relatively uncommon in low-income countries because it demands considerable administrative capacity in order to measure accurately assets and incomes and counteract the potential for fraud and abuse, although means testing based on land ownership may be feasible where land holdings are closely correlated with income and readily observable [Besley and Kanbur (1990), Glewwe (1992), Lipton and Ravallion (1995), Barrett and Dorosh (1996)].[47] Recent work suggests that several simple-to-collect indicators collected by a mixture of methods (e.g., dependency ratio, number of unique foods consumed, rooms per capita) can identify the food insecure with sufficient accuracy to generate cost savings, improved coverage, or both [Haddad et al. (1994), Chung et al. (1997)].

Because of the various problems associated with means tests as a method of FAP targeting, various other ICAT methods have been tried based on correlates of food insecurity other than assets and income. This is often referred to as "indicator targeting" [Kanbur (1987), Glewwe (1992), Lipton and Ravallion (1995)]. One approach is to identify at-risk groups demographically. For example, in the United States, poverty associated with chronic food insecurity is disproportionately a phenomenon of households headed by single, nonelderly women. Moffitt (1992) reports that better than 30 percent of such families received food stamps in 1984, versus less

---

[46] Besley and Kanbur (1990), Glewwe (1992), and Lipton and Ravallion (1995) offer excellent treatments of targeting issues related to poverty alleviation.

[47] Means testing can have undesirable disincentive effects on labor supply, although the empirical evidence suggests these are of relatively small magnitude (discussed below).

than 4 percent of two-parent nonelderly families. By publicizing FAPs and distributing benefits through facilities frequented by the target demographic group (e.g., day care centers, women's health clinics), awareness increases disproportionately among the target population, with the likely effect of increasing program participation. Data on WIC participation in the U.S. and on early childhood supplementary feeding programs in developing countries suggest demographic targeting can be effective [Rush (1987), Beaton (1993), Martorell (1993)]. In the same spirit, the U.S. Food Distribution Program on Indian Reservations and emergency feeding programs for refugees and internally displaced persons (including the homeless in wealthy countries) target FAPs to try to enhance low food security rates among demographically distinct subpopulations.

Supplementary feeding programs generally employ demographic targeting methods, sometimes combined with means-testing in wealthy countries, in an effort to address periodic food insecurity, particularly that associated with the life cycle. Nonetheless, supplementary feeding programs historically have primarily served not infants, preschool children, and pregnant and lactating women – the clientele for which the nutritional impacts appear to be the largest – but rather school children and college students [Beaton (1993), Martorell (1993)]. Supplementary feeding programs have too often been used as high-cost inducements to attend school, with inconclusive effects [Maxwell and Singer (1979)].[48]

Intrahousehold leakages invariably occur. For example, a family may give a child less to eat in the morning and evening than other family members if they know she will be given a full school lunch, and thereby redistribute some of the additional food to parents or other children. Intrahousehold redistribution is inevitable given the dynamics of intrahousehold choice [Beaton and Ghassemi (1982), Beaton (1993), Haddad and Kanbur (1992), Haddad et al. (1997)]. Given the complementarity between Type I FAPs that increase food access, Type II FAPs (e.g., nutrition education and micronutrient fortification), and preventive and curative health care in promoting physical well-being, supplementary feeding programs that are a part of integrated primary health care schemes often seem most effective in improving food security and nutritional status [Gittinger et al. (1986), Rush (1987), Pinstrup-Andersen (1988)].

Another ICAT method is targeting by nutritional status, wherein benefits are given to those exhibiting poor nutritional indicators (e.g., anthropometric measures). Because of insufficient funding to cover all means-tested eligibles, most states in the U.S. use nutritional targeting in WIC to narrow the pool of children (over age one) participating from means-tested eligible families. Many integrated primary health care programs in low-income countries provide supplementary feeding to children showing poor growth. There may be economies of scope in combining nutrition education and complementary health care services with supplementary feeding, but this has not been established empirically outside the United States' WIC program [Rush (1987), Devaney et al.

---

[48] The net effects can be negative if burdening schools with a supplementary feeding mission induces classroom overcrowding and reduces the time teachers spend on educational activities.

(1990)]. While nutritional targeting seems sensible, it can be relatively more expensive because of the labor and supplies needed to evaluate applicants regularly, particularly if an effort is made to identify micronutrient as well as macronutrient deficiencies (e.g., by serum measures of vitamin A or iron adequacy or ultrasonography to check for iodine deficiency). Nutritional targeting may also create perverse incentives, as when households can benefit by systematically depriving one child so as to become or remain eligible for food assistance [Austin and Zeitlin (1981)]. Such behaviors, although uncommon, are a risk.

Time can be a useful indicator. Temporal targeting of price stabilization and subsidy interventions has been common in low-income agrarian nations faced with strong seasonal cycles of food availability. Many governments have operated buffer stocks and panseasonal pricing regimes with the explicit intent of relieving food insecurity pressures during the pre-harvest hungry season. Food security has distinct seasonal patterns in low-income agrarian economies, so there is an obvious logic to temporal targeting [Chambers et al. (1981), Sahn (1989)]. The chief – and oftentimes considerable – problem with such targeting methods is that panseasonal pricing or poorly administered buffer stocks can create enormous disincentives to private food marketing and may thereby create inefficiencies in the food distribution system that pose a far greater long-term threat to food security than is created by the seasonality of agricultural production. Indeed, sharp interseasonal food price variability is generally a signal of weaknesses in the food storage and marketing system, so investments in that sector may provide substantial, if indirect, relief of periodic food insecurity. Nonetheless, temporal targeting can be effectively combined with other methods (e.g., geographical targeting, food-for-work schemes).

Because travel costs can be significant among the poor,[49] thereby inducing self-selection among prospective beneficiaries, all FAPs are *de facto* geographically targeted by the location of supplementary feeding or food distribution centers, of program promotional announcements, etc. Where insufficient attention is given the geography of FAPs, adverse unintended consequences often arise. This is the primary reason why FAP participation rates among eligible rural residents of the United States fell precipitously in the 1980s and rural program participants receive a far smaller per capita share of services and benefits than do urban program participants [Public Voice for Food and Health Policy (1986, 1988)]. Urban bias is just as commonly observed in developing country FAPs [Lipton (1977), Maxwell and Singer (1979)].

This also highlights the possibilities of geographic targeting. Where significant regional disparities in food security can be identified, effective targeting may be achieved simply by locating distribution centers in the middle of the most needy areas. Many governments employ this technique, distributing FAP resources to subsidiary

---

[49] For example, in the U.S., only 22 percent of food stamp recipients drive their own vehicle to the grocery store or food distribution center, as compared to 95 percent of those not receiving food stamps [American Dietetic Association (1990)].

jurisdictions based on spatially disaggregated poverty or nutritional indicators, or locating fair price shops, emergency feeding stations and the like in the middle of disproportionately poor city neighborhoods and rural communities.[50] One prospective hazard of geographic targeting, however, is that it may induce migration to seek better benefits, although little is known empirically about these migration incentive effects [Rosenzweig and Wolpin (1986), Moffitt (1992)]. Moreover, geographic targeting necessarily entails leakage to the food secure in food-insecure regions, and if distribution within a region is ultimately regressive, even progressive distribution between regions may yield high rates of leakage and little net benefit.

The administrative cost of ICAT limits its widespread use in low-income economies. There, self-targeting FAPs may be especially useful. The two most common forms of self-targeting FAPs are subsidies on inferior foods and food-for-work schemes. Subsidies applied to inferior foods and grades of foods – on which expenditures decline as total expenditures increase – can be effectively targeted. Foods most in demand by the poor as a low-cost source of nutrients offering few other redeeming attributes can endogenously direct assistance toward those most needing it without the need for complementary ICAT. In other words, subsidize foods that exhibit high income and (negative) price elasticities of demand among the poor but low income and price elasticities of demand among the rich. Such schemes have met with demonstrable success in Bangladesh, Egypt, Morocco, South Africa, and Tunisia [Grosh (1994), Ali and Adams (1996), Alderman and Lindert (forthcoming)].

There are nonetheless two concerns regarding inferior food consumer subsidies. First, it matters whether the subsidized food is available in restricted or unrestricted quantities to consumers because this determines whether the subsidy is marginal or inframarginal. As Besley and Kanbur (1988, pp. 711–712) note, "infra-marginal subsidies transfer purchasing power independently of current income while subsidies at the margin do so in proportion to current consumption of the commodity in question, and hence (to the first order) in proportion to income. For a given budget, therefore, infra-marginal subsidies are better at alleviating poverty [or food insecurity]". Most food subsidies in the developing world have been inframarginal, using ration cards, fair price shops, and the like [Pinstrup-Andersen (1988), Alderman (1991)]. Inframarginal subsidies are necessarily more costly to implement per unit subsidized, creating a trade-off between administrative costs or leakage to the food secure and open-ended fiscal obligations. In general, limited-access (i.e., inframarginal) food subsidy programs have been more successful in reaching intended beneficiaries with only modest leakage, particularly where subsidies have been on inferior foods [Pinstrup-Andersen (1988), Grosh (1994), Alderman and Lindert (forthcoming)]. The second concern is that one must be careful not to induce people to turn subsidized inferior foods into animal feed. Most inferior staples also double as high quality feed. So subsidies intended to benefit the poor may become an indirect subsidy to rich meat consumers, all the more so for marginal

---

[50] Besley and Kanbur (1988) show why geographic targeting may be particularly cost-effective.

(rather than inframarginal) subsidies. As Timmer et al. (1983, pp. 71–72) put it, "Those concerned with commodity targeting must look in two very different directions: at the consumption patterns of the poor, and at livestock-feeding patterns and the potential for a shift to a subsidized inferior foodstuff. Ways to reach one group without benefitting the other are essential if commodity targeting is to be effective".

In food-for-work schemes, a below-market wage, generally paid in kind, induces those with high (shadow) wage alternatives to self-select out of the pool of participants, thereby minimizing eligibility screening costs. Where minimum wages set a floor on food-for-work compensation rates, these schemes can become oversubscribed, reducing the impact on food security and causing rationing of work [Ravallion et al. (1993), von Braun (1995)]. Where properly designed so as not to compete with the regular labor market, such public employment schemes also minimize the prospective labor disincentive effects of the FAP (discussed below).

Because of intrahousehold variation in food security status, direct targeting of at-risk individuals is generally preferable to household-level targeting. Individual targeting – particularly to vulnerable children more at risk of permanent impairment due to nutrient insufficiency – seems central to the apparent success of the WIC program in the U.S. [Rush (1987)]. But complex intrahousehold resource redistribution patterns complicate both ICAT and self-targeting of particular individuals.[51] For example, public employment programs designed to benefit households suffering due to high unemployment rates may not have much impact on dependent children if benefits are paid in cash and the nature of the work or the wages are such that the scheme employs primarily males. Similarly, supplementary feeding programs – including school meals programs – designed to benefit food-insecure children may induce a reallocation of household food supplies toward nonbeneficiaries and away from the targeted child, thereby reducing the additionality of the program, and in extreme cases causing reduced intake by the child in question.

Overall, the empirical evidence suggests that concerted efforts at targeting can be effective in preventing leakage. The most recent figures indicate that less than 10 percent of U.S. food stamp beneficiaries have incomes above the poverty line, and these recipients receive a disproportionately small share (about 3 percent) of benefits [United States Department of Agriculture, Economic Research Service (ERS) (1995)]. Of course, there is a black market and some counterfeiting takes place, but leakage appears modest overall in the U.S. food stamp program.[52] Similarly, the national WIC evaluation concludes that "the impact of the WIC program on unintended recipients seems to be negligible". The national NPE evaluation likewise found that benefits were reaped disproportionately by senior citizens at or near the poverty line, even though that program is not means-tested.

---

[51] This paragraph draws heavily on Haddad et al. (1997).

[52] In Zambia, by contrast, the food stamp program had to be closed down on account of rampant counterfeiting.

Targeted programs also encourage participation of eligibles, although nonparticipation rates are significant in all programs, targeted or not. For example, only 40 to 70 percent of eligibles participate at any given time in the U.S. food stamp program [Ohls and Beebout (1993), Blank and Ruggles (1995)]. Theory tells us that eligible individuals do not participate in a program only if (1) they are unaware of the program or their eligibility for it, or (2) there are significant costs to participating that outweigh the benefits, such as physical difficulties of applying for or using benefits (e.g., due to disabilities), ill health, distance to program benefit centers, time involved in the application or disbursement process, social stigma, or a desire for self-reliance. Since most of these are not directly observable, it is difficult in practice to distinguish between them, although the order of importance among these clearly matters if participation rates are to be increased among eligibles.[53]

Research on U.S. welfare programs suggests that both lack of information and significant participation costs play a significant role in program nonparticipation rates and patterns [Moffitt (1992)]. Joy et al. (1994) find both factors are important in explaining exceptionally low food stamp program participation by the homeless in the U.S. Levedahl (1995a) finds that outreach programs to improve awareness increased U.S food stamp program participation rates from 59 to 69 percent among targeted populations. Institutional arrangements affecting participant transactions costs likewise appear to affect program participation rates and timing [Lane et al. (1983), Moffitt (1983), Ranney and Kushman (1987), Haddad and Willis (1991)]. A key institutional issue is the way in which it is organized. "Participatory" and "community-led" approaches have come into vogue in the 1990s, although top-down approaches to FAP design and administration still predominate. The limited available empirical evidence does suggest that participation rates of intended beneficiaries and program additionality are positively correlated with the degree of consultation and shared decision-making in program design and assessment [ACC/SCN (1991), Barrett and Csete (1994), Isham et al. (1995)].

In an especially noteworthy study of the dynamics of program participation, Blank and Ruggles (1995) find that a considerable proportion of U.S. food stamp program nonparticipation is accounted for by those who are eligible for only a brief period. These eligibles tend to be older, white, nondisabled, better educated, have fewer children, and have higher expected future nontransfer earnings. For them, stigma costs and sensitivity to institutional arrangements may be higher (in part due to neighborhood effects) and the expected short duration of benefits receipt makes it undesirable to incur the sunk costs of initiating program participation.[54] The empirical evidence also suggests that participation rates are influenced by benefit levels and the rate at which benefits are reduced as participant nontransfer income increases [Moffitt (1992)]. Food stamp

---

[53] It should also be noted that these variables appear only to affect program participation, not food consumption and expenditure patterns conditional on program participation [Ranney and Kushman (1987)].

[54] Initial certification costs are invariably higher than the ongoing costs of recertification.

participation in the U.S. thus appears low in part because coupon amounts are low. When food stamp purchase requirements were eliminated in 1979, program participation rates jumped.

Self-targeting programs fare no better in ensuring high participation rates of intended beneficiaries. For example, food-for-work programs screen out not only the food secure but also the disabled, those too old or young to work, and households suffering labor shortages (including many households headed by single women in agrarian communities). Similarly, subsidization of inferior foodstuffs does not help the poor living in remote areas poorly serviced by private food marketing channels. Because undercoverage is a serious problem in all targeting schemes, the complementary redundancy principle again applies. Self-targeting mechanisms can reduce the scope, and thus the cost, of complementary ICAT activities, and the two together can provide a comprehensive safety net at minimal cost [Drèze and Sen (1989)].

This raises the issue of program overlap. Where multiple programs exist, beneficiaries tend to participate in multiple programs [Lane et al. (1983), Blank and Ruggles (1995)]. Smaller FAPs, like The Emergency Food Assistance Program (TEFAP) complement the main programs, like food stamps, by reaching a somewhat different beneficiary group (e.g., homeless persons) and by promoting awareness of eligibility for other, more substantial forms of assistance. Smaller FAPs also supply the rapidly growing network of private emergency food providers, demand for which has soared in the U.S. over the past twenty years [American Dietetic Association (1990)]. But program redundancy likely adds to aggregate FAP costs. However, since all programs undercover intended beneficiaries, there is surely a (largely unmeasured) trade-off between coverage of eligibles and potential savings from lower administrative costs. The extent of overlap in participation or benefit levels has been under-researched.[55]

Many governments have attempted to use public distribution to enhance the effectiveness of targeting. This has almost always failed. Except in extreme cases of social disruption (e.g., in areas severely affected by natural disasters or war), the private sector food distribution system tends to be relatively cost-effective in reaching even the most needy, provided they have purchasing power. Hence the conversion in the 1930s of the U.S. food stamp program from a public food delivery scheme to a system of coupons redeemable through private food retailers. Targeted price subsidies in several developing countries have likewise used private marketing channels to distribute subsidized rations [Pinstrup-Andersen (1988)]. Where the private food marketing system appears inefficient or noncompetitive, the returns are almost always higher to investing in improving the competitiveness and efficiency of the private food marketing system than to establishing and operating a parallel, public system.

On some occasions, FAPs employ negative or exclusionary targeting, whereby particular groups are explicitly excluded from receiving benefits. A recent, well-

---

[55] Census data suggest that about 90 percent of AFDC recipients also receive food stamps and that 50 percent of food stamp recipients also participate in another FAP, primarily the National School Lunch Program [Smallwood (1993)].

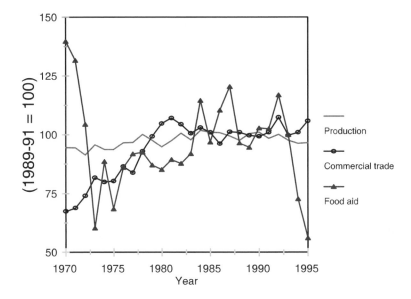

Figure 6. Data source: FAO, *Production Yearbook*, *Trade Yearbook*, and *Food Aid in Figures*, various issues.

publicized example is the exclusion of nearly one million otherwise-eligible legal immigrants from receiving food stamps in the U.S. in the wake of the 1996 welfare reforms. Exclusionary targeting of this sort is almost always driven by political motives rather than a concern to enhance food security in a cost-effective manner, and is thus qualitatively different from the other targeting methods discussed.

3.3.3. Intertemporal variability

To provide effective insurance against transitory food insecurity, FAP transfers should move countercyclically with exogenous business and food production cycles, increasing when employment or crop and livestock output fall. Moreover, as Section 2 discussed, variability in transfers, including FAPs, may add to food insecurity. Intertemporal variability in benefits can offset the otherwise positive effects of food assistance by creating additional risk, particularly if benefits move procyclically.

The literature on food aid points out that because most donors budget food aid on a monetary basis, food aid flow volumes generally covary negatively with international market prices and donor country food inventories [von Braun and Huddleston (1988), Taylor and Byerlee (1991), Clay et al. (1996)].[56] As a consequence, food aid volumes are far more volatile than are food production or trade volumes (Figure 6). Available

---

[56] Because the EU food aid budget is fixed in volume terms rather than expenditure terms, there is no discernible correlation between world food prices and EU food aid flow volumes [Clay et al. (1996)].

food aid volumes tend to shrink precisely when importing countries most need concessional food flows – when food prices rise – causing both food import volumes and food import unit costs to increase. Program food aid disbursement patterns may thereby destabilize food availability and prices in recipient nations. While the shift from program to humanitarian aid supposedly pushes food aid toward a more countercyclical disbursement profile, Barrett (2001) shows that U.S. PL 480 flows – including Title II emergency assistance – are essentially unrelated to (cross-sectional or intertemporal) variation in recipient country nonconcessional food availability, partly due to the politics of food aid, and partly to delivery lags.

This finding from food aid applies to domestic food distribution programs as well. When stocks fall and prices rise, vulnerable subpopulations' need for food assistance increases while the availability of donated commodities decreases. The phenomenon is muted somewhat, but not completely, in the case of domestic FAPs other than FDPs. Because food stamps are denominated in monetary terms and eligibility and benefits are adjusted for a general cost of living index, the real purchasing power of food stamps is as volatile as the difference between staple food prices and the consumer price index. WIC coupons, by contrast, are denominated in physical volume terms and are thus impervious to price fluctuations for individuals who maintain eligibility. However, because WIC (unlike food stamps) is not an entitlement program and is budgeted on an expenditure basis, program coverage in aggregate covaries negatively with food prices. In general, where inflation rates are high and volatile, food assistance denominated in monetary terms (e.g., food stamps) will provide beneficiaries less stable real purchasing power than will FAPs extended in real terms (e.g., supplementary feeding programs).

3.3.4. Direct and indirect costs

The direct costs of FAPs stem from three distinct activities: the distribution of benefits, the targeting and screening of eligible beneficiaries, and general administrative support. There is considerable variation in direct costs across alternative FAP modalities. Food distribution programs, including international food aid, tend to involve significant distribution costs (for transport, storage, and handling) not incurred by programs that provide cash or vouchers (e.g., food stamps, WIC, cash assistance). For example, Clay et al. (1996) find that EU food aid generated counterpart funds valued 23 percent lower than the financial cost of the aid to the donors. Schultz (1960) estimated the value of U.S. PL 480 food aid delivered to recipients at only 37 percent of the total costs to the United States. In the United States, food aid transport costs are inflated by the requirement, under the Merchant Marine Act, that at least 75 percent of U.S. food aid shipments be transported on vessels registered in the U.S. This adds to the costs and lags in delivering food aid [U.S. General Accounting Office (1990)]. In general, tied aid is an inefficient means of providing support, and food aid is often doubly tied, both to a geographic source and to a particular basket of commodities [Abbott and McCarthy (1982), Clay et al. (1996)]. Local purchases, triangular transactions, and cash grants are usually less costly ways of providing budgetary support than direct food aid in kind. This principle carries over into domestic FAPs, where commodity distribution programs are far more costly than food stamps, WIC, or other transfer systems based on negotiable instruments.

As Section 3.3.2 discussed, effective targeting usually adds to FAP cost, although self-targeting mechanisms keep these extra costs to a minimum. Targeting may require additional labor to receive and screen applications where eligibility is means tested, or extra facilities where the FAP employs geographic targeting. Direct costs per beneficiary increase with active targeting efforts, but program costs per intended beneficiary often simultaneously fall as leakage lessens. Surprisingly little empirical research has been done to estimate the marginal costs and related benefits of alternative targeting methods [Alderman (1991), Grosh (1994), Alderman and Lindert (forthcoming)].

The general administrative costs of FAPs similarly vary widely, depending on the efficiency of the responsible government agency and the type of intervention fielded. Where fraud is common, FAPs often become a trough at which many who are ineligible for program benefits feed. Nonetheless, the direct operating costs of FAPs are often far less than commonly believed. For example, nonbenefit costs of the U.S. Food Stamp Program (i.e., including targeting costs) have consistently represented merely 5 to 10 percent of total program costs over the past decade, well below the equivalent figure for most charitable organizations. Unfortunately, many FAPs have kept direct costs down by neglecting program monitoring and evaluation activities necessary to establish the additionality of the program and the effectiveness of its targeting. Given the billions of dollars spent each year worldwide on FAPs, this seems short-sighted economizing.

In addition to – and even less well measured than – the direct costs of FAPs, there may be indirect costs as well. In the absence of lump sum taxes, redistributive programs generally have distortionary effects associated with mobilizing resources to finance interventions. If distortionary taxes retard investment and economic growth, excessive pursuit of public FAPs to provide short-term food security can impede the employment and income growth necessary to ensure food security in the longer term. Furthermore, FAPs funded primarily by direct or indirect resource transfers from the poor (e.g., policies that discourage employment of unskilled labor) may have negative net impacts on food security.

The costs of FAPs are especially difficult to assess in the presence of farm income support programs like those run in the European Union and the United States over the past forty years. Where FAPs stimulate consumer food demand, they put upward pressure on market prices, thereby permitting some reduction in deficiency and other domestic farm support payments. Smith and Lee (1994) report USDA/ERS findings that U.S. food aid shipments of wheat are estimated to have boosted domestic U.S. wheat prices 1 to 5 percent in the mid- to late-1980s. Martinez and Dixit (1992) estimate that domestic FAPs increased farm prices less than one percent on average. Given the modest estimated producer price effects of FAPs, it seems unlikely that they have appreciably reduced government payments to farmers. Moreover, given the dramatic changes enacted in farm income support policies during the 1990s, these effects are likely rapidly approaching zero.

Some FAPs may also entail indirect costs due to regulation. The most obvious example is micronutrient fortification requirements levied on food processors. Governments usually cover only a small portion of fortification costs, primarily for monitoring and quality control. This may be socially optimal, in that the benefits of micronutrient fortification accrue chiefly to private individuals in the form of improved productivity and health [Behrman (1995)]. But fortification programs do impose added social costs not commonly noted.

The literature on food price policy shows that the indirect effects of macroeconomic distortions (e.g., exchange rate overvaluation, high tariffs, or quotas) tend to overwhelm the direct effects of subsidies and taxes [Krueger et al. (1988)]. The analogous situation may prevail with respect to food security as well – that the indirect effects of the tax, regulatory, and farm policies that support FAPs may partially or wholly offset the food security additionality of FAPs – although this point has yet to be considered, much less empirically researched, in the literature on FAPs.

3.3.5. Incentive effects

FAPs may have another sort of indirect cost, in the form of disincentives to produce food, to reform failed policies, to work, or to demand locally grown food [Maxwell and Singer (1979), Maxwell (1991)]. The literature on food aid focused heavily on (dis)incentive effects for twenty or so years following the Cochrane (1959)–Schultz (1960) debates over PL 480. There has been less research on the incentive effects of domestic FAPs, although the incentive effects of cash transfer programs – particularly Aid to Families with Dependent Children (AFDC) in the U.S. – have received considerable scholarly attention.[57]

Schultz (1960) emphasized that if food aid is additional and recipient country consumer demand for food is not perfectly price elastic, then food aid deliveries will increase local food supply, thereby depressing prices and discouraging local production. The existence and magnitude of these price disincentive effects has been heatedly debated for better than three decades. Some have claimed that food supply is highly price inelastic in poor countries, so these disincentive effects are likely small [Khatkhate (1962)], although the long-run price elasticity of food supply in developing countries is much higher than is commonly believed [Chhibber (1989)]. Others have countered that the income effects of food aid transfers will largely mitigate price disincentives [Sen (1960)], although income elasticities of food are low. Fisher (1963) pointed out that the manner of food aid distribution heavily conditions the degree of price disincentive effects. Food aid liquidated on an open market will generally depress prices more than food distributed directly to those who would not otherwise purchase food or who

---

[57] Moffitt (1992) offers an especially good survey.

would purchase food in a distinct market not integrated with the producer market (i.e., where there is geographic or intercommodity market segmentation). If transfers are made directly to the poor, who are generally believed to have higher income and price elasticities of demand for food, demand-side income effects may offset the price effects of a supply increase.

This is widely believed to have been the case with food aid distributions to India in the 1960s, long the world's leading food aid recipient and the subject of most empirical studies on food aid's potential price disincentive effects. In India, food aid was directed almost exclusively to food-for-work schemes, such as the Maharashtra Employment Guarantee Scheme, or to means-tested "fair price" shops. With effective targeting of food aid to the food insecure, who have a high marginal propensity to consume food out of income transfers, the result was that the additional component of food aid (i.e., accounting for displaced commercial imports) was almost entirely absorbed through increased consumption by the poor, with little or no effect on domestic food prices and producer incentives. The Indian experience, while not exceptional, has been better than many [Isenman and Singer (1977), Maxwell and Singer (1979), Singer et al. (1987), Ruttan (1993))]. The available evidence suggests that an appropriate mix of policy tools (e.g., demand expansion, market differentiation, producer price supports) can mitigate any product market price disincentives brought on by food aid [Maxwell and Singer (1979)].

More recent studies have recognized that food producers in food aid recipient countries both consume and produce food, so household modeling techniques [Singh et al. (1986)] are a more appropriate analytical method for investigating the production incentives created by food aid. The basic implication of these studies is that food aid may have factor market effects that mitigate, or even overshadow, the product market effects that concerned previous scholars. Bezuneh et al. (1988) employ a separable household model and find that food-for-work schemes in rural Kenya increase food production by program participants by fostering on-farm investment by capital-constrained households. Mellor (1978), Dearden and Ackroyd (1989), and Dorosh et al. (1995) obtain similar results. Mohapatra et al. (1999) generalized this to consider factor and product market effects in the context of nonseparable household models.

The price incentive effects caused by domestic FAPs in wealthy countries (food aid donors) may work in the opposite direction. FAPs that stimulate consumer demand by increasing beneficiary purchasing power (e.g., food stamps, WIC) or through government purchase for direct distribution (e.g., TEFAP today), stimulate commodity prices. Where Schultzian disincentives work by expanding supply, analogous incentives may be created by expanding demand. The greater the additionality and coverage of FAPs that increase beneficiary purchasing power in the private market, the greater the stimulus to producer prices. The irony is thus that FAPs in wealthy countries enjoying substantial aggregate food surpluses may engender positive incentives to food production, while in poor countries, where aggregate food availability is often insufficient and FAPs are primarily supplied by food aid flows, FAPs may discourage food production if not managed properly.

Schultz (1960) also claimed that food aid discourages recipient country governments from investing appropriately in expanding agricultural production, i.e., food aid may create policy disincentives. Often the core problem underlying food insecurity is poor policies, the distribution of resources, or both, and some have argued that food aid allows governments to postpone or avoid politically difficult but economically necessary reforms. As such, food aid may perpetuate the very power relations, inequities, and failed policies that foster food insecurity. Casual scrutiny of the data certainly suggests a positive relationship between food aid receipts and the maintenance of deleterious agricultural policies – little investment in agricultural research and extension, state control of food marketing, explicit and implicit taxation of agriculture in an effort to stimulate industrialization – in many recipient nations until the late 1970s. One generally overlooked, prospective policy disincentive effect relates to "Dutch disease", the term given to real exchange rate appreciation attributable to a windfall of foreign exchange.[58] If food aid significantly displaces commercial imports (i.e., if the additionality of food aid is low), then unless the government sterilizes the foreign exchange windfall, food aid receipts may foster (modest) real exchange rate appreciation injurious to tradables sectors, perhaps including food agriculture. The 1980s, however, marked the onset of international aid and lending with strict conditionality related to policy reforms, and food aid was no exception to that pattern. As a result, the more recent history of food aid's relationship to recipient country policies is probably the relevant one, but it has received less thorough scholarly review.

On balance, the appropriate general conclusion seems to be that food aid has often been "sucked in by poor agricultural policy rather than itself being responsible for the vacuum which it fills" [Maxwell and Singer (1979, p. 225)]. Well-targeted, well-executed FAPs, including food aid, can improve both short-run and long-run food security when enacted in an appropriate policy environment, but many FAPs have been poorly targeted or executed, or both, or launched against overwhelming odds due to poor general food policies.

These issues apply to domestic FAPs as well. Surplus disposal programs make it easier, both politically and fiscally, to maintain farm programs that cause substantial excess local food supplies. Cheap food policies fostered by generalized subsidies may also create their own domestic political constituency and a host of perverse incentives [Alderman (1991), Pinstrup-Andersen (1993), Barrett (1998b)].

Microeconomic theory is reasonably clear in its suggestion that transfers or consumer subsidies will increase consumer welfare, generating income effects that reduce labor supply [Leonesio (1988)]. These disincentive effects may impact on FAP outcomes. In particular, the additionality of a FAP, as measured by food expenditures or nutrient intake, should fall as labor supply becomes more elastic because a greater share of the welfare gains will be taken in the form of leisure.

There has been relatively little empirical research, however, on whether FAPs create labor disincentives in practice and whether such disincentives are costly in terms of

---

[58] See Edwards and Van Wijnbergen (1989) for a good treatment of Dutch disease.

either foregone additionality or deadweight welfare losses. In his thorough review of the incentive effects of transfer programs generally, Moffitt (1992, pp. 18–19) concludes that "the lack of research on the effects of in-kind transfer programs on labor supply is a serious problem in light of the critical role such transfers have played in the development of the transfer system [in the U.S.]". The one published study on the labor disincentive effects of the U.S. food stamp program finds only very modest disincentive effects, lowering the average hours worked by single-female household heads by one [Fraker and Moffitt (1988)]. Sahn and Alderman (1996) use a selectivity model to study the labor market disincentives of consumer rice subsidies in Sri Lanka, distinguishing between the effects on labor market participation and on days worked conditional on participation. They find no economically significant effect on labor market participation, but they find significant disincentive effects on hours worked, particularly for women. In a less formal treatment of the issues, Jackson (1982) likewise finds significant labor market disincentives from food-for-work projects in various developing countries. On the other hand, Stevens (1979) and Maxwell et al. (1994) found little evidence of labor market disincentive effects from FAPs in various places in sub-Saharan Africa. Still different results emerge from a model of food-for-work distribution in rural Kenya, wherein program participation permits on-farm capital accumulation that increases labor productivity and thereby stimulates additional (rather than less) on-farm employment [Bezuneh et al. (1988)]. The limited and contradictory empirical evidence as yet offers no clear answer to the question of labor (dis)incentive effects of FAPs.

There is little denying that FAPs have the potential to cause significant microeconomic and macroeconomic disincentive effects of various sorts. This was more likely a problem when FAPs, especially food aid, were driven primarily by surplus disposal and geopolitical concerns. The significant shift in emphasis among virtually all FAP types toward enhancing food security may have lessened disincentive effects, although this hypothesis remains to be tested empirically. Moreover, disincentive effects are avoidable. Experience shows that appropriate policies can mitigate, even reverse disincentives, and the major food aid practitioners today appear to have learned most of those lessons. Overall, the empirical evidence suggests that effectively managed FAPs rarely generate significant disincentive effects.

4. Conclusions

Widespread hunger and malnutrition persist today despite considerable progress in per capita food availability over the past century. This has prompted an evolving conceptualization of food security and of mechanisms to attain and maintain food security. Where food security was once roughly equated with food availability, a second generation view came to focus on individuals' access or "entitlements" to food, and an emerging third generation perspective emphasizes uncertainty, vulnerability, and nonfood complementary inputs like health services, sanitation, education, and public infrastructure. Given food security's unobservability and complex etiology, there is no simple, single indicator one can use reliably either to identify the food insecure or to estimate the prevalence or intensity of food insecurity.

For the same reason, there is no single pathway to food security for all. Not long ago, there was widespread confidence in states' abilities to rid the world of hunger and malnutrition. But the palpable need to do something is not a charter for government intervention. Students of food security increasingly recognize that successful FAPs complement rather than crowd out markets and private charitable initiatives, and that they are not financed by implicit taxes or subsidies that counteract the palliative effects of the direct intervention. Moreover, food security in the aggregate and in the long-term probably responds best to broad-based, steady growth in productivity, employment, and incomes. Nevertheless, considerable evidence suggests state-sponsored FAPs can indeed be effectively targeted to improve food consumption, nutrient intake, food sufficiency, and nutritional status at reasonable cost in terms of leakage to unintended beneficiaries, administrative expenditures, and price, policy, or labor supply disincentives. The operative word is "can".

Despite considerable careful research that has significantly advanced our understanding of food security and FAPs, that understanding remains limited in several important respects. First, the empirical evaluation literature generally employs only one or a few – and not necessarily the best – indicators of food security and too rarely acknowledges the importance of dynamics and uncertainty. Second, because the underlying motivations and modalities of assistance programs have been changing rapidly over the past decade, historical experience may not be an especially accurate predictor of future performance. Hence the need for continued data collection and replication of past studies using more current data sets to see whether changed institutional arrangements have affected FAP performance. Third, little comparative empirical work has been done toward establishing the appropriate portfolio of FAPs necessary to achieve desired levels of food security. The trade-offs and complementarities between instruments – e.g., on food subsidies, public works schemes, tax cuts to stimulate private employment, and investment – remain largely unknown. Policymakers need to know how to allocate scarce public resources for maximal effectiveness.

Because domestic FAPs can be effective but food availability remains limited in a variety of low-income settings, there remains an important place for international food aid and food-related financing to overcome market impediments despite the well-documented problems of food aid. The dramatic, recent turn away from program food aid – an expensive, untargeted venture that primarily served geopolitical and surplus food disposal goals over the past fifty years – toward project and humanitarian assistance, and the increasing reliance on local purchases and triangular transactions demonstrate that food aid practitioners have learned key lessons from the history of food aid. General budgetary support is more efficiently provided by cash transfers, but food security can be effectively supported by in-kind transfers, even across borders, when integrated into an appropriate policy environment.

Ultimately, both domestic and international FAPs must be judged by whether they improve long-term (short-term) food security among vulnerable groups without unduly compromising short-term (long-term) food access. Improvements in food production and distribution to help bring down the real costs of food to the poor, in incomes among the poor, particularly through increased labor productivity, employment, and wages, and in human health and education are crucial to long-term food security. At aggregate levels, these dimensions can be summed up as equitable economic growth. In the shorter run and at individual and household levels, however, there is a need for safety nets in the form of publicly provided FAPs as a complement to fill the inevitable gaps left by markets and charitable food assistance systems. Domestic and international FAPs are therefore most necessary where production and distribution systems are weak and leave many people food insecure. But it must be recognized that market weakness is strongly and positively associated with government weakness. Where markets and food production systems are weak, the most effective strategy is therefore not to abandon them – to states that are likely also weak –, but rather to build them up through necessary investment. The ultimate objective of FAP managers should be to make themselves unnecessary to as many clients as possible in order to improve their capacity to service well those subpopulations that will always need at least temporary food assistance.

Acknowledgements

This work has benefitted substantially from conversations with and comments from an anonymous referee, Harold Alderman, Peter Basiotis, Mesfin Bezuneh, Rebecca Blank, Michael Carter, Jim Chalfant, Jean-Paul Chavas, Ed Clay, Layne Coppock, Joanne Csete, Chris Delgado, Pat Dexter, Paul Dorosh, Cheryl Doss, Marcel Fafchamps, Bruce Gardner, Craig Gunderson, Wolfgang Herbinger, Thom Jayne, Judit Katona-Apte, David Lee, Peter Little, Peter Matlon, Dan Maxwell, Jon Moris, Rob Paarlberg, Gordon Rausser, Tom Reardon, Shlomo Reutlinger, Vern Ruttan, T.N. Srinivasan, Frances Stewart, Peter Timmer, Michael Trueblood, and Patrick Webb, and from seminar audiences at Michigan State University and the University of California at Riverside. Sandeep Mohapatra and Shane Sherlund provided excellent research assistance. Most of the work on this chapter was completed while I was on the economics faculty at Utah State University, with the generous support of the Utah Agricultural Experiment Station. At Cornell University, this work has been supported by the Cornell University Agricultural Experiment Station.

References

Abbott, P.C., and F.D. McCarthy (1982), "The welfare costs of tied food aid", Journal of Development Economics 11:63–79.

Achterberg, C. (1992), Effective Nutrition Communication for Behavior Change (Nutrition Foundation and USAID Office of Nutrition, Washington).

Acker, D. (1989), "Food aid programs, food consumption, and incentives for the agriculture of less developed countries and the United States", in: J.W. Helmuth and S. R. Johnson, eds., Proceedings of the 1988 World Food Conference (Iowa State University Press, Ames).

Administrative Committee on Coordination/Subcommittee on Nutrition (ACC/SCN) (1991), Managing Successful Nutrition Programmes (World Health Organization, Geneva).

Alamgir, M., and P. Arora (1991), Providing Food Security for All (New York University Press, New York).

Alderman, H. (1987), "Allocation of goods through non-price mechanisms: Evidence on distribution by willingness to wait", Journal of Development Economics 25:105–124.

Alderman, H. (1991), "Food subsidies and the poor", in: G. Psacharopoulos, ed., Essays on Poverty, Equity and Growth (Pergammon Press, Oxford).

Alderman, H. (1993), "New research on poverty and malnutrition: What are the implications for policy?", in: M. Lipton and J. Van Der Gaag, eds., Including the Poor (World Bank, Washington).

Alderman, H., M.G. Chaudhry and M. Garcia (1988), "Food security in Pakistan: The ration ship system", Working Papers in Food Subsidies No. 4 (International Food Policy Research Institute, Washington).

Alderman, H., and M. Garcia (1994), "Food security and health security: Explaining the levels of nutritional status in Pakistan", Economic Development and Cultural Change 42:485–507.

Alderman, H., and K. Lindert (forthcoming), "Self-targeting of food subsidies: Potential and limitations", World Bank Research Observer.

Alderman, H., and C.H. Paxson (1992), "Do the poor insure? A synthesis of the literature on risk and consumption in developing countries", World Bank Policy Research Working Paper WPS 1008 (World Bank, Washington).

Alderman, H., and J. von Braun (1984), "The effects of the Egyptian food rationing and subsidy system on income distribution and consumption", Research Report No. 45 (International Food Policy Research Institute, Washington).

Ali, S.M., and R.H. Adams Jr. (1996), "The Egyptian food subsidy system: Operation and effects on income distribution", World Development 24:1777–1791.

American Dietetic Association (ADA) (1990), "Position of the American Dietetic Association: Domestic hunger and inadequate access to food", Journal of the American Dietetic Association 90:1437–1441.

Arrow, K.L., and A.C. Fisher (1974), "Environmental preservation, uncertainty, and irreversibility", Quarterly Journal of Economics 88:312–319.

Athanasios, A., M. Bezuneh and B.J. Deaton (1994), "Impacts of FFW on nutrition in rural Kenya", Agricultural Economics 11:301–309.

Atkinson, A.B., and J.E. Stiglitz (1980), Lectures on Public Economics (McGraw-Hill, New York).

Austin, J.E., and M.F. Zeitlin (1981), Nutrition Intervention in Developing Countries (OG&H Publishers, Cambridge, MA).

Babu, S.C., and P. Pinstrup-Andersen (1994), "Food security and nutrition monitoring", Food Policy 19:218–233.

Ball, R., and C. Johnson (1996), "Political, economic, and humanitarian motivations for PL 480 food aid: Evidence from Africa", Economic Development and Cultural Change 44:515–537.

Barrett, C.B. (1996a), "Urban bias in price risk: The geography of food price distributions in low-income economies", Journal of Development Studies 32:830–849.

Barrett, C.B. (1996b), "On price risk and the inverse farm size-productivity relationship", Journal of Development Economics 51:193–215.

Barrett, C.B. (1997), "Heteroscedastic price forecasting for food security management in developing countries", Oxford Development Studies 25:225–236.

Barrett, C.B. (1998a), "Immiserized growth in liberalized agriculture", World Development 26:743–753.

Barrett, C.B. (1998b), "Food aid: Is it development assistance, trade promotion, both or neither?", American Journal of Agricultural Economics 80:566–571.

Barrett, C.B. (1998c), "The value of imperfect ENSO forecast information: Discussion", American Journal of Agricultural Economics 80:1109–1112.

Barrett, C.B. (1999a), "The microeconomics of the developmental paradox: On the political economy of food price policy", Agricultural Economics 20:159–172.

Barrett, C.B. (1999b), "Stochastic food prices and slash-and-burn agriculture", Environment and Development Economics 4:161–176.

Barrett, C.B. (2001), "Does food aid stabilize food availability?", Economic Development and Cultural Change 49:335–349.

Barrett, C.B., and M.R. Carter (1999), "Microeconomically coherent agricultural policy reform in Africa", in: J. Paulson, ed., African Economies in Transition, Vol. 2: The Reform Experience (MacMillan, London).

Barrett, C.B., and J. Csete (1994), "Conceptualizing hunger in contemporary African policymaking: From technical to community-based approaches", Agriculture and Human Values 11:38–46.

Barrett, C.B., and P.A. Dorosh (1996), "Farmers' welfare and changing food prices: Nonparametric evidence from rice in Madagascar", American Journal of Agricultural Economics 78:656–669.

Barrett, C.B., S. Mohapatra and D.L. Snyder (1999), "The dynamic effects of U.S. food aid", Economic Inquiry 37:647–656.

Basiotis, P., M. Brown, S.R. Johnson and K.J. Morgan (1983), "Nutrient availability, food costs, and food stamps", American Journal of Agricultural Economics 65:685–693.

Beaton, G.H. (1987), "Energy in human nutrition: A reconsideration of the relationship between intake and functional consequences", in: J.P. Gittinger, J. Leslie and C. Hoisington, eds., Food Policy: Integrating Supply, Distribution, and Consumption (Johns Hopkins University Press, Baltimore).

Beaton, G.H. (1993), "Which age groups should be targeted for supplementary feeding?", in: United Nations ACC/SCN, Nutritional Issues in Food Aid (World Health Organization, Geneva).

Beaton, G.H., and H. Ghassemi (1982), "Supplementary feeding programs for young children in developing countries", American Journal of Clinical Nutrition 35:864–916.

Becker, G. (1965), "A theory of the allocation of time", Economic Journal 74:493–517.

Behrman, J.R. (1988), "Intrahousehold allocation of nutrients in rural India: Are boys favored? Do parents exhibit inequality aversion?", Oxford Economic Papers 40:32–54.

Behrman, J.R. (1993), "The economic rationale for investing in nutrition in developing countries", World Development 21:1749–1771.

Behrman, J.R. (1995), "Household behavior and micronutrients: What we know and what we don't know: Agricultural strategies for micronutrients", Working Paper #2 (International Food Policy Research Institute, Washington).

Behrman, J.R. (1997), "Intrahousehold distribution and the family", in: M.R. Rosenzweig and O. Stark, eds., Handbook of Population and Family Economics, Vol. 1A (North-Holland, Amsterdam).

Behrman, J., and A.B. Deolalikar (1987), "Will developing country nutrition improve with income? A case study for rural South India", Journal of Political Economy 95:492–507.

Behrman, J., and A.B. Deolalikar (1988), "Health and nutrition", in: H. Chenery and T.N. Srinivasan, eds., Handbook of Development Economics, Vol. 1 (Elsevier, Amsterdam).

Behrman, J., and A.B. Deolalikar (1989), "Is variety the spice of life? Implications for calorie intake", Review of Economics and Statistics 71:666–672.

Behrman, J., and B. Wolfe (1984), "More evidence on nutrition demand – income seems overrated and women's schooling underplayed", Journal of Development Economics 14:105–128.

Benson, C., and E.J. Clay (1998), "Additionality or diversion? Food aid to Eastern Europe and the former Soviet Republics and the implications for developing countries", World Development 26:31–44.

Besley, T., and S. Coate (1991), "Public provision of private goods and the redistribution of income", American Economic Review 81:979–984.

Besley, T., and R. Kanbur (1988), "Food subsidies and poverty alleviation", Economic Journal 98:701–719.

Besley, T., and R. Kanbur (1990), "The principles of targeting", Policy, Research and External Affairs Working Paper 385 (World Bank, Washington).

Bezuneh, M., and B. Deaton (1997), "Food aid impacts on safety nets: Theory and evidence – a conceptual perspective on safety nets", American Journal of Agricultural Economics 79:672–677.

Bezuneh, M., B.J. Deaton and G.W. Norton (1988), "Food aid impacts in rural Kenya", American Journal of Agricultural Economics 70:181–191.

Binswanger, H., and M.R. Rosenzweig (1993), "Wealth, weather risk and the composition and profitability of agricultural investments", Economic Journal 103:56–78.

Blackorby, C., and D. Donaldson (1988), "Cash versus kind, self-selection, and efficient transfers", American Economic Review 78:691–700.

Blank, R.M. (1996), It Takes a Nation (Princeton University Press, Princeton, NJ).

Blank, R.M., and P. Ruggles (1995), "When do women use aid to families with dependent children and food stamps? The dynamics of eligibility versus participation", Journal of Human Resources 31:57–89.

Bliss, C., and N. Stern (1978a), "Productivity, wages and nutrition. Part I: The theory", Journal of Development Economics 5:331–362.

Bliss, C., and N. Stern (1978b), "Productivity, wages and nutrition. Part II: Some observations", Journal of Development Economics 5:363–398.

Bouis, H.E. (1991), The Determinants of Household-Level Demand for Micronutrients: An Analysis for Philippine Farm Households (International Food Policy Research Institute, Washington).

Bouis, H.E. (1994), "The effect of income on demand for food in poor countries: Are our food consumption databases giving us reliable estimates?", Journal of Development Economics 44:199–226.

Bouis, H.E., and L.J. Haddad (1992), "Are estimates of calorie-income elasticities too high?", Journal of Development Economics 39:333–364.

Bouis, H.E., L.J. Haddad and E. Kennedy (1992), "Does it matter how we survey demand for food? Evidence from Kenya and the Philippines", Food Policy 17:349–360.

Bouis, H.E., and M.J. Novenario-Reese (1997), "The determinants of demand for micronutrients: An analysis of rural households in Bangladesh", Food Consumption and Nutrition Division Discussion Paper No. 32 (International Food Policy Research Institute, Washington).

Bread for the World Institute (1995), Hunger 1995 (Washington).

Butler, J.S., J.C. Ohls and B. Posner (1985), "The effect of the food stamp program on the nutrient intake of the eligible elderly", Journal of Human Resources 20:405–420.

Caldwell, J., P. Reddy and P. Caldwell (1986), "Periodic high risk as a cause of fertility decline in a changing rural environment: Survival strategies in the 1980–83 South Indian drought", Economic Development and Cultural Change 34:677–701.

Calloway, D.H. (1995), "Human nutrition: Food and micronutrient relationships", Working Paper on Agricultural Strategies for Micronutrients No. 1 (International Food Policy Research Institute, Washington).

Campbell, C.C. (1991), "Food insecurity: A nutritional outcome or a predictor variable?", Journal of Nutrition 121:408–415.

Cane, M.A., G. Eshel and R.W. Buckland (1994), "Forecasting Zimbabwean maize yield using eastern equatorial Pacific Sea surface temperature", Nature 370:204–205.

Carroll, C.D. (1992), "The buffer stock theory of saving: Some macroeconomic evidence", Brookings Papers on Economic Activity 2:61–155.

Carter, M.R. (1997), "Environment, technology, and the social articulation of risk in West African agriculture", Economic Development and Cultural Change 45:557–590.

Chambers, R. (1989), "Vulnerability, coping and policy", IDS Bulletin 20:1–7.

Chambers, R., R. Longhurst and A. Pacey (eds.) (1981), Seasonal Dimensions to Rural Poverty (Frances Pinter, London).

Charlton, M.W. (1992), The Making of Canadian Food Aid Policy (McGill–Queen's University Press, Montreal).

Chavas, J.-P. (1995), "The microeconomics of food security", Mimeo (University of Wisconsin-Madison, Department of Agricultural and Applied Economics).

Chavas, J.-P., and K.O. Keplinger (1983), "Impact of domestic food programs on nutrient intake of low-income persons in the United States", Southern Journal of Agricultural Economics 15:155–163.

Chen, R.S., and R.W. Kates (1994), "World food security: Prospects and trends", Food Policy 19:192–208.

Chhibber, A. (1989), "The aggregate supply response: A survey", in: S. Commander, ed., Structural Adjustment & Agriculture: Theory and Practice in Africa and Latin America (Heinemann, Portsmouth, NH).

Chung, K., L. Haddad, J. Ramakrishna and F. Riely (1997), "Identifying the food insecure: The application of mixed-method approaches in India" (International Food Policy Research Institute, Washington).

Clay, E.J. (1986), "Rural public works and food-for-work: A survey", World Development 14:1237–1252.

Clay, E.J., S. Dhiri and C. Benson (1996), "Joint evaluation of European Union Programme food aid: Synthesis report" (Overseas Development Institute, London).

Coate, S., and M. Ravallion (1993), "Reciprocity without commitment: Characterization and performance of informal insurance arrangements", Journal of Development Economics 40:1–24.

Cochrane, W.W. (1959), "Farm technology, foreign surplus disposal, and domestic supply control", Journal of Farm Economics 41:885–899.

Cook, J.D. (1983), "Iron fortification: What must be considered?", in: B.A. Underwood, ed., Nutrition Intervention Strategies in National Development (Academic Press, New York).

Corbett, J. (1988), "Famine and household coping strategies", World Development 16:1099–1112.

Cornia, G., R. Jolly and F. Stewart (eds.) (1987), Adjustment with a Human Face, 2 vols (Clarendon Press, Oxford).

Cuddington, J.T. (1992), "Long-run trends in 26 primary commodity prices: A disaggregated look at the Prebisch–Singer hypothesis", Journal of Development Economics 39:207–227.

Dasgupta, P. (1993), An Inquiry into Well-Being and Destitution (Clarendon Press, Oxford).

Davies, J.E. (1994), "Giffen goods, the survival imperative and the Irish potato culture", Journal of Political Economy 102:547–564.

Davies, S. (1996), Adaptable Livelihoods: Coping with Food Insecurity in the Malian Sahel (St. Martin's Press, New York).

Davis, B., and V. Tarasuk (1994), "Hunger in Canada", Agriculture and Human Values 11:19–27.

Dearden, P.J., and P.J. Ackroyd (1989), "Reassessing the role of food aid", Food Policy 14:218–231.

Deaton, A. (1986), "Demand analysis", in: Z. Griliches and M.D. Intriligator, eds., Handbook of Econometrics, Vol. III (Elsevier, Amsterdam).

Deaton, A. (1997), The Analysis of Household Surveys: A Microeconometric Approach to Development Policy (Johns Hopkins University Press, Baltimore).

Deaton, A., and G. Laroque (1992), "On the behavior of commodity prices", Review of Economic Studies 59:1–23.

Deaton, A., and G. Laroque (1996), "Competitive storage and commodity price dynamics", Journal of Political Economy 104:896–923.

DeGarine, I. (1972), "The socio-cultural aspects of nutrition", Ecology of Food and Nutrition 1:143–163.

de Gorter, H., and J. Swinnen (2002), "Political economy of agricultural policy", in: B.L. Gardner and G.C. Rausser, eds., Handbook of Agricultural Economics, Vol. 2 (Elsevier, Amsterdam) Chapter 36, 1893–1943.

Delgado, C.L., and C.P.J. Miller (1985), "Changing food patterns in West Africa", Food Policy 10:55–61.

Devaney, B., L. Bilheimer and J. Schore (1990), "The savings in medicare costs for newborns and their mothers from prenatal participation in the WIC program" (Mathematica Policy Research, Washington).

Devaney, B., and T. Fraker (1989a), "The effect of food stamps on food expenditures: An assessment of findings from the Nationwide Food Consumption Survey", American Journal of Agricultural Economics 71:99–104.

Devaney, B., and T. Fraker (1989b), "The dietary impacts of the school breakfast program", American Journal of Agricultural Economics 71:932–948.

Devaney, B., and R. Moffitt (1991), "Dietary effects of the food stamp program", American Journal of Agricultural Economics 73:202–211.

Devereux, S. (1993), Theories of Famine (Harvester Wheatsheaf, New York).

DeWaal, A. (1989), Famine that Kills (Clarendon Press, Oxford).

Diakosavvas, D. (1989), "On the causes of food insecurity in less developed countries: An empirical evaluation", World Development 17:223–235.

Dixit, A.K., and R.S. Pindyck (1994), Investment under Uncertainty (Princeton University Press, Princeton, NJ).

Dorosh, P., C. Ninno and D.E. Sahn (1995), "Poverty alleviation in Mozambique: A multi-market analysis of the role of food aid", Agricultural Economics 13:89–99.

Doss, C.R. (1996), "Intrahousehold resource allocation in an uncertain environment", American Journal of Agricultural Economics 78:1335–1339.

Drèze, J., and A. Sen (1989), Hunger and Public Action (Clarendon Press, Oxford).

Drèze, J., A. Sen and A. Hussain (eds.) (1995), The Political Economy of Hunger: Selected Essays (Clarendon Press, Oxford).

Duncan, R.C. (2002), "Food security and the world food situation", in: B.L. Gardner and G.C. Rausser, eds., Handbook of Agricultural Economics, Vol. 2 (Elsevier, Amsterdam) Chapter 41, 2191–2213.

Edirisinghe, N. (1987), "The food stamp scheme in Sri Lanka: Costs, benefits, and options for modification", Research Report No. 58 (International Food Policy Research Institute, Washington).

Edwards, S., and S. Van Wijnbergen (1989), "Disequilibrium and structural adjustment", in: H. Chenery and T.N. Srinivasan, eds., Handbook of Development Economics, Vol. II (Elsevier, Amsterdam).

Eele, G. (1994), "Indicators for food security and nutrition monitoring", Food Policy 19:314–328.

Fafchamps, M. (1992a), "Cash crop production, food price volatility, and rural market integration in the Third World", American Journal of Agricultural Economics 74:90–99.

Fafchamps, M. (1992b), "Solidarity networks in pre-industrial societies: Rational peasants with a moral economy", Economic Development and Cultural Change 41:147–174.

Fafchamps, M., C. Udry and K. Czukas (1998), "Drought and saving in West Africa: Are livestock a buffer stock?", Journal of Development Economics 55:273–305.

Fair, R.C. (1986), "Evaluating the predictive accuracy of models", in: Z. Griliches and M.D. Intriligator, eds., Handbook of Econometrics, Vol. III (Elsevier, Amsterdam).

FAO (Food and Agriculture Organization of the United Nations) (1974), World Food Conference: Appraisal of Prospective Food Deficits and Food Aid Needs (FAO, Rome).

FAO (Food and Agriculture Organization of the United Nations) (1996), "Food fortification: Technology and quality control", FAO Food and Nutrition Paper No. 60 (FAO, Rome).

Fisher, F.M. (1963), "A theoretical analysis of the impact of food surplus disposal on agricultural production in recipient countries", Journal of Farm Economics 45:863–875.

Fogel, R.W. (1991), "New sources and new techniques for the study of secular trends in nutritional status, health, mortality, and the process of aging", National Bureau for Economic Research working paper No. 26 (Cambridge, MA).

Fogel, R.W. (1994), "Economic growth, population theory, and physiology: The bearing of long-term processes on the making of economic policy", American Economic Review 84:369–395.

Food and Consumer Service (FCS), USDA (1997), "Charting the course for evaluation: How do we measure the success of nutrition education and promotion in food assistance programs?", Summary of Proceedings (Washington).

Foster, J., J. Greer and E. Thorbecke (1984), "A class of decomposable poverty measures", Econometrica 56:173–177.

Foster, P. (1992), The World Food Problem: Tackling the Causes of Undernutrition in the Third World (Lynne Rienner, Boulder, CO).

Fraker, T.M. (1990), The Effects of Food Stamps on Food Consumption: A Review of the Literature (U.S. Department of Agriculture Food and Nutrition Service, Washington).

Fraker, T.M., A.P. Martini and J.C. Ohls (1995), "The effect of food stamp cashout on food expenditures: An assessment of the findings from four demonstrations", Journal of Human Resources 30:633–649.

Fraker, T., and R. Moffitt (1988), "The effect of food stamps on labor supply: A bivariate selection model", Journal of Public Economics 35:25–56.

Gaude, J., A.Guichaona, B. Martens and S. Miller (1987), "Rural development and labor-intensive schemes: Impact studies of some pilot programs", International Labour Review 126:423–446.

Gavan, J., and I. Chandrasekera (1979), "The impact of public food grain distribution on food consumption and welfare in Sri Lanka", Research Report No. 13 (International Food Policy Research Institute, Washington).

Gittinger, J.P., J. Leslie and C. Hoisington (eds.) (1986), Food Policy: Integrating Supply, Distribution, and Consumption (Johns Hopkins University Press, Baltimore).

Glantz, M.H. (ed.) (1987), Drought and Hunger in Africa: Denying Famine a Future (Cambridge University Press, Cambridge).

Glewwe, P. (1992), "Targeting assistance to the poor: Efficient allocation of transfers when household income is not observed", Journal of Development Economics 38:297–321.

Glomm, G., and M.G. Palumbo (1993), "Optimal intertemporal consumption decisions under the threat of starvation", Journal of Development Economics 42:271–291.

Gordon, A.R., B.L. Devaney and J.A. Burghardt (1995), "Dietary effects of the national school lunch program and the school breakfast program", American Journal of Clinical Nutrition 61:221–232.

Graham, C. (1994), Safety Nets, Policies, and the Poor: Transitions to Market Economies (Brookings Institution, Washington).

Grilli, E.R., and M.C. Yang (1988), "Primary commodity prices, manufactured goods prices, and the terms of trade of developing countries: What the long run shows", World Bank Economic Review 2:1–47.

Grootaert, C., and R. Kanbur (1995), "The lucky few amidst economic decline: Distributional change in Côte d'Ivoire as seen through panel data sets, 1985–88", Journal of Development Studies 31:603–619.

Grootaert, C., R. Kanbur and G.-T. Oh (1995), "The dynamics of poverty: Why some people escape from poverty and others don't: An African case study", World Bank Policy Research Working Paper No. 1499 (Washington).

Grosh, M. (1994), Administering Targeted Social Programs in Latin America: From Platitudes to Practice (World Bank, Washington).

Guthrie, H., and J. Scheer (1981), "Validity of a dietary score for assessing nutrient adequacy", Journal of the American Dietetic Association 78:240–244.

Habicht, J.-P., and L.D. Meyers (1991), "Principles for effective surveys of hunger and malnutrition in the United States", Journal of Nutrition 121:403–407.

Haddad, L., and J. Hoddinott (1994), "Women's income and boy–girl anthropometric status in the Côte d'Ivoire", World Development 22:543–553.

Haddad, L., J. Hoddinott and H. Alderman (eds.) (1997), Intrahousehold Resource Allocation in Developing Countries: Models, Methods and Policy (Johns Hopkins University Press, Baltimore).

Haddad, L., and R. Kanbur (1990), "How serious is the neglect of intrahousehold inequality?", Economic Journal 100:866–881.

Haddad, L., and R. Kanbur (1992), "Intrahousehold inequality and the theory of targeting", European Economic Review 36:372–378.

Haddad, L., E. Kennedy and J. Sullivan (1994), "Choice of indicators for food security and nutrition monitoring", Food Policy 19:329–343.

Haddad, L., and T. Reardon (1993), "Gender bias in the allocation of resources within households in Burkina Faso: A disaggregated outlay equivalent analysis", Journal of Development Studies 29:260–276.

Haddad, L., and C. Willis (1991), "Factors affecting early enrollment in the Women, Infants and Children Program in Massachusetts", Ecology of Food and Nutrition 26:313–321.

Hanes, S., J. Vermeersch and S. Gale (1984), "The national evaluation of school nutrition programs: Program impact on dietary intake", American Journal of Clinical Nutrition 40:390–413.

Hardaker, J.B., R.B.M. Huirne and J.R. Anderson (1997), Coping with Risk in Agriculture (CAB International, New York).

Heckman, J.J., and T.E. Macurdy (1986), "Labor econometrics", in: Z. Griliches and M.D. Intriligator, eds., Handbook of Econometrics, Vol. III (Elsevier, Amsterdam).

Heckman, J.J., and J.A. Smith (1995), "Assessing the case for social experiments", Journal of Economic Perspectives 9:85–110.

Heckman, J.J., J. Smith and N. Clements (1997), "Making the most of programme evaluations and social experiments: Accounting for heterogeneity in programme impacts", Review of Economic Studies 64:487–535.

Henry, C. (1974), "Option values in the economics of irreplaceable assets", Review of Economic Studies 41:89–104.

Hicks, L., R. Langham and J. Takenaka (1982), "Cognitive and health measures following early nutritional supplementation: A sibling study", American Journal of Public Health 72:1110–1118.

Higgins, P.A., and H. Alderman (1997), "Labor and women's nutrition: The impact of work effort and fertility on nutritional status in Ghana", Journal of Human Resources 32:577–595.

Hoagland, W.G. (1982), "The nutritional effectiveness of three federal child nutrition programs: United States 1971–74", American Journal of Economics 64:131–139.

Hoffman, W.L., B.L. Gardner, R.E. Just and B.M. Hueth (1994), "The impact of food aid on food subsidies in recipient countries", American Journal of Agricultural Economics 76:733–743.

Huang, K.S. (1996), "Nutrient elasticities in a complete food demand system", American Journal of Agricultural Economics 78:21–29.

Huang, K.S. (1997), "How economic factors influence the nutrient content of diets", Technical Bulletin No. 1864 (U.S. Department of Agriculture Economic Research Service, Washington).

Hubbard, R.G., J. Skinner and S.P. Zeldes (1995), "Precautionary saving and social insurance", Journal of Political Economy 103:360–399.

Huddleston, B., D.G. Johnson, S. Reutlinger and A. Valdés (1984), International Finance for Food Security (Johns Hopkins University Press, Baltimore).

International Conference on Nutrition (ICN) (1992), Nutrition and Development – A Global Assessment (FAO and WHO, Rome).

International Federation of Red Cross and Red Crescent Societies (IFRCRCS) (1996), World Disasters Report 1996 (Oxford University Press, Oxford).

Isenman, P.J., and H.W. Singer (1977), "Food aid: Disincentive effects and their policy implications", Economic Development and Cultural Change 25:205–237.

Isham, J., D. Narayan and L. Pritchett (1995), "Does participation improve performance? Establishing causality with subjective data", World Bank Economic Review 9:175–200.

Jackson, T. (1982), Against the Grain: The Dilemma of Project Food Aid (OXFAM, Oxford).

Johnson, D.G. (1997), "On the resurgent population and food debate", Australian Journal of Agricultural and Resource Economics 41:1–17.

Joy, A.B., M.L. Fujii, L. Garcia, C. Lamp, J. Sutherlin and E. Williamson (1994), "Hunger in California: What interventions are needed?", Journal of the American Dietetic Association 94:749–752.

Kakwani, N. (1989), "On measuring undernutrition", Oxford Economic Papers 41:528–552.

Kanbur, R. (1987), "Measurement and alleviation of poverty", IMF Staff Papers.

Kanbur, R., and L. Haddad (1994), "Are better off households more unequal or less unequal?", Oxford Economic Papers 46:445–458.

Kennedy, E.T., and H.H. Alderman (1987), Comparative Analyses of Nutritional Effectiveness of Food Subsidies and other Food-Related Interventions (International Food Policy Research Institute, Washington).

Khatkhate, D.S. (1962), "Some notes on the real effects of foreign surplus disposal in underdeveloped countries", Quarterly Journal of Economics 76:186–196.

Krueger, A.O., M. Schiff and A. Valdés (1988), "Agricultural incentives in developing countries: Measuring the effects of sectoral and economywide policies", World Bank Economic Review 2:255–271.

Lane, S., J. Kushman and C. Ranney (1983), "Food stamp program participation: An exploratory analysis", Western Journal of Agricultural Economics 8:13–26.

Leibenstein, H. (1957), Economic Backwardness and Economic Growth: Studies in the Theory of Economic Development (Wiley & Sons, New York).

Leonesio, M. (1988), "In-kind transfers and work incentives", Journal of Labor Economics 6:515–529.

Levedahl, J.W. (1991), The Effect of Food Stamps on Household Food Expenditures (USDA ERS, Washington).

Levedahl, J.W. (1995a), "How much can informational outreach programs increase food stamp program participation?", American Journal of Agricultural Economics 77:343–352.

Levedahl, J.W. (1995b), "A theoretical and empirical evaluation of the functional forms used to estimate the food expenditure equation of food stamp recipients", American Journal of Agricultural Economics 77:960–968.

Levin, H.M. (1986), "A benefit-cost analysis of nutritional programs for anemia reduction", World Bank Research Observer 1:219–245.

Lipton, M. (1977), Why Poor People Stay Poor: Urban Bias in World Development (Temple Smith, London).

Lipton, M., and M. Ravallion (1995), "Poverty and policy", in: J. Behrman and T.N. Srinivasan, eds., Handbook of Development Economics, Vol. 3B (Elsevier, Amsterdam).

Maizels, A., and M. Nissanke (1984), "Motivations for aid to developing countries", World Development 12:879–900.

Martinez, S.W., and P.M. Dixit (1992), Domestic Food Assistance Programs: Measuring the Benefits to Producers (USDA Economic Research Service, Washington).

Martorell, R. (1993), "Enhancing human potential in Guatemalan adults through improved nutrition in early childhood", Nutrition Today 27:6–13.

Maxwell, D.G. (1996), "Measuring food insecurity: The frequency and severity of 'coping strategies' ", Food Policy 21:291–303.

Maxwell, S. (1991), "The disincentive effect of food aid: A pragmatic approach", in: E. Clay and O. Stokke, eds., Food Aid Reconsidered (Frank Cass, London).

Maxwell, S. (1996), "Food security: A post-modern perspective", Food Policy 21:155–170.

Maxwell, S., D. Belshaw and A. Lirenso (1994), "The disincentive effect of food-for-work on labour supply and agricultural intensification in Ethiopia", Journal of Agricultural Economics 45:351–359.

Maxwell, S., and T.R. Frankenberger (1992), "Household food security: Concepts, indicators, measurements", Technical Review (UNICEF, New York).

Maxwell, S.J., and H.W. Singer (1979), "Food aid to developing countries: A survey", World Development 7:225–247.

Maxwell, S., and G. Templer (1993), "The monetization of project and emergency food aid: Project-level efficiency first!", Food Policy 19:9–15.

McLean, W.P. (1987), "Nutritional risk: Concepts and implications", in: J.P. Gittinger, J. Leslie and C. Hoisington, eds., Food Policy: Integrating Supply, Distribution, and Consumption (Johns Hopkins University Press, Baltimore).

Mellor, J.W. (1978), "Food price policy and income distribution in low-income countries", Economic Development and Cultural Change 27:1–26.

Merrigan, P., and M. Normandin (1996), "Precautionary saving motives: An assessment from UK time series of cross-sections", Economic Journal 106:1193–1208.

Miller, J.R., and F. Lad (1984), "Flexibility, learning, and irreversibility in environmental decisions: A Bayesian approach", Journal of Environmental Economics and Management 11:161–172.

Moffitt, R. (1983), "An economic model of welfare stigma", American Economic Review 73:1023–1035.

Moffitt, R. (1989), "Estimating the value of an in-kind transfer: The case of food stamps", Econometrica 57:385–409.

Moffitt, R. (1992), "Incentive effects of the U.S. welfare system: A review", Journal of Economic Literature 30:1–61.

Mohapatra, S., C.B. Barrett, D.L. Snyder and B. Biswas (1999), "Does food aid really discourage food production?", Indian Journal of Agricultural Economics 54:212–219.

Morduch, J. (1994), "Poverty and vulnerability", American Economic Review 84:221–225.

Morduch, J. (1995), "Income smoothing and consumption smoothing", Journal of Economic Perspectives 9:103–114.

Newbery, D.M.G., and J.E. Stiglitz (1981), The Theory of Commodity Price Stabilization (Clarendon Press, Oxford).

Ohls, J.C., and H. Beebout (1993), The Food Stamp Program: Design Tradeoffs, Policy, and Impacts (Urban Institute Press, Washington).

Oldham, E.A., C.B. Barrett, S. Benjelloun, B. Ahanou and P.J. Riley (1998), "An analysis of iodine deficiency disorder and eradication strategies in the high Atlas Mountains of Morocco", Ecology of Food and Nutrition 37:197–217.

Oliveira, V. (1997), "Food-assistance spending held steady in 1996", Food Review 20:49–57.

Payne, P., and M. Lipton (1994), How Third World Rural Households Adapt to Dietary Energy Stress (International Food Policy Research Institute, Washington).

Perrings, C. (1989), "An optimal path to extinction? Poverty and resource degradation in the open agrarian economy", Journal of Development Economics 30:1–24.

Phillips, M., T. Sanghvi and R. Suarez (1996), "The costs and effectiveness of three vitamin A interventions in Guatemala", Social Science and Medicine 42:1661–1668.

Pinstrup-Andersen, P. (ed.) (1988), Food Subsidies in Developing Countries (Johns Hopkins University Press, Baltimore).

Pinstrup-Andersen, P. (ed.) (1993), The Political Economy of Food and Nutrition Policies (Johns Hopkins University Press, Baltimore).

Pitt, M.M., and M.R. Rosenzweig (1985), "Health and nutrient consumption across and within farm households", Review of Economics and Statistics 67:212–222.

Pitt, M.M., M.R. Rosenzweig and M.N. Hassan (1990), "Productivity, health, and inequality in the intrahousehold distribution of food in low income countries", American Economic Review 80:1139–1156.

Platteau, J.-P. (1991), "Traditional systems of social security and hunger insurance: Past achievements and modern challenges", in: E. Ahmad, J. Drèze, J. Hills and A. Sen, eds., Social Security in Developing Countries (Clarendon Press, Oxford).

Platteau, J.-P. (1994a), "Behind the market stage where real societies exist – Part I: The role of public and private order institutions", Journal of Development Studies 30:533–577.

Platteau, J.-P. (1994b), "Behind the market stage where real societies exist – Part II: The role of moral norms", Journal of Development Studies 30:753–817.

Ponza, M., J.C. Ohls and B.E. Millen (1996), "Serving elders at risk: The older Americans act nutrition programs", National Evaluation of the Elderly Nutrition Program 1993–1995 (Mathematica Policy Research, Washington).

Popkin, B.M. (1981), "Community-level considerations in nutrition planning in low income nations", Ecology of Food and Nutrition 10:227–236.

Price, D.W., D.A. West, G.E. Scheier and D.Z. Price (1978), "Food delivery programs and other factors affecting nutrient intake of children", American Journal of Agricultural Economics 60:609–618.

Public Voice for Food and Health Policy (1986), Rising Poverty, Declining Health: The Nutritional Status of the Rural Poor (U.S. Government Printing Office, Washington).

Public Voice for Food and Health Policy (1988), Patterns of Risk: The Nutritional Status of the Rural Poor (U.S. Government Printing Office, Washington).

Ram, N. (1995), "An independent press and anti-hunger strategies: The Indian experience", in: J. Drèze, A. Sen and A. Hussain, eds., The Political Economy of Hunger: Selected Essays (Oxford University Press, Oxford).

Ranney, C.K., and J.E. Kushman (1987), "Cash equivalence, welfare stigma, and food stamps", Southern Economic Journal 53:1011–1027.

Ravallion, M. (1987), Markets and Famines (Clarendon Press, Oxford).

Ravallion, M. (1990), "Reaching the poor through rural public employment: A survey of theory and evidence", World Bank Discussion Paper No. 94 (World Bank, Washington).

Ravallion, M., and L. Dearden (1988), "Social security in a 'moral economy': An empirical analysis for Java", Review of Economics and Statistics 70:36–44.

Ravallion, M., G. Datt and S. Chaudhuri (1993), "Does Maharashtra's employment guarantee scheme guarantee employment? Effects of the 1988 wage increase", Economic Development and Cultural Change 41:251–275.

Reardon, T.P. (1997), "Using evidence of household income diversification to inform study of the rural nonfarm labor market in Africa", World Development 25:735–748.

Reardon, T., P. Matlon and C. Delgado (1988), "Coping with household-level food insecurity in drought-affected areas of Burkina Faso", World Development 16:1065–1074.

Reardon, T.P., and J.E. Taylor (1996), "Agroclimatic shocks, income inequality, and poverty: Evidence from Burkina Faso", World Development 24:901–914.

Reutlinger, S., and M. Selowsky (1976), Malnutrition and Poverty (Johns Hopkins University Press, Baltimore).

Riddell, R.C. (1987), Foreign Aid Reconsidered (Johns Hopkins University Press, Baltimore).

Rogers, B.L., and N.P. Schlossman (eds.) (1990), Intrahousehold Resource Allocation: Issues and Methods for Development Policy and Planning (United Nations University Press, Tokyo).

Rose, D., C. Gunderson and V. Oliveira (1997), "Socio-economic determinants of food insecurity in the United States: Evidence from the SIPP and CSFII datasets", Technical Bulletin (U.S. Department of Agriculture, Economic Research Service, Washington).

Rose, D., and V. Oliveira (1997), "Validation of a self-reported measure of household food insufficiency with nutrient intake data", Technical Bulletin No. 1863 (U.S. Department of Agriculture Economic Research Service, Washington).

Rose, D., and J. Weimer (1995), "The ES/WIC nutrition education initiative: Progress in the first year", USDA/ERS staff paper AGE-9515 (U.S. Government Printing Office, Washington).

Rosenzweig, M. (1986), "Program interventions, intrahousehold distribution, and the welfare of individuals: Modeling household behavior", World Development 14:233–243.

Rosenzweig, M. (1988a), "Labor markets in low-income countries", in: H. Chenery and T.N. Srinivasan, eds., Handbook of Development Economics, Vol. 1 (Elsevier, Amsterdam).

Rosenzweig, M. (1988b), "Risk, implicit contracts and the family in rural areas of low-income countries", Economic Journal 98:1148–1170.

Rosenzweig, M., and K. Wolpin (1986), "Evaluating the effects of optimally distributed public programs: Child health and family planning interventions", American Economic Review 76:470–482.

Rosenzweig, M., and K. Wolpin (1993), "Credit market constraints, consumption smoothing, and the accumulation of durable production assets in low-income countries: Investment in bullocks in India", Journal of Political Economy 101:223–244.

Rush, D. (1987), The National WIC Evaluation: An Evaluation of the Special Supplemental Food Program for Women, Infants, and Children (WIC), 3 vols. (Research Triangle Institute, Washington).

Ruttan, V.W. (1993), Why Food Aid? (Johns Hopkins University Press, Baltimore).

Ruttan, V.W. (1995), United States Development Assistance Policy: The Domestic Politics of Foreign Economic Assistance (Johns Hopkins University Press, Baltimore).

Sahn, D.E. (ed.) (1989), Seasonal Variability in Third World Agriculture: The Consequences for Food Security (Johns Hopkins University Press, Baltimore).

Sahn, D.E., and H. Alderman (1988), "The effects of human capital and the determinants of labor supply in a developing country", Journal of Development Economics 29:157–183.

Sahn, D.E., and H. Alderman (1996), "The effect of food subsidies on labor supply in Sri Lanka", Economic Development and Cultural Change 125–145.

Sahn, D.E., and J. von Braun (1989), "The implications of variability in food production for national and household food security", in: J.R. Anderson and P.B.R. Hazell, eds., Variability in Grain Yields (Johns Hopkins University Press, Baltimore).

Saran, R., and P. Konandreas (1991), "An additional resource: A global perspective on food aid flows in relation to development assistance", in: E.J. Clay and O. Stokke, eds., Food Aid Reconsidered: Assessing the Impact on Third World Countries (Frank Cass, London).

Schultz, T.W. (1960), "Impact and implication of foreign surplus disposal on underdeveloped economies: Value of U.S. farm surpluses to underdeveloped countries", Journal of Farm Economics 42:1019–1030.

Scrimshaw, N., C. Taylor and J. Gordon (1968), Instructions of Nutrition and Infection (World Health Organization, Geneva).

Select Committee on Hunger (SCH), U.S. House of Representatives (1989), "Food security and methods of assessing hunger in the United States", March 23 (1989), Hearing (U.S. Government Printing Office, Washington).

Sen, A. (1981), Poverty and Famines: An Essay on Entitlement and Deprivation (Clarendon Press, Oxford).

Sen, A. (1983), "Development: Which way now?", Economic Journal 93:745–762.

Sen, A. (1989), "Food and freedom", World Development 17:769–781.

Sen, S.R. (1960), "Impact and implication of foreign surplus disposal on underdeveloped economies – the Indian perspective", Journal of Farm Economics 42:1031–1042.

Senauer, B., and N. Young (1986), "The impact of food stamps on food expenditures: Rejection of the traditional model", American Journal of Agricultural Economics 68:37–43.

Sethi, R., and E. Somanathan (1996), "The evolution of social norms in common property resource use", American Economic Review 86:766–788.

Shapouri, S., and M. Missiaen (1990), "Food aid: Motivation and allocation criteria", U.S. Department of Agriculture Economic Research Service Foreign Agricultural Economic Report 240.

Shaw, J., and E. Clay (1993), World Food Aid: Experiences of Recipients & Donors (Heinemann, Portsmouth, NH).

Silberberg, E. (1985), "Nutrition and the demand for tastes", Journal of Political Economy 93:881–900.

Singer, H.W. (1989), "The African food crisis and the role of food aid", Food Policy 14:196–220.

Singer, H.W., J. Wood and T. Jennings (1987), Food Aid: The Challenge and the Opportunity (Oxford University Press, Oxford).

Singh, I., L. Squire and J. Strauss (eds.) (1986), Agricultural Household Models (Johns Hopkins University Press, Baltimore).

Smallwood, D.M. (1993), "Multiple participation in domestic food assistance", USDA ERA Agriculture Information Bulletin 664–666.

Smith, L.C. (1998), "Can FAO's measure of chronic undernourishment be strengthened?", Food Consumption and Nutrition Division Discussion Paper 44 (International Food Policy Research Institute, Washington).

Smith, M.E., and D.R. Lee (1994), "Overseas food aid programs", in: M.C. Hallberg, R.G.F. Spitze and D.E. Ray, eds., Food, Agriculture, and Rural Policy into the Twenty-First Century: Issues and Trade-Offs (Westview Press, Boulder, CO).

Southworth, H.M. (1945), "The economics of public measures to subsidize food consumption", Journal of Farm Economics 27:38–66.

Srinivasan, T.N. (1981), "Malnutrition: Some measurement and policy issues", Journal of Development Economics 8:3–19.

Srinivasan, T.N. (1992), "Undernutrition: Concepts, measurements and policy implications", in: S.R. Osmani, ed., Nutrition and Poverty (Clarendon Press, Oxford).

Stevens, C. (1979), Food Aid and the Developing World: Four African Case Studies (Croom Helm, London).

Stewart, F. (1998), "Food aid in conflict: Can one reconcile its economic, humanitarian and political economy roles?", American Journal of Agricultural Economics 80:560–565.

Stiglitz, J.E. (1976), "The efficiency wage hypothesis, surplus labor, and the distribution of income in L.D.C.s", Oxford Economic Papers 28:185–207.

Strauss, J. (1986), "Does better nutrition raise farm productivity?", Journal of Political Economy 94:297–320.

Strauss, J., and D. Thomas (1995), "Human resources: Empirical modeling of household and family decisions", in: J. Behrman and T.N. Srinivasan, eds., Handbook of Development Economics, Vol. 3A (Elsevier, Amsterdam).

Strauss, J., and D. Thomas (1998), "Health, nutrition, and economic development", Journal of Economic Literature 36:766–817.

Subramanian, S., and A. Deaton (1996), "The demand for food and calories", Journal of Political Economy 104:133–162.

Taylor, D., and D. Byerlee (1991), "Food aid and food security: A cautionary note", Canadian Journal of Agricultural Economics 39:163–175.

Thornton, P.K., W.T. Bowen, A.C. Ravelo, P.W. Wilkens, G. Farmer, J. Brock and J.E. Brink (1997), "Estimating millet production for famine early warning: An application of crop simulation modelling using satellite and ground-based data in Burkina Faso", Agricultural and Forest Meteorology 83:95–112.

Timmer, C.P. (ed.) (1991), Agriculture and the State: Growth, Employment, and Poverty in Developing Countries (Cornell University Press, Ithaca, NY).

Timmer, C.P., W.P. Falcon and S.R. Pearson (1983), Food Policy Analysis (Johns Hopkins University Press, Baltimore).

Toole, M. (1993), "Protecting refugees' nutrition with food aid", in: ACC/SCN, Nutritional Issues in Food Aid (United Nations, New York).

Townsend, R.M. (1994), "Risk and insurance in village India", Econometrica 62:539–591.

Townsend, R.M. (1995), "Consumption insurance: An evaluation of risk-baring systems in low-income economies", Journal of Economic Perspectives 9:83–102.

Tucker, K., D. Pelletier, K. Ramussen, J.-P. Habicht, P. Pinstrup-Andersen and F. Roche (1989), Advances in Nutritional Surveillance: The Cornell Nutritional Surveillance Program 1981–1987 (Cornell Food and Nutrition Policy Program, Ithaca, NY).

Udry, C. (1994), "Risk and insurance in a rural credit market: An empirical investigation in Northern Nigeria", Review of Economic Studies 61:495-526.

Underwood, B. (ed.) (1983), Nutrition Intervention Strategies in National Development (Academic Press, New York).

United Nations (UN) (1974), Report of the World Food Conference (New York).

United Nations Children's Fund (UNICEF) (1994), Small Salt Producers and Universal Salt Iodisation (UN, New York).

United Nations Children's Fund (UNICEF) (1995), The State of the World's Children 1995 (UN, New York).

United States Department of Agriculture, Economic Research Service (ERS) (1995), The Economics of Food Assistance Programs (USDA, Washington).

U.S. General Accounting Office (1990), Cargo Preference Requirements: Their Impact on U.S. Food Aid Programs and the U.S. Merchant Marine (Government Printing Office, Washington).

von Braun, J. (ed.) (1995), Employment for Poverty Reduction and Food Security (International Food Policy Research Institute, Washington).

von Braun, J., and B. Huddleston (1988), "Implications of food aid for price policy in recipient countries", in: J.W. Mellor and R. Ahmed, eds., Agricultural Price Policy for Developing Countries (Johns Hopkins University Press, Baltimore).

Watts, M.J. (1983), Silent Violence: Food, Famine, and Peasantry in Northern Nigeria (University of California Press, Berkeley).

Watts, M.J., and H.G. Bohle (1993), "The space of vulnerability: The causal structure of hunger and famine", Progress in Human Geography 17:43–67.

Webb, P., and T. Reardon (1992), "Drought impact and household response in East and West Africa", Quarterly Journal of International Agriculture 3:230–246.

Webb, P., and J. von Braun (1994), Famine and Food Security in Ethiopia: Lessons for Africa (John Wiley, London).

Weber, M.T., J.M. Staatz, J.S. Holtzman, E.W. Crawford and R.H. Bernsten (1988), "Informing food security decisions in Africa: Empirical analysis and policy dialogue", American Journal of Agricultural Economics 70:1044–1052.

Weiss, T.G., and R.S. Jordan (1976), The World Food Conference and Global Problem Solving (Praeger, New York).

West, D.A., and D.W. Price (1976), "The effects of income, assets, food programs, and household size on food consumption", American Journal of Agricultural Economics 58:725–730.

Williams, J.C., and B.D. Wright (1990), Storage and Commodity Markets (Cambridge University Press, New York).

World Bank (1986), Poverty and Hunger: Issues and Options for Food Security in Developing Countries (World Bank, Washington).

World Bank (1992), World Development Report 1992 (Oxford University Press, Oxford).

World Bank (1994), Enriching Lives: Overcoming Vitamin and Mineral Malnutrition (Washington).

Wright, B.D. (2001), "Storage and price stabilization", in: B.L. Gardner and G.C. Rausser, eds., Handbook of Agricultural Economics, Vol. 1 (Elsevier, Amsterdam) Chapter 14, 817–861.

Zeller, M., G. Schreider, J. von Braun and F. Heidhues (1997), Rural Finance for Food Security for the Poor: Implications for Research and Policy (International Food Policy Research Institute, Washington).

Chapter 41

FOOD SECURITY AND THE WORLD FOOD SITUATION

R.C. DUNCAN

National Centre for Development Studies, The Australian National University, Canberra, Australia

Contents

Abstract

The major food projection agencies see per capita food supplies continuing to increase and real prices of foodstuffs continuing to decline. This trend in food prices has made, and will continue to make, achievement of food security possible for a greater proportion of the world's population. Therefore, projections of an impending or even distant global imbalance between population and food supplies are seen as unfounded. The major problems in the food supply system are either man-made (bad policies) or can be corrected through institutional developments. In particular, increasing water supplies will be difficult and costly; but much can be done to make the use of existing supplies more efficient. Water is too often unpriced to farmers and other users; despite the political difficulties, this has to change. Establishing long-term, secure access to land for farmers is the most urgent need in many developing and transition countries and will make a significant contribution to their food security as well as to global self-sufficiency.

Keywords

global prospects, modeling, property rights

JEL classification: Q11

1. Introduction

Food security is usually defined in terms of the means to gain access to sufficient food to at least maintain a healthy lifestyle. Achievement of food security is ultimately measured by indicators of human health such as infant mortality and life expectancy, for without food security no gains can be made in human well-being, even with adequate levels of other contributors such as clean water, sanitation, and control of disease. However, lack of progress in the provision of clean water, sanitation, and other means of controlling infectious diseases can negate the benefits of improved access to food. Measuring improvements in food security at a country or global level, therefore, is a matter of measuring improvements in human well-being.

As made clear by Sen (1981), food security is basically about access to income, and therefore food security problems may be country, region, income-group, or demographic-group specific. Given unrestricted trade between countries and regions, food sufficiency is only relevant in a global sense, i.e., whether global food production is able to meet the demands of the world's population at given income levels. The issues of food security and food sufficiency are separate issues, except where a country elects to cut itself off from international trade, or where a region may be so inaccessible that trade with other regions or other countries is impossible, or where a war or drought abruptly reduces food supplies or access to food supplies. In these cases, food security and food sufficiency are closely linked. But even here, individuals or households may have more power over resources, and therefore have greater access to food than others.

This chapter tries to make a clear distinction between concerns about food security and concerns about food sufficiency. Except for the situations mentioned above, concerns about food security are seen as being specific to countries, regions, or sub-groups of people, while concerns about food sufficiency relate to the global food situation.

In this chapter progress in food security in the post-World War II period is assessed in terms of country-specific indicators of well-being, while the world food outlook is examined through the eyes of forecasters – past and present – and observers of developments in the natural resources on which food production is based. In the analysis of the world food outlook, there is coverage of the impact of major demand-side variables such as incomes and population growth and, on the supply side, changes in crop yields, cropped area, and fertilizer and water use. In analyses of the world food outlook, usually most attention has been paid to production possibilities and likely threats to future production growth; the effects of rapid income growth in the most populous parts of the world and the sharp decline in population growth rates over most of the globe have been neglected. These demand-side factors have been very important and will continue to have significant impacts on world food production in the future.

Past efforts at forecasting the world food situation are discussed. Perspectives on the future food situation have often been driven by perceived limitations of the agricultural resource base or by concerns about rapid population growth. In many cases there has been a failure to take account of the impact of forecast price movements on input and output substitution. The differences between the analytical frameworks used and the forecasts of the world food situation made by those who are optimistic about world food prospects and those who are pessimistic often come down to the importance given to the role of substitution. Concerns about constraints on food production, primarily environmental concerns, are examined in the light of recent projections which have been made by the major economic modeling groups. Reasons for differences in projections are discussed, focusing on the major variables such as yield growth, population growth, crop area, income growth, and prices. Underlying the assumptions made about these variables are basic assumptions about the effectiveness of agricultural research in making the agricultural resource base more productive and about human responses to income and price in terms of dietary patterns and family size.

Finally, besides the environmental and population growth concerns that have dominated debate over the world food situation, there are also the more recent concerns about the impact of agricultural trade liberalization on food security through increasing price volatility, and the concerns of countries, such as Japan earlier and now China, over the use of restrictions on food trade for political leverage if they do allow themselves to become more dependent on international trade. Are these concerns legitimate and, if so, what policy measures may be appropriate?

2. Improvements in global food security

We commonly hear figures quoted of 1.3 billion people in absolute poverty and 800 million malnourished. Over 70 percent of these desperately poor and malnourished people are said to be in South and East Asia [see, e.g., World Bank (1990), Pinstrup-Andersen (1995)]. However, these figures are difficult to reconcile with the progress that seems to have been made in terms of per capita food production, per capita income, and health indicators. The data in the following paragraphs are from FAO (Food and Agriculture Organization of the United Nations) (2000).

World output of cereals, the main food source (directly or indirectly) for most people, has increased by about 2.7 percent per annum since 1950, while population has grown by about 1.9 percent per annum, i.e., almost a one percent per annum per capita increase. Cereal yields have increased more rapidly than world population since 1950 – at 2.25 percent per annum. This increased cereal production has allowed per capita calorie consumption in developing countries to increase by about 27 percent since the early 1960s.

Total food production in industrial countries increased by 37.6 percent in per capita terms over the 1961 to 1996 period, according to the FAO food production index estimates. In developing countries it increased by 52.3 percent. Within developing country regions, Asia experienced the largest increase (71.2 percent), followed by Latin America (31.5 percent). The food situation in sub-Saharan Africa is the main exception to these improvements, with many African countries experiencing stagnant or even declining per capita food production. Population growth in sub-Saharan Africa as a whole was about 3 percent per annum over this 30-year period, while food production grew by about 2 percent per annum.

Within the populous Asian region, food production performances have been extraordinary. China increased per capita food production by 159.8 percent in the 1961–96 period as the result of rapid increases in aggregate food production and population growth of only 1.8 percent per annum. Indonesia experienced an increase of 81.3 percent in per capita food production, even though its population grew at the relatively rapid rate of 2.3 percent per annum. The increasing proportion of better-fed people in the world is largely due to the gains in Asia, which is home to approximately 60 percent of the world's population. Africa, which has had the poorest performance, accounts for only about 12 percent of the global population; however, its share is growing because of its higher population growth rate.

As more food has become available in developing countries on a per capita basis, prices of foodstuffs have been falling relative to prices of other goods such as manufactures, while incomes have been rising. The World Bank's constant price index for food commodities (commodity prices deflated by the prices of manufactured exports from high income to developing countries) fell by 78 percent from 1950 to 1993. From 1960 to 1990, real per capita GDP of developing countries increased by an average 162 percent.

So, with greater food availability at lower prices relative to other goods and with incomes increasing, how has this improved food security been reflected in human health indicators? Changes in basic health indicators over the periods 1970 to 1993 and 1970 to 1995 are shown for the seven most populous developing countries in Table 1. These seven countries have a total population of around 3 billion people, three-fifths of the global population. Life expectancy at birth and infant mortality per 1,000 live births have improved significantly in all seven countries. The most impressive performance is by Indonesia, with life expectancy rising by more than 30 percent and the infant mortality

Table 1
Health indicators for major developing countries, 1970, 1993 and 1995

| | Life expectancy at birth (years) | | | | Infant mortality rate (per 1,000 births) | |
| | Females | | Males | | | |
	1970	1993	1970	1993	1970	1995
Bangladesh	43	56	45	56	140	79
Brazil	61	69	57	64	95	44
China	63	71	61	68	69	34
India	49	61	50	61	137	68
Indonesia	49	65	47	61	118	51
Nigeria	45	52	41	49	114	80
Pakistan	49	63	50	61	142	90

Source: World Bank (1995, 1997).

rate falling by nearly 60 percent. The three South Asian countries have experienced improvements almost as impressive.

It is more difficult to achieve the same percentage gains in life expectancy from a higher age level than from a lower age level, and in the infant mortality rate from a lower rate than from a higher rate. Therefore, Nigeria's improvement in life expectancy of 15 percent for women and 20 percent for men from base ages of 45 years and 41 years, respectively, pales by comparison with the around 30 percent increase for females and males achieved by Indonesia from base age levels of 49 for females and 47 for males. Similarly, China's 51 percent reduction in its infant mortality rate from a 1970 level of 69 deaths per 1,000 births outshines the performance of all other countries.

What explains the lack of reconciliation between the improvements in food availability, incomes, and health indicators with the widely quoted numbers of absolute poor and malnourished? Basically, the problem appears to lie with the estimates of absolute poor made by the World Bank and others, which are based on estimates of GDP (whether at market exchange rates or purchasing power parity exchange rates). National account estimates greatly underestimate the value of subsistence food production and other informal activities, especially where the majority of the population is agriculturally based. This can be illustrated easily by comparing the cost of purchasing a least-cost diet for human sustenance at international prices with per capita GNP estimates for the least-developed countries.[1]

3. Forecasts of global food sufficiency: Why so wrong?

The world's ability to feed its growing human population is seriously questioned from time to time, usually when there is a sharp increase in cereal prices. In recent years, however, there has been a consistent drumbeat of concern, led by the Worldwatch Institute, about the adverse impact of population and income growth on global food production capacity through the depletion and degradation of soils, water, and air. The most recent heightening of concern was as a result of Lester Brown's (1995) gloomy forecasts of grain consumption and production prospects in China, and the sharp run-up in grains prices in the year ending in June 1996. Brown put forward scenarios wherein China's grain production declines from the 341 million tons produced in 1990

---

[1] In what appears to be the first use of linear programming outside of the derivation of least-cost feed mixes for livestock, Stigler (1945) in a paper on "The Cost of Subsistence" derived the least-cost diet for sustainable human consumption. It was not a very palatable diet, consisting of wheat flour, cabbage, spinach, navy beans, pork liver, evaporated milk, and 'pancake' flour. In 1939 prices, the annual cost was US$40; in 1944 prices it was US$60. Projecting these prices to 1996 using the World Bank's food price index, the cost of the 1939 diet is US$325, while the cost of the 1944 diet is $280. The difference is due to the variability of the prices of the commodities between 1939 and 1944. World Bank (1997) PPP estimates of GNP per capita are much more reasonable than its non-PPP estimates. However, its estimate of 29.4 percent of China's population living on less than $1 a day in PPP terms [World Bank (1997), Table 1, Basic Indicators] appears to be nonsensical, given that food costs alone are around US$300 a year.

to 272 million tons by 2030, basically because of competition for agricultural land from industrial and urban uses. Consumption is projected to grow from the 346 million tons of 1990 to 479 million tons by 2030 under a scenario in which there is no increase in per capita consumption and therefore total consumption increases due only to the increased population; under another scenario, consumption increases to 641 million tons by 2030, with China's per capita consumption increasing to 400 kilograms – about the same as Taiwan's presently, and one-half that of the United States. The zero per capita consumption growth scenario leads to annual grain imports of 207 million tons by 2030, while the second consumption scenario leads to grain imports of 370 million tons. The first scenario would mean that China would be importing the equivalent of global grain trade today, while the second scenario would nearly double global grain trade.

Earlier forecasters of global food disasters have so far been proven badly wrong. A consistent forecaster of global disaster due to population and income growth has been Paul Ehrlich, who in 1968 wrote:

> Americans are beginning to realise that the undeveloped countries of the world face an inevitable population-food crisis. Each year food production in undeveloped countries falls a bit further behind burgeoning population growth, and people go to bed a little bit hungrier. While there are temporary or local reversals of this trend, it now seems inevitable that it will continue to its logical conclusion: mass starvation [Ehrlich (1968), p. 17].

Almost 30 years later none of what Ehrlich foresaw has occurred; indeed, the trend has been in the opposite direction. But Ehrlich, and others [see, for example, Brown and Kane (1994)], still urge population control measures in developing countries to forestall a claimed growing imbalance between population growth and food production.

Why have the pessimistic forecasts been wrong so far? As is generally recognized, Malthus in his "Essay on the Principle of Population as it Affects the Future Improvement of Societies" in 1798 did not take sufficient account of the impact of improved agricultural technology in expanding the production possibility frontier. What about the more recent doomsayers? Agricultural technology has been extremely important in keeping food production growth ahead of global population growth in the post-World War II period – the period of most rapid population growth the world has ever seen. Increased availability of water, with the irrigated area more than doubling from 1950 to 1980, has also been an important contributor to the production increase. But, say the pessimists, the rate of growth of crop yields is slowing down (for numerous suggested reasons, e.g., declining crop response to fertilizer applications, limits being reached on water availability or declining water and soil resources, and limits being reached on the spread of high-yielding crop varieties). However, what does not appear to be realized is that food production does not need to grow as fast as it did previously.

During the 1980s, world cereals consumption growth slowed to 1.7 percent per annum from the 2.7 percent increase averaged in the 1970s. In part, the slowdown was due to the slower economic growth in many developing countries during this difficult period; however, consumption growth also slowed in many Asian economies that did not have slower income growth during this period. In China, for example, real GDP grew substantially faster during the 1980s than during the 1970s, yet consumption of cereals grew by an average of 2.3 percent per annum during the 1980s compared to 5.2 percent per annum during the 1970s.

Behind this slowdown are two important factors. First, the stage of most rapid increase in total food demand for most of the world's population is past. Per capita consumption in total volume terms has risen to levels which are adequate for most consumers. The average level of per capita calorie supplies in developing countries has exceeded the FAO's estimated minimum daily requirements since 1980. While the world's average per capita cereals consumption has not increased appreciably since 1978, in developing countries the average has not increased since 1984. Shifts from cereals consumption to other foods such as meats, vegetables, and fruits will continue, but the decline in the rate of growth of total food consumption per capita can be expected to continue.

The second reason for the decline in the rate of growth of cereals consumption is the declining rate of population growth. The fast rates of growth of population seen in recent decades in developing countries are the result of a unique event, i.e., the demographic transition in response to sharply reduced infant mortality. Clean water and better sanitation have reduced the impact of infectious diseases around the world, reducing infant mortality rates and increasing life expectancy at birth. But it takes some time for fertility rates to adjust to this new situation. So, for a period, the fertility rate remains high and the population growth rate increases sharply. But as the fertility rate adjusts, the population growth rate falls. For those countries experiencing more rapid income growth, the fertility rate falls further as the opportunity cost of procreation increases (with the increased income-earning opportunities for women and the increased costs of education of children). Those developing countries that have had rapid per capita income growth in recent decades have completed their demographic transition and now have much lower population growth rates. (Thailand's total fertility rate was 5.5 in 1970 and 2.1 in 1993. Malaysia's has fallen from 5.5 to 3.5 over the same period. Hong Kong now has the same total fertility rate as Germany, and the Republic of Korea has the same rate as France and Denmark.)

As a result of lower infant mortality and increased longevity, the global population growth rate increased from 1.79 percent in the 1950–55 period to 2.06 percent in the 1965–70 period, but subsequently fell as fertility rates declined to 1.74 percent in the 1985–90 period. The World Bank (World Population Projections, 1991–92) projects that it could fall to between 0.57 and 1.41 percent by 2020–25 – admittedly a very wide range. The uncertainty underlying this large range is due to demographers' uncertainty about the rate at which the fertility rate will decline in those countries undergoing the demographic transition from high to low fertility rates [Bongaarts (1995)]. As the rate of decline is faster the more rapid the income growth rate, faster income growth in those African and South Asian countries still with high population growth rates should push the world population growth rate to the lower end of the World Bank's forecast range. Population growth rates by region are shown in Table 2.

Table 2
Population growth rates, by region, 1950–55 to 2020–25

	Africa	Latin America	North America	Asia	Europe	Oceania	Former Soviet Union
1950–55	2.21	2.73	1.80	1.89	0.79	2.25	1.71
1955–60	2.38	2.75	1.78	1.95	0.80	2.18	1.77
1960–65	2.53	2.79	1.49	2.18	0.92	2.09	1.49
1965–70	2.64	2.60	1.13	2.44	0.66	1.97	1.00
1970–75	2.66	2.48	1.06	2.27	0.59	1.81	0.94
1975–80	2.88	2.29	1.07	1.86	0.45	1.49	0.85
1980–85	2.94	2.17	1.00	1.86	0.32	1.51	0.88
1985–90	2.99	2.06	0.82	1.87	0.25	1.48	0.78
1990–95	3.02	1.91	0.71	1.84	0.23	1.36	0.68
1995–00	2.97	1.76	0.61	1.68	0.23	1.24	0.64
2000–05	2.89	1.62	0.55	1.43	0.15	1.13	0.61
2005–10	2.74	1.49	0.54	1.23	0.08	1.03	0.57
2010–15	2.50	1.36	0.51	1.10	0.03	0.96	0.52
2015–20	2.19	1.24	0.44	0.96	−0.01	0.86	0.48
2020–25	1.90	1.12	0.34	0.89	−0.05	0.76	0.47

Source: United Nations (1993).

It can be seen there that an important role in the increased global population growth rate between 1950–55 and 1965–70 and the decline to 1985–90 was played by the Asian region. Moreover, the expected decline to 2020–25 in world population growth is due in large part to the more than halving of the growth rate in this region.

4. Analysis of the world food situation and outlook

Basically, the volume of food produced and the prices at which it is sold are determined by the interaction of demand and supply. Demand is principally a function of population and per capita incomes, while agricultural food supply is a function of the area of land farmed and yields. Global agricultural models are basically aggregations of country or regional supply and demand functions with other equations modeling trade, prices, and perhaps stocks. Price may be determined as a function of the interaction of supply and demand or as a function of stock levels or changes in stock levels. Complexity can be added to the model in the form of government interventions, which may be incorporated exogenously or endogenously.[2]

In analysis of past behavior in food markets or in projecting future performance, the dynamics of the major variables become of importance. It is with respect to

---

[2] Policy interventions of usual interest relate to output or input price effects but, as in the case of China's population growth, policy affecting this variable has been extremely important in increasing the rate of increase in per capita food production in that country.

these dynamics that the debate over the world food situation takes place, debate that is based in part in ignorance and part, necessarily, in uncertainty. There are also significant deficiencies in analysis of the world food market due to the neglect of important interactions among agricultural productivity, income growth, and population growth, especially in developing countries. However, while very important, these are interactions not easily taken into account because of the direction and/or size of their effects.

In low income, largely agriculturally based countries, increased agricultural productivity is a primary determinant of incomes, food consumption, and population growth rates.[3] As the share of agriculture in the economy declines, agricultural productivity becomes a less important determinant of incomes, food consumption, and population growth. In high income countries, it is quite unimportant. This changing interrelationship has not been captured in modeling work to date. Moreover, little has been done to capture the impact of changes in the demographic profile of countries (particularly the age composition) on the demand for food and for different kinds of food. Few efforts have been made to capture the impact of changes in income elasticities as income levels increase. From the discussion in the previous section it is clear that changes in income elasticities, especially in cases where incomes are increasing rapidly from low levels, has been one of the most neglected issues in discussions of the world food outlook.

Ignorance of these various interrelationships is reflected in the following statement:

Everyone agrees that the world's population will exceed 8 billion people by 2025.... Most everyone agrees that world food supplies will have to more than double by 2025, because of increases in income and urbanization in addition to population growth. Given this widespread agreement on the needs or demand side of the equation and its magnitude... why is there so little agreement on the ease or difficulty of generating the supply to meet that demand? [McCalla (1994)].

Such statements ignore the critical interrelationships between the demand for and supply of food. As well, they demonstrate a neglect of the dramatic changes which have already taken place in population growth rates[4] – and which seem set to continue – and in rates of per capita food consumption growth as incomes have grown rapidly for a large part of the developing world. The global modeling work discussed below which attempts to capture these relationships shows that it is not at all clear that global food supplies will have to double by 2025. Nor does the increase in food supplies needed to meet expected demand appear so difficult to achieve.

In the absence of endogenizing the relationships between agricultural productivity, incomes, population growth rates, and food consumption, projections of the world food

---

[3] Boserup (1965), for example, found that under certain circumstances increased population density could lead to increased agricultural productivity through more labor-intensive farming and demands for more secure access to land for farming.

[4] As explained previously, as the agricultural sector share declines and incomes increase, the population growth rate becomes less dependent upon what happens in the agricultural sector.

situation are made using exogenously projected values of population growth rates, per capita incomes and, in some cases, income elasticities – exogenously set values that usually are not based on an understanding of the kinds of interrelationships described above.

The future world food situation is then seen in the way in which McCalla sees it. That is, given exogenously set food demand, how well will the agricultural production process do in meeting this demand? Within a model of food markets there is a price determination process which equates supply and demand. On the supply side, the variables of interest are cultivated area and yield. Underlying yield growth is the impact of investment in fixed inputs (such as fencing, irrigation, and soil conservation measures) and variable input use (such as fertilizers, pesticides, and water), as well as that of improved technology, which may be embodied in the fixed or variable inputs, or may be incorporated in new farming practices or new or improved plant varieties or livestock breeds.

Concern over the world food outlook is mainly manifest in pessimism about the ability of the agricultural research system to maintain its significant performance of the post-World War II period (whether because of doubts about the potential for further scientific breakthroughs or doubts about the willingness of governments to fund agricultural research at an appropriate level), pessimism about the future status of the agricultural resource base (soil erosion or degradation, or declining water quality), pessimism about supplies of cultivatable land or water, and generally, pessimism about the responsiveness of production and consumption to price changes.

Taking an extremely pessimistic position in the spectrum of views on the world food outlook, Brown and Kane (1994) argue that there is a shrinking backlog of unused agricultural technology while there is declining public investment in agricultural research, the demands for water are pressing against hydrologic limits, there is a declining response of crops to additional fertilizer applications in many countries, and there is substantial loss of cropland to industrialization and urbanization. Moreover, they see fish production as having reached its biological limits, and the carrying capacity of rangelands as having been exceeded, which places an extra burden on cropland in providing increased food supplies. These perceived constraints on increases in food production lead Brown and Kane to project that global import needs will greatly exceed exportable supplies by 2030 – a perception of the food market that somehow sees no role for prices in equilibrating the two.[5] How realistic are these concerns?

---

[5] A tendency for export supplies to exceed import demands would have a large variety of price response effects on both consumption and production. Increasing trade prices would lead to reduced consumption within the existing food basket, as well as substitution from more expensive commodities to less expensive commodities. This could mean shifting from meat to cheese, or from meat to cereals, or from cereals to tubers. These demand shifts would have supply-side implications. In the longer term, the supply-side response to higher prices would reflect research results that would increase yields. Or land at the extensive or intensive margin could be brought into production. All of these effects would tend to dampen the price increase and bring export supplies and import demands into equilibrium.

4.1. Limited water supplies

It is widely recognized that increasing water supplies poses difficulties, both in terms of the higher cost of additional supplies and the declining quality of existing supplies [Rosegrant (1997), Rosegrant and Ringler (1997)]. But as these papers point out, water is too often available free or at highly subsidized prices. Its scarcity value has to be recognized so that farmers and other users are induced to use it in an efficient manner.[6] However, raising the price of water is often politically difficult. Adding to the difficulties of attaining efficient use of water resources is the fact that often the property rights to water are not well or easily defined, as in transborder situations, and until such difficulties are resolved water use will usually be sub-optimal. Developing the appropriate institutional mechanisms presents challenges of enormous proportions, particularly with regard to water resources shared among countries.[7]

4.2. Land availability and land degradation

On the basis of estimates by Buringh and Dudal (1987), less than one-half of the world's land area suitable for crop production is currently being used for this purpose. Much of the presently uncultivated area, however, is located in remote parts of Africa and South America. But it is possible that with the slower production growth needed in the future, the additional requirements for cropland will be relatively minimal. As far as the claims of substantial degradation of arable land (through erosion or chemical degradation) are concerned, Crosson and Anderson (1992) reviewed the various reports on soil loss and degradation and concluded that they were exaggerated; they point to situations where the losses claimed are counter to increased yields over sustained periods. Rosegrant and Ringler (1997) reviewed the more recent studies on the impact of land degradation on crop productivity and reached similar conclusions.

From study of long-term data on soils in China and Indonesia, Lindert (1996) finds that soil organic matter and nitrogen appear to have declined on cultivated lands in both countries while total phosphorus and potassium have generally risen. Alkalinity and acidity have not worsened nor has the topsoil layer become thinner. Though its soil and organic matter and nitrogen have declined, China's yields do not appear to have been adversely affected; presumably because nitrogen fertilizers can substitute. Lindert points to three aspects of development which may improve soil quality: (i) taking all soil-farming feedbacks into account, the shift in food demand away from staples towards legumes and animal products is likely to replenish soil nutrients; (ii) development

---

[6] Rosegrant and Ringler (1997) state that water-use efficiency in irrigation in much of the developing world is only in the 25–40 percent range. That is, only 25 to 40 percent of water in the system reaches the growing plants. They also claim that in major metropolitan areas in developing countries, often up to 50 percent of water is lost from the system.

[7] Worldwide there are around 200 shared river basins; most of them are shared between only two countries. There are 12 major river systems shared between more than two countries.

means cheaper capital and clearer property rights, which improve conservation; and (iii) urbanization and industrialization raise the productivity of soils at the urban fringe.

4.3. Depletion of marine stocks

The depletion of fish and other marine-based stocks is basically due to the absence of effective property rights to marine resources and the consequent common access problem, resulting in over-fishing [for discussion, see Iheduru (1995), Williams (1996)]. But it is clear that, even with effective marine property rights and management controls to ensure optimal harvest rates, the world's demand for seafoods cannot be met from unfarmed resources that allow no increases in productivity. In response to the increasing prices of seafood products, the farming of fish and crustaceans has boomed, backed by scientific breakthroughs in breeding and farming methods.

4.4. Prospects for crop yield increases

With global population growth moving to a much lower level and a large percentage of the populous Asian region now past the rapid consumption growth phase, the best estimates of the crop yield growth needed over the next few decades are in the 1.5–1.7 percent per annum range [see Alexandratos (1995), Agcaoili and Rosegrant (1995), and Mitchell and Ingco (1995)] – allowing for only minimal increase in farmed area. This is much less than the 2.25 percent per annum increase in cereals yields achieved since 1950. The pessimistic view is that this rate of yield growth, due in large part to the introduction of semi-dwarfing genes into rice and wheat, was fortuitous and may well not be repeated. In that case, we would have to manage with previous rates of breeding progress in the 0.5–1.0 percent per annum range [Fischer (1996)]. This is an extremely pessimistic view, given the outstanding performance of science in the twentieth century. Unlike the situation with seafoods, where price increases triggered the search for a regime shift in forms of production, there has been no sustained increase in prices of agricultural products signaling the need for a major increase in research effort on crop yields, or for a search for land-substitution practices, or even for a shift back from livestock consumption to direct cereals consumption.

Yield increases can be achieved either by extending the use of known technology or by the development of new technology such as improved varieties, improved fertilizers, and improved farming practices. Large gaps between on-farm and experimental yields exist in many developing and transition economies due to the lack of application of existing technologies. Closure of these gaps should be greatly enhanced by better agricultural institutions and policies – particularly more secure property rights to land, lower taxation of agriculture, and freeing up of markets, particularly for fertilizers.

There is ample room for new yield-increasing technologies as theoretical maximum yields – determined by photosynthetic potential, land quality, length of growing season, and water availability – are many times higher than actual yields [Plucknett (1995)]. The challenge is for research to provide the knowledge to reduce this gap. Despite concern about the loss of biodiversity from developmental activities such as forest clearing, very substantial stocks of germplasm of the major food crops are held by research bodies in various countries [Wright (1996)]. Research applying biotechnology techniques holds the potential to improve crop yields through introducing higher plant resistance to pests and diseases, higher tolerance to adverse weather (such as drought) or soil conditions (such as salinity), and improved responses to fertilizers. Plant breeding can in these ways substitute for declining availability of good quality land, just as research into soil nutrition can increase the availability of arable land.

4.5. Fertilizer responses

Research into improvement in fertilizer responsiveness should have a high pay-off as levels of application of fertilizer in relatively favorable farming areas in Asia are now quite high and response rates appear to be slowing. Crop productivity can be raised without increased fertilizer use by improving nutrient uptake efficiency and nutrient balance [Rosegrant and Pingali (1994)]. Improved efficiency of fertilizer use is also needed to reduce the impact of fertilizer run-off on water supplies and coral reefs. Fertilizer pollution of water supplies is a problem largely in high income countries. Except for intensively cultivated areas of East Asia, developing countries use too little fertilizer, which leads to reduced soil fertility and soil erosion [Rosegrant and Ringler (1997)]. Under-utilization of fertilizer can often be attributed to import restrictions that provide privileged interests with monopoly rents through raising domestic prices above world prices.

4.6. Improved policies and institutional arrangements

In consideration of the perceived limitations to food production from the actual or potential degradation of the agricultural resource base, it is clear that institutions – particularly those providing clear property rights – and policies have an important role to play in preventing degradation and even improving resource quality. In most cases, the most appropriate management of these resources will be achieved by institutional developments which internalize the external costs associated with their use. This may well mean that marginal lands will be farmed no longer or not farmed as intensively, or that water will be priced at full cost and its agricultural use reduced. But, overall, resource allocation and social welfare will be improved. Moreover, the impact of any reductions in resource use as a result should be more than offset by the improved productivity coming from institutional developments which give farmers more secure access to land and water. More secure access to land and water should lead to greater investment in land, including investment promoting soil and water conservation, which in turn should lead to higher production and less instability in production.

　　Insecurity of property rights for farmers is of major concern in many developing and transition countries. The Russian Federation's recent poor agricultural performance is in large part a result of the absence of long-term security of land tenure. By comparison, the extension of reasonably long-term land use rights to farmers in China and Vietnam was the key reason, together with higher prices and liberalization of markets, for the substantial turnaround in their agricultural productivity [see McMillan et al. (1989), Pingali et al. (1997)]. But a good part of the period of the leases created in these countries has expired, and the government should be ensuring farmer confidence to invest by creating much longer-term leases or making them automatically renewable and fully transferable.

Many government actions serve to reduce global food sufficiency and country food security. Interventions having an indirect impact on the agricultural sector in developing countries, such as over-valued exchange rates and protection of the industrial and service sectors, have been shown to have a greater adverse impact than direct policies such as restrictions on agricultural exports or inputs such as fertilizers [see Krueger (1992)]. Taxation of agriculture to provide raw materials at low cost for industrial development or to provide low-cost food for urban consumers has been frequently used in the former centrally planned economies and in developing countries. It is doubtful that the net result from taxing agriculture in this way gives a positive outcome for the economy as a whole. Certainly, the rural sector is adversely affected, and in most developing countries this is where the majority of the poor are to be found.

But self-sufficiency policies or farm income support policies can also be damaging to farmer interests and to food security in the country as a whole. For example, the rice or grains self-sufficiency policies presently being pursued by China and Vietnam, which rely on restrictions of trade and restrictions on land use by farmers, reduce farmers' incomes by reducing the scope for diversification, and at the same time reduce the scope for risk reduction. Reliance on trade restrictions to increase food self-sufficiency in fact damages food security because the variability of a single country's production is greater than global production variability (because of the offsetting global climate effects).

5. Results from modeling the global food outlook

Short-run fluctuations in prices and production – due mostly to weather fluctuations and disease outbreaks – seem to give rise to most of the concern among the general public, as can be seen from the reactions to news about sharp increases in prices and decreases in stock-to-consumption ratios. But it is the uncertainties about yield growth (or more basically, the pay-off to research), changes in the resource base (soils, water supplies, and germplasm resources), income and population growth rates, and government policies that affect agriculture that are most relevant to the world food situation over the long term. To take all these factors into account effectively in assessing the world food outlook, it is necessary to incorporate them within a multi-market framework or even an economy-wide general equilibrium framework, which prevents inconsistencies in assumptions about the many exogenously defined variables involved and equilibrates functions describing markets through the price mechanism.

Table 3
Comparison of results of global cereals projections to 2010 (million tons, with rice milled)

Production	World	Former centrally planned economies	Industrial countries	Developing countries		
				South Asia	China[a]	Total
Actual 1989–91	1,726.5	266.0	579.8	202.8	326.8	862.7
Projected to 2010						
Alexandratos	2,334.0(1.5)[b]	306.0(0.5)	710.0(1.1)	292.0(1.8)	473.0(2.0)	1,318.0(2.1)
Agcaoili and						
Rosegrant	2,405.0(1.7)	389.0(1.5)	785.0(1.3)	297.0(2.2)	426.0(1.6)	1,232.0(1.9)
Mitchell and						
Ingco	2,311.0(1.5)	324.0(0.2)	733.0(1.0)	282.0(1.6)	475.0(1.6)	1,253.0(1.8)
Net Trade						
Actual 1989–91		−37.2	129.7	−3.2	−14.7	−88.8
Projected to 2010						
Alexandratos		5.0	157.0	−10.0	−15.0	−162.0
Agcaoili and						
Rosegrant		8.0	151.0	−10.0	−14.0	−161.0
Mitchell and						
Ingco		15.0	195.0	−31.0	−22.0	−210.0

Source: Islam (1995).
[a]In Mitchell and Ingco's study, Taiwan is separated from China and is included in other East Asia and Pacific countries. In the other two studies Taiwan is included with China. Taiwan's data for 1989–91 was: production, 1.9 million tons; total use, 8.1 million tons; and imports, 6.1 million tons.
[b]Figures in parentheses are rates of growth from 1989–91 to 2010.

Sets of projections of the world cereals situation, derived from global models, have been made available in recent years by major institutions with extended experience in analysis of primary commodity markets. Long-term food outlook projections of the Food and Agriculture Organization of the United Nations (FAO), the International Food Policy Research Institute (IFPRI), and the World Bank are presented in Islam (1995) by Alexandratos (1995) from the FAO, Agcaoili and Rosegrant (1995) from IFPRI, and Mitchell and Ingco (1995) from the World Bank. IFPRI projections are also presented in Rosegrant et al. (1995). Mitchell and Ingco's projections are presented in greater detail in Mitchell et al. (1997).

Generally, the three sets of projections to year 2010 are fairly close (see Table 3). World cereal production and consumption are projected to grow by 1.5 to 1.7 percent per annum. Industrial country production is expected to grow by 1.0 to 1.3 percent. For the developing countries a rate of growth of between 1.8 and 2.1 percent is projected. While this is well below the 3.1 percent per year growth achieved in the 1970–80 period and the 2.7 percent growth achieved in the 1980–91 period, it should be remembered that population growth in developing countries is projected at 1.7 percent or even much less by this time. The role of the industrial countries as exporters is projected to grow in importance in supplying developing country imports of 160–210 million tons by 2010. The former centrally planned economies of the former Soviet Union and Central and Eastern Europe are projected to shift from being major importers of cereals up until the early 1990s to becoming major exporters. The projections of production for these countries justifiably have the widest variation among the three sets of projections. It is conceivable that agriculture in these countries could be revolutionized under appropriate policies, but under poor policy regimes could continue to perform dismally. Two factors strongly support projections of a shift from importing to exporting, however. First, cereal consumption in the former Soviet Union and the Eastern and Central European countries was heavily subsidized, to the extent that total per person calorie consumption was higher than in the richest industrial countries. With the movement towards world market prices in these countries, per person consumption of cereals has declined and wastage in consumption will be reduced. Second, while several of these economies have resource endowments favoring agricultural production, their agricultural production, harvesting, and storage practices under central planning were highly inefficient. With the shift to market pricing, production efficiency should improve. Further, yields, including livestock feeding ratios, should also increase [see Tyers (1994) for a comprehensive discussion].

The higher world production figure projected for 2010 by Agcaoili and Rosegrant (1995) is basically due to their more optimistic projection for the former centrally planned economies – 1.5 percent compared to 0.5 percent growth projected by Alexandratos (1995) and 0.2 percent projected by Mitchell and Ingco (1995). The high degree of uncertainty attaching to this projection has to be accepted – an uncertainty that flows over into the net trade projection.

There is substantial agreement on the outlook for China. None of the projections give any support to the very pessimistic forecasts made by Brown (1995). Mitchell and Ingco project net imports of 22 million tons by 2010, while Alexandratos, and Agcaoili and Rosegrant, see no increase in cereal imports over the 1989–91 level. These latter projections indicate an acceptance that the Chinese government will enforce its recently declared policy of "95 percent grain self-sufficiency".

The three sets of forecasters see food prices continuing to decline in real terms. Agcaoili and Rosegrant (1995), Rosegrant et al. (1995), and Mitchell et al. (1997) carry out various simulations with changes in basic assumptions to test the sensitivity of their models of the food supply system. As stated earlier, the main factors assumed to influence the global food system are population growth, income growth and changing income elasticities, and yield growth. In their baseline simulations, all forecasters assume that the population growth rate will slow in line with the UN's medium variant projection. Yield growth is largely driven by trend variables, which give declining percentage rates. The income growth assumptions are basically those provided by the World Bank, of which the most important feature is the rapid growth forecast for the East and South Asian economies, particularly China and India. This assumes continuing income convergence for the bulk of the world's poor population.

Agcaoili and Rosegrant (1995) undertake three sensitivity tests of interest to these basic assumptions: (i) a 20 percent increase in the population growth rate; (ii) a 15 percent increase in the per capita GDP growth rate; and (iii) a 25 percent reduction in the yield growth rate. All changes lead to higher real prices than the baseline projections. As might be expected, the 25 percent reduction in the yield growth rate is the most important change, giving rise to higher real prices for all commodities than in the base year. Higher prices would have the most severe impact on developing countries, particularly sub-Saharan Africa and South Asia. The increased population growth rate assumption also translates into real price increases, but not by as much as the yield reduction. The increased per capita GDP scenario also leads to price increases, but these have a different pattern to the other two scenarios as the higher incomes affect most the income-elastic commodities such as meats. The need for these kinds of sensitivity tests illustrates the problem discussed earlier of there being no inter-relationship within the models between agricultural productivity, income growth, and population growth.

Mitchell et al. (1997) also carry out sensitivity tests on their model for so-called "minor variations" of (i) higher GDP growth (10 percent), (ii) higher population growth (the UN's high variant), and (iii) a temporary doubling of energy and fertilizer prices (similar to the impact of the "oil price shock" of the early 1970s); and for "major variations", of zero yield growth after 1990 and much more rapid consumption growth in the developing countries. Grain prices rise relative to the baseline real price path under each of the minor variations, but prices still continue to trend downwards over the long term. However, there are temporary increases in prices, especially with the oil price shock, before they adjust to each of the changes.

Both of the major variations put the global food system under considerable pressure. Under zero yield growth, prices rise in real terms rather than fall, while consumption and production increase, but by less than under the baseline; exports from high income to developing and former centrally planned economies increase. The production and trade increases are made possible by land that had been idled from agriculture being brought back into production and new land brought into production. The main consumption impact falls on the developing countries where consumption has been growing fastest.

The rapid consumption growth scenario assumes about a 50 percent increase in developing economies. This is equivalent to twice the size of existing world food trade. Most of this increase would have to come from domestic production and would assume an increase in the rate of growth of production of 3.7 percent per year. This is obviously infeasible. These "minor variation" sensitivity tests do show, however, that the world food system is quite robust in the face of substantial pressures.

Of course, food prices will remain volatile in reaction to short-lived shocks such as temporary shortfalls in major producing countries. A new concern has arisen, however, over the prospect of agricultural liberalization; in particular, that Uruguay Round-agreed reductions of price support programs in the European Union and the United States will reduce public stocks in these countries, leading to lessened cushioning of international price stability and food shortages, and reduced availability of food aid [see, for example, Islam and Thomas (1996)]. Several points can be made in response to these concerns. First, there has in fact been little reduction of protection of agriculture to date through multilateral processes [see, for example, Hathaway and Ingco (1995)]. Second, public stocks crowd out private stocks, so there is no reason to believe other than that private stocks will increase to take the place of public stocks. Moreover, private stocks should be more efficient than public stocking policies in stabilizing markets. Indeed, while most world market instability arises from weather shocks in large-producing countries, on occasion the instability has been attenuated by policy measures in large-producing countries such as the United States. For example, the large public stocks held in the United States at the time underlay the policy measures in the 1985 Farm Bill, which sharply depressed world agricultural prices.

Second, while the stocks-to-consumption ratio of recent years may be lower than in the past, this is not necessarily cause for alarm as, given advances in transportation facilities and inventory-holding practices, the optimal stock level may well be lower than in the past – just as in other activities where inventories are held. Third, more openness to trade by food-importing developing countries should reduce their quantity risk exposure by being able to take advantage of global trading opportunities when domestic shortfalls arise. China has expressed concern about the possibility for international political leverage if it becomes more dependent on food imports. History does not lend much support to such concerns. For example, in previous periods of food shortages in China during the Cold War, there was no attempt made to exert such leverage. Further, as experience with the U.S. embargo on grain sales to the former Soviet Union showed, an embargo is ineffective unless total international cooperation can be achieved. Nevertheless, it may still be useful to have in place an international treaty which obliges countries to refrain from using food trade as a political weapon.

Fourth, most low income, food-importing countries have policies which directly (e.g., taxes) or indirectly (e.g., over-valued exchange rates) inhibit agricultural development. Better policies including agricultural trade liberalization would increase agricultural productivity, dampen production risks, and generally improve food security. Finally, while the forms of delivery of food aid have improved in recognition of the adverse impacts it can have on domestic food production and on consumption patterns, it has to be recognized that basically the availability of food aid has been determined by production behavior under price support in donor countries, not by demand in the recipient countries.

Of greater concern for the food production systems in developing countries is the demise of state marketing and price support/stabilization agencies that has been part of the trend towards liberalization of marketing arrangements. In many cases, this has left farmers, traders, and exporters completely exposed to international price risks. Those without sufficient creditworthiness to access futures markets or other financial instruments, where available, in order to diversify their risks, are likely to reduce their level of activity or engage in other activities with less risk and lower returns. In response to these developments, the United Nations Conference on Trade and Development (UNCTAD) and the World Bank have been working with developing countries in efforts to improve accessibility to commodity options and futures markets and to set up mechanisms such as warehouse receipts systems which securitize commodity stocks so that credit is more easily available to farmers and traders [Duncan and Rutten (1996)].

The FAO, World Bank, and IFPRI models discussed above have been primarily concerned with assessing the future world food situation and not so much concerned with the effects of policy changes, although policies have been assessed indirectly through simulating the impacts of changes in factors affecting farmed area or yield. The inclusion of agriculture in the GATT Uruguay Round gave rise to a considerable amount of agricultural modeling – mostly in a CGE format – of a direct policy nature. Much of this work was reported in Goldin and Kundsen (1990). Major global modeling studies that presented results on the impact of trade liberalization in agriculture included the partial equilibrium models of Anderson and Tyers (1990) and Zietz and Valdés (1990), and general equilibrium models of Frohberg et al. (1990) and Burniaux et al. (1990). Comparison of these partial and general equilibrium models showed the trade-offs involved between being able to define the complexities involved in the interaction between the various agricultural commodities and the different forms of government intervention, which is possible in a partial equilibrium framework, and the possibility of allowing for intersectoral movement of labor and capital, which is only possible in a general equilibrium context.

Probably the most important finding from these trade policy studies of relevance to the world food situation, and particularly to food security, is that while developing country food exporters will benefit from agricultural trade liberalization in the high income countries, they will benefit even more from liberalizing their own agriculture. Moreover, rather than losing from trade liberalization in high income countries due to agricultural prices being higher than they otherwise would be, food-importing developing countries would gain if they also liberalized their agricultural policies [see particularly Anderson and Tyers (1990), and Goldin and van der Mensbrugghe (1995)].

6. Conclusion

As far as the world food outlook is concerned, the recent upsurge in concern seems poorly based. With incomes rising in the most populous areas of the developing world and population growth continuing to slow, and the most rapid phase of growth in food consumption now past for most of the world's population, the rate of growth of food production needed to meet the expected growth in demand is much lower than it has been for the past 40 years. Hence, the declining yield growth rates may be more a reflection of the declining rate of growth in demand, rather than being due to a drying-up of research breakthroughs or a degrading agricultural resource base. A significant challenge for agricultural research and policy appears to lie in adapting to the changing dietary patterns resulting from the rapidly increasing incomes over much of the developing world. The global food system appears to be robust in the face of substantial shocks; it is likely, therefore, to continue providing improved diets for greater numbers of people at lower real prices.

Other global challenges for ensuring continuing and sustainable growth in food production are to provide appropriate property rights over land, water, and new technology to ensure that these resources are used most efficiently. In particular, more secure access to land, which will lead to greater investment in soil and water conservation, will lead to more stable and higher production. The availability of water for expanded production appears to be a critical issue requiring attention. Full-cost pricing of water needs to be introduced to ensure its more effective use, though it is recognized that tackling this difficult issue will require political courage. Developing countries also have much to gain from reducing direct and indirect taxation of their agricultural sectors. This should lead to increased agricultural productivity which, especially in the low income countries, is also likely to make an important contribution to increasing incomes, reducing population growth, and improving food security.

Acknowledgements

My thanks to Rod Duncan and to the book's editors and referee for their very helpful comments. I would also like to record my appreciation to Don Mitchell and Merlinda Ingco for all that I learned while writing *The World Food Outlook* with them.

References

Agcaoili, M., and M.W. Rosegrant (1995), "Global and regional food demand, supply and trade prospects to 2010", in: N. Islam, ed., Population and Food in the Early Twenty-First Century (IFPRI, Washington, DC).

Alexandratos, N. (1995), "The outlook for world food and agriculture to year 2010", in: N. Islam, ed., Population and Food in the Early Twenty-First Century (IFPRI, Washington, DC).

Anderson, K., and R. Tyers (1990), "How developing countries could gain from agricultural trade liberalization in the Uruguay Round", in: I. Goldin and O. Kundsen, eds., Agricultural Trade Liberalization: Implications for Developing Countries (OECD, Paris).

Bongaarts, J. (1995), "Global and regional population projections to 2025", in: N. Islam, ed., Population and Food in the Early Twenty-First Century (IFPRI, Washington, DC).

Boserup, E. (1965), Conditions of Agricultural Growth: The Economics of Agrarian Change Under Population Pressure (Aldine, Chicago).

Brown, L.R. (1995), Who Will Feed China? Wake-up Call for a Small Planet (Norton, New York).

Brown, L.R. (1991), State of the World: A Worldwatch Institute Report on Progress Towards Sustainability (Norton, New York).

Brown, L.R., and H. Kane (1994), Full House: Reassessing the Earth's Population Carrying Capacity, The Worldwatch Environmental Alert Series (Norton, New York).

Buringh, P., and R. Dudal (1987), "Agricultural land use in time and space", in: M.G. Wolman and F.G.A. Fournier, eds., Land Transformation in Agriculture (Wiley, New York) 9–43.

Burniaux, J.-M., D. van der Mensbrugghe and J. Waelbroeck (1990), "The food gap of the developing world: A general equilibrium modelling approach", in: I. Goldin and O. Kundsen, eds., Agricultural Trade Liberalisation: Implications for Developing Countries (OECD, Paris).

Crosson, P., and J.R. Anderson (1992), "Resources and global food prospects: Supply and demand for cereals to 2030", World Bank Technical Paper 184 (World Bank, Washington, DC).

Duncan, R.C., and L. Rutten (1996), "Managing commodity price instability in newly liberalised economies", Global Economic Institutions Working Paper Series No. 9 (Centre for Economic Policy Research, London).

Ehrlich, P.R. (1968), The Population Bomb (Ballantine Books, New York).

FAO (Food and Agriculture Organization of the United Nations) (2000), FAOSTAT: Agriculture Data – Agricultural Production Indices, http://apps.fao.org/, on February 22, 2000.

Fischer, R.A. (1996), "Food for the Next Quarter Century – Will There Be Enough?", Address to the Australian and New Zealand Association for the Advancement of Science Conference, 1 October, Canberra.

Frohberg, K., G. Fischer and K.S. Parikh (1990), "Would developing countries benefit from agricultural trade liberalization in OECD countries?", in: I. Goldin and O. Kundsen, eds., Agricultural Trade Liberalisation: Implications for Developing Countries (OECD, Paris).

Goldin, I., and O. Kundsen (eds.) (1990), Agricultural Trade Liberalisation: Implications for Developing Countries (OECD, Paris).

Goldin, I., and D. van der Mensbrugghe (1995), "The Uruguay Round: An assessment of economywide and agricultural reforms", presented at the Uruguay Round and the Developing Economies Conference (World Bank, Washington, DC).

Hathaway, D.E., and M.D. Ingco (1995), "Agricultural liberalization and the Uruguay Round", presented at the Uruguay Round and the Developing Economies Conference (World Bank, Washington, DC).

Iheduru, O. (1995), "The political economy of Euro–African fishing agreements", The Journal of Developing Areas 30:63–90.

Islam, N. (ed.) (1995), Population and Food in the Early Twenty-First Century: Meeting Future Food Demand of an Increasing Population (IFPRI, Washington, DC).

Islam, N., and S. Thomas (1996), "Foodgrain price stabilization in developing countries: Issues and experiences in Asia", Food Policy Review 3 (IFPRI, Washington, DC).

Krueger, A.O. (1992), The Political Economy of Agricultural Pricing Policy, Vol. 5, A Synthesis of the Political Economy in Developing Countries (The Johns Hopkins University Press, Baltimore, MD).

Lindert, P. (1996), "Soil degradation and agricultural change in two developing countries", Proceedings of Conference on Global Agricultural Science Policy for the Twenty-First Century, 26–28 August, Melbourne.

McCalla, A.F. (1994), "Agriculture and food needs to 2025: Why we should be concerned", Sir John Crawford Memorial Lecture, International Centers Week, Consultative Group on International Agricultural Research (World Bank, Washington, DC).

McMillan, J., J. Whalley and Lijing Zhu (1989), "The impact of China's economic reforms on agricultural productivity growth", Journal of Political Economy 97(4):781–807.

Mitchell, D.O., and M.D. Ingco (1995), "Global and regional food demand and supply prospects", in: N. Islam, ed., Population and Food in the Early Twenty-First Century (IFPRI, Washington, DC).

Mitchell, D.O., M.D. Ingco and R.C. Duncan (1997), The World Food Outlook (Cambridge University Press, London).

Pingali, P.L., Nguyen Tri Khiem, R.V. Gerpacio and Vo-Tong Xuan (1997), "Prospects for sustaining Vietnam's re-acquired rice exporter status", Food Policy 22(4):345–358.

Pinstrup-Andersen, P. (1995), "The challenge for a 2020 vision: Extent of today's human suffering and a view toward 2020", in: A 2020 Vision for Food, Agriculture, and the Environment, Conference jointly hosted by the International Food Policy Research Institute and the National Geographic Society, Washington, DC.

Plucknett, D. (1995), "Prospects for meeting future food needs through new technology", in: N. Islam, ed., Population and Food in the Early Twenty-first Century: Meeting Future Food Demand of an Increasing Population (IFPRI, Washington, DC).

Rosegrant, M.W. (1997), "Water resources in the twenty-first century: Challenges and implications for action, food, agriculture, and the environment", Discussion Paper No. 20 (IFPRI, Washington, DC).

Rosegrant, M.W., M. Agcaoili-Sombilla and N.D. Percy (1995), "Global food projections to 2020: Implications for investment, food, agriculture and the environment", Discussion Paper No. 5 (IFPRI, Washington, DC).

Rosegrant, M.W., and P. Pingali (1994), "Policy and technology for rice production growth in Asia", Journal of International Development 6:665–688.

Rosegrant, M.W., and C. Ringler (1997), "Environmental and resource policies: Implications for global food markets", Paper presented to the 41st Annual Conference of the Australian Agricultural and Resource Economics Society, Pan-Pacific Hotel, Gold Coast, January 20–25.

Sen, A.K. (1981), Poverty and Famines: An Essay on Entitlement and Deprivation (Clarendon Press, Oxford).

Stigler, G. (1945), "The cost of subsistence", Journal of Farm Economics 27(2):303–314.

Tyers, R. (1994), "Economic reform in Europe and the former Soviet Union: Implications for international markets", Research Report No. 99 (IFPRI, Washington, DC).

United Nations (1993), World Population Prospects: The 1992 Revision (New York).

Williams, M. (1996), "The transition in the contribution of living aquatic resources to food security, food, agriculture and the environment", Discussion Paper No. 13 (IFPRI, Washington, DC).

World Bank (1997), World Development Report 1997 (published for The World Bank by Oxford University Press, Oxford).

World Bank (1995), World Development Report 1995 (published for The World Bank by Oxford University Press, Oxford).

World Bank (1990), World Development Report 1990 (published for The World Bank by Oxford University Press, Oxford).

Wright, B. (1996), "Crop genetic resource policy: Towards a research agenda", Discussion Paper No. 19 (IFPRI, Washington, DC).

Zietz, J., and A. Valdés (1990), "International interactions in food and agricultural policies: Effects of alternative policies", in: I. Goldin and O. Kundsen, eds., Agricultural Trade Liberalisation: Implications for Developing Countries (OECD, Paris).

Chapter 42

POLICY-RELATED DEVELOPMENTS IN AGRICULTURAL ECONOMICS: SYNTHESIS OF HANDBOOK VOLUME 2

BRUCE L. GARDNER

Department of Agricultural and Resource Economics, University of Maryland, College Park

D. GALE JOHNSON

Department of Economics, University of Chicago

Contents

Handbook of Agricultural Economics, Volume 2, Edited by B. Gardner and G. Rausser

Abstract

Extension of factual and analytical work to policy issues has been a feature of agricultural economics from its beginnings, but only in recent decades have these efforts become part of the scientific core of what agricultural economists do. At the same time, the range of policy analysis has expanded to cover environmental economics, issues in rural economic development, and the range of market imperfections and economic analysis of politics. This chapter reviews the accomplishments and remaining tasks to be undertaken, as discussed in Volume 2 of this *Handbook*.

Keywords

political economy, environment, world food problem, economic development

JEL classification: Q10

1. Introduction

Volume 1 of this *Handbook* treated developments in production economics, agribusiness behavior, and commodity markets. Agricultural economists have also long been strongly committed to the analysis of broader societal issues. Some of these, such as the economics of education, research and innovation, and food safety, were addressed in Volume 1. Volume 2 concentrates on further aspects of the broader agenda. The topics covered range from the fundamentals of welfare economics as applied to agricultural markets (in Innes)[1] to data-based assessments of world hunger and the prospects for future food shortages (in Duncan). The approaches taken range from austerely conceptual to nakedly descriptive, and from strictly positive economics (even of political action) to normative assessments of policies aimed at economic growth, trade, poverty reduction, and development assistance. Rausser and Goodhue outline an overarching framework that brings together the main analytical contributions of the directly policy-related chapters in four dimensions: policy incidence, policy design and implementation, political economy, and governance structure.

This overall synthesis chapter briefly discusses the individual chapters and relationships among them, and then addresses what they add up to as a group. We close with implications for the prospects of agricultural economics as an academic discipline capable of usefully contributing to the analysis of important ongoing issues and policy alternatives.

2. Highlights of the chapters

The chapters of Part 3 address the interface between agriculture and the environment. Resource conservation and management, particularly of land and water, are a longstanding concern, but only in the last three decades has there been sustained research on environmental externalities associated with agriculture. The economics of natural resources and the environment is a vast subject that has already been treated in a three-volume Handbook in this series [Kneese and Sweeney (1985)]. Our aim in this Handbook is not to revisit material from that effort, some chapters of which were written by agricultural economists, but rather to focus on selected topics that have been on the front burners of recent scientific investigation and policy debate.

The chapter by Ramon Lopez covers environmental aspects of agriculture in developing countries. Central in this context is the relationship between environmental degradation and economic growth. The issue is not so much disutility from air and water pollution that industrialization or expanded agriculture may generate, but rather the question whether environmental degradation might render the economic growth process

---

[1] Chapters in this Handbook are referenced by citation of the author's name only, and are not included in the reference list.

itself unsustainable.[2] Agriculture is particularly important because it is natural-resource intensive and because the key agriculture resource, soil, is fragile in tropical areas and soil degradation is not readily reversible. The same is true of tropical forests, which are cleared to increase land for agriculture.

Lopez links the process of growth to environmental damage in a model with the characteristics of traditional land- and labor-intensive agriculture using tropical soils. He brings out the crucial role played by institutions in determining the kind and extent of damage that is external to decision-making households. In developed economies, soil erosion or fertility depletion on a farmer's own land can be expected to be optimized, except for external damage such as downstream or downwind siltation of eroded topsoil.

Under open-access farming, the further problem arises that the farmer may be led to over-exploit soils from the standpoint of his or her own farm. Similar problems arise with open-access forested land. Institutions establishing resource ownership and determining the legal scope of an individual's land use are therefore crucial. Lopez analyzes conditions under which inefficiencies resulting from sub-optimal use of natural resources bring economic growth to a halt, and assesses the prospects for resource privatization and government regulation to forestall adverse consequences of over-exploitation.

The scientific contribution of the work that Lopez discusses has two components: assessing the plausibility of the idea of environmental constraints as an impediment to growth; and providing evidence, from either statistical data or telling case studies, that such constraints are binding or threaten to become so. Achievements in economic research are more visible in the former (conceptual) area than in the latter (evidential) one. It has become fairly clear what types of events and situations are likely candidates for causing problems, but it is less clear to what extent such events and situations have already caused or are causing problems. There are apparently too many other causal factors at work simultaneously.

Erik Lichtenberg's chapter addresses a range of environmental issues that are notably different from those emphasized by Lopez. Lichtenberg considers resource limitation as a source of problems under economic growth, but here the problems are not loss of forests or soil, but rather of open space and other environmental amenities associated with agriculture. These problems become more acutely felt as urbanization encroaches on rural areas. His chapter pays most attention, however, to externalities created by production activities of commercial agriculture.

The models reviewed by Lichtenberg primarily analyze externalities arising in static optimization, rather than the growth context that Lopez emphasizes. The main issues are chemicals used in soil fertilization or protection of plants from weeds, insects, and disease that leave the farm and pollute water or air or contaminate agricultural products.

---

[2] Examples are the Chernobyl nuclear reactor explosion of 1986, which has destroyed the agricultural usefulness of large tracts of land in Ukraine, and salinization of large tracts of land in India, Uzbekistan, and elsewhere as the result of irrigation.

Lichtenberg's analysis has a strong policy focus, mainly concerning optimal policy instruments for control of externalities. Taxes or fees on the production of crops that are heavy users of polluting chemicals, or more directly taxes or fees on the chemicals themselves, have been proposed as remedies.

Lichtenberg shows the difficulties of designing and implementing such instruments when farms are heterogeneous in technology, and he is not optimistic about their being welfare-increasing in practice. He pays particular attention to the situation when farmers have information that is hidden from the regulatory authority, and emphasizes the difficulty of implementing a (second-best) optimal policy regime for pollution control, mainly because it involves nonlinear pricing that is hard to maintain against incentives for black markets or other arrangements made among those who face different regulated prices for chemicals they buy or sell.

The chapter by Ostrom considers the conditions under which self-governing institutions evolve that are capable of defeating the "tragedy of the commons" that characterizes the most serious environmental problems addressed by Lopez. Ostrom draws on a body of experimental economics in a laboratory setting as well as field experience in developing countries. She lists conditions under which such institutions can form, function effectively, and adapt to correct problems that emerge over time. She pays particular attention to the role of the size and heterogeneity of the group forming a self-governed common-pool resource. Communication and trust among individual resource users ("appropriators") are key elements.

Both Lopez and Lichtenberg address institutional issues, but in ways notably at variance with Ostrom. Lopez mentions "traditional common property management" but is pessimistic about the capabilities of localities in developing countries to adapt institutions endogenously to optimize resource use under economic growth. He is led rather to emphasize privatization, and/or legal and regulatory authorities beyond the local area. Lichtenberg is quite brief on the nature of regulatory institutions but goes into detail on the crucial subject of how such institutions can specify and implement rules leading to optimal resource use under informational constraints.

Heal and Small synthesize the issues under the rubric of agriculture as both consumer and producer of "ecosystem services". These services are products of "natural capital". Heal and Small accept the view that agriculture is playing a key role in environmental destruction worldwide, and that governmental institutions are currently unable to achieve efficiency in the use of ecosystem services. Analytically, they focus on the problems that arise in the incorporation of ecosystem services in the economic analysis of agricultural production. They emphasize the conflation of ecosystem services with land services in the agricultural economy, and note the consequence that the rental value of land substantially measures the value of ecosystem services. With respect to policy, they note the absence of policies that would optimize the provision of ecosystem services, and give considerable weight to ideas of harnessing appropriate incentives through market mechanisms such as trading rights to omit global-warming gases.

Useful as the developments discussed in these chapters may be for future development of environmental policy, the general absence of arguably optimal policies in most if not all countries is telling. Apart from practical difficulties of specifying and carrying out optimal environmental policies, the political forces brought to bear on any regulatory regime may defeat economists' social efficiency objective anyway. These considerations lead back to Ostrom's focus on localized self-governing institutions, which can actually be seen on the ground working. Yet the limited scope of current operation of localized institutions, and their likelihood of not being able to cope with the strains imposed by economic growth, do not inspire confidence in a long-term future for these approaches in coping with many serious and widespread environmental problems associated with resource use and nonpoint pollution. The comprehensive framework that Rausser and Goodhue provide in their synthesis of Part 5 suggests societies may have to change at the fundamental constitutional level if ecosystem-efficient policies are to be attained. But what is the path toward attaining the appropriate governmental institutions when they are not already in place? We have no answer. Altogether not a hopeful picture, but one that leaves plenty of room for further economic research both conceptual and empirical.

The chapters of Part 4 are addressed to agriculture in its macroeconomic context. While much of agricultural economics began as farm management, from which it has evolved principally as an applied branch of neoclassical microeconomics, the economics of agriculture also has paid early and continuing attention to the interactions between agriculture and the economy as a whole. "The ploughman feeds us all" is a Y1K saying [Aelfric, quoted in Lacey and Danzinger (1999, p. 10)] that one finds echoed to the present day, with particular urgency in development economics. Beyond the fundamental fact of nutrition as the fuel of the labor force as well as the means of subsistence, agriculture has been seen in more subtle ways as crucial. Quesnay became famous as an exponent of the view that agricultural land is the foundation of an economy's wealth. In a more modern vein, the World Bank (1997) sees rural development as crucial in economic growth for low-income countries. Much of the analytical support for this view is described in Peter Timmer's chapter and assessed in that of de Janvry, Murgai, and Sadoulet.

The other side of the coin is how events in the macroeconomy affect agriculture. Economists and others concerned about chronic economic problems of farmers have hypothesized various macroeconomic sources of these problems. One line of thought emphasizes the relative lack of market power of farmers as compared to the buyers of their products and suppliers of inputs and credit to farmers. Such issues of imperfect competition are not macroeconomic in the full sense, and have been addressed in Volume 1 of this Handbook by Sexton and Lavoie. More properly macroeconomic is the view vigorously asserted in the U.S. by the Populists of the 1890s, that farmers suffered under tight monetary policy (the "cross of gold" of William Jennings Bryan), believing that general inflation would be good for farmers by increasing real commodity prices and lowering interest rates. The more sophisticated body of theory and empirical work that has evolved from these ideas is the subject of the chapters by Schiff and Valdes and by Ardeni and Freebairn.

The chapters of Part 4 lay out the quite disparate ways economists have undertaken to place agriculture in the context of the whole economy. The chapter by Abbott and McCalla integrates and assesses the other chapters in one key respect: the predominance of macroeconomic causes of events in agriculture as compared to agricultural causes of macroeconomic events. The former are more important in high-income countries, where agriculture accounts for a small share of the whole economy, than in low-income economies where agriculture accounts for over half of the labor force and a large share of economic activity.[3] Abbott and McCalla note that accordingly the Ardeni-Freebairn chapter covering developing economies devotes most of its discussion to macroeconomic effects upon agriculture, while Timmer's chapter pays a lot of attention to agriculture's role in the whole economy's growth process.

It is striking, and departs substantially from theoretical correctness, that none of the chapters, except Tom Hertel's on general equilibrium, treats agriculture explicitly as part of a simultaneously determined system in which each sector is affected by, and affects, all the others. Seeing the economy as composed of markets, each of which comprises producers and consumers behaving as rational maximizers under constraints of fixed resources and competition, leads to a neoclassical general equilibrium view of the whole economy. Agriculture as a sector within that general equilibrium is in principle analyzable in the same way as any other sector. This approach is a natural one for extending the predominant supply-demand modeling of a single sector to a whole-economy context.

A problem though is that modeling all the sectors brings in an unmanageable quantity of data and structural equations, and even so cannot hope to encompass all the economic activity of a country, suitably disaggregated, with precision. Sargent (1987) sees the problem as follows: general equilibrium

> instructs the user to employ all of the available data on all of the model's variables… the model itself does not say that its predictions are to be taken more seriously in some directions than in others. On the other hand, in order to make general equilibrium models tractable, their preferences, technology, and endowments have been so simplified, and so much has been abstracted, that it is often difficult to take their predictions in some directions seriously. The internal logic of general equilibrium modeling then creates a difficulty in taking *any* of the model's predictions seriously. (p. 7, Italics in original)

Much of the literature underlying Hertel's chapter can be seen as an evolving attempt to home in on specifications that will allow general equilibrium effects to be taken into account, while not causing the results to be skewed by misspecifications of parts of the economy about which little is known. The analytical choices turn on what is seen as fundamental in the functioning of the economy overall as well as specifically in

---

[3] Despite industrial growth in many countries, it remains the case that a majority of the worldwide labor force remains in agriculture, according to estimates of the World Bank (1997).

agriculture. Hertel's chapter crystallizes a long line of work that has brought general equilibrium concepts down to earth for quantitative analysis of interactions between agriculture and the overall economy.

General equilibrium models are macroeconomic in the sense that they deal with the whole economy, but in crucial ways the approaches that Hertel reviews neglect macroeconomic phenomena. The models treat the relative prices of factors of production and agricultural goods as compared to other sectors, rather than agriculture as related to whole-economy aggregates. General equilibrium models typically deal quite superficially with inherently macroeconomic concepts such as inflation and interest rates, and these models notoriously do not explain business cycles or fluctuations in unemployment. Such topics are addressed in a more specialized literature, two closely related aspects of which are taken up in the chapters by Ardeni and Freebairn and by Schiff and Valdes.

Ardeni and Freebairn divide their discussion into two parts, covering "backward" and "forward" linkages, and in each case distinguishing monetary and real effects. The focus on transmission mechanisms gives the analysis a dynamic and recursive flavor quite distinct from that of general equilibrium models, where prices and other sectoral variables are simultaneously determined. The empirical work is accordingly largely concerned with leads and lags in time series. The main substantive findings involve the relationship between the aggregate price level (and hence expansionary macroeconomic policy) and agricultural commodity prices. The long-standing Populist idea that farmers gain from inflation, reflected in models in which agricultural prices are more flexible than nonagricultural prices, is generally borne out for short-term changes. But in the longer term agricultural relative to nonagricultural prices are typically found to be unrelated to overall inflation, so that monetary policy is long-run neutral in that sense.

General equilibrium models were developed in the context of a closed economy with fixed resources. Because of the importance of both international trade and endogeneity of land and other agricultural resources, a good deal of the work that Hertel reviews has involved extending general equilibrium ideas to specifically quantified ("computable") models of economies linked by trade. But the models that incorporate trade still tend to treat financial markets and currency exchange rates as fairly superficial add-ons, if at all.

Schiff and Valdes go into detail on a particular macroeconomic determinant of agricultural prices and profitability in the context of trade, the exchange rate between domestic and foreign currencies. Ardeni and Freebairn also discuss this linkage, particularly with reference to agriculture-exporting developed countries, where Schuh (1975) argued strongly for the importance of exchange rate effects. Schiff and Valdes focus on the situation in developing countries. They review an extensive literature indicating that an overvalued exchange rate, attributable to "Dutch disease" or other policy-related causes, has imposed a substantial tax on agriculture in many developing countries. The issue of what constitutes "over-valuation" of an exchange rate is tricky and is defined differently by different authors, and too often is not explicitly defined at all. Overvaluation is paradigmatically the result of macroeconomic policy or regulation, but the term is also used to refer to a market-driven rise in the value of a country's currency in the short or intermediate run that cannot be sustained in the longer run. Schiff and Valdes give particular attention to changes in capital flows driven by either policy or market events.

Because some features thought to be important for agriculture are scanted in general equilibrium models as developed to date, economists who want to take seriously the full range of agricultural economic issues have to resort to special-purpose modeling and ad hoc hypotheses.[4] It is instructive to see the different ways this has been done in the chapters by Timmer in the context of agricultural development, de Janvry, Murgai, and Sadoulet in the context of rural development, and Brooks and Nash in the context of transition economies of the former USSR.

Timmer is concerned with agriculture's role in the process of economic development. His conceptual framework embraces the whole economy, with emphasis on changes over time in per capita income. He analyzes the agricultural and nonagricultural sectors separately, and devotes considerable attention to linkages between them, especially effects originating in agriculture and influencing the economy's overall income per capita. It is striking how little use Timmer makes of parameters that are key in neoclassical general equilibrium models – elasticities of substitution in production within each sector, elasticities of substitution in consumption between products of the sectors, factor shares, and other coefficients representing the production technology. Instead, he follows neoclassical growth modeling, with emphasis on saving, investment, technical change, human capital formation, and various aspects of "structural transformation". However, even in his treatment of commodity markets, Timmer pays more attention to disequilibrium and instability than to trends or comparative statics.

Timmer's choices of emphasis evidently are conditioned by his long experience in several countries, particularly his sense of what the real engines of and constraints upon growth are. His experience is probably also responsible for his emphasis on the traditional economic development modeling literature, featuring *ad hoc* sectoral economics based on "dual economy" models and the classic work of Johnson and Mellor (1960), rather than proceeding by adding particular assumptions to a standard general equilibrium model that begins with all sectors having the same economic specification.

The chapter by de Janvry, Murgai, and Sadoulet contains much that is neoclassical, but they go even further than Timmer in finding it necessary to move beyond the confines of standard models of markets. They highlight the importance of the rural sector in a geographical sense as opposed to agriculture as a commodity-based

---

[4] In addition to its omission of key macroeconomic phenomena, it is notable that general equilibrium modeling has been much further developed for the analysis of comparative statics than for economic dynamics including investment, technology adoption, endogeneity of resources (rather than fixed resource constraints) and risk management.

sector. Since people in rural areas produce many goods and services, agricultural and nonagricultural, it is difficult to specify a general equilibrium model that will provide an appropriate analytical framework for spatial development economics.

De Janvry, Murgai, and Sadoulet place a major emphasis on the role of agrarian institutions, largely embodied in rural communities, that govern control over productive resources (land and water), transactions in credit (including loan security and penalties for nonpayment), and household economics (notably the role of women). The forces that establish and change these institutions are seen to be crucial in economic development. These forces are complex and they are economic, but their supporting political and social determinants go well beyond what standard economics covers.

The complexity is illustrated by a comparison of de Janvry, Murgai, and Sadoulet with the review article by Binswanger and Deininger (1997). The two cover a lot of the same ground, in a similar general spirit, but the specifics are very different. Both search for the loci of promise and pitfalls in market institutions as a means to foster economic development, and both point to ways in which entrenched power relationships in rural areas can forestall progress and subvert gains that market-based economic relations could generate – a species of market failure that is based on social and political factors rather than technical interdependencies or transactions costs (although the latter are not neglected). Both however lack the data-based detail that Timmer features. The two more general reviews provide many arguments that are plausible in explaining a broad range of events, but do not leave the reader with a stock of specific events that have been explained. Timmer explains some specific events but one wonders about the range of applicability and robustness of the findings he cites.

The chapter by Brooks and Nash is geographically focused on the transition economies of the former Soviet sphere and China. While the other chapters that have been discussed tend to be theoretically specific and factually disparate, Brooks and Nash are factually specific with the conceptual framework left implicit. In part this probably reflects the same impatience with the limitations of standard models that has led other chapters to "roll their own" conceptual approach to reflect their own thinking, rather than utilize a standard, general model. The former Soviet Union is a particularly challenging case for a theory of economic growth in agriculture to confront. The failure of large-scale collective farms reinforced confidence in some basic tenets of neoclassical economics – that incentives are crucial, and that distortions of market prices can have large economic costs. Now that the apparent sources of the worst distortions of prices and incentives – central planning of prices and resource allocation – have been removed for a decade, it is striking how little that alone has accomplished. Of course, plenty of distortions remain, and from the beginning economists have said that institutional reforms were also essential, most importantly the establishment of appropriate and well-functioning legal institutions for property and contracts. These reforms have hardly begun in much of the former Soviet Union, and are far from complete even in countries like Poland and Hungary that have moved furthest on the path to reform.

Two analytical issues appear central at present. First, what is the connection between property, contracting, and other legal institutions and economic growth? Is it the case that even if these institutions had been reformed to the Western norm, remaining limitations of credit, input supply, marketing infrastructure, and macroeconomic instability would have precluded economic improvement in agriculture? We have no useful theory of how these factors all fit together, or which are most important. And surprisingly, the multi-country experience reviewed by Brooks and Nash does not yet appear to have provided data evidence that would suggest a more focused conceptual approach. The Great Depression provided the experiential underpinnings for Keynesian macroeconomics and price-supporting regulation in agriculture. High inflation in the 1970s, along with high unemployment rates, gave oxygen to monetarist macroeconomics around the world. The collapse of Communist economies resulted in the replacement of central direction of economies by decentralized market forces. The problems that followed, as Brooks and Nash say, have not led any country to attempt the restoration of a communist economic system. But what is the most promising positive agenda from this point forward?

No theoretical standpoint has achieved predominance as a basis for developing and implementing a development program that looks like a near-term winner. The frustration, for both theorists and practitioners, is that it remains unclear exactly what the lessons of the last decade are. Brooks and Nash cite two factors that appear favorable for success of reforms. One is for new reforming governments to move quickly during a honeymoon period. The other is that the prospect of accession to the European Union facilitated reforms in Central Europe that were seen as necessary to the process of joining Western Europe and sharing in its wealth. These are both political factors, illustrating the importance of a second set of analytical issues, the politics of economic policy.

Theories of politics are not lacking, and Rausser and Goodhue's synthesis provides a framework for considering political economy and governmental institutions; the question is what theory helps most in understanding recent events. The two political observations cited by Brooks and Nash are observations for which, as they say, "one does not need sophisticated theories of political economy" (p. 65). One could say the same for the explanations that have been put forth for some perhaps surprising obstacles to reform. An example is the seemingly visceral and dominant aversion to the idea of transferable private property rights in agricultural land that has been expressed in many countries.

Abbott and McCalla tie together some of the main points of the chapters in Part 4 in their section on the "structural transformation" of agriculture in the process of economic growth. The main overall economic feature of this transformation is movement from an agrarian society to an industrial/service economy. Abbott and McCalla follow Timmer in attributing cardinal importance to the work of Johnson and Mellor (1960) and related literature, in particular the importance of economic progress in agriculture as a cause of growth for the whole economy (as opposed to the more passive role of being a backward sector serving as a source of low-cost labor for industrial development). T.W. Schultz (1964) forcefully championed a similar view, with a more intense focus on specifics of how the transformation of agriculture from traditional (poor but efficient) to modern could be achieved.

Agricultural economists have paid less systematic attention, almost four decades after these seminal writings, to evidence on how the agricultural economies of developing countries actually have functioned. A myriad of studies of rural households and villages, some of which Timmer discusses, have sought to explain microeconomic behavior in developing country agriculture. Their authors use similar models, and with similar explanatory success, as has been achieved in explaining microeconomic household behavior in urban and industrial-country settings. That is, roughly, hypotheses derived from microeconomic theory are often not rejected; but at the same time one does not feel confident that puzzles about why people do what they do have been solved. It is nonetheless a real contribution to have amassed considerable evidence that the Schultzian view of the rural poor as rational, efficient optimizers given the constraints they face has prevailed.[5]

At the market supply level, research such as that reviewed by Mundlak (Volume 1 of this Handbook) has similarly been as able to explain short- and long-run supply response to price in developing countries as in industrial-country agriculture. But tests of hypotheses about agriculture's role in economy-wide economic growth have not been pursued with as much success. The problem is not lack of variation in the achievement of economic growth across countries. In sub-Saharan Africa the prevailing story is of agricultural stagnation, and also of slow overall economic growth, but with many episodes of more promising experience. South Asia saw highly successful introduction of new technology in the green revolution of the 1960s, but generally these changes appear not to have made agriculture an overall engine of growth. The most striking success stories are of the "Asian Tigers", which still are amazing performers notwithstanding the financial crises that set them back in the late 1990s. The causes of growth here appear to lie in manufacturing, not agriculture. But these are impressionistic observations, not conclusions from systematic investigation.

Part 5 of this Volume focuses attention explicitly on policy: effects of policies, optimal choice of policies, and the political process itself. The standard conceptual framework for normative analysis of policies is welfare economics, with the central issue being the Pareto optimality of unregulated market prices as the coordinating signal for production and consumption decisions. Markets fail when prices other than market prices can generate a welfare gain for at least one person without making anyone else worse off. The existence and scope of market failure in agriculture has been long debated. The chapter by Innes reviews likely market failures with specific consideration of three areas: nutrition, credit, and commodity programs. He emphasizes the importance of identifying the underlying economic source of market failure (as

---

[5] Today *Transforming Traditional Agriculture* reads as a summary of research findings that confirm what most economists would expect. It is therefore worth a reminder that on its appearance the book was dismissed by the *Economic Journal's* reviewer as "ill-informed and potentially mischievous" and "unscientific" [Balogh (1964)].

opposed to the simple finding that a market failure exists). A key source of market failure is seen to be incomplete markets, the underlying cause of which is hidden information. Pareto-improving policies may consist of institutional arrangements that perform the functions that missing markets leave unperformed, or they may be subsidies or regulations chosen to correct marginal distortions that missing markets cause. In nutrition policy, Innes considers food subsidies targeted at poor people via low prices as compared to vouchers (food stamps). Given the incentives for non-poor people to attempt to obtain subsidies, and for poor people to sell their subsidized access to the non-poor, he finds a clear preference for the voucher approach.

In farm credit policy, Innes focuses on asymmetric information between lenders (banks or investors, for example) and borrowers (farmers). The result is too little investment in agriculture as compared to the first-best situation in which all parties have full information about their behavior and characteristics that influence the probability of debt repayment. His analysis opens the possibility of welfare-increasing subsidies to entrepreneurial borrowers in agriculture, but complications are cited which may negate this possibility. His point nonetheless is to challenge the premise of "free market utopia in credit markets". Besides credit subsidies, the main policies attempting to improve the functioning of credit markets are bankruptcy laws and targeted provision of state credits. The history of state credits in the transition economies of the former USSR, both before and after the watershed of 1989–91, is an example of political pitfalls that confront targeted subsidies.

Innes also analyzes how the absence of contingent claims markets in which farmers can deal (he argues that existing options markets are not sufficient) changes the consequences of standard commodity policy instruments, using the example of a deficiency payment approach. It is possible to obtain such an unexpected result as farmers losing from an increased support price. He does not claim factual relevance for this finding, but rather emphasizes that the welfare economics of standard policies gets considerably more complicated in cases of stochastic production by risk-averse farmers.

Other market failures play a large role in debate on agricultural policy, notably monopoly power of businesses that buy from and sell to farmers, and the impracticability of farmers capturing the full gain from market information or productivity-increasing innovations they make or fund (because of a lack of property rights in intangible capital or because the optimal scale of investment for some information and innovation is beyond the capabilities of an individual farmer, and voluntary collective provision cannot overcome free-rider problems). Monopoly power and sub-optimal information provision have been cited as justifications for interventions in commodity markets to increase and stabilize farm commodity prices.

Two issues that arise in proposals for governmental action to remedy market failures are the discovery of appropriate interventions, and political forces that may prevent the adoption or efficient carrying out of appropriate interventions. Discovery of optimal mechanisms of intervention is addressed in the chapter by Chambers. He focuses on policies that will be optimal in pursuit of the government's objectives given that people whose activities are regulated by the policies have their own objectives and can hide relevant information or action from the government. Chambers illustrates optimal mechanism design for cases where the government has a preference for (or against) small or inefficient farms as compared to large or efficient ones, and where each farmer knows, but the government does not, whether that farm is efficient or inefficient. He considers the possibility of the government achieving its objectives by offering different contractual arrangements (in the case of commodity price support) or regulatory alternatives to each type of farm, and allowing each farmer to declare which type of farm it is and contract for the corresponding payment schedule or regulatory alternative. An analytical feat of the approach Chambers develops is a method of finding the specifications of optimal contracts for the achievement of the government's objectives, given the hidden information constraint. The approach also provides an analytical basis for determining how far the optimal policy given hidden information falls short of the "first best" policy (with no relevant hidden information).

Chambers considers how the approach could be applied to payments made to farmers under commodity programs, and derives the optimal payment schedule (payment made and quantity on which the payment is made) for each type of farmer, with the government's objective function weighting different types differently. The situation is similar to Innes's food aid problem, but while Innes pays a going market price for food that is sold to different types of consumers at different price-quantity pairs, Chambers charges consumers a going market price for products that are bought from different types of farmers at different price-quantity pairs.[6] Chambers then applies the mechanism design approach to the provision of crop insurance, an area of agricultural policy where, under the headings of moral hazard and adverse selection, hidden action and information issues have long been seen to be important. Chambers adds the further complication that farmers may use an input in managing production risk that generates an environmental externality (and the government does not regulate pollution directly but only indirectly by influencing state-contingent output). A general finding is that optimal insurance only partially offsets farmers' risks, and that farmers consequently produce a less risky state-contingent output mix than they would if fully insured under a "first best" with full information.

Mechanism design provides notable advances in deducing optimal policies given the government's preferences, particularly in allowing for different weighting of rewards accruing to different people in the government's objective function. A major issue remaining to be analyzed is determining where the government's preferences come from. Farmers behave strategically to maximize their interests given the policies that

---

[6] Innes and Chambers are parallel in paying close attention to the incentives of one type of agent to falsely claim to be the other type. Innes also considers the incentives of the subsidized type to sell its subsidy (to resell goods acquired at a subsidized price or sell its vouchers for cash). In Chambers' payment set-up, the analogous problem would be the incentive of producers getting low prices to sell directly to consumers or to non-government black marketeers.

they are confronted with, but they also attempt individually and together with other farmers to influence what the policies are.

The question is principally one of positive rather than normative economics. Chambers considers a situation of democratic voting in which the group favored, in a set of two groups, is the more numerous. But for most contexts, and in much descriptive writing on agricultural policy by political scientists in both industrial and developing countries, it is striking how little of the government's apparent preferences can be explained by a principle of majority rule. In recent years a substantial body of work has addressed this and related issues, in an area of investigation called "political economy" in the literature covered in the chapter by de Gorter.

There is an element of normative economics in political economy, evident in the term "government failure" used as a concept to contrast with market failure. However, there is not a settled and rigorous definition of government failure. A practical way to think about government failure is in terms of departure from Pareto optimality caused by policies. Thus we have deadweight losses of commodity policies, as comparable to social losses of monopoly. The chapter by Alston and James reviews a large literature on the estimation of producer and consumer gains and losses, and resulting deadweight losses, generated by agricultural policies.

Second-best analysis, reviewed in the chapter by Innes, can in principle take both market failures and deadweight losses from intervention into account together to specify a set of policies that meets the marginal conditions that define Pareto optimality. But once we have brought political economy into the picture, we have to take seriously the fact, underlying the analyses developed by Alston and James as well as Chambers, that much of what governments do is *aimed* at making some people better off (for example through subsidies) at the expense of others (for example through taxes). In this context it is much less clear what government failure means.

Given that policy aims to redistribute well-being, mechanism design again provides a framework for doing so most efficiently. Moreover, as developed in the chapter by Chambers, mechanism design addresses how to implement optimal policies given the government's distributional objectives and the additional complexities resulting from the fact that individuals affected by policies can be expected to act strategically in their own interests in a context where information is imperfect and individuals have knowledge or can take action hidden from the government. We could then say that government failure is the shortfall in attainment of the government's objectives resulting from not implementing the optimal mechanism.

But, given that optimal mechanisms have been specified in implementable detail only for highly simplified examples, in the state of our empirical knowledge today we cannot meaningfully estimate the extent of government failure. And if we could, there remains the question whether we should accept whatever government preferences reveal as beyond criticism. Preferences of dictators are hard to credit, and economists from Arrow onward have raised cogent reasons for questioning the preferences even of well-functioning democracies. The gravamen of some political economists, such as

James Buchanan, is that government failure exists in a quite fundamental sense in the absence of constitutional restrictions on governments that exist nowhere.

A first step in applying analytical tools to government action is to discover concretely what the government's objective function is. The chapter by de Gorter reviews an extensive literature by agricultural economists attempting to use observable data to draw inferences about the government's objective, or policy preference function. This task proves rather more difficult than one might at first suppose, and despite ingenious efforts it is doubtful that any government's objective function underlying its agricultural policies is sufficiently well known to estimate quantitatively the government's success in achieving it.[7]

More fundamentally, even if we knew the government's objective function precisely, and could accurately estimate the shortfall between its actual attainment and its potential attainment if an optimal policy mechanism had been implemented, we would still be in no position to make judgments about government failure in an objective way. As just discussed, we lack criteria for evaluating the government's objective function.

What we can do is press on with the program of positive political economy, the main subject of de Gorter's chapter, and seek to understand why the government makes the policy choices it does. A principal reason why the political economy of agriculture has become the subject of intense scholarly interest is the quite strong evidence that a group being large, even a majority, is no guarantee of government favor; and that being a very small numerical minority is no obstacle to political success.

De Gorter reviews the wide cross-country evidence that agriculture in general is taxed in developing countries where farmers are numerous, while farmers are subsidized in industrial countries where they are few. The specifics of policies reviewed by Alston and James further indicate that agricultural policies tend to favor the interests of landowners much more than labor in agriculture. Similar findings, inconsistent with the simplest theory of what should happen under democracy, are common for other economic policies, too, generating a broad research program by economists as well as political scientists to explain the political power of economic interest groups. Observation and theory both focus on lobbying as central to government choice, and since lobbying is costly, that suggests disproportionate influence by the rich. In addition, lobbying is a voluntary collective activity, the results of which are not fully appropriable by those who fund it, and that indicates free rider problems that further complicate the political prospects of different groups.

In de Gorter's presentation, a key issue is the extent to which government policies are the expression of autonomous government preferences as opposed to government being

---

[7] The clearest demonstrable cases of government failure are those in which the government repudiates or cancels its own previous decisions, such as occurred widely in the former USSR and China, and in less drastic policy reforms in the United States and many other countries. But in some cases it can be argued that the original policy was suitable for its time, but had become obsolete. Another set of observable failures occurs when governments announce the goal of policy, and the goal is then not achieved. But these cases also require careful case-by-case investigation, because the world may have changed since the announcement, or the announced goal may not have been the real one.

a passive instrument reflecting the outcome of a lobbying competition. All investigators find lobbying important, but the role of autonomous governmental preferences is less well accepted. An approach that provides some unification of views is the "protection for sale" model advanced by Helpman and Grossman (1994) and subsequent papers. Here the government, or more precisely the political organizations that provide the government's elected and politically appointed officials, does not have substantive preferences for issues or people, but offer redistributional policies to interest groups in exchange for the groups' political support.

In applied work on the political economy of agricultural policies, although many observers have strong priors that differ by country, it has so far not been conclusively demonstrated which of these views – policy preferences generated through decision-makers seeking to best serve their own or their parties' overall conception of what government should do, or policy preferences generated by interest-group lobbying with decision-makers just registering the sum of political pressures – provides the best explanation for agricultural policies in the many countries that have them. A substantial number of studies have been carried out that explore statistical relationships between characteristics of commodities, voters, political systems, and outcomes in terms of agricultural support programs, and as de Gorter summarizes the findings it is apparent that a variety of forces is at play.

In traditional welfare economics, and political economy stemming from it, there is a sharp distinction between policies that respond to market failures and policies that create deadweight losses as a by-product of redistributing income to politically successful interest groups (called PERTs and PESTs respectively in Rausser and Goodhue). The literature on lobbying groups generally makes no distinction between the two types of policies. Whether a policy is overall welfare-increasing or deadweight-loss generating, its success depends on lobbying groups mobilizing support for it. But the autonomous-government view leaves scope for the government even with no lobbying to undertake policies that increase the well-being of all or most people.

In the political economy section of their synthesis chapter, Rausser and Goodhue focus on the policy process as a bargaining game that results in a political preference function, revealed as an objective function of the government that weights the disparate interests of the governed. Modeling political bargaining as a cooperative game generates a presumption that the outcome will be Pareto optimal, and this in turn implies that governmental choices about income redistribution can be used to estimate the relative political weight placed on those among whom the redistribution takes place. In a series of papers Bullock (1995, for example) emphasizes the necessity in such empirical work of assuming Pareto optimality of policies in place. De Gorter's chapter reviews the literature of lobbying as a noncooperative game, in which outcomes that are not Pareto optimal abound. Yet many noncooperative games also generate Pareto optimal results, especially when repeated play, communication, and coalitions are allowed.

Game theory is a powerful tool in detailing how political processes might work, but remains weak in specific application to observed policies. It can explain almost any observation in some way; but this is also its weakness. Game theory also helps in normative analysis of politics in the way that price theory functions with respect to commodity markets. In both cases one sees the likelihood of desirable results increased by competition, information, and learning.[8] But one typically cannot characterize *a priori* the actual results of the political process.

These considerations lead to explicit consideration of applied welfare economics, asking what are the gains and losses of policies that actually exist, and how do they add up to gains or losses for society as a whole. The chapter by Alston and James addresses this issue conceptually for a range of commodity policies, and the chapters by Karp and Perloff and by Sumner and Tangermann consider policies more specifically in the context of international trade.

Two general conceptual issues underlie the literature covered by Alston and James: the measurement of gains and losses to individuals that result from agricultural policies, and assessment of overall social gains or losses from the programs. The two issues are closely related, especially since the overall net gains are the sum of individual gains. But social accounting is more controversial in that measured net social gains more readily lend themselves to a normative interpretation while individual gains can easily be left as a matter of positive economics. The normative interpretation of empirically estimated social gains (or deadweight losses) is fraught. To put one key issue starkly, deadweight losses can be taken to reveal a violation of Pareto optimality, or they can be taken as consistent with Pareto optimality. Deadweight losses can be taken as consistent with Pareto optimality because the policy that generates the deadweight loss may be the least-cost way to accomplish the income redistribution that the policy causes (so we could not make the loser better off without making the gainers worse off). Deadweight losses can be taken as inconsistent with Pareto optimality because we could make the losers better off at no loss to the gainers, by paying lump-sum transfers instead of the distorting policy that generated the deadweight loss. But then one has to consider the feasibility of the relevant lump-sum transfers.

Measurement of individual gains from taxes and regulation, referred to as the "incidence" of these policies, is the subject of a large literature with a complex history. Alston and James take as sufficient for their purpose aggregations of consumers' surplus and factor owners' rents or quasi-rents. They show how elasticities of supply and demand affect the incidence of policy instruments that have been widely used in agricultural price support programs – government purchases, payments to producers, acreage controls, input subsidies. Drawing on a large literature expanding on the basic findings for a competitive industry with one product and two inputs in a closed economy, they consider the implications of international trade, simultaneous use of several policy instruments, and distortions caused by taxes used to raise revenue for spending on commodity programs. They pay detailed attention to complications introduced by

---

[8] By "desirable results", we don't mean just Pareto optimality (which might be well achieved through a political monopoly so strong as to cause all others to refrain from lobbying) but a combination of efficiency and recognition of the redistributional preferences of all the interests in a society.

producers' responses to output or acreage regulation, including "slippage" caused by idling a farmer's least productive land, the incentive to produce lower-quality product, and "cheating" by producing more than the regulations permit. The effect of many of the complications is to increase the losses incurred by consumers or taxpayers in order to generate a given level of gains to producers.

Analysis of costs to losers relative to gains of winners leads naturally to calculation of the sum of gains and losses – deadweight loss – as an overall indicator of program efficiency. A major issue in economists' writing on agricultural policy is how far calculations of deadweight loss can legitimately be taken as the basis for an objective critique of farm programs.

One outcome of the debate stemming from the three postulates of Harberger (1971), which Alston and James cite as the touchstone of their approach to policy assessment, is that approximation errors that may look innocuous relative to the size of consumers' surplus or rents can nonetheless be substantial relative to the size of sums of surpluses. Nonetheless, criticism of Marshallian surpluses and rents, as opposed to compensating or equivalent variations (or Hicksian surpluses), can be fended off as hairsplitting given the imprecision with which the relevant demand and supply functions are known. But this imprecision also implies large potential errors in estimated deadweight losses.

Apart from the preceding technical considerations, it is a further large step to give normative social significance to deadweight loss as the sum of consumer and producer gains and losses. The main issues involve the completeness and appropriateness of interests summed. Environmental externalities and other nonmarket goods are likely exclusions from the accounting.[9] On appropriateness, it makes a substantial difference, when large countries are concerned, or when the policies of many countries are considered simultaneously for traded commodities, whether one takes a nationalistic or worldwide viewpoint. Variable import levies of the Common Agricultural Policy of the European Union are argued to drive down and destabilize prices received by developing country exporters. Lower world prices moderate the loss of consumers' plus producers' surplus that the import levies generate within Europe, for net imported commodities, so that import levies could conceivably be a first-best policy for the perpetrator as Karp and Perloff discuss. Nonetheless, the normative ground for economists to exclude non-EU gains and losses from the tally is not firm. Indeed the "bottom line" in the trade liberalization analyses summarized by Sumner and Tangermann is a worldwide sum of gains and losses.

For those interests that are included in benefit-cost calculations, summing gains and losses weights all interests equally, while appropriate normative calculations arguably might place a larger weight on $100 gained by a person whom that money might save from starvation than on $100 lost by a millionaire who might then choose to buy fewer

---

[9] Alston and James consider other omissions from sum-of-surplus calculations that are quite likely to make a substantial practical difference, most notably the deadweight losses caused by raising tax revenues necessary to carry out policies, the consequences of cheating through noncompliance with output regulations, and the administrative and monitoring costs of the policies.

expensive cigars. Of course, compensation principles argue for adding gains and losses up, and evening things up as redistribution norms require with lump-sum redistribution. But given the practical world of policy we inhabit, the possibility of lump-sum transfers doesn't cut enough ice to make the summing-up (deadweight loss) approach obviously right.

What are the implications for what economists have accomplished? And how might we in future most productively direct our efforts in policy research? Alston and James are quite pessimistic in their assessment of what has been accomplished empirically. They distinguish two types of studies: those that model generic policy instruments for an aggregate of many crops, or the entire agricultural sector; and those that focus on particular policy instruments for a particular commodity during a particular time period. The former, without exception, specify both policy instruments and market parameters (elasticities) that are too loosely connected with the facts to provide plausible estimates of incidence. The latter typically have at least some policy instruments quantitatively tuned to the actual situation, but are weak on the parameters most crucial to estimating incidence of such policies, namely the elasticities of supply of inputs to the particular commodity. The result is that we have little econometric support for even the findings about agricultural policy incidence that are most commonly asserted and most readily derived from economic models, such as the conclusion that landowners capture most or all of program benefits.

Alston and James state that "we cannot make the broad generalizations that we may wish to make, such as that farm program benefits are ultimately capitalized into land, based on theory alone". It is obviously true that theory as a system of unquantified tautologies has no empirical implications. But theory can have empirical content. The model of Floyd (1965) that is the basis for much of the subsidy-incidence literature has strong exclusion restrictions – it says that only a few parameters determine income distributional results, and that tens of other economic parameters that a layperson might believe relevant are not. The Physiocrats, and Henry George, had theories about land that contained empirical predictions, and so do some papers cited in the synthesis chapter by Rausser and Goodhue. The systems of equations that Alston and James use have implications that could possibly be tested – that commodity prices equal average costs for example. An interesting theory that can be expressed in their model, but is more general than that model, is that if land is the only specific factor in agriculture, then land gets all the producer benefits of price support programs. They label as "extreme" the hypothesis that this theory actually applies, but it is not obviously wrong or even implausible for a long-run context. Moreover, Alston and James's quoted point omits an important use of economic theory in policy analysis, which is to provide discipline to the formulation of hypotheses, and thus provide a more satisfactory basis for assessing the land-gets-the-benefits view than is expressed for example in Cochrane (1985).

Alston and James are actually optimistic in general about the appropriateness of the conceptual framework based on consumers' surplus and factor owners' rents, suitably expanded. This optimism is shared by the authors of the two chapters addressed to agricultural trade. Karp and Perloff consider generalizations of the framework to cover several complications that arise in trade policies. These include possibilities for second-best interventions to offset existing distortions or missing markets (e.g., for risk management), optimal intervention for countries with market power in determining world prices of commodities they sell or buy, and possible economies of scale justifying protection of a domestic industry. They pay particular attention to strategic interaction between countries whose policies affect each other's markets. Karp and Perloff see a general consensus among agricultural economists that more liberal trade is welfare-increasing on a worldwide basis and for the individual countries that restrict trade (virtually all). They are critical of the conceptual and evidential support that economists have provided for this consensus. But they do not dissent from "the general agreement within the profession that government policies over the last several decades have been tremendously wasteful" (p. 69).

Sumner and Tangermann focus more closely on a particular issue in international trade, recent international negotiations on agricultural policies culminating in the 1994 Uruguay Round Agreement on Agriculture. They accept the consensus that liberalized trade is welfare increasing, but rather than addressing the general point they assess the large body of empirical work done in quantifying the consequences of liberalized agricultural trade, with specific reductions in trade barriers under the conditions of actual commodity markets in the 1980s and 1990s. This effort is perhaps the largest-scale attempt by agricultural economists collectively to remedy the empirical shortcomings criticized in both the Alston–James and Karp–Perloff chapters. The studies carried out include multimarket general equilibrium models such as some reviewed by Hertel, smaller-scale models with a single or a few related commodity markets using generic policy instruments (such as the "producer subsidy equivalent"), and analyses of changes in single policy instruments being negotiated (commodity-specific tariff or export subsidy levels).

Sumner and Tangermann arrive at a somewhat hedged commendation of agricultural economists' accomplishments (p. 82). They compare the findings of seven projections of market price effects of the Uruguay Round agreement, and four sets of estimates of income effects. The estimated effects on commodity prices tend to be small and positive for most commodities. Estimated income effects of agricultural reform are larger, ranging from gains of $3.5 billion to $58.3 billion annually. The qualitative findings are largely consistent across studies (but one study estimates a price decline for feed grains and another one for cotton); but the common findings, as Sumner and Tangermann say, "could have been made with no model, and any model that produced a contrary result would likely have been considered suspect" (p. 60). That does give one pause about the value-added of the multiplicity of studies. It is not clear why many of the estimated effects differ as they do.

Sumner and Tangermann provide a summary assessment as follows: "The models we use are, on the one hand, complex enough to defy comprehension of what drives the results, and on the other hand, so simple that they cannot incorporate crucial features of a complex policy reform" (p. 67). This critique of trade liberalization studies is strikingly parallel to that of Alston and James's on domestic policy analyses. Yet in all three of the applied policy chapters, the authors believe that agricultural economists have made a positive contribution to understanding the effects of policies and to informed policy debate. Why?

A broader historical context, beyond the purview of these chapters, helps in comprehending a sense of achievement in the profession. Agricultural economists have since the inception of farm subsidy programs been supporters as well as critics of them. Some authors, notably Pasour (1988), have taken support for farm commodity programs as an occupational hazard of employment of U.S. agricultural economists by Land-Grant Universities. Nonetheless, the prevalence of writings by agricultural economists sympathetic with governmental assistance to agriculture and critical of deadweight-loss arguments [such as Clodius (1960), Brandow (1977), Boggess (1995)] has diminished over time. Especially notable are cases of economists such as Willard Cochrane (1985), who evolved from proponent to opponent of commodity programs. In the broader contexts of economic growth in agriculture, rural development policy, and food policy, the chapters by Timmer, de Janvry–Sadoulet–Murgai, Brooks–Nash, and Barrett all indicate a consensus more favorable to markets and less favorable to governments as price-setting institutions. The sense of achievement arises from a shift in the terms of debate in politics and in actual policies that parallels the prevailing views of agricultural economists. Causality running from economists' views to policies has not been established, but some degree of connection is plausible.

Arguably the greatest area of influence of economists is international trade policy. The Uruguay Round of GATT negotiations represented an important beginning in the effort to reduce the trade restrictions affecting agricultural products, as well described by Sumner and Tangermann. The Uruguay Round was the first of the GATT negotiations that seriously addressed issues related to agricultural products.

The Uruguay Round agreement resulted in the near elimination of quantitative import quotas, placed limits on the use of export subsidies, imposed reductions in measures of protection of agriculture, and required nations to permit minimum levels of imports of agricultural products. But as Sumner and Tangermann point out, except for bringing export subsidies under a significant degree of control, there is less here than meets the eye. It was agreed that quantitative import quotas would be eliminated and replaced by tariff rate quotas. The tariff rate quotas were set at approximately the same level as the previous import quotas. Imports in excess of the tariff rate quotas would be permitted, but at tariff rates that were supposed to be no higher than the degree of nominal protection under the former quantitative import quotas, and then subject to a negotiated reduction. However, in the majority of the cases the tariffs were established at rates substantially in excess of the degree of nominal protection actually provided by the import quotas. Even with the reductions planned, the level of the tariffs in most cases will remain so high that tariffication will not result in any higher level of imports than was formerly permitted by the import quotas.

The commitment to reduce the level of nominal protection 20 percent by 2003 was largely an empty one. The measure used – the Aggregate Measure of Support (AMS) – is not an accurate measure of the amount of protection provided in a given year since the international prices used for comparison with domestic prices are fixed at their 1986–88 levels. Moreover, a large percentage of the agricultural subsidies paid by governments, especially in the United States and the European Union, were excluded from the measurement of the AMS.

The chapters by Barrett on food security and food assistance and by Duncan on the world food situation cover topics that are particularly amenable to economists' influence, in that the main relevant interest groups – the poor in developing countries, advocacy groups in developed countries, and a worldwide constituency for global food availability – are either politically weak or else too nearly universal to have serious opposition. It is consequently easier to carry on a policy debate centered on the economic merits of alternative approaches. This does not however imply a lack of contention.

Since the end of World War II there has been an enormous improvement in the per capita supplies of food in the world, in the developing as well as in the developed countries. Per capita food production in the developing countries increased by almost 51 percent between 1961 and 1996, with Asia experiencing an increase of an unprecedented 70 percent. Only in Africa has there been a failure to achieve significant increases in food supplies. Yet throughout this period the public's attention to the world food situation has primarily been dominated by foreboding and predictions of disaster. Paul R. Ehrlich wrote in 1971: "The battle to feed all of humanity is over. In the 1970s and 1980s hundreds of millions of people will starve to death in spite of any crash programs embarked upon now. At this late date nothing can prevent a substantial increase in the world death rate" [Ehrlich (1971, p. xi)].

Lester Brown stated in 1981: "Recent trends indicate the potential for a continuing rapid rise in crop yield per hectare may be much less than has been assumed in all official projections of the world food supply. The postwar trend of rising yields per hectare has been arrested or reversed in the United States, France, and China, each the leading cereal producer on its respective continents. Aside from the biological constraints on raising land productivity, a combination of pressures to extract even more food from the land plus poor land management is leading to the slow but progressive deterioration of one-fifth to one-third of the world's cropland" [Brown (1981, p. 86)].

What actually occurred was that between 1974–77 and 1990–92 grain yields in China increased by 108 percent, in France by 68 percent, and in the United States by 43 percent. Obviously yields did not stagnate and there is very little credible evidence that there has been "progressive deterioration of one-fifth to one-third of the world's cropland". In fact, the one systematic study of changes in the quality of agricultural land over time indicates that for two of the world's most populous countries – China and Indonesia – there has not been a significant change in land quality over the past several decades [Lindert (1996)].

Ron Duncan notes the remarkable similarity of recent projections by researchers from three major international institutions: the Food and Agricultural Organization, the International Food Policy Research Institute, and the World Bank. Each projected a faster rate of growth of supply than of demand over the period from the mid-1990s to 2010 or 2020. Consequently it is expected that real grain prices will continue to decline.

In response to the argument that the rate of growth of grain yields from 1960 to 1990 was high by historical standards, and thus it should not be assumed that future yield increases will be at the same high rate, Duncan emphasizes that future rates of yield increases need not be as high as those of the past three decades because future growth rates of demand and consumption will be lower than in the immediate past. The primary reason for this is that the rate of population growth has slowed and is expected to slow even further. Population grew at an annual rate of 1.9 percent from 1960 to 1990; it is projected to grow at about 1.3 percent for 1990–2020. This is the median UN projection made in the early 1990s; subsequent projections have indicated an even lower rate of growth. From 1960 to 1990 the annual growth rate of world grain use was 2.46 percent; per capita grain use increased by 0.56 percent annually. Consequently population growth accounted for about three-quarters of the annual increase in grain use.

It is unlikely that future grain yield increases will match those of the past, but the probable reason is economic rather than biological. With demand growing so much more slowly than in the past, past rates of output growth would push grain prices to such low levels that output growth would be slowed by the lack of profitability of grain production. Duncan points to limitations of current world food market models. Many models assume that the growth of supply and the growth of demand are independent of each other, except as both are influenced by prices. In fact, as he notes, there are important interactions between agricultural productivity, income growth, and population growth. Population growth affects supply as well as demand, in that an increase in the labor force in rural areas contributes to an increase in output. Improvements in agricultural productivity affect not only output but the incomes of farmers, which in turn affects demand. Duncan notes that the effects of population growth on productivity and output may work through providing incentives for technological change and for changes in institutions, citing Boserup's important work on the historical relationships between population growth and agricultural productivity.

Neoclassical growth models tend to suffer from these same defects. Productivity change, the savings or investment rate, and population growth are taken as exogenous variables and there is no interrelationship or feedback among them. In such models it is always the case that more people result in lower per capita real incomes. An increase in the labor force, with constant capital and rates of productivity improvement, can only result in a lower real marginal product of labor. Yet the experience of the world since 1950 is at variance with this result. The world has had both the most rapid population growth *and* the most rapid growth in real per capita income in its entire history. Before the twentieth century, the world had a very low rate of population growth; it also had a very low rate of real per capita income growth [Maddison (1995)].

By themselves these juxtapositions of similar rates of population and per capita income growth prove nothing but they do suggest that it may be wrong to assume that there is never a positive relationship between population growth and real income growth.

Kremer (1993) makes a reasonable case that historically the rates of world population growth and real per capita income growth have been positively related, and that there is a probable causal relationship running from population growth to real per capita income growth. Serious consideration of population growth and the improvement in the well-being of the world's population during the twentieth century impels questioning the validity of the widespread view that population growth has negative effects on human welfare. During this century the world's population will have nearly quadrupled – increasing from 1.6 billion to about 6 billion. Yet in this century most, if not all, measures of human well-being have shown improvement, not by a little but a lot. In the developing world life expectancy has increased from approximately 30 years to 65 years. The improvements in life expectancy and related measures were in large part the result of increased productivity and higher real incomes that made possible dramatic improvements in the conditions of living. The dramatic improvements included creation of safe water and sanitation systems, in both urban and rural areas, and major increases in the quantity and quality of the food supply. The developing countries also saw significant decreases in infant and child mortality, as well as large increases in life expectancy and in per capita food supplies.

Barrett's exhaustive review of food security and food assistance programs is cautionary in summarizing a large body of work by economists indicating how difficult it is to do good. His review also indicates that in numerous cases it is difficult to know if one has done good, in that we know relatively little about the effects of either programs of international food aid or of domestic assistance programs. There are some notable exceptions, such as studies of the effects of the Women, Infants and Children program (WIC) in the United States. But even here a significant part of the positive improvement in nutrition that was achieved seemed to be due at least as much to the educational aspects of the program as to the actual food distributed.

The counting of individuals who suffer from food insecurity, hunger or malnutrition is a very difficult task. Estimates based on actual measurements of people are relatively expensive to collect and repeated sampling over time of the same population is quite rare. The available estimates on malnutrition or food insecurity indicate a remarkable reduction in the number of chronically undernourished people in the developing world. Between 1968–71 and 1988–90 the percentage of the Asian population that was seriously malnourished declined from 40 percent to 19 percent; in the Near East from 22 to 12 percent; and in Latin America, from 19 to 13 percent. Only in Africa was there no change.[10]

---

[10] Barrett accepts an estimate, attributed to Bread for the World, that 20 million people die from hunger each year. This figure seems highly unrealistic. In the first half of the 1990s the average annual number of deaths in the world was 50 million. If the figure for the number dying from hunger were correct, this would mean that hunger was the cause of two out of every five deaths. Given that live expectancy at birth for the world is now estimated at 67 years (65 years in the developing countries), it seems most unlikely that hunger is responsible for such a large share of the deaths that occur.

Barrett makes the point that lack of food availability is not the primary cause of food insecurity. Nutrient deficiencies other than energy and protein now seem to loom very large. Major problems arise due to deficiencies of iron, iodine, and vitamin A. Where there is a modern marketing system for food, such as exists in developed countries, it is possible to provide the iodine and vitamin A through fortification of certain foods. But when large percentages of food come from the household's own production or that of one's neighbors, such fortification is not possible. Consequently the deficiencies will probably be overcome only as real per capita incomes increase and more food passes through a formal marketing and processing system that permits fortification at relatively low cost.

It is, of course, not only the amount of food ingested that determines the state of malnutrition. In developing countries the incidence of dysentery and malaria are high and each adversely affects the utilization of the food actually eaten. If a child has four or five attacks of dysentery a year, which is not unusual in some low income developing countries, the child may well be stunted and wasted even if the caloric intake were adequate for a healthy child.

Barrett emphasizes that successful food security strategies should emphasize three points: (a) availability of an adequate level of income; (b) access to finance, food markets, and storage to permit consumption smoothing in the face of shocks to income; and (c) safety nets for those who suffer adverse shocks that cannot be offset by the economic system. The production of food in a particular area has a secondary role if markets are permitted to function and if adequate purchasing power exists or is made available. Obviously, the overall supply and prices of food play a role, since food security is enhanced by a growing per capita supply of food at declining prices. And this has been the experience of the world since World War II. Based on Barrett's analysis, it is reasonable to conclude that in today's world, food insecurity is due far more to variable and low levels of income than to the lack of available food supplies. However, it needs to be remembered that in rural areas one of the sources of low and variable incomes is variability in agricultural production. The loss of entitlements in a particular community or region can be due to low crop yields with an adverse effect not only on the supply of food from local resources but also on the income of farm families. Where a large percentage of food supplies of families comes from their own production, the market may take some time to bring in food to offset the loss of local production.

3. Assessment of the state of knowledge

Applications of economic theory have suggested many interesting hypotheses in agricultural economics; but, seeking to improve our knowledge of the range of subjects covered in this *Handbook*, a recurring theme of its chapters is the necessity of data-based empirical work. The scientific value-added of much of the empirical work has been questioned in the *Handbook* and elsewhere. In such work, three quite different approaches to improved understanding of the agricultural economy, and agricultural policies, have been important. In assessing accomplishments made it may be helpful to distinguish among them and to outline their strengths and weaknesses. The approaches are: econometric models, simulation models, and descriptive analysis.

Econometric models provide estimates of relationships between variables of economic interest, in which the parameters that relate the variables to one another are obtained by statistical analysis of data. Paradigms of this approach in agricultural economics are commodity demand and supply models. Agricultural economists in the period up to roughly 1960 were pioneers in the development of such models, and productive work on them continues to the present day as covered in several chapters of Volume 1. The appropriate specification and testing of econometric models has been the bread and butter of graduate-level training in agricultural economics, and the ideal for an article in a professional journal of agricultural economics in most of our minds is likely to be an innovative hypothesis about behavior that is formalized in an identifiable econometric model that is then estimated using appropriate data.

What is perhaps surprising is the relative scarcity of econometric findings in the literature on resources, environment, rural development, and policy that is reviewed in Volume 2. Econometric studies are not absent – this Volume reviews many on topics in agricultural development, macroeconomic policy effects on agriculture, nutrition, and political causes of government decisions, for example. Timmer spells out details of some such modeling in his chapter. What is striking though is how seldom econometric studies have been decisive in determining the state of scholarly opinion, and in contrast, how much of the work that these chapters discuss derives from ideas, inferences, models, and observations that have not been confirmed, refuted, or even seriously confronted with statistical data.

Why? Two good reasons that appear important are (a) lack of data on key variables, and (b) even when data are available, inadequacy for the purpose at hand. For work on fundamental topics such as demand and supply, agricultural economists have been blessed with fairly carefully constructed data on prices and quantities of inputs and outputs for many commodities in many countries over substantial periods of time under a variety of market conditions. Even in these cases accurate estimation of econometric parameters is no picnic, as Volume 1 of this Handbook, especially the chapter by Just and Pope, makes clear. In Volume 2, Alston and James discuss the importance of knowing the relevant labor and land supply elasticities, but find virtually no reliable econometric evidence to draw upon, for any country.

How much worse the situation must be for variables needed to estimate parameters further removed from standard supply and demand analysis – exchange-rate effects on farm incomes, effects of price stabilization on agricultural investment, effects of food aid on food security. Most problematic are the data on global soil degradation, environmental damage from pesticides, and others of the ecosystem services discussed by Heal and Small. In the literature they cite, the tendency is to emphasize decline and loss. But where we do have some relatively solid data, as in the United States, indicators of soil erosion, and of populations of deer, beaver, bald eagles, ducks, alligators and other wildlife, are improving. Where the problems appear most resistant to improvement, in water quality and loss of undeveloped land, reliable data on the situation and trends are needed before appropriate economic and policy analysis can be carried out.

On the subject of explaining commodity policy actions or votes on farm legislation, de Gorter cites several econometric studies but does not use their findings to draw conclusions about causes of policy. The main reasons seem to be that data measuring the key concepts in theories of policy are not available, and the data that investigators are forced to use as proxies are insufficiently convincing. It is then hard to take the results seriously as tests of the theories (and the results tend not to yield high explanatory power or robust significance of effects even on their own ground).

Even when relevant data can be obtained, the historical experiments embodied in them are often inadequate for the purpose at hand. For example, an issue underlying the Cairns Group's push for agricultural trade liberalization in the Uruguay Round was their belief that their agricultural exports and hence their real incomes would increase as trade barriers were removed. Estimating the effects of increased exports on commodity revenues in those countries could test an aspect of this belief. Relevant post-1995 data are available, but they have not been generated by a clear enough natural experiment in which exports increase because of changed trade policies or events abroad (rather than endogenously in response to price changes), and we can identify the effects – at least no studies claiming to have estimated such effects are cited in our chapters on trade. A prevalent problem is the one so exhaustively explored in recent years of spurious regression in times series; and in agricultural economics the identifying strategies generated by econometric theorists have so far yielded little.

The category "simulation model" encompasses the use of systems of equations that quantify economic relationships in order to simulate effects of changing variables of interest, without econometric estimation of the equations. A paradigm of this approach is general equilibrium models. Often there is no hope of estimating them econometrically. There are too many endogenous variables, too few exogenous variables, and too much missing data in too few observations over which the economic structure can reasonably be assumed to have remained constant (but too little data to estimate structural changes). So, we obtain plausible estimates for a simplified set of parameters, and simulate the equilibrium of the system. Hertel provides a lucid and judicious review of the use of this approach in agricultural economics, and Sumner and Tangermann discuss the use of findings from this approach in the context where most has been made of it, the analysis of trade liberalization effects. One has to conclude from the discussion that the empirical value of this approach has not yet been demonstrated.

The less complex topic of domestic price support policy for a single commodity, or aggregate farm output of a country, would seem more amenable to an econometric approach. But the chapter by Alston and James covers a literature consisting mainly of simulation models: the structure consists of equations relating the simultaneously determined prices and quantities, typically for one product produced by two inputs in a competitive market. The exogenous variables are policy instruments, and typically omit variables such as consumer income, population, or nonagricultural prices that might be used to identify the equations in an econometric model. Two problems that arise in the use of such simulation models: where does the analyst obtain appropriate parameter values (mainly elasticities because the models are specified in log-linear form); and how confident can we be that the model is appropriately congruent with the facts? The discussion in Alston and James encourages pessimism on both scores.

A different body of literature that fits under the heading of simulation models for policy is research on optimization by governments given their objectives and the constraints they face. The chapter by Chambers shows how optimal policies can be specified given quite general objectives and with constraints that are difficult for governments to cope with, notably hidden information on the part of the governed. The question again arises of whether the objectives and constraints are in fact as assumed, and how sensitive the optimal choice of policy is to changes in the constraints. Lichtenberg in his chapter considers the possibility of a mechanism for chemical-use regulation derived from such optimization, but considers it a non-starter for practical reasons that can be summarized by saying that the specifications of the hidden information model are too far from the actual situation. A problem is, when we are working with non-data-based models we do not have a systematic way to assess how well a model fits the situations to which it ostensibly applies.

Descriptive analysis relies on expert-observer perceptiveness from the start. It is not a systematic research program, but rather an approach we are driven to by the lack of results in which we can be confident from econometric evidence or simulated models. Especially in matters of choosing between policy options when some action is imperative, analysts are not in a position to make no call, or wait for more data (although we can, and often do, and sometimes with success, call for a pilot program or slow rate of program start-up when the consequences of alternative policy options are highly uncertain). An example of such a situation is agricultural policy in the transition economies of the former Soviet sphere in the 1990s. Should former collective farms be broken up and the land sold or distributed to individuals who would then become private owner-operators, even in the absence of well-functioning input or credit markets or macroeconomic stability? In 1991 such decisions had to be made, but no econometric findings or quantified models could be plausibly called upon to provide answers about what would happen. Economic advice was given by World Bank and other experts who visited the area, collected information, made comparisons with situations they had seen in other countries, and evaluated the outcomes of experiments in the economic organization of agriculture in those countries. Analysis of this kind is the main analytical basis for the judgments reviewed in the chapter by Brooks and Nash.

Even after a decade of experience in formerly socialist agriculture, it is difficult to make firm assessments of what the best approach was in 1991 (or what it was in 2001), and Brooks and Nash are suitably cautious. But even here economists have something to contribute, and it is striking after reading the chapters on developed country farm policies and internationally negotiated trade policies that descriptive analysis really doesn't have much less to offer than the large investments in more formally worked-out analyses have achieved.

The outlook for world food availability is a subject that might be thought to lend itself better than most to econometric or simulation modeling, and it may therefore be surprising how little modeling of either type is drawn upon in the chapter by Ron Duncan. Why doesn't the extensive accumulated econometric evidence on commodity supply, demand, and price forecasting lend itself directly to projecting food scarcity in the future, thus allaying or confirming neo-Malthusian fears? Long-term projections like the ones we cited earlier turn not so much on elasticities or other standard estimated parameters as on the evolution of variables usually taken to be exogenous in commodity market econometrics, notably population and technology. The future course of these variables is uncertain, and itself is in part a function of economic variables as the chapter by Sunding and Zilberman and others in Volume 1 of this Handbook have discussed. But these variables change more slowly and persistently than prices, tempting commodity modelers to replace them by trends, not ultimately satisfying for either understanding the past or forecasting the future.

Econometric forecasting of long-term trends has not been a success story. The most serious and well-funded current attempts by agricultural economists to forecast many years ahead are the 10-year "baselines" published annually by the Economic Research Service of the U.S. Department of Agriculture. Their approach is an ad hoc blend of expert opinion, supported to varying degrees for different commodities by piecemeal econometrically estimated equations, simulation using multipliers the empirical support for which is obscure, and adding-up of supply-use components to get a consistent picture of the whole sector at each future point in time [see United States Department of Agriculture (USDA) (1999)]. Why not formal multi-equation, multi-commodity models? They have been tried, and died.

Assessments of such forecasting/policy analysis models have been published, such as Taylor, Reichelderfer and Johnson (1993) and some chapters in Marvin Duncan (1981). These assessments have found plenty of problems with the models they discuss, but do not reach bottom-line findings that reject such modeling efforts, generally holding out hope for improvements in further work. Nonetheless, in the last ten years none of the formerly flourishing commercial agricultural models (DRI, Chase Econometrics, WEFA) or public-sector ones in USDA or the Land Grant Universities have been functioning, or if functioning not publishing projections. Their place has been taken by aggregation of independently estimated segments, using small-scale models and expert opinion (notably in bringing foreign demand for U.S. products into account). Two notable current U.S. examples are models of the multi-university Food and Agricultural Policy Institute, and the mobilization of economists by USDA in the World Agricultural Outlook and Situation Board and Economic Research Service. However these analytical efforts are sufficiently diffuse that one would not call them a model. So the grand modeling approach appears to have been interred without a proper funeral. Christopher Gilbert (1996) prepared a nice memorial for international commodity price stabilization schemes, but this task seems to have been neglected for econometric multi-commodity models.

4. Implications for what we know and future directions of productive research

Each of these chapters cites and discusses problems about which scholars have developed a great deal of fact and analysis. A question that can be raised, however, is the value of the results achieved. Many of the chapters have found quite pronounced shortcomings to be pervasive over a wide range of what agricultural economists have done. But the authors disagree on the nature and provenance of the shortcomings. A notable disagreement is between two chapters that focus on agricultural policy analysis. Alston and James devote their chapter to a large literature that treats agricultural policy as a standard subject in applied welfare economics, with emphasis on the economic gains and losses generated by particular policy instruments from the large menu that has been drawn upon in both industrial and developing countries. When they move on to evaluation, they rate policies principally according to the deadweight losses they generate. Chambers finds unacceptable both the limitation to a given list of policy instruments and deadweight loss as a criterion. He develops for simplified cases a more general method for discovering optimal pricing and regulatory policies when the government prefers providing assistance to one group of farmers as compared to another. This becomes a considerable analytical task because such preference makes hidden information that farmers may have important, the main practical problem being that a less favored farmer may wish to qualify for the benefits of the more favored farmers.

Chambers' critique is pushed quite far. He finds the practical relevance of traditional welfare-economics studies of alternative policies or policy instruments to be low. More fundamentally for the academic industry, he believes that the value of further such work is essentially nil ("beneficial for the length of policy economists' publication lists"). The approach of mechanism design encompasses a much smaller body of studies, which means their value added per study is likely to be higher, *ceteris paribus*. But some of these studies go back 15 years or so, and the question may be raised of why their approach hasn't generated more usable empirically based work or proposals. Lichtenberg's negative assessment of a nonlinear pricing approach to regulating polluting inputs in agriculture indicates one area of difficulty that may be hard to overcome.

The general literature on the economics of taxation and public finance has a similar split. Many economists continue to analyze tax incidence using traditional welfare economics (but perhaps with more concentration on general equilibrium approaches as discussed in Hertel for agriculture) and to develop these tools to incorporate market failures [as in Innes or Parry (1999) for agriculture]. The mechanism design approach to tax policy does not appear to have had the influence that the traditional approach to tax analysis has. Perhaps surprisingly, the main empirical application has been to suggest reasons for policies that are already in place rather than designing improved ones. For example, the demonstration that random tax rates can be optimal has been used not to suggest new approaches to taxation but rather to explain why some states have both income taxes and state-run lotteries [see Pestieau, Possen and Slutsky (1998)]. Other distinctive results, such as the finding that the top income should not be taxed, have been neither politically digestible nor helpful in explaining actual policies.

However, what counts as influence and where to look for it are open to question. The main arenas of influence are governmental departments (but not so often legislative bodies), advisers to governments, and international institutions such as the World Bank or the WTO which offer policy advice. From these circles there remains plenty of demand for traditional analysis of gains and losses from taxes on farmers, import barriers, or price supports for farm products. And the study of fairly convoluted combinations of policy instruments meets a demand, too, because such combinations have in fact been tried. Indeed, a heavy criticism launched by Sumner and Tangermann at trade policy simulation work concerning the Uruguay Round is that the studies woefully lacked the detailed specificity of policy instruments needed to provide estimates of trade liberalization effects of the GATT agreement. In her assessment of models for assessing policy alternatives, Reichelderfer stated that "The demand for the services of the existing stock of agricultural sector models is strong" (1993, p. 328). In recent years that demand has weakened, although not as much for models of policy alternatives as for large forecasting models.

Rausser and Goodhue in their synthesis distinguish four dimensions of economists' policy research: policy incidence, policy design and implementation, political economy, and governmental institutions. They state that "only by formally recognizing each of these dimensions is it possible to design and implement public policies that are sustainable and robust". This is a call for a more comprehensive research strategy than is followed in any of this Handbook's chapters or the papers cited in them, and Rausser and Goodhue are accordingly critical of all of them. Yet they do mention with favor some papers that focus on particular aspects of the issues. Our general sense of the literature is that in both theoretical and empirical work, the research that has been most instructive has been quite narrowly focused and has made hugely simplifying assumptions in order to obtain definite results or has ignored the bulk of facts about a situation in order to zoom in on a few key elements, like the deadweight loss of a policy.

Nonetheless, in looking for common ground on which future discussion of policy research can proceed, all parties can agree, for example, on the limitations of deadweight loss as a criterion for choice of policy. It is far too confining to rule out income distribution among citizens as an objective of policy. And, when we consider income distribution as an objective of policy, the issue comes to the fore of criteria for favoring one group over another, both as a matter of normative theory and political fact. Such considerations lead us back to the broader research agenda and the necessity for the more comprehensive approach that Rausser and Goodhue recommend.

An example of an issue that requires consideration of all four dimensions of policy research is the question of why lump-sum transfers are not used more, e.g., to compensate the losers from trade liberalization. Such transfers are an obvious way of dealing with distributional politics that impede aggregate income-increasing policies. Several obstacles to lump-sum transfers have received discussion. One is that they are costly to implement. In the case of farmers growing import-competing crops, say sugar beets and cane, the implementation costs might be small if all farmers got the same payment, but a moment's reflection on the diversity of farmers casts grave doubt that uniform payments would ever be chosen. The closest approximation might be a *pro rata* arrangement wherein each farm got a payment proportional to the farm's base commitment to sugar crops, somehow measured. But there will be other losers, for example workers who harvest and market the domestic sugar crops. What about them? In addition, farmers will try to influence the government's assessment of their losses, and each individual of their base commitment to those crops. We shouldn't just assume that the costs of working these matters out are trivial. Moreover, producers may see any particular proposal to differentiate among them in payment as a scheme to divide and conquer their aggregate interest in payments.

A second argument for why lump-sum transfers aren't used is the government's preferences. As reviewed by de Gorter, several economists have argued that the government considers its own interests and not just those of farmers or consumers. The pursuit of these interests leads to complicated laws and obscure regulations; lump-sum transfers is the last thing the government wants, according to this view. It can be argued that political competition will promote policy efficiency, but in politics the actors are political parties and organized interest groups that differ greatly in cohesion and attention to farm policy. Their strategic interaction could again lead to payments with an arguable social purpose, which are unlikely to be lump-sum transfers.

Becker (1983) places his focus on deadweight losses in redistributional schemes, finding that policies with less deadweight losses will replace those with greater deadweight losses. While this hypothesis has received some empirical support, it remains controversial, as de Gorter discusses, and takes us back to where we were a few paragraphs ago.

Thus, the situation and outlook for agricultural economics in application to societal issues – agricultural policies and broader issues of economic growth and rural development – is notably fragmented. Several agendas of theoretical development, empirical investigation, model building, and normative argument, are being pursued by different groups of economists. Cross-fertilization or even recognition between some of these groups is surprisingly limited. Nonetheless, progress is being made on many fronts, aided immeasurably by an accumulating body of evidence on results of policy experiments and economic shocks. Agricultural economists of all persuasions thankfully retain a feeling of obligation to occasionally check what they are finding in their academic work against actual events.

References

Balogh, T. (1964), "Book review of *Transforming Traditional Agriculture* by T.W. Schultz", Economic Journal 74:996–999.

Becker, G.S. (1983), "A theory of competition among pressure groups for political influence", Quarterly Journal of Economics 48:371–400.

Binswanger, H., and K. Deininger (1997), "Explaining agricultural and agrarian policies in developing countries", Journal of Economic Literature 35:1958–2005.

Boggess, W.G. (1995), "The poverty of applied policy analysis", Journal of Agricultural and Applied Economics 72:1–12.

Brandow, G.E. (1977), "Policy for commercial agriculture", in: L. Martin, ed., A Survey of Agricultural Economics Literature, Vol. 1 (University of Minnesota Press, Minneapolis) 209–292.

Brown, L.R. (1981), "The worldwide loss of cropland", in: R. Wood, ed., Future Dimensions of World Food and Population (Westview Press, Boulder, CO).

Bullock, D.S. (1995), "Are government transfers efficient: An alternative test of the efficient redistribution hypothesis", Journal of Political Economy 103:1236–1275.

Clodius, R.L. (1960), "Market structure, economic power and agricultural policy: A proposal for forward production control", Journal of Farm Economics 42:413–425.

Cochrane, W. (1985), "The need to rethink agricultural policy in general and to perform some radical surgery on commodity programs in particular", American Journal of Agricultural Economics 67:1002–1009.

Duncan, M. (ed.) (1981), Modeling Agriculture for Policy Analysis in the 1980s (Federal Reserve Bank, Kansas City).

Ehrlich, P. (1971), The Population Bomb, Revised Edition (A Sierra Club/Ballantine Book, New York).

Floyd, J.E. (1965), "The effects of farm price supports on the returns to land and labor in agriculture", Journal of Political Economy 73:148–158.

Gilbert, C.L. (1996), "International commodity agreements: An obituary notice", World Development 24:1–19.

Harberger, A.C. (1971), "Three basic postulates of applied welfare economics", Journal of Economic Literature 9:785–797.

Helpman, E., and G. Grossman (1994), "Protection for sale", American Economic Review 84(4):833–850.

Johnson, B., and J. Mellor (1960), "The nature of agriculture's contribution to economic development", Food Research Institute Studies 1:335–356.

Kneese, A., and J. Sweeney (eds.) (1985), Handbook of Natural Resource and Energy Economics (North-Holland, Amsterdam).

Kremer, M. (1993), "Population growth and technological change: One million B.C. to 1990", Quarterly Journal of Economics, 108(3):681–716.

Lacey, R., and D. Danzinger (1999), The Year 1000 (Little Brown, New York).

Lindert, P.H. (1996), "Soil degradation and agricultural change in two developing countries", Working Paper Series No. 82 (Agricultural History Center, University of California, Davis).

Maddison, A. (1995), Monitoring the World Economy (Organization for Economic Co-operation and Development, Paris).

Parry, I. (1999), "Agricultural policies in the presence of distorting taxes", American Journal of Agricultural Economics 81:212–230.

Pasour, E.C., Jr. (1988), "Financial support and freedom of inquiry in agricultural economics", Minerva 26:31–52.

Pestieau, P., U.M. Possen and S. Slutsky (1998), "The value of explicit randomization in the tax code", Journal of Public Economics 67:87–103.

Rausser, G.C. (1982), "Political economic markets: PERTs and PESTs in food and agriculture", American Journal of Agricultural Economics 64:821–833.

Reichelderfer, K.H. (1993), "Utility of models for policy analysis and decision making", in: C.R. Taylor, K.H. Reichelderfer and S.R. Johnson, eds., Agricultural Sector Models for the United States Ames (Iowa State University Press, Ames) 328–346.

Sargent, T.J. (1987), Dynamic Macroeconomic Theory (Harvard University Press, Cambridge, MA).

Schuh, G.E. (1975), "The exchange rate and U.S. agriculture", American Journal of Agricultural Economics.

Schultz, T.W. (1964), Transforming Traditional Agriculture (Yale University Press, New Haven).

Taylor, C.R., K.H. Reichelderfer and S.R. Johnson (eds.) (1993), Agricultural Sector Models for the United States (Iowa State University Press, Ames).

United States Department of Agriculture (USDA) (1999), "Agricultural baseline projections to 2008", Staff Report WAOB-99-1 (Office of the Chief Economist).
World Bank (1997), Rural Development: From Vision to Action (World Bank, Washington, DC).

AUTHOR INDEX

n indicates citation in footnote.

SUBJECT INDEX

HANDBOOKS IN ECONOMICS

1. HANDBOOK OF MATHEMATICAL ECONOMICS (in 4 volumes)
   Volumes 1, 2 and 3 edited by Kenneth J. Arrow and Michael D. Intriligator
   Volume 4 edited by Werner Hildenbrand and Hugo Sonnenschein

2. HANDBOOK OF ECONOMETRICS (in 6 volumes)
   Volumes 1, 2 and 3 edited by Zvi Griliches and Michael D. Intriligator
   Volume 4 edited by Robert F. Engle and Daniel L. McFadden
   Volume 5 edited by James J. Heckman and Edward Leamer
   Volume 6 is in preparation (editors James J. Heckman and Edward Leamer)

3. HANDBOOK OF INTERNATIONAL ECONOMICS (in 3 volumes)
   Volumes 1 and 2 edited by Ronald W. Jones and Peter B. Kenen
   Volume 3 edited by Gene M. Grossman and Kenneth Rogoff

4. HANDBOOK OF PUBLIC ECONOMICS (in 4 volumes)
   Volumes 1, 2 and 3 edited by Alan J. Auerbach and Martin Feldstein
   Volume 4 is in preparation (editors Alan J. Auerbach and Martin Feldstein)

5. HANDBOOK OF LABOR ECONOMICS (in 5 volumes)
   Volumes 1 and 2 edited by Orley C. Ashenfelter and Richard Layard
   Volumes 3A, 3B and 3C edited by Orley C. Ashenfelter and David Card

6. HANDBOOK OF NATURAL RESOURCE AND ENERGY ECONOMICS
   (in 3 volumes). Edited by Allen V. Kneese and James L. Sweeney

7. HANDBOOK OF REGIONAL AND URBAN ECONOMICS (in 4 volumes)
   Volume 1 edited by Peter Nijkamp
   Volume 2 edited by Edwin S. Mills
   Volume 3 edited by Paul C. Cheshire and Edwin S. Mills
   Volume 4 is in preparation (editors J. Vernon Henderson and Jacques-François Thisse)

8. HANDBOOK OF MONETARY ECONOMICS (in 2 volumes)
   Edited by Benjamin Friedman and Frank Hahn

9. HANDBOOK OF DEVELOPMENT ECONOMICS (in 4 volumes)
   Volumes 1 and 2 edited by Hollis B. Chenery and T.N. Srinivasan
   Volumes 3A and 3B edited by Jere Behrman and T.N. Srinivasan

10. HANDBOOK OF INDUSTRIAL ORGANIZATION (in 3 volumes)
    Volumes 1 and 2 edited by Richard Schmalensee and Robert R. Willig
    Volume 3 is in preparation (editors Mark Armstrong and Robert H. Porter)

FORTHCOMING TITLES

HANDBOOK OF LAW AND ECONOMICS
Editors A. Mitchell Polinsky and Steven Shavell

All published volumes available